THE SUPPORT ECONOMY

WHY CORPORATIONS ARE FAILING INDIVIDUALS
AND THE NEXT EPISODE OF CAPITALISM

THE SUPPORT ECONOMY

WHY CORPORATIONS ARE FAILING INDIVIDUALS
AND THE NEXT EPISODE OF CAPITALISM

Shoshana Zuboff
and James Maxmin

ALLEN LANE
an imprint of
PENGUIN BOOKS

ALLEN LANE
THE PENGUIN PRESS

Published by the Penguin Group
Penguin Books Ltd, 80 Strand, London WC2R 0RL, England
Penguin Putnam Inc., 375 Hudson Street, New York, New York 10014, USA
Penguin Books Australia Ltd, 250 Camberwell Road, Camberwell, Victoria 3124, Australia
Penguin Books Canada Ltd, 10 Alcorn Avenue, Toronto, Ontario, Canada M4V 3B2
Penguin Books India (P) Ltd, 11, Community Centre, Panchsheel Park, New Delhi – 110 017, India
Penguin Books (NZ) Ltd, Cnr Rosedale and Airborne Roads, Albany, Auckland, New Zealand
Penguin Books (South Africa) (Pty) Ltd, 24 Sturdee Avenue, Rosebank 2196, South Africa

Penguin Books Ltd, Registered Offices: 80 Strand, London WC2R 0RL, England

www.penguin.com

First published in the USA by Viking Penguin, a member of Penguin Putnam Inc. 2002
Published in the UK by Allen Lane The Penguin Press 2003
1

Set in Stempel Garamond
Printed in England by Clays Ltd, St Ives plc

ISBN 0–713–99320–0

Every young and growing people has to meet, at moments,
the problem of its destiny. . . . The fathers are dead, the prophets
are silent, the questions are new, and have no answer but in time. . . .
The past gives no clue to the future. The fathers, where are they?
And the prophets, do they live forever? We are ourselves the fathers!
We are ourselves the prophets!

John Hay,
secretary of state and formerly President Lincoln's private secretary, speaking to Congress in affirmation of the new movement toward corporate capitalism, February 27, 1902

The composition of this book has been for the author a long struggle
of escape, and so must the reading of it be for most readers
if the author's assault upon them is to be successful,—a struggle
of escape from habitual modes of thought and expression. . . .
The difficulty lies, not in the new ideas, but in escaping from the
old ones, which ramify, for those brought up as most of us have been,
into every corner of our minds.

John Maynard Keynes,
from his preface to *The General Theory of Employment, Interest and Money*, 1935

Once in a while you get shown the light in the strangest of places
if you look at it right

The Grateful Dead, "Scarlet Begonias"

Acknowledgments

We owe an immense debt of gratitude to Jeff Cronin of the Harvard Business School. He has been an indefatigable colleague and a loyal friend as he helped coordinate literature searches and locate the thousands of documents that have been used to define the pattern and weave the fabric of this book. Christine Fajors, also of the Harvard Business School, was nothing less than heroic in her ability to organize these many research materials while remaining resolutely cheerful.

Many readers have helped us with useful comments as our argument developed. We owe special thanks to Tom McCraw for his characteristically painstaking and deeply insightful reading of the manuscript at a critical stage. We also want to thank readers George Fisher, Richard Broyd, Gene Gendlin, Jim Austin, Claudio Ciborra, Shibani Sain, Herb Kelman, Robert Schrank, and John Staudenmaier for their reactions to all or part of the manuscript at various stages.

We want to thank the special people in our lives who have over these many years provided us with the "deep support" we needed to complete this undertaking: Mary Dee Choate Grant, Laura Waltz and Frank Waltz, "Uncle Dick" Chadwick, John Jicha, and Melanie Mayes.

We are grateful to our editor, Janet Goldstein, and the professional team at Viking Penguin who stood by us as we brought this project to completion.

Most of all, we want to thank our two young children, Jacob Raphael Maxmin and Chloë Sophia Maxmin. When they were very small they carved out their corner of Mom's writing cottage, which they filled with the markers and colored pencils that brought forth magnificent drawings to adorn the walls. As they grew, their projects turned to writing their own books. They have been our cheerleaders, especially as they have supported Mom's daily writing. Jacob always made sure to turn on the light that illuminates the path back up to the house at night, as he waited to greet Mom at the door. Chloë showered Mom with notes of love. This book belongs to them.

Contents

PART THREE
Emergence: The New Enterprise Logic

Preface

This book was born in silence.

For many years after the publication of *In the Age of the Smart Machine*, it was clear to me that management theory and management practice were fated to move on tragically separate paths. Conceptually, the criteria for excellence in management were well articulated, and had been for some time. Practically, good management is highly contingent. It depends upon so many variables—involving leadership, governance, and markets—being well aligned for a long enough period of time to make a difference. In research generously funded by the Harvard Business School between 1988 and 1994, I followed a group of visionary top managers and watched each one fall prey to corporate politics, self-interested boards, and the whims of financial analysts reacting to short-term fluctuations in a company's earnings. What possible contribution can theory make, when the realities of business are determined by endogenous forces fully dedicated to system survival, or at least to the perpetuation of the interests that govern the system, frequently at the expense of the consumers and employees whom the system should be serving? Worse yet, in the field of management the true nature of these forces is too often regarded as undiscussable, and is therefore rarely addressed in the theories. The problem wasn't management, per se, but the institutionalized practices and logic that shaped managers' work.

I chose not to publish anything for a long while, rather than to simply add one more voice to the well-known critique of this status quo. I wanted, instead, to find a way through to a new conversation. I turned to history, immersing myself in the origins and evolution of the corporation, as we know it. This work helped me to clarify the internal "systems principles" of managerial capitalism and the conditions that enabled it to prosper. It also allowed me to begin to understand underlying societal changes that held the potential to challenge the system beyond its limits and in so doing, set into motion the forces capable of laying the foundation for a new episode of capitalism based on a new "enterprise logic."

For a theoretician interested in practice, I was blessed to share my life with a brilliant practitioner. When I first met Jim Maxmin, he was known as the kind of CEO who cared deeply about people but also possessed such mastery of the complexities of managing a large commercial enterprise that he could legitimately turn failing companies into profitable businesses. What had struck me most about him, though, was his profound conceptual appreciation of his own work. Unlike any other businessman I had ever met, he also spoke the language of philosophy. From the start, a relentless exploration of the theory and practice of management characterized our life together. Oddly, the rhythms of our lives led us each into questioning our most basic assumptions about these matters at around the same time. And so it was that out of years of reading and thinking and searching conversation, we came upon the insight that would change everything for us—the Copernican inversion that locates all value in the end consumer and redefines commercial activity as advocacy for individuals in what we eventually came to call "individual space." In this new commercial system, supporting end consumers is not an occasional event, but a necessary condition of being in business.

Once we had seen our way through to the origins of this new enterprise logic, I knew that a new conversation was possible, after all. It was then, in 1996, that I began the years of research and writing that would bring this book to fruition. As the writer in the family, I went to work on the historical and sociological themes that set the stage for the new enterprise logic. Jim immersed himself in the new technologies of the Internet and their commercial application. His work deeply informed our understanding of the shortcomings of the e-commerce of the 1990s, as well as the critical role those new technologies would play in the new enterprise logic. Later, we collaborated closely on thinking through the principles of a new "distributed capitalism," and how they could be implemented in the service of a support economy. Jim's profound grasp of commerce ensured that the exposition of the new enterprise logic never succumbed to science fiction, but rather was sensible, practical, feasible, and, above all, capable of producing immense wealth.

While a good deal of scholarly work underlies the critique and propositions offered here, I have endeavored, however imperfectly, to write this book for a wide audience. The ideas we have developed are not just for the professionals to ponder. They concern every woman and every man who values their own individuality and is frustrated by a world of institutions still fitted out for the old mass order. They concern everyone who is a consumer, everyone who is trying to raise a family, everyone who has a career, and everyone who has been frustrated by a commercial system that is too often indifferent to the very people who depend upon it for consumption and employment.

Many individuals have inspired me along the way. Whether or not they suspect it, it is they who kept me going during these years of solitary writing. I am grateful to the men who shared their truth with me in the course of my leadership study over a decade ago. You know who you are. I have drawn strength and insight from the men and women who have participated in my *ODYSSEY* program at the Harvard Business School during the last ten years. They have taught me so much about the new society of individuals, and each of them carries a piece of my heart. I have been inspired by my husband, his courage and genius. Most of all, I have learned from our children, Chloë and Jacob, from what they expect and what they deserve. I hope this book accrues to making theirs a better world.

Shoshana Zuboff
June 23, 2002

The birth and evolution of this book has been a magical experience for me. For twenty years as a CEO, I struggled to enter into true relationship with my customers and provide them with an outstanding experience all the time. I also endeavored to provide a meaningful and enriching work environment for all my colleagues. No matter how I tried, I knew that I always fell short of my expectations. I worked with great people, each of whom taught me an enormous amount. We were all intelligent and well-intentioned, with ample resources at our disposal. We all agreed that truly satisfied and engaged customers were the keys to our long-term success. And we all knew that this goal eluded us.

Over time, I began to distill some conceptual understanding of my experiences. I had always had a strong sense that value resides in the individual end consumer. I also believed that when a company imposes upon itself the discipline of managing for cash flow, rather than being seduced by financial engineering, it is forced into measuring itself by the true reactions of its customers. But over time, I was compelled to admit that the modern com-

mercial enterprise did not easily lend itself to these practices. The financial
metrics that managers employ, and the institutional pressures that most
CEOs face, make sustained alignment with the end consumer nearly impossible. Long-term wealth creation is usually sacrificed to short-term gains, no
matter how poorly this serves the firm's constituencies or suboptimizes its
real wealth-creating potential for investors. Shoshana and I spent many
hours talking about these intuitions, which allowed them to grow into
better-defined ideas. Still their larger significance eluded me.

Shoshana insisted that the answers lay in a better understanding of history, specifically the history of managerial capitalism. As she read and wrote
on this subject, and as we talked and argued, a new perspective opened up to
me. Through the lens of history, I began to see the interconnections and the
dynamics that created so many of the problems I dealt with on a daily basis
as a CEO. I began to understand the hold that the logic of managerial capitalism had on my effectiveness as a manager, on the quality of my work life,
and perhaps most of all, on my experience as a consumer. Things began to
fall into place like some giant metaphysical jigsaw puzzle. As we began to
explore the relationships among the three forces we write about in this
book—markets, technologies, and a new enterprise logic—I developed a
more trenchant understanding of my past experience. It also became possible
to envision a new kind of commerce, truly aligned with today's society; one
that can not only create more wealth but can also give us back our lives.

I want to thank the many individuals I have endeavored to serve around
the world during my career. As we developed the ideas for the support economy, I heard your thousands of comments and suggestions ringing in my
ears. I remembered the letters you wrote in praise and despair. We all deserve more than we are getting, and it is a pity that all the effort and resource
directed at trying to make things work can so often fall so wide of the mark.
Like many others, I have worshiped at the altar of transactions and earnings
per share, simply because I knew no better. I now regard that as time spent
with false idols. It is my fervent hope that the ideas set forward here can help
the next generation of management to be more productive and fulfilled as
they learn that a future of wealth and prosperity depends upon celebrating
today's individuals and learning to see the world from their perspective.
That is the promise of the support economy.

None of this would have been possible were it not for the years of
thinking, research, creative conceptualization, synthesis, and writing that
represent Shoshana's devotion to this book. She made our ideas and discussions come alive in a way that I never could have achieved. She has opened

my mind and heart to new ideas and perspectives. She has made me think and think again, and for this, along with millions of other things, I am eternally grateful.

Jim Maxmin
June 23, 2002

INTRODUCTION

ONE

Bridging the Chasm

People have changed more than the business organizations upon which they depend. The last fifty years have seen the rise of a new breed of individuals, yet corporations continue to operate according to a logic invented at the time of their origin, a century ago. The chasm that now separates individuals and organizations is marked by frustration, mistrust, disappointment, and even rage. It also harbors the possibility of a new capitalism and a new era of wealth creation.

THE CHASM

In the second half of the twentieth century a new society of individuals emerged—a breed of people unlike any the world has ever seen. Educated, informed, traveled, they work with their brains, not their bodies. They do not assume that their lives can be patterned after their parents' or grandparents'. Throughout human history the problem of identity was settled in one way—I am my mother's daughter; I am my father's son. But in a discontinuous and irreversible break with the past, today's individuals seek the experiences and insights that enable them to find the elusive pattern in the stone, the singular pattern that is "me." Their sense of self is more intricate, acute, detailed, vast, and rich than at any other time in human history. They have learned to make sense of their lives in unique and private ways, to forge the delicate tissue of meaning that marks their lives as their own.

In all other times and all other places, psychological individuation was unimaginable. It was, at best, the emotional precinct of an elite group of artists and spiritual seekers—rare, elusive, precious. But today that unique human capacity for individuation has been put within the reach of millions of people. Their individualism, long regarded as the basis for political self-determination, has also become the foundation for the one sure thing they have in common: a deep and abiding yearning for psychological self-determination.

The new individuals are remaking their societies as they demand the right to psychological sovereignty, but they continue to be invisible to the commercial organizations upon which they must routinely rely. Long distant from the land and far removed from age-old traditions of household production, the new individuals protect, sustain, and nurture themselves and their families in the only way that is available—through the modern processes known as "consumption." But corporations continue to be dominated by a commercial logic based on assumptions about human beings and their approach to consumption that is more than one hundred years old. That commercial logic, known as managerial capitalism, was invented for the production and distribution of things. It has been uneasily adapted to the delivery of services. But neither goods nor services adequately fulfill the needs of today's markets.

In search of psychological self-determination, the new individuals want something that modern organizations cannot give them: tangible support in leading the lives they choose. They want to be freed from the time-consuming stress, rage, injustice, and personal defeat that accompany so many commercial exchanges. As a result, a chasm has opened up between the new individuals and the world of business organizations. Too many people, consumers and employees alike, feel that businesses are failing those whom they should be serving—capitalism's past is in bold confrontation with the realities of human life today.

Companies invest billions in endless cycles of quick fixes to "rediscover" their end consumers. But the chasm that separates the new individuals from their commercial organizations cannot be bridged within the terms of today's business models. Instead, we will argue, that chasm reflects an enterprise logic that has outlived the society it was once designed to serve. It matters little whether companies think of their end consumers as wallets, eyeballs, anonymous marks on a ledger, "cognitive real estate," "personalized relationship targets," or "individually addressable data packets." In every case, what is most important about today's individual end consumers cannot be perceived by the modern enterprise as we know it. Corporate indifference has resulted in a weary mistrust—frequently shading into disgust—among end consumers, as well as a new determination to find alternatives to the status quo of today's marketplace.

We will explore these propositions in depth in the coming chapters. For now, consider but a few points:

◆ Fifty-seven percent of Americans say they do not trust corporate executives or brokerage houses to give them honest information. "The public feels pretty good about themselves," says the architect of the poll, "but they're disappointed [that] . . . our institutions are failing us." A majority of Americans believes that companies should put the interests of employees (31 percent), their customers (27 percent), and their communities (19 percent) first. Many fewer identify stockholders (14 percent) or executives (3 percent) as the appropriate focus of corporate decision-making. Evaluations of actual corporate behavior show just the opposite. A plurality of 43 percent believes that top executives are the primary beneficiaries of corporate decisions, with 37 percent saying that shareholder interests come first.[1] Sixty percent of investors believe that well-known corporations are using questionable accounting practices, while 28 percent believe there is an "epidemic of deceptive accounting practices" among well-known corporations.[2]

◆ Trends in British public opinion show a dramatic decline in people's faith in corporations. In 1970 the public agreed by a majority of two-to-one that "the profits of large companies help make things better for everyone who buys their products and services." By 1999, the situation was reversed. Surveys showed an equally decisive rejection of that statement by the same two-to-one majority. That year, four-fifths of the British public agreed that "As they grow bigger, companies usually get cold and impersonal in their relations with people."[3]

◆ The April 2002 Eurobarometer Survey (a semiannual public opinion survey of the fifteen EU member states) queried the public's trust in institutions. Trust in "big companies" was least widespread. Only 33 percent of the sample indicated a tendency to trust corporations. They ranked last behind the army (70 percent), the police (67 percent), the United Nations (59 percent), charitable or voluntary organizations (56 percent), the national legal system (51 percent), religious institutions (44 percent), nongovernmental organizations (42 percent), and trade unions (39 percent).[4]

◆ In order to divert the U.S. Congress from a debate over a passenger bill of rights, the airline industry executed the Airline Customer Service Commitment in June 1999. The plan detailed numerous customer service improvements to be undertaken immediately. Despite the commitment, the U.S. Department of Transportation (DOT) found that customer complaints more than doubled in 1999 over the prior year, and complaints for the first four months of 2000 were up by 74 percent over 1999. They also estimated that the airlines themselves received as many as 400 complaints for every one complaint received by the DOT.[5]

◆ More than half of all Americans are not satisfied with the availability of their doctors and the amount of information they receive in an office visit, which now averages seven to ten minutes. As a result, they are breaking new ground in the $1 trillion health-care industry. Fifty-two million adults now use the Internet as their primary source of health-care information.[6] Between 1990 and 1997 the number of visits to alternative medicine practitioners increased 47 percent. By 1997, visits to alternative practitioners exceeded the number of visits to all U.S. primary care physicians by 243 million, and the total out-of-pocket expenditures for these services was about $27 billion, comparable to the out-of-pocket payments to all U.S. physician services that year.[7]

◆ A U.S. Department of Education report concludes that the number of children being home-schooled increased by 100 percent to 200 percent between 1990 and 1996. By 2000, the number of children in home-schooling was estimated to be between 1 million and 1.7 million. Given the turnover in home-schooling, as much as 6 percent to 12 percent of the school-age population is now likely to have had some home-schooling by the age of eighteen.[8] Home-schooling families can now avail themselves of thousands of new consumption options, including textbooks, videos, software, seminars, camps, and distance-learning programs, all aimed at enabling them to design a unique approach to their child's education.

◆ Demographers have concluded that the hallmark of population movements in the United States in the late twentieth century was a pattern known as "deconcentration," in which people left the regimentation of city and suburb to forge a new kind of life, infused with a greater sense of well-being and personal control, in rural America. In a demographic turnaround without historical precedent, rural net migration gain was 3.6 percent during the 1990s, compared to 1.8 percent in the cities.[9]

Today's individuals have a hard time believing in the corporate institutions of managerial capitalism, even the best among them. As end consumers and as employees, they find it increasingly difficult to trust that their interests are being served. The evidence we will present suggests that not only are the new individuals forced to absorb the consequences of corporate indifference, they are also ready to blaze new trails. As their needs go unheeded, they are pioneering wholly new kinds of consumption experiences, hoping to find what they are after. The industrial economy is no longer adequate to their demands. The service economy cannot fulfill their needs. But as we will argue in the coming chapters, this depressing scenario harbors an electrifying possibility: Everything about the new individuals that is ignored today is waiting to become the focus of a new "support economy," based on a new "distributed capitalism."

The chasm between today's individuals and today's commercial organizations is what we call the *transaction crisis*. On the surface, this appears to be merely a source of irritation. Indeed, consumption itself is belittled by conservatives and progressives alike. Both tend to conceive of consumption narrowly, as if it were only about people running through shopping malls like rats in a maze. In consumption they see moral vacuity and self-indulgence. Progressives blame this on manipulation by corporations and their advertisers. Conservatives blame the loss of values and communal purpose. In fact, consumption these days is only incidentally about tossing away discretionary income at the mall.

In an advanced industrial society, consumption is a necessity, not a luxury. It is what people must do to survive. It is the way that individuals take care of themselves and their families, much as hunting and gathering or growing crops were for people of earlier societies. For today's women and men, consumption decisions encompass everything from education to health care, insurance, transportation, and communication, as well as food, shelter, clothing, and luxuries. Through the consumption of experience—travel, culture, college—people both achieve and express individual self-determination. No one can escape the centrality of consumption. There is no distinct class of consumers. Everyone is a consumer, no matter what their status or income level. Corporate executives and their employees, entrepreneurs and their investors, students and their teachers, artists and their agents, retail magnates and their clerks, telecommuters, factory workers, farmers, small business owners, public officials, professionals, civil servants, and stay-at-home moms are consumers all. Far from being a trivial irritant or a complaint of the spoiled rich, the transaction crisis has far-reaching consequences for a majority of individuals, families, firms, and economies.

Small wonder that at the first signs of recession, political leaders exhort people to spend money. Consumption has come to define economic well-being in an advanced economy. By 1993, nearly two-thirds of all jobs in the U.S. economy were directly or indirectly dependent upon consumer expenditures, making consumers responsible for more than 79 million jobs that year, a number that is expected to increase to 92 million jobs by 2005. Consumer spending generates employment in all but ten of the 195 industries that are tracked by the Bureau of Labor Statistics (BLS) (the ten are either government related or special industry categories designed for input-output accounting conventions). Every one of the 278 occupations used in the BLS industry-occupation matrix has become more dependent upon consumer spending since the mid-twentieth century.

The fastest-growing industries have also been those with the highest dependency (100 percent) upon consumer spending, such as health care and educational services. Consumption-related employment growth in computer and data-processing services increased by nearly 500 percent between 1977 and 1997. In management and public relations, that growth was about 250 percent. Indeed, U.S. Labor Department figures indicate that nearly two-thirds of all managerial and executive positions are directly consumer related.[10] In 1998 consumption accounted for nearly 67 percent of the U.S. Gross Domestic Product. Trends in Europe were similar, if not everywhere quite as dramatic. For example, in 1998 consumption as a percentage of Gross Domestic Product ranged from a high of 71.7 percent in Greece to a low of 49.8 percent in Norway, with the United Kingdom slightly above the mean at 65 percent.[11]

So here is today's new problem with no name: People have changed more than the commercial organizations upon which they depend. And here is the new opportunity: In the chasm that now separates individuals and organizations lie the keys to a new economic order with vast potential for wealth creation and individual fulfillment. The marketplace of a support economy and the associated possibilities of a new distributed capitalism are emerging from the disappointments, frustrations, and all-too-frequent humiliations to which today's new individuals are routinely subjected at the hands of the old organizations. Fortunes will be made, as a new kind of commercial enterprise learns how to make money by authentically supporting the new individuals in their quest for psychological self-determination.

IN SEARCH OF A NEW
ENTERPRISE LOGIC

The chasm between individuals and their organizations is not limited to the business world. It describes citizens and their public institutions and, for many people, worshipers and their religious institutions. It describes dilemmas that afflict not-for-profit as well as for-profit organizations. It accounts for many of the agonies associated with "the employment relationship," assumptions about which also bear the limitations of an earlier era. Our focus in this book, though, is on the chasm that separates consumers and the practice of commerce. The reason is this: New patterns of consumption have historically played a powerful role in changing the *enterprise logic*, or deep structure, of business organizations—the internally consistent set of practices, attitudes, and assumptions on which they are based.

Epochal shifts in the logic of commerce—and of capitalism itself—have typically begun in response to underlying changes in the nature of society as they were expressed in new approaches to consumption. The record of the last quarter-century shows that business organizations do not easily change from within. Instead, the changes occurring outside the organization—in the nature of consumption today—are most likely to be the source of the next fundamental transformation in the nature and purpose of business, as well as in the underlying logic of capitalism itself.

There is another reason to train our focus on business organizations. In the past, new approaches have tended to emerge in the private sector and then migrate to other kinds of organizations in the public and not-for-profit sectors. Obvious examples include the spread of many aspects of the mass-production model to such disparate contexts as farms, hospitals, and schools. There is a likelihood, then, that fundamental changes in the organization of commerce will pave the way for change in the enterprise logic of many kinds of organizations and institutions.

Despite the centrality of consumption for an advanced economy and the fact that everyone is a consumer, people have come to accept that their consumption experiences will be largely adversarial. The reason lies in the deep structure of today's enterprise, an enterprise logic inherited from the early-twentieth-century era of the "mass." In that era, mass consumption begat the innovative logic of mass production, which in turn gave rise to the revolutionary new principles of managerial capitalism. These inventions ruled the commercial world with incredible success during most of the twentieth century, when people were willing to follow the rules as consumers.

Most people had little and desired much. They assumed they had to do whatever was necessary to earn and maintain their place in a new society of plenty. As mass consumers, their choices were as circumscribed as their expectations.

The enterprise logic associated with managerial capitalism—what we call the *standard enterprise logic*—was created to serve the demands of these mass consumers, and it continues to dominate commercial life today, sustained by a variety of institutional, economic, and social-psychological factors. It relies on an economic framework we call *transaction economics*, which assumes that value is created by producers in *organization space* (the internal world of the organization), and lodged in the products and services they sell. That *transaction value* is maximized as firms seek the most profitable terms in their exchanges with end consumers, thus perpetuating the adversarialism between buyers and sellers. In this book we argue that the standard enterprise logic and the framework of transaction economics have outlived their relevance. The organizations operating this way simply do not have the capability to perceive individuals, let alone to respond to their needs for psychological self-determination, even as a perpetual drumbeat of consumer-oriented rhetoric claims the opposite.

Economic revolutions have occurred in the past, when new human yearnings changed the nature of consumption and created new kinds of markets. Ultimately, these new markets were addressed by new technologies linked to new organizational forms. Taken together, these elements created a new kind of commercial pattern or enterprise logic. The contributions of some of history's greatest entrepreneurs—pottery maker Josiah Wedgwood in the eighteenth century, automaker Henry Ford in the twentieth—were in precisely this arena. They did not simply stimulate new demand. They typically did not invent new technologies. Instead, they discovered the possibility of a new kind of convergence between consumers' desires, technological capabilities, and organizational innovations. These three elements were combined in a new enterprise logic.

Take Ford, for example. In the early twentieth century, the automobile industry was an industrial sideshow, a playground in which rich men made fancy toys for their rich friends. Ford alone perceived a mass market of "ordinary people" willing to pay for the convenience of a plain but reliable automobile. He invented a new way of organizing technologies and people to produce a vehicle at a cost that farmers, shopkeepers, and even factory workers could afford. That invention of a new enterprise logic not only created the modern automobile industry but set the pattern for most modern organizations, in virtually every sector. In forging this wholly different pattern, Ford unleashed vast new sources of wealth and began the process of reinventing capitalism for his century. Such is the opportunity upon us now, and such are its rewards.

A SHARED CAPITALISM: AN OVERVIEW

The historic achievement of psychological individuality is laden with consequences for the nature and purpose of commercial activity. These are as explosive as the emergence of mass consumption was in Ford's day. And today's new individuals are as invisible to the radar of today's commercial organizations as Ford's farmers and shopkeepers were to other automobile makers a century ago. The challenge for a new generation of entrepreneurs will be to grasp the meaning of the new society of individuals as it expresses itself in the dreams and yearnings of today's new people and the kinds of markets they comprise.

The new individuals express a very different orientation toward consumption as compared with the generations that preceded them. We call their new approach the *individuation of consumption*. It means that people no longer want to bend to antiquated rules of business. They do not want to be the objects of commerce, treated like anonymous pawns in the exploitative games of market segmentation, penetration, and manipulative pseudo-intimacy. Instead, they want to "opt in" and make their own choices, controlling their destinies and their cash. They want their voices to be heard, and they want them to matter. They want to be the subjects of a new commerce in which they are recognized as the origins of a new form of economic value that we call *relationship value*.

Relationship value cannot be created or destroyed by managers in organizations linked in value chains. Rather, this new form of value is latent in the subjective experience of each individual, a psychological destination that we call *individual space*. Relationship value is realized in individual space, rather than created in organization space. It is at the center of a new economic framework called *relationship economics*. This framework redefines the commercial process from the point of view of individual space. It recognizes the individual as the origin of all value and the source of all cash. In this new perspective, all commercial processes are aligned with the individual end consumer, a principle enforced by a critical operational requirement: No one gets paid until the individual releases cash. In this way, *realized relationship value* translates into immediate cash flow.

Today, relationship value is invisible. It is frozen in place because it cannot be perceived, let alone responded to, in the context of current economic frameworks. There are, of course, plenty of tactics in the management arsenal that purport to address the value of customer "relationships." There has been a good deal of discussion of "embedded customer value," the "cost of customer acquisition," the "share of customer," and even the "value" of customer relationships. These and other concepts point to the economic rationale for customer retention. We will explore such initiatives in detail in Chapter Nine. For now, let's just say that we regard these as important insights that are ultimately doomed, because they remain constrained by the standard enterprise logic, with its economic assumptions and methods of value creation.

Relationship value realization does not revolve around the acquisition of products or services. The individuation of consumption means something more. For the new individual, the purpose of consumption is life itself—the acquisition of the time and support necessary to pursue a life of psychological self-determination. Products and services continue to have a role to play in this new kind of consumption, but they become secondary to the broader and more inclusive new commercial purpose that we call *deep support*. Individuals want honest assistance in meeting the challenges of their intricate lives, not subterfuge, patronization, or the false solicitude widely regarded as the best that can be hoped for in a commercial exchange. In providing deep support, enterprises assume full accountability and responsibility for every aspect of the consumption experience. Deep support provides ongoing relationship based on advocacy, mutual respect, trust, and the acute alignment of interests.

The new digital technologies are essential to the successful consolidation of this new enterprise logic. In the past, organizations were in some respects forced to ignore individuals because they did not possess technologies capable of managing individual complexity. Indeed, most commercial technologies have been dedicated to the goal of simplification. Their focus has been on how to eliminate complexity in order to make things ever more efficiently, so more people could buy more and buy it more cheaply. But today there is a wholly new technological infrastructure based on information. The physical world of atoms is translated into digits, where it can be coordinated and communicated intact with nearly infinite degrees of complexity and detail. The networks that link people around the globe continue to develop in speed, intelligence, accuracy, and breadth. The new information technologies have reshaped business processes in many industries. Until now, however, they have been bent to the purposes of the old consumption, according to the principles of the old capitalism. They have continued to be used to do more and to do it more efficiently. If there is some disappointment over what they have yielded, this is why.

The revolutionary potential of the new technologies will be ignited only when they are married to a new commercial destiny expressed in a new enterprise logic. Here for the first time is a technological medium that can enable the coordination of nearly limitless and detailed complexity. The new medium makes it possible to eliminate the replication of effort across organizations, merging infrastructure activities and linking enterprises in new *federations* oriented toward the support of individual moments of individual lives. We view federations as dynamic enterprise partnerships and alliances that can eliminate traditional industry boundaries to support individuals and particular constituencies of individuals in unique ways.

Federations have the potential to share a radically redefined cost structure that achieves *infrastructure convergence*. That means eliminating the replication of costs associated with the basic activities and functions enacted by every company—accounting, payroll, warehousing, logistics, etc.—as well as eliminating interfaces between enterprises. We anticipate the merger of infrastructure activities as they migrate to ubiquitous Web-based or distributed platforms. These common digital platforms will link federation enterprises and their respective networks, integrating a federation's strategically designed approach to deep support, along with a constant flow of products and services. Infrastructure convergence enables federations to lower infrastructure costs and levels of working capital by many orders of magnitude. This new cost structure makes it possible to offer various levels of deep support to individuals at every income level. Deep support is not a premium for the wealthy. It relies on a combination of human and automated systems to provide nourishment and advocacy for anyone, to the degree and in the form they choose.

In the coming chapters, we argue that the new individuals and their markets for deep support create the conditions for the next episode in economic history, which we call *the support economy*, based on the principles of *distributed capitalism*. Under managerial capitalism, ownership and control were separated for the first time in commercial history. Ownership was dispersed among many shareholders, but control was concentrated at the top of the managerial hierarchy. This made sense when value was "created" inside organizations, lodged in products and services, agglomerated in supply chains, and delivered to customers. Administrative oversight and top-down direction were required in order to achieve the standardization, efficiency, and low unit costs upon which a successful response to mass consumption depended. But in the new world of individuated consumption, value is dispersed. It is lodged in individual space and realized in relationships of deep support.

Once value is deemed to reside in individuals, everything changes. Firms no longer "create" value; they can only strive to realize the value that already exists in individual space. In this way, distributed capitalism further expands the concept of ownership. Not only is share ownership dispersed, but value itself is dispersed. Individuals "own" the sources of value, as all value originates in their needs, and all cash flows from the fulfillment of those needs. The dispersion of value necessitates the dispersion of control. Relationship value realization cannot be achieved through the hierarchical oversight of a central management structure. Instead, it will require the real-time collaboration of *advocates* and individuals in individual space. As the origins of value and the source of all cash flow, individuals can no longer be written off as anonymous "consumers" who sit at the far end of the value chain, devouring the value created by managers and underwritten by shareholders. Instead, they are preeminent stakeholders in the new collaborative structures that are fundamentally aligned with the requirements of relationship value realization.

In contrast, then, to managerial capitalism, distributed capitalism means that ownership *and* control are dispersed, shared by individual end consumers and their federation advocates. We liken this development to the shift from subject to citizen wrought by the spread of democracy and universal enfranchisement. Distributed capitalism announces a similar shift from consumer to individual. No longer an anonymous abstraction, the individual as the originator of all value and the source of all cash enjoys structurally based opportunities for the expression of voice and participation in governance—hence the emphasis on the distributive characteristics of the new capitalism and the collaborative processes that imbue the new enterprise logic. This critical tenet creates constant pressure to align all behavior around successful relationship value realization as the primary source of wealth creation.

The call for a further evolution of capitalism is not a sign of its weakness. Just the opposite is true. Crises of capitalism have been regularly predicted, with little accuracy. Instead, capitalism has proven to be vastly plastic and extraordinarily versatile. As an economic system, capitalism's capacity to evolve has been the source of its robustness and success. Capitalism has avoided devastating crises, not because it is permanent, but because it changes. Such change has meant that specific expressions of capitalism during a particular historical period have given way to newer, more comprehensive forms as social and technological conditions changed, leading to new strategic imperatives. Indeed, the various historical episodes of capitalism—mercantile, proprietary—have exhibited something like a beginning, a middle, and an end, as markets, technologies, and the organizational means of harnessing the two have shifted. In other words, the specific forms that capitalism takes have a limited range of adaptation. That these forms have changed with the centuries, however, is the heart of capitalism's strength and endurance.

In our view, the standard enterprise logic of managerial capitalism has by now traversed a similar arc, reaching the farthest borders of its adaptive range. The addition of new tools and techniques that translate into superficial change at the margins of the enterprise is simply not an adequate response to the historic challenges it faces in the new society of individuals. The demands associated with their new approach to consumption, coupled with the opportunities represented by the new technologies, now point to the urgent need for a new kind of capitalism that incorporates, but is much more than, what has gone before. In this process of what scientists call "hierarchical integration," a new framework is not merely a linear extension of its predecessor but integrates old elements in a new, more expansive and complex pattern. In this way, the support economy integrates the capabilities of earlier economies into a new and more capacious pattern, just as distributed capitalism integrates many of the elements of managerial capitalism into a new worldview.

I VALUE

Consider a young family in the not too distant future, as they learn to rely upon the deep support available to them in the new world of distributed capitalism. Lillian and Carlos Acero—she is a librarian and he is a software engineer—make use of several federations, including one that automates all their routine purchases and payments, such as telecommunications and utilities services. They also have one advocate, David, who supports their more complex consumption needs through a second federation. For example, when they travel, David monitors in-journey care, home oversight, communications, and cash-flow management, each according to instructions from the couple and subject to their daily input and control. When David arranges a business trip, Lillian elects to have the concierge service, which means that she is supported throughout the journey: Cancellations or other deviations from the schedule are managed proactively with alternative reservations, in-air food selections, and reading or video material; ground transportation and hotel accommodations are assigned and monitored; Lillian's luggage is shipped separately, and her clothes are stowed in her hotel room before her arrival.

When Lillian and Carlos decide to buy a new desktop computer for their nine-year-old daughter as a birthday present, they are discouraged by confusing Web sites and a manufacturer's 800 number that requires more than seven minutes in an automated decision tree. Instead, they decide to opt into help from their federation. Carlos finds several Web pages provided by the federation that are devoted to purchasing a computer, replete with advice, product information, and links to buyers' comments. In fewer than five minutes he completes a needs analyzer. The federation instantly offers three alternative packages, complete with technical details, prices, and links to independent evaluations and chat rooms where user information is available. Each alternative carries the federation's 100 percent guarantee, along with life-of-the-product support that includes child-content supervision, automatic quarterly software upgrades, firewall installation and maintenance, component upgrades, and technical service. Carlos selects his preferred package and receives an instant message from David that the unit will be delivered by 3:00 the next afternoon. He debates whether to request the "drop off" or "delivery, setup, and removal" option and finally chooses to simply have the unit left at his door.

The computer arrives on time, only two days before the birthday, and a federation e-mail is received that hour, asking for delivery confirmation. Carlos unpacks and sets up the computer, to check it before presenting it to his daughter. To his surprise, the unit produces an acrid smell that becomes more intense after an hour of use, when the monitor suddenly goes blank. Carlos contacts the federation "guarantees port" by e-mail. After describing the problem he receives an immediate response that a technical assessor will be in touch with him within thirty minutes. Twenty minutes later, he receives an e-mail from the assessor asking him to hold down the Start button on the hard drive for ten seconds and report back. Carlos quickly reports that nothing happened. There is an instant message that the power drive is probably faulty. A new unit will be delivered the next day, with complimentary setup and removal of the faulty equipment. Carlos responds with a note underscoring the importance of on-time delivery of a working unit so that he will be able to present the computer to his daughter on her birthday. The new unit is delivered the next afternoon, set up, and tested. There is also a

$100 voucher for additional software and a yellow teddy bear with a birth-day card from David attached to its large red bow. Carlos reckons he spent less than a half-hour dealing with the problem of the faulty computer and is glad he used the federation for his purchase.

Lillian learns that her mother has been diagnosed with an unusual blood disorder. After meeting with her mother's physician, she, her mother, Carlos, and the doctor contact David, who has also provided much of the older woman's deep support. David immediately puts the federation's systems to work on their behalf. They quickly receive up-to-date information on the disease, information on hospitals and doctors that specialize in relevant research and treatment, and descriptions of relevant clinical trials for experimental drug treatments. They are able to compare this information to that received from their physician's medical information hub. David directs them to an electronic dialogue conducted by people who have the disorder and their relatives. With a few structured queries to this constituency, they are able to identify individuals with experience in each of the key medical centers or physician groups that treat the disease. To save time, David assists them in carrying out more queries to these individuals. He also accesses other data that rate and evaluate physicians and medical facilities, including those recommended by their doctor.

Within two days they have assembled enough information to confer again with the mother's physician, plan a course of action, and narrow their choices to two specialists. Using the federation's health-support technologies, the physician's staff electronically sends all relevant medical tests and records to both specialists. David works with their offices to arrange video conferences with the family and their doctor. They decide, based on what they learn about each physician's practice and related medical facilities, to begin treatment with one of the specialists. David finalizes an appointment, and relevant insurance coverage is confirmed. Though the treatment center is in another state, David quickly coordinates the family's travel arrangements, along with complete in-journey concierge care. Lillian's sister comes to stay with the children, but David monitors and assists in the smooth functioning of the household. Even as treatment begins, David begins to explore the in-home care that Lillian's mother will require.

Does this seem too good to be true? If so, it is because our expectations as end consumers are already shaped by the anticipation of indifference and conflict. In fact, it could be like this. The new individuals are ready. Their needs are there. The markets for deep support exist. The technological cap-abilities are well developed. All that is missing is the new enterprise logic capable of reclaiming capitalism for all its constituencies as it builds a new bridge between the individual and the organization and reaps the wealth of a new era. The new enterprise logic will have to stake out new territory as it forges a new model spacious and strong enough to supersede antiquated institutional barriers, outmoded economic assumptions, and self-protective mentalities. It can accomplish this in much the same way that the movement toward managerial capitalism successfully reconfigured institutional boundaries more than a century ago: by offering more people more hope for a way of life that does a better job of fulfilling their needs and speaking to their dreams.

WHY "ORGANIZATIONAL CHANGE" IS NOT THE ANSWER

A policeman sees a man on his hands and knees under the lamppost, obviously searching for something. "What have you lost?" he asks.

"I have lost my keys," replies the man.

"Are you sure you dropped them under the lamppost?" the policeman queries.

"No," says the man. "I lost them over there," motioning toward the darkness.

"Then why are you looking for them here?" asks the bewildered policeman.

"Because," the man continues steadily, "this is where the light is."

The light is shining over our organizations, and it is there managers seek solutions, using the management tools, old and new, available to them. They try everything in the kit, from amputation to bolting on a new appendage. They streamline the plumbing, enhance the superstructure, custom-configure their products, put the marketing department on steroids, spin off an e-business, or put inventory on the Internet. They merge, they downsize, they experiment with new pricing regimes, integrate the supply chain, try to manage knowledge, or reconceptualize the organizational chart—it's a diamond, a shamrock, a blueberry pancake, a pepperoni pizza, an orchestra, a team of astronauts. It's clicks; no, it's bricks; it's bricks and clicks. . . .

All of this activity is what there is to do—because that's where the light is shining. And it's okay, unless there is a bona fide discontinuity. At those times, shoring up, paring down, adding on—none of it makes enough difference. Customer solutions developed in organization space merely perpetuate the fundamental problems whose symptoms they seek to address. Another cautionary tale comes to mind—something about rearranging the deck chairs on a very large steamship that is only a few miles from a fatal mountain of ice. Here is what we can learn: When we face discontinuity, the answers we seek cannot be found under the light from the lamppost. They are not here, but over there—in the darkness, through the looking glass, on the other side of what is known.

Organizations, indeed whole economies, are like all living systems—they seek stability and predictability, not crisis or revolution. Today, many biologists, life-span psychologists, organizational theorists, and institutional economists share a new perspective on how organisms change. Evolution is no longer regarded as simply a gradual process of adaptive change, fed by random mutation. The new perspective recognizes that every living system has its own unique "deep structure," a highly durable order that expresses its internal organization as well as the basic activities that define its existence and govern its interactions with the environment. One theorist suggests thinking of deep structure as the design of the playing field and the rules of the game.[12] Organisms live through extended periods of equilibrium during which they may experience many adaptive changes, but those changes do not affect their deep structure. During periods of stability, it is the deep structure that allows the organism to persist, to reproduce itself, and to limit change; "it generates a strong inertia, first to prevent the system from generating alternatives outside its own boundaries, then to pull any deviations that do occur back into line."[13]

Occasionally, however, equilibrium is punctuated by intense periods of qualitative, metamorphic change—revolution. Revolutionary periods derive their momentous character from the fact that the deep structure itself is what undergoes change. The system experiences a wholesale transformation of its deep structure, which must be disassembled in order for any fundamental changes to be accomplished. To contrast adaptation with revolution, let's return to the game analogy. In a game of tennis, adaptive change during a stable period might involve changing the material composition of the racket and the height of the net. But if the rackets and the net were eliminated entirely? That is a revolution. The first sort of change leaves the deep structure intact. The second dismantles it. Adaptive change can occur at the margins of the system, without affecting the deep structure. Revolutionary change alters the basic structures and therefore affects every premise, assumption, and activity that derives from or depends upon those structures. Revolutionary change is systemic and irreversible. Nothing can be the same again.

For nearly thirty years, we have heard about the end of the industrial economy and its prototypical enterprise logic. Revolutionary transformation has been posited in many different ways: a postindustrial economy, a service economy, an information economy, a knowledge economy, a digital economy. In the heat of global competition, managers have been exhorted to move beyond the mass-production model and rediscover their customers through so-called revolutionary innovations in marketing, quality, reengineering, customization, personalization. Each new "revolution" has been followed up by scores of books, articles, and academic studies telling firms how to change from what they were to what they must become. Often there are examples of the "pioneers" who have throttled history to be new. Sometimes it is only a matter of months before the pioneers are derided as failures. The pronouncements all begin to sound the same. They rail against the same mass-production mentality and with some alteration of vocabulary prescribe the same kinds of remedies—less hierarchy, more teams, open and visionary leadership, shared knowledge, and a customer orientation that is flexible, innovative, creative, customized, educational, family friendly, and so on. Change management itself has become a global industry, swelling the ranks of consultancies around the world.

While many are prepared to say that the mass-production model of organization is dead, few seem willing to confront the fact that mass production and managerial capitalism are twin born. They find their joint expression in the standard enterprise logic of today's approach to commercial activity that aims to create value through the production of goods and services in organization space. Its purpose was to harness technology to meet the needs of expanding markets. Its goal was to drive high volumes of transactions by providing products at ever-lower cost. Its methods depended upon replacing market mechanisms with administrative coordination that was able to yield lower costs, higher productivity, and steadily increasing profits. To accomplish this it required a new managerial hierarchy with a relentless internal focus on the control and measurement of production and distribution. Managers and engineers inherited the task of planning and overseeing a minute division of labor to accomplish the standardization, increased throughput, and reduced unit costs necessary to meet the new demands of mass consumption. In this new structure, massive capital requirements forced the diversification of ownership through public shareholding, and salaried managers assumed the rights to determine policy and oversee operations.[14] The system evolved as a hierarchy of orbiting interests, with professional managers at its center and successive orbits inhabited by shareholders, employees, suppliers, business customers, and finally, in the farthest orbit of all, end consumers. In this hierarchy, value is regarded as a zero-sum game in which competing interests plot the tug-of-war games that will yield them the greatest economic return, typically at the expense of the other groups and their respective interests.

By now, the standard enterprise logic has become so deeply taken for granted that it is no longer visible. People do not question assumptions that they no longer see. If the changes that have been prescribed were inevitable, or even likely, they would not be preoccupying so many smart people for such a long time. A brilliant European sociologist, Norbert Elias, wrote a history of manners called *The Civilizing Process*.[15] He figured out how people conducted themselves in the intimate matters of daily life many centuries ago by reading what the authors of etiquette books were telling them not to do. Why write books telling people not to defecate in public, he reasoned, if that's not exactly what people were doing all the time? And so it is today. Change management would not be the industry it is if organizations were changing. Change management is huge precisely because organizations are *not* fundamentally changing.

Like other living systems, the standard enterprise logic is organized to reproduce itself at all costs, even when it is commercially irrational to do so. It is through these processes, so often undiscussable, that organizations defy change, even when they say they are changing.[16] Neither the growth of service businesses, the preeminence of knowledge-based work, nor the shift from atoms to digits have transformed the deep structure of the firm under managerial capitalism, as many have predicted they would. Rather, they have been used by it as opportunities for self-extension and reproduction. These innovations, no matter how dramatic, have been absorbed into the rules of the same old game.

The truth of these matters has thus far surfaced in fragments, strained and refracted through the grid of the current enterprise logic and the larger framework of managerial capitalism that it expresses. There is a good deal of rhetoric concerning a new awareness of consumers as individuals and the role that new technologies might play in addressing their needs. However, most of the responses to this sense of historic change have taken conventional forms, leading to adaptation, not revolution. There has been downsizing and streamlining to improve operational excellence and lower costs—supposedly to better serve the end consumer. Some firms have shifted their advertising strategies to appeal to the new sense of individuality. Organizations have invested heavily in new information technologies and electronic commerce. Some marketing departments have been updated with an emphasis on gathering more data on customers, customer-focused information systems, and

so-called one-to-one marketing. Some manufacturing units have used technology investments to increase their ability to customize products, an approach known as "mass customization." It is not uncommon to see initiatives
occurring on several of these fronts, led by different teams and unrelated to
one another.

We believe that these innovations, important as they may be, barely
constitute a tug on the sleeve of the deeply entrenched economic and organizational logic that undergirds the firm today. Each such innovation is a fragmented reflection of the historical forces that are engulfing us. Each is an
effort to adapt to these new forces at the margins of the organization, without disturbing its deep structure. As a result, neither individually nor collec-
tively do they constitute a serious basis for a new enterprise logic.

Consider an old Yiddish joke about a man who went to the tailor to
have his suit altered. The shoulders were too tight, the left sleeve too long,
the right pant leg too short. The man put the suit on and stood in front of the
mirror. The tailor walked around him, clucking knowingly, shaking his head
at the ill-fitting garment. First, the tailor counseled the man to pinch his
shoulders together. The jacket no longer felt too tight! Next, he told the man
to lift his left arm and bend his elbow. The left sleeve didn't look too long
anymore! Finally, he advised his customer to lift his left leg and bend his knee.
Amazingly, the legs now appeared to be the same length! With his shoulders
pinched together, his left arm raised and bent, and hopping on his right foot,
the man contemplated his suit. It was now a perfect fit! He gratefully paid
the tailor's bill and, looking like a cheerful exotic bird, hopped out of the
tailor's shop. The problem arose as he went to run for the bus.

The innovations we have mentioned create the corporate equivalent of
the man with the ill-fitting suit. Customer relationship management systems?
"Just pinch your shoulders together." Mass customization? "Hold your left
arm up." One-to-one marketing? "Left leg bent at the knee, please." A move
to the Internet? A wireless platform? "Now, hop!" These are attempts to
make the suit fit without cutting into the cloth or fundamentally altering its
design. These innovations do not produce the standard enterprise logic transformed and reborn. Rather, they reveal today's commercial organizations at
the breaking point—strained, cracked, and stretched to their very limit as
they attempt to confront challenges that they were never designed to address
and that are in conflict with their nature and purpose.

We have concluded that there is no methodology, no silver bullet, no
amount of heroic leadership that can transform an organization as long as
the tightly woven web of precepts, assumptions, and practices of managerial
capitalism remain intact. We regard most managers as extremely capable and

often brilliant. But we know that as long as they are imprisoned within today's enterprise logic, they are no more likely to transform themselves into what we need for tomorrow than the business owners at the turn of the last century were able to transform themselves into the worldly professionals who administer business today.

INTO THE DARKNESS

Yet revolutions do occur. Though rare, revolutionary change can be triggered when a system's deep structure does not provide the necessary resources to meet the challenges it faces. In a very different context, Thomas Kuhn illustrated this sort of process in his work on the structure of scientific revolutions.[17] Scientists use paradigms in their normal research. But sometimes their normal accomplishments make the paradigm they are using obsolete by running up against puzzles or observations that the paradigm can neither solve nor accommodate. That is when a paradigm shift becomes necessary. Sadly, Kuhn's work has frequently been misappropriated, especially in the business literature, where normal adaptive change is routinely hailed as a "paradigm shift." In fact, a paradigmatic shift occurs only when there is change in the deep structure. In the business world, changes in the deep structure of commercial activity—what we call the enterprise logic—have occurred in cycles of more or less one hundred years since the first industrial revolution in the eighteenth century.

Consider a vital issue. A challenge to the deep structure does not necessarily result in revolutionary change. That is only one among many possibilities. More typically, people do not see what's coming. Events are not read as an indication that people should change what they are doing or how they are thinking. On the contrary, challenging events are often regarded as a signal that people should do the same thing they already know how to do, only even more assiduously than before. Sometimes these responses to grave challenges are deeply unhealthy and actually weaken the person, group, or conceptual system, but people feel compelled to reproduce what they already know how to do. Consider Detroit's elite families in the first years of the twentieth century. They were heavily invested in a variety of automobile companies, each trying to produce a more elaborate and expensive vehicle that would impress and appeal to their social peers. They lost much capital and eventually lost all their investments in the industry because they could not and would not consider other strategies. Producing cars for ordinary people was beneath them. Henry Ford alone saw the opportunity to change the pattern and change capitalism too.[18] As one theorist succinctly put it, "groups and organizations may rely more heavily on old routines when faced with decline."[19]

It seems prudent, then, to regard the challenge of discontinuity with some reverence. The standard enterprise logic that has ruled the century continues to dominate the practical and imaginative life of today's managers. As a result, most of the efforts that come to be regarded as paradigmatic change are merely incremental adaptations that occur at the margin of the standard enterprise logic but leave its core undisturbed. These innovations are inherently fragile and difficult to sustain because they are fundamentally at odds with the deep structure of the organization. New remedies are always needed to shore up the last round of fixes. Managers are thrown into a perennial search for the next silver bullet, as eager and needy as they are cynical. Firms gyrate like out-of-control bulimics, purging themselves of employees and customers, then bulking up in order to drive growth again.

No such remedies are presented in this book. Indeed, the challenges and opportunities we discuss are of a different order. We argue that the discontinuity represented by the new society of individuals and their markets for deep support present an insurmountable challenge to the standard enterprise logic of managerial capitalism. This is precisely the sort of challenge that has led to economic revolutions in the past. If the newly minted mass markets of a century ago gave impetus to a revolutionary new enterprise logic called managerial capitalism, then it is reasonable to conclude that the new society of individuals of the twenty-first century, with wholly different needs and expectations, might also stimulate the invention of a fundamentally different approach to wealth creation. Thanks to the deeply institutionalized forces of inertia that have today's commercial organizations in their grip, new market forces are stirring in opposition, searching for alternatives outside the circle of light from the lamppost. In these new markets lies the opportunity for revolutionary change.

So what is it that must change? What are the pieces from which a new kind of capitalism can be fashioned, truly suited to a new society of individuals, with its individuated approach to consumption and its new markets for deep support? There is no one thing that must change, and so the light is not shining where we want to look. It is not the marketing or the manufacturing functions that must change. It is not even the organization itself. It is not top-management leadership, governance, customer service, the Internet strategy, shareholder relations, the information architecture, accounting principles, the supply chain, or customer relationships. It is not the employment contract, career ladders, or the organization of work and its relation to the family.

What must change is the systemic logic that defines each of these pieces and holds them together in one particular way. This logic is not unalterable. It is not divinely ordained and beyond human grasp. It is the result of very canny commercial inventions intended to make money by way of fueling mass consumption. It is a logic that has been developed, perfected, and diffused over the last one hundred years or so. It is a spectacularly successful historical construction that has now outlived its purpose, even as it maintains an iron grip on the way economic, social, and psychological life is conducted. Miraculously, it manages to do all this while accompanied by a ceaseless cascade of claims testifying to its transformation. The kind of change we describe will not occur under the lamppost. Instead, it requires the courage to explore what has been left in darkness.

To summarize: Now, at the dawn of the twenty-first century, people have new dreams. In spite of the heterodoxy and diversity that mark the advanced societies, we observe a common source for many of these dreams. It is expressed in a psychological awareness of one's own complex individuality. Today's people experience themselves first as individuals and share a common longing for psychological self-determination. There are many who have lamented this, seeing only an erosion of community and the spread of narcissism. We, on the other hand, celebrate this psychological achievement as an important milestone in the evolution of humanity.

As a result of these new dreams, a chasm has opened up between people and the organizations upon which they depend. People have undergone a discontinuity in mentality, but organizations have not. Business organizations, and other institutions too, continue to treat the new individuals according to the terms of the older mass society. Individuals reach out from the intricacy of their lives in search of understanding, accommodation, and support, but the complexity of their needs and desires is ignored. Instead, they are greeted by the metaphorical equivalent of the assembly line, expressed in the internally consistent set of practices, attitudes, and assumptions we call an enterprise logic.

But the chasm between new individuals and old organizations also contains the seeds of the next economic revolution. History suggests that the next great era of commercial innovation will require more than the production or exploitation of new technologies, however creative that undertaking may be. The next revolution in wealth creation will draw life, first and foremost, from a profound grasp of the new society of individuals and its expression in a new kind of consumption. Only the full force of this understanding can ignite the entrepreneurial innovation capable of leading such a revolution and paving the way toward a support economy and a new episode of capitalism. That innovation will entail discontinuity. It will be as radical a break with the past as the break that today's people have made with the lives of their grandparents and great-grandparents. It will be as radical a break with the past as managerial capitalism was a break with the practices of proprietary capitalism and craft production that preceded it.

THIS BOOK

This book proceeds in three movements: "challenge," "crisis," and "emergence." Part One, "Challenge," reaches back over the last one hundred years to explore the structure of earlier economic revolutions and the rise of the standard enterprise logic. It investigates the rise of the new society of individuals, individuated consumption, and the new markets for deep support. It examines the explosive challenges that these new developments present to the status quo of managerial capitalism, and the opportunities for wealth creation they represent.

Part Two, "Crisis," focuses on what happens when the new individuals in their roles as end consumers confront the old organizations. It examines the resulting transaction crisis and considers why it is that the standard enterprise logic has been unable to overcome it. This initiates a journey through the social psychology of the modern organization, particularly as it helps explain the adversarial relations between the worlds of "producers" and "consumers." Finally, it critically inspects a range of recent innovations aimed at "transforming" the organization and its relationships with end consumers.

Part Three, "Emergence," addresses the opportunity for economic revolution—commercial inventions that reflect our times as they speak to the yearnings of the new individuals and their needs for deep support. The recent history of electronic commerce is explored in order to understand how the new technologies can be recast as an important part of the bridge across the chasm of the transaction crisis and thus grow into their critical role in the construction of a support economy. Here we lay out the metaprinciples that can point the way toward a new enterprise logic as they redefine the purpose of commercial activity and express the deep structure of a new distributed capitalism. Here too is an examination of the kinds of commercial inventions that will be necessary to meet the demands of the new markets for deep support and so bring to life dramatic new possibilities for wealth creation.

A warning: This is not a dispassionate book. It expresses a theory of the future based on an analysis of the past and a diagnosis of the present. A theory of the future does not begin with worshipful and awestruck forecasts of new technologies. That is the sort of reasoning that led "futurists" a century ago to envision twenty-first century people flying to work powered by their own propellers. A theory of the future depends upon engaging with the deeper currents of human yearning. Ours is a way of exploring the future that looks deeply into the present. It suggests that history does not run in straight lines but more often in spirals and Möbius loops as possibilities fulfill themselves and become something altogether different from, and sometimes even antithetical to, their origins. Our style of prophecy does not want a crystal ball or even a crow's nest. It wants unflinching observation of the lines of force that already shape us, and the grit to follow their cracks and fissures as they spread and swell and rupture what was once true.

Let's remember what's at stake: *People have changed more than the organizations upon which their well-being depends.* The chasm that now separates them conceals the resources for a support economy based on the enterprise logic that we have named distributed capitalism. It is this magnitude of invention that will unleash the next leap forward in wealth creation, even as it frees today's individuals from shouldering more than their share of the burden of historical change.

PART ONE

CHALLENGE

NEW PEOPLE, NEW MARKETS

TWO

Dreaming Economic Revolution

During the last decade of the twentieth century, the concept of a "new economy" gained credence. Its proponents were hard to resist, as they inevitably cited the marvels of new information technologies. The jewel in the crown was the Internet, which, it was said, was transforming the nature of business. The new technologies were finally beginning to demonstrate their long-promised impact upon the nation's productivity, unleashing the possibility of unabated economic growth.

THREE INGREDIENTS FOR ECONOMIC REVOLUTION

There were "new economy" naysayers too. They typically disputed information technology's role in productivity growth and questioned the real significance of the Internet for the broader economy.[1] While the balls of this debate were lobbed back and forth, with many spectators riveted on the game, something else happened. Too many new economy companies failed to deliver on inflated promises and their valuations plummeted. As suddenly as it all began, old economy companies began to look like the real pros after all. The proselytizing icons of the new economy were left with a lot of explaining to do, but they seemed as dazed and confused as the people who had followed their advice.

In fact, new economy enthusiasts, cynics, and their eager spectators were only the latest generation to be seduced by the fantasies of extreme transformation associated with a new technology. Things that we can see, touch, and measure have a way of taking precedence over other less well defined matters of daily life like attitudes, feelings, tastes, needs, desires, and dreams. Hard drives out soft, or so runs the cliché, and it certainly tends toward truth in the business world. And so it is when we think about the big changes in economic history. We point to the "hard" things—technologies like the steam engine and the power loom, the railroad, the factory and the assembly line, or the computer and the Internet—when we want to explain the great leaps forward in wealth creation that have accompanied those fertile periods of discontinuous innovation known as industrial revolutions. But just because it's easier to count hard things doesn't mean that they always deserve their status. More often than not, letting the hard drive out the soft eliminates crucial sources of insight.

As evidence of this tendency, our attention has typically focused on the "industry" in industrial revolutions. New machines and new methods of production have been the center-stage attractions in most accounts of those great turning points in history. But during the past twenty years, a new school of historians has begun to reveal a much more complex reality. The new history shows that people, not just machines, make economic revolutions. In fact, history suggests that the best way to imagine the future of an economy is to ground your thinking in a deep appreciation of its people and their dreams. How do people yearn to live their lives? What do they long for?

The last two major economic revolutions worked just this way. In the late eighteenth century in Britain, and again in the late nineteenth and early twentieth centuries in the United States, dramatic changes in what people yearned for brought forth radically new organizational conceptions that harnessed technologies in new ways. These inventions resulted in a cornucopia of new consumer goods, provoked enduring changes in the nature of capitalism, and enabled the great leaps forward in wealth creation associated with the first and second industrial revolutions.[2] Some have even argued that these changes in consumption were responsible for capitalism itself.[3] Even Max Weber emphasized in his *General Economic History* that "the decisive impetus toward capitalism could come only from one source, namely a mass market demand."[4] "Why is it," one historian asked, "that consumption, which is the linchpin of our modern system, has never been the linchpin of our theories explaining modernity?"[5]

The idea of a new economy based on new digital technologies like the Internet, or whatever succeeds it, is a classic example of "hard driving out soft." The old misconceptions about the origins of an industrial revolution were repeated as the dramatically visible presence of new digital technologies—speeding up production, transactions, and communication while reducing their associated costs—led many people to the conclusion that "newer, faster, and cheaper" also meant "different." The belief was that these new technologies were sufficient to create a third industrial revolution. But history-making entrepreneurial breakthroughs do not come from new technologies alone. They are not simply better executed or more dazzling incarnations of the old capitalism on a new technological platform. Instead, they emerge as a response to people and the new lives they yearn to live. In each era, the breakthroughs that become the vanguard of a new economy are once-unimaginable solutions designed to use technologies to fulfill the dreams of people as they are expressed in a changing approach to consumption.

Economic revolutions, then, arise from the complex interplay of three forces: a new structure of consumption, technologies aligned with the new consumption, and a new enterprise logic capable of linking people, technologies, and markets in a new way. In this book, we will address all three forces, but in Part One we intend to concentrate on the first crucial component for a new economy: the growing presence of new kinds of people who yearn to live differently than people lived in the past. We will argue that, however varied their reasons, today's people share new dreams of psychological self-determination that in turn create new markets characterized by wholly new approaches to consumption. These dreams are the seedbed for a new enterprise logic that will bend new technologies to a new set of purposes. Herein lies the opportunity for the kind of economic revolution that gives way to a new era of capitalism and provides the foundation for a support economy. The best way to anticipate these possibilities is to consider how these dynamic forces have converged in the past.

THE FIRST FIELD OF DREAMS

The first industrial revolution took root in mid-eighteenth-century England. That "new economy" is now viewed by many historians as the result of a "consumer boom . . . a convulsion of getting and spending . . . such as to bring about as great a change in the lifestyle of the population as was brought about by the Neolithic revolution in agriculture which began some eight thousand years before the birth of Christ."[6] The English upper classes indulged in what has been described as an "orgy of spending" trained on domestic luxuries from mansions to jewels, pottery, gardens, and zoos. But the epicenter of the consumer boom was located in the middle classes. They began to buy the sorts of things that previously only the rich had enjoyed.[7]

It was a time when luxuries were reinterpreted as "decencies," and decencies became necessities.[8] The new middle-class thirst for material improvement, fashion, and luxury was emulated by working-class families too.[9] In 1767 the political economist Nathaniel Forster worried that "fashionable luxury" was spreading "like a contagion," as he complained of the "perpetual restless ambition in each of the inferior ranks to raise themselves to the level of those immediately above them."[10]

The prosperity that fueled this democratization of consumption arose from a source that is familiar to us today. Family incomes rose as women (and children) left the drudgery of their cottages and fields—where they had worked long hours without wages—and streamed into the emerging industrial centers, becoming the dominant workforce in the new textile mills. For the first time, many women became independent wage earners, and to a lesser extent, so did their children. Historians estimate that, as a result of these new sources of income, the number of working-class families able to afford consumer goods rose from about 15 percent to 25 percent between 1750 and 1780 alone.[11]

This explains why so many of the great fortunes of the first industrial revolution arose from small items of household consumption—items that represented the commercialization of women's needs and desires. First, families had to buy the things that women once made at home: clothes, beer, candles, pottery. Then there was an increased demand for goods dominated by female consumer choice: clothes, curtains, linens, pottery, cutlery, furniture, brass and copper for the home, buckles, buttons, and all manner of fashion accessories. Remember, Adam Smith used the manufacture of pins as the basis for his famous description of the division of labor. The first modern study of business was based on an analysis of the factory of Peter Stubs, a nail maker. Birmingham's prosperity was built on the fabrication of buttons, buckles, and candlesticks. Sheffield grew wealthy on the profits of cutlery, Staffordshire on crockery, and Manchester on textiles. Other areas prospered on hats and gloves, belts and wigs, shoes and dresses, copper saucepans, chairs and tables.[12]

Eighteenth-century observers, and many who came later, tended to ignore this new consumption story and the women behind it. Some disapproved of it; others simply didn't understand its importance. Then, as now, social critics complained about the breakdown of the family, the loosening of morals, the threat to authority, the loss of femininity. Nevertheless, these changes in women's experience, income, needs, and dreams fueled the economic revolution in eighteenth-century Britain.[13] As one scholar of the subject observed, "If the entrepreneur is rightly seen as the most important human link between the non-economic variables and the production end of the economy, then the female consumer should be seen as the most important human link between them and the demand side of the economy."[14]

The entrepreneurs bent on responding to the new democratization of consumption faced the need to invent a new kind of enterprise capable of increased production. This led to the rise of the factory system.[15] The enterprise logic that emerged from their efforts was a dramatic contrast to the traditions of household production and forced labor that characterized the preindustrial world. Josiah Wedgwood stood out then and now as an innovator whose inventions were widely adapted. He understood the powerful urge among the middle classes to improve their quality of life through acquiring goods that imitated their social superiors. Wedgwood revolutionized salesmanship and achieved enormous commercial success with his energetic determination to understand and meet the needs of diverse consumer groups. He won commissions of his "creamware" to royalty and gentry and used royal patronage to cunningly market his wares to "the Middling Class of People . . . infinitely superior in number to the Great."[16]

Wedgwood also won acclaim for the exacting standards of organization that he imposed on an ever-reluctant workforce in his famous Etruria works. He increased production by standardizing and simplifying his methods, utilizing many interchangeable handles and ornaments, and substituting engine-powered lathes for some handwork. He devised a more efficient division of labor and trained his own workers, as it was not possible to hire people with the specialized skills required by his approach. He insisted on labor discipline and punctuality, including rigorous use of the factory bell, a clocking-in system, clerks to oversee production, and detailed guidelines addressing every aspect of the manufacturing process and the exacting behavior it required. He pioneered the financial analysis of manufacturing, and in the process he came to understand the difference between fixed and variable costs and the effects of each on profit.[17] He cleverly controlled production levels, limiting the supply of many of his popular lines in order to keep his prices high.[18]

Wedgwood's innovations were widely copied, but even they were only part of a larger scene teeming with pathbreaking innovation and invention. In 1769 when Wedgwood opened his pottery factory at Etruria, James Watt patented the steam engine (his patent for the locomotive would follow fifteen years later) and Richard Arkwright invented the water-powered spinning frame. Within another three years James Hargreaves patented the spinning jenny, and by 1776 Adam Smith systematized and extended much of the economic thinking that animated the new enterprises in his treatise on political economy, *The Wealth of Nations*. His work helped to consolidate the new enterprise logic that would come to be known as "proprietary capitalism."[19]

That new enterprise logic opened up new ways of connecting with consumers—inventing new sales and distribution channels, brand awareness, and marketing communications. It drew people from cottages and fields to a central production site in order to exploit power sources that eliminated the age-old dependence on animal power and plant growth. It relied upon increasingly mechanized equipment, breaking the ancient links between production and the limitations of the human body. It emphasized rationality and eventually science, breaking the vice of inherited tradition that had governed craft production.[20] It experimented with a more specialized division of labor and devised new methods to impose labor discipline on a labor force driven more by compulsion than by choice.[21] Centralization, mechanization, and organization made it possible to meet the rising levels of demand, increasing the size of the workforce along with its efficiency and volume of production.

Most significantly, the new approach concentrated the ownership of once-fragmented commercial processes—including marketing, recruitment, factory organization, product design, production planning, accounting, finance, labor supervision, and often the invention or design of new equipment.[22] The prevailing view was that only ownership could assure the honest and productive use of capital.[23] This view was elaborated by Adam Smith and many others writing at the time.[24] Successful management, it was believed, was a function of the direct involvement of ownership; delegation doomed a business to failure. This perspective guided the centralization of once disparate commercial activities within the new industrial concern. It also encouraged owners not to enlarge their firms beyond the point at which they could oversee things themselves. While some of the new works employed a small number of clerks or foremen, the concept of management as we know it today did not yet exist.

But there remains a puzzle in all of this. If the democratization of consumption ignited the first industrial revolution, how do we explain why middle- and working-class people decided to spend their money rather than save it, as they had tended to do in the past? Somewhere along the way, consumption had developed a new meaning. We need to grasp how this occurred, because it is essential to understanding the powerful consequences of the new consumption that confronts us today.

THE INVENTION OF MODERN PLEASURE

The acceleration of industrialization followed the rise of the human capacity for imaginative daydreams, longing, and fantasy.[25] The capacity to long for a better, more pleasurable quality of life is not simply indigenous to human beings. This kind of longing is as modern as the once startling claims set forward in the U.S. Declaration of Independence to "life, liberty, and the pursuit of happiness." It was introduced to the human scene with the nascent experience of individuality that first took root in the early eighteenth century and has been gathering strength ever since. Only when human beings learned to imagine pleasure and experience it as an inward emotion did they begin to long for the kinds of objects and experiences that could stimulate and prolong those feelings. This longing is the human core of what in modern economics are called "markets." It helped to ignite the explosions of industrialization that occurred first in the mid-eighteenth century and then again in the late nineteenth and early twentieth centuries.

For people in ancient societies, whose consciousness was fixed by myth, ritual, and social precedent, pleasure seems to have had a very different meaning. The ancient pattern was to value experiences for the pleasurable sensations and emotions attached to them, and the list of pleasures was pretty short—eating, drinking, sex, socializing, singing, dancing, games, and spectacles. Pleasure was not located in the meaning that a person attached to an experience, but rather in the objects of that experience. In ancient Rome, for example, pleasure was considered to be located in a lavish banquet or an exciting spectacle at the Coliseum. Judging the degree of pleasure in a feast was straightforward. It hung upon the presence of dining couches, the number and variety of boiled, sugared meats, the complexity of their sauces, the diversity of fruits, the strength of the wine, the quality of the music, dancing, and other entertainments, the status of the assembled guests.

The absence of the right elements also meant an absence of pleasure. This is because people thought of pleasure—and all emotions—as located in things outside themselves, not in the subjective experience of those things. Pleasurable sensations were attached to certain objects, and objects were valued in terms of their intrinsic pleasure quotient. The more of those objects that were present, the more pleasure there was to be had. This helps to explain the endless parade of delectables and the forced vomiting in order to be able to have more pleasure. It would have been difficult to sit at a poorly laid table and feel compensatory pleasure from, say, an illuminating conversation or a bit of successful networking. As one historian observes, the ancient Romans were strangers "to modern subjectivism, to our thirst for experience. Standing apart from the world, we choose to experience something in order to see what effect it has, not because it is intrinsically valuable."[26] In the modern result, people are willing to pay for brand names and designer labels out of all proportion to their actual "value." That is because value itself is now a subjective, rather than an objective, proposition. It arises from the meanings with which we invest things, not from the things themselves.

It was not until the eighteenth century that people began to think of meanings and emotions as "inside" rather than linked to objects in the external world. Sociologist Max Weber called this the "disenchantment" of the world and regarded it as the threshold separating traditional from modern life. This disenchantment accompanied people's growing self-consciousness of themselves as individuals. What fed this new self-awareness? While there are many detailed analyses of this important development, for our story we need only mention a few of the highlights.

Most historians agree that the Protestant Reformation had a critical role to play in the early experience of subjective individuality and the relocation of emotions inside people rather than outside in the world. Protestantism insisted on personal meaning to supplant the external symbols and institutional authority of the Church. The philosophers of the Enlightenment also made the eighteenth century a turning point in the movement toward individual political rights, as expressed most prominently in the French and American Revolutions. Literacy was another powerful force in the rise of subjectivity, as it gave people the means to privately manipulate language and its meanings. By the mid-eighteenth century, the novel had become a hugely popular form of expression and communication, especially the romantic novel with its female readership. Novels enhanced people's creative capacity, and they invested a new legitimacy in the imagination of the common person.

Changes in family life also contributed to the rise of a subjective sense of individuality. The traditional family was deeply enmeshed in the community. In colonial America, much as in pre-modern Western Europe, there were few boundaries between what people today think of as public and private life. If a person transgressed some important social rule—not paying debts, some forms of infidelity—it wasn't the family that enacted discipline so much as the villagers or townspeople. In some parts of Western Europe, a person who violated the law or an important convention could expect a crowd to show up in the middle of the night wearing masks, banging pots and pans, and blowing on cow horns. Maybe they dragged him outside to jeer at his poor, shivering body. Maybe they burned him in effigy, making sport of his humiliation. In colonial America he might have spent a day in the stocks being insulted by his fellow townspeople, or a woman might have been forced to wear the scarlet letter.[27]

It wasn't until the eighteenth century that people slowly began to place more importance on their own feelings and intimate relationships, and less on their conformity to communal norms—a development that family historian Edward Shorter has called "the great transformation."[28] This sea change in human experience was expressed in three arenas. The first was the growing belief in romantic love as people began to want to choose their own marital partners. Romantic love detached the couple from the supervision of the community and turned it inward. The second arena was mother love. As infant mortality declined, women began to regard their babies as unique creatures requiring nurturing, safety, love, and comfort.[29] Mothers became more emotionally attached to their infants and began to put their welfare ahead of other obligations. As women turned their energies toward their children, they too shifted their attention away from communal activities.

The third arena was "domesticity," a word that describes the new emphasis on the privacy and intimacy of the nuclear family. People began to rely more on family members for emotional, not just material, support. The family became more of a closed circle in which people assumed they had more in common with each other than with their neighbors. This new domestic solidarity completed the nest created by the loving couple and the mother-child bond. It drew the family away from the community and into the emotional shelter of the home.[30] By the middle of the eighteenth century, especially among aristocratic and upper-class families, homes were reorganized into public and family rooms, expressing a new code of manners that emphasized the nuclear family unit. As families were freed from community regulation and surveillance, the foundations were laid for the gradual emergence of the psychological individual from the defining context of the group, and eventually from the family itself.[31] All of this led to a new dimension of human experience that today is thought of as "private life."

This new possibility of individuality spread modestly, throughout the eighteenth and nineteenth centuries, primarily in the United Kingdom, Western Europe, and the United States. It was reflected in a variety of new and subtle developments that are entirely taken for granted in these societies today. For example, people increasingly turned away from the strict rules governing the transmission of family names in order to bestow unique names upon their children. More people became able to sign their names, and initials began showing up on clothing and accessories. There was a new appreciation of animals as pets became popular and were regarded as individual creatures worthy of human sentiment. The looking glass had been an aristocratic luxury, but by the nineteenth century mirrors appeared in more ordinary homes, and for the first time many people had an opportunity to see their own image. Portraiture migrated from the upper to the middle classes, a trend later accelerated by the invention of photography, which meant that for the first time common people could possess images of themselves. Tombstones were newly carved with individual epitaphs and often included small portraits embedded in the stone.

There was also a new interest in, and growing knowledge about, the body—its internal organs and their functions, its hygiene, health, and grooming. As hygiene and overall health improved, infant mortality decreased and people began to live longer. As a result, they also became more attached to one another as special, irreplaceable individuals, and death became an occasion for a deeper and lasting grief.[32] The reproductive process was better understood too, and rudimentary contraceptive devices were invented. These new developments formed the context in which, by the end of the nineteenth century, the human psyche itself became the object of intense scrutiny, debate, and inquiry.[33]

With this new capacity for subjectivity, the experience of pleasure gradually shifted from concrete objects to imagined ones. Pleasurable experiences could be imagined, and that very act of imagination was pleasurable. Modern pleasure-seeking was freed from the concrete world to expand limitlessly in the world of imagination. Once people learned to recast pleasure in this way, they wanted their dreams to come true. The desire to experience in reality the pleasures already enjoyed in imagination motivated people to buy things. This new psychological motivation helps explain the propensity toward consumption that played such a crucial role in the economic explosion of the mid-eighteenth century and that continued to fuel subsequent waves of economic growth.[34]

But as fashion designers have known for 300 years, reality is never as satisfying as dreams, and purchases are easily set aside in the pursuit of fresh desire. A new and restless dynamic was thus established, animated by an unquenchable eagerness to embrace the promise of ever new pleasures. The modern attitude toward longing was born in this interplay between fantasy and reality.[35] In this way, the nascent stirrings of individuality brought forth a new human capacity for subjectivity that relocated pleasure and fulfillment in the imagination. And it was this new imaginative life—above all, among women—that also became the motivating force behind that very modern phenomenon that interests us now: the thing we call consumption.

THE MASS PRODUCTION OF DREAMS

The second industrial revolution was characterized by the rise of mass production and the new enterprise logic of managerial capitalism. It too was born in response to changes in the character of human yearning and the consequences for a new kind of consumption that has come to be called "mass consumption." More than anything else, it was the desire to live a different quality of life that set fire to mass consumption in the United States during the nineteenth century and ultimately created the vast new opportunities for commerce associated with mass production. Between 1820 and 1860 alone, urban growth increased at three times the rate of the general population. The rise of the city meant that people who once had made their own household objects, or bought them locally, were now exposed to and increasingly dependent upon mass-manufactured goods. The certainties of traditional rural life were supplanted by the pleasures of new goods and a new standard of living that had once been reserved for the rich. "It is the reduction of old pleasures that forces the consumer to resort to new pleasures to make up for the loss of old ones," counseled one enthusiast of the new consumption in 1892.[36]

The new consumption also reflected the social aspirations of the rising urban majority. In the America of the eighteenth century, gentility had been the province of the upper classes, who fashioned themselves and their surroundings after the manners and styles of European aristocracy. But by the nineteenth century, this structure of privilege was challenged by many new sources of turmoil and confusion. As people left the established hierarchies of their traditional rural communities, and urban strangers replaced lifelong acquaintances, conveying one's status became a real problem. Appearance and manners took on a new importance as the way to establish a family's social position in a confusing new world.[37] "All who aspired to simple respectability had to embody the marks of the genteel style in their persons and their houses."[38] These were the same decades in which business moved decisively out of the house. As men departed from their parlors, libraries, and home offices for the new factories, commercial office buildings, and state capitols, women were left to cultivate their homes as havens of gentility.

Women's dreams again led the way toward a new capitalism. Through consumption a wife could aim her family toward respectable society and enhance its standing in the emerging social order of an urban industrial nation.[39] More than ever, consumption became women's work. Once again, women fueled the emergence of a rapidly expanding mass market for hundreds of items like carpets, mahogany furniture, tableware, fabrics, brooms, candlesticks, buckles, buttons, hats, books, and so on. Early in the nineteenth century, hundreds of small producers established workshops to meet the new demand. Over time, they were replaced by manufacturers and retailers whose new production methods helped to put manufactured goods within the reach of the ordinary household budget.[40] Their methods came to be known as the "American system" of manufacture. They relied principally on a much greater use of specialized machinery and a more detailed division of labor. In some cases, the new factories began to achieve the standardization of parts that would become an important component in the eventual triumph of mass production.[41] Railroads sped the new goods across the nation. Yankee peddlers established elaborate distribution systems, bringing merchandise manufactured in the east to every state and region. Women's needs and desires were thus an important vanguard of mass consumption that stimulated these nineteenth-century efforts at expanded production and set the stage for the industrial explosion of the early twentieth century.[42]

A new enterprise logic takes hold at crucial turning points in history and redefines commercial success because it connects to the yearnings of people who have already made a psychological break with the past, however latent and poorly articulated that break might be. It is contested and shaped by opposing interests, but ultimately it wins converts in much the same way as any social movement does—because it offers more people more hope of fulfilling their dreams than do earlier ways of organizing economic resources.[43] Perhaps no one in modern history intuitively understood these dynamics better than Henry Ford. Though Ford was lionized in his time, his biography is not a pretty one. His record as an anti-Semite is well known. Historians have revealed his sadism, paranoia, and capriciousness, including the heartbreaking way he treated his only son, Edsel. His autocratic behavior undermined the health and development of his company, frequently threatening its very survival. Some have even called him a madman.[44] These tragic limitations, however, do not alter the fact that he helped to midwife a new enterprise logic with the sheer ferocity of his conviction. His lasting contribution had little to do with any single technological invention. Instead, Ford's brilliance lay in his recognition of a new kind of market arising from the needs of "ordinary" people and his unfaltering belief that responding to them would require a new approach to manufacturing—one that would help lay the foundation for a new economics and a new kind of capitalism.

DISCOVERING MASS PRODUCTION

Back at the turn of the last century, Detroit's established elite invested heavily in the production of luxury cars. In many cases they either became executives or were demanding participants on boards of directors. One historian has cleverly anointed this syndrome "conspicuous production," because these wealthy men set out to make cars that their peers would want to buy, "a gentleman's car, built by gentlemen." Indeed, the great majority of automobile companies before World War I were aimed at the luxury market, and that proportion only increased after the war. They typically "allowed their prices to soar as they endeavored to present a car worthy of the high social status they sought or already possessed."[45] But none of these elitist companies could develop a sufficient volume of business, and most were sold or shuttered within a few years. Of the fifteen top automobile companies in Detroit before 1925, Ford's was the only company to persist in the mass market before 1920 and to remain committed to that market after World War II.[46] His historic success had more to do with his unique social orientation than his prowess as an engineer. He was the entrepreneur who broke through because he alone proceeded from his identification with, and intuitive understanding of, how the new mass consumers wanted to live.

Henry Ford was an outsider to Detroit's business establishment and deeply antipathetic to its values and behavior.[47] Ford perceived the enormous potential of the demand represented by ordinary working people. Some of his biographers have called his dedication to their interests a compulsion; others have called him a visionary.[48] Most agree that Ford had an intuitive grasp of the widespread yearning among the nation's farmers and shopkeepers for a robust, well-made, inexpensive automobile.[49] He held fast to his vision, even as everyone around him doubted that it could ever be turned into a profitable business.[50] He sneered at received wisdom, fighting his partners and his bankers, leaving two companies and eventually starting his own with $28,000 raised from a host of small investors.[51]

At the heart of Ford's contribution was a daring inversion of the way automakers had thought about the relationship between cars and customers.

Until then, automobiles had been highly diverse, taking into consideration the whims and fancies of individual wealthy customers. But in aiming himself at the still untested mass market, Ford wanted to make one kind of car that would suit all his customers. Purged of any fashion content, it would be a utilitarian appliance. Herein lies one of the great paradoxes of industrial history. Ford championed mass consumers, but in order to serve them, he focused relentlessly on the standardization of his product and its production.

Ford wanted to make as many cars as possible at the absolute lowest price, but he did not know how to do it nor what the car should look like. "Ford merely had the idea; he had no picture in his mind as to what the car would be like, or look like," recalled his production chief, Charles Sorensen.[52] What he did know were some of the principles behind the car that would eventually be marketed as the Model T. By standardizing the product, Ford believed he could maximize profits by driving up volumes, decreasing costs, and thus widening demand. This was a production equation that had not yet been proven and for which no economic theory existed. Until that time, most national manufacturers had not been able, or willing, to translate either increased volumes or increased standardization of parts into dramatically lower prices.[53] No one had yet achieved what Ford set out to do, and he himself did not know how to do it.[54]

Ford and his engineers culled many ideas from other production experiences. They knew that the interchangeability of parts would be essential to achieve speed, reduce labor content, and lower costs. Absolute standardization required an unprecedented number of specialized precision machines. The idea of continuous-flow production had arisen from observations of the Chicago meatpacking plants, as well as from flour-milling operations, canneries, and brewers.[55] But from 1903, when the Ford Motor Company was founded, to April 1, 1913, when the first moving assembly line (it was for the assembly of flywheel magnetos) brought the mass-production concept to fruition, the name of the game at Ford was open-ended and carefully documented experimentation.[56]

As historian David Hounshell tells it in his detailed chronicle of the Ford Motor Company, on that April day the first moving assembly line seemed simultaneously to be just another "step in the years of development at Ford yet somehow suddenly dropped out of the sky. Even before the end of that day, some of the engineers sensed that they had made a fundamental breakthrough."[57] Improvements to the line over the next year reduced the amount of time to assemble a flywheel from twenty man minutes to five. As moving assembly lines were adapted to every phase of Model T production, the gains were ever more astonishing. By April 1914, a "perfectly synchronized" chassis assembly line was the crowning achievement of Ford's engineers. It reduced chassis assembly time to ninety-three man minutes per unit, down from twelve hours and twenty-eight minutes before the moving line.[58] These accomplishments overwhelmed the most seasoned manufacturing veterans.[59] Productivity increases across the plant ranged from 50 percent to as much as ten times the output of the fixed assembly methods.[60]

Ford engineers had significantly reduced labor costs and increased the speed and volume of production with specialized machinery to produce interchangeable parts that eliminated skill requirements. Now the moving assembly line went even further. In the case of the flywheel magnetos, for example, a man who had stood at his own workbench and pieced together an entire flywheel magneto assembly from sixteen magnets, supports, clamps, bolts, and other parts was now instructed to place just one part in the assembly or perhaps merely start a few nuts or tighten a few bolts, continuously, all day. In this way, the work of production was radically simplified, broken down into what has come to be known as a "minute division of labor." Machines now did the work of production and the line set the pace. Workers were meant to be part of this machine process—appendages, really. Their job was to tend, feed, and support the vast machinery of production. Few factories would match the extreme mechanization of the Ford works for many decades. Nevertheless, the principles of work organization pioneered there—de-skilling, simplification, and fragmentation in the service of speed, efficiency, and cost reductions—became standard operating procedure for most lower-level jobs, spreading across factories as well as to the burgeoning back offices of the new corporations.[61]

With the consolidation of mass production based on interchangeable parts, standardization, continuous flow, labor substitution, and the minute division of labor, Ford achieved the levels of speed, regularity, efficiency, and cost reduction that enabled him to fulfill his goal of manufacturing "the *lowest* priced automobile and to use continuing price reductions to produce ever greater demand."[62] (Italics in original.) This in itself was an enormous accomplishment—a first. For example, in 1908 when the Model T was initially produced, it sold for $825. At a time when sales of 1,000 units made an automobile a huge success, 5,986 Model Ts were sold. By 1916, more than 565,000 Model Ts were sold at a price of only $360. Within a year, 1.5 million Model Ts were sold, and the price continued to drop as demand climbed.[63] In 1924 the price had fallen to $260, the lowest price in history for a four-cylinder automobile.[64]

Until Ford, there was no economic theory to account for these relationships between supply and demand, because no theory took into account the possibility of unlimited supply associated with mass-production methods. The prevailing theory of monopoly assumed that supply would always be limited, while demand was, in theory, unlimited. The contraction of production in order to maintain high prices, as practiced by Wedgwood, does indeed yield maximum profit under those conditions. But mass production lifted the traditional limitations on supply. Supply, not demand, became theoretically unlimited. That meant that maximum profit could be achieved through maximum production, with dramatically lower costs translating into the low prices that would stimulate demand. Management scholar Peter Drucker long ago credited Ford with being the first to understand this reversal of supply and demand, crediting him with a "revolution" in economics.[65]

Even as Ford achieved "true mass production" and a historic breakthrough in economic reasoning, all the key elements of the new enterprise logic of managerial capitalism were not yet in place.[66] Mass production would necessitate three other crucial components of what would become the standard enterprise logic in the twentieth century—a new employment relationship, a professional managerial hierarchy, and the corporate form of ownership. The first of these concerns the relationship of employees to the enterprise. In the twentieth century this employment relationship was characterized by a trade-off in which regular effort and obedience on the job were exchanged for higher wages and more leisure time. This quid pro quo was born with Ford's famous five-dollar day.

THE FIVE-DOLLAR DAY AND ITS (HIDDEN) THEORY OF CONSUMPTION

Ford's fabulous production innovations created misery among his workers. Their jobs had been depleted of skill, autonomy, and control. They were subjected to the speedup of the line and driven by often capricious foremen to maintain a constant pace. With no voice to influence plant organization, they simply left in droves. In 1913, the year of the first moving assembly line, turnover reached 380 percent. By the end of that year, if the company wanted to add 100 men to the line, it was necessary to hire 963.[67] There were growing signs of unionization, and other auto companies were experiencing strikes. A series of labor reforms and wage increases were initiated, including raising the minimum daily wage to $2.34 for all workers, but nothing really modified the rising levels of dissatisfaction and acrimony in the plant. While there are many accounts of the deliberations that led to the five-dollar day, we know that Ford and his financial chief, James Couzens, decided to adopt it on January 5, 1914.[68] It offered most workers five dollars each day, paid out partly as wages and the rest as profit sharing for those who met the company's criteria.[69] It also reduced the workday from nine to eight hours.

The five-dollar day was a shot heard around the world.[70] It was, first of all, an extraordinary amount of money, far beyond the wage standards of the time. Moreover, it was offered voluntarily, though admittedly to solve what appeared to be an intractable conflict between workers and the new work. It accomplished all sorts of things for the company, including, for a while, stemming the excessive rates of turnover. It made Ford an international hero, and it heaped free advertising on the company.[71] It also sent two powerful messages that remained essential to the standard enterprise logic for most of the twentieth century. First, it set the terms of the employment relationship: Workers would submit to the terms of production defined by their superiors in return for more money and time off. This would become the basic approach of business trade unionism in the United States for decades to come, acknowledging management's prerogatives to organize and control work.[72] Eventually another, parallel kind of implicit contract would come to characterize the dominant employment relationship for white-collar professionals and managers, one that traded salary increases, seniority-based promotions, and job security for loyalty and submission to the corporation and its requirements.[73]

Second, the five-dollar day sent the message that workers were now consumers too. Higher wages would return as profits because they contributed to healthy consumer demand, enabling workers to buy the products of mass production. But of most importance for our story is the way the employment relationship also concealed a specific interpretation of consumption and consumers. The implicit conception was one of anonymous consumers whose interests were fulfilled by the conjunction of decent wages and cheap goods. As long as consumption was based on an anonymous cash transaction, a person needed only cash to be a successful consumer, and a company had only to supply well-priced goods or services to be a successful producer.

What mass consumption required of work above all, then, was efficiency. In that context, it appeared perfectly reasonable to segment a person's economic roles. Work was inside the organization, and consumption was outside. Workers were supposed to, more or less, check their brains at the door, and with them their own consumption experiences. They were asked to bow to managerial prerogatives and, like Ford himself, focus exclusively on the product and its production. It was assumed that the only thing workers needed to do for consumers was to get them the goods at the right price, and that meant sacrificing everything to the requirements of efficient production. There was no thought that workers' own consumption experiences might usefully influence work practices, or that there might be an alternative to the rigid division of "economic labor" between production and consumption.

The simplicity of the consumption relationship was thus mirrored in the simplicity of the employment relationship. Both were based on a transaction: in one case, cash for goods; in the other, cash for compliance. All of this may seem somewhat antique, far from the realities of a service society. But as we will suggest in our discussion of the transaction crisis in Chapter Seven, the core assumptions of the classic employment relationship—and its consequences for the segmentation of the roles of people as consumers and employees—remain surprisingly intact. They have in most respects survived the service economy, but they cannot possibly survive the passage to a support economy. In a world of individuated consumption, end consumers want more than just efficient workers; they want people who can provide them with advocacy and deep support. The very notion would have driven Henry Ford wild. But a new consumption led to a new kind of worker then, and the same potential force for change exists today.

THE MANAGED CORPORATION

Even the audacity and sweep of the five-dollar day could not successfully complete the new enterprise logic that Ford had set into motion. The Ford Motor Company remained privately owned, increasingly an anomaly at a time when most large enterprises were adopting the corporate form. Ford was stuck in the behaviors of proprietary capitalism, though he had outgrown its economics and methods of operation.[74] He eschewed the kind of management infrastructure that would be necessary to coordinate and control complexity on the grand scale that he had brought to life. Despite a labor force now gutted of craft knowledge and responsibility, he was reluctant to hire the managers who were now needed to oversee, plan, and coordinate the new work. He continued, instead, to typify a nineteenth-century owner-manager. He insisted on making the decisions that affected every aspect of his business, from production planning to product design, marketing, and distribution. The last thing he wanted around him was a group of managers, as he was convinced that they would turn his business into a mere backdrop for their own career ambitions.

Ford boasted of the lack of formal organization, managerial titles, and orderly career paths in his company. All that, he reckoned, was nothing more than a platform for individuals to compete over power and influence. He believed that such competitive career dynamics would shift everyone's attention from the real work at hand, which was production. "This habit of making the work secondary and the recognition primary is unfair to the work. It makes recognition and credit the real job. . . . It produces the kind of man who imagines that by 'standing in with the boss' he will get ahead."[75] As far as he was concerned, it was the product and its production that should command everyone's full attention, not organizational structure or career advancement. "To my mind there is no bent of mind more dangerous than that which is sometimes described as the 'genius for organization,' " he complained.[76] "It is not necessary to have meetings to establish good feeling between individuals or departments. It is not necessary for people to love each other in order to work together."[77]

Business historians have shown persuasively that this lack of attention to organization and management led to the disastrous results at the Ford Motor Company by 1927, when its market share collapsed.[78] The company had saturated its markets with more than 15 million Model Ts that sold at ever lower margins. In 1924, the profit per car had dropped to only $2; most of the company's revenue derived instead from sales of parts and other ancillary activities.[79] The central paradox of Ford's contribution—a unique appreciation of mass consumption coupled with a single-minded focus on his product—now nearly cost the company its survival. Ford had lost sight of the growing complexities of consumer demand, complexities that he had helped to create by satisfying basic needs for an automobile and creating a thirst for more powerful and beautiful vehicles. Consumers now demanded more from a company than a single product, and they had the purchasing power to follow their new dreams.[80]

Ford faced the need for a sudden, unprecedented changeover to more diverse automobiles in a gargantuan manufacturing facility in which every machine, conveyer belt, gauge, and jig had been specifically designed for Model T production. Ford's company did not have the management expertise or planning capacity to tackle the changeover in a rational and systematic way. With these shortcomings, it fell into a frenzy of firing and hiring as it embarked upon a chaotic, capricious, and nearly fatal effort to change from Model T to Model A production. During this period the Ford Motor Company lost its preeminence in the automobile market and would spend a good part of the century fighting to regain it.

In contrast to the dire predicament at Ford, its rival, General Motors, had already begun to anticipate and plan for annual model changes. In the early 1920s, General Motors, led by Pierre du Pont and later Alfred Sloan, had begun to outline a new, more complex approach to mass production that incorporated consumers' interests in novelty, fashion, and comfort.[81] Sloan recognized that the new ingredients necessary to sustain a firm's growth and financial success included marketing, new product development, and more complex pricing, sales, and distribution strategies. To accomplish these new goals, he needed to be able to attract managerial talent and devise organizational structures and practices that enabled strategy formulation, planning, and implementation.[82]

The combined pressures of mass production, vertical integration, and more complex markets blasted the owner-manager's role into a hundred fragments, each of which materialized in a new tier of management or a new set of specialized staff functions. The new organizational structures developed to accommodate these new activities gradually came to dominate the economic landscape. They were led by a still nascent but fast-growing cadre of professional managers. "A managerial hierarchy had to be created to supervise several operating units and to coordinate and monitor their activities."[83] With this invention, the new enterprise logic of managerial capitalism would be nearly complete.

General Motors made the greatest single contribution to developing and refining this new management organization. GM executives frequently described their organizational innovations in the new management journals of the day. This helped to make theirs the standard according to which other firms shaped their organizational structures and practices.[84] Sloan created the multidivisional structure. The divisions were headed by middle managers, who reported to a general office of senior managers, who were in turn supported by large administrative and financial staffs. Senior managers oversaw the divisions, monitoring the balance of supply and demand and ensuring comparable policies in all the functional areas—personnel, purchasing, research, etc. Top managers also evaluated divisional performance, but most important, they concentrated on planning and resource allocation.[85] With the creation of these new systems and methods, "the basic organizational structure and administrative procedures of the modern industrial enterprise were virtually completed."[86] But there is still an important element of the new enterprise logic left to account for: What gave managers authority over their businesses? In the new structure, salaried managers could assume the rights to determine policy and oversee operations because they had been vested with authority derived from the property rights of their shareholders.[87] How did this occur?

The diversification of ownership through public shareholding was well established by World War I.[88] The corporate form had been developed for large-scale public works, like the Erie Canal, that required immense amounts of capital. In the private sector, it was first fully exploited by the railroads. Their unprecedented capital requirements led to the consolidation of the U.S. money market in New York City, and from the 1850s to the 1890s Wall Street was almost exclusively dedicated to railroad finance. Thanks to the U.S. government, the opportunity to diversify—and extend the corporate form—appeared in the guise of antitrust legislation.

The year 1890 saw the passage of the Sherman Antitrust Act, which forbade interfirm cooperation in restraint of trade. Firms that had colluded in monopolistic practices to form cartels or trusts were now challenged to find profits in competition. The result was a shift from an emphasis on monopoly, in which one firm or a combination of firms dominated an entire industry, to oligopoly, in which several large firms competed within an industry. New incorporation laws made it possible to form holding companies in which a number of firms could trade their stock for equity in a larger enterprise, thus creating the framework for the new large-scale industrial corporation.[89]

By the 1890s, businesses in every major industry were adopting the corporate form. There was a wave of historic mergers that defined much of American "big business" for the coming century. These included the formation of Standard Oil, American Tobacco, United States Rubber, Pittsburgh Plate Glass, American Cereal (later Quaker Oats), General Electric, United States Steel, National Biscuit, United Fruit, International Paper, International Harvester, DuPont, and many others.[90] As the merger movement gained momentum, it too looked toward Wall Street's investment bankers and stockbrokers to unite participants, agree on terms, oversee the exchange of stock, execute legal arrangements, and, importantly, underwrite and market the new securities, often with substantial opportunities for successful speculation.[91]

The mergers were typically motivated by an interest in establishing legal combinations to achieve market control, as well as by the enticing prospect of the profits that would accrue to those who promoted and financed the deals. Gradually, though, the new economic and regulatory environment forced more corporate leaders toward a crucial lesson. Sustained market power could derive only from lower unit costs, which in turn necessitated determined exploitation of the new economies of scale that the mergers had made possible.[92] They would have to work for dominance and the wealth it promised. Their goal would be efficiency; their tools would be administration, centralization, vertical integration, and rationalization—in other words, management. Substantial capital was necessary to finance the relocation and redesign of old facilities, the building of new plants, the design and purchase of equipment, and the other investments necessary to exploit economies of scale. The Wall Street men who mediated the flow of capital took on an even more central role, typically joining the boards of the new industrial enterprises.[93]

The corporate form offered many attractive legal advantages, many of which had been inherited from its original role in enabling large-scale public works. These included limited liability, the right to own stock in other companies, and the separation of ownership, which was dispersed, from control, which was concentrated.[94] Boards of directors typically included senior members of the salaried hierarchy and sometimes founding family members who were also in top management. But they also included "outside directors" who represented major stockholders, the interests of the capital markets, and the interests of founding family members not involved in the management of the firm. As operations grew ever more complex, however, it was the inside directors who "increasingly controlled the *instruments* of power." (Italics in original.) While outside directors retained their legal rights, the authority associated with their property rights was ceded to those with the information and skills to make the enterprise successful.[95]

As in the case of General Motors, the complexity of mass production and distribution in the new industrial enterprises of the twentieth century necessitated extensive hierarchies of managers and immense amounts of capital. Each of these features required full exploitation of the corporate form as it offered access to capital, rights to control, and the other legal advantages we have mentioned. The shift toward managerial capitalism was decisive as the corporation became the taken-for-granted form for commercial enterprise, and salaried career managers took charge of the large multi-unit firms that would dominate the American economy for decades to come.[96]

MANAGERIAL CAPITALISM
AS A ROAD TO DREAMS

Ford's success remains a cautionary tale. It reminds us that people, not just machines, make economic revolutions. Automobiles in and of themselves did little to contribute to the early-twentieth-century industrial explosion. Nor did the equipment that produced them. The motor vehicles and equipment industry was not even listed in the Standard Industrial Classification indices in 1899. Only when cars were made for new people in new ways and for new purposes did they set into motion the forces of economic growth capable of producing the modern automobile industry. Ford's mass production was not a system of machines, but a system of principles arrayed in a wholly new pattern featuring labor substitution, a minute division of labor, standardization, and the migration of control to engineers and managers.[97] By 1914 the auto industry ranked fifteenth among all classifications in number of workers, seventh in wages, sixth in value added, and ninth in the value of products. But by 1935, with all the elements of the new enterprise logic firmly in place, it was first in all categories, except the number of workers, where it was third.[98] Experts from around the world came to the United States to try to understand how the economic miracle had been achieved. The Germans called it *Fordismus*. In Russia, Henry Ford was honored above all other foreigners.

Ford's ability to unite mass production and mass consumption was so successful that it helped fuel the shift in manufacturing from proprietary capitalism to a new enterprise logic derived from managerial capitalism. That shift was completed as it was exposed to the refining fires of Alfred Sloan's leadership at General Motors; his brilliant administrative inventions included the clear establishment of a managerial hierarchy, the multidivisional structure, the emphasis on vertical integration, and the establishment of a centralized bureaucracy to oversee and coordinate decentralized operations.[99] The new enterprise logic was further elaborated and consolidated within many other large corporations, including DuPont, Standard Oil, and General Electric.

The purpose of the new enterprise logic was to produce affordable products for mass consumption at a profit. Its means depended upon economies of scale, standardization, and high volumes to lower unit costs. Its methods replaced market mechanisms with administrative coordination able to rationalize competition, balance supply and demand, drive down costs, and harness technology to improve productivity. Its success required a new managerial hierarchy with a relentless internal focus on the control and measurement of production and distribution. Managers and engineers inherited the task of planning and overseeing a minute division of labor to accomplish the increased throughput and reduced unit costs necessary to meet the new demands of mass consumption while steadily increasing profits.[100]

Ultimately, the rise of managerial capitalism can be attributed to its success as a social movement.[101] That new approach was a radical break with the past, replete with costs and benefits for a variety of groups.[102] It did not appear full-blown. It was constructed over time by people in the clash over opportunities foreclosed and found. The new enterprise logic served many interests, but it is doubtful that it would have gained ascendancy had it not first and foremost served the interests of the society through mass consumption. The regulatory efforts of the government—the Sherman Antitrust Act (1890), the Federal Trade Commission (FTC) Act (1914), and the Clayton Antitrust Act (1914)—reflected this. They were intended to foster new kinds of intercompany competition conducive to innovation and increased efficiency. Theodore Roosevelt himself made the distinction between a "good trust," one based on cost reduction, and a "bad trust," one based on collusion to achieve monopoly. This distinction influenced the way regulations were enforced by the FTC, the Justice Department, and the courts.[103]

Against this background, the new enterprise logic was regarded as a progressive force in society, with appeal to members of every class, as reflected in the quote from John Hay at the beginning of this book. The new capitalism was more capacious than the old. It could integrate and accommodate much of what had gone before, combining the interests of many groups in a new pattern. Small producers could enjoy more stable prices and markets as well as an opportunity to merge with larger firms and diversify their holdings. For the middle class there was an opportunity for investment and, more significantly, the prospect of employment in a meritocracy, where promotion did not depend upon being a member of the founding family.[104] For labor, there was increased regularity and security of employment, and better wages. Early accommodations to limited collective bargaining, primarily in craft industries, also set the stage for later widespread though hard-won success in unionization.[105] The new capitalism was able to attract support from people up and down the class structure, who saw in it the promise of greater affluence, social mobility, and dreams fulfilled. It succeeded because it was capable of commanding the loyalty of successive generations in their roles as consumers and employees. "For many Americans," observed economic historian Martin Sklar, "the corporation became the new frontier of opportunity that the western lands had once symbolized."[106]

All this helps to explain why the shift toward managerial capitalism was relatively swift and, though not uncontested, generally peaceful. Eventually the new enterprise logic spread across every sector of the economy, from manufacturing to services and even to agriculture. Many of its principles were adopted by smaller firms in non-oligopolistic industries (fine furniture, machine tools), even when they could not fully apply mass-production techniques.[107] It created unprecedented wealth as the new managerial hierarchy learned to guide a complex organization and an always evolving complement of new technologies to serve, stir, and exploit the new cravings and requirements of mass consumption.[108]

But the influence of the new enterprise logic was not restricted to the formal operations of business. Indeed, America's burgeoning industrial society absorbed the new worldview associated with managerial capitalism like a thirsty sponge. Its norms and values came to imbue organizational life in every dimension of society, from schools to hospitals, government, and civic organizations. And beyond the concrete policies and administrative principles of organizational life, that worldview animated a new mass order— marked by large work units, urban agglomeration, class identification, and mass media—that engulfed every aspect of American society and eventually spread across the industrializing world. This was the heyday of the mass as it flung itself headlong into the business of economic growth and forged the rules of production and consumption that would dominate life throughout the twentieth century. It was animated by people who had little and wanted much. Their dreams of a better quality of material life helped to make them willing participants in the demands of the new mass order, feeding a hunger for, and belief in, everything that was mass and modern.

Those generations created a new world of material abundance. That wealth was produced by our great-grandparents, our grandparents, and our parents and was shared across the new American middle class, particularly during the decades from 1940 to 1970. Many people sacrificed their bodies in hard physical work. Most accepted the terms of mass society, playing by the rules of large hierarchical organizations when it came to earning a living and acquiescing to the rules of consumption when it came to spending their money. But what these generations did not know was that they were also setting into motion a set of world-historical forces that would irreversibly transform the mass order, along with the very character of their descendants. In other words, it was the success of the standard enterprise logic, and the new mass order it helped to shape, that gave birth to the new society of individuals. Yet today's organizations remain loyal to the standard enterprise logic and stuck in the old worldview. We need to understand something about the worldview of this older mass society for two reasons: first, to see in what ways its assumptions and perspectives continue to animate today's organizations; and second, to appreciate how different the new society of individuals really is. Just how much have our dreams really changed?

THE NEW MASS ORDER
AND THE UGLY INDIVIDUAL

The worldview associated with the new standard enterprise logic assumed a deep connection between knowledge, especially scientific knowledge, and rational action. Centralized authority, it was believed, could exercise effective command as long as it possessed the correct data and the correct administrative structures. Scientific knowledge would guide bureaucracy as it administered the actions and interactions of the myriad groups under its control. The core processes of society were no longer thought of as an infinite number of personal interactions. Instead, the nervous system of the new society was composed of groups in a state of "continuous pressure" upon one another. The most important thing a person could do, or teach his children to do, was to effectively adapt to group life. "The individual was meaningless as a unit for investigation; only men's social behavior deserved analysis."[109]

The emphasis on the collective and the social extended to every aspect of life, from business to labor and government. "Individualism was increasingly hollow . . . beckoning more toward a past . . . than affirming the present."[110] The values of a democratic civilization would be reinterpreted for the new mass industrial society through the power of the group. From the Supreme Court, which had adjudged corporations to be "persons" within the meaning of the Fourteenth Amendment, to writings of social theorists and philosophers, the task of making sense of social change dominated every consideration. "With few exceptions, the individual . . . received only perfunctory attention. Much like their contemporaries on the Court, theorists concerned themselves with the rights and needs of the individual only when they could not avoid him. Engrossed in the sweep of impersonal forces, they could not tarry long with one man."[111]

Certainly by 1920, the debates over modernization had shifted. No longer was it viewed as something that could be forestalled, derailed, or avoided. Modernization had garnered a new sense of inevitability, even though many of its primary beneficiaries in the new middle class also had to contend with a growing sense of individual helplessness. "In the town," as one historian observed, "power was personal." Any interested citizen could figure out how things worked and how to influence them. "When they moved to a broader arena, however, they soon found that they could neither see, know, nor even know about the people upon whom they had to depend. . . . The system was so impersonal, so vast, seemingly without beginning or end."[112]

It was such middle-class men and women, frustrated with the sprawling inertia and headless complexity of the emerging society, that formed the vanguard of a reform movement loosely known as Progressivism. Their aims were manifold, but their methods shared a common approach. They established organizations—"associations"—of informed citizens with common interests. The leaders of these new entities used the political weight of group solidarity to raise awareness of critical issues, field and elect candidates, design administrative procedures, lobby legislative bodies, and collaborate on public policy. Like the businessmen whom they often opposed, they believed in "organization" and "administration" as the antidotes to chaos and as the ways to eliminate the grim, "unintended" consequences of modernization. The new associations were single-minded in their efforts to select and support political candidates. They commanded the votes of their members, and "when an office-seeker accepted their support, he was expected in return to abide by their platforms and their ideals."[113] Membership in such groups offered solace, order, and connection for men and women living through the turmoil of the modernization process. It offered a means to exert influence and reestablish a sense of personal control in the new mass order.

Solidarity and association were everywhere. From the 1870s through the 1910s, associations multiplied, new chapters of preexisting organizations proliferated, and these groups increasingly established statewide and national organizations. In small towns and large cities, Americans organized clubs, churches, lodges, and veterans groups. Across the United States, voluntary associations grew more rapidly than the population.[114] Half of all the largest mass-membership organizations in two centuries of American history were founded in the decades between 1870 and 1920.[115] During the 1920s, membership in these organizations increased sharply and continued to climb for the following four decades, with the exception of a brief period of decline during the Depression. As part of this trend, women joined clubs, political associations, and professional groups in unprecedented numbers, mobilizing around the issues of suffrage and temperance, forcing new questions about their role in society onto the public stage. Beginning in the last years of the nineteenth century, they founded the League of Women Voters, the Parent-Teacher Association, the Girl Scouts, the Hadassah, the Red Cross, the Campfire Girls, and the American Association of University Women, along with thousands of church groups, book clubs, service clubs, and bridge clubs.[116]

Men founded fraternal groups (the Knights of Columbus), expanded many that had been established decades earlier (the Masons, the Odd Fellows), and established new service groups (the American Legion, Rotary, Lions, Kiwanis, Jaycees). They founded or extended professional organizations, chambers of commerce, and labor unions. One historian has calculated that by 1910, a third of all adult males belonged to a fraternal order.[117] Similarly, participation in unions was rising rapidly. Between 1897 and 1904 nationwide union membership nearly quadrupled from 3.5 percent to 12.3 percent of the nonagricultural workforce. Union membership continued to grow, rising dramatically after passage of the National Labor Relations Act (Wagner Act) in 1935 and encompassing 70 percent of the manufacturing workforce by 1946.[118] It is striking that organizations as disparate as the Masons and the International Ladies Garment Workers Union attracted people for very similar reasons. Individuals sought empowerment and protection through group membership. "Working for the union and empowering the delegates to do battle with the boss was a reassertion of the individual's power over his environment."[119]

The protections provided by the family were no longer sufficient to compensate for the potential disasters of this new industrial world, no matter where one stood in the class structure. Only the group, it seemed, could protect the weakened individual from being crushed between the shifting tectonic plates of past and future. The unions, lodges, and fraternal orders offered people security in the form of mutual aid, reciprocal relations, and social connection, all of which mitigated against the trauma of crisis and dislocation. For those in the growing ranks of management, the corporation provided these benefits and protections, offering both financial security and a coveted social network.

A new fascination with psychology was turned into standardized tests used to "weed out misfits" from schools and workplaces, and to assess workers' and consumers' motivations in order to manage them more effectively. As psychological concepts invaded the professions of social work, management, advertising, mental health, and education, they emphasized successful adjustment to group life and organizational requirements.[120]

As a result of progressive reforms, child labor underwent a sharp decline during this period, and many states adopted laws to eliminate it entirely. In

1889 only 75 percent of school-age children were enrolled in public or private schools, but by 1926 that number had climbed to nearly 90 percent.[121] Where there had once been a wide range of different ages represented in any given school grade, the educational process became increasingly regimented, with age grading leading to more homogeneous experiences within age cohorts across the country.

While the children went to school, their older brothers and sisters went to work, many of them in large factories and offices.[122] By the late 1920s, these new mass organizations—schools, workplaces, unions, and associations—were fully established and had taken up much of the responsibility, once lodged in the family, for teaching the new behavioral norms of modern industrial life and enforcing conformity to those norms.[123] According to one historian, "the establishment of the schools was the disestablishment of domesticity."[124] It was in school and work that sons and daughters would be whipped into shape and molded for the orderly new worlds of production, administration, and consumption.

The family lost its major role in shaping the life course of its offspring, but it learned how to guide them toward the appropriate channels for adaptation and success in the wider society. Success, viewed in market terms, generally translated into some combination of status and consumption. Successful men made money, or they skillfully ascended the hierarchy in one of the new bureaucratic organizations, whether it was a corporation, a union, or a government agency. They were expected to be the breadwinners whose wages and salaries would equip the family for participation in the new consumption-oriented economy. Successful women—well, they married successful men.

According to many contemporary observations, women enjoyed primary authority over household expenditures, an authority that grew as their husbands vanished into the public world of careers and jobs. Now women were widely considered to be the "purchasing agents" for their families, and the great majority of advertising was aimed directly at their control of the "purse strings."[125] Successful women looked forward to presiding over an ever more ample budget, capable of realizing ever more desire. As one historian wrote, "The activity of parents became directed less at ensuring that their children should *be* more than themselves than that they should *have* more than themselves."[126] (Italics added.) The family itself was gradually redefined as a haven for emotional intimacy among couples and their children, as well as the primary arena for personal consumption. As the bureaucratic world increasingly emphasized rationality and objectivity, the family offered a counterpoint, a place where people could express themselves and find satisfaction in sexual romance, familial affection, and consumption.

The mass society was not uncontested. In addition to political controversy, there was a fierce cultural debate over the passing of the old order. The 1920s, for example, saw an outpouring of books and articles that tried to reconcile past and present. High- and low-brow authors echoed the same question: Were mass society and civilization compatible? One of the outcomes of these debates was a campaign of popularization of culture that included the *Reader's Digest*, the Book-of-the-Month Club, and scores of outlines of history, science, and philosophy, some of which actually made the best-seller lists. Cartoons and comics, visual advertising, motion pictures, and even tabloid newspapers were innovative ways of informing the new "masses."[127] Aldous Huxley published his *Brave New World* in 1932 attempting to shock his readers into realizing the dangerous destination of a mass society. Upton Sinclair's *Flivver King*, in 1937, portrayed the brutality of mass-production work. For those who weren't reading Huxley or Sinclair, there was Charlie Chaplin's *Modern Times*, released in 1936, in which the Little Tramp was driven mad by a factory inspired in real life by Chaplin's tour of Ford's gigantic River Rouge plant.[128]

THE PAYOFF AND ITS DISCONTENTS

The devotion to managerial capitalism and the new mass order paid off. Even working-class people were able to afford goods and amusements that had only decades earlier been out of reach. The housing, electrical appliance, and automobile industries boomed. By 1929 there were more than 25 million car registrations, and almost 70 percent of American homes had electricity. In 1909 a factory worker had to work 22.2 months to earn the cost of a basic Model T; by 1923 it took him only three months. Radio sales rose 1,400 percent between 1922 and 1929, reaching nearly $1 billion.[129] The automobile companies also introduced installment buying, legitimating credit and stoking the growing fires of consumption.

These developments were slowed but by no means extinguished when the Depression engulfed the economy in 1929, and they reasserted themselves with even greater force during the economic reconversion of the early postwar period as mass consumption and the new enterprise logic were more fully diffused and more deeply institutionalized across the economy and society. Between 1945 and 1960, the gross national product grew by almost

250 percent, and per capita income by 35 percent. Housing starts exploded after the war, peaking at 1.65 million in 1955 and remaining at more than 1.5 million a year for the rest of the decade. The increase in single-family home ownership between 1946 and 1956 exceeded cumulative increases during the preceding century and a half. By 1960, 62 percent of American families owned their own home, compared to 43 percent in 1940.[130]

Many middle-class families moved to the suburbs, and many working-class families moved to the middle class. The number of salaried workers increased by 61 percent between 1947 and 1957, and by the mid-1950s nearly 60 percent of the population was considered middle class, compared to only 31 percent in the prosperous 1920s. Women led the consumption boom again, as the biggest increases in consumer spending were in household goods like furniture and appliances, which rose by 240 percent in the five years after World War II, compared with increases of 33 percent for food and 20 percent for clothing. By 1960, membership levels began to peak in most of the mass associations founded earlier in the century. Perhaps this was because so many of their objectives had been achieved: That year 70 percent of all families owned their homes, 80 percent had a television, 75 percent had a car, and the number of people with discretionary income had doubled in the ten years since 1950.[131]

The new and improved nuclear family appeared to thrive in its new middle-class affluence. Man and woman were united in affection and consumption, as loyal to the domestic institution of marriage as they were to the commercial institutions of managerial capitalism. Rates of divorce and illegitimacy were low. A *Fortune* magazine survey of women between the ages of twenty and thirty-five was conducted in 1943. According to the magazine's editors, "The most interesting aspect of their opinions is the close approach to unanimity that a great variety of women achieve on a great variety of points." For example, 74 percent of the women said they would rather be married and run a home than have a successful career and not be married or have a successful career and be married. Among single women, 79 percent were confident that they would be married; "even the unattractive turned in thumping majorities expecting to catch a husband."[132] According to a 1955 study of marriage, fewer than 10 percent of those surveyed believed that an unmarried person could be happy. The advice in one popular book counseled, "The family is the center of your living. If it isn't, you've gone far astray."[133]

By the 1950s a massive baby boom turned America into a child-oriented society: Births rose from a low of 18.4 per 1,000 during the Depression to 25.3 per 1,000 in 1957. Between 1940 and 1960, the birth rate for third children

doubled; for fourth children, it tripled. Even theoretical sociologists of the
stature of Harvard's Talcott Parsons and Robert F. Bales now regarded the
nuclear family structure as essential to modern industrial society. To function
effectively, they proclaimed, the family had to abandon its traditional functions and wider kinship networks. Instead, the family was expected to specialize in the activities of emotional nurturance and child-rearing and, above
all, to concentrate on the development of a modern personality in its children—one that would predispose them to success in the larger organizational
world. "Nuclear families," they warned, were the " 'factories' which produce
human personalities. . . . In the 'normal' case it is both true that *every adult* is
a member of a nuclear family and that every child must begin his process of
socialization in a nuclear family."[134] (Italics added.)

But even during these seemingly monolithic and harmonious decades,
hairline cracks were beginning to appear in the seamless unity of family life,
mass consumption, and organizational devotion. Subordination to domestic
and career institutions had a dark side too, but the discord underneath those
shiny surfaces was rarely discussed. One recent study of so-called schizophrenic women in the San Francisco Bay area during the 1950s reports that
institutionalization and electroshock treatments were the therapies recommended for women who refused their domestic roles. In those years, women
continued to be excluded from many professions. They were often denied
the right to serve on a jury, have a credit card, enter into contracts, or establish a residence. In 1949, *Life* magazine wrote that "suddenly and for no
plain reason" American women were "seized with an eerie restlessness." In
1953 a physician wrote that under a "mask of placidity" and a feminine appearance, there was often an "inwardly tense and emotionally unstable individual seething with hidden aggressiveness and resentment."[135]

A number of large-scale surveys suggested that many married people
were not happy, and that women especially had settled for "working marriages" rather than real happiness. Tranquilizers were developed in the 1950s
in response to a need that physicians explicitly saw as female. Tranquilizer
consumption rose from zero in 1955 to 462,000 pounds in 1958, and then to
1.15 million pounds in 1959. By 1960, almost every major new journal was
using the word "trapped" to describe the feelings of the American housewife. When *Redbook*'s editors asked readers to provide them with examples
of this feeling, they received 24,000 replies in a matter of days.[136] Betty
Friedan's *The Feminine Mystique* rocked the world in 1963, because it set
the match to a fire that was already laid.[137]

While men tended to be more satisfied than women, they too harbored
private misery. Unmarried adult males were viewed suspiciously and could

be denied jobs or promotions because they didn't have the right kind of private life. Popular culture frequently parodied the hapless, gullible man susceptible to the cunning "gold digger" and seduced into a marriage in which he was destined to play the fool. These caricatures suggested the guilt and shame that dogged men who didn't fit the cultural stereotype and tormented fathers who didn't always know best. A host of now famous books endeavored to shine a light on the unsavory, injurious, and mean-spirited political cultures of the large organization. In cool prose, they revealed a world that demanded the surrender of spirit, will, and judgment to the explicit dictates and informal norms of managerial capitalism. With titles like *The Organization Man, Men Who Manage*, and *The Lonely Crowd*, they quoted men who could not identify meaning and purpose in their lives much beyond the realities of conformity itself.

Slowly, as the century progressed, the forces of modernity unleashed by managerial capitalism widened these hairline cracks into fissures that began to spread, creating new ravines, eruptions, and irregularities in the once smooth surfaces of conformity and devotion. Managerial capitalism's success eventually helped to unleash the large-scale forces—of mass education, information access, broad-based labor force participation, improved health, knowledge-based work, and mass travel—that would alter the terms of social and psychological experience for hundreds of millions of people in the United States and around the world. These were the forces that would lead the way to a new society of individuals with its own field of dreams, new individuals who are now groping their way toward yet another frontier and yet another new capitalism. That is where this story leads, as the next chapters consider managerial capitalism's success and the new people it birthed.

THREE

How Managerial Capitalism Made New People

From the beginning of human history most people would have agreed on this: Destiny is written in blood. The future was dictated by the circumstances of birth: Parents, grandparents, kin, ancestors, religion, language, native geography, gender, physical stamina—these were the factors that circumscribed a life before it was ever lived. It was not until the late twentieth century that this ancient canon came to be contested on a large scale. By then, the achievements of managerial capitalism had introduced many people to new qualities of experience that left them facing a more liberating but anxiety-ridden question: "Who am I?" That question had always been simply resolved: "I am my father's son. I am my mother's daughter."

I AM I

By the late twentieth century "I am I" became the only adequate response to the question of "Who am I?" even as it framed a new riddle. As Erik Erikson, the psychoanalytic pioneer of this quest for identity, first set it out in the book that catapulted him to fame in 1950, *Childhood and Society*, "The patient of today suffers most under the problem of what he should believe and who he should—or . . . might—be or become; while the patient of early psychoanalysis suffered most under inhibitions which prevented him from being what and who he thought he knew he was."[1]

The opportunity to forge an identity from a sense of psychological individuality is the hard-won fruit of the twentieth century, a century in which the agonies of war, modernization, and displacement were matched by unparalleled prosperity and the gradual spread of democratic forms throughout much of the world. For millions of people today, life is no longer foretold, but rather is an open canvas waiting to be painted by individual choice. Indeed, the late twentieth century is likely to stand for this mounting and, in some parts of the world, finally decisive psychological break with the feudal past. This discontinuity has affected many people around the globe, though its consequences have been most profound in those societies that form the industrial core of the global economy. In such societies, self-determination, the hard-won right of a people to govern itself, has become the defining project of each individual person. Because psychological individuality blossomed and spread in the second half of the twentieth century, many who grew up with it have a hard time appreciating just how profoundly new it is. We can observe something of the pervasiveness of the new psychological individualism by looking where one might least expect to find it—the U.S. armed forces as they try to reconcile the claims of psychological self-determination in the late twentieth century with the ancient and authoritarian culture of war.

SOLDIERS OF THE SELF

The Vietnam Veterans Memorial in Washington, D.C., consists of 140 slabs of black granite polished like mirrors. Inscribed on its granite walls in chronological order are the names of the 58,000 Americans who died in the Vietnam War. Designed by Maya Ying Lin as a young architectural student at Yale University in 1981, the memorial was controversial from the start. It departed from all the norms of commemorative monuments. Conventional memorials lionize one interpretation of the past. They tell people what to think and how to feel. They explicitly depict an event through statues and inscriptions intended to evoke the same experience for the whole community, affirming and producing social cohesion. After all, the word monument comes from the Latin *monere*, which means "to remind," but also "to admonish," "warn," "advise," and "instruct."

Lin's approach was just the opposite. Her intention was to support an individual experience rather than to deliver a sermon. The Wall, as the memorial has come to be called, is designed to memorialize the life and death of each lost soldier, and it avoids any glorification or fixed interpretation of the war itself. But its reversal of perspective does not stop there. The Vietnam Veterans Memorial also addresses the individuality of those who come to visit and mourn. Rather than attempting to persuade them of the "truth," it is a "quiet place for personal reflection and private reckoning," a home for many truths. The wide, shallow area encompassed by the Wall was meant to allow for a singular experience for each visitor. The silence of the memorial—physical silence produced by the private quality of the experience[2] and formal silence produced by the absence of inscriptions and explicit storytelling—invites people to discover their own interpretations of the past.[3] When visitors look at the Wall, they are met with their own reflections in its polished surfaces. The only meanings encountered are the ones they make.

The Wall was controversial from the start, precisely because it showed no trace of the traditional commemorative impulse.[4] But neither its promoters nor its opponents foresaw the public's extraordinary response to the Wall. It quickly became and has remained the most visited memorial site in Washington, D.C., attracting between 12,000 and 15,000 visitors each day.[5] The Wall has become the object of intense emotion for millions of people in ways that have superseded the original intentions of its most avid supporters. As they touch the Wall, some weep. There is an overwhelming sense of solemnity. The names on the Wall are caressed, traced by fingertips, rubbed with pencil on paper to be taken home. And something from home is often left at the Wall: a statement of questioning or protest, a letter or poem, an article with significance to the dead soldier. As one scholar put it, the Wall itself has become a kind of "debating forum—a repository of diverse opinions about the very war that occasioned its construction."[6]

If the Vietnam Veterans Memorial expresses any overarching meaning, it is the powerful way it testifies to the rise of psychological individuality. There are no more anonymous soldiers, only specific human beings whose individuality is conveyed in the most unambiguous way possible—by their names. Visitors to the memorial are not regarded as so many sheep, ready and willing to be told what to think and how to feel. Each visitor creates the meanings that the Wall has for him or her; even when those meanings are patriotic in the traditional sense, they are meanings that have been opted into by the individual, rather than imposed by the memorial. Meanings are chosen in a way that only individuals can choose them, and there is nothing traditional about that.[7] The public's powerful response to the Wall demonstrates how deeply this memorial resonates with the new realities of psychological self-determination. The Wall is about, by, and for the new society of individuals. It makes it possible to imagine, in a not so distant time, memorials of future generations in which every victim and every soldier is equally honored for his or her unique, spent humanity, irrespective of their nationality or which "side" they were on.

Military life has always been, above all, about the suppression of individuality in favor of obedience to authority, anonymous self-sacrifice, and group solidarity. Yet even there, the realities of the new individualism are redefining centuries of tradition. Evidence of this shift in human sensibilities can be found in the public's—and therefore politicians' and military commanders'—deep reluctance to put soldiers' lives at risk. Consider the way soldiers were depicted during World War II and the way they have been treated by the press, politicians, and the public in more recent conflicts, such as those in Kosovo and Afghanistan.

In the 1940s, war correspondent Ernie Pyle created the mythic figure of GI Joe, the common man who routinely revealed uncommon bravery. In hundreds of dispatches from Europe, North Africa, and the Pacific, he made sure the reading public knew that at the raw heart of the Allied triumph in World War II lay the courage and grit and mutual devotion of millions of such men. He had many names for them, all written in affection: "your average doughfoot," "our kids," "our boys," "our swell boys," "the mud-rain-frost-and-wind boys." Sometimes they were simply "our troops," "the tired soldiers," and, finally, "dead men."

He described the daily agonies and hard-bitten heroism of frontline soldiers, sailors, bombers, medics, mountain fighters, engineers, artillery men, and brass hats. In Pyle's reporting one senses the vast wartime apparatus that engulfed, transformed, and directed the flow of humanity that became its fighting force. Approaching the invasion of Sicily with the U.S. armada, he wrote of an anonymous young skipper on a nearby vessel whose voice could be heard through the darkness: "Some young man who shortly before had perhaps been unaware of any sea at all—the bookkeeper in your bank, maybe—and then there he was, a strange new man in command of a ship, suddenly a person with acute responsibilities, carrying out with great intentness his special, small part of the enormous aggregate that is our war on all the lands and seas of the globe." That young skipper, like millions of others, had traded one role in society for another and was ready to sacrifice everything to do his part. "We were all men of a new profession out in a strange night caring for each other."[8]

Only occasionally in Pyle's dispatches does the name of a soldier appear, usually with his exact street address. Those tiny fragments of detail cut like a knife. They stand out in shocking contrast to the relentless recounting of masses of anonymous men trapped in the titanic machinery of battle. They forced readers to reckon with something that was almost impossible to grasp—those soldiers were individual human beings with birthdays and with dreams.

Ernie Pyle was killed by a Japanese machine-gun bullet just three weeks before VE Day. In his last column, never published by his editors at Scripps-Howard, he darkly summarized his experience of the war: "Dead men by mass production—in one country after another—month after month and year after year. Dead men in winter and dead men in summer. Dead men in such familiar promiscuity that they become monotonous. Dead men in such monstrous infinity that you come almost to hate them."[9]

Nearly sixty years later, U.S. soldiers would again find themselves on a European battleground. This time it was in Kosovo that they joined with troops from other nations to block Serbian aggression against ethnic Albanians. But President Clinton and his advisers knew that most Americans would not support the incursion if it meant American casualties. They had to promise a "clean" war that would rely on a punishing air campaign and avoid the deployment of ground troops. And so it was with a sense of shock that reporters learned how, during the afternoon of Wednesday, March 31, 1999 (7:30 A.M. EST), three American soldiers traveling in a Humvee military vehicle along the Macedonia-Kosovo border had come under fire and were missing. The soldiers had been assigned to a NATO mission that had been on patrol in that area since 1993 and intended as the vanguard of a proposed UN peacekeeping unit once the war there ended. Reporters also learned that the president as well as each of the soldiers' families had been notified early Wednesday morning, shortly after the incident had occurred. By Wednesday evening in the United States, it was reported that shortly after the American soldiers had radioed their distress, ninety more troops representing NATO forces from several nations, U.S. Blackhawk helicopters, and British helicopters had been dispatched in a comprehensive search effort.[10]

Shortly after midnight, in the early hours of April 1, CNN broadcast videotape from Serbian television showing three men in Serbian custody wearing U.S. military camouflage. One of them was obviously scratched and bruised. The three were identified as Staff Sergeant Christopher Stone, Staff Sergeant Andrew Ramirez, and Specialist Steven Gonzalez—the missing soldiers. That morning the talk shows featured as much information as they could about the three—their ages, their families, their hometowns in east Texas, northern Michigan, and East Los Angeles. Later the president, the secretary of defense, and other top military brass gathered with U.S. servicemen and their families in a huge aircraft hangar at Norfolk Naval Base. To thunderous applause, the president warned Serb leader Slobodan Milosevic that the United States would hold him responsible for the three soldiers' safety and well-being. (Top aides reported that the president was "very disturbed" at the apparent maltreatment of the soldiers.) "All Americans are concerned about their welfare," he said. "President Milosevic should make no mistake: The United States takes care of its own." The secretary of defense went on to assure the gathering that he would spare no effort to secure the safe return of the three men. Around the same time, heads of state and military commanders from across the NATO alliance weighed in with their concern for the three. Even Serb military leader Zeljko Raznatovic, himself sought by a war crimes tribunal for offenses in Bosnia, praised the three to the BBC as brave soldiers and thanked God they were alive.[11]

Later that afternoon, a Pentagon spokesman began his news briefing. There was news about the conflict, but reporters wanted to know about only one subject: What had happened to the three soldiers? It was learned that the initial search effort had actually included nearly 200 troops as well as French and Italian helicopters alongside those from the United States and Britain. By that evening Rosie Gonzales, Steven's mother, was on television talking about her son. The world learned that she and her husband were employees in the Texas prison system and that prisons across that state would display yellow ribbons until the men were released. "They don't deserve this," she complained. "They're young men with their whole life ahead of them and they were put in a bad situation."[12]

By the morning of April 2, a mere forty-eight hours after the initial incident, reporters had fanned out across the hometowns of each of the three. Media outlets from the morning news shows to the *New York Times* were determined to learn as much as they could about each of the young men, however mundane the information. Parents, siblings, cousins, colleagues, neighbors, teachers, coaches, acquaintances, and simply fellow townspeople—everyone had something to contribute. And even when there was little to say to distinguish the individuality of a twenty-year-old, they found something: "He was an average student, and an average athlete, but he had one superior quality, he never quit," reported Christopher Stone's cross-country coach and history teacher.[13]

The interest and intensity did not abate until the Reverend Jesse Jackson and a nineteen-member delegation of American Christian, Jewish, and Muslim leaders undertook an unofficial mission to Belgrade and secured the soldiers' release one month later on May 2, 1999. According to the *Los Angeles Times'* eyewitness reports: "When the three soldiers were released . . . there were hugs, tears—even some Yugoslav authorities seemed moved." The men were given cell phones to call their families and then traveled by bus to Croatia, where they were "picked up by a U.S. Army hospital jet and flown to Germany in the company of generals, psychiatrists and doctors—all of whom were giddy, joyful and deeply moved to be welcoming the men. . . . Everyone who greeted them—hardened Army generals and everyone who was there—had tears in their eyes."[14]

It took the grim atrocities of September 11, 2001, to persuade Americans that soldiers' lives must be put at risk in a retaliatory effort in Afghanistan. Still, President George W. Bush and Secretary of Defense Donald Rumsfeld were forced to sound a constant drumbeat, reminding the public that all wars could not be clean, that ground troops would be needed, that the risk of death must be incurred. Not even the cold determination to combat terrorism, however, could extinguish the public's loyalty to the individuality of soldiers, rescuers, and victims. If anything, the grief and anger that accompanied the tragedy intensified the awareness of each person's uniqueness. For example, the mourning over the attacks on the World Trade Center and the Pentagon quickly took the form of celebrating individual lives. Within twenty-four hours of the attacks, journalists were plumbing the narratives of individual victims and heroes, interviewing their families, broadcasting their final words as recounted by the loved ones they called on their cell phones or as captured by the tape of an answering machine.

By September 12, the whole world knew the faces of the flight attendants and the pilots who crewed the hijacked planes, along with their spouses and children. The biographies of many other victims in the planes and targeted buildings became well known just as quickly: the professor traveling with her family to a university post in Australia, the Orthodox Jewish man in the World Trade Center who perished because he insisted on staying with his best friend confined to a wheelchair, the students and their teacher en route to a conference, the Pentagon clerk who, moments before the plane hit her wing of the building, had left a tender message on her daughter's answering machine, and hundreds more. In some cases, the world actually heard the last words of the dead—their final declarations of love, their terrified screams—and watched the faces of their families contorted in grief.[15] Some shows broadcast the names and phone numbers of the missing; many showed their pictures; others followed family members for days as they searched for their husbands and wives and sons and daughters and friends and lovers, endlessly reliving the intimate details of their last morning alive.[16]

There was an insatiable interest in these individuals as their stories continued to unfold over the following days, and weeks, and months. The *Wall*

Street Journal quickly began a daily feature titled "Tales from the Inferno," in which it chronicled the lives and deaths of men and women who had died on September 11. One month after the attack, the *Journal* presented another commemorative series of in-depth narratives.[17] The *New York Times* embarked upon an unprecedented feat of reporting as it launched its daily "Portraits of Grief": astute, nuanced, tender, and insightful cameos of each of the victims of the terrorist attack.[18] "Everyone is unique," the *Times'* editors told journalist Robin McNeal for a PBS feature on their work that aired in December 2001. On September 23, the *New York Times* also printed the names and pictures of each of the 343 firefighters reported missing or listed among the dead.[19]

Indeed, from the moment the first plane hit the first tower on September 11, there was nothing anonymous about any of the dead, from the most prominent executives to the police and firefighters, to the cooks and custodians, to the so-called ordinary men and women who rushed the terrorists and averted the murderous flight path of United flight 93. The focus on individuals did not abate as the first deaths were reported from the Afghan conflict. Once again, the American public instantly demanded and received information about each fallen individual, his family, his childhood, and his aspirations.[20]

Since the days of Ernie Pyle something profound has changed in the self-understanding and public conception of the soldier as well as the citizen. This change reflects the march of human consciousness in the wake of modern wealth, technology, and education. The new social sensibilities that recognize the sanctity of personhood cannot be escaped, not even in war. The military, in order to maintain the support of both politicians and the public it serves, can no longer regard its soldiers as nameless interchangeable parts in the immense machinery of war. Gone is the unending supply of anonymous fodder for the pitched battles of Gallipoli or Verdun or Normandy. Today each man and woman is first of all an individual. He or she has a name, a rank, a serial number, a cell phone, a fax number, an e-mail address, and a hard drive with a Pentium processor. Each has family and friends, a subjective sense of identity, multiple loyalties, opinions, rights, claims to self-determination, and access to the global community through television and the Internet. Each has dreams, and we can know all about those dreams, in vivid detail and instantly. They are us and, knowing that, we are reluctant to sacrifice even one.

As a society we are not willing to let individuals die by mass production, in "monstrous infinity." And as individuals, they are no longer willing to do so. This is why every branch of the armed forces is now struggling with the problem of how to more effectively attract and retain recruits. Even during the emotional two months that followed the September 11, 2001, attacks on the World Trade Center and the Pentagon, the U.S. Army Recruiting Command in Fort Knox, Kentucky, reported "minimal impact" on recruiting, and most National Guard stations continued to struggle to meet their quotas.[21] How do you turn individuals imbued with a hunger for psychological self-determination into soldiers? Is it even possible? In 2001, struggling with this question, the U.S. Army abandoned its twenty-year-old advertising slogan "Be all that you can be." In its place a new advertising campaign was launched with the headline "An Army of One." In the first television ad, a soldier runs alone through a vast desert. "I am an army of one," he says. "Even though there are 1,045,690 soldiers just like me, I am my own force. . . . The might of the U.S. Army doesn't lie in numbers; it lies in me."

As the pundits, journalists, and ad critics took aim at what appeared to be a blatantly dishonest bit of seduction, the secretary of the army, Louis Caldera, defended the new campaign. It had been based on extensive market research by the likes of management consultants McKinsey & Company and the RAND Corporation. Their surveys and interviews showed that the target group of eighteen- to twenty-four-year-olds regarded the army as dehumanizing and soldiers as "nameless, faceless people in green uniforms crawling through mud." The surveys showed that young people wanted control over their lives; they wanted to date, they wanted free time, they wanted to see immediate benefits from signing up. Thus the new ad campaign stressed "212 different ways to be a soldier." As Secretary Caldera put it, "What we are telling them is that the strength of the army is in individuals. Yes, you're a member of the team and you've got support from your fellow teammates, but you as an individual make a difference. . . . You've got to let them know that even though it is about selfless service, they are still individuals." Like a man with a foot in each of two rowboats drifting in opposite directions, the army's chief executive struggled to reconcile the ancient demands of warfare with the new society of individuals that will shape its future.[22]

In the United States today, there are many who are exhilarated by this social evolution and its potential for a more enlightened and humane future. Others use it as an opportunity for commercial exploitation, cynically addressing themselves to the new individuals by using the slogans of self-improvement to market thousands of products, publications, and experiences. Still others despair at what they regard as an erosion of communal bonds and mutual responsibility. But within the diversity of views one truth stands out: Even these varied and contradictory convictions are the result of individuals who have the education, the information, and the sense of psychological entitlement to form their own opinions. The very presence of so many perspectives is an expression of the new society of individuals at whose very heart lies the claim to psychological self-determination. No society has traveled here before.

TWENTIETH-CENTURY WEALTH AND ITS CONSEQUENCES

What happened in the twentieth century that propelled us into these new chapters of human history? How did the mass society of managerial capitalism give birth to this new society of individuals? While there are many answers, chief among them is this: In the United States and other Western economies, a new enterprise logic known as managerial capitalism created more wealth than had ever been imagined possible. That wealth—in conjunction with democratic politics expressed in labor unions, minimum wage laws, progressive tax codes, etc.—helped to unleash discontinuous change in nearly every aspect of society. New world-historical forces were set into motion that offered millions of people new physical, intellectual, and psychological experiences, from university education to world travel, mass media, abstract work, improved life expectancy, global communications, access to information, and hyperconsumption, to name just a few.

These are precisely the kinds of experiences that have helped to nourish psychological individuality on an unparalleled scale. These encounters exposed more people to more complexity, intensity, and diversity of experience, propelling them toward more intricate and self-authoring lives. Education and the growing abstraction of work increase mastery of language and thought, giving people the tools to create their own meanings and form their own opinions.[23] Communication, information, consumption, and travel all stimulate individual self-consciousness and imaginative capabilities, informing perspectives, values, and attitudes in ways that extend beyond tradition and group solidarity. Improvements in health, and especially the quality of an extended life span, provide the time for people to develop deeper moorings in their own capacities for selfhood and increase the society's willingness to value and invest in individual life.

The seeds of psychological individuality were planted in the eighteenth century, and their shoots continued to grow, but gradually, modestly, for nearly 200 years. It was only in the last four decades of the twentieth century, as people were exposed to the vast new social changes made possible by wealth, that psychological individuality came into full flower on a grand scale. These social changes have been the driving force behind the metamorphosis of mass society into a new society of individuals intent on sowing an utterly new field of dreams, as they seek the commercial equivalent of the Vietnam Veterans Memorial Wall. What follows, then, is a brief chronicle of some of the most important and discontinuous social changes that have helped to shape the new society of individuals.[24]

WEALTH

The twentieth century was characterized by a stunning increase in material prosperity, led by the United States, Western Europe, Japan, and the Commonwealth nations. By the second half of the twentieth century, the U.S. economy in particular had become a bountiful cornucopia of affordable goods, dependent on consumer expenditure for the economic growth that swelled the middle class. Economist J. Bradford DeLong has analyzed the U.S. economy from 1890 to 2000. He describes its most outstanding feature as the nearly continuous "broad upward sweep" across the century of the growth in gross domestic product (GDP) per worker.[25] (The single exception is the Great Depression, which temporarily wiped out income growth until the economic mobilization for World War II and then the ensuing peacetime reconversion.)[26] DeLong's comparison of GDP per worker in the early and late twentieth century, based on the standard measurement procedures, concludes that the "material standard of living and potential economic productivity at the start of the third millennium was nearly five times what it had been only 110 years before: a rate of per-worker real economic growth of 1.4 percent per year." Adjusted for the decline in working hours since 1890, that becomes a six- to sevenfold increase in measured per-hour real GDP. That means a family with six or seven times the median income back in 1890 would be able to buy as many 1890 goods and services as would an average American household today.[27]

But even such comparisons, he cautions, dramatically understate the real magnitude of economic growth, because they don't take into account the fact that about 45 percent of the value of what middle-class consumers in an advanced economy use is derived from goods and services that were not invented, or were not widely available, a century ago.[28] One hundred years ago, people spent most of their money on food, shelter, and clothing. The real discontinuity came in the second half of the twentieth century, when innovations in consumer goods, unmatched by anything that had occurred in the nineteenth century, transformed the character and quality of life. Most of the consumption opportunities that bring real value to people's lives today—medicine and medical technology; health insurance; higher education; microprocessors; software; air travel; unlimited access to information; mass-produced clothing and footwear; music, films, and entertainment; mass media; plastics; year-round access to high-quality fruits and vegetables; home appliances; health and beauty aids, to name but a few—simply did not exist one century ago. The richest man in the first half of the nineteenth century was Nathan Rothschild; like so many others, he died of an infected abscess because there were no antibiotics.[29] Some economists suggest that the standard measures of economic growth simply fail to capture the true magnitude of this economic discontinuity. Measures such as "per capita output growth" would show an even more pronounced rise in the twentieth century if they took into account the true values of new and improved goods and services.[30]

Based on the Boskin Commission's* work on consumer prices and economic growth, as well as other studies of new goods and services, DeLong concludes that economic output per worker can more accurately be considered to have multiplied by a factor of 16 since 1890.[31] This astonishing increase in material wealth has defined the economy of the United States, and similar trends characterize the rest of the Western industrial world. But DeLong also calculates that even today's average inhabitant of less wealthy countries, such as Mexico, Thailand, Botswana, has three to five times the productive potential of the average U.S. inhabitant in 1900. And he calculates that in even poorer countries, with a level of material output less than that of the United States in 1900, today's inhabitants are living about five times better than their counterparts of a century ago.[32] "Thus," he concludes, "not just in the United States, but worldwide, the twentieth century is unique in its pace of economic growth. Such rapid growth in standards of living has never been seen before, anywhere."[33] That fact alone is riveting. But it marks the beginning, not the end, of our story. That is because it is this material prosperity that has set the stage for the kinds of social developments that have shaped the new society of individuals.

A CONSUMER ECONOMY

By 1993, nearly two-thirds of all jobs in the U.S. economy were directly or indirectly dependent upon consumer expenditures, making consumers

*A presidential advisory commission established in 1995 to study the consumer price index and recommend needed changes.

responsible for more than 79 million jobs that year, a number that is expected to increase to 92 million jobs by 2005. Since the early 1970s, people have spent significantly more on their health, their homes, their computers and other electronic gear, travel, and recreation than in prior decades.[34]

Women continue to be at the front line of consumption. In 1996, some 84 percent of women in a large national survey said that they took care of the family's checkbook and paid all the bills.[35] In another large-scale survey in 1994, nearly 52 percent of women said that they "always" or "usually" did the shopping, while only 5 percent said that the man in the family "usually" or "always" shopped.[36] During the 1980s purchases of many consumer durables and services increased dramatically "as the growth in labor force participation of women spurred a need for more time-saving devices and the peak earning years of baby-boomers provided the wherewithal to buy them." Families spent significantly more on timesaving devices like telephone answering machines, home entertainment like VCRs and cable television for tired parents, and services to help augment Mom's traditional role, like restaurant meals, child care, and housekeeping.[37] All of this suggests that the commercialization of women's needs and desires continues to be a principal theme in economic growth.

Consumption in the twentieth century clearly reflects the long march from necessities to decencies to luxuries that began in the eighteenth century. However, the intensity and complexity of modern life, combined with the sophisticated experiences of the new individuals, worked a new kind of magic: Luxuries, once achieved, were routinely reinterpreted as necessities. Consumption was no longer only a matter of buying what you could not grow or make. Nor was it primarily a case of purchasing more luxurious versions of those early necessities as a means of expressing refinement, gentility, and class. Consumption now centered on new goods and new services whose function and meaning were gradually converted from being special to being necessary. Such was the trend for goods like automobiles, medical technology, and health insurance. Eventually stereos, laptop computers, running shoes, and a trip to Machu Picchu began to look pretty essential too. Victorian sensibilities that denounced the corrupting effects of consumption found new voice on both sides of the political spectrum in well-respected social observers from David Riesman and John Kenneth Galbraith at mid-century to Christopher Lasch, Daniel Bell, and, more recently, Juliet Schor.[38] But these did little to interrupt the continuous expansion of human yearning.

As consumption became the dominant force in economic growth, researchers began to appreciate it as an important and complicated social process in its own right. Consumption can be an expression of community, an outlet for spiritual expression and the preservation of ethnic heritage, a way of constructing one's identity, a means to achieve personal growth and self-renewal, an expression of values and meaning, an action that generates personal energy, an opportunity to express free choice, a way of elaborating self-concept, a means of expressing fantasies, feelings, and having fun, a way to demonstrate motherly love, a rite of passage, and an expression of imagination, to name but a few of the findings that have emerged from this new field of study.[39] In other words, the processes and objects of consumption contribute to a more complex world and help develop more complex people. Consumption both develops and expresses psychological individuality.

EDUCATION

Secondary education in the United States was the dramatic educational story of the first half of the century,[40] and it paved the way for another drama—the accelerated expansion of college education that followed World War II. In 1900, only 2.3 percent of all the U.S. adults between ages eighteen and twenty-four were enrolled in college. By 1940, that proportion had grown to 9.1 percent, but by 1999 it had exploded to 55.7 percent. There is another even more startling way to appreciate the twentieth century's educational accomplishments. Consider that in 1640 only 0.1 percent of the population in the American colonies attended a university. By 1900, that number had edged up to only 0.3 percent of people in the United States. By 1940 it had grown to 1.1 percent but by 1999 it was 5.4 percent. This means that from the seventeenth to the twentieth century this proportion grew by a factor of 3. But during the twentieth century alone, it grew by a factor of 18!

In 1996, 23.6 percent of all adults in the United States had college degrees, as compared to 6.2 percent in 1950. The disruption of World War II and the educational benefits that accompanied the postwar GI Bill added considerable thrust to this trend. It helped universalize access to higher education (half of those who used the GI benefits came from families in which neither parent had gone to college). It also forced an increase in the supply of higher education as total enrollments increased by 1 million students, from 1.5 million in 1940 to 2.5 million in 1949, and college gradually came to be viewed as an entitlement of high school graduates.[41]

More bachelor's degrees, in turn, paved the way for another educational explosion in advanced degrees, the number of which increased by a factor of 218 in the twentieth century. In 1900, a mere 1,965 people received master's or doctorate degrees, compared to 30,021 in 1940 and 428,900 in 2000. If you consider these numbers as a percentage of the total population, the increases are even more dramatic. In 1900 only .003 percent of the total U.S. population attained an advanced degree. In 2000 that proportion was 2.0 percent. While that may still seem like a tiny percentage, consider that this proportion increased by a factor of 667 in just one century. Professional degrees showed a similarly explosive growth curve during the century.[42]

One of the most sensational features of this education story is the rise in the numbers of educated women. Between 1910 and 1960 there was a significant gap between the number of degrees granted to men and to women. By 1980, women outnumbered men at college graduations. That year, more than 50 percent of all master's degrees and nearly 30 percent of all doctorates were conferred upon women. In 1900, women received 16.5 percent of the few advanced degrees awarded. In 1940 that proportion was 35 percent, and by 2000 it was 56 percent.[43] The last quarter of the century also saw a revolution in the numbers of women receiving professional degrees. This is particularly significant, given how recently the gender barriers to professional education were removed. The U.S. Census Bureau reported only ten women attorneys in 1870, seventy-five in 1890, and just over 1,000 in 1900.[44] Harvard Law School did not begin to admit women until the 1950s. The story is only slightly brighter for the women who pioneered in medicine. The few female doctors in the late nineteenth century faced intense prejudice and hostility. The need for medical personnel during the Civil War increased their numbers to 2,500 by 1880, and by 1920 there were about 8,800 women doctors practicing in the United States.[45] A similar pattern was repeated in other professions such as the clergy, architecture, dentistry, engineering, and business.[46]

It was not until the late twentieth century that women's entry to the professions changed decisively. For example, in 1970 5.4 percent of all law degrees and 8.4 percent of all medical degrees were awarded to women. In 1990 women garnered nearly 41 percent of the degrees in law and 33 percent of the degrees in medicine. In 1960, some 5,000 men were awarded MBA degrees, compared to only 200 women, a ratio of 25:1. At that time most business schools, including Harvard Business School, did not even consider female applicants. In the subsequent thirty years, however, there was a 10-fold increase in MBAs for men, and a 150-fold increase for women. By 1990, the ratio of men to women among MBAs had dropped to 5:3.[47]

HEALTH

The combination of wealth and better-educated people increased human life expectancy. During the twentieth century, infant mortality rates in the United

States shrank from 162 to 7 babies dying for every 1,000 born.[48] Average life expectancy climbed from 47.3 years in 1900 to 76.4 years in 2000.[49] As infant deaths fell below 30 per 1,000, life expectancy also began a clear upward trend. It was precisely during those years that higher education enrollments began to show steep increases and personal recreational expenditures began to climb. There were many specific reasons for these increases, and each is independently related in some way to increases in wealth. But it may also be true that just as eighteenth-century families deepened their attachments to their children once more of them began to survive infancy reliably, so U.S. society began to invest more in the long arc of education as people became convinced they could live longer and well.[50]

THE CHANGING NATURE OF WORK

As the century progressed, work became more abstract. This trend arose from higher levels of automation that marginalized workers from the physical aspects of their tasks. But it also expressed a deeper shift in employment toward white-collar knowledge and service-oriented activities.[51] Indeed, along with all of its other remarkable achievements, the twentieth century was the first to see a society, such as that of the United States, in which a majority of the workforce was exempt from the excesses of physical exertion that had been work's implacable companion since the beginning of time. The rapid progress of computerization since 1980 further accelerated this already well-defined trend.[52] By the century's end, the labor force was dominated by technical and professional work. The professional class accounted for only single-digit percentages of the 1900 labor force, but by the year 2000 managers, professionals, and technicians accounted for 27 percent of the working population.

Manufacturing work had once ruled the economy, but it declined to about 18 percent of employment at the end of the century, while service work exploded to comprise more than 70 percent of employment. Between 1996 and 2006, services are expected to account for 11.3 million of the 17.6 million new jobs that are projected, or 64 percent of all job growth. Employment in this sector is projected to grow at a rate of nearly 3 percent, more than twice the rate for other jobs. Moreover, the fastest-growing industries within this sector are also those that are highly knowledge-intensive, namely "business" and "health" services, which together account for nearly 60 percent of all projected job growth in services. When two other knowledge-intensive industries are added to this tally—"social services" and "engineering, management, and related services"—78 percent of all new service-job growth is accounted for.[53]

At the same time, computerization transformed work in every sector and at every level of the organization, increasing the intellectual content of work for blue and white collar alike. By the mid-1990s, some 30 percent of those with only a high school education and 60 percent of those with a college education or more were using computers daily as part of their job.[54] The broader distribution of information, and sometimes knowledge too, created a new dynamism inside organizations in which more people had more information, more insight, and more opinions about what to do. This challenged organizational hierarchies, and also created a good deal of resistance and dysfunction as managers frequently endeavored to maintain their sources of authority at work.[55]

WORKING WOMEN

In 1936, a *Fortune* magazine survey found that 54 percent of male and 41 percent of female respondents disapproved of women working outside the home. By 1960 the scene hadn't changed much. The University of Michigan Survey Research Center found that 46 percent of its survey respondents thought it was a bad thing for a wife to have a job.[56] Despite these seemingly intractable attitudes, the feminization of the labor force became one of the big headlines of the U.S. and other industrialized economies in the twentieth century. And as in the eighteenth century, an explosion in the number of women at work helped fuel their preeminence in the new consumption, while their difficulties and successes on the job helped to shape their desire for psychological self-determination.

For the first half of the century in the United States, women tended to enter the labor force in their late teens, depart at around age twenty-five to have their families, and then sometimes reenter in their late thirties or early forties for a few years before retirement. For example, in 1950 about 45 percent of all twenty-year-old women were working, compared to only about 30 percent of twenty-five-year-olds. The numbers climbed back up to near 40 percent for middle-aged women and then declined sharply after age fifty-five. This gave rise to what statisticians call the "M" curve of women's labor force participation, and it compares to the inverted "U" curve for men, in which they join the labor force in their late teens and twenties, and remain working through to retirement in their sixties. As recently as 1967, fewer than 25 percent of mothers with children under age three were in the labor force.[57]

By 1987 the pattern of women's labor force participation had begun to change. Labor economists called it the "flattening M," because the "M" was turning into an inverted "U," just like the men's pattern. That year the labor force participation rate for twenty-year-olds was about 73 percent, 72 percent for those twenty-five to thirty-four years old, 74 percent for those thirty-five to forty-five years old, and 67 percent for those forty-five to fifty-four years old. For women with no children under the age of eighteen, the participation rate was nearly 90 percent. It fell to 82 percent for moms with teenagers and ratcheted its way down to 57 percent of moms with children under age six. As one economist summarized, "The fact that more than half of all mothers with toddlers were in the labor market in 1987 indicates the magnitude of social and economic change in recent years."[58]

By the late 1990s the same trend was even more strongly in evidence in the United States, and it was projected to strengthen further by 2010.[59] In 1997, for example, 60 percent of all U.S. women were working, up from only 33 percent in 1950 and accounting for 46 percent of the entire U.S. labor force. By that year, 64 percent of all moms with children under six remained in the labor force.[60] These trends also receive firm support among young adults. Indeed, nearly 90 percent of adults between eighteen and thirty-four consider a woman's career to be as important as a man's. They expect mothers to work and believe that working mothers can have just as good a relationship with their children as full-time moms.[61]

Similar patterns have been identified in other industrialized countries. The United Kingdom, Australia, Canada, Sweden, and the Netherlands all experienced significant increases in the labor force participation of married women since 1960. In the United Kingdom, for example, only 33 percent of married women worked in 1960, compared to 74 percent in 1998. There have also been substantial, though less dramatic, increases in France. Only in Germany and Italy have formal measures of married women's entry into the labor market shown little change.[62]

Harvard economist Claudia Goldin deepens this analysis with a specific look at the experiences of college-educated U.S. women in the twentieth century. Between 1908 and 1917, women who finished college faced a choice of having a family or a career. Half of them chose careers, typically as librarians, nurses, teachers, or social workers. They never married or had children. Their stark choices reflect more than personal inclination. They were also an expression of the marriage bars that existed both formally and informally in many organizations that refused to either hire or retain married women. A second generation attended college between 1940 and 1960. Imbued with the reigning ideology of the nuclear family and strictly enforced gender roles,

they tended to have families first, then seek a job, typically in female occupations such as teaching or clerical work, once their children were grown. A
third cohort was born during the peak baby-boom years and graduated from
college by 1979. Goldin found that the majority of these women joined the
labor force and about 43 percent of them developed careers. But Goldin's
analysis also reveals that only between 13 percent and 17 percent were able
to achieve a combination of family and career. Many of the career women
postponed marriage and childbirth into their late thirties and early forties,
while many others rejected marriage, or children, altogether. The peculiar
stresses on the educated women who tried to "have it all" were also evidenced in their rates of divorce that were as much as 20 percent to 30 percent
higher than for the larger group of college-educated women in the same age
cohort.[63]

The dramatic increases in women's education and professional training
that characterized the last decades of the twentieth century have also
strengthened women's abilities to find employment and establish careers
outside of the traditionally female occupations. The long trend toward the
abstraction of work has operated in favor of widening women's employment
opportunities, and this trend too has been accelerated as the process of computerization penetrates virtually every corner of the labor market. Many
jobs in manufacturing and the trades that were once closed to women because of their physical requirements now depend upon computers. As the
physical component of work vanishes, so too do the traditional gender barriers. One economist estimates that as much as 50 percent of the growth in demand for women workers since the mid-1970s can be accounted for by the
spread of computerization.[64]

There are many stories behind these statistics. Women work because
they can, they work because they want to, and they work because they have
to. There is compelling data that suggests most of the increase in women's
full-time employment since 1978 has been due to financial necessity.[65] As a
counterpoint, it is worth noting that another national survey found that the
vast majority of women in every age cohort said they would continue to
work even if they had enough money to live as comfortably as they liked for
the rest of their lives.[66] Of course, as new consumer goods and services are
constantly redefined as "necessities," the concept of "financial necessity" itself becomes a lot more complicated.

It's a good thing for the United States, as well as for the global economy,
that working women were not deterred by the traditions of prejudice they
faced because their earnings are largely responsible for the enormous expansion of the consumer economy. Women are the sole sources of income in

many families today, and in many more families their incomes are no longer supplemental but vital to the family's standard of living. In fact, it is now clear that the standard of living would have fallen for many middle-class families, who have seen little growth in their real income since the early 1970s, were it not for the contribution of women's earnings. Only families composed of married couples with two wage earners consistently managed to escape income stagnation during the last decades of the twentieth century.[67] A 1995 survey showed that in most families, a woman's income accounted for half or more of the total family income. In only 44 percent of families was the woman's income contributing less than half of the family's total earnings.[68]

There continue to be many important problems associated with women's participation at work. Women have tended to be segregated in less remunerative and more subordinate jobs. They have also received less pay than men for the same work. There are well-documented "glass ceilings" in most occupations that unjustly limit what women can achieve. But for this part of our story, we want to concentrate on one set of facts: The women who helped shape the mass markets of the early twentieth century mostly did not work. When they did, it tended to be for a few years, until they had children, and later for a few more years after their children were grown. In contrast, today's women mostly do work, even when they have young children at home.[69] They have been left to fend for themselves as they explore a new range of human experience, juggling their commitments to family and to work in an occupational world that was built by and for men. The quiet heroism of this undertaking is exactly the sort of experience that acts upon the human personality to create a more differentiated and complex self. This puts women in the vanguard of the new society of individuals, even as it amplifies their role in consumption. Once again, it suggests that the commercialization of women's dreams will be an important factor in the next economic revolution, defining the new structure of consumption as the mass order fades.

INFORMATION AND COMMUNICATION

The democratization of information sharply intensified in the second half of the twentieth century. Like education, this is a powerful force that contributes to an individual's ability to form opinions and exercise informed choice. One-way "broadcast" technologies like television, radio, cable, satellite, and recording have become just about universal.[70] This means that experiences that were once highly restricted on the basis of income, expertise, or

location are now accessible to all. It is easy to overlook the fact that the opportunity to listen to a talented orchestra perform a great symphony is now
within the reach of anyone with a radio or a CD player. At the start of the
twentieth century, only the elite would have had access to such an experience, and it would have been confined to a particular concert hall on the date
of the symphony's performance. Similarly, astronomical events could be
viewed only by astronomers on modest telescopes. Political events could be
experienced only by actually attending them. Eventually, newsreels began to
spread important information about such experiences to a wider audience.
But even that could not compare with real-time coverage in the media and
on the Internet of a moon landing, a hostage taking, a bombing campaign, an
exploration of the surface of Mars, or a terrorist attack.

Over the course of the century, more people wrote books and magazine
articles, and more people read them. In 1903 there was one publication for
every 10,000 people. As the U.S. population grew, that ratio declined to
1:12,640 in 1920, and it decreased further to 1:13,721 in 1950. Only in the
second half of the century did these ratios dramatically reverse, with 1:5,650
in 1970 and 1:4,618 in 1989.[71] Book sales also reached new levels, with 1.7
billion volumes sold in the United States in 1995, an increase of about 430
million over 1982. As people have become wealthier, more educated, more
skilled, experienced, and informed, and therefore more individual, so too
have their interests. In the 1950s, when Americans were more of a common
mind, periodicals like the *Saturday Evening Post, Life, Time,* and *Newsweek*
all thrived. But by late century, a new style of magazine had begun to dominate the newsstands. In the mid-1980s, special-interest magazines accounted
for 80 percent of the 1,300 titles in a typical Barnes & Noble bookstore.[72]
Special-interest offerings nearly doubled the number of magazine titles between 1986 and 1996, from 2,400 to 4,200. In 1986 the twenty-five highest-
volume retail magazines accounted for 52 percent of sales, but by 1996 that
number had fallen to 35 percent of sales.[73] "There are a lot of people out
there with unique passions," one publishing executive told the *New York
Times,* "and less and less time to pursue them."[74] These readers want magazines that speak directly to them and to their interests. Enter *American
Patchwork and Quilting, True Crime, Brew Magazine, Coffee Journal,
Northern California Bride, Dressage and CT Magazine, Walking, Fly Fish-
erman, Combat Handgunner, Modern Ferret,* and *American Cheerleader.*

Broadcast television has undergone a similar metamorphosis, from a
handful of network channels catering to the masses, to scores of cable and
satellite channels directed to ever-narrower audiences. In 1980, fewer than
20 percent of U.S. households had cable service, but by 1995 that number

had grown to 63.4 percent. It's no longer merely the Food Channel or the History Channel. Now it's the Discovery Wings cable channel for aviation buffs, Discovery Health for those eager to follow the latest medical news, Discovery Home and Leisure for do-it-yourselfers, and Discovery Civilization for kids with a homework assignment on ancient Egypt.[75]

Since the mid-1990s the Internet has dramatically multiplied communications and information access, removing it from the domain of centralized broadcasters and placing it in the hands of a worldwide network of individuals. A few figures are illustrative. According to Jupiter Communications, in 1996 only about 10 percent of U.S. households were online. That percentage had climbed to 50 percent by 2000 and was expected to reach about 63 percent by 2003. That would mean a 500 percent increase in just seven years. In 1991 in the United States there were about 3 million Internet users—a number that multiplied more than 40 times to just over 121 million by the end of the decade. During the same period, non-U.S. Internet users increased by a factor of 60, from about 4.5 million in 1991 to 263 million in 2000.[76] The World Wide Web now provides even once-isolated individuals instant access to every major newspaper, as well as to books, financial analysis, and information on virtually every subject.

Even as commercial fortunes rise and fall on the Web, the appetite for electronic community and person-to-person communications appears to be insatiable. People talk to each other for business and pleasure, forming and communicating opinions, forging and deepening relationships, doing deals and enjoying gossip. Market-research firms estimate that in 2000 there were nearly 10 billion e-mail messages sent daily from between 450 and 570 million e-mail accounts worldwide, about 55 percent of which were in North America. The number of accounts was expected to grow to over 1 billion by 2005. More people now use the Internet for e-mail than for "surfing the Web." In 2000, about 60 percent of those messages were business-based, and the rest were from personal accounts.[77]

RECREATION AND TRAVEL

People in the United States are spending more on recreation than they have in the past. Personal consumption expenditure on recreation as a percentage of total personal consumption rose steadily throughout the century, with a particularly smooth upward growth curve since mid-century. Between 1970 and 1994 the total national expenditure on recreation increased from $94 billion to $370 billion, a rise of 294 percent. Recreational expenditures as a percent of total personal expenditures nearly doubled, from 4.3 percent in 1970 to 8.3 percent in 1994.[78] Between 1990 and 2001 alone, consumer spending per person per year on media entertainment (television, radio, recordings, newspapers, books and magazines, videos, movies, Internet access, and software) also nearly doubled, increasing from $365 to $685.[79] A 1997 study by MIT economist Dora Costa analyzed recreation expenditures since 1888. She concluded that "leisure is now less of a luxury" as Americans of all income levels were able to spend more of their money on recreation by the century's end. This was due to the rising percentage of discretionary income for families at all income levels, as well as significant decreases in the cost of recreation and entertainment.[80]

Most Americans now have routine access to experiences that until quite recently were reserved for the elite. Across the United States, in cities and small towns, people are drinking gourmet coffees and seeking out sophisticated foods. They can find sauces and condiments from all over the world in their local supermarkets, along with salad greens and exotic fruits from Europe, South America, the Middle East, and Asia. *Bon Appetit* magazine now sells nearly one-third of its 1.1 million copies each month in the heartland states, long considered a culinary wasteland. In 1997, 27 percent of the nation's highest rated restaurants were in rural areas, as compared to only 19 percent as recently as 1993. The number of nonprofit professional theater companies in the United States has grown to more than 800 today, compared to fewer than 60 in 1965. More than 110 American symphony orchestras have been founded since 1980—including the Louisiana Philharmonic in New Orleans and the Northwest Symphony near Seattle. Opera attendance is up 34 percent since 1980; there are now more than one hundred professional opera companies in the United States, thirty-four of which were founded since 1980. Public radio stations specializing in classical music and extensive news analysis have more than tripled since 1980 to about 700.[81] In 2001, *Newsweek* magazine offered extensive coverage of a boom in museum construction and expansion, "symbolizing the aspirations of communities" across the country.[82]

In 1936 a prestigious London publishing house produced an authoritative study of the worldwide tourist industry by a learned professor of industrial economics from the University of Pretoria. In considering U.S. tourism, he concluded that the development of the national parks, the political pressure for a more equitable distribution of wealth, the weakening of U.S. ties to Europe, and the country's bent toward isolationism would "weaken rather than strengthen the desire on the part of U.S. citizens to visit distant overseas countries."[83] Such is the nature of discontinuity that it is visible only in the rearview mirror. In this case, overseas travel, once reserved for wealthy families who made "the grand tour," has become the object of an insatiable appetite for millions of people. The jet airplane speaks to the dreams of people who now have the cultural exposure, self-confidence, disposable income, and curiosity to travel abroad. In turn, it has exposed them to more diversity, complexity, dissonance, and discovery than ever before—precisely the sorts of experiences that contribute to individualized sensibilities.

In 1929 there were 517,000 overseas trips from the United States, and by 1950 that number had increased only modestly to 676,000. From 1950 to 1996 the number of international trips increased 3,500 percent to 20 million. That means one trip for every 235,000 people in 1929, one for every 225,000 in 1950, and one for every 13,275 people in 1996.[84] Travel has contributed to the long-term processes of psychological individuation, and the new individuals already have had a considerable effect on the consumption of travel. Some of the largest growth in the industry now comes from "special-interest" travel. For example, adventure travel has become one of the fastest-growing industry segments, netting $100 billion in revenues in 2000, up 14 percent from 1998.

Adventure travelers pay thousands of dollars to visit a traditional healer and attend a voodoo ceremony in places like Togo and Benin, or to learn the skills of hunting with eagles in the mountains of western Mongolia, to live with nomads, to balloon over Cappadocia and trek in the Pontic Alps in Turkey, to cruise the Straits of Magellan in southern Chile while game-spotting guanacos and nandus, or to crawl inside a polar bear den in the subarctic tundra. In Bolivia, the government has promoted "Che Guevara Adventure Tours" that follow the path of that infamous guerrilla leader. At Victoria Falls, between Zimbabwe and Zambia, bungee jumpers, whitewater rafters, and kayakers compete for space with the helicopters, sky divers, and light planes that whoosh overhead. In 1987 about 70,000 people visited the falls; by 1997 it was 300,000, and by 2006 one million visitors are anticipated.[85]

There are also travel agents who specialize in helping "volunteer vacationers" hook up with not-for-profit agencies around the world for holiday trips that provide meaning as well as an opportunity to see new places.[86] Some do short Peace Corps–like stints, hooking up with communities in need; others work on environmental projects in remote areas of the globe.[87] Prior to September 11, 2001, U.S. travel firms ran sell-out tours to the Gaza Strip, Northern Ireland, and Haiti to a new kind of tourist seeking "war-zone" travel. There is also "eco-travel," which takes people deep into natural environments like rain forests and mountain jungles, where they can enjoy

ecologically sound accommodations that blend with local wildlife and vege-
tation. In 1997, some 15,000 people visited Antarctica. Some wildlife areas
have even had to ration the number of tourists they can accept, in order to
protect indigenous animals and people.

Americans are not the only ones clamoring down the jetways. In 1925
just over 30,000 people came to the United States for a "pleasure visit"; in
1985 that number had grown to nearly 7 million, and by 1996 it had increased to more than 19 million![88] According to the World Tourism Organization, in 1996 travelers took some 595 million trips abroad, 77 percent
more than they had in 1986. And, the WTO predicts, that number will grow
to 937 million by 2010. The World Travel and Tourism Council estimated
the total economic value of goods and services attributable to tourism in
1996 at $3.6 trillion, or 10.6 percent of the gross global product for that year.
It calculated that in 1996 tourism sustained more than one in ten jobs around
the world, providing work for 255 million people, and that it could create
another 130 million jobs by 2006.[89] By that year some 15 percent of the
world's population could be traveling abroad, creating something of a permanently rotating global population. The number of people roaming around
the world for business and pleasure is certain to rise and fall with the intensity of concerns over personal safety and airport security, reflecting the competitive and regulatory responses to those concerns. Nevertheless, the twin
pressures of individualization and globalization suggest that the trajectory of
these long-term trends will remain strong.

FAMILY

By the end of the twentieth century, the American family had exploded into
dozens of new and variegated forms. It was clear that the new individuals
could no longer be contained by the traditional structures of the family and
its prescribed roles, norms, and duties. Such was the intensity of this explosion that even the U.S. Census Bureau, normally given to understated analysis, was moved to introduce its 1996 report "Family Composition" with this
caveat: "The increasing diversity of household types continues to challenge
our efforts to measure and describe American society. The typical household
is an illusion."[90] In 1950 nearly every household—88 percent—contained a
married couple.[91] By 2000 the percentage had slipped to 51.7 percent.[92] In
1950 just over 44 percent of homes had children in them.[93] By 2000 just over
23 percent did.[94] These patterns are even more pronounced among young
adults ages twenty-five to thirty-four. In that group, only 12.1 percent fit the
profile of the "traditional household" (married couple with children, only

the husband works), compared to more than half in 1970.[95] In 1950 about 9 percent of all households were made up of single people, and by 1995 that number was up to 25 percent, with women outnumbering men by a ratio of 1.5 to 1.[96] In 1963, some 83 percent of women ages twenty-five to fifty-five were married; by 1997 that figure was down to 65 percent.[97]

Many women, and men too, no longer regarded marriage as a necessary component of a fulfilled life. A poll conducted in 2000 showed that only 34 percent of women and 41 percent of men thought they would settle for someone less than their "perfect" mate.[98] Among households with children, about 27 percent were headed by single parents in 1998, compared to 11 percent in 1970.[99] In 1998 women outnumbered men in single-parent families by a ratio of 6 to 1.[100] According to the 2000 Census figures, the number of single mothers increased by 25 percent between 1990 and 2000 to 7.6 million or 7.2 percent of all households.[101] The rate of increase in unmarried couples living together has also been significant. The rate per 1,000 households was 8.3 in 1970 and 34.6 in 1992. But among those under age twenty-five, the rate increased from 12.8 to 136.0 during that period. Additionally, of the more than 3 million unmarried-couple households in 1992, just under 5 percent were same-sex partnerships.[102]

Other developments that stumped the census takers: Households are shrinking; more people live alone; more children live with their grandparents; more unrelated people live with one another. Families have changed in character, as divorce rates quadrupled between 1970 and 1996 to result in more than 18 million divorced adults, and about 50 percent of all marriages now result in divorce. There are blended families and stepfamilies and many variations of living arrangements among them.[103] So extensive have been these changes that many schools have had to expunge Mother's Day and Father's Day celebrations from their annual calendars. They have learned to avoid certain kinds of assignments like asking students to create their "family tree."[104] When it comes to families, what could once be taken for granted is now an arena for society-wide experimentation and innovation.[105]

Nor are these developments confined to the United States. While the numbers are most dramatic there, other Western countries, including Canada, France, Denmark, Germany, Italy, the Netherlands, Sweden, and the United Kingdom exhibit the same trends, with some moving much faster than others. Divorce rates are increasing. Married-couple households are declining in share, as are married-couple households with children. Single-parent and one-person households are on the rise. There has also been a rapid increase in the numbers of unmarried couples living together, and in some countries the idea of "consensual unions" without marriage has gained considerable legitimacy.[106] In 1998 about 38 percent of British births and 41 percent of French births occurred outside marriage.[107] By 2001, the nuclear family was no longer considered the norm in most of the world. A majority of people in North and South America, Europe, and the Asia-Pacific region disagreed with the statement "Families can only be formed through blood, marriage, or adoption; friends and live-in lovers don't count."[108] Even Britain's royal family had to reconcile itself to the claims of psychological self-determination as it reluctantly accepted the divorces of its princes Charles and Andrew.

RUPTURE AND MUTATION

The structure of human experience has changed qualitatively throughout the centuries, reflecting changes in the conditions of material life. For example, the concept of childhood as a separate and unique stage of life developed only in the eighteenth century, as babies more reliably survived beyond infancy.[109] Similarly, an American during the colonial period would have been hard-pressed to identify what was meant by the terms "middle-age," "lifestyle," or "self-realization." There was neither enough wealth, enough life, nor enough leisure for the experiences associated with these concepts to take shape.[110] Yale historian John Demos observed that these sorts of "deep structure" alterations in the mentality of a people can occur within the space of a single generation.[111]

In the last half of the twentieth century we have seen just this sort of rupture and mutation in the mentality of people. The consequences of managerial capitalism—wealth, education, science, and all that has followed from those developments—have wrought a new mentality that is a true discontinuity with the past. They worked their way into the hairline cracks that had been barely visible in the old harmony between the mass and its organizations. Those hairline cracks were the early expression of a still inchoate, unnamed, but expanding sense of individuality that could no longer be contained by the old structures. Eventually the one-time unity was not only ruptured but transformed, producing the people born around mid-century and after, who possess an abiding sense of their own uniqueness and who believe they are entitled to personal self-determination. They have established a new mentality of psychological individuality that would have been an unnatural act of hubris for their parents or grandparents. They share a new mentality that can no longer be reconciled with mass society. And they constitute a new kind of marketplace, still awaiting the invention of an appropriate new enterprise logic.

As a result of this social discontinuity, the family today is more than the place from which people are channeled into organizations to learn how to succeed. Today one expects to "grow" in special ways in relation to other family members. Not only do husbands and wives expect to contribute to one another's self-realization, but parents now regard it as their responsibility to help facilitate the growth and self-fulfillment of their children. French historian Antoine Prost, in considering his country's revolution in mentalities during the second half of the twentieth century, sums it up for many people in many countries when he writes, "A half century ago the family took precedence over the individual; now the individual takes precedence over the family. The individual once was an intrinsic part of his or her family. Private life was secondary, subordinate, and in many cases secret or marginal. Now the relation of individual to family has been reversed.... Now the family is judged by the contribution it makes to the individual private lives of its members."[112] One need only read Henry James's observations of the old European families or contemplate the fate of Victor Hugo's daughter Adele, ruthlessly forced into isolation in order to protect her father from shame, to appreciate the accuracy of Prost's assessment.

Not only are families now expected to contribute to the individual, but what and how they contribute may be severely judged. Parents are expected to nurture their children toward self-realization, rather than infect them with competitive anxieties and unfulfilled ambitions. One columnist from *Time* addressed the allegedly rising levels of anxiety among children, counseling parents to "keep your expectations for your children reasonable. Many highly successful people never attended Harvard or Yale."[113] Another respected career counselor who taught a Radcliffe adult education program has devoted an entire book to a subject she calls "hand me down dreams." "Because I believe that much happiness derives from finding meaningful work that expresses our unique creative selves," she writes, "... this book concentrates on the ways our families influence our careers ... [and] the barriers families may wittingly or unwittingly construct on our path toward satisfying work lives." Her advice to readers is to "decode" the messages received from our families, "redefine" our responsibilities to them, and "rediscover" our own dreams.[114]

Mike Nichols told the story that best captured the essence of this reversal of fortune in his wildly popular 1967 film, *The Graduate*.[115] Benjamin, played by the young Dustin Hoffman, was the newly educated individual. His graduation from college turned him into a graduate of the old order and with it all that remained of the Victorian family and its conventions and organizations. After college, he returns to his parents, only to discover that he no longer feels connected to the very kinship circle that launched him into the world. He sleepwalks through their revelry and affection, upending sexual norms and social conventions, attuned only to his private search for meaning.

Benjamin's future feels like a gathering storm of questions until he meets Elaine, played by the ingenue Katherine Ross. Romantic love, freely chosen and against the odds, becomes a sacred source of self-definition. But Elaine hasn't quite "graduated" yet. She allows her family to arrange a loveless but socially useful marriage. Just as her wedding vows are being spoken, Benjamin appears in the church. He bellows like a wounded animal, crying out to her from the very depths of his soul. Like Dostoyevsky's Jesus to the Grand Inquisitor, his grief testifies to a deeper truth—a personal truth known only to those with a psychological awareness of their own individuality and felt to have a legitimacy that runs deeper than the rules of organizations and families. At that moment, in response to his tormented wail, Elaine's own pilgrim soul is finally and irreversibly ignited, and she screams out his name.

Elaine and Benjamin flee the church in a violent melee, using a crucifix to fight off their families. Once liberated, they gleefully escape onto a passing bus that will take them to their futures. But after only a few moments of euphoria and exhilaration, they face each other with dismay. The anxiety that settles over them is palpable, and their looks of triumphant happiness fade to discomfort. They sit dazed and silent, as a voice begins to whisper, *"Hello darkness, my old friend."*[116]

Under the relentless gaze of the other bus passengers, Benjamin swallows hard and Elaine stares into space, each struck with the enormity of what they have embarked upon. They have succeeded in ripping their lives free from every tradition. But in order to win the right to self-authorship, they have also forfeited their rights to inherited knowledge of the road ahead. Who would help them now? Who would love them? How would they find their way? The world had suddenly shrunk to just two, and all the maps had vanished. *"In restless dreams I walked alone . . ."*[117]

FOUR

The New Society of Individuals

And so it is that millions of people in the global society of the late twentieth century have enthusiastically followed Benjamin and Elaine onto their own private bus, realizing later that it is they who must do the driving, across uncharted terrain, toward a place they cannot know.

THE RISE OF THE NEW INDIVIDUAL

Managerial capitalism helped to create a world of unprecedented abundance. With that plenty came education, health, opportunity, information, and experiences of ever-greater complexity. New people emerged from this rich stew. We call them "individuals." The new individuals seek meaning, not just material security and comfort. They enjoy their things but place an even higher value on the quality of the lives they lead, in which those possessions play a part. They insist on self-expression, participation, and influence because they share the certain knowledge that the singularity of their own lives cannot be deduced from the general case. No longer born to a biography, their identities must be invented as they go—cobbled together from personal initiative and private judgment.

These new voices rise from the United States to the United Kingdom, from Canada to New Zealand, and across Western Europe. They have gathered force in the offices and classrooms of Santiago, Istanbul, and Prague. They form a new society of individuals who share a claim to psychological self-determination—an abiding sense that they are entitled to make themselves. Managerial capitalism and its now standard enterprise logic were designed to meet the needs of their parents, grandparents, great-grandparents. Today its rules persist, but they are woefully inadequate when it comes to responding to the realities of life in the new society of individuals. This is not a mere failure of marketing but a fundamental challenge to commerce as we know it—because what the new individuals want most cannot be bought or sold in today's commercial world.

It is vital to understand the new individuals now, because it is from their dreams that a new enterprise logic and a new capitalism will need to be constructed. They are not only the source of future wealth, they hold the key to how that wealth can be created. In this chapter we describe the new individuals and the effect they are having upon society—its values, laws, and patterns of association. Then, in the following two chapters, we explore some of the consequences of the old organizations for the quality of life of the new individuals at work (Chapter Five) and the new approaches to consumption they are inventing (Chapter Six).

PSYCHOLOGICAL INDIVIDUALITY AROUND THE WORLD

What began in American life as the self-conscious assertion of political individuality has mutated into a widely experienced sense of psychological individuality. But is this a uniquely American phenomenon? While these ideas tend to describe many people who live in the United States and other centers of the world economy, there are many others too, in more slow-moving regions, for whom exposure to education, information, mass media, and consumption has been sufficient to awaken a subjective sense of their own individuality. Indeed, individuality is becoming a shared feature of psychological awareness throughout much of the world. Nor is it limited to the upper, upper-middle, or even middle classes in the most economically developed societies. Those class distinctions may still make sense in some contexts, and certainly people in higher income brackets tend to get more exposure to the large-scale forces we cite. But nearly everyone in an advanced society gets far more exposure to these forces than did anyone in the society of 1900, even in the then most developed parts of the world. That is why psychological individuality reaches across the traditional boundaries that defined mass society, such as class, nation, gender, race, political affiliation, and ethnicity.

Sociologists have written persuasively about this phenomenon using many different vocabularies that include such terms as "self-identity," "the post-scarcity order," and "reflexive modernization"—all of which have been described as essential features of "late modernity" throughout the West. German sociologist Ulrich Beck, for example, observes the German case when he describes the rise of an "individualized post-class society." "People demand the right to develop their own perspective on life and to be able to act upon it," writes Beck, and "these claims . . . arise from the actual conditions of life in Germany as they have developed in the past three decades."[1] He observes the relationship between the success of managerial capitalism and the emergence of the new society of individuals when he comments on the "high speed industrial dynamism" that is "sliding into a new society without the primeval explosion of a revolution, bypassing political debates and decisions in parliaments and governments. . . . Not only indicators of collapse, but also strong economic growth, rapid technification, and high employment security can unleash the storm that will sail or float industrial society into a new epoch."[2]

International research efforts have also generated a good deal of insight into the emergence of the new society of individuals throughout the West. In 1990, a two-decade, twenty-four-nation study of the evolution of values in the late twentieth century published by University of Michigan political scientist Ronald Inglehart found a prominent shift toward "postmaterialist" values, a result of the unprecedented and sustained economic and physical security of the postwar era.[3] These values emphasize the right to individual voice and influence in political and organizational life, the importance of self-actualization, and the heightened significance of issues associated with the quality of life. Such values were found to be associated with the "more highly educated, more articulate" generations of the late twentieth century who have grown up with affluence and choice.

When considering Western Europe and the United States, where postmaterialist values were expressed with the greatest intensity, Inglehart noted a "cross-national consistency that is almost breathtaking."[4] His analysis of postmaterialist and materialist value clusters showed a pattern of intergenerational replacement, as people born after mid-century entered adulthood in successive waves.[5] Writing in the late 1980s, he predicted that the year 2000 would be something of a "tipping point," especially in Western Europe, as by that time about one-half of the adult population would have been "replaced" by a younger cohort. Even when the ratio of materialists to postmaterialists approached 1:1, he cautioned that educated and articulate postmaterialists would have the larger impact on politics, culture, and commerce.[6]

In 1997 the World Values Survey, conducted in 1981 and 1982 in twenty-five countries, was expanded to forty-three societies representing 70 percent of the world's population, including countries as diverse as Japan, South Africa, China, Russia, India, and Nigeria. Inglehart's original findings about postmaterialism were strengthened, and he broadened them into a framework called "postmodernization."[7] The study documents the ways in which new societal goals were replacing those that dominated Western society since the second industrial revolution in many countries around the world. Modernization, the study suggests, helps a society move from poverty to economic security, but that is not the end of development. The successes of mass society lead to a fundamental shift in basic values—a shift in "what people want out of life."[8] Postmodernity values autonomy and diversity over authority, hierarchy, and conformity. "Postmodern values bring declining confidence in religious, political, and even scientific authority; they also bring a growing mass desire for participation and self-expression. . . . Today, the spiritual emphasis among mass publics is turning from security to significance: from a search for reassurance in the face of existential insecurity to a search for the significance of life."[9]

Inglehart compared time-series data for twenty-one countries in which values surveys were administered in 1980 and 1981 and in 1990. He found positive shifts toward postmaterialism in eighteen of the twenty-one countries, including double-digit shifts in the Netherlands, Canada, Sweden, West Germany, Britain, France, Belgium, Ireland, Argentina, the United States, Japan, Italy, Spain, and Northern Ireland. In 1981, only Finland showed a higher percentage of postmaterialist than materialist values. But by 1990, postmaterialist values appeared to have gained a majority in nine of the countries, including Finland, the Netherlands, Canada, Sweden, West Germany, France, Belgium, the United States, and Italy.[10]

These new attitudes arise from the experience of material security that is in turn linked to economic growth and its consequences. As Inglehart concludes, "We find persisting generational differences that seem to reflect the enduring legacy of the distinctive formative experiences of given generations."[11] These values are not simply a function of age; they do not represent youthful idealism that dissipates as people grow older. Instead, they reflect the material circumstances in which a person is shaped, and they endure across the stages of life, though as individuals mature they develop more of the emotional and cognitive resources needed to successfully enact the values associated with psychological self-determination.[12]

It makes sense that the rise of psychological individualism, with its emphasis on meaningful self-expression, personal self-determination, and the quality of life, is strongest in the West, where variants of managerial capitalism have driven growth for more than a century, and where democratic principles have influenced the distribution of wealth and its conversion to public goods. Those trends contributed to a strong middle class—a powerful market for education, science, information, and all that follows from it. The democratic political culture of individual citizens also enables and legitimates the newer culture of psychological individualism. But Inglehart stresses that the rise of the new values is not a uniquely Western phenomenon, nor can it be explained as simply a process of Westernization. His data reveal important intergenerational shifts toward postmaterialism in much of Eastern Europe, China, Turkey, East Asia, and parts of Latin America, even where democratic processes are poorly developed or nonexistent.[13] This implies that democratic processes are not a necessary precursor to the rise of psychological individualism or postmaterialist values. In some cases, democratization may be the result of the new demand for psychological self-determination rather than its precondition, because as societies become more wealthy—and begin to produce "individuals"—those new people are more likely to demand democratic government.

Even a superficial reading of Western history reminds us that there is nothing about psychological self-determination that is particularly indigenous to Western culture. English, European, and American laws have until very recently emphasized the necessities of public order, conformity, and social solidarity over any concern for individual self-determination and its associated rights claims.[14] For example, dissent from the doctrines of established Christianity had been regarded as a dangerous threat to civil society in England (as well as most of Europe) well into the twentieth century. Religious zealotry in Tudor England produced civil war, regicide, and large-scale executions. Public dissent was repressed across the centuries, with the first published discussion of religious tolerance appearing only in the late seventeenth century. Brief efforts at tolerance, which excluded many groups anyway, reliably led to new eras of repression. Not until the nineteenth century did it even become lawful to deny the Trinity. Only in 1858 did the British Parliament finally drop the religious oathing requirements that excluded Jews from public office and other occupations. In 1880, with 16,000 Anglican clergy petitioning against it, the Burial Laws Amendment Act for the first time granted non-Anglicans the right to burial in English churchyards. The Blasphemy Act of 1698 was not revoked until 1967, although a British poet teaching in the United States was successfully prosecuted in 1979 for writing a poem that depicted Jesus as a homosexual.[15]

The British colonists in America imitated the intolerance of the society they fled, establishing dominant religions in their communities and criminalizing dissent. The important exception to this pattern was the disestablishment principles of Roger Williams's Rhode Island, which linked civil liberty with complete liberty of conscience. Even after the American Revolution, the colonies' legal framework of intolerance survived in the laws of the new states—that is, until the Fourteenth Amendment was ratified in 1868 and Williams's principles finally superseded the autocratic and theocratic tendencies of other states. Right through the mid-nineteenth century, there are many examples of people prosecuted for blasphemy, some successfully. It was only gradually, through the late nineteenth century and into the twentieth, that the U.S. Supreme Court came unequivocally to the defense of freedom of conscience and freedom of speech. And it was not until 1968 that the Supreme Court made it totally clear that the "First Amendment mandates governmental neutrality between religion and religion, and between religion and non-religion."[16] Nevertheless, the state of Pennsylvania attempted, though unsuccessfully, to prosecute a blasphemy case in 1971.[17]

It is easy to lose sight of the fact that the rights of all individuals—including racial minorities, the unpropertied, and women—to full participation in the institutional and political processes of Western societies have been established for only a few generations. For most of American history, for example, women had no legal status. The laws and the courts perpetuated the view of English law, in which "by marriage, the husband and wife are but one person in law, that is, the legal existence of the woman is suspended during marriage, or at least is incorporated into that of the husband, under whose protection and cover she performs everything."[18] In 1848, when Elizabeth Cady Stanton and others convened the first women's rights convention in Seneca Falls, New York, the "unalienable rights" promised by the U.S. Declaration of Independence could be enjoyed only by white males.

Cady Stanton and other nineteenth-century U.S. women lived under a regime of laws and social norms that differed only in small degree from the current limitations on women that exist in many Muslim societies. Women could not vote but were required to abide by the laws made by others. They lost their civil rights upon marriage. A woman was legally required to accept her husband as her master, and she lost all rights to her children if her husband divorced or separated from her. With marriage, women lost their property rights, including legal entitlement to their own wages. A woman was not allowed access to higher education or most occupations; when she did work, her wages were low. These legal limitations say nothing of the cultural proscriptions imposed on women's "moral" behavior.[19] While the modern mind recoils from these circumstances, it must be remembered that even Cady Stanton did not see the reversal of most such laws during her lifetime. Women did not attain the right to vote in the United States until 1920. The first legal reform allowing women to own certain forms of property was enacted in New York State in 1848, but many other vestiges of this legal perspective—the denial of access to credit or the right to enter into a contract—continued well into the 1960s. During that same period African Americans went from slavery to segregation, enforced in the South by a cruel regime of "Jim Crow" laws. It was not until the passage of new civil rights legislation in the 1960s and 1970s that even legally established rights for women and minorities could—more or less—be exercised reliably.

The repression of difference, among groups and individuals, has in fact been a salient force in Western culture and law, right down to very recent history. It shaped the rancorous peace accords after World War I and promoted visions of the "good society" that punished difference and dissent, visions that found their ultimate expression in the grotesque evil of Nazi Germany and later in the totalitarian regimes of the former Soviet Union and its Eastern European satellites. And in the years leading up to World War II, one did not have to travel to a battered Germany to hear the testimony of intolerance. It was comfortably ensconced in the most elite precincts of American society, including the well-appointed lecture halls of the University of Virginia, where only applause greeted the honored T. S. Eliot when he shared his prescription for the good society:

> The population should be homogeneous; where two or more cultures exist in the same place they are likely either to be fiercely self-conscious or both to become adulterate. What is still more important is unity of religious background; and reasons of race and religion combine to make any number of free-thinking Jews undesirable. . . . And a spirit of excessive tolerance is to be deprecated.[20]

Nor can intolerance in the name of social harmony and traditional values be regarded as somehow a relic of the past. The new individuality remains deeply contested in many quarters, even as it continues to grow.[21] Bernard Lewis, V. S. Naipaul, and others have described the deep conflicts over these issues in the Muslim world and the violent rejection of the new values among its most extreme elements.[22] Consider too the Orthodox Jews in Israel who use parliamentary power to exert their theology over the secular majority, or conservative groups in the United States who seek to ban books and films from school curricula, and antiabortion groups who intimidate and sometimes resort to murder in their campaigns on behalf of the unborn.

Despite these conflicts, the new human sensibilities associated with psychological individualism have taken root in many parts of the world. As legal scholar Thomas Franck cautions, if these values have a Western provenance, it is only in the most narrow chronological sense, in that they first found general acceptance "in societies spread around the North Atlantic littoral. But the same could be said of gravity, or Mendel's Law, neither of which are today thought to be particularly 'Western.'"[23] The same could also be said of the enterprise logic of managerial capitalism, which, though first developed in the West, took root in the industrialization processes of much of the globe, even where the larger political culture did not embrace capitalism or democracy.

Psychological individualism, then, whenever and wherever it emerges, is the hard-won and still contested culmination of a long struggle to rise above the ancient norms of hierarchy and conformity that characterize traditional society and that survived, albeit in new forms, in the organizational mandates of the industrialized mass order. It is the human voice that emerges from a new world of material prosperity, education, and the challenges of a complex, specialized, fragmented life that inevitably incites opinion and requires choice. Though the claims of psychological self-determination find their strongest expression in the West, it is clear that they are not limited to those societies but are in fact part of a new universal culture increasingly shared by those who live in the aftermath of scarcity.[24] These claims have already had a profound impact upon the theory and practice of U.S. and international law—especially as they bear upon notions of individual rights—just as we expect them eventually to have a transforming effect upon the theory and practice of business.

NEW LAWS FOR NEW INDIVIDUALS

The rise of psychological individualism is reflected in a wide range of recent developments in international law.[25] Since World War II, modern law has increasingly embraced individual claims to personal self-determination. The law now views individuals as having legitimate claims to the right to choose and creatively assemble—from "dependent" variables such as lifestyle, group affinities, taste, economic self-interest, beliefs, opinions, values, spiritual orientation, geographic preference, occupational interests, sexual orientation, and other dimensions of personal experience and judgment—aspects of identity that were until recently imposed by destiny in the guise of national origin, ethnicity, patrimony, race, gender, age, and so on. This is true of the development of law in the West, as well as in the general evolution of international law, particularly in the arena of human rights. There are, for example, significant instances of courts and legislators moving in this direction in non-Western countries such as Turkey, Pakistan, and Singapore, despite the continued strength of traditional norms and autocratic politics in those societies.[26]

Societal recognition of the new individualism is manifested in a range of human rights entitlements that have won near-universal legitimacy in recent decades. For example, "freedom of conscience" has come to be regarded as an "irresistible claim" in most national and international courts.[27] Similar acceptance has been granted to individual claims to personal autonomy in matters such as the choice of one's name, the choice of sexual identity, the choice of career, and the right to privacy.[28]

The new rights claims assert that each individual is empowered to make the question of identity a central enterprise, if not *the* central enterprise, of life.[29] As individuals compose their identities they are also now free to choose multiple allegiances for the first time in history.[30] Transnational loyalties and multiple loyalties are not only tolerated but have, for many educated individuals who operate in the global economy, become the norm. Consider, for example, international confederations of lawyers, doctors, and scholars, transitional corporations and political parties, or supranational political institutions such as those dedicated to environmental protection and human rights. These institutions have become the object of personal allegiance alongside many more traditional loyalty referents such as nation, birthplace, or family. Today, people from across Europe vote to elect members of the European Parliament, or take property and human rights claims against their own governments to the European Court of Human Rights. They carry their European passports across unguarded national frontiers. NATO troops are deployed under the command of the United Nations, while Canadian and Argentine election monitors safeguard fragile democratic processes in places like El Salvador and Nicaragua.

The new social acceptance of self-designed identity is also expressed in the degree to which legal systems now honor claims to dual citizenship. Consider the evolution of U.S. law. Through most of the twentieth century, dual nationality was regarded as a "conceptual oxymoron." Citizenship was a validation of identity, and so a person could have only one nationality.[31]

The 1907 Expatriation Act asserted that citizens expatriated themselves if they took an oath of allegiance to any foreign state. In 1940 a new statute withdrew citizenship from anyone taking an oath to a foreign state, serving in its armed forces, or voting in its elections. By the late 1950s and into the 1980s, a series of cases began to erode the legitimacy of this statute. By 1986, Congress had repealed many of its provisions, putting the onus on the government to prove that a person intended to renounce his or her citizenship.

In 1990, the State Department publicly accepted the premise that U.S. citizens may intend to keep their U.S. nationality even when they obtain citizenship in another state, make a proforma declaration of allegiance to another state, or accept a nonpolicy-level position in another state. The remaining limitations on dual citizenship have not been enforced. There have been numerous recent instances of U.S. citizens in prominent policy positions in other countries—including as prime minister of Yugoslavia, as foreign minister of Armenia, as foreign minister of Bosnia, as chief of the Estonian Army, and as their "other" country's ambassador to the UN—and none of these individuals were deprived of their U.S. passports. The legal systems of many other countries have evolved along similar lines, suggesting that much of the world's population has an interest in, and is establishing the legitimacy of, the individual right to self-determination—as individual choice replaces nation, culture, and genes as the source of identity.[32]

In the second half of the twentieth century, the new legal commitment to the individual as a rights holder is also evidenced in the growth of international, regional, and national legal systems that support human rights and recognize the individual as the repository of those rights. The UN Human Rights Commission emerged in 1945 as a direct response to widespread revulsion toward the crimes against individuals and ethnic and religious groups during World War II. It includes the International Convention on Civil and Political Rights, in which 140 states participated as of 1998. The Convention includes some fifty supplementary instruments covering such subjects as the rights of women and children, racial discrimination, torture, freedom of thought and association, freedom from religious intolerance, and elections based on universal suffrage and secret ballot.[33]

In addition to the universal declarations, conventions, and covenants that make up the global human rights canon, there are regional instruments such as the European Convention on Human Rights, which now also includes Eastern Europe and much of the former Soviet Union. That Convention now maintains a court with full-time judges and jurisdiction over forty states in which claims can be pursued by individuals against their nations.

Increasingly, on both an international and a regional basis, "jurisprudence demonstrates that a radical new idea has gained currency: that individuals can hold their governments accountable before an international tribunal applying globally adopted principles of personal rights."[34]

Many national legal systems have also evolved a tapestry of case law, statutes, and regulations to define, protect, and extend individual rights. In the United States, for example, the American Civil Liberties Union published a series of thirty-five "rights" handbooks between 1973 and 1996. These books illustrate the ways in which existing laws can be extended to protect the rights of individuals who seek self-determination within the new and complex terms of layered, multidimensional identity. They offer guidance on the rights of aliens and refugees; authors, artists, and other creative people; candidates and voters; crime victims; the critically ill; doctors, nurses, and allied health professionals; employees and union members; ex-offenders; families; government employees; Indians and tribes; lawyers and clients; lesbians and gay men; mental patients; people with mental disabilities; mentally retarded persons; military personnel; older persons; parents; patients; people who are HIV positive; physically handicapped people; police officers; the poor; prisoners; racial minorities; reporters; single people; students; suspects; teachers; tenants; union members; veterans; women; and young people.[35]

The postwar expansion of individual rights has proceeded through liberal and conservative governments. In fact, the new centrality of psychological individualism and its reflection in the extension of individual rights cannot be identified with liberal or conservative politics. It is decried by liberals who long for the communitarian ideals of progressive government at least as often as it is denounced by conservatives who pine for the communitarian solidarity of a more traditional society. This is because psychological individualism is not produced by politics alone. It is the result, above all, of wealth and its consequences: a complex society that produces complex human experiences and requires personal choice.

THE OLD GLASS IS HALF EMPTY

Many political leaders and social observers have rejected the new individuals and their claims, in much the same way that they have been ignored and rejected by business organizations. From the political left and the right, the new individuals have been derided as hedonists and narcissists.[36] From the point of view of the old organizations that depended upon group solidarity (unions, political parties, corporations, large civic associations), the new individuals could be seen only as a fall from grace. In the 1970s, internationally renowned political scientists claimed that a crisis of democracy was at hand, ignited by a "democratic surge" that threatened to swamp governmental institutions with demands for equality and participation.[37] The behavior of the new individuals has been regarded as an inappropriately adolescent expression of self-centered indulgence. Its critics view it as an insult to the established norms of social integration and a subversion of communitarian ideals. These concerns have been accompanied by a new wave in the mental-health literature that confirmed narcissism as the personality disorder of the late twentieth century and fretted over its diagnosis and treatment.[38]

Harvard political scientist Robert Putnam breathed new life into the standard jeremiad against individuals with his study *Bowling Alone*, which was eagerly embraced by political leaders who no doubt were yearning for simpler times.[39] Putnam observes that "the life experiences of people who came of age after 1950 were very different from those of people who came of age before 1950." His study documents what he sees as the consequences of those differences—namely, declining rates of group association and political engagement since, more or less, the early 1960s. We want to dwell briefly on his analysis, as it helps to shed a fascinating light on the predicament faced by the new individuals, the reasons they are rejected in politics and commerce, and the opportunities they represent for a new era in the evolution of business.

According to Putnam, the civic associations founded at the turn of the last century saw their greatest rise in membership between 1920 and 1960. During the last third of the century, formal membership diminished by as much as 20 percent, but active involvement "collapsed."[40] Similar trends existed for political parties and campaigns. He regards this as a sign of diminished "social capital," which is, in his view, a critical ingredient of an active democracy. Consistent with our analysis, Putnam regards the decline in civic engagement as largely a consequence of generational replacement, as the new individuals born at mid-century and later have gradually taken over from their more group-oriented parents and grandparents.[41]

Putnam renders his analysis through the lens of the "long civic generation," the members of the old mass order, for whom he clearly harbors a deep reverence and respect. As a result, he can see the new individuals only as a glass half empty. They are responsible for the degradation of civic life and the depletion of social capital. Rather than defining them on their own terms, Putnam defines them only in relation to the past, and therefore as "postcivic"; they are the generation that failed to carry the torch their parents and grandparents fought so well to light. When Putnam does attempt to describe the late-century generations of "baby boomers" and "Generation X'ers," he does so with a barely concealed mix of pity and derision. He describes boomers as voting less, campaigning less, attending political meetings less, contributing less, and in general avoiding their civic duties. After that, it gets worse:

> Boomers were slow to marry and quick to divorce. Both marriage and parenthood became choices not obligations. Although 96 percent of boomers were raised in a religious tradition, 58 percent abandoned that tradition, and only about one in three of the apostates have returned. In their work life they are less comfortable in bureaucracies, less loyal to a particular firm, more insistent on autonomy. . . . Late boomers were less trusting, less participatory, more cynical about authorities, more self-centered, and more materialistic, even by comparison to early boomers. Boomers in general are highly individualistic, more comfortable on their own than on a team, more comfortable with values than with rules.[42]

And when it comes to Generation X, the descriptors are even more harsh. At their hands, civic engagement has continued to "plummet," as they "accelerate the tendencies to individualism found among boomers." They have an "extremely personal and individualistic view of politics" and have "never made the connection to politics, so they emphasize the personal and private over the public and collective." What's worse, they are "visually oriented, perpetual surfers, multitaskers, interactive media specialists."[43]

The wayward qualities of these generations could only have arisen from chaos and tragedy. And so it is, according to Putnam, that the boomers' failings are a result of too much television, the civil rights movement, political assassinations, the traumas of Vietnam and Watergate, overcrowded schools that deprived them of extracurricular activities, and competitive pressures within their cohort. As for the X'ers, they are the unfortunate products of "an era that celebrated personal goods and private initiatives," slow economic growth and inflation, insecurity arising from divorce, and an absence of "collective success stories"—no D day, no Hitler to triumph over, no marches on Washington in favor of civil rights and against the Vietnam War[44]—some of the very experiences that supposedly contributed to selfish boomers.

Putnam finds an ally in his distress over the new individuals in several studies of suicide and depression, both of which have become more prevalent in the cohorts born after 1940. The figures on suicide are real enough—a quadrupling of the adolescent suicide rate between 1950 and 1995. Putnam quotes psychologist Martin Seligman, who maintains that "depression among young Americans is the result of 'rampant individualism,' coupled with 'events that have weakened our commitment to the larger, traditional institutions of our society.'"[45] He concludes that depression over the last two generations increased "roughly tenfold" over generations born before 1940. Other survey results are also cited that show a "widening generation gap in malaise and unhappiness." "The younger you are," writes Seligman, "the worse things have gotten over the last decades of the twentieth century in terms of headaches, indigestion, sleeplessness, as well as general satisfaction with life and even the likelihood of taking your own life."[46]

Still other survey data reveal more about the value differences between the generations. One survey conducted in 1998 shows that the generations born after 1949 place a higher value on self-fulfillment and material well-being and a lower value on patriotism than do those generations born before 1948.[47] A Yankelovich study conducted from 1997 to 1999 asked people, "In what ways do you get a real sense of belonging?" Those born before and after 1948 all rated family, then friends, then co-workers as the successively most important sources of their feelings of belonging. However, the generations born after 1946 gave significantly lower rankings to community ties such as neighbors, religious groups, and other associations than did the older cohorts.[48] Clearly, the "postcivic" generations are quite different from those who went before, but are they responsible for the "national slump in civic engagement," as Putnam suggests?[49]

THE NEW GLASS IS HALF FULL

We agree with Putnam that the generations born since the mid-twentieth century represent a new mentality. In our view, they are characterized, above all, by a deep and abiding subjective sense of individuality and an unmitigated yearning for psychological self-determination. But we do not regard this individuality as an unfortunate degradation of an earlier mentality. Nor is it simply the tragic result of chaotic and disillusioning events like political assassination, Vietnam, and Watergate that have marked the last forty years. Rather, the new individuals are the more or less predictable product of wealth and its consequences.

Managerial capitalism begat prosperity and a more complex, differentiated society. It unleashed a range of world-historical forces from campus life to adventure travel that exposed people to more information, more knowledge, more conflict, more cultures, more diverse people, more surprises, more cognitive dissonance, more opinions, and more choices, while simultaneously dissolving the frameworks of traditional society. These new exposures increased the probability of the kinds of experiences that induce human development. Small wonder that the field of "adult development" has flowered during precisely this same fifty-year time frame, beginning with Erik Erikson's essays on identity in 1950 and proceeding to the many important clinical and longitudinal studies that have revealed predictable patterns of change and growth in adulthood.[50] Life is throwing more developmental experiences at people, and a longer life means that there is more time to experience development. At the same time, the values of psychological self-determination that exist within a particular generation motivate more people to engage in the kinds of developmental experiences that build the capacity to act on those values.

As a result of this important new work in psychology, we now know that normal healthy human development in adults tends to proceed from a reliance upon group identification and compliance with group norms toward increasingly internalized values, more reliance upon one's own judgment, a deepening sense of self, a growing need for self-authorship, and a deeper capacity for empathy, deep personal connection, and non-instrumental qualities of relationship. Even when a generation embraces the values of psychological individualism, each person in that generation will not be equally capable of enacting those values. But as adults develop, they garner more of the cognitive and emotional resources that enable them to implement their claims to personal self-determination. That is when they are truly able to fashion identities from their own subjective meanings, rather than depending upon the group, authority, tradition, or institutionalized rules and norms as sources of meaning.

As human beings acquire these characteristics of psychological individuality, they also become more capable of perceiving others as individuals. That means there is a greater capacity to appreciate others in terms of their own meanings, rather than simply as reflections of their social role or hierarchical status. Psychological individuality is also typically associated with powerful drives toward interdependence, affiliation, and community-building, but in ways that no longer depend upon a priori criteria such as kinship or geography. A heightened sense of individuality is not a sign of narcissism or self-indulgence. It reflects the material and cultural circumstances in which a life is shaped and becomes an increasingly integral aspect of behavior throughout the course of a dynamic and fully lived adulthood.

There is much to suggest that these new sensibilities are driving the new individuals to redefine political action in much the same way that—as we shall see in Chapter Six—they are seeking new consumption choices that can redefine commerce. The new individuals want to make a difference, they want to be heard, they want to have direct influence. In short, each wants voice, and each wants to matter. Their new political choices begin with an apparent dilemma for leaders. The new individuals are educated, opinionated, rights-claiming, and keen to act. They have concepts, ideals, and information. All of these characteristics ought to make them avid participants in the political process, but despite these credentials, the political participation of the "postmaterialists" is, by conventional measures, lower than that of the more materialistic older generation.

This apparent dilemma fades, however, once we consider the kinds of organizations that mobilized political participation in the first half of the twentieth century. Typically, they were headed by a small number of leaders or bosses who mobilized a mass of disciplined troops. These hierarchical organizations were effective when the goal was to bring large numbers of uneducated, untrained, but newly enfranchised citizens to the polls to effect social change. Such "elite-directed" organizations could organize a lot of people efficiently, but the kind of participation they produced was pretty perfunctory.[51]

In contrast, the values surveys of Ronald Inglehart indicate that the new postmaterialists demand true voice.[52] Theirs is a *psychological reformation* that suggests some interesting parallels to the religious reformation of the sixteenth century. Today's individual rejects organizational mediation, seeking instead to have a direct impact upon matters that touch his or her life, just as the early Protestants rejected priestly mediation of their relationship to God. In the early twentieth century people joined organizations as a way to reestablish a sense of influence and control in a world that was spinning away from individuals. But the new individuals do just the reverse. Now it is those very organizations that make them feel "out of control." They shun those associations in favor of an unmediated relationship to the things they care about. The new individuals thus demand a high quality of direct participation and influence. They have the skills to lead, confer, and discuss, and they are not content to be foot soldiers. As one political scientist put it, "legitimacy based on inclusion is replacing legitimacy based on hierarchical authority."[53]

The preference for unmediated influence is evident in a 1998 survey of attitudes toward leadership and social action conducted among a cross section of young Americans ages eighteen to thirty. Their views contrasted with those of earlier generations in that they rejected many of the traditional measures of civic responsibility in favor of a "distinctly personal" outlook, "with a heavy emphasis on direct, one-on-one individual service . . . [and] a model of leadership that is best characterized as 'bottom up' rather than 'top down'—young adults place a premium on the efficacy of small groups of people working together to effect change in tangible ways." And they showed a strong preference for leadership "that emphasizes the collective participation of many individuals over the strong leadership of just a few." Ninety-four percent regarded "being able to see a situation from someone else's point of view" as the most important leadership quality, with 79 percent believing that "average people," not the experts, "have the resources and practical know-how to solve most of their problems in their community."

The researchers also reported that these young people were "extremely concerned not only with respecting individual differences, but also with reaching out to connect to and work with people from different backgrounds to address problems and formulate solutions." They preferred direct action, such as mentoring a younger person or working on a local issue, to other forms of social engagement. In fact, a robust 68 percent reported this sort of direct involvement during the three-year period leading up to the survey. These individuals placed enormous emphasis on the power and value of human relationships, with 87 percent rating with a value of 8 or higher (on a 10-point scale) the statement "Making a difference in the life of someone close to you is important."[54]

This rejection of mediated influence also helps explain the growing interest in the concept of "direct democracy" as a natural evolution of representative democracy. As the argument goes, representative democracy reflects earlier historical conditions when most citizens were not literate, let alone educated and informed. It also reflects the sheer practical impossibility of getting everybody to vote on everything. In today's world, however, most citizens are relatively well educated and are, or can be, informed on issues. Further, new electronic networking technologies mean that the idea of continuous electronic voting is no longer political science fiction.[55] The new impulse toward direct democracy has been carried furthest in Switzerland and Italy but is also expressed in many U.S. states that rely heavily on state-sponsored referenda and citizen-sponsored initiatives to decide policy issues.[56] Clearly, the political participation of the new generations of individuals will rise on the strength of radically new participatory formats for exerting voice and influence on particular issues. The old mass forms of participation—and the political organizations in which they are embedded—do not serve the new people.

New forms of voice are emerging that appear to be far more satisfying to the new individuals.[57] Grassroots activism enjoyed an extraordinary rate of growth during the last third of the twentieth century, spreading across and within societies. By the end of the 1990s, participation in "unconventional political activity" had increased among every subgroup of the U.S. population, with the most significant increases reported "among the self-employed, citizens between 30 and 49 years of age, and especially women, the major new entrants in the public politics of contention." There were also marked increases in grassroots activism across Europe, especially in Denmark, Iceland, Norway, Switzerland, Belgium, Britain, Germany, Ireland, the Netherlands, France, and Italy.[58]

Social activism has evolved into a wider variety of forms, even as it has abandoned many of its traditional and more rigid vehicles. It includes self-help groups (for example, women's groups), cooperatives and service organizations, new social movement organizations, new political parties (for example, the Greens), public-interest organizations, and a variety of temporary coalitions mobilized for large-scale public performances (for example, Earth Day). Political scientists have noted that even groups with well-established institutional means of political access have embraced direct action, from French farmers overturning wagonloads of produce to protest the import of Spanish wine, to British matrons blocking shipments of calves to the Continent, to Italian milk producers cutting off access to Milan's airport with their tractors in order to protest EU limits on subsidies.[59]

The movement known as "socially responsible investing" is another example of individuals finding a new means to directly express their values. They seek to influence corporate decision-making by including social and ethical criteria in their investment choices. According to the Social Investment Forum, a nonprofit organization that promotes social investing, the total level of socially and environmentally responsible investing in the United States grew by 8 percent, from $2.16 trillion in 1999 to $2.34 trillion in 2001, despite a significant stock market decline during that period. In 2001, these funds accounted for nearly 12 percent of the total $19.9 trillion in investment assets under professional management in the United States. For those who don't want their choices mediated by even as much as a fund manager, there is a Web site that offers data on how more than 1,000 firms are doing on issues ranging from human rights to labor practices and animal testing.[60]

Increasingly, the new individuals are reaching across localities and national frontiers to join with others who share similar values in an activism dedicated to the solution of national and international problems. The rise of the Green Party demonstrates how the new individuals reach across old boundaries to share values and influence action.[61] New communities are fostered in cooperative efforts on behalf of Amnesty International, the World Wildlife Fund, the Red Cross, or Human Rights Watch. The Internet has helped to nurture these global affinities, even as it has enabled all sorts of more informal virtual communities, some dedicated to activist goals and others based simply on the pleasures of shared interests and communication.

The rise of nongovernmental organizations, or NGOs, is another illustration of how new individuals are finding new forms of participation. Some of these organizations are "expert participants in the intergovernmental diplomatic process by which new policies are formulated, implemented, and enforced." Others "rally individuals to influence the domestic politics that affect global and national agendas."[62] During the same period in which the large civic organizations have seen their memberships dwindle, the number of NGOs has increased dramatically. Only five such organizations existed in 1850, and only 176 in 1909.[63] The 1985–1986 *Yearbook of International Organizations* listed 18,000 NGOs, 1,000 of which had obtained consultative status with the United Nations. The 1993 *UN Human Development Report* described an explosion of participatory movements of nongovernmental organizations, noting that "people's participation is becoming the central issue of our time."[64] Indeed, by 2000, the *Yearbook of International Organizations* listed a total of 27,898 NGOs worldwide.[65]

A powerful example of this new form of participation for individuals involves the work of medical professionals. The NGO Médecins Sans Frontières (MSF; known in English as Doctors Without Borders) was founded in 1970 as a "ragtag band of anti-establishment French doctors." Today MSF has become the extreme sport of the new volunteerism, with more than 2,500 doctors and nurses from several dozen nations and twenty-three offices serving in more than eighty countries, presiding over an annual budget of nearly $200 million. The group was created as a reaction against traditional humanitarian organizations, like the International Red Cross, that maintain strict neutrality and a reverence for diplomatic protocol. "When we saw people dying on the other side of the frontiers," recalls one of the group's founders, "we asked ourselves, 'What is this border? It doesn't mean anything to us.' "[66] "It was a medical adventure," recalls another founder, "but also a political one against conformism and the way the borders are built."[67]

The patterns of social and political action forged by the new individuals impart an important lesson about the way society develops. First, it suggests that the future is not just more of the past. Society does not develop in a linear way in which, for example, modernization simply begets more modernization. On the other hand, social evolution is not an abrupt sequence in which later patterns have no connection to earlier patterns. It is more useful to think of social development in a pattern of "hierarchical integration." That means development leads to greater complexity and a broader framework of meanings—what comes later builds on, but is both different from and more than, what went before. Earlier concerns may be included in the new framework, but they take on new meanings and new status. Clearly, not everyone in a society shares the same outlook or personal claims. But a dominant set of values and psychological expectations determines the larger framework within which other perspectives find their place in relation to a new whole. This, we believe, is the effect that the claim of psychological self-determination is having today.

In this way, continuity exists within discontinuity. For example, it cannot be said that the new individuals do not care about the "other." It is, rather, that what it means to care is different, and the way in which one expresses or acts on that caring may be different too. Some of the studies we have reviewed suggest that caring is less anonymous, more intensely personal, and immediate. In the new society of individuals, people may still experience a special pride and identification with their countrymen, for example, but those feelings of connection and sympathy with fellow citizens may not be regarded as exclusive of other feelings of connection toward people who come from different countries.

Instead of complaining that the new people are different, or worse than, the old, we need to understand the new meanings they bring to social life and the new frontiers of human experience they pioneer. There is grandeur in the new sensibilities they have achieved; indeed, it is an important milestone in the development of civilization. We regard it as a cause for celebration. It is a glass that is, at the very least, half full.

CELEBRATING THE NEW INDIVIDUALS

The new individuals seek true voice, direct participation, unmediated influence, and identity-based community because they are comfortable using their own experience as the basis for making judgments. Such a person is deeply aware of his or her own subjectivity. Maybe it's this new capacity that leads people to acknowledge depression or malaise, thus leading to the increases in those two conditions that so concerned Robert Putnam. This is precisely the conclusion of one of the very few in-depth studies to compare the subjective experiences of mid-century and late-century U.S. adults. This survey—sponsored by the University of Michigan's Survey Research Center and the National Institute of Mental Health—compared national samples of "normal" adults in 1957 and 1976. The objective was to achieve a more precise understanding of the changes in how Americans subjectively "experienced life."

The study, published under the title *The Inner American*, compares the most salient conclusions from the two surveys. The researchers in 1976 found adults, especially young adults, to be much more uncertain about their futures than were their counterparts in 1957, when there were fewer choices, less diversity, and far more conformity to an accepted framework of social norms. However, what is so interesting is how those 1976 adults chose to handle their uncertainties. It is described as "a shift from a socially integrated paradigm for structuring well-being, to a more personal or individuated paradigm for structuring well-being. We see the 1957 population," observed the authors, "taking much more comfort in culture and the 1976 population gathering much more strength in its own personal adaptations to the world."[68] In other words, in 1957 more people looked outside themselves for the answers. By 1976, more people looked within. The authors of *The Inner American* were sensitive to what they call the "bandwagon to indict the current population for their 'narcissism,'" and took great pains to situate their findings in a broader historical context. They understood this new "inner American" to be the result of a more affluent, complex society in which ritualized solutions to life are supplanted by an endless horizon of choices. This new psychological orientation was seen as the basis for a more open and dynamic society as well as for significant improvement in the quality of subjective well-being.[69]

The authors found, for example, that in 1976 people were far less likely to evaluate themselves in terms of how well they lived up to standard role definitions. Accordingly, marriage and parenthood no longer represented the standards for judging successful personal adjustment. "Americans have become more open to more individualized and abstract bases for well-being."[70] Adults in 1976 tended to judge the success of their adjustment in terms of opportunities for self-expression and self-direction. They were far more likely to be dissatisfied with their work, for example, if it did not provide these opportunities, as compared to respondents in 1957.

Another prominent finding concerned a "shift from integration through social organizations to integration through interpersonal intimacy." In other words, people moved away from relying on formal participation in large organizations as their way of connecting with society toward more intimate, one-to-one relationships. For example, instead of seeking support from formal groups, people in 1976 talked more openly to friends and others in their intimate support system about their worries and periods of unhappiness. Parents showed more concern in 1976 with the quality of their intimate relationships with their children. They judged themselves on that basis rather than in terms of the former criteria of physical care and financial support. In 1976, people belonged to fewer organizations and fewer people participated in "ritualized" visiting with family and friends, but more people referred to the intimate dimensions of their relationships as a source of satisfaction. While divorce rates climbed, more husbands and wives reported themselves happy in their marriages.[71]

In 1976, people were also much more likely to understand their own behavior in psychological terms and therefore were more likely to acknowledge personal problems and to seek professional help with their feelings and uncertainties.[72] This fact alone probably goes a long way toward explaining the rise in cases of depression and "malaise" that Putnam cited. Recall that depressed women in the 1950s were labeled as having "adjustment" problems. They received tranquilizers and in some cases electroshock therapy. By late century, people had learned how to name their feelings in psychological terms. Mental-health issues like depression or anxiety were no longer regarded as a source of shame or a sign of illness. People became far more willing to discuss their problems or their children's problems with their doctors and to seek appropriate care from mental-health professionals. Indeed, a study of depression published in the *Journal of the American Medical Association* in 2002 stimulated national headlines when it reported that the number of people treated for depression increased from 1.7 million in 1987 to 6.3 million in 1997. But the doctors who conducted the study were unruffled, attributing the increase to "broader changes in attitudes toward the treatment of depression and a decrease in stigma."[73] People were no longer ashamed to say they felt depressed, and their willingness to seek treatment was reflected in many new and less onerous treatment options.

But suppose, just for the sake of argument, that the new individuality really is associated with more depression and malaise. How else might we explain that correlation? One clue comes from psychologist Seligman, who accounts for the increasing incidence of depression this way: "Individualism need not lead to depression as long as we can fall back on large institutions. . . . When you fail to reach some of your personal goals, as we all must, you can turn to these larger institutions for hope."[74] In a similar vein, Canadian historian Edward Shorter, in his in-depth study of psychosomatic illness since the eighteenth century, suggests that loneliness is the Achilles' heel of psychological individualism. He sees it as the likely source of this epoch's psychosomatic complaints of fatigue and physical malaise, much as hysteria and fainting represented a late-nineteenth-century woman's unconscious protest against the suffocating culture of the Victorian family. Now, as the solidarity of the family gives way to the importance of the psychological fulfillment of each member, relationships become more tenuous and fragile. More young people live alone. More elderly people live alone. More people divorce and find themselves alone before forming new relationships. The literature on health and loneliness strongly suggests that solitude creates a vulnerability to depression and somatic distress.[75] If people can no longer fall back on the Victorian rendition of marriage and family, then why don't they look to other forms of association, civic or religious, to fill the void?

Here Putnam's analysis provides another vital clue. Remember that the "institutions of civil society," which the new individuals have been so chastised for neglecting, were formed between roughly 1880 and 1910, and saw their greatest rise in membership between 1920 and 1960. These large organizations were created by and for an earlier generation, with its own distinct mentality, needs, and dreams. They were patterned on the enterprise logic of managerial capitalism and do not provide adequate mechanisms for the new individuals to experience a meaningful sense of connection, participation, and influence. As a result, they do not provide sustenance and reassurance when a person must cope with loneliness, conflict, crisis, or any of the many other problems that routinely afflict people in their daily lives today. The old organizations are indifferent to the new individuals, leaving them nowhere to turn but toward themselves and each other.

The theme was brought home again in a 1999 *New York Times* survey that asked a random national sample how much importance they attached to each of fifteen values. In light of our discussion of the new individuals, it is not surprising to find that the top five values included "being responsible for your own actions," "being in good health," "being able to stand up for yourself," "being able to communicate your feelings," and "having faith in God." Among the five least important values were "being religious," "being involved in the community," and "having a lot of friends." The surveyors questioned a subset of respondents as they tried to understand the disparate meanings that were imputed to "having faith," as opposed to "being religious." As one respondent put it: "Religion to me means belonging to a specific congregation or denomination, and that is not very important to me.

Faith means something I found myself, not something I learned in grade school or something someone told me I had. It's very much a personal thing."[76]

Those words echo the findings of other studies of suburban American culture in which people expressed a "quiet faith" in matters of the spirit, though relatively few attended regular worship or otherwise involved themselves in organized religion.[77] Similarly, a market-research survey that assessed issues related to the Christian religion asked people for the source of the principles or standards on which they based their moral and ethical decisions. The survey was conducted shortly after the September 11, 2001, terrorist crisis, when presumably more people would have been seeking comfort from "traditional sources." Nevertheless, only 13 percent of the survey's respondents cited the Bible as their source of moral principles and only 14 percent cited their parents. The largest group by far, 25 percent, cited their "feelings" as the basis for these important decisions.[78] For the new individuals, even spirituality, morality, and ethics fall under the sway of psychological self-determination.

THE OLD ORGANIZATIONS HAVE FAILED
THE NEW INDIVIDUALS

Once again, we see the chasm that separates the old organizations from the new individuals who bring new needs, new desires, and new dreams into the world. The new people reach out from the complexity of their unique lives and encounter organizations ruled by a logic invented for the mass. The older forms of association do not support the need to develop and sustain psychological individuality. Instead, they try to foist old patterns on new people, with little capacity to perceive or relate to those dimensions of experience that individuals now hold most precious.

The old organizations have become sufficiently insulated and self-congratulatory to ignore the chasm that has formed between their practices, invented for a mass society, and the new people it has spawned. This insularity has afflicted political and civic organizations and is an important explanation for their loss of membership and declining levels of active participation. We think that business organizations have been infected with the same stubborn inward focus. For reasons we shall visit in depth, especially in Part Two, they have refused to reckon with discontinuity, preferring what was to what was needed next. As a result, individuals have also been left on their own to absorb the shocks of historical change in their economic lives as consumers and employees. If there is malaise, it is because without a new organizational logic that takes the individual as its compass, each person is forced to walk alone. If, despite the grandeur of their achievement, the glass remains only half full, it is because the new individuals bear the burden of these historic social developments without aid, chastised and ignored by the very organizations upon which they have depended for civic action, political expression, spiritual communion, consumption, and employment.

We conclude that the new individuals are being blamed for the problems of the old organizations, when the facts suggest the opposite. It is not the new individuals who have failed the old organizations, but rather the old organizations that have failed the new individuals. If there is narcissism here (a self-involved and self-perpetuating inward focus, impermeable to real connection and transformation), it is lodged in the organizations themselves, not in the new individuals. In the civic, the political, the religious, and the commercial realms, organizations have failed to reinvent themselves in ways that respond to the new dreams of new people. These changes in human beings reflect the evolution of the human spirit, and they deserve celebration. Bemoaning the new individualism is like chastising children for growing out of last year's clothes. When the old clothes no longer fit, make new ones.

FIVE

The Individual as History's Shock Absorber

What happens to the new individuals when they are spurned by the old organizations? How can the chasm between them lead to new wealth? In order to answer these questions, we need to understand the daily effort to reconcile new dreams with the seemingly intractable realities of managerial capitalism, especially as they have been intensified under the new regime of economic globalization.

THE EMPLOYMENT RELATIONSHIP GOES GLOBAL

We begin with an exploration of the new individuals' experiences inside the organization, in their lives as employees. There we see them squeezed between past and future, anonymity and individuality, the rules of the mass and the impetus toward psychological self-determination. Paradoxically, it is in the agony of this crush that we can begin to discern the origins of a new kind of marketplace and the next frontier of wealth it represents.

Each day the new individuals gather up their claims to psychological self-determination—along with its associated values of self-expression, participation, self-authored identity, meaning, and quality of life—and they go to work. There they encounter old organizations based upon the standard enterprise logic of managerial capitalism. While corporations are larger and more sophisticated than they were in 1920 or 1960, today's individuals still find their companies intent upon maximizing profits from largely anonymous transactions through the "efficient" production of goods and services. They also find large chunks of the old employment relationship, somewhat disfigured but still surviving, with its implicit theory of consumption intact.

First, what has changed in this relationship? For many decades, job security and seniority-based promotions were an important part of the employment quid pro quo for many blue- and white-collar employees. Today neither effort, nor compliance, nor loyalty can guarantee these comforts.[1] A new virus of uncertainty invaded the blue-collar world in the early 1980s, and by the 1990–1991 recession it was clear that even white-collar managers and professionals were not immune. The sources of this uncertainty are well known. The high-quality, low-cost Japanese imports of the early 1980s (in autos, steel, consumer electronics, and other products) announced a new era of intense global competition. Many U.S. companies were caught off guard, having become complacent about the need to cut costs (they were passed on to consumers) and introduce higher-quality, more-differentiated products. At the same time, large shareholders of public companies, distrustful of the managers who had allowed earnings to dwindle, instituted shareholder lawsuits and forced executives to reduce fixed costs, deploy new financial metrics, and institute compensation plans linked to the firm's share price.[2] Senior managers' jobs were suddenly on the line as they became pressed to maximize profits that translated into shareholder value.

Firms whose administrative apparatus and local-market dominance had once insulated them from excessive competitive pressures now found themselves at risk. Flexibility and agility replaced long-term planning in importance, and with that shift, long-term employees seemed to be more of a liability than an asset. The new idea was to bulk up and slenderize the workforce as competitive conditions dictated, firing and hiring employees in order to continuously attain the best mix of critical skills. These new strategies unleashed a contagion of cost-reduction programs that relied heavily on automation and labor substitution, "outsourcing," a shift to offshore labor markets, "downsizing," "reengineering," "rightsizing," twenty-four-hour shifts, and an expanded reliance on temporary employees and nonstandard work arrangements that reduced fixed labor costs.[3]

It is now considered the responsibility of individual employees to ensure they have the skills employers seek. From the factory floor to the office suite, people have found themselves exposed to the fickle winds of the labor market, as internal training, development, and promotional systems give way to perpetual churn. When labor markets are tight, there is turnover as employees seek better deals elsewhere. When labor markets are slack, people are fired so new people, with more relevant skills, can be hired. Job security, internal career ladders, and lifelong and even long-term employment have largely become relics of the preglobal past.

Many researchers have noted that while employee commitment and morale has worsened significantly during this twenty-year period, it has not obviously correlated with firm performance. One reason is that many people, maybe as much as half of the labor force, never had much job security anyway; for them, not much has changed. Those who have undergone changes recognize that most large firms have adopted similar employment practices; there is no place to go for a guarantee of better treatment. Instead, employees' perceptions of injustice and frustration continue to grow, while they simultaneously feel even more pressure to adapt to performance standards, knowing that they risk being unemployed themselves.[4] There is a new intensity to daily life on the job, often accompanied by a sense of fear and vulnerability, especially during those periods when labor supply exceeds demand.

But not all has changed in the classic employment relationship. There are many aspects of the old deal that have survived. Employers still control the key variables that determine the nature of their relationship with employees. They retain, for example, their prerogatives over the organization and pacing of work, career paths, the structure of compensation, and investments in training. The extent to which employees have any say in these matters remains widely contested; it varies by industry, company, division, occupational status, and individual boss. Unions, which once played a key role in negotiating these issues for millions of workers, have been frequently forced to accede to managerial requirements in the face of new competitive conditions, even as they see their own ranks dwindle.

Another survivor of the new competitive pressures is the old theory of consumption implied by the five-dollar day. Employers continue to regard their responsibility to end consumers as centering on the efficient production of goods and services. As we discussed in Chapter One, organisms under threat tend to respond by doing what they already know how to do, only with more intensity and rigor. Thus it is that the standard enterprise logic, its inward focus, and its value of efficiency (which had become more rhetoric than reality in many companies during their decades of dominance) are now embraced with a new urgency as the key to personal and organizational success.[5] Wages are still traded for compliance with, and submission to, these heightened standards of efficiency. Employees are asked to focus on wringing out cost and sometimes on increasing quality. Efficiency, it is still assumed, is what consumers most want from producers. It is viewed as serving the greatest good, whether in the coverage of insurance claims, the practice of health care, or the production of toasters. Employee turnover is necessary in order to secure the optimum mix of skills to support and extend these new product- and process-oriented efficiencies, together with new technology applications, software, production techniques, financial practices, marketing methodologies, and so on.

With these assumptions intact, organizations continue to enforce the segmentation of economic life. A person is an employee at work and a consumer on her own time. As an employee, one is expected to demonstrate attitudes and behaviors that are usually quite different from what one might hope to encounter in one's own experiences as a consumer. Employees' allegiance must be first of all to the authority of the firm, its efficiency norms, products, and procedures. The relationship of employees to consumers is largely adversarial, though rarely acknowledged to be so. There are, of course, plenty of exceptions to this, but few that arise as a result of policies.

The new pressures of the workplace in a global economy are not responsible for the new society of individuals, but they have accelerated its growth and deepened its roots. Complexity and conflict are just the sort of experiences that help breed psychological individuality, and the changes people are experiencing at work hold plenty of each. Moreover, these changes have occurred during precisely the same decades when the labor force itself has undergone a decisive transformation. No longer is it just the male breadwinner off to do battle with the forces of globalization, then pampered at home by a dutiful wife. Today Mom and Dad are both at work, forced to accommodate the new realities of personal and family life to the new demands of employment. We call these employees "history's shock absorbers," because the burden of simultaneous adaptation to history's most recent curveballs—psychological individuality and a global economy that has intensified the application of the standard enterprise logic—falls squarely on their shoulders. In the U.S. case, at least, while there has been some progress in parental leave, health insurance, and tax policy, the federal government has not been inclined to do much to ease the burden that falls on these individuals. Overall, precious few societal or organizational resources have been dedicated to their support.

This brings us back to the heart of our story. Today's individuals seek psychological self-determination. Years of effort to improve "the quality of work life" have paradoxically yielded an even more pressured work environment. The common parlance for this syndrome is "the time squeeze," in concert with a growing vocabulary of time troubles: "time famine," "time bind," "time crunch," "time deepening," "quality time," "24/7," "multitasking," "trip-chaining," "hurry sickness," and "work/life balance." Individuated lives require time, but the contemporary experience of work is marked by a deepening conflict between how one wants to live and how one must live. With few alternatives, people seem to feel more than ever that they must keep silent and comply.

The data that we review in this chapter suggest that there are tens, perhaps hundreds, of millions of these new time-choked individuals. They are the red-hot core of the new society of individuals and its markets for deep support. We have already suggested that the new individuals seek more from producers than mere efficiency; they seek support in their efforts at psychological self-determination. For those infected by the new uncertainties at work, the yearning for self-authorship is painfully thwarted on a daily basis. Powerless to change the pressures of work, they turn instead to life outside of work to seek fulfillment of their new dreams. That is, they turn toward the other domain of their lives—as consumers—where their dreams are magnified in proportion to their sense of helplessness and frustration at work. In this way, as we shall see below, the malaise of the workplace in this age of globalization is helping to fuel the new markets for deep support and fortify peoples' determination to restructure consumption in their own image.

THE DAILY GRIND

Discussions of the time squeeze typically begin with a historical analysis of working hours. What would seem to be a pretty straightforward calculation is, in fact, fraught with controversy. In the early 1990s Harvard economist Juliet Schor's *The Overworked American* garnered attention as it argued that since 1969 Americans were working more and enjoying less leisure. She concluded that "just to reach their 1973 standard of living," production and nonsupervisory employees "must work 245 more hours, or 6-plus extra weeks a year." Salaried workers also had to work more hours to keep up with their lifestyle demands. Among both groups, Schor argued, women were hardest hit, as they increasingly opted for full-time employment while facing continued unpaid labor demands for housework and child care.[6] This theme of women's increased time burden was also popularized in sociologist Arlie Hochschild's books *The Second Shift* and *The Time Bind*.[7]

The debate expanded with the 1997 publication of *Time for Life*, by sociologists John Robinson and Geoffrey Godbey.[8] They used information from special data-gathering devices called "time diaries" to analyze Americans' use of time. In contrast to Schor's work, and many other studies that had been based on self-reports of time use, Robinson and Godbey concluded that work hours had actually declined slightly since the mid-1960s, while free time had increased considerably for both men and women. Since 1997, a range of new studies has endeavored to combine diverse methodologies and new analytic frameworks to reconcile these very different conclusions. So far the answer to the objective question of work hours appears to be something like: It depends. It depends on the time frame, age, occupation, income, gender, and marital, parental, and educational status of the group in question.

Economists from the U.S. Bureau of Labor Statistics, for example, concluded that the average length of the workweek for many groups has changed little since the mid-1970s, but the distribution of work hours among groups has changed considerably.[9] They show a decline between 1976 and 1993 in the number of people working 40-hour weeks (from about 45 percent to 40 percent), and an increase in those working more than 49 hours a week (from about 13 percent to 18 percent). This increase becomes more marked during the peak earning years (from ages twenty-four to fifty-four), when the number of men working more than 49-hour weeks increased from 22 percent to 29 percent, and the number of women more than doubled from 5.7 percent to 12 percent. Between 1985 and 1993, the number of people with long workweeks increased by 5.1 million. About half of that gain is attributed to an overall growth of employment. Another 8.1 percent is due to growth in occupations that favor long workweeks, such as managers, professionals, sales, and transportation workers. The rest of the increase was due to the increase in the share of long workweeks across all occupational categories.

When these researchers focused on the question of gender differences, their findings were more dramatic. They found a 15 percent increase (193 hours) between 1976 and 1993 in the number of hours women worked each year, and a 3 percent increase (62 hours) in that number for men. When they narrowed that calculation to only those persons ages twenty-five to fifty-four, the average hours per year rose 45 percent for women, from 888 to 1,290 hours, while for men their average was unchanged at just over 1,900 hours. Women's annual work hours have increased because more women up and down the economic scale now work in full-time, year-round jobs.

The gist of these findings is echoed in another recent study by economists Jerry Jacobs and Kathleen Gerson.[10] Their calculations conclude that the "average" American worker is putting in about the same amount of time on the job as he did thirty years earlier. However, the increased participation of women in the paid labor force, the rise of dual-career families, and the growing number of single-earner families headed by women means that more households are missing the one factor that had kept everything afloat: a full-time wife. As a result, more "average" Americans are experiencing time pressure, even if their hours of paid work have not increased. In this way, the sense of a "daily grind" has settled over a large segment of the population, even when its formal hours of work have not increased.

That study goes on to look more deeply at differences among groups of workers. It finds an increasing split in the workforce between those who work exceptionally long hours and others who work the same or fewer hours compared to earlier decades. This split can be defined by occupation and educational level. For example, more than one-third of the men in professional, technical, or managerial occupations work 50 hours per week or more, compared to only 20 percent of men in other occupations. For women the figures are 17 percent, compared to fewer than 7 percent. So as the ranks of those long-hours occupations keep growing, the number of people still at work at 7:00 P.M. on Wednesday, or on Sunday afternoon, is likely to grow with them.

The numbers are even more striking if viewed through the lens of educational attainment. About 40 percent of men with at least a college education work 50 hours or more each week, compared to about 12 percent of those with less than a high school degree. For women the numbers are 20 percent compared to fewer than 5 percent. The authors hypothesize that to some extent the split in the U.S. workforce between those working longer and those working the same or less can be explained by the way firms manage labor costs to save money. On one end of the split, they hire more part-time workers who do not receive benefits, creating a low-hours, low-pay workforce. At the other end of the spectrum, full-time employees, especially those on salary, often find themselves under pressure to work as many hours as possible. Jacobs and Gerson also found that the United States stands out among the Organisation for Economic Co-operation and Development (OECD) countries for having the most people working long-hours workweeks. Only in the United States and Australia does the number of men working 50-hour weeks exceed 20 percent, with Japan and the United Kingdom following close behind.[11] In most countries the number is between 10 percent and 20 percent, while in Sweden, the Netherlands, and Luxembourg the numbers are well below 10 percent. American women also have the highest proportion of long workweeks and the lowest rates of part-time work.

The 1997 National Study of the Changing Workforce (NSCW), conducted by the Families and Work Institute, is a comprehensive national survey that also illuminates the question of work hours.[12] Its findings include some comparisons with the results of *The Quality of Employment Survey*, conducted in 1977 by the U.S. Department of Labor. The survey reports that both paid and unpaid work hours were greater in 1997 than in 1977, with the men's workweek increasing by 2.8 hours and the women's by 5 hours. Further, 63 percent of all people surveyed said that they would prefer to reduce their workweeks by about 11 hours. When Jacobs and Gerson did an even more detailed analysis of these data, they found that more than 80 percent of the men and women working more than 50 hours per week preferred shorter schedules. Those working between 50- and 60-hour weeks wanted to cut back by about 12 hours, while those working more than 60 hours wanted to cut back by 20 hours.

Instead of reduced workweeks, though, the survey suggests that work pressures are increasing and that work has colonized more of people's lives than it did twenty years ago. A majority of *NSCW* respondents said that within the previous three months they sometimes, often, or very often did not have enough time for their family or other important people in their lives (58 percent), did not have enough energy to do things with family or friends (57 percent), did not have enough time for themselves (65 percent), and were not able to get everything done at home (65 percent). Between 1977 and 1997, the amount of time for personal activities available to fathers and mothers declined on workdays as well as on days off. Mothers reported the least amount of time in 1997, with less than one hour to themselves on workdays and about two and a half hours on days off.

This trend is abetted by computer technologies and the underlying abstraction of work, which makes many jobs inherently more portable: It's a lot easier to bring home a diskette, a bunch of papers, an e-mail, or a telephone contact list, than to tote around your piece of the factory. Recent analyses suggest that between 25 percent and 65 percent of jobs in North America and Europe are portable in this way.[13] According to the 1997 *NSCW*, 31 percent of employees said that they bring work home at least once a week, compared to 20 percent in 1977, while those who say they never bring work home decreased by 16 percent. In three related measures of job pressure, 68 percent of *NSCW* respondents in 1997 agreed that their jobs require them to work very fast, compared to 55 percent in 1977; 88 percent agreed that their jobs require them to work very hard, compared to 70 percent in 1977; and 60 percent agreed that there is never enough time to get everything done on the job, compared to 40 percent in 1977.

The increase in job pressure has not been accompanied by a comparable increase in the flexibility of work arrangements. About 45 percent of *NSCW* respondents say that they can choose, within some range of hours, when they begin and end their workdays, but only 25 percent can change their daily schedules as needed. An overwhelming 74 percent say that they do not, and would not be allowed to, work at least part of their regularly scheduled work hours at home. It is interesting to note that, despite the obvious potential threat to job security and career progression, nearly 30 percent of respondents said that they would give up a day's pay for an extra day of free time each week, and about 25 percent said they would sacrifice professional advancement for more control over the timing of their work.

The 1999 "Work Trends" survey underscored the gap between what people want and what organizations offer.[14] For example, nearly half of the workers surveyed said that telecommuting (the use of computing and communications technology to support working from home) is important, but only 17 percent of employers offered that opportunity. The study found that 8 percent of all workers telecommuted for some part of their job, but 59 percent said that they would telecommute if given the opportunity, despite concerns about its effect on advancement. Nearly all systematic studies of telecommuting, as well as the anecdotal evidence on the subject, report significant productivity increases and exorbitant increases in job satisfaction. There is some research to suggest that a sizable proportion of would-be teleworkers are willing to take a cut in pay from 5 percent to 10 percent for the privilege of telecommuting.[15] Despite the widespread interest, positive outcomes, and the new portability of so much work, most research estimates suggest that somewhere between 1 percent and 10 percent of the U.S. workforce has the opportunity to telecommute, even on a temporary basis.[16] While some reports noted a renewed interest in telecommuting after the September 11, 2001, attacks in New York City and Washington, D.C., it is doubtful that this alone will stem the tide of resistance to the concept among employers, especially large companies.[17] As a result, the great majority of telecommuters come from firms that have fewer than one-hundred employees and that typically are geared toward some kind of professional service.[18]

ENCOUNTERS IN CAREER TAXIDERMY

The art of taxidermy is to take something that is dead and make it appear alive. Much of the anguish associated with the daily grind is the result of just this sort of practice, but the dead animal's head hung above the mantelpiece is not that of a moose, but of a career. More specifically, it is a conception of career norms developed by and for the men who once dominated corporate life. Statistically speaking, the work patterns of these men formed an inverted "U" curve, discussed in Chapter Three. That is, they went to work in early adulthood, worked throughout their adulthood, and retired in their sixties. Sociologically speaking, the men worked while their wives raised their children and attended to home and hearth. Biologically speaking, men worked through what are regarded as the peak years in the male life cycle. It was generally believed that a man's career plateaued somewhere in his fifties, by which time he would have achieved his highest career status. This career norm, perhaps right for its time, no longer reflects the realities of today's individuals, who live longer and healthier lives and tend not to have a domestic partner fully dedicated to minding home and family. Nevertheless, the old moose has been artfully embalmed to appear alive and relevant; it is the cause of much grief associated with the daily grind.

The first casualties of career taxidermy are the more than 60 percent of all women who work, the 78.3 percent of women with children between the ages of six and seventeen who work, and the 63.9 percent of all women with children under the age of six who work.[19] While men continue to dominate management, women have significantly expanded their presence in every sector and occupation, creating new sources of conflict with the moose head on the wall. One of the biggest sources of conflict involves opportunities for well-remunerated and respected part-time work. Obviously, part-time work arrangements are quite important to women during their childbearing and child-rearing years. Their sociological and biological realities have little in common with the old career norms. They do not have wives at home to raise their children and preside over domestic affairs. Another major concern involves the overall structure and pacing of careers. The rhythms of a woman's life cycle do not follow the same patterns as those of her male counterparts.[20] For many women, for example, some of the most productive years occur after their children have become independent, just when men are supposed to be in or approaching their career plateau.

The experience of female attorneys offers a powerful illustration of this confrontation between new individuals and old career norms. In 2000, more than half of incoming law students were women. Yet, according to a 2000 report issued by the Women's Bar Association of Massachusetts, the cultures of most law firms continue to be dominated by a male perspective.[21] That year, women comprised 28 percent of the respondents to the Bar Association survey but 40 percent of all attorneys leaving their firms. Forty percent of the women who left their firms between 1996 and 1998 reported "their firm's policies or approach toward reduced-hours arrangements affected their decision to leave." More than one-third of the respondents to the Bar Association survey said that a reduced-hours arrangement would be detrimental to their careers, and that the firm's negative attitudes and behaviors toward attorneys who made such arrangements "was indicative of how the firm felt towards women generally."

Those women who were willing to run the risks of part-time work did not fare well. Nearly 80 percent reported that their career path toward partnership had been adversely affected. Most of these women felt that they were no longer considered viable for promotion, whether or not that had been explicitly stated by senior partners. But the negative attitudes did find their way into other forms of expression. The women report being ignored by their colleagues, a lack of organizational support for their working arrangements, and deteriorating relationships with other attorneys in the firm who showed skepticism toward the part-timer's "professional commitment." Many reported that their skills were devalued and that the substantive quality of their assignments declined. Most part-timers found that their colleagues expected them to be on call 100 percent of the time, despite the fact that they had accepted a reduced salary in return for a reduced workweek. "I once felt well liked and very much a part of this place," recalls one attorney. "I am now seen as a slacker." "I feel like the partners view me as a problem," says another. "Although they have told me that I am 'on track' [for promotion], they have also told me that I am a marginal case."

The Massachusetts Bar Association findings are echoed in a late-1990s survey of women who graduated from Stanford University's Graduate School of Business during the 1970s through the 1990s. Despite their formidable level of preparation for professional business responsibilities, the numbers of women who worked full-time had dwindled to an astonishing 47 percent. Another 46 percent worked part-time, and 7 percent had given up on paid work altogether. When the women were asked about the disadvantages of corporate life, "male corporate culture" and "lack of flexibility" drew the top rankings. When asked to rank the most significant disadvantages to full-time work, "time pressure" and "high role conflict" were rated as the top two problems. As one respondent, a new mother, elaborated: "In order to be on the fast track, most corporations demand a level of commitment that I was not willing to make. Right now what's important to me is being in control of my time. While I miss being at the center of things, I enjoy the flexibility and a schedule that allows for a family life and for other activities that are important to me."[22]

The women who remain at work suffer the most extreme time pressures at the hands of career taxidermy, but their husbands do not fare much better. They find themselves trapped in the inverted "U" curve, along with their wives. According to Jacobs and Gerson's data, the average couple is working ten hours more each week than in 1970. That "average" increase isn't due so much to changes for each person as it is due to the decline of male-breadwinner marriages and the rise of married working women. In another study, two Cornell sociologists found that between 1972 and 1994, couples' total average working time increased by 7 hours a week.[23] Both sexes reported feeling pressured by the conflicting demands of home and work, with 43 percent of men saying that they work more hours than they want to and 50 percent of women wishing that they could work part-time. As a sign of the historical mismatch between the new individuals and the career norms of the old organizations, only about 10 percent of the couples in the Cornell study preferred traditional husband/wife roles, but a full 25 percent fit that profile. Similarly, only 14 percent said that they wanted both spouses to work full-time, but nearly 30 percent actually did. There simply are too few part-time employment opportunities that offer suitable pay, benefits, and career development.

The 1999 "Work Trends" survey, cited earlier, also showed that workers rated the ability to balance work and family as the most important aspect of a job (88 percent said it was very or extremely important; 97 percent said it was important).[24] In 1993, the DDB Needham Life Style Study found the most dramatic gender-related trend in the last quarter-century to be the increased agreement of women with the statement "I feel I am under a great deal of pressure most of the time." Affirmative responses increased from around 40 percent of women in 1975 to nearly 60 percent in 1993, rising to 65 percent among women who worked full-time. Results from the Needham study in 1996 showed 72 percent of all women between the ages of eighteen and fifty agreeing with the statement "It seems as though everyone in our family is always on the run."[25]

Women's Voices 2000 is another U.S. study of the changing attitudes and experiences of men and women across a wide spectrum of economic, racial, and ethnic diversity.[26] According to its findings, both men and women emphatically listed the dilemma of "combining work and family" as the top problem facing women at work today, significantly outdistancing other important issues like equal pay, discrimination, child care, sexual harassment, health care, job security, retirement benefits, and elder care. In addition, every subgroup of women said that combining work and family was the biggest problem they faced. A whopping 89 percent of the women with children under the age of six said that it was as hard or harder to juggle work and family demands compared to four years earlier. The researchers reported that "time constraints" was the central theme in all their focus-group discussions, and that women "find each moment of their days accounted for. . . . Faced with the prospect of increasing pressures, key words for women are more 'flexibility' and 'control.' " As a result, 71 percent of the women surveyed said they would prefer a job with benefits such as family leave, flexible hours, and child-care assistance to one with higher wages.[27] These findings echoed and amplified the findings reported by this research group in similar surveys conducted in 1992 and 1996.

The old norms have been made to appear alive and relevant, even when they openly contradict the realities of the new people, especially the women among them. Thanks to career taxidermy, dual-career couples who work full-time, especially parents, and most especially mothers, shoulder the greatest burden in the time squeeze. Add to these findings the fact that people with a college education are also working the longest hours, and we have identified the raw heart of this drama: the educated working mother. She is the epicenter of the daily grind, the grande dame of frustrated dreams, and, as we shall see a bit later in our story, the front line of the new consumption.

NO TIME FOR LIFE

These studies of the daily grind—and the way it has been exacerbated by the conflicts between new individuals and outmoded career norms—still do not tell the whole story of today's time battles. The time squeeze suggests the terror of an Indiana Jones caught between two enormous boulders inexorably approaching one another and leaving no way out. The only certainty is that they will gradually and painfully crush the life out of whatever is trapped between them. This is the daily grind. If increased work hours, intensified work pressures, and role conflicts represent one of the boulders, and working mothers and dual-earner couples are caught in the middle, then what's the other boulder?

The second boulder in the time squeeze is composed of all the nonwork activities that create and sustain identity. Whether it's outdoor adventure, travel, building a home, genealogical research, writing a memoir, taking a class, or a shopping expedition—these experiences take time. They are no longer the eccentric amusements of the rich. They are increasingly regarded as necessary by the tens of millions of people embarked on the work of composing their identities. These demands are vastly magnified for parents, especially mothers, who must also dedicate themselves to developing the individuality of their children. The growing literature on this subject suggests that parents rarely translate this obligation into the simple experiences of quiet family time, reading, play, and conversation.[28] Instead, they frequently feel driven to assemble and oversee a complex pastiche of activities designed to develop the child's abilities along multiple dimensions of skill and experience. Parents' dedication is also spurred by the expectation that their investment in the production of exquisitely individual children will help their offspring compete and achieve in the new society of individuals, where people must make themselves. As one mother puts it, "I feel it's part of my job, my obligation, to expose my children to the arts, sports, various activities." And a family researcher observes, "Raising kids becomes like product development. It's competitive parenting, all well intentioned, to develop the kid in every possible way."[29]

Even sociologists Robinson and Godbey, who have ardently defended their data suggesting that working hours have declined, were forced to reckon with the reality of the time squeeze. Their national studies of time use from 1965 through 1995 asked Americans about the feeling of being rushed. They report that the "always feel rushed" response grew from 24 percent of people eighteen to sixty-four years old in 1965 to 38 percent in 1992. In attempting to reconcile these findings with their analysis of decreases in work time and increases in free time, these researchers were forced to conclude, "Free time is expanding, but not as fast as people's sense of the necessary."[30]

The "necessary" today is the work of developing and sustaining psychological individuality for oneself and one's children. It is the second vector of the time squeeze. For many groups, especially dual-earning couples and working mothers, the first vector concerns increased hours of work. For other groups, the first vector may be the increased sense of work pressure and the absence of flexibility. In each case, the individual is now history's shock absorber, trapped between two opposing historical forces, required to absorb the pressures of a new individualism faced off against the very enterprise logic that gave it birth—an enterprise logic that is intensified as it struggles to meet the challenges of global competition. This is the reality of the so-called time squeeze. When these two opposing forces confront each other, they produce a new kind of misery and its name is "stress."

THE NEW STRESS

It was a peaceful early-summer morning on the banks of the Mianus River in Connecticut. Only a handful of cars threatened the stillness as they approached the small section of the Connecticut Turnpike bridge that would carry them across the river. Suddenly and without warning, the air filled with thunder, accompanied by a massive explosion of debris, as a 100-foot section of the bridge that had spanned the river for twenty-five years collapsed without, it seemed, the slightest provocation. When the dust cleared, three people were dead and three more lay critically injured among the scraps of twisted metal in the marshes below.

Later, highway engineers would report that the continual stress of rusting metal had reached a critical structural limit and the bridge simply gave out. "We certainly had no indication of structural problems," avowed Connecticut's transportation commissioner. "The failure mechanism as happened the other day is sudden and catastrophic. It gives little warning," added a prominent local engineer. True enough, there had been no catastrophe—no earthquake, hurricane, tornado, or mud slide—only the chronic unobserved stress of corroding metal. But had there been any warning signs? Residents of homes underneath the bridge said that pieces of concrete and steel had been falling from the bridge for five years. The bridge had also been vibrating and whistling, and in the days before its collapse there had been a strange new sound, "high, piercing, like thousands of birds chirping," said one local. Neighbors had called and written to the state's Transportation Department, as well as to its nearby maintenance shop and to several state representatives. A group of engineers had visited months earlier, but nothing was done. "No one in the Transportation Department has any record of complaints," insisted the governor's press secretary.[31]

Psychologists know that much of the stress that people experience in contemporary life is a result of the repetitive experiences associated with the time squeeze and works in much the same way as the stress on the Mianus River bridge. In earlier centuries, terms like "burden," "grief," and "trial" were synonyms of stress. Stress was thought of as outside people, located in external challenges like a raging storm or a loved one's illness. Suffering stress was a temporary hardship that called forth endurance and tested strength.[32] Certainly this kind of stress still exists. People face catastrophes and alarming or grief-filled events. (In psychological models these are called "stressors," which act on a person, causing "stress," and the response that one has to the experience of stress is exhibited in varying levels of "distress.") But today psychologists have a greater appreciation of a more ubiquitous and insidious kind of stress that afflicts contemporary people. They call it "chronic stress." This is what the bridge was suffering from: continuous and unobserved stress that, when left unchecked, took the structure beyond its limits.

Engineers have long realized that some stress on machines or built structures is a good thing. It actually increases what they call "elasticity," increasing a structure's tolerance and flexibility. Research shows that the same is true for people. A moderate amount of stress tends to stimulate performance, enlarging a person's limits and increasing her capacity to face all sorts of experiences in a constructive way. But too much stress leads to physical and mental distress and eventually, as in the case of the bridge, breakdown. How this works can vary a good deal from person to person. It depends a lot on the meaning that a stressful event holds for someone—psychologists call that the "context"—as well as on the coping resources that a person starts out with—hardiness, optimism, friends, loving family, interests, and activities, versus pessimism, isolation, and poor health.[33]

One stress specialist, sociologist Howard Kaplan, defines chronic stressors as the expression of "problems and issues that are . . . so regular in the enactment of daily roles and activities . . . that they behave as if they are continuous for the individual." Such stressors typically include "excessive task or role demands . . . excessive complexity, uncertainty, conflict, restriction of choice, or underreward." Kaplan emphasizes that this kind of stressor is a regular feature of the social structure; it creates a barrier between one's goals and the means to achieve them; with enough force and continuity it can challenge someone beyond their limits; if not fixed, it will create damage; it undermines valued aspects of personal identity; and it often operates outside of awareness.[34] Psychologist Robert Kugelmann describes this experience of chronic stress as the feeling of being pitted against "a given" that cannot be escaped. "We know that how we live is killing us, leading us into addictions, flaying our most important relationships. . . . Yet we see no way out."[35] Unlike centuries ago, we no longer experience stress as something from the outside that must be escaped, changed, or temporarily endured as a test of strength and character. Today's chronic stress is experienced as "inside"—a more or less permanent feature of subjective experience.

Two more concepts from modern stress theories are crucial to our effort to understand the relationship between the time squeeze, stress, and the latent demand for a new enterprise logic represented by the new markets for deep support. Chronic stress is linked to a well-documented psychological phenomenon: People become anxious and otherwise distressed when their actions or thoughts are subject to interruption. The more organized their activities, and the more severe and constant the interruptions, the greater their distress will be. One of the most important ongoing organized processes in modern life is the establishment and maintenance of identity. As sociologist Peter Burke observes, it involves behaviors, thoughts, and feelings in a "continuously operating, self-adjusting feedback loop." Burke argues that at the heart of modern stress is the experience of failed or interrupted identity. People exhibit anxiety and distress when they cannot control events that undermine or are discrepant with identity maintenance and "self-verification." Their distress is greater when the identity interruptions are severe and frequent, but distress also increases in proportion to the strength of identity organization and the importance vested in that identity.[36] In other words, when a person's experiences impede their self-authoring efforts and contradict their sense of self, they will produce a stress response: anxiety, exhaustion, numbness, rage, and a welter of physical symptoms, from fatigue and depression to immune disorders, ulcers, high blood pressure, obesity, and heart disease. The stress response will be worse if a person has a very clear sense of identity and places a lot of importance on that sense of self.

These relationships are underscored by a recent study based on three national samples of U.S. adults, ages twenty-five to seventy-five, who were analyzed in terms of psychological and physical health. Researchers from Brandeis University found that when people enjoyed a sense of "personal mastery" and did not perceive significant constraints on their scope of action—two dimensions that add up to what we have called psychological self-determination—they were significantly healthier in terms of a wide range of physiological and psychological measures. They had fewer depressive symptoms, higher ratings of life satisfaction, and higher ratings of their health. These findings held true up and down the income scale. In fact, low-income respondents with high ratings in psychological self-determination were characterized by the same positive patterns of health and well-being as high-income respondents with a similar pattern of ratings.[37]

Another nationwide study magnifies this point.[38] A group of elderly people was asked to rank-order the three roles that were most important to them. The researchers questioned the study participants exhaustively, in order to understand all the factors that influenced their ability to carry out their various roles. Then their medical conditions were also studied in detail. Each participant was measured in terms of the degree of control they could exert over each role, as well as their "global feelings" of control. When all the data were analyzed, the researchers found that those with a strong sense of control in the role that was most important to them were less likely to die during the follow-up period than those who did not exercise much control over their most salient role. In fact, a one-unit increase in control over the most salient role was associated with a 7 percent decline in the odds of dying. These effects remained strong even when all the well-known predictors of mortality were statistically controlled. In contrast, global feelings of control did not appear to influence longevity.

These studies suggest that when people can successfully maintain and verify the most valued aspects of their identity, they live longer, healthier, and happier lives.[39] The findings imply that when social experiences affirm, support, and contribute to the activities associated with constructing and maintaining personal identity, people experience the opposite of stress. They encounter, instead, sources of meaning, pleasure, nourishment, and energy. Identity-affirming experiences are, quite literally, life-giving. This study also reminds us that the quest for psychological self-determination is not the same as the need to feel "in control" of everything. Psychological self-determination describes the ability to exert control over the most important aspects of one's life, especially personal identity, which has become the source of meaning and purpose in a life no longer dictated by blood lines and tradition. The sense of a meaningful existence is intimately linked to the possibility of hope and optimism, which have also been shown to be predictors of health.[40] If stress can kill, then psychological self-determination appears to be its opposite—it can quite literally keep us alive.

The final point to be garnered from these theories is that history also has a role to play in the experience of stress. Social change and powerful social events can affect the life course of an entire birth cohort, or of successive cohorts.[41] Think of German Jews in 1938, those coming of age during the Great Depression or World War II, and the cohorts born since the mid-twentieth century who have grown up in the postscarcity cornucopia of the advanced societies.

Some experiences of stress, then, can vary enormously on an individual basis. The wide range of reactions people have to a personal loss would be an example of this kind of stress. But other forms of stress are more chronic. These are often embedded in the regularities of societal and organizational experiences. They are likely to affect large groups of people who are all exposed to similar stressors, though there remain individual variations in the stress response. Finally, some stress may be an inescapable feature of living in a particular place at a particular time in history.

It is no coincidence, then, that the concept of chronic stress has become a central feature of kitchen table conversation, mental health conferences, social-psychological research, and yoga retreats only during the last thirty years or so as the time squeeze began to be experienced as a regular feature of many people's lives. That's the time frame during which whole cohorts began to long for a way of being that was at odds with the demands of the organizations they depended upon for employment and consumption.[42] Thousands of books and articles on stress offer similar prescriptions for the stress associated with the daily grind. They speak to what people feel is missing: the ability to escape, simplify, relax, imagine (take twenty-minute vacations), feel peaceful, feel centered, heal, sleep, find coherence, discover joy, energy, and balance. The message? Find a way to feel self-determining, even if it's only in your head. As Kugelmann observes, people under stress feel the need to make lists. That way they impose some order on the scarce resources of time and energy, and create a feeling of control, however illusory. Otherwise, they are condemned to the whipsaw of adrenaline surges followed by helplessness, exhaustion, numbness, and rage.[43]

In fact, recent research on stress suggests that millions of people are caught in precisely that whipsaw. These studies shed light on the linkages between chronic stress and the time squeeze. They are distinguished by the oppressive uniformity of their results. Millions of people are united in stress, a unity that ignores the old divisions of class and nation. In 1993, a survey titled "Stress Among Working Women" conducted by the New York Business Group on Health found that 42 percent of respondents said they were frequently affected by stress in their jobs. Women who assumed multiple roles had an even higher stress rating. The principal mechanisms women used to cope with stress? They exercised and worked harder.[44] In 1997, Princeton Survey Research Associates conducted a national poll that showed 73 percent of respondents experienced more job-related stress than they had in the past.[45]

In *The 1997 National Study of the Changing Workforce* (NSCW), people were asked, "Have you felt used up at the end of the workday?" The survey found 36 percent of respondents replying "often" or "very often," with another 35 percent responding "sometimes." There was a similar pattern of response to the question "Have you felt burned out or stressed by your work?" with 26 percent saying "very often" or "often" and 31 percent replying "sometimes." The 1999 "Work Trends" survey also addressed the issues of stress—88 percent reported it as their most important issue. In both cases, women and minority respondents showed higher levels of concern than their male or white counterparts. By 1999, the National Institute for Occupational Safety and Health had issued a public health warning that called job stress "a threat to the health of workers." The U.S. public, it reported, was registering the highest-ever levels of stress at work, and "shifting work patterns due to the global economy are aggravating these issues."[46]

In March 2000, a national survey of U.S. women conducted by Gallup showed that among working women with children (29 percent of U.S. women), "time and stress" rated third among their "most pressing concerns," following such megawatt issues as "family" and "money." For working women without children (27 percent of U.S. women), "time and stress" ranked second, following only concerns over "money." That means that 56 percent of American women rated "time and stress" as either their second or third most important life concern.[47] In August 2000, an online Roper Starch survey among 1,000 America Online members, commissioned by a major provider of personal services, found that 62 percent of all respondents and 66 percent of women said that "help getting things done would greatly reduce the stress in my life," and 50 percent agreed that "if I could, I'd pay to have more time for myself or my family."[48] Small wonder, then, that an ABC News prime-time special on women and stress, aired in 2001, featured working moms rushing from their jobs to their children's activities as sensors monitoring their stress-hormone levels registered the equivalent of those of a soldier entering combat.[49]

In Canada, where average work hours have been slightly below U.S. rates, a nationwide survey by Statistics Canada in 1999 found that the "struggle to juggle" was most acute among full-time working parents.[50] The survey classified 38 percent of women between ages twenty-five and forty-four as "time stressed." In 2000, an Ipsos–Reid/CTV survey found that 48 percent of Canadians said they feel "really or seriously stressed" at least once a week, and 16 percent said they felt that level of stress daily. When asked what they do to relieve stress, most people placed exercise and relaxation at the top of their lists.[51]

In the United Kingdom, the only member of the European Union where the number of hours worked increased during the 1990s, the picture is even more grim. In 1998 the Institute of Management and the University of Manchester Institute of Science and Technology produced the first of its reports on a nationwide five-year study.[52] It showed that most managers worked more than 40-hour weeks, and 40 percent worked 50 hours a week or more. Sixty percent reported stress associated with job insecurity, lower morale, and diminished motivation. Another 1998 U.K. survey of financial professionals conducted by financial recruitment specialists Robert Half International found 80 percent of executives reporting that their workplace was more stressful than five years earlier, and more than 70 percent said that their colleagues were suffering from high levels of stress. Their average workweek was more than 47 hours, with 40 percent working more than 50 hours and over 6 percent working more than 60-hour weeks.[53]

In 1999, initial findings from a U.K. government-sponsored nationwide occupational study found 20 percent of all workers suffering from "extreme stress," largely due to long work hours, diminished security, and less flexibility.[54] In 2000, another nationwide survey, by the Institute of Management, found that stress continued to rise above "unsustainable levels," despite more widespread awareness of the subject. More than 90 percent of the managers surveyed reported working in excess of their contracted week, and 37 percent worked more than the 48-hour maximum week mandated by the European Commission. More than 70 percent considered stress to have an adverse impact on their health, including disturbed sleep, rage, headaches, fatigue, and lowered sex drive. Seventy-nine percent considered that stress had adversely affected their marriages, and 86 percent of those who were parents felt it had negatively affected their relationships with their children.[55]

Also in 2000, the Trades Union Congress, a U.K. labor organization founded to protect industrial workers, conducted a nationwide survey of 9,000 health and safety representatives across every industrial sector.[56] Their purpose was to understand the most significant workplace hazards facing British workers. Under the auspices of this quintessential industrial age organization, one might anticipate findings related to unsafe working conditions, poor enforcement of safety regulations, or antiquated plants and equipment. But no. Their survey named "stress" as the number-one workplace hazard in the United Kingdom in all but three of the industries surveyed. It was cited as the top concern in banking, finance, and insurance (86 percent), education and the voluntary sector (82 percent), central government (81 percent), health services (74 percent), and six other industries, including leisure services, transport, energy and water, and agriculture and fishing. Heavy workloads were cited as the major cause of stress by 74 percent of all the respondents across these industries.

An analysis of eight European surveys during the period 1977 to 1996 indicates a gradual increase in the time pressures experienced by employees across Europe that has not been matched by a corresponding increase in job autonomy.[57] A 1999 study of more than 15,000 EU workers reported that 30 percent of full-time employees said that they experienced stress at work.[58] A global survey of 30,000 people in 1999, conducted by Roper Starch Worldwide, found that women consistently reported higher levels of stress in the thirty countries included in the survey, with the highest stress levels reported by full-time working mothers with children under the age of thirteen.[59]

THE VANGUARD OF A NEW CONSUMPTION

Listen and you can hear the piercing sound of thousands of birds chirping. Recall Kaplan's criteria for chronic stress. Each one is fulfilled for tens of millions of women and men up and down the socioeconomic scale. They are experiencing regular features of a social structure and an enterprise logic that have created barriers between their goals and the means to achieve them, while challenging them beyond their limits, undermining valued aspects of their identities, often operating outside of their awareness, and most definitely causing damage. They are plagued by excessive task and role demands, along with complexity, uncertainty conflict, restriction of choice, and underreward.

And the remedies in sight are little more than those offered to the ailing Mianus River bridge. Solutions are inevitably directed toward the individuals experiencing the strain, who are squeezed between history's opposing forces, rather than toward eliminating the stressors themselves. Women are advised to withdraw from the workforce. Employers offer stress counseling to improve an employee's ability to cope with his or her plight. People are admonished to exercise, watch their diets, and develop relaxation skills. These may certainly help stave off the worst health consequences of chronic stress, but they do nothing to affect its source. The two vectors of history, past and future, continue to oppose one another, slowly grinding the life out of whatever stands between them.

The chronic stress people feel today is a more or less permanent feature of experience, when individuals gripped by the sense of entitlement to self-authorship encounter the practices and demands of an organizational world built for the old mass order and especially for the kind of men once at its helm. As the old organizations struggle in the heavy new currents of the global economy, they have learned to reproduce their old logic ever more assiduously, as living systems under threat will often do. Changes at the margins, such as redefining aspects of the employment relationship, do not alter the deep structure of the firm but merely shift more of its risks to employees.

The pervasive conflict in the daily life of the new individuals is succinctly described by German sociologist Ulrich Beck as the desire to "take one's own life in one's hands." "With only slight exaggeration," he writes, "one can say that the daily struggle for 'one's own life' has become the collective experience of the entire western world."[60] That this confrontation is stressful—a "struggle"—is precisely because of the difficulty individuals encounter reconciling their new dreams with the practices of old organizations. As in the study of the elderly we discussed earlier, for whom loss of control of their identity led more quickly to death, the chronic stress experienced by the new individuals signals the thundering absence of what they long for and feel entitled to: psychological self-determination. Because the two poles of existence, the individual and the organizational, have come into conflict, it appears as though it has always been and must always be so. The stress people feel is accepted as a more or less inevitable consequence of "late modern" life.

This story of the daily grind and the stress it produces might end here in a somber realization of depressing facts, were it not for a further crucial contention: The experience of stress is now so widespread that it is exactly the sort of large-scale world-historical force that can transform populations. It does this by forcing people to reckon with complexity and conflict as they endeavor to reconcile the need to adapt with the need to invent. The constant friction between one's own needs and organizational demands invites people to become more aware of themselves in juxtaposition to organizations, rather than as mere extensions of them. Consider that the 2000 U.S. Census counted 82.8 million people (an increase of 32 percent or 20 million from 1990) between the ages of thirty-five and fifty-four—prime years for the stress of the time squeeze. There can be little doubt that tens of millions of people are spinning new dreams that cannot be satisfied within the old enterprise logic, either in their roles as employees or as consumers.

The stress of the daily grind that so many people feel today is thus an expression of the thwarted yearning for psychological self-determination. It signals the absence of what people long for. This signal increases in intensity in proportion to the intensity of desire for a world in which psychological self-determination is affirmed, supported, and nurtured. Today's chronic stress is a cri de coeur announcing a profound longing for a kind of life that is meaningful, pleasurable, nourishing, energizing, and life-enhancing. As a result, many of these new individuals are transmuting their disappointments as employees into new dreams as consumers. These stressed-out, hardworking, complicated, and conflicted individuals, especially the women among them, are the core from which a new structure of consumption and a new framework for capitalism are emerging. They are the vanguard of the support economy.

Longing, as we have seen, is the human core of markets. People long for things that stimulate and prolong their feelings of pleasure. They then desire to experience in reality those pleasures already imagined. This is the process that motivates consumption, and it is the equation that turns dreams into unrealized economic value. Today there are millions of people who are stepping up to history's challenges, despite the absence of a new enterprise logic to midwife their dreams. They are inventing ways to take their own lives in their own hands in order to translate those dreams into reality. Their emerging approach to consumption is one important means toward this end. In the next chapter we follow their trail of stress and struggle in order to learn about the new structure of consumption anticipated in their choices and foretold in their inventions.

SIX

The Individuation of Consumption

In the popular 1950s television show *The Life of Riley*, a group of men piled into a friend's car each morning, clutching their metal lunch boxes on their way to the factory. Their wives remained at home, presumably cooking, cleaning, and completing the errands that kept the household ticking. In 1992, the city of Norfolk, Virginia, spent more than $120 million on a car-pool lane, hoping to ease congestion and speed commuting time on its troubled highway system.

WHERE HAVE ALL THE CAR POOLS GONE?

By 1998, the Norfolk car-pool lane had attracted only one-third of the expected ridership, and the numbers continued to decline. In Norfolk and other cities around the United States, Riley and his pals had vanished, leaving car-pool lanes underutilized by as much as 60 percent. In their place were harried women and men, dropping children off at day-care centers and schools before work and picking them up after work, along with additional stops for dry cleaning, groceries, soccer games, music lessons, and fast food. "People don't want to be bothered with the hassles of carpooling," was the belated observation of a Norfolk-area transportation official. "They want personal rapid transit." "You see the lane there, but you can't use it," protested one solitary New Jersey commuter who frequently found himself creeping along Route 80 next to an empty car-pool lane. "It's like we're being punished."[1] And so we are.

People are routinely punished for being complex psychological individuals in a world still fitted out for the old mass order. In the early twentieth century, organizational affiliation provided shelter from the storms of rapid urbanization and industrialization. In the early twenty-first century, the situation is reversed. Now, it is the very demands of those organizations that have become the storm. Perhaps this is the reason that the problems of the daily grind have produced so little in the way of new political movements. The new individuals are not inclined to seek solutions to these conflicts through more organization. Instead, they are inventing individual self-help strategies expressed in new approaches to lifestyle and consumption.

Companies responding to new competitive pressures with the product-focused efficiency norms of the standard enterprise logic have created stress-weary populations among their employees. Once those employees leave work, they become the target market for a barrage of products designed for the time-embattled. Fast-food restaurants and prepackaged food options proliferate. Consumer-goods companies push "aromatic" products—air fresheners, carpet deodorizers, candles—for women who do not have the time to clean their homes but still want them to smell good. The best-selling cleaning products are those that promise to work "automatically," like Windex Outdoor, hang-in toilet bowl cleaners, wrinkle-releasers, and "self-scrubbing" tile cleaners.[2]

The real needs of the new individuals, however, have little to do with these product gimmicks. Instead, the new individuals are seeking ways to take their lives in their own hands by constructing new approaches to consumption that buffer them from the stress of the daily grind while creating wider opportunities to nourish their sense of psychological self-determination. These new approaches reveal three prominent modalities in the expression of new needs. The first is what we call the *claim of sanctuary;* the second is the *demand for voice.* These expressions of independence, self-control, and self-definition also lead people, paradoxically, to reach out toward new interdependencies in what we call the *quest for connection.* This quest frequently takes the form of seeking out trusted others who can provide the support necessary to fulfill the needs associated with sanctuary and voice. It is also expressed when people seek support from like-minded others in online communities and other forms of association. In this way, the claim of sanctuary, the demand for voice, and the quest for connection translate the needs associated with psychological self-determination into new markets for deep support. They help define the framework for a new structure of consumption that supplants earlier "mass" or "segmented" consumption models. That new structure is what we call the individuation of consumption.

CONSUMING SANCTUARY

Sanctuary is consecrated space. It is imbued with the sacred but is also a place for refuge and protection from which predators are barred. Sanctuary can be a physical as well as a psychological space. It means being centered in my individual space, where I can own my choices, control my time, and shape the quality of my experience. The claim of sanctuary is a claim of psychological self-determination because it declares the individual as the origin rather than the object of action. In individual space, power shifts from the organization to the individual; one acts instead of being acted upon. One can experience one's own uniqueness without battling the forces of the mass order that want to treat all end consumers as anonymous and equivalent transactions. This means devising ways to gain control over activities related to employment and consumption by translating them from the public realm of the organization to the personal realm of individual space.

Seeking sanctuary at home or in the countryside has always been an idealized counterpoint to the pressures of modernization. There are many homilies that tell this story: "A man's home is his castle," "There's no place like home," "home sweet home," and so on. But by the late twentieth century—with even more people swamped by chronic stress—individuals from across the social map had turned the claim of sanctuary into a vital strategy for affirming the psychological individuality of oneself and one's family. As a result, the claim of sanctuary is now associated with a new and growing panoply of consumption activities that endeavor to assert, protect, enable, extend, and enrich the experience of taking one's life into one's own hands. In these activities, individuals invest in and act from their own individual space. There, they trade discretionary money for discretionary time, while selecting and acquiring experiences that support their objectives for an ever more individualized life.

BALI HAI ("YOUR OWN SPECIAL HOPES, YOUR OWN SPECIAL DREAMS")[3]

Sonora, California, is a 5,000-person hamlet tucked among the terra-cotta-colored foothills of the Sierras. An unlikely place, it would seem, for the new Staples office-supply store that opened there, with modest expectations, in 1997. One year later, the store had doubled its employment along with its sales. "Everybody up here does something with computers," explained the store manager. That's partly because a good many of them "up here" were until recently elsewhere. They are part of a growing number of the new individuals who have lost patience with the chimerical Bali Hai of dream life: an ever-distant object of longing, concealed in pale mist just beyond the horizon. These people are ready to embrace their Bali Hai in real life, and in so doing they have created one of the most startling demographic trends of the late twentieth century, known as the "rural renaissance." They are the reason that by the end of the 1990s, about a third of Staples stores were in small towns, compared to fewer than 10 percent at the beginning of the decade.[4]

For most of the twentieth century in the United States, people left the country for the city, where they joined the aspirations, rhythms, and routines of the new mass order. But when the first generation of new individuals came of age in the 1970s, they reversed this pattern in what one prominent demographer, Kenneth Johnson of Loyola University, has described as a "remarkable demographic turnaround," one that is "without historical precedent." They shunned the cities and the suburbs for rural landscapes and small towns to such an extent that nonmetropolitan population gain in the 1970s exceeded that of metropolitan areas for the first time in more than 150 years. This new trend abated during the 1980s, due to prolonged recession and other economic "period effects," but it was back with a vengeance during the 1990s, when the nonmetropolitan net migration gain was 3.6 percent, compared to 1.8 percent in metropolitan areas.[5]

Johnson concluded that this new pattern is the demographic hallmark of the late twentieth century. Known as "deconcentration," it is a long-term process of population redistribution that occurs as people leave the congestion and regimentation of city and suburb to forge a new kind of life in rural America. Most striking in light of our understanding of the new individuals is the news about where they are moving. Many of the biggest gains were in rural areas adjacent to metropolitan centers. This reflects the fact that many of those who are moving "out" still need to commute back "in." Johnson also analyzed counties across the United States according to their primary functions, such as farming, manufacturing, commuting, recreation, retirement, and so on. He found that there was near-universal population growth in the 285 "recreational" counties of the United States. The growth rates in counties that fell into the "recreation" and "retirement destination" categories (101 in all) were the highest of any identifiable group "because the amenities, temperate climate, and scenic advantages which attract vacationers and seasonal residents" also appeal to the new migrants.[6]

It should come as no surprise that these new migrants are people in search of a better quality of life infused with meaning, influence, and self-authorship and consistent with the dreams of self-determination we have been exploring. For these individuals, Bali Hai has become more than a wish. They are laying claim to their sanctuaries here and now, empowered by fax machines, e-mail, the Internet, and overnight shipping—a combination that has also made it easier for a range of companies to shift to the countryside. Johnson conducted focus groups to understand more about why people were moving. Their most frequent responses centered on the very themes that define the claim of sanctuary: They seek unmediated influence ("small towns offer an opportunity for one person to make a difference"), and they want a better quality of life ("we want a safe place to raise our children"). "We don't have to go camping anymore to relax or get away. We are away," observed one recent migrant to small-town Montana. "You just step out your back door, take a deep breath, look at the mountains, and everything is okay." "You have a chance to restore yourself," echoed another.[7]

The changing size and content of houses is another expression of the claim of sanctuary. For many people today, the sense of sanctuary is typically expressed in the physical form of the "house" and in the psychological sense of "home." Their houses are no longer simply a base of operations. They are a retreat, a buffer zone, a countermeasure to the stress of the daily grind. This, we think, is an important reason for the increase in the size and style of homes during the last thirty years—precisely the time frame that stress was on the rise. In 1970, the largest percentage of homes (36 percent) was in the smallest size category measured by the U.S. Census Bureau: less than 1,200 square feet. In 1997, the largest percentage of homes surveyed (31 percent) was in the largest size category: 2,400 square feet and larger. The average new home was 53 percent larger in 2001 than it was in 1970, even as the average family was 15 percent smaller.[8] Along with square footage, amenities have been growing too. In 1970, 52 percent of new homes had one and a half baths or fewer, while in 1997, 50 percent of new homes had two and a half baths or more. In 1970, 65 percent of new homes had no fireplace; in 1997, 61 percent had one or more fireplaces. Similar trends are evident for garages, central air-conditioning, and the number of stories.[9]

In 1996 the annual convention of the National Association of Home Builders promoted a conception of the home as "the ultimate destination for family and friends, a place one never has to leave." Experts in the home-construction field agree. They say that these trends cut across all demographic lines. Children are no longer expected to share a bedroom. Each family member counts on having private space.[10] The more upscale homes are also built to encompass more specialized activities, with high-tech theaters, pools, exercise centers, pubs, wine cellars, wired home offices, and hobby rooms. Even buyers of less expensive homes demand "the stress-busting master suite" ("They're building mini-retreats," says the editor of *Builder* magazine), a wide-open space to accommodate a kitchen and family room, a dedicated laundry room, a huge amount of closet space, and a home office or exercise space. The market for home-exercise equipment grew 75 percent between 1987 and 1997, compared to a 63 percent rise in health club memberships during that time.[11] Designers describe such homes as "destination houses" whose strength lies in the fact that they are self-contained work and entertainment complexes: "You can entertain yourself in this house," says one architect. "You do not have to go out." Or as another designer puts it, "We are no longer selling homes to people; we're selling lifestyles."[12]

At the Concord Group, a California real-estate consultancy, the advice to builders is to beware of buyers' aversion to "cookie-cutter" houses. Instead, they counsel offering dozens of options to change standard floor plans. The space needs to be able to change as people's needs and circumstances continuously develop and change. As a result, many new homes are designed with the recognition that people will want to make new choices, without having to move. Houses are fitted with extra wiring and plumbing to create "swing" spaces that can be easily adapted as bedrooms, offices, playrooms, or areas for other activities like crafts or billiards. "We offer bonus space or extra rooms that people can do with what they want," says a spokesperson for one of the largest building companies in the United States.[13] "Home products" is the third-largest retail expenditure category, totaling more than $585 billion in 2000, when 98 percent of all households made discretionary purchases.[14]

The home office is one important aspect of the claim of sanctuary. People work at home for many reasons—they may have lost their traditional job, want to pursue a business hobby, be fed up with commuting, want to escape the politics of organizations, or they may be trying to create a more flexible kind of work experience that enables them to balance work-life concerns and feel more self-authoring. The surveys we have already reviewed suggest an enormous hunger for self-determining working conditions. Survey respondents consistently want more flexibility than companies will provide. By the mid-1980s, there were sufficient innovations in computer and communications technologies to support these yearnings and their impetus toward sanctuary. As a result, the last decade has seen a return of the office to the home from which it was exiled 200 years ago. Today it's the eighteenth century with wires—and frequently a woman at the desk.

The market research firm International Data Corporation (IDC) estimates that in 2000 there were nearly 37 million home-office households (that's more than one-third of all U.S. households), compared to estimates of about 20 million in 1991.[15] IDC predicts that by 2004 there will be more than 46 million home-office households. That represents a compound annual growth rate of 6.2 percent, about six times greater than the rate of growth of the total number of U.S. households. Among all home-office uses, the one that is expected to grow most dramatically is that of income-generation, with a growth rate of 7.4 percent anticipated by 2004, representing about 27 million homes.[16]

The largest share of all home offices are used by people bringing work home from their corporate offices (26 million). This means that working at home extends the workday, although presumably under more congenial conditions. A growing number of home offices, though, are used for other purposes. For example, IDC estimates that 9.2 million home offices were used by telecommuters in 2000. (They counted people who worked at home at least three days a week.) A few months later, in February 2001, the U.S. Department of Labor's research concluded that there were approximately 19 million telecommuters. (They counted teleworkers based in satellite offices as well as at home.)[17] In 2001 the International Telework Association and Council in Washington, D.C., counted 24 million people who telecommuted either regularly or occasionally.[18] Whatever the exact number, it is clear from the surveys discussed in the last chapter that there are fewer telecommuters than there are people who want to telecommute.

SELF- (DETERMINING) EMPLOYMENT

The home-office boom is the most recent chapter in the complex history of self-employment in the U.S. economy. After nearly a century of decline, self-employment began to increase again during the mid-1970s. The number of workers in nonagricultural jobs who were self-employed in their primary jobs increased by 74 percent between 1975 and 1990, compared to a general employment increase of 33 percent during that period. Not surprisingly, the unique challenges faced by women in the daily grind have made women's increased share of self-employment a striking feature of this story. In 1975, women accounted for one in four self-employed workers, but by 1990, one-third of the self-employed were women. An overall comparison shows that male self-employment increased by 54 percent and female self-employment increased by 63 percent during those years.[19]

Researchers have arrived at substantially different conclusions about the nature and meaning of rising self-employment. Some have seen it as an emancipatory development, fulfilling workers' needs for more flexibility and control over their work life. Others have seen it as a disturbing consequence of a globalization in which more workers are forced to the economic margins, where they face greater insecurity and lower incomes. Some scholars have tried a more nuanced approach, recognizing that the self-employment experience is likely to vary with other considerations, such as socioeconomic status, race, sex, ethnicity, education, and so on.

One recent study of middle-class, professionally trained, self-employed "homeworkers" investigated their motives and experiences in considerable depth. It offers compelling evidence to suggest that much of the increase in self-employment can be understood in terms of the yearning for psychological self-determination and its associated claims of sanctuary. The interviews reported in that study show that self-employed homeworkers were invariably motivated by a desire for self-determination, though what self-determination meant to each varied according to the aspects of their identity that most concerned them (not unlike the study of the elderly discussed in the previous chapter). Mothers wanted the flexibility to care for children, while women without children emphasized self-fulfillment. White men sought independence and an escape from office politics; men and women of color wanted a means to overcome racial barriers and discrimination. Most achieved considerable satisfaction from self-employment, despite ongoing concerns about financial viability. The study concluded that self-employed homework is liberating and revolutionary but also carries the costs of unpredictability and insecurity for careers and incomes.[20] Certainly self-employment can provide an exit from whatever it is that one finds most stressful about one's life as a salaried employee.

Indeed, for many women self-employment has become one coveted antidote to the stress associated with the daily grind. One economist found that women with young children were significantly more likely to be self-employed.[21] Another study by economist Richard Boden also found that women with young children were more likely to choose self-employment. His study went on to analyze the motivations for self-employment among men and women with and without children. From his data it is clear that both sexes choose self-employment for reasons directly related to their needs for self-determination. For example, "enjoyment of being one's own boss" was by far the most commonly cited motive for all respondents of both sexes. Among women with young children, however, about 72 percent also cited a combination of motives, including flexibility, family obligations, child-care problems, and "other personal reasons," while for women without young children only 48 percent cited these secondary motives. Among men, these issues were far less pressing, with only 27 percent citing this complex of motives.[22] While the combined numbers of self-employed persons peaked toward the end of the recession in the early 1990s, women continued to become self-employed at a higher rate than men, and their businesses tended to succeed at a significantly higher rate than business start-ups overall.[23]

Self-employment is not a solution to the stress created by the time squeeze or the practices of career taxidermy. But the fact that it is gaining in popularity, especially among women, is surely an expression of those problems. Self-employed home-based work involves a minority, not a majority, of workers, but their effort and the risks they take are warning signs, like the canary in the mine shaft, that dreams brewing cannot be ignored forever. The very fact that millions of men and women are willing to accept more insecurity and, frequently, less income as the price of self-determination is one powerful statement of the chasm between individuals and organizations. The studies of working hours and stress we reviewed in Chapter Five suggest that behind these millions are tens of millions more who also yearn to take their lives into their own hands. Of course, those who opt out of the classic employment relationship also help create a new dynamic that widens the chasm between individuals and organizations even further. The self-employed can act from their own individuality toward their clients and customers, offering the individuated support and connection that others seek. The more people experience these alternatives, both as employees and as end consumers, the deeper their repugnance toward the status quo ante of the standard enterprise logic, and the wider the chasm grows.

SCHOOLED IN SANCTUARY

In the early twentieth century, public education was a defining characteristic of the new mass order. Primary and secondary education was intended to be a public good, not an object of consumption. But by the end of that century, new individuals had begun seeking approaches to education that reflected their demands for psychological self-determination. These have led to some significant innovations in the public school system, including charter schools, magnet schools, and schools within a school. But for most of the educational organizations of the old mass order, the new demands have been nearly impossible to meet. As a result, individuals have increasingly turned toward new forms of consumption that enable them to take their own (educational) lives in their own hands.

The rise of home schooling is one such example. The home-schooling movement began quietly in the early 1970s, led primarily by parents who wanted their religious beliefs reflected in their children's education. During the late 1970s and early 1980s, a series of legal decisions affirmed parents' rights over their children's education, citing the right to privacy and extending the legislative meaning of "school" beyond that of a formal organization.[24] Buoyed by these rulings, home schooling developed into a bona fide social movement during the 1990s, becoming a legal option in all fifty states. No longer restricted to true believers on the right or left, home schooling penetrated the American mainstream and became an important educational alternative for hundreds of thousands of families.

A recent report from the U.S. Department of Education concludes that "the general size and direction of the homeschooling movement is beyond doubt." The report shows that home schooling more than doubled, and possibly tripled, in the five years between 1990/1991 and 1995/1996, when the home-schooled population reached about 750,000.[25] By 1999, that number had reached 850,000, representing 1.7 percent of the total school-aged population.[26] Other estimates placed the number of home-schooled children at 1.7 million in 2000.[27] Many researchers have also observed that, on average, the home-schooled child is only out of formal schooling for about two years. "If the average turnover rate is 2 years," concludes a Department of Education report, "then the number of children with some homeschooling experience, by age 18, would be around 6–12 percent of the population."[28] According to advocates, home-schooling support groups have also formed in Australia, Canada, New Zealand, Japan, Taiwan, Norway, Germany, and the United Kingdom.[29]

The significant growth of home schooling is one expression of the growing self-confidence of the new individuals and their commitment to psychological self-determination for themselves and their children. Early in the twentieth century, parents proudly sent their children to public schools that promised to turn them into successful members of the new mass order. But the new individual is also a new sort of parent. Studies show that most home-schooling parents are not particularly wealthy, but they do have higher-than-average levels of education, and often one or both parents have professional training.[30] Their own education, wide-ranging experiences, opinions, and access to information naturally incline them to second-guess mass organizations in ways that would have been inconceivable only a few decades earlier. Indeed, in the Department of Education's most recent report, the largest single motive of home-schooling parents was the belief that they could provide their children with a better education at home than they would receive in public school.[31]

While there is little systematic research, the anecdotal evidence suggests that what unites these parents is a passionate desire to see their children treated as individuals. They want to choose the content, structure, and rhythm of the educational experience, tailored to their child's needs, interests, and learning style.[32] As a consequence of these new demands, more people are coming to believe that matters of education should be absorbed into the ever-extending realm of individual choice. In this way, education becomes another occasion for the consumption of psychological self-determination, and in the process the notion of "school" is redefined in terms of the individual and his or her claims to self-authorship.[33] This commitment runs deep enough for parent-educators to overcome the enormous demands of time and responsibility that home schooling entails—especially remarkable in this era of the daily grind.

The increased popularity of private schools is another sign of the defection from the mass consumption of education. The reasons are fundamentally the same as those that animate home-schoolers: Parents want their children to be recognized and treated as individuals. Private schools promise lower pupil-to-teacher ratios, smaller class size, more access to teachers, more flexibility, and greater opportunity to exercise voice over a child's educational experience. "If a kid is in the mainstream, public schools just warehouse him through," complained a bus driver dad from San Francisco who had put his young son in a private school. "We get parents who say they're just too tired to fight the public schools anymore," reported the admissions director of a private high school in that city.[34] While private schools' fees have never been higher, their waiting lists have never been longer. Enrollment in nonsectarian private schools has soared, from 1 percent of total enrollment in 1960 to 6.5 percent in 1999.[35]

The same psychological demands that fuel the interest in home schooling and private schooling are driving the growth in online distance learning. According to one study, online learners express a tendency toward "an internal locus of control."[36] That's a psychologist's way of saying that they want to make their own choices and feel self-determining. They see themselves as actors, not as pawns. As the University of Phoenix Online explains in the introduction to its 54-page course brochure, it is not just selling education, it is selling the experience of control: "You can earn your degree via the Internet whenever and wherever you want—at home in the evenings, at work during lunch, or while traveling.... No commuting. No lines. No wasted effort. . . . You can complete 100 percent of your education at the times and places most convenient to you. . . . You never have to rush."

The National Center for Educational Statistics notes that there are approximately 5,000 postsecondary two- and four-year institutions, with enrollments of about 14.4 million students. In 1997/1998, about 1,700 institutions, or just over one-third of the total number, offered distance education. That represented about a 33 percent increase from just three years earlier in 1994/1995. During that same time period, enrollments in distance education doubled, reaching nearly 1,700,000 in 1997/1998, compared to 753,640 in 1994/1995.[37] In 2000, researchers at International Data Corporation (IDC) reckoned that about 47 percent of all postsecondary institutions offered distance learning, and they predicted an increase to about 87 percent in 2004.[38] They calculated that the number of students enrolled in distance education courses would grow to 2.2 million by 2004. Others have predicted 5 million distance learners in higher education by 2006.[39]

As the allure of distance learning spreads beyond the traditional student group, the number of vendors and students is likely to grow even more dramatically. Today distance learners include traditional and nontraditional students: lifelong learners, adults seeking to finish degrees on a part-time basis, employees and professionals who want to upgrade their skills, home-schoolers, and elementary and high school students seeking tutoring or enrichment courses. Using U.S. Department of Education data, IDC estimated the distance-learning market could actually include 138 million "students" in schools, homes, and corporations, with as many as 230,000 providers of one sort or another already lined up to serve them.[40] IDC analysts also observed that virtually all of the equity capital raised in the education industry in the United States in 2000 came from the online distance-learning segment,[41] and they forecasted an annual growth rate of 95 percent for the online segment through 2002.[42] Indeed, online learning was one of the few areas to emerge as a robust business, even after the Internet stock bubble burst. The University of Phoenix Online, for example, saw revenues increase 76 percent between 2000 and 2001.

OUR BODIES, OUR SELVES

For many people, the determination to take their lives in their own hands has translated into a range of new consumption practices related to health and medical treatment. People are designing ways to become the originators of their own health-care choices rather than the objects of bureaucratic cost-cutting procedures in HMOs, hospitals, and medical practices. This has translated into a tidal wave of protest against the seven-minute office visit that manifests itself in everything from the growing popularity of organic foods to the rise of alternative medicine.

Many people are choosing "self-care" over a conventional doctor-patient relationship. One example is the increase in self-doctoring through the use of the Internet. According to recent studies, 52 million Americans, or 55 percent of those with Internet access, use the Internet for health and medical information. Half of these people say the information they garner on the Web has improved the way they take care of themselves, and 36 percent say it has affected their decision on behalf of a loved one.[43] Self-care is also behind the explosion in the consumption of "natural products." According to recent market research, people who buy vitamins, minerals, and herbal supplements, alternative health care, organic foods, natural health and beauty aids, and natural household products "are those who respond proactively to the sense of alienation and diminished control that many Americans have in a society of ever-larger and more impersonal institutions. For these people, the use of natural products is a way of regaining control over one's physical and emotional self."[44] An article in *Nursing Management* addresses why people are seeking alternative health care. First among all reasons listed is "the desire for more control over personal health."[45]

People are also seeking out practitioners who will provide the deeper quality of support and connection they desire. The numbers are far from trivial, and they have shocked even the normally complacent medical establishment. A 1998 study in the *Journal of the American Medical Association* (*JAMA*) found a 47 percent increase in the total number of visits to alternative-medicine practitioners between 1990 and 1997, from 427 million to 629 million. By 1997, visits to alternative-medicine practitioners exceeded the number of visits to all U.S. primary care physicians by 243 million. Researchers attribute the increase to a rise in the number of people seeking alternative therapies, rather than to increased visits per patient. They found that about 25 percent more adults used alternative therapies in 1997 than in 1990. The use of alternative therapies was also found to be widely distributed across all socio-demographic groups.

The growing use of alternative therapies is all the more impressive considering that most health plans do not reimburse people for these therapies and related professional services. Estimated expenditures for alternative-medicine professional services increased 45 percent between 1990 and 1997, and were conservatively estimated at about $21 billion in 1997, with at least $12 billion paid out of pocket, exceeding the out-of-pocket expenditures for all U.S. hospitalizations. The total out-of-pocket expenditures related to alternative therapies was estimated at $27 billion in 1997, which is comparable to the out-of-pocket payments for all U.S. physician services that year.

Significantly, the *JAMA* researchers found that a substantial portion of alternative therapy use for a principal medical condition (46 percent in 1997) was done on a self-care basis, without input from either a medical doctor or a practitioner of alternative therapy. People are making their own decisions about therapies and treatments involving nutritional supplements, herbal medicines, and vitamins. The research also identified a 380 percent increase in the use of herbal remedies and a 130 percent increase in the use of high-dose vitamin supplements.[46]

Small wonder that 70 percent of consumers told pollsters that the availability of alternative care was a top criterion in their choice of health plan. By 2000, it was estimated that Americans who use alternative health care spend about $500 out of pocket annually.[47] The market for nutritional supplements, or "nutraceuticals," was estimated at between $92 billion and $200 billion in 2000.[48] Market researchers found that about 68 percent of U.S. households used some form of alternative health care during the first six months of 1999. They also estimated that 68 percent of American households used vitamins, minerals, and herbal supplements in the first six months of 1999. "Merely taking assorted vitamins, minerals and herbal supplements on a regular basis inspires a feeling of self-empowerment that contributes to overall wellness."[49] Another survey showed that people prefer self-care because they want "nutritional individualization." Three-quarters of survey respondents said they believed that their own nutritional needs were different from everyone else's.[50]

There is more evidence of the impulse toward health-related self-determination in the foods people want to eat. The U.S. organic-food market doubled every three and a half years since 1990, reaching $5 billion in 2000, while the larger "nutrition" industry was up to $49.5 billion in annual retail sales by 2000.[51] A study by the Food Marketing Institute, "Shopping for Health 2000," found that 37 percent of U.S. shoppers said they used organic foods to maintain their health. One producer of natural meats notes that consumers who buy organic products are smart, have sophisticated palates, and "mistrust the big food companies."[52] According to *Advertising Age*, "While mainstream food marketers have experienced annual revenue growth ranging from 2% to 3%, natural and organic marketers have been seeing revenue growth of 15% to 20% overall and some particularly hot segments, like soy, have even seen annual advances of 50% to 100%."[53] Retail sales of soy-based beverages in mainstream stores exploded by 71.5 percent between 1999 and 2000.[54]

In 1995 the National Institutes of Health founded the National Center for Complementary and Alternative Medicine to fund and legitimate research in this field. By 2001, its funding had increased from $2 million to $89 million. Well-known hospitals across the United States began opening "integrative" clinics that combine traditional and alternative therapies. In 2001, an industry newsletter, *The Integrator*, counted twenty-seven such clinics associated with institutions such as the University of California, Harvard University, and New York's Beth Israel Medical Center. Beth Israel's CEO told *Newsweek* magazine that "the public groundswell of interest in alternative medicine" convinced the hospital to open the center, which is described as "unhurried" and "spalike," "a refuge for patients who've had it with the cold, 10-minute HMO grind."[55]

While patient groups lobby HMOs for more flexibility and choice, a growing number of physicians are developing new practices aimed at the demand for more attentive individualized care. Some are adding deluxe executive physicals. Others are adding an alternative-medicine component to their practices. Others are returning to a direct fee-for-service format, which sometimes bypasses the health insurers altogether. One Seattle-based practice allows patients "unlimited access to a doctor they know who will guide them through the maze of hospitals and medical specialists they may encounter if they do get sick . . . the kind of personal around-the-clock attention that people used to associate with their family doc."[56] This trend toward what some have called "concierge care" has spread to many regions around the United States, including Florida, California, Washington, D.C., and Massachusetts.[57] Other physicians, and some former patients too, are tapping into a growing market for medical support by pioneering a new role called "medical advocate." They specialize in helping patients make their cases for treatment or treatment coverage to doctors, hospitals, and insurance companies.[58]

The doctor's house call largely disappeared in the 1960s. That was around the time that hospitals and insurance companies began what would become a relentless focus on curbing costs—one that frequently took the form of eliminating choice and flexibility in the patient's experience of health care. Medicare set reimbursement rates so low in 1966 that house calls "stopped overnight." Doctors are now expected to see four or five patients in their office in the time it would take to travel to one home. As recently as 1997, Medicare paid skilled nurses more than doctors for at-home care, $100 a visit compared to $60.[59] Nevertheless, a growing number of doctors are returning to the practice of making house calls because their patients want and need home care.

The American Academy of Home Care Physicians saw its membership double to 700 between 1998 and 2000, and it has lobbied Medicare for higher fees. In San Diego, one medical group operates a fleet of seven mobile medical vans and employs eight physicians, plus radiology technicians and nurse practitioners. They visit patients in their homes without forfeiting vital diagnostic and treatment equipment such as X-ray equipment, EKG monitors, cardiac output monitors, and laboratory tests. In 2000, they averaged 1,200 patient visits each month. They claim their $200 house calls save valuable time, money, and patient dignity, compared to a $450 ambulance ride, $1,500 for a visit to an emergency room, and hospital stays that can run $1,200 a day.[60] There are other medical practices specializing in twenty-four-hour house calls in Florida, New York, and other cities. In one model, doctors associated with the practice (often retired MDs who want to work part-time) are dispatched from a call center that fields toll-free calls from its patients.[61] While it's still difficult for these practices to break even, one physician observes, "The market forces are there. It's just a question of when they're going to bubble to the surface and break out."[62]

The enormous hunger for self-determination in matters of medical care is also expressed in the rapidly growing appeal of the total body scan. Medical imaging centers are opening up on Main Streets and in malls all over the United States, designed to appeal to sanctuary-craving individuals who want to be proactive about their health. Most of the centers are designed to feel more like a spa than a doctor's office or hospital, with luxury amenities, waterfalls, and artwork, all designed to impart a sense of serenity. Staff doctors meet with individual clients, carefully reviewing each scan. As one middle-aged woman who took advantage of a Mother's Day Special at a Phoenix-area scanning center confided, "It's kind of nice to be able to take things into our own hands."[63]

The desire to take one's health into one's own hands is also driving the rapidly growing availability of home monitoring and testing devices that measure a range of conditions from blood pressure to pregnancy, ovulation, blood glucose, peak blood flow, hepatitis C, cholesterol, HIV, and drug use. A new category of devices under development can identify the presence of infectious and sexually transmitted diseases, as well as test hormones, proteins, and DNA. New technologies promise over-the-counter tests for *H. pylori*, fecal occult blood, urinary tract infections, and osteoporosis, as well as screening tests for colorectal, cervical, and potentially other cancers. Moreover, these devices are increasingly able to be linked to phone lines or the Internet, enabling monitoring, data analysis, and diagnosis without the patient leaving home.[64] The revenues in this market have shown double-digit growth, increasing from $1.2 billion in 1994 to $1.7 billion in 1997 and reached $3.6 billion in 2001.[65] As one do-it-yourself health consumer who indulged in a battery of home tests put it, "I wanted more control over my health."[66]

The claim of sanctuary asserted in the market for home care extends to the experiences of dying and death. A growing number of people are turning away from the industrialized death of hospitals and funeral parlors, seeking a more serene and meaningful experience for themselves and their families by dying in their homes. The *Wall Street Journal* recently devoted a page-one story to a new kind of service designed to provide sanctuary in the face of death. A new breed of professionals, known as death consultants, is helping people to design a more spiritual, caring, and intimate death. Some of these new practitioners operate like professional "best friends." They are caring listeners and advice givers, and a source of companionship while a person is dying. Others help families through home deaths and home funerals, much as midwives rekindled home and natural childbirth during the 1970s. As the director of the Funeral Consumers Alliance put it, "Baby boomers have written their own wedding vows; now they want to personalize and take control of the death experience as well." One workshop on compassionate companionship in death was offered in 1997 and 200 people attended; in 2000, some 2,500 people signed up for it. "Graduates will be called something like 'midwives for death,' or 'mentors through dying,'" explained its founder. Another project trains volunteers to give support to the dying. Its workshops once drew people who were young and experimenting, but according to the project's director, they now "represent a cross section of Middle America." Some "guides" charge up to $200 for a ninety-minute session with a dying client. Others rely on donations and barely make enough to cover their costs. "This is heart work," explained one home-funeral consultant.[67]

TIME FOR MONEY

People are also finding new ways to moderate the stress of the daily grind by trading discretionary money for discretionary time in the form of a diverse range of home and personal services. This sector is new, highly fragmented, and growing fast. While there is little precise data that permits a careful analysis of its size and development, there is plenty of anecdotal evidence that suggests how important these services are becoming to a lot of people, buyers and sellers alike.

Hardware stores, national franchises, and large national retailers like Sears and Lowe's offer a range of home repair and improvement services from maintenance, landscaping, and plumbing to electrical work, cleaning, construction, and furniture repair. According to market research conducted by the Home Service Store, 80 percent of the home-improvement purchases in families are made by women.[68] As one executive described it, people "want someone they can trust to take care of the yard and the house . . . an HMO—a home maintenance organization, incorporating a one-stop shopping, repair, and replacement service." One customer describes the experience with a local hardware retailer who expanded into home services: "With other places you just get conned, sweet-talked or ignored. I feel so good about having [them] here, because you've got somebody to talk to if the job isn't done right." A study conducted for the National Home Center Institute identified a market of $17 billion for common recurring home-maintenance services and another $23 billion for nonrecurring services like air-conditioner installation and sewer cleaning. More than half the shoppers they polled had hired at least one home-services provider within the past year. Sears has even more ambitious estimates. They calculate the home services market at $160 billion, including the installation costs for things like appliances or vinyl siding.[69]

The demands of stress-saturated individuals have fostered a whole new range of services geared to individual space. Personal services once available only to the rich are now within the reach of many for a modest hourly rate. In one of the few studies of this employment category, the State of Virginia Employment Commission predicted a 20 percent growth rate in local personal-service jobs between 1994 and 2005.[70] Other industry experts call growth "explosive" and anticipate a $40 billion personal services market by 2003.[71] Today in many areas of the United States, it is possible to hire someone to walk and clean up after the dog, chauffeur the kids, organize the closet, do the shopping, prepare the family meals for the coming week, provide fitness training, tend the house plants, do the errands, and pay the bills. There are automobile oil-change services that will come to the house, along with car detailers and mobile repair services. "The trend of treating oneself, of retreating home to lick one's wounds, is growing by leaps and bounds," observes one woman who prepares gourmet meals for the time-embattled.[72] But if those wounds are to heal, the quality of the relationship with these purveyors of sanctuary becomes a critical component of the exchange, tightly coupling the independence of sanctuary with the interdependence of connection. The president of one service firm that performs errands for its clients observes that her business hinges on trust: "We have the keys to our clients' homes and cars and their credit cards. They have to feel that they can trust us."[73]

Women buy time by delegating a range of domestic activities, from cooking to cleaning and running errands. For example, the market for meal preparation was estimated at $100 billion by 1996, including prepared food from a variety of sources such as supermarkets, restaurants, and fast-food takeout. There is even a United States Personal Chef Association that trains cooks in how to start their own small entrepreneurial businesses, preparing meals for ten to fifteen families each week. According to the executive director, the association is unable to train enough chefs to meet national demand despite certifying 1,000 new chefs in 2001. One personal chef observed, "People want to be healthier. They want to go home, de-stress, cocoon, and be comfortable." And a client confessed, "I used to think a chef was too ritzy for a middle-class guy like me, but I was wrong."[74]

In a similar vein, the number of certification workshops for personal fitness trainers tripled, from 96 to 300, between 1993 and 1998, and the number of people taking the American Council on Exercise's personal training exam increased from 3,300 to 15,000. The U.S. Bureau of Labor Statistics counts fitness trainers among the twenty fastest-growing occupations between 2000 and 2010 (behind computer specialists and health care–related personnel), projecting an increase of 40 percent during that period.[75] As their numbers have increased, their prices have decreased. One professional trainer notes, "Ten years ago, this was a service reserved for people with a lot of money. Now we're seeing people with moderate incomes hiring personal trainers. . . . People want to make that investment in themselves."[76] Spending on personal-care services such as health clubs and spa visits increased 62 percent to $77 billion in 2000, from $47 billion a mere eight years earlier in 1992.[77]

Home and personal services have also been consolidated in a new kind of business known as a "concierge service." The concept, derived from traditional concierge service in a luxury hotel, rests on the central themes of time and trust: "We are in the business of giving people back their time," they say; "instead of calling dozens of people you just call one person that you can trust." The industry is young and little aggregate data exist. But dozens of articles suggest that concierge services are proliferating around the country, their growth relatively impervious to fluctuations in the economy.[78] What began as a service directed toward wealthy executives and celebrities now serves stressed-out individuals across the mainstream. The National Concierge Association, founded in the mid-1990s, reported a quintupling of its membership between 1995 and 2000, with one hundred members in 2000.[79]

In one model, residential real estate brokers have begun to offer wide-ranging concierge services to homeowners. In this approach, the agency assembles a large network of prescreened, dependable local vendors of services for a wide range of homeowner needs and offers them at preferred prices, sometimes exclusively to people who buy or sell houses through that agency. Vendors pay the agency for the privilege of being in the network, and customers pay the vendor directly for services rendered. One concierge service, offered by an affiliate of Coldwell Banker, lists nearly one hundred vendor services from accounting and banking to closet organizing and arranging golf course memberships.

Other concierge services cater directly to individuals. These services will undertake almost anything—arranging parties, catering dinners, furnishing a home, waxing a car, or choreographing Christmas, complete with wrapped presents, cards, and a decorated tree. As the owner of one such service described it, "Things get complicated and nobody is able to live their lives as they would like to. I saw that need, and that's how I began."[80] The CEO of an Atlanta-based service observes, "We become an intimate part of these people's lives."[81]

Kathy Lindsey is the founder of the aptly named "Time Machine." Based in Portland, Maine, it was one of the fastest-growing concierge services in 2001, with plans to franchise its approach nationwide. About 20 percent of Lindsey's clientele is upper income, while the rest are middle-class, educated, white-collar employees with moderate incomes—"no multiple homes or fancy cars." Her client base has expanded steadily since the company was founded in 1998, reaching more than 150 households in 2001. Growth rates have remained steady, seemingly unaffected by short-term economic perturbations. Lindsey and her staff have learned to use their own individuality to support others in that all-important intersection between sanctuary and connection:

> The demand we see is stronger and deeper than what's happening short term in the economy. We are committed to the people whose lives are so stressed that they no longer have the choice to go to their child's ball game or take a walk with their friend. We want to respect and honor those individuals, while being individuals ourselves. We listen to them. We ask questions. We pick up subtleties and look for clues about where people are coming from, because sometimes they don't even understand what their needs are.
>
> The rich have always had others to do things for them, but not the middle class. They have assumed that they had to do everything by themselves. Once they realize that we are genuine and trustworthy and

reliable, we find our clients to be ready, needy, hungry for our services, and willing to use us. Eventually consumers will wonder how they ever lived without us, because what we are offering is something that they have never been able to buy and for which there is no price tag— we are offering more time. Once people understand their needs, they realize that it's not a luxury but a necessity. Everyone needs to have someone on their side. We can give them choices again, and they don't have to quit their jobs.[82]

Lindsey's observations are consistent with accounts from others in her industry. In March 2001, the *Washington Post* reported that the demand for personal services continued to grow, despite a softening economy.[83] One of the fastest-growing business models involves companies that contract with corporations to offer "work/life" services as an employee benefit, a market estimated in 2000 at $20 billion.[84] According to one industry executive, 15 percent to 20 percent of all employers use some sort of work/life program, with much greater penetration among the largest U.S. companies.[85] Many of these companies began by offering outsourced administration of traditional employee benefits and then expanded into child care, elder care, educational assistance, wellness training, and a range of referral resources. More recently, many have added concierge services to help employees manage daily responsibilities, as new computer technology and Internet-based applications (referred to in one company as a "cyberbutler") allow these services to be offered at relatively low cost.[86]

CONSUMING VOICE

The exercise of voice is a second strategy for moderating the stress of the daily grind by strengthening the person caught in the crush. The expression of voice is an important means by which individuals create and encounter their own identities. Voice is first and foremost an assertion of uniqueness and an expression of self-worth. It says, "I have a special world to disclose." With the expression of voice one names the world, turning otherwise chaotic experience into something that can be known and understood. In this way the exercise of voice is a way of creating meaning and imbuing experience with a sense of purpose and choice. As psychologists and artists know, voice also contributes to and signals psychological individuality. It is an important foundation for self-knowledge, because human beings make themselves through their expressions. One's sense of self develops as thoughts and feelings are articulated and can become objects of reflection. In this way, voice enriches identity and helps to bolster and elaborate inner resources.

People also seek influence through the exercise of voice. The new individuals cherish opportunities for the expression of voice that are personal and direct, as one's own experience is regarded as a legitimate basis for judgment and critique. And like the claim of sanctuary, the demand for voice is also intimately linked to the quest for connection. Voice may be first of all for the self, but it is always also a voice toward someone else. Voice signals the hope for relationship and communication. It requests, "Please value me enough to listen to me."

The gap between today's new individuals and their organizations means that the craving for voice is rarely satisfied through formal channels. Instead, consumption has become a means of addressing the needs for voice of many people as they invent new ways to fortify and express their personal sense of uniqueness and self-worth. People buy opportunities for self-expression and its attendant possibilities of self-discovery and connection. This provides an important countermeasure to the stress of the daily grind in which one's individuality must constantly do battle with the forces of the old mass order. It helps contribute to the sense that one is finding ways to take one's life into one's own hands.

REACH OUT AND CHAT SOMEONE

For eloquent testimony to the hunger for voice one need look no further than some simple calculations on Internet traffic. As recently as the early 1990s, the words "e-mail" and "chat room" had not even entered the consciousness of most people. Within a few short years, however, people poured their lives into these new communication outlets, swamping all other forms of Internet usage with their eagerness to declare their presence and opinions to each other. For the price of an Internet Service Provider subscription, people are finding new ways to tell their truths and elaborate their personal identities, making connections, giving and receiving advice, and picking up information and insight along the way.

As we saw in Chapter Three, the appetite for electronic community and person-to-person communication appears to be insatiable. According to the International Data Corporation's analysis of e-mail usage in North America, between 1995 and 2000 the number of business e-mail mailboxes increased from 48 million to 134 million, or a factor of 2.8. In comparison, consumer mailboxes increased from 7 million to 113 million, or a factor of 16. Their forecasts predict 252 million business mailboxes and 217 million consumer mailboxes by 2005. That would mean that between 1995 and 2005, business accounts will have increased by a factor of 5 and consumer accounts by a factor of 31. The predictions for the patterns in e-mail usage are even more dramatic. Between 1995 and 2000 business e-mails on an average day increased from 0.2 billion to 3.4 billion (a factor of 17), and personal messages increased from 0.1 billion to 2.7 billion (a factor of 27). The IDC predicts increases to 10.4 and 7.6 billion, respectively, in 2005. That would mean that from 1995 business usage will have increased by a factor of 52 and personal usage by a factor of 76.[87]

Chat room usage is more difficult to measure, but clearly tens of millions of people are online daily engaged in virtual communications through thousands of sites that sponsor episodic or ongoing "chats." There is a growing assortment of sites devoted solely to conversation, many of which offer moderated chats on a wide range of subjects with dozens of daily scheduled events. According to a 2001 survey, 84 percent of Internet users, or 90 million Americans, have used the Internet to contact or get information from a group. That's more people than have used the Internet to search for news or health information or to buy a product. Seventy-nine percent remain in contact with one particular group, and 49 percent say the Internet has helped them connect with groups or people who share their interests. When asked why they communicate online to a group, 76 percent said they want to keep up on membership news and information, while 68 percent want to discuss issues with others, and 49 percent are creating or maintaining relationships with others in the group.[88] Following the September 11, 2001, terrorist attacks in New York City and Washington, D.C., the Internet provided what some have called a "virtual commons" in which one-third of all Internet users read or posted material in chat rooms, bulletin boards, or other online forums, while an even larger group (72 percent) used the Internet "to contact family and friends to discuss events, reconnect with long-lost friends, discuss the fate of victims, and share news."[89]

TO TELL MY TRUTH

The urge to express oneself and tell "my truth" also animates the late-twentieth-century explosion in the genre of autobiography and memoir. The *New York Times* has called this "the age of the literary memoir," *Vogue* said it was "the new age of memoirs," and *Harper's* referred to this literary trend as "the art of self." Most bookstores have added special sections for these books. Universities have hired faculty who specialize in the genre. And publishers are paying record amounts for the recollections of people whom no one has ever heard of. In 1998, Warner Books paid $1 million for the memoirs of a ninety-eight-year-old Kansas woman, composed in a senior citizens' writing workshop in her hometown. One of the most stunning examples of the popularity of the memoir involves a retired high school English teacher, Frank McCourt, whose recollections of a poverty-stricken Irish childhood earned him a Pulitzer Prize, seventy-one weeks on the *New York Times* best-seller list, a Hollywood feature film, and fifty-six printings for a total of more than 1.9 million copies of his first-ever book, *Angela's Ashes*.

The first-person voice, once regarded as unseemly, inappropriate, aggressive, or even vulgar, now elicits trust and immense interest. The titles that tend to grab the most attention are those involving wrenching tales of personal suffering. But the boom in memoirs also includes hundreds of unknown authors who use this form of literature to grapple "out loud" with the meaning of their very individual lives. As one poet and memoirist explains it, "We're faced with an overwhelming amount of manufactured identity. . . . Memoirs are crawling out from under that, saying I really have to understand who I am, not who the culture is telling me I am. . . . It's people claiming their power to talk back to the culture about who they are."[90] Memoirs are no longer the exclusive province of celebrities and world leaders. Instead, the genre has moved in the opposite direction, toward the insights of average people working through life's challenges. The head of the nonfiction writing program at the University of Iowa calls it "the democratization of the memoir," as writers turn their own stories into "a song we can all share."[91]

In the memoir, the writer's exercise of voice becomes an experience of self-discovery for writer and reader alike. "I want to record how the world comes at me, because I think it is indicative of the way it comes at everyone," writes memoirist Philip Lopate.[92] Publishers have been surprised by the depth of the market for these books, as people consume memoirs to ignite their own voices and enrich their own self-understanding. "People like to read memoirs as a kind of reflection on their own lives," says a Barnes & Noble executive.[93] And the author of a book on autobiography, Tristine Rainer, observed, "We're trying to figure out how to live our own lives in a tremendously complicated world with too many choices and no clear guidelines. The only thing we can go on is other people's actual, lived experiences. We don't want to be preached to; we don't want abstract ideas about what we should or shouldn't do."[94]

The value of giving voice to one's personal experience in this way is powerful enough to convert many readers to writers, even if their works are not intended for publication. Throughout the United States scores of memoir clubs have sprung up, where members go to share their own "art of self." The American Association of Retired Persons calls it an "outbreak of memoir fever." "They're exploring the mystery of their lives," says Rainer, who also teaches workshops in autobiography. "Whether their books are published or not, the writers tell me that along with having their children, it was the most meaningful thing they ever did."[95]

Indeed, it appears that today's stressed-out individuals require the experience of voice for their very health and well-being. The research of psychologist James Pennebaker at the University of Texas reveals a strong relationship between written or verbal self-disclosure and a variety of health benefits. In dozens of studies, he and his colleagues have discovered a range of positive measurable physiological and psychological consequences of the exercise of voice. In one study, Pennebaker compared a group of subjects who wrote about a past trauma for four consecutive days to another group asked to write about trivial matters. In "before" and "after" blood samples from each group, he showed that the group writing about difficult events had improved immune system functions, a benefit that continued for six weeks after the experiment. In another study, he found that high-level engineers who lost their jobs were more likely to be reemployed if they wrote about their job loss than those who either did not write about that difficult experience or who wrote on the more trivial topic of time management. Other studies showed that "thought suppression" had a negative effect on the immune system.[96]

TO SAY MY HISTORY

This craving for voice has been intense enough to spawn a new breed of entrepreneurs, known as personal historians. The *Wall Street Journal* has called personal history "a burgeoning cottage industry" whose clients are predominantly women in their forties and fifties.[97] The Association of Personal Historians was formed in 1995 with just a few people and by 1999 counted 120 official members. According to the association's president, "Our membership doesn't reflect the numbers involved. It's far more. The market is just huge. . . . We know there are hundreds of thousands of people doing this, most on their own. Most don't even know there's help out there, and we can save them a lot of work."

Some personal historians simply compile interviews, others compose detailed biographies, and still others produce biographies on audiotape, videotape, or CD-ROM. Personal historians interview one's relatives, charging anywhere from a few hundred dollars to more than $10,000. If the production of a book or videotape is involved, the price can be many tens of thousands higher. Specialty publishing houses print family histories in any quantity, charging from $10,000 to more than $100,000. But many people regard the investment as well worth it. What is the right price for the discovery, elaboration, and preservation of personhood? As one personal historian describes it, "We are careful to try to keep the voice, spirit, tone, and personality of that human being, so future generations will know them as a real person."[98]

The experience of self-discovery associated with writing one's family history often begins with an interest in figuring out the family tree. It's difficult to say who I am without also considering from whence I come. According to a poll conducted by *American Demographics* in 1995, close to half of all American adults were involved in genealogical research. The pollsters estimated that 113 million people were somewhat involved in researching their ancestry, and 19 million of those were deeply immersed in that undertaking. The highest rates of involvement were among those ages thirty-five to forty-four. They are the ones with the least amount of time for such hobbies but the deepest need to understand the roots of their individuality. According to this survey, nearly 60 percent of all those interested in their genealogy have composed a family history or created a family tree. Another 45 percent traveled to their ancestral town or country to collect information about their roots.[99]

Thousands of businesses sell products and services to help amateur genealogists assemble their ancestry; these services range from searching centuries-old passenger lists of immigrants to storing fragile documents. By 1999 roots-seeking ranked with sex, finance, and sports as a leading subject on the Internet. There has been a constant stream of genealogy software, online searches, and databases for family research, with specific Internet-based resources for nearly every heritage, including Cajun, Ukrainian, Chinese, Jewish, African, Hispanic, and dozens more. The Web site Cindislist.com has grown to more than 300 pages with links to nearly 50,000 genealogical sites worldwide. The World Family Tree Project stores millions of family-tree records for use by genealogy researchers.[100]

The widespread hunger for this kind of knowledge has found expression through new Internet tools, helping to turn genealogy into what *Time* magazine called a "national obsession."[101] By mid-1999, some 160 million messages flowed through a site called rootsweb.com in just one month, with 1.7 million unique visitors. The Family History Library of the Church of Jesus

Christ of Latter-day Saints opened its 142,000 square-foot, five-floored library in 1985. By 1999, it included documents touching on 2 billion people, had 3,200 branches in sixty-four countries and eight territories, hosted 800,000 annual visitors, and was fulfilling plans to add 50 million more names each year. It also inaugurated its FamilySearch.org Web site, which contains more than 600 million names. The site went live on Monday, May 24, 1999, designed to support up to 25 million hits per day. On its first day it received 30 million hits, then 100 million on Tuesday, and another 100 million on Wednesday. By Thursday the site had crashed, and IBM was frantically working to upgrade capacity. Once online again, the site received up to 50 million hits per hour, and users were limited to fifteen minutes.[102] Volunteers from the Mormon Church also donated more than 6 million hours to assist in the creation of an Ellis Island Web site, with information on immigrants who entered the United States between 1892 and 1924. The site received 50 million hits during its first six hours of operation in April 2001.[103]

TO WEAVE MY ME

The Internet also offers other opportunities to buy and sell support for the creation and elaboration of personal identity. It has made it easy for people to publish their own writing through self-publishing Internet sites or through e-publishers. New technologies make it possible for musicians to make high-quality recordings of their own music in their home studios and post it on the Internet for downloading by anyone, anywhere. The *New York Times* has called this "a way to speak to listeners one by one . . . the equivalent of private music . . . tapped straight from his mind into yours, with no whiz-bang overdrive music business machinery getting in between."[104] Painters, cartoonists, and filmmakers are doing the same. The traditional gatekeepers of culture debate what, if any, of this new outpouring constitutes art, and in so doing they perfectly miss the point.[105] What these examples have in common is that whether or not they are all art, they are all expressions of voice. Art accrues to the audience, but voice accrues to its source. This has less to do with the so-called democratization of creativity than it does with the democratization of the yearning for psychological self-determination expressed in the embrace of opportunities for unmediated voice.

The "echo-boom" generation of today's early adolescents and teenagers—the largest teen population in history, according to the 2000 U.S. Census—has become known among market researchers for its strong insistence on self-authorship and demand for voice. Marketers are already keenly aware of the ways in which teens' psychological inclinations translate into new approaches to consumption that help shape and express identity. According to one survey by a New York City market-research firm, teens said their most valued traits are "individuality" and "uniqueness"—"being truly uniquely themselves." As a result, explain these researchers, teens want "to customize and personalize their image, dip into different streams of history, iconography, and symbolism, and craft an individual message that communicates uniqueness. . . . The past is not a place to long for, but a huge catalog of raw material to cut and paste into personal statements of identity." They are more interested in friends and family members than celebrities, rejecting the "force feeding of images and specific role models." As consumers, they want to put their stamp on what they buy, customizing their own clothes, shoes, and cosmetics as a form of self-expression and opting into consumption opportunities that allow them to master the quality and form of their purchases, from downloading music to Internet-sourced social and information content.[106]

The same ingenious and determined impulse toward the creation and assertion of individual identity is expressed in the explosive growth of "extreme sports." While participation in most fitness activities has declined since 1985 among Americans of all ages, the fastest-growing sports defy the general trend because they offer an intense opportunity for self-invention and self-expression.[107] The National Sporting Goods Association classifies extreme, alternative, or freestyle sports from snowboarding to street luge as "alternative individual sports." According to their 1998 figures, these were the fastest-growing youth sports of the 1990s, with 69 million Americans participating in the top nine extreme sports: in-line skating, mountain biking, skateboarding, snowboarding, trail running, artificial wall climbing, wakeboarding, mountain/rock climbing, and snowshoeing.

While the popularity of traditional sports with strict rules of play—like baseball, basketball, and volleyball—has waned, the 1990s saw participation in in-line skating and snowboarding increase by 590 percent and 148 percent, respectively.[108] In December 1999, *Sports Business Journal* declared, "The alternative sports world should expect huge growth in the next century." Indeed, snowboarding, skateboarding, and wakeboarding were the fastest-growing sports in 2000.[109] As a sports marketing professor from the University of Oregon put it, "Kids see skateboarding as a way around the rigid rules and hypercompetition of many youth team sports." Skateboarders emphasize individual achievement and are more interested in honing their skills than accumulating trophies in structured competitions. It makes sense, then, that one of the all-time high points in that sport was when skateboarding icon Tony Hawk finally completed a "900" (a leap from a 12-foot ramp into two and a half midair rotations), which he had been attempting for thirteen years. He achieved his goal during the 1999 X Games, on his twelfth try, after "he had broken all the rules, far exceeding his official time limit amid wild cheering from fans and competitors."[110] A *New York Times* survey in 2000 found the X Games to be second in popularity only to the Olympics among six- to seventeen-year-olds.[111]

Ski-industry analysts attribute most of the decline in alpine skiing to the increased popularity of snowboarding, initially despised for its association with unorthodox, rule-breaking "young mavericks" who like to "shred" down the slopes.[112] Yet snowboarding has become one of the fastest-growing sectors of the sporting-goods industry, with more than 7 million snowboarders in 2000, compared to only about 1 million a decade earlier.[113] Skydiving, bungee jumping, whitewater rafting, and other "high risk" sports are all showing substantial increases in participation. The U.S. Parachute Association reported in 1997 that its membership of 33,500 had been growing by 10 percent annually and that between 130,000 and 150,000 people skydived that year. Whereas skydiving was once the sole province of adrenaline-chasing young men who consumed risk for its own sake, the fastest-growing segments of the group's membership were among those forty and older. The American Mountain Guide Association reports similar growth patterns. The U.S. Bungee Association estimates 7 million jumps worldwide since the late 1980s. "People are less satisfied than they used to be with being pigeon-holed by what they do, so they want to change their self-image," says that group's president.[114] In 1998 the X Games included the first skiboarding competition and a few months later in a *New York Times* article on "trend spotting," the cool-hunting guru Tru Pettigrew named skiboarding as a potential Next Big Thing, noting, "It's the individualism of it."[115]

FOLLOW THE LINES OF DESIRE

When urban planners and landscape architects contemplate a new project, they are likely to look for "desire lines" to guide them. These are the routes that people instinctively take through an open space, rather than those marked by paving. We have all seen those dust-brown paths, where the green has been trod under, as scores of people daily find the most efficient trajectory across a grassy lawn to a street or parking lot. Wise planners know how to follow these desire lines through an acre or a city toward a successful design.

And so it may be said of capitalism itself, which for the last 300 years and more has sensed the shifting trajectories of human desire, reinventing itself at crucial turns in order to embrace each new incarnation of yearning. Like a snake shedding its skin, it remains itself, but different. The pattern of new consumption activities undertaken in the quest for psychological self-determination is a map of the desire lines that weave a path from the economies of the past to the support economy of the future. In the proper hands, it is a guide to the latent potential for wealth creation in the decades ahead. But following these desire lines means leaving the light from the lamppost. It means moving beyond the limitations and standard operating procedures of the old capitalism and shedding the skin that has constrained the emergence of a more spacious economic order based upon the real needs of people today. It means a trip into the darkness, where the old maps end.

Today's new individuals know the experience of being history's shock absorbers. They have a profound impulse toward psychological self-determination, but as employees and consumers, they are frustrated and constrained by organizational norms and practices invented for people of another era. Caught between these two conflicting forces and plunged into chronic stress, they seek ways to buffer and transcend the daily grind. As part of that effort, millions of the new individuals, and especially the women among them, are inventing new consumption activities that provide sanctuary, voice, and connection. In this way, however circumspectly, they are finding ways to take their own lives into their hands.

Their new forms of consumption are highly fragmented—from concierges to personal historians, home-schooling Web sites to chat rooms. There is no storefront marquee that reads: BUY SANCTUARY HERE. There is no Wal-Mart for self-expression or connection. Many of the new forms currently exist at the margins of commercial activity. But despite this still-awkward state of affairs, we see a large and growing range of new consumption activities whose message is consistent across an immense diversity of social and economic worlds. The message is this: *"I am willing to buy that which will enable me to live an ever more individuated life. I am willing to buy that which will enable me to make myself, to know myself, and to be myself. I am willing to buy aid and succor in my quest for psychological self-determination."*

The new desire lines reflected in this message reveal a subterranean shift in the structure of consumption to what we call the individuation of consumption. In the standard enterprise logic of managerial capitalism, people must adapt to the terms and conditions of consumption set by producers. But the real essence of the individuation of consumption is an inversion of that logic. It requires the agents of commerce to operate in individual space. There, they form a relationship with the individual who says, *"This is my space where I live and dream. Come to me here. My life is worth lavishing care. Help me make myself. Be of my life."*

We think that this shift has been partially sensed but badly misconstrued. For example, marketing professionals have preached a reorientation away from mass markets, first to segments of mass markets and then to niches within segments. This means that instead of directing a product to "all young men," companies learned to direct their products first to "all well-educated young men," and latterly to "all well-educated young men who wear Nikes, crave pizza, live in North London, and own skateboards." In other words, companies have responded to the emergence of the individuation of consumption by continuing to pursue their traditional purpose: the profitable sale of goods and services. The only difference is that now those goods and services can be cleverly targeted to an ever more differentiated group. In this marketing evolution, companies have acquired many new skills, but nowhere along the way has it been necessary for the snake to shed its skin. The purpose of the commercial undertaking has remained intact. Adaptations have occurred at the margins, but not within the deep structure of the standard enterprise logic.

The new desire lines actually lead in a very different direction. They do not point toward a mass market, a segmented market, or even a niche market. Indeed, they do not lead to any sort of market that can be carved up from afar, like a diagram of a holiday turkey, by marketers and managers. The individuation of consumption is not simply a plea for more variety in products, or even for services tailored to myself or my group. It is a market for deep support whose value can be known and realized only from within individual space. It is a plea for help in living an ever more individuated life in an ever more complex world. The new individuals have assessed the effort required to "take my life in my own hands" and have concluded that such effort is worth paying for. Today's dreamers of psychological self-determination are demanding something altogether different from what the twentieth-century corporation has offered. They want to buy something that has never before been for sale—support in the invention and sustenance of a unique life.

The provision of this support, what we call "deep support," becomes the new, higher-order purpose of commerce. It is of a higher order of complexity because such support includes goods and services but is also substantially more than merely goods and services. The progression from products and services to deep support follows the inner logic of the history of work and consumption. The history of work has proceeded from concrete activities based on manual labor to abstract activities involving administration, information, knowledge, and service. Similarly, consumption has moved from the concrete to the abstract, as hard goods give way to services, and now to the even more comprehensive but less tangible realm of deep support. We have also seen how the history of consumption has consistently redefined ideas about what is a "necessity." In each century, former luxuries are reinterpreted as necessities by new people whose lives are marked by wider experience and choice. And so it is now, as the fiercely held belief in psychological self-determination finds its commercial expression in markets for deep support—once a luxury reserved for the rich, now a requirement for each individual life.

Deep support relies upon a new economic framework and a new technological medium to provide a historical first: accountability and responsibility for the entire consumption experience. For example, in the support economy, one no longer has to buy mere medical treatment. As part of that "purchase," one receives support in the research and vetting that goes into selecting a doctor and deciding on treatment; complete peace of mind as to insurance coverage and payment; logistical aid in acquiring treatment and caring for one's family while absent; confidence that one's doctor will not be distracted by misaligned financial pressures that encourage fragmented communication and service; and assistance through the processes of recovery and rehabilitation or ongoing care.

Deep support enables psychological self-determination. It produces time for life. It facilitates and enhances the experience of being the origin of one's life. It nurtures the experience of sanctuary. It recognizes, responds to, and promotes individuality. It celebrates intricacy. It multiplies choice and enhances flexibility. It encourages voice and is guided by voice. Deep support listens and offers connection. It offers collaborative relationship defined by advocacy. It is founded on trust, reciprocity, authenticity, intimacy, and absolute reliability. It is a living relationship that insists on the possibility of what the philosopher Martin Buber called the "I–You"—that is, a quality of relationship in which people engage each other as fully human. It stands in contrast to the "I–It" relationship, in which the other is experienced as an object: the anonymous data point of market research, the wallet from which cash flows, the eyeballs that watch a screen. The I–You means that one encounters another in the true wholeness of his or her reality. In the I–You, the individual is no longer an economic abstraction—consumer or producer—but a vital, intricate, self-originating, and irreducibly unique life.

To summarize Part One and anticipate Parts Two and Three: Dreams make markets, and new markets combine with new technologies and a new enterprise logic to make economic revolutions. In the twentieth century, managerial capitalism created unprecedented wealth with an enterprise logic invented for the dreams of a mass society. It emphasized consumption and mass production. Its success unleashed the large-scale forces associated with health, education, communication, mobility, and so on. These forces transformed populations. They engendered a psychological reformation that imbued many people around the world, and especially within its industrial core, with an abiding sense of individuality and a deep impulse toward psychological self-determination. This phenomenon has often been derided as narcissism and lamented as a degradation of the social order. It has been largely ignored by the organizations of late-modern society, especially those upon which people depend for employment and consumption.

We celebrate this psychological reformation as a profound evolution of individuals and society toward a world in which each person is valued, respected, and empowered. In it we find cause for jubilation, a triumph over humanity's sorry history of tyranny, enslavement, and the silence of ordinary people. But today's individuals are caught in the cross fire of history, their needs for psychological self-determination thwarted by organizational norms and practices invented for another era. As a result, they are using their new dreams to once again reinvent consumption. Their search for sanctuary, voice, and connection has shifted the structure of consumption toward "the individuation of consumption," characterized by markets for deep support. This presents a challenge to the still-reigning enterprise logic of the old mass order. But it also represents an immense new opportunity for wealth creation and the forging of a new capitalism that can become the foundation for a new support economy.

What happens when the old organizations face this new challenge? To answer this question, it is time to follow our new individuals out from sanctuary, as they bring their complex lives and intricate selves to the threshold of the standard enterprise logic, where they meet others like themselves, still captives of product-focused efficiency norms and cost-reduction mandates. It is necessary to understand what occurs in that encounter. How does the old organization perceive and respond to the new individuals? How do we explain its practices? Is it capable of fulfilling the new dreams expressed in the markets for deep support? And if it cannot rise to this challenge, can we begin to chart a new capitalism, and a new economy, better suited to our times?

PART TWO

CRISIS

OLD ORGANIZATIONS MEET NEW PEOPLE

SEVEN

The Transaction Crisis

When the new dreams of deep support come face to face with the old business organizations, still based on the standard enterprise logic, the result is what we call the transaction crisis. Most people experience the transaction crisis, as consumers and as employees, every day.

BATTLE AT THE BARBED WIRE

The transaction crisis begins when the new individuals in their "leisure-time" roles as consumers meet up with their mirror images—individuals like themselves who are still at work, subordinated to their roles as employees. Both groups are time-choked and stressed, a condition that is only exacerbated by the adversarial relationships in which they must engage, courtesy of the standard enterprise logic. Success as an employee requires primary allegiance to the firm and its product-focused efficiency norms. Incentives and rewards are linked to an employee's achievements in relation to these internal standards of evaluation. When these standards are at odds with the consumer's best interests, it is the consumer who must be jettisoned. This is true even though, in just a few hours, these roles are likely to be reversed.

And so it is that the individual-as-consumer reaches out in search of deep support only to be snagged on the barbed-wire fence that surrounds nearly every commercial exchange. The only thing that can squeeze under that fence is a bit of cash. The rest of a person—all that holds the real complexity of his or her life—is left behind. The individual-as-consumer is shut out, and the individual-as-employee on the other side of the fence is locked in. That fence is woven from economic assumptions, organizational mandates, and psychological dynamics that express and sustain the standard enterprise logic.

The misery associated with commercial transactions has reached crisis proportions gradually over the last twenty years or so. During that time, the new society of individuals flourished, along with the complexity and richness of individuals' needs. Simultaneously, global competitive pressures drove more firms to emphasize productivity improvements and resource reductions as they endeavored to implement the standard enterprise logic with ever-greater zeal and efficiency. Organizations have, as a result become increasingly remote and indifferent to the individual consumers who depend upon them. This is a "thing-world," where end consumers are most often treated like objects to be manipulated or problems to be eliminated. The consequence is what we call the transaction crisis: People reach out in search of sanctuary, voice, and connection only to encounter commercial practices that treat them like anonymous marks on a balance sheet.

A sense of embattlement has become such a permanent feature of the consumption experience that most people now just take it for granted. Do you know anyone who looks forward to calling their insurance agent to make a claim? Do you know anyone who expects to receive what they deserve from an insurance company without a hassle? What about buying a car or having one repaired, staying in a hospital, getting an appliance fixed under warranty, calling an 800 number for help with your personal computer, determining the right choice of medical treatment or adjusting a medical bill, purchasing a computer over the phone, checking late into a hotel, changing your phone service, getting reliable information from your stockbrocker, or querying a credit-bureau rating? Complaints about these experiences are usually interpreted as reflections of substandard customer service, but we think something far more profound is at work. Namely, these inconveniences, hassles, battles, daily diminishments, and bona fide miseries are predictable expressions of the yawning gap between the new individuals and today's business organizations, which are still ruled by an enterprise logic invented nearly one hundred years ago as a response to other people with different dreams.

THE SOCIAL RELATIONS OF THE STANDARD ENTERPRISE LOGIC

As we saw in Part One, the twentieth century was in part the story of how managerial capitalism came to be invented, diffused, elaborated, and consolidated, eventually defining most modern economic activity. It was brilliantly successful at creating wealth in the context of the historical conditions it faced, marked, above all, by the rising tide of mass consumption. That historic shift in the number of people who wanted things—and the number of things they wanted—created the possibility of a mass market and signaled a fundamental change in the structure of consumption. Meeting the needs of that new kind of market required more than just new technologies. It depended upon a new corporate enterprise logic whose production methods succeeded in organizing people and technology to achieve high levels of standardized throughput and low unit costs.

The essential elements of managerial capitalism were first consolidated in that new enterprise logic. First, the new approach required an acute internal focus, as activities and resources that were once scattered over many independent businesses—and prey to the unpredictability of market forces and craft authority—were consolidated within a single enterprise and chain of command. Second, it required a professional, salaried managerial hierarchy to oversee the now internalized administrative coordination of production and distribution. Third, ownership and management were separated. Ownership was distributed across many shareholders, but *control was concentrated* as the authority of ownership shifted to management, which now directed operations and determined long-term policies. Managerial careers consisted of climbing the hierarchy, and managers' policies favored the long-term stability of the organizations that defined their careers.[1]

The corporate enterprise logic became the standard for the vast majority of businesses—and other kinds of organizations too, from government agencies to not-for-profit organizations—as managerial capitalism came to define the logic of wealth creation everywhere that markets operated in relative freedom. Its principles, once contested, gradually came to be seen as the definitive expression of capitalism itself. The roles that people play in a modern economy—consumer or producer, employee or employer, debt holder or equity holder—and the relative importance ascribed to those roles—dominant or subordinate, central or peripheral—came to be defined in terms of one's relationship to this new enterprise logic.[2] Over time, this once revolutionary system solidified into standard operating procedures governed by increasingly tacit assumptions about the purpose, process, and content of commerce. Leading these assumptions was the notion that producers were central to the creation of value, while consumers could be regarded as a distant anonymous abstraction.

One way to explore the tacit assumptions and social relations of this now standard enterprise logic is through the metaphor of a solar system. The laws of the solar system become visible only as continued observation reveals the relations among its elements. Similarly, the standard enterprise logic encompasses a commercial solar system of institutions, their internal principles, and social relations. This system holds all the constituent elements in place and ascribes to each the relative importance of its role in the march toward wealth. The metaphor of the solar system is a useful one because of its essential interdependence—the behavior of each element can be explained only by its place in the system. The secrets of each are unlocked only in relation to all of the other elements.

The center of the commercial solar system is occupied by its most powerful player. Traditionally this was the producer organization that did the final assembly and/or packaging of goods (an automobile manufacturer like General Motors or a consumer goods manufacturer like Procter & Gamble). Increasingly, however, the center of the system may be occupied by a company that retails goods or services to end consumers. Examples include firms like Wal-Mart, McDonald's, Marriott, and American Airlines. These companies at the center are the "sun" around which all other elements in the system are expected to revolve, and for the sake of this discussion we refer to them as the producers. Firms that occupy this position in the system frequently have the advantage of size, but most certainly enjoy the advantages of buying power. Commercial solar systems also overlap in complicated ways. A firm may occupy the central position in one system and a secondary or tertiary position as a supplier or business customer in other systems.

Producer organizations, like other firms, are controlled by managers and boards of directors. They require an inward focus on organization space, where resources are dedicated to producing goods and services and bringing them to market. What claims managers' attention first is the administrative complexity associated with the principles, rules, and procedures according to which production and distribution are successfully accomplished, and the ongoing plans intended to ensure success into the future. Management hierarchies preside over these procedures with the authority of ownership, symbolically vested in them by the shareholders of the company. There are perennial complaints that managers put their own interests ahead of those of the shareholders and other constituencies—as in the recent scandals involving the Enron Corporation, Waste Management, Global Crossing, and others—but this behavior is a more or less predictable consequence of the professionalization of the managerial career and the concentration of control in the managerial role.[3] Managers have urgent personal stakes in the growth and long-term stability of the firm, even when it comes at the expense of other constituencies. Scandals erupt when this disposition toward self-interest becomes too audacious and where the losses to other constituencies are significant enough to provoke a backlash. But even without the extreme behavior that leads to scandal, there is a natural antagonism between the interests of managers and other constituencies in the commercial solar system.

Typically, only certain organizational members in specific functions are required in the course of their daily activities to pay attention to people and constituencies outside the corporate organization. For example, marketing departments were created in the 1950s to attend to market trends, but their relationship to actual end consumers is mediated by advertising agencies and market-research firms. Top executives meet with their counterparts among suppliers or industry partners. They occasionally meet with important business customers, but their engagement with end consumers generally is mediated by marketing and public relations. A sales force is designated to meet with business customers, though rarely with end consumers. The chief executive and often the chief financial officer are designated to interact with the board and shareholder representatives, financial institutions, and analysts. These interactions tend to be highly orchestrated and artificial. Increasingly, there are contacts across the supply chain among lower-level managers, but these are typically over specific transactions or procedures designed to improve efficiency.

Even when information is collected from outside constituencies, it is interpreted through the lens of the organization. For example, managers will ask, how can we exploit a market trend? How can we improve our product over that of a competitor? In this way, organizational members up and down the hierarchy engage problems in organization space, and it is there that they attempt to craft solutions. Indeed, most of the twentieth century's classic tomes on management, organization, administration, and production—not to mention entire disciplines such as organizational behavior, administrative science, and organization development—have almost nothing to say about events and people outside the firm, except occasionally as abstract "environmental" factors or resources to be controlled or exploited in ways that best support the organization's purposes.

In the closest orbit around this central "sun" are its large institutional shareholders, financial analysts, and investment bankers who control access to the equity markets and other sources of capital. Small shareholders may be the nominal owners of the firm, though they have become largely anonymous abstractions of share price, mediated by market analysts and fund managers. Nevertheless, when members of the producer organization must look beyond their own internally focused substantive and political preoccupations, the "interests of shareholders" or "shareholder value" are generally the first additional set of criteria to win their attention. This tendency has been amplified by the trend to link executive compensation to share options and to specific targets for earnings per share. A similar process holds in reverse: When shareholders want to evaluate their investments, they look toward the "sun"—the producer organization at the center of the system. They want to know about the tangible and intangible assets of the business. They rely on measures such as earnings per share, net profit, gross margins, and cash flow, all of which refer to processes that are internal to the organization.

In the next orbit are the firm's employees. Traditionally, middle managers were not regarded as members of this group. However, in the recessions of the past twenty years, many middle managers have found themselves as vulnerable to business cycles, and the inevitable downsizing that accompanies them, as are production workers and lower-level staff. There are many reported cases of middle managers who are asked to design restructuring plans, only to find themselves restructured out of employment. When economic downturns or other failures drive out profits and earnings, employees must be shed in order to "save the business."[4] While in every era there have been a small number of progressive firms that seek to ensure employment security for their workers, the vast majority rely upon this "cyclical" business logic. This logic does not necessarily reflect the personal attitudes of top executives, but rather a fundamental tenet that insists on the survival of the institution over and above the fates of some of the individuals who work for it.

Today, perhaps more than at any time since World War II, employers are insisting upon only limited commitment to employees at all levels, especially in the arena of job security. But that is only part of what accounts for the distance between employees and the center of the firm. From the point of view of employment law, which is solidly reflected in human resource practices, firms retain the greatest share of rights in determining the structure, content, and pacing of the employment experience. These rights, whose origins lie in the rights of ownership as ceded to management, are lodged in the center of the commercial system, with the executive management of the firm. It is true that decades of unionism have won greater protection for many hourly workers. But, however much public policy and the courts have created a new awareness of the potential limits of firms' rights, no government regulations, court opinions, or political movements have fundamentally altered the balance of power between salaried or hourly employees and the firms that employ them. Responsibility for the policies that most affect employees—for example, compensation and benefits, work organization, career structure and pacing, training—remains squarely within management's prerogatives.[5]

Suppliers occupy the next orbit in the system. For most of the twentieth century, the relationship between a large producer and the first-, second-, and third-tier firms that make up its supply chain was an adversarial one, and it continues to be so. The "channel master" that tops the chain seeks the most at the least cost from its suppliers. The need to control the costs of components and raw materials has become so great that it has led many firms toward vertical integration—ensuring ownership of some or all of the supply chain. Japanese competition in the early 1980s sparked an interest in "just-in-time" practices that required closer relationships with suppliers. In this alternative to either vertical integration or fragmented market transactions, the supplier was intended to be a partner, sharing information on production requirements and quality standards. In many cases, shared information systems have allowed suppliers and producers to jointly monitor logistics and inventories.

Sustained partnership between lead producers and members of the supply chain, though, has been difficult to achieve. As one group of consultants describes it, "Sourcing has been viewed as transactional and functionally competitive: Winners cannot exist without losers. This mind-set has long been evident in the behavior of 'supply chain bullies' that forcibly extract price reductions or service enhancements from their suppliers without any return."[6] Channel masters seek to reduce working capital by "playing the float," dunning customers and taking as long as possible to pay suppliers. As another supply chain consultant put it, "The whole idea behind supply chain improvement is to get somebody else to carry the can."[7]

While the automobile industry has been touted as the textbook case of supply chain transformation by just-in-time practices, partnership has been elusive. For example, in the economic downturn of early 2001, Daimler-Chrysler unilaterally decreed a 5 percent price cut across all product lines from all of its suppliers, many of whom had not seen a price increase in fifteen years. With volume dropping and inventories at risk, the OEMs (original equipment manufacturers) "pass on the problem to suppliers by demanding they take the cost off their products," notes a senior research analyst for the automobile industry. Analysts at Forrester Research concur:

"While the [automobile] industry likes to call its suppliers 'partners,' that's just talk. . . . This is not a chain of relationships, but one company mandating something to another company, which pushes it to another company, on down the line. . . . One automaker . . . fines its suppliers tens of thousands of dollars for every hour they're late delivering in a just-in-time environment."[8]

The persistence of conflict and distance in the supplier relationship is another predictable consequence of the standard enterprise logic. Producers and suppliers remain independent legal and financial entities with separate boards of directors, different sets of shareholders, and therefore distinct motivations and incentives. Their success or failure is ultimately judged on the basis of their individual performance, even where they have forged productive partnerships. Conflicting strategic and financial objectives involving working capital, stock turn, profit margins, and so on inevitably lead to an element of distrust. Even when improving relationships and performance across the supply chain is the goal, the explicit focus tends to be toward the "sun"—the most powerful producer organization and its financial criteria. The senior partners in Cap Gemini Ernst & Young's global supply chain practice advise executives that improving supply chain efficiency is the most effective way to increase a company's stock price and bring their options "above water."[9] Small wonder that real collaboration among producers and their suppliers is not sustainable, as suppliers remain orbiting at some distance from the self-interested priorities of producers.[10]

The next orbit in the commercial solar system is filled by its business customers. These relationships tend to mirror the difficulties of the relationships between producers and suppliers. There are chronic tensions that arise as each party struggles over working capital and profit-taking. Again, producers and their business customers are independent entities, judged with distinct criteria by different sets of shareholders. As in other parts of the supply chain, power tends to trump partnership as profit-taking is shaped by the strongest players in the relationship.

The orbit at the furthest remove from the center of the system—let's call it the last rock from the sun—is inhabited by end consumers. Advertising and public relations firms extol the primacy of the end consumer precisely because just the opposite is true. The relationship between producers and end consumers has more typically been characterized by disdain and conflict. If the current tidal wave of platitudes about customer service and satisfaction were true, then the frustration, stress, and anxiety that is the transaction crisis would have long ago disappeared. Instead, they are growing with each passing year.

End consumers revolve around producers from a great distance. They must conform to producers' rules, procedures, standards, requirements, and schedules, rather than the other way around. Moreover, it is not uncommon for end consumers to be caught in the crush between two or more solar systems whose most powerful players are at odds with each other, neither aligned with the end consumers' best interests. A prominent example of this can be found today in health care, as the profits of insurance companies are pitted against the profits of the pharmaceutical companies, with consumers caught in the middle, fighting for coverage and frequently unable to afford the escalating cost of the medicines they need.

Productivity investments reduce producers' costs, but the cost of an end consumer's time never enters the calculation. Consider a range of everyday trivia: You call back to reconfirm your restaurant reservation on the day you plan to dine; you call the hotel to confirm your arrival time and accommodations; you pursue the staff at the bank to have your statement corrected; you must file, check, and manage the paperwork to have an insurance claim honored; you call the airlines to see if your flight is on time and pray it has not been overbooked; you wait for months for a piece of furniture; you wait for hours in unnecessary queues while renting a car; you spend an entire evening checking your telephone and hospital bills for bogus charges; you set aside an afternoon to plod your way through an automated system when the personal computer you ordered by phone fails to arrive. End consumers must conform to producers' rules, spending their time as well as their money.

It is common to read now that "power is shifting to the consumer." What does that really mean? It often means that consumers can access more information about their purchases. The Internet has helped to make prices and other product information transparent across an array of competitors. This accelerates the commoditization of goods and services and creates pressure for everyone to keep prices low, though there are real questions as to whether most people even have the time to make use of the new opportunities to garner enough information to make a difference in the tug-of-war between producers and consumers. Sometimes the "new power" means that end consumers can access producer information systems. This is a result of productivity enhancements that off-load more of the labor and time invested in a transaction to end consumers, as they track their own parcels, do their own banking online, book their own travel, etc. Though such innovations might provide some information benefits that increase consumers' influence, they are clearly intended to reduce producers' costs.

More "power" sometimes means more choices. There are more products and services to choose from, as well as more channel, format, and price alternatives from one-click electronic shopping to electronic auctions, hundreds of mail-order catalogs, and the vast array of physical consumption experiences like outlet villages, Wal-Mart, Main Street, Nike Town, or Neiman Marcus. End consumers can withdraw their purchasing power from one seller and invest it in another. But all of this yields only marginal increments in consumer power, as all sellers are locked into the same logic, in which the price of purchase includes conforming to producers' rules and procedures. Some of these developments may represent an overall gain for a beleaguered economic citizenry whose earning and spending is now essential to a healthy economy. Nevertheless, these small increments of influence do not alter the ranking rules of the standard enterprise logic.

The end consumer still stands alone and apart, with freedom primarily to buy or not to buy. Once end consumers do decide to buy something, they discover that producers still make most of the rules to which they must conform, and those acts of conformity are so deeply woven into the fabric of everyday life that most people are barely conscious of them. They swallow the frustration, take responsibility, and make themselves smaller to fit the required patterns. They know they must protect themselves and their families, so they bend or do battle. This compromise seemed inevitable to the mass consumers whose dreams revolved around acquiring new goods. But for today's individuals, this fitful compromise has boiled over in chronic disappointment and barely suppressed rage. Most people don't make more of their anger and frustration only because they know there is nowhere to turn for a fundamentally different experience. It would be like complaining about the price of automobiles before Henry Ford hit upon a whole new way of producing cars that actually made them affordable for people with average incomes.

Because solutions to the transaction crisis have not yet been invented, people assume they must engage on the only available battleground. At best, they can search the margins of the economy for those few and fragmented commercial experiences that seem to point in a new direction because they honor sanctuary, voice, and connection. Or they can try to avoid the worst excesses of the transaction crisis by shifting more of their purchasing to an electronic medium. They don't make this shift, as some have said, because it's *more* personal, but rather because it is *less* so; it frees consumers from the wasted time and the many other more degrading inconveniences and insults that plague so much of the consumption experience. When a "nicer" producer comes along, people flock to it, making great success stories out of the likes of UPS, or Starbucks, or Southwest Airlines. But being "nicer" rarely outlasts a bad financial season. The real challenge is transforming the enterprise logic that rules the commercial solar system and relegates end consumers to the frozen netherworld of distant space, where their new dreams are inevitably stillborn.

A TALE OF TWO ECONOMICS

The persistence and ubiquity of the transaction crisis reflect the notion of value at the heart of the standard enterprise logic—what it is and how it is created.

TRANSACTION ECONOMICS

The subject of "value" bears a long and tortured history in the field of economics.[11] When managers and business economists today speak of "value creation," or for that matter "value destruction," they refer primarily to what has come to be known as "shareholder value." Shareholder value is reflected in the wealth that accrues to investors over and above their investment and the cost of their capital to the firm. A firm's success is measured—primarily, if not exclusively—in terms of its ability to create more wealth for investors. "Value-creating" activities are those that increase profits and earnings per share. "Value-destroying" activities are those that inadvertently decrease profits—for example, poor judgment in acquiring new businesses, overburdening business units with expensive central administration, or poor operational execution.[12]

The financial assumptions associated with the standard enterprise logic can be viewed as constituting an economic paradigm that we call "transaction economics." This perspective assumes that business is comprised of transactions between sellers and buyers. Each transaction is a wholly contained unit of analysis—an end in itself. Transactions are regarded as the building blocks of market activity that exist in an abstract, two-dimensional framework of costs and revenues. Most transactions are regarded as anonymous, binary, episodic encounters. As a result, each transaction occurs as though it had no body, no history, no context.

Within this paradigm, the value that is maximized in order to produce shareholder wealth is what we call *transaction value*. The end consumer is either a means or a troublesome obstacle in the effort to maximize transaction value. In today's enterprise logic, measures of transaction value creation and shareholder wealth are formally indifferent to the consequences that may exist for other constituencies in the commercial solar system. Increasing profits is an assumed good, even when those profits come at the expense of end consumers, employees, business customers, supply chain "partners," or even the long-term wealth of the organization. In this game with rules, the winner must create the maximum current value from a transaction, whether that transaction is the acquisition of a large business or a single sale to an end consumer.

Given these assumptions, it follows that transaction value is maximized by "managing" each transaction to yield the highest possible levels of profit. There are perennial arguments as to how managers should achieve this goal. Typically, these arguments can be understood in terms of two divergent perspectives. The most popular of these, and probably the easiest, emphasizes resource reductions—that is, reducing the use of financial, physical, and human resources. Managers who emphasize resource reduction tend to focus on lowering costs and limiting capital and employee expenditures as well as reducing working capital. They view each transaction as an opportunity to achieve greater levels of efficiency and productivity. Managers in this camp tend to rely on strict financial and organizational control systems to oversee costs. The salience of this point of view accounts for much of what has been most enthusiastically received in the management world, particularly in the last quarter-century of accelerated globalization and competitive pressure: automation, reengineering, downsizing, outsourcing, the focus on achieving operational excellence, and the attractiveness of new financial measures such as EVA (economic value added) and MVA (market value added).[13]

The second perspective emphasizes revenue enhancement by opening new markets, new channels, and new points of distribution, and/or developing new products and services. Members of this camp warn that managing for cost alone is a short-term proposition. They argue that robust and sustainable value creation depends upon expanding revenues in new ways, which in turn leads to an emphasis on strategy, innovation, education, people-management skills, and better service. This perspective requires more diversified financial measures, such as the "balanced score card" approach, which weighs outcomes among a variety of stakeholders, not just the firm's investors.[14]

These two points of view have existed throughout the history of managerial capitalism.[15] They frequently exhibit a compensatory relationship. A firm will be managed with a strict emphasis on cost and productivity for a period of time. The consequences of that approach create problems, often in the form of disgruntled customers, exhausted employees, and depressed growth, which then lead to compensatory efforts that emphasize innovation and revenue enhancement.[16] Indeed, these pendulum swings have become fairly predictable within firms and even within the economy as a whole as organizations oscillate from one pole to the other, looking for the change program that will produce more profit. Thus, nearly a decade and a half of zeal for labor-substituting automation, streamlining organizations, and reducing costs led finally in the mid-1990s to a renewed interest in growth, customer service, business "transformation," and innovation. These remedies, which tend to require a lot of skill and patience, in turn provoked an onslaught of enthusiasm for e-commerce, which in the late 1990s appeared to many to be the last word in automation and cost reduction. Each perspective provides a corrective for the other. These roller-coaster rides are exacerbated by the impatience of the financial markets and the hasty criticisms of its analysts, whose knee-jerk response to a single quarter of missed profit targets is usually to advocate deep and determined cost reductions.[17]

These perspectives on cost and revenue constitute different practical approaches within the larger paradigm of transaction economics. Both seek to maximize the value that can be created from the firm's transactions with its various constituencies—employees, suppliers, business customers, and end consumers. Each regards the prospects for "maximization" with contrasting assumptions, but both assume that value is there to be created or destroyed by the firm in the way it manages transactions. Each generation produces new management experts and practitioners associated with one or the other point of view, as well as new methods, techniques, and concepts that translate the old arguments into contemporary terms.

The relentless focus on transactions as an end in themselves affects managers' conduct with other businesses and also helps explain much of the dysfunction in today's supply chains, where each organization's management applies transaction economics to the decisions it makes. Each is judged according to _its_ success in creating transaction value. Each is rewarded for increasing _its_ shareholders' wealth. These standards and rewards are in force, irrespective of the performance of the rest of the supply chain. Despite much rhetoric to the contrary, each firm in the supply chain is striving to maximize a different value—the value that derives only from _its_ transactions and accrues only to _its_ shareholders. This applies to profitability as well as to profits—that is, to cash and capital employed. Decisions on alliances and partnerships, acquisitions and divestitures, resource allocation across business units, or investments in research and development, training, and education are made separately, according to each firm's standards for judging how to convert its transaction value into wealth for its shareholders. This inevitably produces friction, conflict, contradiction, and misalignment within the supply chain and frequently between levels of management within a single organization.

But in today's world, the worst consequences of transaction economics are reserved for the end consumer. There are myriad ways that managers "create" value and increase profits that either ignore end consumers or actually cause them pain. Similarly, "value destruction" refers to the moves that reduce profits, even if those moves are in the interests of end consumers and contribute to building long-term relationships. In this game, profits can increase even when end consumers suffer, because measures of one do not depend on measures of the other. End consumers are regarded as independent agents at the margins of the commercial solar system who are responsible for protecting themselves from the excesses of value creation. The standard enterprise logic dictates that interactions with end consumers are inevitably a means to a limited end, as value is sucked from the transaction for the sake of the organization. The warning "caveat emptor" (buyer beware) has deep roots in the history of trade and continues to capture the essence of the consumption experience. Today, it is the warning label that accompanies transaction economics, comparable to the surgeon general's warning on a pack of cigarettes.

RELATIONSHIP ECONOMICS

But what if the straitjacket of transaction economics and the ferocious pursuit of transaction value—reasonable criteria of excellence in the context of the standard enterprise logic—prevented managers from even noticing other, possibly more fertile forms of value? This is precisely what occurs in the transaction crisis. As the character of consumption shifts from mass consumption to the individuation of consumption, each transaction also carries with it the possibility of interdependence. When an individual engages with an enterprise, needs for deep support often rise to the surface and cry out for attention. Typically, though, those cries are choked off at their very source.

Embedded in that impetus toward interdependence is a still undiscovered form of economic value that we call *relationship value*. This new form of value cannot be created by managers in organization space. Rather, it is latent in individual space and can only be realized there, in the process of understanding a person's needs and providing him or her with the necessary support to fulfill those needs. Relationship value is the ultimate expression of the individuation of consumption and the untapped wealth associated with the new markets for deep support. But here is the queer situation we face today—the activities associated with the creation of transaction value can, and usually do, freeze the impetus toward interdependence and thus abort the possibility of realizing relationship value. Transaction value creation typically translates into relationship value destruction, as individuals in search of deep support lay their complex and elegantly differentiated lives on the line, only to be read the rules and treated like objects as they confront the stern face of transaction economics.

In fact, the realization of relationship value cannot be achieved within the context of transaction economics. It requires a higher-order economic paradigm, one that can absorb transaction economics into a broader and more comprehensive conception of value. We call this new paradigm relationship economics. It reflects the ways that power really has shifted to the end consumer. This shift is not a theoretical fantasy or a public relations ploy. It is not the result of technological innovations that can be obstructed or subverted. It is not the result of competitive strategies or managerial philosophies that can be reversed. Rather, it is a verifiable consequence of the long-term historical processes associated with the individuation of consumption that cannot be controlled, undermined, corrupted, or suspended by producers. As a result of this historic and irreversible shift, we think the next leap forward in wealth creation depends upon the realization of a new form of value—relationship value—that is lodged in individual space. It does not depend upon products, however new or customized. It does not depend upon the customized delivery of services. Rather, it is realized through the activities associated with deep support, in which products and services are included but subordinated to new forms of advocacy and assistance that enable individuals and their families to pursue their goals of psychological self-determination.

WHAT'S CUSTOMER SATISFACTION GOT TO DO WITH IT?

The dominance of transaction economics helps explain why it is so difficult to use current measures of customer satisfaction to illustrate the growing urgency of the transaction crisis. The problem is that measures of customer satisfaction implicitly reflect customer expectations. These expectations are, in turn, universally shaped within the framework of transaction economics.

As a result, customer satisfaction data are best understood as testimony to the conflicting strategies that firms employ to maximize transaction value, especially the ongoing pendulum swings between approaches that emphasize resource reduction versus those that emphasize revenue enhancement.

One group of economists from the University of Michigan's business school has shown that customer satisfaction and productivity will tend to "move in opposite directions for a profit-maximizing firm" when customers are seeking a "customized" approach.[18] Since the need for tailored responses tends to be greater for services than for products, their study shows that the trade-offs required between productivity and customer satisfaction will be greater for service-based than for product-based businesses. In a sampling of firms, they found that those service businesses with the highest return on investment (ROI) were also those that scored high in customer satisfaction but low on productivity. This implies higher levels of investment in front-line personnel and operations in order to deliver on customer satisfaction and garner healthy returns. In other words, these firms tended toward the revenue-enhancement perspective for transaction value creation.

A lead author of these studies, Claes Fornell, was the key figure in establishing the American Customer Satisfaction Index (ACSI) in 1994. Its purpose was to measure "the quality of the goods and services as experienced by the customers that consume them."[19] Specifically, Fornell wanted to demonstrate clear empirical links between financial performance within individual firms and the economy as a whole, on the one hand, and customer satisfaction, on the other. For example, one ACSI study demonstrated a positive association between the index and ROI.[20] It estimated that a one-unit change in the ACSI was associated with a $654 million increase in the market value of equity above and beyond the book value of assets and liabilities. Another study showed that stock-trading strategies based on the ACSI or its Swedish counterpart, the Swedish Customer Satisfaction Barometer, delivered portfolio returns well above market returns.[21] The ACSI has consistently shown a relationship between customer satisfaction and corporate earnings, such that one financial quarter's movements in nationally aggregated customer satisfaction scores predict the next quarter's movements in corporate earnings.[22] Yet despite these important correlations, many firms within the ACSI surveys continue to post earnings gains as their customer satisfaction scores stagnate or decline.

Since the early 1990s, technology-driven productivity improvements have tended to upgrade the overall quality of manufactured goods while decreasing the quality of services, where they result in the off-loading of time and labor demands to end consumers.[23] By 1994 customer satisfaction with most services was in decline, but satisfaction with manufactured durables and nondurables remained significantly above national averages for the economy as a whole. The success of manufactured products is even more outstanding when compared to those service industries with low levels of competition, like the airlines. Indeed, the ACSI scores that have been recorded since 1994 show some service industries (for example, the airlines) and some service companies (for example, BankAmerica, US West, Commonwealth Edison Company, Northwest Airlines, Pacific Gas & Electric) in a customer satisfaction free fall.[24] The differential impact of productivity improvements in goods and services underscores the fact that the standard enterprise logic was invented in order to manage the production of things. Its inward focus and control systems were consequences of the demands of mass production. They are much less suited to the requirements of a service business, and as we will argue extensively in the next chapters, they are even more inimical to the prospect of a support economy.

The overall consistency of the annual aggregated national customer satisfaction score (it was at 74.2 in 1994 when the index was initiated, fell to 70.7 in 1997, climbed back to 72.2 in 1998, and has fluctuated modestly in that range ever since, with fourth-quarter 2001 results at 72.6) is more significant than its changes.[25] In theory, as Fornell puts it, "the market economy provides buyers with the freedom to choose. . . . In markets where there are many buyer alternatives . . . one is more likely to find a strong relationship between customer satisfaction and profitability. This is not the case in the monopoly situation, where profits could be high and customer satisfaction low, as there is no incentive to treat the customer well."[26] This certainly helps to explain why some industries fare better than others in customer satisfaction, and why some industries with little competition, like the airlines, can survive while treating their customers so poorly.

But the relative consistency of customer satisfaction scores reflects the uniformity of consumer expectations. When Fornell and his colleagues measured consumer expectations, they found less than a 1 percent variation between 1994 and 1999, while perceived quality (of services more than goods) had declined by nearly 3 percent in that period.[27] We think this is explained by the fact that even under conditions of healthy competition for transactions, nearly all firms are defined by the standard enterprise logic and its reliance on transaction economics. This suggests that the destructive excesses of monopolistic industries like the airlines are only a small part of the problem. The larger conundrum is that the standard enterprise logic imposes a "supermonopoly" on the economy as a whole, and therefore on all transactions within it. This supermonopoly limits consumer expectations and sets

the standard for customer satisfaction across all industries. It is reflected in
the modest aspirations of consumers, whose expectations have been trained—
and whose imaginations have been constrained—by the universality of the
standard enterprise logic. Dissatisfied customers are driven to the margins of
the economy, where they can safely be regarded as deviations from the norm
until, as in the case of alternative medicine, the sheer size of the markets they
represent begins to attract attention.

Within the mainstream economy, then, firms are distributed in terms of
their propensity to emphasize resource reduction versus revenue enhancement in the race to create transaction value. The ACSI and other work on
the subject of customer service, satisfaction, and loyalty try to move the
mean of that distribution toward the pole of revenue enhancement. They
hope to persuade more companies that investing in the customer experience—which also means investing in employees, training, work design,
etc.—is good business.[28] But revenue-enhancing strategies are extremely
vulnerable to the short-term pressure for transaction value creation that is
more easily and quickly achieved through resource reduction. And so it is
that a few quarters or years of emphasis on one strategy give way to corrective measures that lead toward the other end of the distribution.[29]

Moving the mean of the distribution toward one or the other approach
does nothing to undermine the supermonopoly of transaction economics and
the standard enterprise logic. As such, "moving the mean" must always be a
temporary solution to the unfortunate excesses of the resource-reduction
strategy and the toll it can take on end consumers and employees alike. Neither transaction value strategy brings the organization any closer to perceiving, let alone realizing, relationship value. In other words, relationship value
cannot be derived from current measures of customer satisfaction any more
than deep support arises from good service. The relationship value embedded
in the new markets for deep support cannot be realized by shifting the mean
of the current distribution of business practices toward the more progressive
strategies of revenue enhancement. Instead, a new model of wealth creation is
required, one that jumps the curve entirely.

LITTLE MURDERS

So it is that too many acts of so-called value creation are more accurately revealed as acts of relationship value destruction when examined from the perspective of relationship economics. We think of them as "little murders," the

daily indignities—some small, some grave—that deny the need for psychological self-determination and freeze the impetus toward interdependence. Each of these little murders can be read in today's world as just another customer-service debacle, but that's not what makes them interesting to us. Instead, we want to call attention to them as they shape the transaction crisis by suffocating relationship value before it finds a voice. When this occurs, the relationship value that could have been realized over months, years, and decades remains invisible.

There are several forms that these little murders can take. We call them: *starvation, inflation, tyranny,* and *mimicry.* These forms are not perfectly distinct. Still, each emphasizes a slightly different aspect of the transaction crisis. Taken together, they give us a more nuanced appreciation of the collision between the new dreams and the standard enterprise logic. The examples we use here have been gathered from colleagues and acquaintances, but most people have had experiences like those we cite. They are meant to be illustrative rather than exhaustive and to provoke the reader's reinterpretation of their own battles across the barbed wire.

TRANSACTION STARVATION

One of the most obvious ways in which so-called value creation destroys relationship value concerns a firm's zealous commitment to resource reduction at the front line of the organization, which is also the point where organizations and their end consumers meet. The most prominent way that managers starve transactions is through determined efforts to squeeze out costs. For most of the postwar era, companies relied upon price increases to maintain their profits as wages rose. But by the 1980s, this strategy was no longer viable. Globalization supercharged the competitive environment. Discount retail strategies experienced enormous success. Continuous price increases were no longer viable. By the mid-1990s, the electronic markets introduced by Internet-based commerce demonstrated a powerful tendency to commoditize a vast array of products, exacerbating the already significant downward pressure on prices. Price stabilization has been most striking in product markets, but the consumer expectations created in those markets have also influenced the pricing behavior of many service providers.

The reluctance to raise prices has sparked a greater than usual degree of attentiveness to automation and cost reduction, which are frequently targeted at the front lines of the firm, where, in turn, they accelerate the transaction crisis. All too frequently, the front lines of the organization are starved of resources, when these are the very places where organizations confront end consumers' pent-up demand for deep support. One of the most vivid expressions of transaction starvation occurs in the arena of customer communications. This includes the mundane ways in which firms can maintain points of contact with their end consumers. It is instructive, then, to examine the zealousness with which these interfaces, particularly the telephone, are targeted for cost reductions as they eloquently convey the social relations of the standard enterprise logic.[30]

The telephone is often the primary means through which end consumers interact with the firms from which they seek goods and services. It is not unusual to have exclusively telephone-based contact with a host of figures, from insurance agents, financial brokers, and health-care administrators to travel agents, airline representatives, and bankers. Increasingly, entire transactions occur over the telephone. When there is a problem with the purchase of goods or services, it is inevitably to a customer-service phone number or e-mail address that one must turn. Cost is eliminated from this customer interface with automated answering systems and fewer human operators. Those who do remain to answer the phones are at the bottom of the totem pole, with little useful information, training, or authority to really help the customer.[31] They are monitored and measured—the objects of an ever-escalating pressure to answer more calls per minute and spend less time with each caller.

In fact, the telephone interface has come to be viewed as such a costly activity that more and more companies are choosing to create even more "value" by outsourcing it entirely. Why be troubled with those pesky and annoying calls from customers when the whole set of problems can be outsourced to a low-wage labor force that can be expensed as a variable cost or, even better, automated entirely? From the point of view of relationship economics, the mere thought is inconceivable. It is value suffocation par excellence. But within the terms of today's enterprise logic, it is merely another reasonable opportunity for value creation through resource reduction. An announcement from AT&T's consumer division illustrates how a desperate search for transaction value can blind a company to the vast hidden reserves of unrealized relationship value. In this case, the company announced it would pay consultants $2.6 billion to reduce the cost of customer service by more than half. The goal was to use interactive voice response and the Internet to shift 35 percent of its customer transactions to self-service. Talking with people was just too expensive.[32]

Enter the "tele-services" industry—one of the fastest-growing occupational opportunities in the Western world.[33] Its focal point is the call center, where "savings are possible because call-center outsourcers are experts at shaving seconds from the time an agent spends on the phone with a customer."[34] Here is an antidote to all those brazen customers, trying to worm their way into the center of the commercial solar system, stealing time and attention that should be devoted to other, more important matters. One study claimed that companies that outsourced customer service grew faster and created more shareholder wealth than companies that either had no call centers or kept them in house. "Look at the direct cost of operating an internal call center," urges the author. "Could those assets be used elsewhere to enhance core responsibilities?"[35]

The same taken-for-granted sense of priorities is echoed by the *Financial Times* in an article on the spread of call centers throughout the United Kingdom: "There is a powerful logic behind the growth of call centres. Dealing with the vast numbers of queries and requests for help . . . can tie up central staff . . . to an unacceptable degree. Outsourcing the responsibility to a third party frees people and telephone lines for more productive activities."[36] The theme appears again in the *Times'* coverage of the spread of call centers in the United Kingdom. Its article quotes the recipient of the UK Call Centre Manager Award: "By outsourcing a service which is not its specialty, a company can concentrate on its core business."[37]

Matrix, a subsidiary of Cincinnati Bell, has been one of the largest players in the tele-services industry in the United States, United Kingdom, and Europe. A large portion of the *Fortune* 100 number among its clients. Matrix operators answer calls on everything from Microsoft support to kitchen blenders, CD-ROMs, Gatorade, and health care. Matrix has claimed to have the highest revenues in the business.[38] According to *Los Angeles Times* writer Charles Fishman, who worked "undercover" in a Matrix call center and wrote up his extensive observations in a lengthy and poignant article, most call centers "impersonate their client companies—handling orders, complaints, credit card numbers and records—without callers ever realizing they aren't talking to the company itself. (If you ask, the customer service reps on the phone are often instructed to lie and insist they are.)"[39]

"The call center world can be secretive, even paranoid," writes Fishman. You think you've reached the company that sold you something, "but you haven't. They ask for your phone number, but they already know it. . . . What plays out over the phones is a strange, richly American tapestry: People talking about their breast cancer or about why their doll's arm came off. Both kinds of callers have taken a leap of faith: They believe the stranger who answers the toll-free line will actually be able to help them. . . . Americans dialed toll-free numbers 27.6 billion times last year—more than 75 million calls a day. All that dialing is fed by a convergence of trends: the increasing complexity of the products we buy, our insistence on immediate help with those products, our own restless mobility, which makes us unlikely to turn to a neighbor or a neighborhood merchant for advice." All that dialing also represents 30 billion searches initiated for interdependence, support, and relationship, searches that found their way to an agent's cubicle in North Dakota or New Delhi because a firm's "real" employees were too busy with "core responsibilities."

There is probably no arena where the conflict between transaction value creation and relationship value destruction is more grievous than that of health care. To be sure, health care was plagued with the consequences of a fragmented, overspecialized, and poorly administered medical system long before it became widely subjugated to the disciplines of managerial capitalism. Doctors sought to maintain their professional authority, and substandard care was too often protected by colleagues and hospital administrators. End consumers traditionally had little valid information with which to make informed treatment choices.[40]

Today, however, these problems have been exacerbated by the fact that medical care has been largely subordinated to the standard enterprise logic and, with it, transaction economics. Most doctors are now governed by a complex web of administrative and insurance regulations that value productivity over patient care. There are productivity standards for office visits per day, as well as for surgeries and other procedures. There is hardly a person who doesn't know the feeling of being rushed out of the doctor's office without the time to ask questions, let alone pursue any in-depth discussion of problems. Many hospitals subject their physicians and "business" units to batteries of financial measures that in some cases overtly demand increases in the volume of procedures, reductions in the quality of supplies and staffing levels, limits on treatment options, and even withholding care from uninsured patients.[41] In a replay of the customer service outsourcing model, new businesses that specialize in "disease management" are being hired by insurers and employers. In these companies, employees armed with software and telephones provide information and advice to hundreds of thousands of patients with serious conditions whose doctors cannot afford the time to answer their questions or monitor their progress.[42]

Insurance companies also hire productivity consultants to set standards for medical procedures. Their influence has led to limits on hospital stays, irrespective of the physician's judgment and the patient's needs. In many cases, mothers are limited in their hospital stay after giving birth, and mastectomies are treated as walk-in procedures. These patients and their doctors plead for extensions, citing the necessary learning curves for new mothers or for patients tending to their own surgical wounds. They also cite the need for psychological adjustment that requires emotional and medical support. Oncologists estimate that as many as 9 percent of all mastectomy patients develop unnecessary infections and other complications because they were forced home too abruptly. Doctors look for ways to do an end run around the insurer's regulations, even resorting to lodging patients in nearby motels in case problems arise.[43]

One of the most comprehensive studies of these issues, published in the *Journal of the American Medical Association*, concluded that investor-owned firms provide a lower quality of care than not-for-profit HMOs.[44] The researchers found that as the medical market is shaped by insurers, whose interests are not the same as the individuals they insure, efficiency is systematically rewarded over quality. In-depth knowledge of patients, de-tailed clinical examinations, and patient education—all hallmarks of preven-tive medicine and, for that matter, deep medical support—are discouraged in these settings. As the researchers conclude, "Although costs are similar in investor-owned and not-for-profit plans, the latter spend more on patient care." A holistic, prevention-focused, integrated orientation to the deep sup-port of individual wellness seems impossible as long as each member of the "value chain"—the hospital, the specialists, the HMO, the insurers—focus exclusively on transaction value. The problem isn't that each entity wants to make a profit; the problem is that each wants to make a profit based on transaction value, and the primary means used to achieve that goal is transac-tion starvation.

The transaction crisis within the health-care system, and its vast but un-tapped resources of relationship value, are vividly illustrated in the case of families who must shoulder the responsibility of caregiving for chronically ill children, spouses, and parents. Carol Levine, a medical ethicist, compiled one of the few comprehensive studies of family caregiving.[45] Her interest was triggered when she and her husband were in a car accident that left him paralyzed and with severe brain damage. As she worked to rebuild their lives, she was overwhelmed with the demands entailed by everything from battling the bureaucracy for key supplies to finding a new apartment and renovating it to accommodate a wheelchair.

Levine struggled with her transformation from wife to home nurse with no help from doctors, insurers, managed-care companies, or government agencies. "There was something basic not happening here, and I couldn't be-lieve I was the only one who felt that way."[46] "Families need emotional sup-port," she writes. "They frequently bring a patient home to a living space

transformed by medical equipment and a family life constrained by illness. . . . The intricate web of carefully organized care can unravel with one
phone call from an aide who is ill, an ambulance service that does not show
up, a doctor's office that cannot accommodate a wheelchair, an equipment
company that does not have an emergency service. There are generally no
extra hands to help out in a crisis and no experienced colleagues to ask for
advice. Friends and even family members fade away. . . . I feel that I am challenging Goliath with a tiny pebble. More often that not, Goliath just puts me
on hold. . . . No one advocates on my husband's behalf except me; no one
advocates on my behalf, not even me."[47]

The number of people who provide care to adult family members is estimated at between 24 million and 28 million. Calculations based on modest
wage assumptions translate their activities into revenues of $196 billion to
$288 billion annually.[48] But even these estimates of potential transaction
value must fall far short of the unrealized relationship value embedded in the
needs for deep support associated with these families. Advances in medical
research and technology have exploded the numbers of people who will live
longer lives than at any other time in human history. New treatments are
also responsible for prolonging the lives of people with chronic illness, no
matter what their age. Yet once again the individual plays shock absorber,
with disproportionate responsibility to absorb the implications of these historic developments.

Insurers are focused on creating transaction value through resource reductions; employers are loath to offer their employees the flexibility and
benefits they need to sustain their caregiving responsibilities; and so the issues turn intensely political, with new congressional mandates for unpaid
leave, increased HMO regulation, and a legislative initiative for a "patients'
bill of rights."[49] To quote Levine: "In terms of the health care system, there
is a void."[50] In that void, made even larger by transaction starvation, lie the
new economic opportunities associated with this burgeoning market for
deep support.

It would be possible to explore similar conflicts in virtually every service
industry—travel, banking, telecommunications, utilities, and so on. For example, long before the September 11, 2001, terrorist attacks in New York
City and Washington, D.C., sent the airline industry into chaos, per-passenger
spending on domestic flights by the twelve big U.S. airlines had plunged by
one-third, from $4.76 in 1991 to $3.03 in 1997, while industry profits hit
record highs.[51] This pattern of transaction starvation persisted, despite evidence that many, perhaps even a majority, of air travelers care deeply about

many factors other than cost.[52] When you find yourself unable to get a call through to an airline or are forced to wait on the phone for twenty minutes, or when you must join a long line in the air terminal to have your ticket amended, it is because your time is free to an airline, but an employee's time is expensive. It's transaction starvation. When you find airline personnel unable or unwilling to solve your problem, you receive no help in boarding, there is no food to eat, or you discover that there is plenty of software to track fare yields on your flight but none to track your lost bags, it's transaction starvation. Do not assume that these misfortunes are customer service oversights. They are intentional and well-constructed efforts to increase transaction value. If this occurs at the expense of the end consumer, destroying relationship value on the way, then that is merely consistent with the standard enterprise logic.

As an illustration of this predicament, consider the Airline Customer Service Commitment, executed in June 1999 as a way of diverting the U.S. Congress from a debate over the treatment of airline passengers and specifically, a "passenger bill of rights." Despite the major airlines' public commitment to detailed customer service improvements, the U.S. Department of Transportation found that customer complaints more than doubled in 1999 over the prior year, and complaints for the first four months of 2000 were already up by 74 percent over 1999. They also estimated that the carriers themselves received 100 to 400 complaints for every one complaint filed with the DOT. The problems appear intractable because they do not have their origin in failures of customer service. Instead, they derive from the deep structure of the firm that we have called the standard enterprise logic and its overreliance on transaction starvation in the drive toward transaction value creation.[53]

When transactions are starved through cost reductions, there are also secondary and tertiary forms of starvation that are set into motion. Each of these helps foster the goals of transaction value creation while intensifying the process of relationship value suffocation. As investments are channeled away from the consumer, so too are information, skill, authority, and commitment. Resources are invested in information systems that help manage cost, rather than in those that help support end consumers. Employees who conduct transactions with end consumers lack more than information for problem solving and support. They are typically regarded as the bottom of the organizational totem pole. Their pay is low or stagnant. The investments made in their training and education are perfunctory. Little authority is ceded to them, so that even if they find the right information and figure out what to do with it, they are so tightly circumscribed in their discretionary power that they remain helpless. When anything goes wrong in the transaction, the end consumer is seen as an aggravating reminder of the employee's powerlessness. Front-line employees are caught in an impossible situation, knowing the customer's demands and knowing that the organization they represent cannot or will not meet those demands.[54]

This is why study after study over the past twenty-five years has identified front-line employees—customer service, sales, etc.—as having among the most stressful jobs in the entire economy.[55] In one of the most comprehensive studies of customer service representatives, they were found to match or exceed the levels of burnout characteristic of well-known high-stress professionals such as the police, medical residents, or mental-health workers.[56] Specifically, there are three dimensions of burnout: "emotional exhaustion," "a reduced sense of personal accomplishment," and a tendency to "depersonalize" the people one must deal with on the job. In the case of customer service representatives, they ranked the fourth highest of all professions in "emotional exhaustion," behind only infant-care workers, child-care workers, and lawyers. They ranked third highest in "reduced personal accomplishment," behind public contact employees and welfare workers, and they ranked highest of any occupation on the dimension of "depersonalization."

A woman tells a story of her day in an airport that amply demonstrates how companies, in their zeal for transaction value creation, can be systematically indifferent to individuals as they reach out for sanctuary, voice, and connection. It illustrates the ways in which transaction starvation can strip the front line of information, power, training, and ultimately the motivation to care. By that time, depersonalization becomes the only means an employee has to defend him- or herself from the frustration and stress of the position they fill.

> It had been a long overseas trip. I missed my kids like crazy, and I couldn't wait to get home. My husband had hurt his back trying to fix our washing machine. Our baby-sitter had left halfway through my trip, when her mother fell ill. I had a sinus infection and was desperate for some antibiotics. I was overjoyed when my plane touched down in Boston, and I made my way to the commuter connection, where I would catch my plane to northern Vermont. I arrived at the counter with time to spare and went to check in. It was the middle of the day and the gate area was nearly empty. The agent barely looked up at me as I waited. When she did, her message was blunt. The flight had been

canceled. There was no explanation, and I suspected it was simply that there were not enough passengers to make it worthwhile for the airline to fly that plane. I asked her if that was the case, and she looked away, muttering, "It looks that way."

The next flight was hours away, and my family had already left for the airport to meet me. Was there any other flight? "Yes," she offered. There was another airline with a flight leaving in twenty minutes that had seats available. She told me the gate number, and I made a quick calculation. Not only was it leaving from another terminal, but the gate I was standing at and the one I needed to get to were at the two farthest points from one another. Could she get me a cart to speed me over there? "No." Could she call and have them hold me a seat? "Yes." So I sprinted across two terminals and arrived at the gate breathing heavily and drenched in sweat. I presented my ticket at the counter, only to be met by a blank stare. There were no seats on the plane; the last seat had been given away seconds before. But hadn't the gate agent called to have a seat held for me? "No."

I struggled to keep my composure. There was another flight in one hour. I could book on that. I waited. The hour came and went. Finally it was announced that the flight had been canceled. No explanation was given. There were no more scheduled flights for several hours. Then they announced that an earlier commuter connection that had been canceled was now rescheduled for departure in twenty minutes. The full implications of this information had barely sunk in as I lunged at the counter and asked them to please call my original airline to hold my seat. They said they would. So there I was, sprinting across two terminals again. I arrived back at the gate I had started from, breathing heavily and drenched in sweat. "Not so fast," they said. "You have to go standby and we don't know if there will be a seat. Sit and wait. You are number eight."

"But I have my ticket, my seat assignment, you said the flight was canceled. My kids are waiting for me!"

"Too bad," they said. "We signed that ticket over to another airline, and now you have lost your seat. Wait." So I waited. The plane boarded. Standbys were called. One, two, three, four, five, six, seven. Silence. The door was being closed. I tried one more time: "Please, I really need to get on that plane." A stony glare was the only response. I walked over to a window, dropped my bags, and with my face turned away from the now crowded gate area, I began to weep.

Why did she cry? When asked the question, the woman reflected,

> Yes, I was exhausted. Yes, I was frustrated. But there was something else. No one who could have helped me did help me. I realized that throughout that long and stressful afternoon, no one had cared about my situation. I tried to connect with someone on the other side of the counter, but I could not. I kept thinking about the phrase "caveat emptor." I knew that according to the rules, I had no right to complain. I was on my own, just as I was meant to be. But in treating me that way, the people on the other side were also being mistreated. I felt that something violent and ugly had occurred. I was not a person there, barely even a thing, and it was the same for them.

When transactions are starved of all resources—money, information, skill, and authority—the coup de grâce is this loss of care. In the face of marketing rhetoric and cheesy slogans that glorify the customer, firms use their most powerful means of communication—resource allocation—to demonstrate the priorities dictated by the standard enterprise logic. In the case of the woman who cried, the gate agents were not given the tools, resources, or motivation to notice her needs, let alone to help. The only thing visible at the gate that day were problems that had to be controlled. Some of those problems were travelers and some of them were employees.

We cannot overemphasize our view that this state of affairs cannot be explained away as a failure of customer service and cannot be permanently improved by better service management. The actions that constitute transaction starvation are successful and efficient applications of transaction economics intended to create transaction value. They are statements of what really matters, as they acknowledge the rightful place of end consumers at the furthest reaches of the commercial solar system. Along the way, they also tell employees that they are worth barely more than those whom they would serve. When employees lack any meaningful way to support customers, they must choose between perpetual frustration or simply withdrawing their care. That loss of care is the final phase of decline and depletion, when what has been starved turns cold and lifeless for everyone involved.

TRANSACTION INFLATION

Another way in which transaction value creation results in relationship value suffocation is what we call transaction inflation. Where transaction starvation is aimed at squeezing out costs, transaction inflation intends to squeeze the maximum revenue from each transaction, irrespective of its real value, real cost, or the consequences for any potential relationship with the end consumer. This is another tactic that recognizes only an eternal present of transactions. There are no relationships, no history, and no future. One form of transaction inflation is represented by new pricing structures that assign extra fees to aspects of service that were once considered part of the routine exchanges between end consumers and the firm. These surcharges create transaction value, but they also mask inefficiencies within the firm or its supply chain.

By 1999, for example, the U.S. banking industry could boast eight years of record profits, driven by giant consolidations and automation.[57] How did it achieve that success? Each new merger promised the consumer dramatic economies of scale leading to lower costs and a broad range of one-stop-shopping financial services. But these promises did not temper the astonishment of bank customers as noninterest service fees continued to climb, ultimately accounting for one-third of industry profits and 40 percent of revenues in 1998. In a study of 470 banks, the U.S. Public Interest Research Group (USPIRG) found that consumers paid 15 percent more to maintain a regular checking account at a big bank than at a small one, and that big banks' surcharges averaged $1.35 more than those of smaller banks. The cost gap between large and small banks for a no-frills account increased 39 percent between 1997 and 1999.[58] New fees are being invented to further bolster revenue. For example, the USPIRG documented new fees to call a computerized call center and new annual and monthly fees for ATM cards and ATM mini-statements. Wells Fargo offered a checking account that included three free calls and then charged customers 50 cents to use its automated voice-response telephone lines or $1.50 to speak to an agent to shift funds or ask questions. First Chicago charged $3.00 for a visit to a live teller, and Banc One charged its own account holders for use of its cash machines.[59] In 1998, John Reed, then chairman of Citibank, remarked to the press that checking accounts were "criminally profitable."[60]

The U.K. banking industry is equally skilled at transaction inflation.[61] Banks pushed for a massive shift toward electronic banking, in the face of ample customer skepticism. A consumer survey by the magazine Which? found that one in eight of its readers had spotted an error in their bank account during the prior year, and only half were satisfied with the way it was handled. Automation was supposed to lower costs for banks, and so presumably for their end consumers. However, the Sunday Telegraph has reported on the detours in this equation. For example, the bank clearing system, unchanged from the 1950s, can still take up to seven days to clear a check. In the meantime, the banks make about £1 million a day on the £4 bil-lion stuck in the system, and another £20 million annually on the day's inter-est charged on payments made by standing order. Customers who want their checks to clear more quickly, even if they are transferring money from one credit account to another, must pay up to £15 for express check clear-ance. Banks charge customers up to 33.8 percent for overdrafts, while paying only 0.25 percent on credit balances in current accounts. In many cases, charges are rising far more quickly than national inflation. The mere request for a borrowing facility, even if it isn't utilized, costs £30 at NatWest in "overdraft arrangement fees." In the mid-1990s First Direct charged £25 for exceeding the agreed overdraft plus £6 each time the overdraft was increased. By 1999 that charge had increased by 40 percent to £35, and the additional charge for exceeding the overdraft jumped to £8.50. One bank, the TSB, in-creased those unauthorized-overdraft charges from £6 per month to £5 per day.[62]

Examples of transaction inflation are rampant in other service indus-tries. The *Wall Street Journal* has reported on these practices in the rental car business, noting that "the industry as a whole has slipped in every cate-gory, including service, convenience, and availability, since 1995."[63] The top consumer complaint is having to wait in long lines. The troubles stem in part from old fleets, old computer systems, and understaffing, all bona fide examples of transaction starvation. But the biggest reason for the lines has to do with bogus charges. Profits, when they do exist, are increasingly derived from "extras" that the companies think up in order to maintain competitive positions with their basic daily rates. It appears that the real creativity in the industry is now trained upon how to concoct these extra fees. Sometimes these charges are simply buried in an already indecipherable bill: "In recent years, Hertz and others started charging $5.00 fees to corporate clients who rent a car for just one day. . . . In Seattle, Boston, and New York, Budget ex-perimented with imposing the full-day rate on people who make weekend reservations but fail to show up. In California, rental companies now charge customers as much as $1.95 a day to pay for their own vehicle-licensing fees. In Newark, they charge 75 cents a day for the new tram. In Miami, Avis im-poses a $2.05 road tax and 9 percent airport fee."

Other rental car charges depend upon "up-selling" to unsuspecting cus-tomers, which in turn requires a face-to-face encounter—thus the long lines. As the *Journal* reported, "Rental car companies long ago proved they can provide fast, lines-free service to their frequent-renter club members. So why can't everyone get a car quickly? Because those lines at the counter often add up to extra dollars."[64] Rental car companies covet the face-to-face opportunity to sell upgrades and extras to infrequent renters. Counter clerks are motivated by commissions to pitch more expensive cars, a tank of gas, a damage waiver, and other add-ons like a global positioning system or cellular phone. It's called "up-selling" in the trade and is reported to account for as much as 20 percent of the revenue of some rental car companies.

Similar acts of transaction inflation are multiplying in many domains. Take the restaurant business: A Zagat survey of diners in New York and Los Angeles found hidden charges for things like a basket of bread, bathroom attendants, coffee refills, salad dressing, uncorking a bottle of wine, and even cutting a cake. Diners can be charged for bottled water they did not order, for splitting a meal, and even for the chips set down on the table with cocktails.[65] When was the last time you made a purchase and had it sent to your home? Did you notice the ubiquitous "shipping and handling" charges? Perhaps a reasonable case can be made for extra shipping charges, but what exactly is "handling"? Aren't those overhead costs already reflected in the price of the goods purchased? Bell Atlantic's cellular service charges hefty fees for roaming as well as for incoming calls. And what about telephone information: 411? For years customers were told that these prices were high because the work was still so labor-intensive. But the more automated telephone services become, the higher the fees climb. And look closely at your hotel bill—have you noticed the range of extra service charges that have appeared in recent years, including hotel surcharges for electricity, theater tickets, bottled water, breakfast substitutions, gym usage, telephone calls, resort amenities (the spa, the newspaper, housekeeping), and even surcharges to cover hotel renovations?[66]

PRODUCT TYRANNY

In the case of product tyranny, the rules of the transaction are derived solely from the firm's analysis of how to maximize revenues from a product. This exclusive focus leaves no room for consideration of the needs of the end consumer or of past interactions between the firm and the end consumer. Product tyranny derives from the analytical framework with which the firm judges revenue and profitability. When products or lines of business are the unit of the analysis, there is no way to perceive individual end consumers, let alone the relationship value they may represent. While the strength of product tyranny may vary with the strength of the economy, reflecting short-term fluctuations in demand, it does not vary with the strength or potential strength of a relationship.

One illustration of product tyranny is the practice of yield management, made successful by the airlines. The price of a seat on a typical flight can vary as much as 80 percent depending upon how far in advance of the flight the seat is purchased. So, for example, business travelers, who are the airlines' heaviest users, but who often cannot book their travel far in advance, typically pay substantially more than the once-a-year vacationer who books a flight six months ahead. In transaction economics, it makes perfect sense to exploit your best customers in this way, especially when it is the product, not the individual, that is the focus of service and pricing decisions.[67]

Such revenue-management systems have spread to other industries as well. For example, hotels use similar systems to extract more revenue on a nightly or weekly basis. The Omni Par West, located in a booming area east of the Dallas–Fort Worth airport, prices its rooms as high as $199 on a strong-demand night and as low as $59 on a humid weekend in August. Marriott officials estimate that yield management results in an additional $400 million a year in revenue, much of which flows straight to the bottom line as profit. Industry analysts report that revenue-management systems are the main reason hotels have been able to jack up their room rates by an average of 6.4 percent a year since 1995, more than twice the rate of inflation during that period.[68] Once again, pricing is not embedded in relationship, in knowledge of the end consumer, or in the long-term contribution of that individual to enterprise revenues. Prices are a function of a product-based revenue model that is formally indifferent to the individuals using the product, any revenue they have contributed in the past, or any they might contribute in the future.

Many hotels have joined this chorus of relationship value suffocation in other ways. Some indulge in product tyranny by imposing length-of-stay restrictions, especially on peak nights, and overbooking rooms. Even frequent visitors to a Four Seasons Hotel can find themselves unable to book a room for fewer than two nights. As one Omni hotel manager explained, "The idea is to maximize revenue over a week, not just on one particular day."[69] But what if a person wanted to stay for only one night this week, and three nights next week, and two nights the week after, and one night for each of the next four weeks, and then bring the kids and the grandparents and have three rooms for five nights? No one asks. As a result, "hotel rage" has joined "air rage" in the growing list of consequences of the transaction crisis. A 2001 marketing survey showed that hotel customer complaints had increased by 22 percent in only two years, and the U.S. Bureau of Labor Statistics reports assaults on hotel workers increased by 47 percent between 1997 and 1998, with at least 10 percent of them initiated by frustrated customers.[70]

RELATIONSHIP MIMICRY

As the family sits down to dinner, the phone rings. You hesitate, then decide to answer. The voice announces itself as from your long-distance telephone company, and it asks for a garbled version of your name. In an animated but strangely impersonal style, the voice launches into selling you a new long-distance service. It doesn't take you long to realize that not only doesn't this person know your name, he doesn't know how many phone lines you have, or your telephone numbers. In fact, he doesn't know anything about you at all. You are on the list, and the list is the job. You decline the new service. Several evenings later the phone rings again. This time it's for yet another version of your name. It's the same pitch. In this way you become familiar with the company's "relationship marketing" strategy.

Relationship mimicry is designed to seduce, and it often succeeds. In the case of this little murder, the transaction is presented to look like a relationship. For example, many firms have tried to convert transactions into relationships with the promise of "after-care" to support new products. This may take the form of an 800 number for technical support, or even a technical service contract priced as an add-on to the product. But as long as after-care is subordinated to transaction economics, it frequently turns into relationship mimicry instead. This was the case for a man who bought his daughter a computer.

> The objective was a new personal computer and printer for my daughter as a Christmas present. I chose a company famous for its ability to customize your personal computer choices. A magazine ad with great prices drew my attention, so I went to the Web site. But the site would not accept the product codes from the magazine. Nor could it provide information on the printer options. After a couple of hours, I gave up and called their 800 number to order the computer rig from a person.
>
> I spoke with Steve. He was congenial and very helpful, walking me through the options. I made the choices, including a twenty-four-hour home-service option, agreed on the price, and was given a delivery date three weeks before Christmas. Steve gave me his direct number and encouraged me to call him if I needed further help. It was easy and pleasant.
>
> The gear arrived on time but without the printer. I made several phone calls to Steve, but none were returned. On Christmas Eve, someone called to say the printer would be delayed until late January. I began to complain, and she hung up on me.

We unpacked the computer on Christmas Day, set it up, and plugged it in. The next day, we could not turn the unit back on. We called Steve—no answer. We left a message. No return call. We called the 800 number and waited for over half an hour. When I finally reached someone, they said it was a faulty component, not a faulty computer, and we would have to ring the company that sold the component. After some arguing, they gave me a trouble-shooting routine. It was then concluded that we had a faulty power drive. Since I had the twenty-four-hour home-service contract, they told me someone would be calling me by 1 P.M. the following day to arrange a service call for that afternoon. The next day came and went, but no call. Once again, I had to ring the 800 number. This time I was given another number to call. That person gave me another number, and that person gave me still another number. Four calls later I was speaking with someone who said the new component had never even been ordered. Three days later, someone finally showed up to fix the thing.

January came and went, and still no printer. Six more phone messages to Steve went unanswered. I tried getting a sales supervisor, but he said he did not deal with delivery issues. I tried the 800 number, and they told me I would have to call the printer company directly. I calculated that I had already spent twelve hours on the problems related to this purchase. I felt really bitter and would have liked to send the whole rig back, if it were not for all the hassle involved in even doing that! Who would I send it to? That afternoon, I went to Wal-Mart and bought my daughter a great printer. I never did hear from the computer company.

People also invest in special credit and frequent buyer cards, in the belief that they are entering into a relationship with a firm that will treat them as especially valued customers. Firms tout their commitment to these premium customers. How do you know if it's relationship mimicry? What happens when the "relationship" hits a pothole and the ensuing conflict hits the profit-and-loss statement? In relationship mimicry, the veneer of relationship peels away as soon as commitment begins to have a cost. At that point the end consumer is face to face with the raw heart of the transaction crisis. The disaffection that follows is far worse than if those false expectations had never been aroused in the first place. One frequent business traveler with ample needs for interdependence was willing to pay the $300 annual fee for a platinum card for the additional support he thought its services might provide. This is how he discovered relationship mimicry:

I found that the front-line personnel working for platinum services were well trained. They found me a way out of Malaysia when my own flight was canceled. They had helped me with lost luggage and a stolen passport. For eight years it seemed that maybe this was the real thing, until the first dispute arose. When checking my statement I found that an airline ticket had been double-charged to my account. One ticket had been canceled and a new one purchased, but both showed up as charges on my statement. The total airfare amounted to less than the annual fee, but I wanted the charge removed. I expected it to be easy, but it certainly wasn't. There were several frustrating phone calls, arguing with successive layers of accounting management. They demanded more and more paperwork from me. Finally I exploded. I told them I was simply going to rip up my platinum card, despite heavy usage over the past eight years. They had absolutely no response. I ripped up the card and never heard from anyone in that company again!

The airline industry offers the promise of relationship to its travelers with frequent-flier miles and gold cards. Today, there are more than 3 trillion frequent-flier miles lodged in customers' accounts, but the annual redemption rate has remained steady, averaging about 200 billion redeemed miles a year. The cost to an airline of honoring a free ticket is only about $20, but the profits from selling frequent-flier miles are enormous.[71] In addition to the miles directly awarded to passengers, the airlines generate about $1.5 billion a year "selling miles" to marketing partners, who sell them on to their customers through credit card purchases, hotel stays, and the like.

The sine qua non for frequent fliers is the gold card, said to distinguish its holders for special treatment. At least that's what Jon Wiener believed. He was a gold card holder at American Airlines when a letter arrived informing him one day in October that unless he racked up 548 more miles in his account by December 31, he would lose his membership status. "They reminded me that I belong to an exclusive group that enjoys a number of benefits. They reminded me that these things have to be earned. . . ." Gold card points could be derived only from actual flying. So Jon decided to fly round-trip from Los Angeles, where he lived, to Orange County, 36 miles away. Since each flight segment carried an award of 500 mileage points, one round-trip flight would put him solidly into "elite" status for another year.

Jon arrived at the airport only to learn that fog had canceled his flight. A van was hired to take the four passengers to the Orange County airport. He made sure that he would get his mileage credit anyway. Of the four people in the van, two were there solely to qualify for their gold miles. By the time

Jon reached his destination, it was time for him to check in for his return flight. It too was canceled. Once again, he was shepherded toward a van. This time there were only two people traveling, Jon and another man, both traveling only to qualify for gold. "The other guy was just starting out, and he needed three times what I needed—four segments with five hundred miles credit for each would give him more than he needed. When he found out they were putting us in a van, he had a bold idea: He called AAdvantage Gold Customer Service in Dallas–Fort Worth and asked to make a deal: If he could stay home and still get the miles, the airline could keep his money for the ticket. He had bought a ticket, he had checked in, now could he go home, please? They told him no deal: Rules are rules. You earn qualifying miles only by actually flying or, in this case, taking the van."[72]

Jon eventually arrived back at the Los Angeles airport; it had been a long day on the freeway. What appeared to be a relationship was actually a transaction cynically decked out in the paraphernalia of relationship. It was relationship mimicry that promotes transaction value as it suffocates relationship value, wildly ricocheting between hope and disappointment.

A HAMMERLOCK ON CHANGE

Commercial organizations continue to operate on the aging premise that the purpose of business is to make a profit on transactions for products or services. An individual's complexity and yearning for psychological self-determination are imperceptible in these commercial transactions. The markets for deep support to which they give rise are equally invisible. Customer satisfaction may or may not figure prominently in the equation, depending on where a firm sits in the distribution between resource-reduction and revenue-generating strategies. But in either case, the transaction crisis is perpetuated as generally well-intentioned men and women do the "right" thing, based on a now tragically limited set of assumptions about value and consumption that have their origins in an earlier social and economic universe. It matters little whether their limited mandate is achieved with a smile or stony indifference, with a lot of sophisticated concepts and technology or none at all. Under none of these circumstances is the borderland into individual space ever traversed. Each time an individual's needs for deep support are ignored, firms lose an opportunity for wealth creation. Multiply this effect across the economy and ponder the unrealized relationship value and lost wealth associated with the vast new and wholly uncharted markets for deep support.

Transaction economics, however, is not the only legacy of managerial capitalism to maintain a hammerlock on the current enterprise. If managerial capitalism is limited by its own economics, it is also prisoner to its own psychology and social dynamics. Specifically, the "inward focus" dictated by the standard enterprise logic is responsible for a range of chronic behaviors and attitudes that help maintain the status quo and foster the distance between producers and consumers. In the next chapter we will explore this social psychology of the standard enterprise logic in order to better understand why the transaction crisis appears to be both ubiquitous and intractable—even in the face of new opportunities for wealth creation—and why relationship value remains invisible. That understanding necessarily takes us back to the crucible of today's enterprises, where the habits and frames of mind that govern modern organizational life were forged.

EIGHT

Organizational Narcissism: Products, Pyramids, and the Legacy of Contempt

In the waning days of the twentieth century, the *Wall Street Journal* published an in-depth account of the multibillion-dollar settlements and jury verdicts facing the General Motors Corporation over fuel-system fires in its "A" cars produced during most of the 1970s and early 1980s.[1] In these cases, the plaintiffs' lawyers argued that General Motors knew the safety risks of their fuel systems. These safety risks, it was held, were regarded as less important than the profitability of the automobiles in question. The accidents under inspection included heartbreaking instances of death and disfigurement as men, women, and children were consumed in flames when a rear-end collision sparked the explosion of their fuel tanks, placed without protection or support under the trunk, just 11 inches from the rear bumper.

US

According to the *Journal*'s account, well-paid engineers and executives who had spent their careers working together on fuel-system design, cost-benefit analysis, and production planning could not recall each other's names, memos they had authored, or reports they had read. Beyond the stonewalling one has come to expect, what interests us specifically here is the language used in these professionals' notes and memos, and the implicit assumptions about the standard enterprise logic it conveys. For example, one infamous memo written by an engineer noted the rising number of deaths each year "where bodies were burnt." He estimated that "fuel-fed fires were costing General Motors $2.40 per vehicle," based on a calculation that each human life "has a value of $200,000." "This cost," he wrote, "will be with us until a way of preventing all crash-related fuel-fed fires is developed."

In one of the trials, General Motors' lawyers offered to set up a crash test for a disputed vehicle. The company was confident, they said, that the car would pass the test and demonstrate its safety. But lawyers for the plaintiffs later discovered notes written by the crash-test engineer based on directives given to him by a GM attorney. The notes revealed the attorney's instructions to create test conditions that favored a positive outcome for the test car. For instance, with the fuel tank under the trunk, it would be more likely to survive a rear collision if the rear-colliding car rode over the test car rather than submarined under it. The engineer's notes, later disclosed in court, read: "Override is good for us."

We want to call attention to the word "us" used by both engineers. Who is "us"? "Us," of course, is the General Motors Corporation, everyone from GM's CEO and top executives to the people whom the *Journal* described as "low-level engineers." Who was not included in "us"? Well, everyone else, but most painfully GM's end consumers. Not only were they excluded from "us," but in not being one of "us," they were dehumanized. Their deaths, their disfigurement, their grief were encapsulated in an inconsequential dollar amount and referred to by another engineering analyst as simply "a cost of doing business."

The underlying social psychology of the situation is this: The importance of "us" (our success, our solidarity) eclipses any value assigned to "them" (their safety, their well-being). Further, the importance of preserving one's membership and status in "us" takes precedence over any other consideration. The focus on "us" is necessarily an inward gaze. Members of "us" are transfixed by the shared goals and social machinations within organization space at the center of the commercial solar system. Their continued membership and the satisfying of their ambition depend upon the results achieved in this domain.

The exposure of unscrupulous financial practices at the Enron Corporation provides another illustration of this syndrome. When Chief Financial Officer Andrew Fastow was first questioned by the firm's attorneys about his role in controversial outside partnerships, he showed no concern over the potential consequences for Enron's investors, employees, or consumers. Instead, he defended the partnerships as "good for the company" and blamed any criticism on "a rival's efforts to get his job."[2]

In fact, this inward focus and its powerful social-psychological dynamic of "us" and "them," inclusion and exclusion, has been a necessary component of the standard enterprise logic from its inception. Early in the twentieth century, corporate capitalism was hailed by many as a progressive force in U.S. society, precisely because it appeared capable of addressing the needs, fulfilling the dreams, and healing the rifts among disparate groups— labor and capital, consumers and producers.[3] The new corporate form replaced the fragmentation and ruthless competition of proprietary capitalism with the stability of professional administration and predictable measured growth. But by its very nature, these tasks, and the managerial hierarchy they necessitated, demanded managers' scrupulous and unwavering attention trained on the internal matters of command, control, and career. Gradually that inward focus insulated the organization from the very markets it had been invented to serve, as production and consumption became distinct realms separated by attitude, experience, and sex.

A measure of the distance that now separates the firm and its markets is the extent to which the modern corporation has developed the behavioral, attitudinal, and financial means to insulate itself from the little murders of its own end consumers. This self-insulating posture is what we call *organizational narcissism*. The historical factors that originally shaped organizational narcissism have by now produced an elaborate construction of habits, behaviors, expectations, norms, attitudes, and values that have a life of their own. People enter these already constructed situations and "learn the ropes," accepting them as givens, when in fact they have their origins in specific organizational inventions designed to achieve economic success under wholly different societal and market conditions.

Organizational narcissism is not an economic concept but a social-psychological one. It links the predilections of organization members to the wider economic, social, and organizational structures they inhabit. Over the last fifty years such concepts have helped to explain aspects of human behavior that cannot be easily reduced to purely "rational" considerations. Such was the contribution of social philosopher Hannah Arendt's insight into "the banality of evil,"[4] and social psychologist Stanley Milgram's work on "obedience to authority."[5] In both cases, these essentially social-psychological concepts provided a way to understand the otherwise inexplicable behavior of the apparently ordinary people who perpetrated atrocities like the Holocaust.

In that tradition, the notion of organizational narcissism is intended to illuminate a range of managerial choices and activities that, while typically framed as though they derive exclusively from economic considerations, cannot be wholly reduced to those rational motives. Organizational narcissism helps to explain why the new individual's consumption needs have been overlooked and why the opportunities associated with relationship value remain invisible. In other words, organizational narcissism is at the heart of the social-psychological drama that undergirds the transaction crisis. It protects enterprises, their leaders, and their members from the full force of the changes in the society that surrounds them, and it suppresses the emergence of genuine alternatives in the economy at large. Indeed, it is possible to pick up any business publication and find similar tales of organizational narcissism sometimes crippling great companies, sometimes even destroying them, on more or less every day of every week.[6]

It is our view that most innovations in the theory and practice of management, and each periodic "rediscovery" of the primacy of the end consumer, including those that preoccupy practitioners today, have sooner or later fallen victim to the centripetal forces of organizational narcissism and its uncanny ability to reproduce the status quo. It is difficult for organization members, swept up as they are in the urgencies and dramas of organization space, to notice or understand, let alone ground themselves in, individual space, where relationship value is lodged. They assume that value is under the lamppost—where they are.

A new enterprise logic based on the higher-order principles of relationship economics can be established only outside the range of these centripetal forces. But in order to do this, one must have one's eyes wide open. This requires a critical appreciation of the deep social structure of the situations we inhabit in order to understand the sources of their tenacity. What are the social-psychological roots of this inward focus on organization space, and how do they continue to flourish today?

Organizational narcissism is actually the nexus of several historical factors—most importantly, an orientation toward the product and its production, a preoccupation with the organization politics that arise from the professional managerial hierarchy, an inherited tradition of contempt for consumers, and a twentieth-century sexual divide that injected that tradition of contempt with a supercharge of acrimony and estrangement. The next sections explore these factors in order to define the legacy that has shaped organizational narcissism in today's organizations and continues to find expression in the everyday lives of individuals in their various roles as managers, employees, and consumers.

PRODUCTS FIRST

Organizational narcissism is a consequence, first and foremost, of the preoccupation with making things that characterized the growing complexity of mass-production operations. It was the rigorous attention to innovation in production that made possible the great breakthroughs in increased throughput and lowered unit costs that defined the mass-production marvel. Henry Ford described it in his autobiography as "modern methods applied in a big way."[7] In fact, the Ford Motor Company was paradigmatic not only in pioneering these modern methods but in articulating this exclusive focus on the product and translating that inward focus into a new enterprise logic that was widely emulated.[8] According to James Couzens, one of Ford's early partners, before the era of mass production it was assumed that "selling started with the customer and worked back to the factory—that the factory existed to supply what the customer asked for."[9] But this system frustrated Henry Ford. Satisfying the needs of individual customers made it impossible to achieve the scale and scope that mass production promised. In 1909, as Ford recounted it, his sales force was badgering him for a more diversified product line. "They listened to the 5 per cent," he complained, "the special customers who could say what they wanted, and forgot all about the 95 per cent who just bought without making any fuss."[10]

In spite of the pressures to further diversify his range of models, Ford went ahead and announced that rather than increase the product range, he would reduce it, building only one model on only one chassis. The difference in these strategies pivoted on Ford's insight into the true immensity of the mass-market opportunity and what it would mean for production. While the sales force at Ford Motor Company continued to regard the automobile as a high-priced luxury item whose design should cater to the desires of individual wealthy customers, Ford anticipated the tidal wave of demand that only mass-produced products would be able to fulfill. "The selling people could not of course see the advantages that a single model would bring about in production. More than that, they did not particularly care. They thought that our production was good enough as it was and there was a very decided opinion that lowering the sales price would hurt sales. . . . There was very little conception of the motor industry."[11]

The truly profound innovation by Henry Ford was not the moving assembly line, the minute division of labor, or any one of the many production breakthroughs for which his factories became world-renowned. Ford's single-minded act of brilliance was to take a process that began with the customer and invert it. His unusually canny insight into the then-changing structure of consumption, combined with his unique imperviousness to the opinions of others, led to this historic invention: a classic Copernican inversion of periphery and center that would form the template for modern industry in the twentieth century. Years later, Couzens would be the one to state it most clearly:

> What the Ford company really did—although not in so many words—was to reverse the process. We worked out a car and at a price which would meet the largest average need. In effect, we standardized the customer. We set the price of the car as a goal to reach and depended for profit upon the economies that we might effect in volume manufacturing.[12]

Ford's truth would be held as self-evident for decades to come. It shaped the assumptions and daily practices of chief executives and managers the world over. It guided textbook writers and management experts. In 1943 an influential management thinker, Lyndall Urwick, chided his readers: "To allow the individual idiosyncrasies of a wide range of customers to drive administration away from the principles on which it can manufacture most economically is suicidal—the kind of good intention with which the road to hell or bankruptcy is proverbially paved."[13] The same antipathy toward the unique needs of unique individuals would eventually permeate the production and delivery of services. This attitude helped to consolidate transaction economics as the dominant framework for judging commercial success in product and service businesses, a dominance that remains in force today.

THE MANAGERIAL PYRAMID

The rapid growth of the managerial hierarchy has been one of the truly dramatic developments in the U.S. labor market of the twentieth century. In

1900 managers accounted for less than 1 percent of the labor force. By 1930 that figure had risen to 7.5 percent and by 1970 to 10.5 percent; by 1990 the figure was approaching 14 percent.[14] This occupational growth needs to be understood in relation to other occupations. For example, between 1900 and 1940 the population of the United States increased by 73 percent, the labor force by 81 percent, the ranks of direct labor by 87 percent, and the numbers of administrative personnel in business enterprises—those engaged in managerial decision-making, coordination, supervision, planning, record-keeping, buying and selling—by 244 percent. From 1897 to 1947 the ratio of administrative personnel to direct labor grew from 9.99 percent to 22.2 percent.[15]

In a landmark study of this phenomenon published in 1951, Seymour Melman of Columbia University concluded that this trend in the growth of administrative overhead appeared to be consistent across businesses and industries.[16] Moreover, it was not a function of size, mechanization, technical complexity, or any one of a host of other variables that many had assumed were responsible. Instead, he hypothesized, it was due to the perpetual addition of new functions and activities, a process propelled by managers' attempts to control more of the factors that bore upon the performance of the firm. This meant both more staff engaged in record-keeping and data analysis, and more executive management to address an increasing proliferation of activities related to marketing, strategic planning, finance, and the like. Others have noted that "a central aspect of managerial employment systems was the strong bias toward continually increasing managerial employment."[17] The United States leads the world in managerial intensity, with Canada, Britain, and Australia not far behind. Some scholars have argued that this pattern can be attributed to patterns of executive compensation that tend to link salary increases to increases in the size of the unit that a manager oversees.[18]

Melman's analysis appears to have withstood the test of time. Between 1960 and 1977 the ratio of managers, including line and staff, to establishments increased by 280 percent, while the average number of production employees decreased by about 50 percent.[19] During the fifteen years between 1975 and 1990 the numbers of managers in the manufacturing sector alone more than doubled, from approximately 1.2 million to more than 2.5 million, in spite of well-publicized attempts to eliminate excessive layers of hierarchy in these industries.[20] Between 1986 and 1996 managerial employment grew by about 28 percent.[21] Despite the recessions of the 1980s and early 1990s, managers continued to experience employment growth. However, middle managers, especially in the early years of their careers, did become more vulnerable to displacement than in any other decade and experienced more "churning" in their careers than had previously been associated with the managerial role.[22] The U.S. Bureau of Labor Statistics, in its projections of occupational employment to the year 2006, predicts that executive, administrative, and managerial occupations will increase their share of total employment over the 1996–2006 period by a healthy 17 percent.[23] Between 2000 and 2001 alone, as recession reduced total employment by 1.36 percent, managerial employment actually rose by 2.54 percent.[24] In 1958 there were 120 graduate business programs established to fill the ranks of the managerial hierarchy. By 1998, there were 750 such programs in the United States alone.[25]

The growth of the managerial hierarchy was motivated by technical requirements and economic opportunities, but it never was the realm of pure rationality upon which its reputation rested. From the start, it was enmeshed in the intrigues of any social hierarchy, fully burdened with thrills and terrors. Managers developed a common outlook and code of conduct together with behavioral norms, language, values, and collective standards of dress and grooming. In short, the growth and diffusion of the professional managerial hierarchy gave rise not only to managerial capitalism but to managerial culture.

LIFE AT COURT

The presence of hierarchy in human affairs always points to an unequal distribution of authority, power, and influence. In this respect, the modern corporation differs little from the courts of Henry VIII or Louis XIV. In fact, it was precisely there, in the rarefied precincts of court society, that men first learned to control their impulses toward violence and direct expression in favor of the subtleties of interpersonal influence, persuasion, and manipulation aimed at advancing their political fortunes. It was there for the first time that social position began to depend upon a more precise observation of others, vigilant self-control, and a deeper understanding of human interactions in terms of longer series of motives and causal connections, "a lengthening and broadening nexus of interdependence."[26] In other words, such courts were where men learned to be psychological observers and to observe and control the expression of their own psychological life. It is worth understanding the deep symmetry between the early experiences of court society and the political life of the modern organization. That symmetry helps illuminate the inward focus that arises within a social group when hierarchically oriented interpersonal influence is a critical skill for individual success. It suggests the regularities of behavior that such hierarchies produce and the organizational narcissism that results.

"Life at court," wrote Jean de La Bruyère, an observer of French court society in the seventeenth century, "is a serious, melancholy game, which requires of us that we arrange our pieces and our batteries, have a plan, follow it, foil that of our adversary, sometimes take risks and play on impulse. . . . A man who knows the court is master of his gestures, of his eyes and his expression; he is deep, impenetrable. He dissimulates the bad turns he does, smiles at his enemies, suppresses his ill-temper, disguises his passions, disavows his heart, acts against his feelings."[27] Consider this description of court behavior, and let your mind wander to the daily life you have experienced or observed in any modern organization:

> Life in this circle is in no way peaceful. Very many people are continuously dependent on each other. Competition for prestige and royal favor is intense. . . . The sword . . . is replaced by intrigue, conflicts in which careers and social success are contested with words. . . . Continuous reflection, foresight, and calculations, self-control, precise and articulate regulation of one's own effects, knowledge of the whole terrain, human and non-human, in which one acts, become more and more indispensable preconditions of social success.
>
> Every individual belongs to a "clique," a social circle which supports him when necessary; but the groupings change. He enters alliances, if possible with people ranking high at court. But rank at court can change very quickly; he has rivals; he has open and concealed enemies. And the tactics of his struggles, as of his alliances, demand careful consideration. The degree of aloofness or familiarity with everyone must be carefully measured; each greeting, each conversation has a significance over and above what is actually said or done. They indicate the standing of a person; and they contribute to the formation of court opinion on his standing.[28]

And like the nobles drawn to the king's court by the promise of power, influence, titles, and land, those drawn to the corporate hierarchy tend to have a natural ardor for the rewards of status, power, and wealth that it can bestow. The climb through the hierarchy, motivated by these incentives, came to be known as a "career," and the most successful careers were those that carried men toward the top of the organizational pyramid. Career advancement, much as Ford had feared, became an intensely political game, with rules that demanded exquisite levels of interpersonal skill, studious observation of behavioral subtleties, particularly of superiors, and unflinching attention to group norms, values, and standards of conduct. To play this game well required relentless concentration on the unique political dynamics that unfold within organization space—in other words, an intense inward focus.

These demands of personal politics were evident from the earliest days of professional management. In 1902 a "how-to" book written for young aspirants to business success warned, "Be manly, and look it. Appear the gentleman, and be a gentleman."[29] The fact that there were few objective criteria for judging the future potential of managers contributed to the political charge of everyday behavior. When success was equated with the ownership of a large enterprise, many books outlined the qualities of character associated with that single-minded achievement. But as success came to depend upon rising to the managerial elite, the criteria were less clear. The message began to shift from an earlier emphasis on character to a new concern with "personality." To get ahead one had to "get along with others, conquer self-created fear, and develop personal efficiency."[30]

The classic text among the early advice literature for aspiring managers was by Dale Carnegie. Originally published in 1926 as *Public Speaking: A Practical Course for Business Men* and reissued in the 1930s as *Public Speaking and Influencing Men in Business*, his book was used as the official text for training aspiring management recruits in such major organizations as the New York Telephone Company and the American Institute of Banking. Carnegie told his readers that their success or failure depended upon the impression they made in four areas: "We are evaluated and classified by four things: by what we do, by how we look, by what we say, and how we say it." By 1938 Chester Barnard, an executive with a forty-year career at AT&T who went on to many top public-service jobs, including president of the National Science Foundation and assistant secretary of the Treasury, would advise his readers that political skill and fealty were critical to career success. "Learning the organizational ropes" was a matter of learning the "who's who, what's what, why's why, of its informal society. . . . The most important single contribution required of the executive . . . is loyalty, domination by the organization personality. . . . This, as a personal qualification, is known . . . in religious organizations as 'complete submission' to the faith and to the hierarchy of objective religious authority."[31]

As professional managerial hierarchies grew in size and proliferated across industrial sectors and geographic boundaries, this new political universe developed a life all its own. Meetings, socializing, and paperwork dominated the lives of executives and managers. By the 1950s sociologists had turned their attention to unraveling the cultural mysteries of this new and powerful group. Books like C. Wright Mills's *White Collar*,[32] William H. Whyte's *The Organization Man*,[33] and Melville Dalton's *Men Who Manage*[34] became classic studies of the executive manager at mid-century. "You're always selling," an executive observed to Whyte. "Everything I do is subject to review by all sorts of people, so I have to spend as much time getting allies as I do on the project. You have to keep pace with people on all levels. Sometimes I get worn to a frazzle over this." "You've got to endure a tremendous amount of noncontributory labor—this talking back and forth, and meeting, and so on," lamented another. "The emptiness and the frustration of it can be appalling. But you've got to put up with it."[35]

Whyte concluded that this intense involvement with others according to a prescribed set of norms and values was at the heart of the manager's work—getting things done through other people. The further up the pyramid one climbed, the more demanding the political role. Success put a premium on the theatrics of conformity, managing the impressions of subordinates, peers, and superiors at the expense of one's own tastes and opinions. Executives worked long hours and submerged themselves in the business of the corporation to the exclusion of family or leisure pursuits. Skills in communication and interpersonal influence were deemed critical to the success of line and staff alike. Dalton likened these conformity tactics to the protective camouflage that other species use to evade predators: "In today's vast systems of rationality, the individual conforms as he evades their schemes of detection. Some members find room for personal choice and ingenuity as they strain and thrill in meeting appearances. Others conform to avoid conflict and to maintain the demanded tranquillity and uniformity."[36]

Today it is chic to say that the "organization man" is dead, but nothing could be further from the truth. Indeed, the facts suggest just the opposite. The organization man is not dead; everyone is now an organization "man." Physical labor has receded so far into the recesses of our economy and our culture that it is no longer the standard by which other, "newer" forms of work are judged. Nearly everyone takes for granted that work is meetings, work is talk, work is interpersonal influence, communication, and implementing ideas through the efforts of other people.

Most of the ethnographies of corporate life, books on executive leadership, and primers on change management written in the last quarter-century echo the themes not just of Whyte, Dalton, Barnard, and Carnegie, but of La

Bruyère himself.[37] In them we see a fiercely political world in which the stakes are high—my career, my identity, my livelihood, my wealth. It is a game with rules, and those rules derive from the peculiar properties of the managerial hierarchy. It is a game whose intensity is heightened by the nature of the very people that can be drawn into it. Too often their personal equilibrium depends upon at least being in the game and, at best, "winning." Strip away today's sleek business suits and stow the laptops, and you discover the deep social structure of life at court preserved intact.

Consider, for example, a savvy consultant's advice to his executive clients, as related in David Nadler's *Champions of Change: How CEOs and Their Companies Are Mastering the Skills of Radical Change*. Nadler summarizes the "twelve action steps" that his consulting firm views as critical for leading change. Consider the top three: Build the support of key power groups, use leader behavior to generate support, and use symbols and language deliberately. The others are just as inwardly focused—build participation, reward behavior, use multiple leverage points, and so on. Nadler underscores the significance of the leader's behavior: " 'Everything counts,' says Henry Schact [then CEO of Lucent Technologies and one of Nadler's clients]. 'Every signal counts—little signals, big signals, intentional signals, unintentional signals.' Managers have to be keenly sensitive to the possible ramifications of everything they do and say because people will try to read signals even when no signals are being sent. I have seen inadvertent grunts, grimaces, and symptoms of indigestion by senior executives misread and widely misreported as opposition to change."[38] It is La Bruyère for modern times.

GOOD GUYS CREATE . . .

Let's begin with these words: "produce" and "consume." A quick trip to the *Oxford English Dictionary* tells a disturbing story. "Produce," it informs us, means "to lead, to bring forth." Its most general form of usage relies on meanings in play since the early sixteenth century: "to bring into being or existence . . . to give rise to, bring about, effect, cause, make." The chief synonyms offered up by Roget's *Thesaurus* are these: "create, originate, make, invent." And what about "consume"? Its primary meanings extend back to the early fourteenth century: "to take up completely, make away with, eat up, devour, waste, use up destructively, spend." Roget's is more colorful: "devour, eat up, lick up, gobble up, swallow up, engulf, absorb, squander,

run through." The story in these words is clear. Producers are good and consumers are bad. Producers create, which takes skill and hard work. There is
honor and value in their effort. Consumers merely destroy. Consumption
requires no skill, only appetite. There is no honor, no value, in it—only the
vanity and selfishness of uncurbed desire. These meanings well reflect the
sentiments of one well-known economist who opposed the notion of consumers' sovereignty with the declamation, "Any schmuck can consume!"[39]

In 1776, Adam Smith argued for a new system of political economy. He
wanted to challenge the policies and assumptions of Britain's mercantile system, which in his view were limiting economic growth. Prominent among
these was the contempt that producers held for consumers. "Consumption,"
he wrote, "is the sole end and purpose of all production; and the interest of
the producer ought to be attended to, only so far as it may be necessary for
promoting that of the consumer. The maxim is so perfectly self-evident that
it would be absurd to attempt to prove it. But in the mercantile system, the
interest of the consumer is almost constantly sacrificed to that of the producer; and it seems to consider production, and not consumption, as the ultimate end and object of all industry and commerce."[40] In contrast, Smith's
vision of a new capitalism based on firms competing freely in the marketplace was one that would reject this legacy of contempt and rationally embrace the real interests of consumers.

What Smith could not foresee is that the success of the very principles
he immortalized—free markets, competition, the division of labor—would
set into motion a chain of consequences that led eventually to managerial
capitalism and with it new sources of contempt for consumers. The inward
focus on the product, together with the swirling dramas of power and influence associated with managerial career advancement, dramatically widened
the distance between producers and consumers. But that distance was never
merely neutral; it was never just a question of producers being simply too
busy, too disciplined, too preoccupied, or too efficient to look up from their
demanding work and connect more directly with their end consumers. Instead, that distance was all too frequently charged with contempt, which in
turn served to rationalize and legitimate the commitment to an organization-
ally defined "us." Managers pledged their identities and disavowed their
lives beyond the limits of organization space. They did it in order to succeed
in the world bequeathed by managerial capitalism, even when they knew
better. They did it because they felt they had to. They did it because the alternatives were not obvious.

Once the standard enterprise logic was completed with the consolidation of the managerial hierarchy, the new distance between producers and

consumers presented itself not as something to be overcome but as something to be managed. By the mid-1920s, it had already become clear that producers and consumers had split off into two different sectors of the economic universe, and the obvious questions presented themselves—what did producers need to know about end consumers, how could they find out, and what should they do with that information? Already by 1923, the *Saturday Evening Post* featured an article whose headline trumpeted, "The Producer Goes Exploring to Find the Consumer."[41]

The one who would do the most to pioneer a philosophy of and approach to the new "customer research" was one Henry "Buck" Weaver, who worked for Alfred Sloan at General Motors.[42] He had already received the Harvard Award for Scientific Research in Advertising in 1925 for his studies of purchasing power. His articles were published in the *Harvard Business Review*. The fate of Weaver's work inside General Motors is instructive because it shows how one of the largest and certainly most paradigmatic corporations in the world confronted and finally rejected the opportunity to reintegrate the end consumer into the producer's orbit. Instead, General Motors chose distance and contempt, a straight-line inheritance from the world that Adam Smith had once decried. GM's choices foreshadow the contemptuous attitude toward end consumers that would continue to define the standard enterprise logic throughout the twentieth century.

WHAT BUCK KNEW

The Great Depression, and the anti-big-business sentiment that flourished during those years, forced General Motors, along with many other companies, to seek out the consumer's goodwill and loyalty as never before. Positive consumer attitudes were seen as the company's best hedge against government intervention in commercial activity. In that context, Weaver's work acquired more prominence within GM. Sloan commissioned Weaver to come up with a comprehensive proposal on consumer research, and he announced to a GM stockholders meeting that customer research was now "an operating philosophy" within the company that "must extend through all phases" of the business. In GM's internal magazine, Sloan went even further, observing that the company's operations had become too big and dispersed to rely upon anecdotes and personal impressions of the public's attitudes. By combining the "practical experience" of customers with "the technical skills of General Motors engineers and production experts, the gulf between the customer and those responsible for guiding the destiny of the institution" could be bridged.[43]

Weaver grasped the potentially profound implications of his work. "I am convinced," he wrote, "that the approach of running a business from the customer viewpoint is perhaps bigger than any of us really realize." He predicted "an even greater and more secure prosperity" by "recognizing the ultimate consumer as the hub about which all our activities revolve and cementing all of our public relations with a more liberal measure of human understanding."[44] If Henry Ford's genius had been to put the product in the center of the universe, then perhaps GM could engineer a revolution in reverse, once again putting the end consumer at the hub.

Indeed, Weaver believed that his research could establish GM as "a democratic institution by playing up the importance of the consumer instead of playing up the importance of the producer." Here was not merely a technique but a philosophy of business—a corporation operating entirely in the service of its customers, much as a democratically elected political body was meant to govern in the service of its constituents. Following the customer survey distributed in 1934, entitled "Your Car as YOU Would Build It," GM's ads announced that "more than a million car owners" had " 'sat in' on our conferences, so to speak" and that new design changes unequivocally reflected "what people want." Weaver's program bore some kinship to modern concepts called "mass customization," though he assumed that consumer desires could be satisfied with a few models and designs.[45]

By 1938, Weaver's work was the subject of a *Time* magazine cover story. In 1939, *Fortune* credited Weaver and his operation for greatly enhancing mutual understanding between the "immense corporation" and the "small consumer." It concluded that Weaver was leading a campaign to "preserve the right of the individual to be heard and serviced in an increasingly collectivized society." Had Weaver found the way to bridge the growing distance between producers and consumers? Well, not exactly.

A close reading of Weaver's own internal communications shows that he was from the beginning well aware of the "propaganda" value of his surveys. He observed that the research questionnaire proved to be "a potent tool for bringing the dormant prospect up-to-date, dissatisfying him with his old car, making him more intelligent on questions of design," even as it paved the way "for a more effective sales effort."[46] His notes reflect his uphill battle within the GM hierarchy. He regretted that his research offered "nothing sufficiently spectacular to force its attention upon our own people." He attempted to keep the results of his work in front of company executives by passing along mimeographed excerpts from his daily mail. He feared the contemptuous attitudes of the "real" car men—the technicians and designers who planned the new automobiles. As early as 1932, he had sought to face this problem directly by citing the criticisms of a GM engineer who had complained: "The general tone of the questionnaire reflects a respect for the engineering knowledge of the consumer which is out of line with the facts of the case."[47]

In public, Weaver stressed that the value of the public's responses was to impart information on their psychological and aesthetic reactions to stylistic and mechanical features. But privately he went further in reassuring the executives, explaining that "from a psychological standpoint" he had found it necessary "to inject a harmless note of flattery in order to offset the resistance [of the customer] toward answering the ordinary type of questionnaire." He confirmed that expectations should be limited to insight into the layman's "reactions to engineering developments" as they affected "his physique, his nerves, his temperament, and . . . his pocket book."[48] One senses Weaver trimming his sails, relinquishing his grand dreams of reclaiming the still nascent standard enterprise logic for consumers, as he perceived the threat to his career and his credibility within General Motors.

Were GM executives really convinced that this sort of information was useful, let alone vital? According to the autobiography of the first great public relations guru, Edward Bernays, GM officials "thought they knew what the public wanted and considered the survey Weaver's play toy."[49] And years later, when Alfred Sloan would write his own account of General Motors, he made clear what he thought really counted in the product development process:

> In General Motors there are thousands of persons—in addition to production workers—involved in the creation of the new models: they include style artists, and engineers; scientists; financial and marketing experts; members of the technical staffs of the various divisions; and the general executives and staff technicians of the corporation. . . . The problem of co-ordinating their varied activities is extremely complex. On the average about two years elapse between the time we make the first decision on the new models and the time the cars appear in dealers' showrooms. Ordinarily, the sequence of events during these two years is determined principally by the requirements of body production. . . .
>
> General Motors . . . is obliged to invest millions of dollars to devise new products, which cannot, however, be sold until a long period of time has elapsed. Meanwhile, the consumers' taste, income, and spending habits may all have changed radically. For that matter, we cannot

even be certain that the new model is "right" at the time it is first conceived. Responses to sketches, and to survey questions, are often undependable. It is an axiom of marketing research that automobile customers never know whether they like the product well enough to buy it until they can actually see the real thing. But by the time we have a product to show them, we are necessarily committed to selling that product because of the tremendous investment involved in bringing it to market. Every automobile manufacturer has on occasion been caught off base by the consumer. Nevertheless, in the nature of things, we must plan and co-ordinate our efforts in order to get to market with a new model.[50]

From Sloan's authoritative voice, it is difficult to imagine the carnage that would engulf GM by the early 1980s at the hands of Japanese competitors. Yet GM's failures were due to precisely the all-encompassing preoccupation with organization space that Sloan embraces with such certainty. The company assumed that consumer input was inherently undependable and thus could be ignored in favor of the by now well-entrenched inward focus on the product and the technical and political complexities of managing its journey from design to sales. It faced an opportunity to genuinely alter the standard enterprise logic by providing a structure for consumer voice and influence, linking two orbits that had already lost contact. Then it rejected that opportunity in favor of a marketing gimmick. Peter Drucker's judgment can be felt haunting Sloan's paragraphs. General Motors' managers already knew the answers, and when they did not, they surely knew where to look to find them. They looked in the mirror.

ADVERTISING CONTEMPT

In the absence of a structural solution that would bridge the growing distance between producers and consumers, the new discipline of marketing was created. It included the subsidiary functions of advertising and public relations. Its principal responsibilities were persuasion and logistics. If persuasion worked, then the distance between producers and consumers, and especially the contempt that helped to maintain that distance, would be adequately camouflaged. If logistics worked, then consumers would be so awash in plentiful, well-priced products that they would not be motivated to complain. Why protest a system that produced a cornucopia of affordable goods such as the world had never seen?

During the first half of the century, it was only the large corporations that even established marketing departments. In those firms, marketing was relegated to specialists, which allowed the rest of management to stay focused on what was happening inside organization space. Only the marketing group had the formal responsibility to look outward, across the distances of the commercial solar system toward end consumers. Their charge was consistent with Sloan's later summation—to both stimulate and manipulate consumer demand, thus ensuring that the company could sell the products it had already invested in. The new specialists conducted market research and analysis, managed relations with advertising firms, designed public communications, and led the way in forecasting and budgeting sales.

By the mid-1920s, some businesses had publicly begun to worry about overproduction. There was an increasing recognition that high-velocity consumption was critical to the well-being of their firms. Advertising firms came to be seen as the experts who knew how to stimulate that velocity.[51] Professional marketers began to delegate most of the responsibility for communicating with the public to these "ad men." Total advertising volume in the United States increased from $682 million in 1914 to about $1.5 billion in 1919, to nearly $3 billion in 1929. The ratio of advertising to total distribution costs nearly doubled in the ten years between 1919 and 1929, rising from 8 percent to 14 percent. National magazine advertising increased 600 percent between 1916 and 1926. Business leaders, even the secretary of labor, claimed that advertising would bring an end to business downturns and prevent future depressions.[52] The ultimate evidence of advertising's new economic power came in 1927, when a surly Henry Ford, who a year earlier had eliminated all advertising from his budget, announced a massive ad campaign in support of the new Model A.[53]

In the 1920s advertising also shifted from the fact-based "factory viewpoint," with its emphasis on communicating product characteristics, to a more evocative psychological approach meant to stimulate a desire for consumption. Advertisers saw an opportunity to cast their products as solutions to the many new discontents of an urban mass society.[54] Yet for all the success of this new profession, the "ad men" looked upon their newly established role with ambivalence. In social class, education, and value orientation they identified with their clients and the "production ethic" of the business world. Yet they had been hired to do the "dirty work" of attending to the very end consumers whom their clients wished to avoid, work that required them to proselytize the hedonism and lower-class impulse toward self-gratification they despised.[55]

Advertisers felt debased by having to communicate with an "irresponsible public" whose "tabloid minds" demanded a diet of frivolity and emotional appeals. The president of the American Association of Advertising Agencies wrote in 1927, "Average intelligence is surprisingly low. It is so much more effectively guided by its subconscious impulses and instincts than by its reason."[56] Throughout the trade literature of the period, in the articles that advertisers wrote for one another, they warned that the average mental age of the consumer was between nine and sixteen years old. Their colleagues in the popular press reinforced this image of an unintelligent public. *Time* magazine, in describing to a trade audience its own editorial approach, proclaimed its unwillingness to dilute its news content with a "multitude of features dedicated to Mr. and Mrs. Moron and the Little Morons."[57] Closely related to the notion of limited intelligence was the assumption of public lethargy. One prolific advertising writer, in his book about the profession, noted that "man in the mass," except when caught up in emotion, "won't exert himself beyond the line of least resistance."[58]

Advertisers themselves suffered from the same inward focus that they were paid to compensate for in their client firms. They lived their own professional and private lives within a narrow circle, socially, intellectually, and culturally separate from the mass of consumers. Many articles within their own trade journals tirelessly sermonized on the importance of knowing one's audience. Copywriters were urged to go out and sell something, mingle, and "slum." Such rebukes say more about the ad agencies' anxieties than they do about their actual practices, much as today's managers are urged toward greater customer responsiveness.[59]

. . . AND BAD GIRLS DESTROY

Producers' and advertisers' contempt for consumers has also expressed a strong sexual charge. This sexual acrimony is another important source of organizational narcissism. Many aspects of this story have been well documented by historians, but there has been little recognition of the role this sexualized contempt has played in fixing the horizons of the standard enterprise logic. It permeated the age-old mistrust between buyers and sellers, further alienating producers from end consumers. It nourished the already prominent tendencies toward self-insulation, and, most important, it cost managers a foothold in the changing structure of consumption in the late twentieth century.

The story of sexual contempt begins at home. In the eighteenth century, the home was the seat of power; it was the center of commercial and political life as well as the sphere of private and domestic life. This pattern held at every level of society, whether it was the home of a craftsman with his workshop attached or situated across the yard, or the home of a wealthy merchant or politician in which the parlor and study were dedicated to their commercial and public affairs. George Washington, Thomas Jefferson, Benjamin Franklin—each took the lead in designing their homes and ordering the furniture that would grace the rooms in which they conducted their business. Other business sites simply did not exist; the world's work was conducted at home, where dignified surroundings reflected the importance of the work that transpired there and the relationships upon which it depended. "Command of the house signified command of all its power functions, and understandably men retained control of these places where significant business occurred."[60]

During the nineteenth century, the role of the home changed dramatically as business moved out. State capitols were constructed, and governors and their assistants began to conduct public business in those imposing new structures. (Only the White House retained its dual role as private dwelling and public office.) One of the most significant architectural developments was the office building, a new structure uniquely dedicated to the conduct of business. Factory cupolas and bell towers, private offices layered with mahogany and rosewood, hushed executive dining rooms replete with potted palms, marble floors, and oriental carpets—these were intended to transfer the dignity and importance of the home to a new public space. The power associated with commerce and politics followed men out the door to work, while the home was gradually redefined as a place devoted to family and culture. Women were left in charge of this genteel domain, but at the expense of their physical separation from economic and political activity.[61]

These developments also had consequences for the separation of production and consumption. Men, women, and children had once been bound together in the work of producing and consuming. The family was the source, and the home was the center, of most of the activities associated with growing and making things. Goods were traded and bartered, or purchased from other members of the community. Factory-made consumer goods became available only gradually, to be purchased in a general store, or later from a mail-order catalogue. Until the late nineteenth century, most people knew where all of their things came from because they had produced them or knew who did. They knew the value of goods because they understood the effort necessary to bring them to life.[62] With the emergence of mass production in the early twentieth century the separation of home and work became all the more definitive.[63] Men were required to enter the world of production to provide for their families with wages and salaries, while women ran the household and managed most of the work associated with consumption.

By the 1920s and 1930s there were ample statistics to show that women did the bulk of the nation's retail buying. Women were referred to by the ad agencies as the "purchasing agents" for their families. The advertising trade journals commonly attributed 85 percent of all consumer spending to women. The end consumer was routinely referred to as a "she." As one ad in *Printer's Ink* succinctly put it, "The proper study of mankind is *man*. . . . But the proper study of markets is *woman*." (Italics in original.) In 1937 a *McCall's Magazine* ad ran in the trade journal *Advertising Age*, intended to persuade potential advertisers that *McCall's* was the best vehicle for reaching consumers, as consumers were, by definition, women. The ad featured a picture of a woman preparing a meal at an in-store demonstration, while a man stood by her table, eagerly eyeing the food. The copy read: "This young man is getting nothing to eat because he's not a 'consumer.' Actually, he could consume the whole demonstration and feels hungry enough to try it! But, categorically, he's a producer. Man is always the producer . . . woman, the consumer. And this demonstrator, who is smart enough to know that *Madam* is her market, plays straight for a woman's attention."[64] The male advertising elite shaped the content of its communication on the steadfast assumption that it was engaged primarily in talking to masses of women. The advertiser-audience relationship was, at heart, a sexual one.[65]

Women's new role posed some special challenges. In addition to the actual work involved in consumption—shopping meant absorbing many of the transportation and distribution functions once performed by producers—they were required to seek out and recognize value. Yet many women were now entirely removed from the processes of production. How were they to evaluate the prices of so many diverse consumer goods, from food to shoes to bedding to medical services? They had to learn how to read through the enticements and analyze the claims of manufacturers and advertisers, department store merchants and shopkeepers. They also needed to be able to distinguish between the individual desires that they and other family members may have felt, and the real needs of their families, and somehow to strike the correct balance among those conflicting claims.[66]

The salience of women's role in consumption spread across the lines of nation and class.[67] Working-class women in the United States, the United

Kingdom, France, and other industrializing countries were expected to be good household managers. Studies of U.S. working-class families between the wars reveal the importance of the mother's role as a good manager and "a miracle worker of consumption." Her adeptness at financial management was regarded as the critical factor that would shape the family culture and its social position. Mothers were required to do much with little, and through their efforts they not only provided a stable environment for their families but created a platform for their children's social mobility. These women often dipped in and out of employment when the family needed extra funds to get by or to improve the quality of life.[68] Other studies document the frequent state of nutritional deprivation that mothers endured as providing for their families took precedence over their own needs.[69]

This sexual division of labor appears benign enough. Men produced to earn a livelihood for their families, and women invested those wages in consumption to meet their families' needs for sustenance, comfort, and improvement, once again taking up their place in the vanguard of consumption. In fact, this division was anything but benign. From the start, the tradition of contempt that charged producers' attitudes toward consumers had a fiercely misogynistic bent. Advertisers drew upon these attitudes, already embedded in Western European and American culture, that regarded women as "fickle and debased consumers." They spoke with scientific certainty of women's "well-authenticated greater emotionality" and "natural inferiority complex."[70] George Gallup, as a young man employed by the Young and Rubicam agency, wrote that he could not account for the amazingly low level of taste displayed by the typical female newspaper reader, and noted that his interviews found "stupid women" in city after city.[71]

Advertisers cast their project as a therapeutic one, helping the bewildered consumer with the plethora of choices that now confronted her. The woman in a Parke, Davis and Company advertisement fretted: "I used to be all confused. I would go into the drug store and see rows and rows of products, all different. I suppose most of them were good—but how could I know? . . . I almost wore my mind out trying to decide."[72] According to one historian of the subject, advertisers became increasingly committed to a view of consumers as "an emotional, feminized mass, characterized by mental lethargy, bad taste, and ignorance."[73] The attitudes of the ad men reflected their identification with the clients who employed them. Those men looked back with derision from their new perches in the masculine world of production. Once they traded homes for offices and factories, they belittled the importance of what they had left behind. Consumption had become feminine, and as such it did not merit the time or attention of the men who had set out to make a new world.[74]

When Henry Ford capitulated to the need to style and market his automobiles, he complained sourly to the press that he was now in "the millinery business." Nearly twenty years later, Henry Dreyfuss, who designed appliances for General Electric, spoke to the Canadian Manufacturers Association at a meeting in Toronto in 1952, assuring them that men still retained control over product design. He announced that it was a good thing industrial design had entered the home "through the back door," into the kitchen, where "wear and tear were faster" and the housewife, "a gadget-conscious mammal," could be persuaded to have her house brightened up with handsome machinery.[75]

The context for his remarks was a campaign mounted by Canadian women to influence the design of kitchen stoves. They formed the Canadian Association of Consumers to work closely with the National Industrial Design Council. After extensive research, they offered detailed design suggestions that would better reflect the ways they actually worked in their kitchens. In the end, however, their suggestions were ignored. According to a wonderful history of the whole affair, GE's Henry Dreyfuss found women users "too mercurial, or disingenuous, or hedged in by their relationships to the men in their lives to provide reliable information about what they really wanted."[76] He dismissed the patterns of kitchen work women had developed as "retrograde." The editor of a product design journal, who would later become Ontario's minister of consumer and corporate affairs, stated the view plainly: "It would be advantageous to General Electric and to industry as a whole to educate people to understand what they should want. In other words, to give them what they need rather than what they want."[77]

The retailers of electric appliances were just as determined to ignore the insights of their female customers. They insisted on male salesmen, but the men knew nothing about cooking. Manufacturers organized cooking schools for salesmen, but by all reports these attempts were farcical. The solution to the salesmen's dilemma came another way—the elaborate accessorizing of stoves. These accessories not only provided manufacturers with a way to differentiate "one brand of white metal box from another," but the features provided content for their sales pitch. As the manufacturers cheerfully informed the salesmen: "A stove with twice as many features has twice as much for you to talk about—dozens of special sales features which mean added advantage to you in the days ahead."[78]

The story of AT&T's early choices of advertising imagery is also instructive. From its inception there was ample evidence that the telephone was used, especially by women, for purposes of sociability. They used the telephone to stay in touch with friends and family members. The sales advertising of the Bell System companies, however, emphasized the telephone's business uses. When it did locate the telephone in the home, ads underscored its practicality in case of emergencies or other aspects of home management. According to one study, the telephone facilitated "an activity that women typically both enjoy and are good at."[79]

But AT&T's managers, most with engineering backgrounds, regarded those activities as too undignified and foolish to deserve positive recognition. They also believed that their monopoly status as a nationwide utility supplying a vital service was a good reason to avoid any association with what they regarded as pointless self-indulgence. In 1909 a Seattle telephone manager announced his determination to reduce the "unnecessary use" of the telephone for "purely idle gossip," despite the fact that a sampling of calls showed that the largest proportion were for this strictly sociable purpose. Local phone companies even attempted to set time limits on calls as an explicit effort to stop people chatting when there was "real business" to be conducted.[80] Over the first ten years of AT&T's advertising, images of male consumers outnumbered those of women by more than ten to one. Men were shown talking to one another, and occasionally to women. Not until 1934, after twenty-five years of monthly advertising, did AT&T finally depict two female subscribers conversing with one another.[81] As a historian of this subject concluded, "The people who developed, built, and marketed telephone systems were predominantly telegraph men . . . [who] considered telephone 'visiting' to be an abuse or trivialization of the service."[82]

More than any other invention of the early twentieth century, the department store was designed to cater to women. These stores were fabulous worlds unto themselves, offering a lavish and elegant atmosphere of light and color, fantasy, luxury, and abundance, where women could appear in public without embarrassment. They offered extraordinary levels of service—valets, credit cards, home delivery, gift wrapping—along with many amenities, such as restaurants, lounges, tea rooms, and concerts, as well as fantastical playgrounds and zoos staffed by nurses to care for children while their mothers shopped. Edward Filene once called his store "an Adamless Eden," because his customers were all women. But this was not quite right—all of his department managers were men. And the same was true in every other department store. It was here, in this world of spectacular merchandising catering almost exclusively to women, that the sexual charge of producers' contempt was particularly vehement.[83]

The same managers who invented this sumptuous atmosphere—with its munificent levels of service, all of which were intended to transform women consumers into loyal shoppers—deeply resented their own customers. These women had a power as consumers that outweighed their power in society. Managers resented having to kowtow to women in the store, when they could dominate women on the streets and at home.[84] Department store managers longed for male customers, even though it was well known that they bought less, because "they found a male style of making a discrete purchase personally more appealing and less disruptive of store operations."[85]

These attitudes were not lost on Christine Frederick, a well-known home economist and early marketing consultant, who complained in her famous book *Selling Mrs. Consumer*, "Mrs. Consumer is often regarded as so much coal in a chute, passive and stupid, and shunted about the store as if she were an inanimate object with no feeling, and all the time in the world." She cites marketing surveys that showed that when consumers ceased to trade with a store, it was usually because of "the indifference of the salespeople who waited upon them." Frederick counseled retailers to concentrate on "making a customer" rather than "making a sale."[86] Her counsel sounds all too familiar, just as difficult to implement then as it is today, and for the same reasons: Organizational narcissism and the sexual contempt it harbored drove managers to ignore relationship value and its grounding in the real needs of individuals.

Across the world in Australia, training materials for retail managers bluntly tell a similar tale. According to a study of Australian sales literature between 1900 and 1930, various frameworks were put forth for judging customer types and manipulating them effectively. Among them they produced quite a variety of profiles meant to describe their (mostly female) customers, and few of them were flattering—sanguine, nervous, phlegmatic, calmly indifferent, prejudiced, logical, emotional, overcareful, grumpy, overbearing, argumentative, frigid, procrastinating, vacillating, hesitating, quiet, quick-tempered, doubting, the customer who cannot say yes, and the customer who is just having a look around. Psychologists and anthropologists were brought in to advise retailers. They emphasized women's primitive instincts; one classical scholar advised that women's predilection for hats and jewelry was evidence of their affinity with savages. Women were depicted as creatures of instinct, impulse, and emotion, lacking any sort of social, moral, or economic self-control in their lust for change, pleasure, and possession. "The female customer was constituted in retail discourse as 'other': at best, unpredictable and childlike . . . at worst, frigid, highly-strung, primitive or kleptomaniac."[87]

TO BE A MAN

The evidence suggests that men not only departed the worlds of home and consumption but felt an urgent need to denigrate those domains, largely because they were now identified as only and merely female. Their ambivalence toward the customers they were required to serve shaded into contempt, not only because of the typical suspicions that have always reigned in the marketplace, but because men felt acutely uncomfortable having to serve the very women they dominated in the society at large. Our sensibilities today incline us to wonder why the need to distance and diminish "the feminine"—and with it the possibility of relationship value—was so strong.

To answer that question one needs to appreciate something of the "crisis of masculinity" that accompanied the shift toward modern industrialization and the growth of large corporations.[88] Men had been accustomed to working on their own account, not reporting to "superiors," who in turn reported to other "superiors" in the endless chains of command that formed the corporate bureaucracy. The old standards of masculinity extolled the self-owning, self-acting, independent man. Life in the new hierarchy created some bosses and many subordinates, in a world where the very notion of subordination was feminine. Even in manufacturing, where self-employment had been the norm, the shift to wage-earning status during the first decades of the century was dramatic. In 1880 there were only 2.7 million wage-earning employees in that sector; by 1920 the number had nearly tripled to 8.5 million. Managers across the economy became the backbone of a new salaried class, distinct from the merchants, tradesmen, and entrepreneurs of an earlier generation. During these years, the nation also shifted from being predominantly rural to urban. By 1920, more than 50 percent of the population lived in an urban community of more than 2,500 people.[89] It was feared that these new circumstances threatened the "manly" qualities associated with a more aggressive and independent outdoor life.[90]

During this period, the nature of work underwent wrenching change, especially for this new group. As late as the 1950s William Whyte's organization man complained about the amount of "noncontributory labor" in his workday. Even five decades after the United States had become an urban nation, many men continued to think that only hard, physical "direct labor" qualified as "real work." In comparison, managerial office work seemed abstract, subtle, and often pointless, even to the men who performed it. What did it mean to spend one's productive years in meetings, writing and reading memos, talking on the telephone, and immersed in the politics of the pyramid?

For all the responsibility entailed in their jobs, it's not difficult to imagine how "feminine" this new office work must have seemed, especially in cases where the job seemed superfluous to or distant from the actual processes of production. One expression of this anxiety was the way the print media began to portray the image of the executive as "steely-eyed and square shouldered, with a broad sharply etched jaw," and the qualities of command and dominance they routinely associated with business leaders.[91]

With the growth of the modern firm, the traditionally male clerk morphed into a manager and quickly found himself surrounded by an entirely new species of employee: the female clerk. The new clerical positions—stenographers, typists, file clerks, secretaries—were filled by women. This was the first time that women entered the business world in large numbers. Between 1880 and 1890, when the typewriter was introduced, the numbers of female clerical workers increased more than tenfold, from 7,000 to 76,000. During the same period the enrollment of women in commercial schools jumped from 2,770 to 23,040, an increase of 732 percent, compared with an increase of only 140 percent for male students in that decade. By 1920, some 92 percent of all stenographers and typists were women. Sixty-nine percent of the change in female nonagricultural employment between 1910 and 1920 was due to the increase in the number of female clerks.[92] Not only was office work sexually suspect, but it was now work that also entailed being engulfed in a sea of women!

One former clerk at Equitable Life Insurance derided the changes in office work created by this new female presence. "Nowadays one is surrounded by an ocean of permanent waves and one's requests (not orders) are received with a smile while one's vocabulary has been refined to such an extent that 'Oh well' is about as near as one can come except that the 'Old Timers' occasionally relapse in the old version." In his view, women had altered the "vigorous, independent masculine office relation beyond recognition." In this and other accounts, the male manager is portrayed as having lost his manhood in the newly feminized office. They were mocked by one prominent management educator who wrote, "There is something a bit silly in seeing a husky man in an office chair so helpless that there isn't a paper . . . or a utensil he knows how to lay hold upon, without asking a frail little woman on the other side of the room to go get it for him."[93]

Private offices were introduced around 1920 and "set those who possessed them apart from other workers, and in very visible ways emphasized the individualism and masculinity of their occupants."[94] As the bureaucracy evolved, higher-level positions came to be associated with masculine qualities, and lower-level, or "subordinate," positions with feminine qualities. "A woman manager was expected to adopt masculine business behaviors and beliefs . . . [and] a male secretary, attributes increasingly defined as feminine." By 1930, the situation had evolved even further, with separate promotional tracks, pay scales, and status levels for men and women. In this way, even men who were in "subordinate" positions could look forward to job advancement, while women remained locked in what came to be known as the clerical "ghetto."[95] The longed-for masculinity of the new managers depended on this sort of systematic and institutionalized separation from women.[96]

Another tactic for sustaining a sense of masculinity involved the kind of women that were hired into these offices. When the Bureau of Vocational Information hired current and former secretaries from the Metropolitan Life Insurance Company, they were struck by an odd pattern. There seemed to be a preference for women who were younger and less well educated, rather than women who were older and possessed education, training, and experience. One secretary observed, "There is not a little prejudice . . . against the college girl; she's less easily blindfolded and men don't like to be 'seen through.'" Another claimed that "some of the men in the concern like to have high school graduates; they enjoy the feeling of superiority over their secretaries." And still another wondered, "Whereas when I started out I was turned away for lack of experience, today I notice the advertisement calls especially for the inexperienced." Young women were so prevalent in these offices that the term "girl" quickly became shorthand for "clerical worker."[97]

The masculinity of department store executives was even more suspect than that of the white-collar managers. They were not bona fide producers, but merchants. Worse still, they had to pander to a fickle public and demonstrate a dependent, servile attitude toward their customers, who were "always right." Even more humiliating was the fact that these customers were overwhelmingly women. The better-known among these executives assiduously cultivated their reputations for seriousness and hard work. Macy "worked indefatigably" and was known as a "hard-bitten economizer." Field "maintained a penchant for austerity, a contempt for frivolity," and a "steely cold" disdain for any decision not based on fundamental business principles.[98] The department store managers shielded themselves from their irksome customers by employing women at their sales counters, who would be assigned the distasteful task of encountering the feminine public.[99]

The story of a threatened masculinity and its contribution to sex segregation in the workplace is not new. Nor is the fact that men and women were even more broadly segregated in the worlds that have come to be known as production and consumption. We know that men sought refuge in their offices, there to find themselves "at home" in a different way, in the emerging male culture of managerial capitalism. Some historians have already begun to explore the derisive attitudes of businessmen toward the women who consumed their goods and services. But here is what is new: In distancing themselves from women, managers also distanced themselves from the dreams and yearnings and deeply felt needs of their most important end consumers. In deriding women, they turned their backs on the true nature of their markets, relegating the consumer-housewife to a distant orbit, the last stop in a long chain of distribution that emanated from the stronghold at the center of the commercial solar system, also, and not ironically, known as "the firm." The need to emphasize and embrace their difference and separateness from women cost corporate managers a front-row seat in the changing structure of consumption and may yet cause them to forfeit their leadership in the next episode of capitalism.

THE CONSEQUENCES OF
ORGANIZATIONAL NARCISSISM

The distance that arose between producers and end consumers was created on practical grounds. It was a consequence of the inward focus on production and control necessary to manage the new complexities of the corporation under managerial capitalism. But that distance has been nourished and sustained for less savory and more intractable reasons. First, it was animated by a contemptuous attitude toward end consumers. While that attitude reflected the age-old mistrust between sellers and buyers in every marketplace the world has known, it was intensified by the repugnance an educated elite felt toward the increasingly powerful but unpolished urban masses. It was also a uniquely twentieth-century expression of a newly problematic, anxious, and uncertain masculinity defining itself through opposition to what it most feared. That anxiety resulted not only in the well-documented practices of sexual domination within the organization, but also in the sexual dominion of producers over consumers.

We propose that this second form of dominion, expressed in the aversion of male producers to the consuming female, has had far-reaching consequences for lost wealth and retarded economic growth. It cemented the notion that the worlds of producers and consumers were not only separate but unequal. It helped deny the end consumer a legitimate structure for voice and participation in the industrial enterprise. It defined value creation as something that occurs in organization space, thus confining the modern enterprise to the light under the lamppost, where it became vulnerable to rigidity, arrogance, and indifference toward the human beings it was intended to serve. The comforts of belonging to a group of men called "us" deprived managers of a deep understanding of the changing world around them, changes marked by the emergence of the new society of individuals and the women who are its vanguard, their needs for deep support, the expression of those needs in the individuation of consumption, and the rising significance of relationship value for the next leap forward in wealth creation and a new episode of capitalism.

Twenty years ago, Harvard sociologist Harrison White pointed out a puzzle in producers' behavior. He noted that decisions about production should, according to neoclassical economic theory, be based on an analysis of consumer demand. Instead, such decisions tended to be based on the firm's already established criteria for reducing costs. He found that only an understanding of the social relations among producers and consumers could resolve the puzzle. "Markets are not defined by a set of buyers, as some of our habits of speech suggest," he reasoned, "nor are the producers obsessed with speculations on an amorphous demand. . . . Markets are tangible cliques of producers observing each other. Pressure from the buyer side creates a mirror in which producers see themselves, not consumers."[100]

When producers look into that mirror, they see themselves and they see one another. In other words, they see "us." According to White, the "market" is best thought of as any other ecosystem, where creatures seek out a niche in which they can survive and, of course, reproduce. In sociological terms, the market is just such a place or space, in which firms find a niche in order to continue reproducing their practices. Managers tend to regard their markets as things to be "penetrated" or "dominated," with spoils to be won and jealously guarded, thus increasing the size of their niche and precluding others from enjoying its resources. The sexual dramas that help sustain organizational narcissism are well-enough reflected in these routine metaphors of marketing and sales. Looking in the mirror that buyers provide, managers see the challenges of self-reproduction, positioning, and dominance. What they do not see are the real needs that dwell on the other side of the looking glass and the demands for interdependence that arise from those needs. Here is the myth of Narcissus at the heart of the transaction crisis. Producers see themselves, not consumers. The new individuals remain hidden in the darkness, harboring needs for sanctuary, voice, and connection that wait to be fulfilled.

NINE

Rediscovering the End Consumer, Over and Over Again

Announcements of "paradigm shifts" and "transformational change" have kept the business press churning in recent decades. In some cases, there have been solid innovations with real benefits to end consumers. But there is no evidence that anything like a paradigm shift in the standard enterprise logic has occurred. The most eloquent testimony to this observation is the fact that since the days of Buck Weaver, the business community has been regularly stirred up by the so-called rediscovery of the end consumer. This call to rediscovery occurs at least once, sometimes more often, each decade. It is, after all, end consumers' relegation to a faraway orbit that makes them available for rediscovery, like the sighting of some distant star by an astronomer with chronic amnesia. It's always new. Producers feel the need to rediscover their end consumers, because the deep structure of the standard enterprise logic insists that they must always lose them.

LOOK, A DISTANT STAR!

In this chapter we investigate some of the most prominent efforts during the last fifty years that have aimed at "healing" the transaction crisis and "rediscovering" the end consumer. The results remind us that living systems do not necessarily fare well when faced with the need for discontinuous change.

In most cases, as we have discussed, organisms that confront system-threatening challenges tend to keep doing what they know how to do successfully, only with more vigor. During this half-century period—and especially during the last twenty years, which have been marked by the vivid and relentless competitive pressures of the global economy—companies have applied transaction economics and enacted organizational narcissism with increased determination and frenzy. As a result, most of the techniques intended to improve competitive positioning have actually heightened the alienation of end consumers. These "solutions" have intensified the transaction crisis, suffocating relationship value ever more violently. Each time a new remedy is proposed to halt this destructive cycle, it is applied in organization space, where it is sucked down the maw of transaction economics to become just another feature of the standard enterprise logic's life support.

There are several reasons why this is the case, each of which leads home to one big reason. First, it has been assumed that the way to bond more effectively with the new individuals as end consumers is through more differentiated or more customized products and services. Second, it has been assumed that business organizations can undertake systemic "transformational" change in order to make them more responsive to end consumers through customization and other relationship-oriented practices. Third, it has been assumed that these changes are possible within the framework of transaction economics. And fourth, efforts at rediscovery have ignored the social psychology of managerial capitalism and its predisposition toward organizational narcissism.

The one big reason? All of the activity associated with rediscovering the end consumer has been directed at symptoms, not their cause. These innovations fail to take into account that the transaction crisis is a chronic symptom, arising from the collision between the new individuals and the standard enterprise logic, with its emphasis on the production of products and services in organization space, its long-standing sexually charged aversion to end consumers, its allegiance to transaction economics, and its hierarchy of orbiting interests that puts end consumers last. If a new enterprise logic capable of truly supporting individual end consumers is to be forged, it will have to claim new territory outside the gravitational field of these powerful forces. That means a change in the deep structure of the enterprise, a real discontinuity that necessarily points beyond the adaptive range of the standard enterprise logic. But none of the proposed remedies to the transaction crisis have addressed the causes of this chronic symptom, which necessarily involve the deep structure of the standard enterprise logic. None have proposed an alternative to that deep structure.

The tenacity of the transaction crisis leaves firms always on the prowl for new techniques that might help them bridge the distance to their end consumers. Then, the "acceptable" solutions that firms do embrace are intrinsically incapable of resolving the dilemma. This is because the standard enterprise logic—like any other living system—will not and cannot host solutions that interfere with its ability to reproduce. Thus, even when a solution arises from a really good insight into the problem, it must be cloaked in the assumptions of the standard enterprise logic in order to gain acceptance, the way parents once crushed a baby aspirin in applesauce. As a result, every glimmer of insight into the new individual as end consumer has been refracted through the prism of the standard enterprise logic, its purposes, economics, and social psychology. Innovations fade or fail to fulfill their potential, assuring that end consumers remain available once again for rediscovery, and that managers will remain an eager market for the next round of techniques.

THE MARKETING CONCEPT

By the early 1950s, with the explosion of postwar consumption, the business community was once again ready to rediscover the end consumer. General Electric announced the importance of putting the customer first in its 1952 annual report. Much as GM's Alfred Sloan had declared twenty years earlier, the customer orientation was to redefine every phase of the business. GE called its new approach "an advanced concept of marketing":

> This . . . would introduce the marketing man at the beginning rather than the end of the production cycle and would integrate marketing into each phase of the business. Thus marketing, through its studies and research, would establish for the engineer, the designer and the manufacturing man what the customer wants in a given product, what price he is willing to pay, and where and when it will be wanted. Marketing would have authority in product planning, production planning and inventory control, as well as the sales, distribution and servicing of the product.[1]

In 1954, Peter Drucker published an influential book called *The Practice of Management*. His message was strikingly similar. In his opinion, it was not enough to move from selling to marketing. Marketing was not even to be considered a specialized activity, but rather a way of seeing the whole business from the customer's point of view.

> It is the customer who determines what a business is. For it is the customer, and he alone, who through being willing to pay for a good or service, converts economic resources into wealth, things into goods. What the business thinks it produces is not of first importance. . . . What the customer thinks he is buying, what he considers "value," is decisive.[2]

John McKitterick was the manager of the Marketing Services Research Service at GE and the Buck Weaver of his generation, writing articles and speaking at professional conferences to spread the gospel of advanced marketing. In 1957, he wrote in a prominent marketing textbook: "The principal task of the marketing function . . . is not so much to be skillful in making the customer do what suits the interests of the business as to be skillful in conceiving and then making the business do what suits the interests of the customer."[3]

Other large corporations—including IBM, Procter & Gamble, and General Foods—made well-publicized commitments to a business strategy based on this so-called marketing orientation. In 1960, a Pillsbury executive described that company's evolution from an emphasis on sales to a marketing orientation and ultimately, he hoped, to what he called "marketing control." He claimed the "marketing concept" had transformed Pillsbury:

> No longer is the company at the center of the business universe. Today the customer is at the center. Our attention has shifted from problems of production to problems of marketing, from the product we can make to the product the consumer wants us to make, from the company itself to the market place. . . . Soon it will be true that every activity of the corporation—from finance to sales to production—is aimed at satisfying the needs and desires of the consumer. When that stage of development is reached, the marketing revolution will be complete.[4]

A good deal of innovation arose from this new thinking. Consumer goods companies invented brand management and used market research to finely tune their market-segmentation strategies. Many more companies established marketing departments, staffed with professionals trained in the research techniques—surveys, focus groups, test marketing—that would become the hallmark of their trade. There were many more instances where marketing reported directly to the CEO or division chief, rather than to the head of the sales function. But by the 1970s, it was clear that the so-called marketing revolution had not, after all, made a very big dent in the practice of business as usual. Several studies published around that time underscored the limited adoption of the marketing orientation. The job of marketing continued to be "to sell what the factory could produce."[5]

The champions of the "total customer orientation" had predicted a blurring of the boundaries between the traditional management functions. Instead, the period between 1950 and the 1970s saw those boundaries grow stronger and more variegated than ever before. Indeed, the fact that marketing grew in popularity as a management function was part of the problem. As a staff function, marketing would always be a cost center, not a profit maker. And by bunching the responsibility for customers into one staff department, other managers were freed to focus on their own narrow domains, knowing that someone else had been delegated the messy tasks of worrying about end consumers. As one marketing historian points out, most CEOs have had a hard time putting the customer first, even if they have said they will. The continued emphasis on return on investment and quarterly earnings per share quickly communicates to the rest of the organization the real yardsticks against which they will be evaluated and rewarded.[6] Under these pressures, the exuberant hurricane of renewed interest in "the market" was downgraded to the routine, and often marginalized, exercise of marketing.

THE QUALITY MOVEMENT

In the 1980s the rapid advance of global competition caught many U.S. and European industries by surprise as consumers rejected their products in favor of Japanese imports they regarded as superior in quality. Those shocks led to a decade-long emphasis, especially in manufacturing companies, on "total quality management" as the newest and best route back to the end consumer. The new quality "paradigm" was referred to as a "market-in" orientation in which every effort would be made to internalize customer preferences.[7] "Quality circles" quickly became standard practice for *Fortune* 500 companies, though, as one scholar of the movement observed, "they were totally divorced from any strategic corporate initiatives and certainly didn't challenge fundamental beliefs and objectives."[8]

As quality circles failed to deliver on the goals of the movement, they rapidly lost popularity. Managers turned to more comprehensive approaches to quality, the most popular of which was the Crosby method, designed by Phil Crosby, a former vice president of quality for ITT. His 1979 book, *Quality Is Free*, was intended to legitimate quality concepts by translating them from the Japanese context into a distinctly American approach. Crosby set up his own training institute, and by 1985 his firm was grossing $20 million a year. In 1990, some 20,000 managers attended his training programs, paying a total of $84 million for the privilege. All in all, managers from more than 1,500 companies had received Crosby training by that time.[9] In 1992, a Boston Consulting Group study concluded that companies were paying out $750 million annually to 1,500 third-party providers of advice and materials on quality improvement.[10]

In spite of this enormous level of effort, results were questionable. In 1992, a survey by Arthur D. Little of 500 U.S. manufacturing and service companies found that only one-third of their total quality programs were considered to have "a significant impact" on competitiveness. Another survey by A.T. Kearny of more than 100 U.K. firms found that only 10 percent believed their quality programs had yielded "tangible results." The U.S. electrical utility company Florida Power & Light was the first non-Japanese company to win the Deming Prize for quality work in 1989. It had 85 full-time quality employees, 1,900 quality teams involving three-quarters of its workforce, and a rigorous quality-review system. But according to FP&L's own managers, the improvements in customer service were trivial, especially when compared to the magnitude of the firm's quality effort. By 1992, a new head of quality had dismantled the department and disbanded the quality teams in order to refocus the firm on "the customer." "Customers now count for everything," he vowed.[11]

In his exhaustive study of the quality movement, sociologist Robert Coles documents the new activities, relationships, practices, and forms of discourse that eventually helped American managers to institutionalize and routinize quality procedures and a quality-oriented mentality. He also observes the many ways in which this process of institutionalization fell short of the original "market-in" goals of the quality movement. "Given the enormous quality challenge facing many manufacturing firms during the early 1980s and the looming sense of crisis," he wrote, "it is crucial to understand how managers looking for radical solutions to their problems ended up implementing very conservative ones."[12] Coles's research found that even quality zealots determined to make radical change found they lacked a supportive culture. The only argument they had that carried any clout among their peers was the notion that the cost of nonconformance to quality standards was typically 20 percent of total operating costs. Here was a justification that went straight to the bottom line and met with far less resistance. As a result, many quality efforts devolved into the idea that "change" meant getting employees to follow agreed-upon standards and procedures more assiduously.

What happened to the end consumer in all of this? As Coles observed, the logic that had finally won the day had a serious blind spot: "You could have a perfectly conforming product in which customers had little interest because it was the wrong product. . . . Managers ended up setting the rules for the agreed upon requirements . . . using traditional criteria and without strong efforts to meet external customer needs."[13] Despite improvements in quality, the call for revolution had become one more turn around the clock face, as conformance to standards became the hallmark of effective quality practices, and once again the end consumer was left waiting for the next round of rediscovery.

REENGINEERING

There wasn't long to wait. The concept of reengineering was introduced to the public in a 1990 *Harvard Business Review* article by Michael Hammer[14] and was most prominently elaborated in a 1993 book he coauthored with James Champy, *Reengineering the Corporation*.[15] They defined reengineering as a radical reinvention of the corporation, indeed a "reversal of the Industrial Revolution."[16] That radical reinvention was meant to be conducted from the "outside in," with an orientation toward the marketplace and the needs of customers. "Reengineering ignores what is and concentrates on what should be," they intoned.[17] It demanded a "fundamental rethinking and radical design of business processes to achieve dramatic improvements in critical, contemporary measures of performance, such as cost, quality, service, and speed."[18]

Hammer and Champy stressed that each customer counts and that reengineering required employees who "deeply believe that they work for their customers, not their bosses."[19] "It isn't about making patchwork fixes," they insisted. "It does mean abandoning long-established procedures and looking afresh at the work required to create a company's product or service and deliver value to the customer."[20] Hammer argued that strict command-and-control leadership and the leverage offered by new information technologies would make it possible to drastically reduce bureaucracy and with it administrative overhead by as much as 75 percent.[21] Statements like "those who are deliberately trying to obstruct the reengineering effort . . . need the back of the hand"[22] and "don't try to forestall reengineering; if senior management is serious about reengineering they'll shoot you"[23] represent only a tiny sample of Hammer's typical exhortations on behalf of strong leadership. He predicted that market-oriented, technology-enabled teams would replace middle-management hierarchies in an all-new, streamlined, process-based organization, as a result of this "clean slate," "top-down" change program.

While many researchers have acknowledged that reengineering drew on earlier managerial techniques, in the early 1990s it appeared to be an idea whose time had come. In a 1993 survey of 224 North American senior executives, reengineering emerged as the most important issue facing managers, and 72 percent of those surveyed had a program already underway in their organizations.[24] The major consultancies rapidly expanded their practices in this area. As early as 1993, a senior partner at Andersen Consulting was quoted as saying, "God bless Mike Hammer," after their consultancy work in "business process reengineering" that year yielded worldwide company revenues of $700 million.[25] A 1994 survey of U.K. firms showed that about 60 percent were planning or already undertaking reengineering activity.[26] That year, U.S. businesses were estimated to have spent about $30 billion on reengineering, with plans underway for spending an additional $50 billion by 1996. By 1995, more than 80 percent of the *Fortune* 500 companies had introduced some form of reengineering activities.[27]

By the second half of the 1990s, though, new studies routinely suggested that 70 percent of reengineering efforts had failed. Champy himself indicated that $20 billion of the $30 billion spent on reengineering in 1994 was invested in programs that were likely to fail.[28] In a 1995 interview, he complained that too many companies had failed to get the focus right. "What they've done is to do what they have always done: taken an internal view of the process. . . . Companies will plaster the walls of their offices with detailed process charts and sit and stare at the walls to find where it is they might save some money or reduce some time or improve quality instead of reengineering from the outside in. . . . You have to go to the marketplace. You have to talk to people who are your customers. . . . Then we look back into our company and identify the processes . . . that actually will create some different business results."[29]

Here, of course, was a description of the quicksand of organizational narcissism. It explained precisely the way in which one great company, Levi Strauss, badly lost its way in the reengineering process.

In the late 1980s and early 1990s it was not only an economic powerhouse but widely regarded as a model of progressive employee-centered management.[30] Employees enjoyed good food, beautiful fitness facilities, endless cappuccinos, flexible hours, generous pay and benefits, casual Fridays before they were de rigueur, and principled managers. It appeared to be about as far from the "us" vs. "them" General Motors–style corporate culture as one could get.

Many Levi Strauss watchers believed that as a privately held company (it was taken private in a leveraged buyout in 1985), free from the demands of declaring quarterly earnings, it would be able to make the high-quality decisions that would ensure its long-term success. At first glance it would seem that private ownership could have paved the way to eliminate or at least diminish the transaction crisis. Without the constant pressure of public shareholders and their claims on wealth, it should have been easier to reach across the boundaries of the standard enterprise logic to connect in new ways with end consumers and enable the realization of relationship value. But even private ownership did not alter the standard enterprise logic, with its economic assumptions and inward focus.

In 1990 Levi's first convened the group known as CSSC (Customer Service and Supply Chain) committee, intended to serve as a platform for critically reviewing the firm's supply chain and ability to serve its business customers. The company's visionary chief information officer, Bill Eaton, saw the CSSC as the wedge that would initiate a substantial "reengineering" of the firm's business processes in order to make it dramatically more responsive to its retailers and end consumers.[31] An early meeting of the committee was opened with drumrolls, fanfare, and high hopes, until one of the most senior managers at the table stood up to pronounce, "I don't see why we even need this effort; we're already the best."[32] That sour note was an early clue to a process that would be doomed from inception as it too fell hostage to the ravenous forces of organizational narcissism.

By 1999 Levi Strauss had laid off one-third of its workforce and announced plans to close twenty-two plants and slash 30 percent of those remaining—another 5,900 jobs. That made a total of twenty-nine plants and 16,310 jobs eliminated since 1997.[33] In March 1999, the company also began a well-publicized search for new senior managers. The brief to the headhunters was to find outsiders, who would bring objectivity to their analyses and be able to lead real change.[34] In 1998 sales had dropped 13 percent. *Fortune* magazine estimated that since another leveraged buyout in 1996 the company's market value had shrunk from $14 billion to $8 billion in 1999.[35]

What went wrong? Certainly Levi Strauss paid a price for a noble effort to maintain U.S. domestic manufacturing in an industry where virtually all competitors were sourcing from lower-cost offshore plants. But that accounts for only a small piece of the puzzle. To find some of the other pieces one must return to the CSSC committee and what had seemed to be the right venture at the right time. The committee had eventually agreed upon two major goals: First, they wanted to reduce the fifteen months it took to bring a new product to market down to three months; second, they sought to reduce the time needed to restock a pair of jeans into a retail outlet from three weeks to seventy-two hours. By June 1993, some 200 of the company's best people, joined by another 100 Arthur Andersen consulting employees, began designing a new supply chain. High-level middle managers assigned to the project left their own groups without leadership, even as their colleagues were forced into double duty on the work left behind.

The CSSC group commandeered an entire floor of the headquarters building. They quickly developed an identity as missionaries and zealots, proselytizing revolutionary change. "It created huge battle lines," Levi Strauss's COO told *Fortune* magazine. "There were Moonies and there were nonbelievers, and they avoided each other and said bad things about each other. But there was no way to get out of it. It was like quicksand." The CSSC committee expanded its charter to redesign jobs throughout the company. More than 600 new job descriptions were written, and people had to reapply for their positions. Many employees broke down in distress; others quit.

"Everything had to go into a corporate process, so nothing ever got resolved," former Levi Strauss executive Robert Siegel later told *Fortune*, in language that echoed William Whyte's managers a half-century earlier. "Almost half my time was spent in meetings that were absolutely senseless." By the time the board of directors put an end to the project in 1995, the reengineering team's budget had ballooned by 70 percent to $850 million. J.C. Penney, Levi Strauss's biggest customer, reported that in the fall of 1998, Levi Strauss delivered its all-important back-to-school line forty-five days late. As for restocking basic product, Penney's standard in 1998 was twenty days, while Levi Strauss's average that year was twenty-seven days. Tom Kasten, a capable and intelligent executive who had headed the Levi Strauss manufacturing operations for women's wear before being tapped to head up the reengineering effort, reflected: "I don't think we fully accomplished anything, to be honest."[36]

Many customers agreed. One put it this way: "I've sold Levi's in my retail store for 20 years. . . . Levi's stayed the same, never recognizing the market change and fashion overhaul that was occurring. So as Levi's showed up at J.C. Penney and Sears, the demand died, and the name was not the 'instant sale' it once was. Now Levi's is closing plants and laying off thousands of Americans and going overseas for production. This is a perfect example of American businesses' arrogance, ignoring the market, ignoring the needs of wholesale customers, and ignoring the insight and fashion trends of its core customers. It's no fluke when a company like Levi has more than 40% of the denim market and the share dwindles to less than 20%. And it's not due to labor costs. It's due to arrogance and ignorance."[37]

To be fair, there was nothing ignorant about Levi Strauss's managers. On the contrary, they were probably one of the most intelligent, sensitive, principled, and talented management groups in the world. In fact, what makes Levi Strauss a worthy example is that it was a highly respected and successful company run by brilliant people. But even their extraordinary talents did not protect them from being engulfed by the standard enterprise logic and its inward focus. In fact, their very intelligence drove them to execute that logic better than anyone else, and in the end it was the logic itself that doomed them.

In fact, as more research emerged on reengineering it became clear that the whole effort was, more often than not, a disaster for the individual end consumer. Careful analyses of reengineering efforts show that change agents paid little attention to organization politics, what we have called the "deep social structure" of managerial capitalism, or to the wider economic frameworks in which managers operate. As a result, middle managers found ways to torpedo or resist the incursion of the reengineers. Where reengineering did produce results, they were almost entirely in the realm of cost-cutting and other resource reductions.[38] Reengineering had quickly become a cover for a dramatic swing of the managerial pendulum toward a vast undertaking in corporate downsizing that left fewer employees doing more work, experiencing more stress, and leaving more customers "on hold."[39] A review of seventy-nine case studies from the reengineering literature found that only 25 percent of the companies studied said that they had undertaken reengineering because of customer demands or with any sort of customer benefit in sight.[40]

Not even the paroxysm of spending and disappointment associated with reengineering could bring closure to the century-long pastime of rediscovering the end consumer. In a special issue dedicated to the subject of "The Tough New Consumer" during the winter of 1993, *Fortune* magazine warned its readers, "Instead of choosing from what you have to offer, the new consumer tells you what he wants. You figure out how to supply it."[41] And in a 1996 report called "Rediscovering the Customer," the Conference Board trumpeted the news:

In the past several years, intensifying competition has awakened many companies to the fact that satisfying customers may not be enough. Equally important is the need to retain customers and attract new ones by providing "value." Customer value is the outcome of a process that begins with a business strategy anchored in a deep understanding of customer needs. . . . For many companies, this new awareness of the need to deliver customer value is a natural extension of their experience with Total Quality Management. For others, it is an urgent new initiative focused on keeping pace with or pulling ahead of marketplace demands.[42]

Once again, "market-oriented" champions, now armed with new concepts such as "mass customization," "one-to-one marketing," and electronic "personalization," threw themselves at the barbed wire surrounding the organization, intent on transforming the business practices that had erected those barriers in the first place.

MASS CUSTOMIZATION

Many of the original ideas behind mass customization are commonly ascribed to business consultant Stan Davis's 1987 book, *Future Perfect*.[43] During the late 1980s, there was already a general belief that new information technologies applied to manufacturing and engineering were opening the way to a degree of customization unprecedented in most industries since the logic of mass production had established its dominance. But it was Davis who linked this new general capability to an opportunity to connect more effectively with the end consumer. His reasoning stemmed from an important, though unelaborated, insight: The "individual customer" was the building block for the market in the "new economy."[44] That insight, perhaps because of the lack of analysis preceding it, immediately yielded to an assumption. Davis asserted that the individual would become a source of wealth creation only as the "ultimate logic of internal differentiation" drove companies from strategies based on mass markets, to market segmentation, to "units of one." "In the same way that segments and niches are reached on a mass basis," he wrote, "individuals can now be reached on a basis that is simultaneously mass and customized."[45]

In this linear march toward increased product variety, the individual remained a formal abstraction "out there." In order to provide the varied and unique products that these individuals supposedly wanted, companies would once again have to focus "in here" to develop manufacturing and service technologies capable of producing variety at the same low costs that mass production had achieved. There was little analysis of the nature of demand for mass customization. It was simply assumed that because individuals were unique, they would want unique, "customized" products. The focus thus remained under the lamppost, trained on products and how to produce them. Despite its call for "revolution" and "transformation," mass customization was in perfect consonance with the standard enterprise logic and its internal focus on organization space.

The mass-customization model was further developed in a 1993 book called *Mass Customization*, by Joseph Pine.[46] Once again, organizations were called upon to rediscover the now "heterogeneous" customer. And as in Davis's writing, it was assumed that the individuality of the new consumer would be satisfied by increased product variety and more tailored service. True to the inward focus of the standard enterprise logic, most of Pine's discussion concerned the new manufacturing principles and organization structures that would contribute to customer responsiveness. Successful mass customization called for nothing less than the "total transformation of the organization" from the "tightly integrated networks that form the backbone of the continuous improvement organization" to a collection of "loosely linked autonomous modules" that are constantly reconfigured in response to customer demands."[47] The mass-customization organization was "integrated," "dynamic," and "flexibly specialized." It relied on the "integration of thinking and doing." It required every function, unit, and person to be focused on the individual customer, as each does "whatever is necessary to develop, produce, market, and deliver low-cost customized products or services." All functions must "reach out to customers," he urged.[48]

Despite the individual end consumer's status as *the* causal element in the whole argument for a shift to mass customization, Pine offered almost no analysis of that consumer.[49] He asserted that demand had become "fragmented," resulting in "market turbulence," "unstable and unpredictable" demand levels, "uncertain needs/wants," "heterogeneous desires," and "quickly changing needs/wants." As he put it in a 1993 article, "Leaders of mass-customization organizations never know exactly what customers will ask for next. All they can do is strive to be more prepared to meet the next request."[50]

In fact, if just about everything about the "new demand" seemed uncertain, unpredictable, and quixotic, it probably had more to do with the methods of perception than with the real people at the far end of the commercial solar system. It is difficult to understand those new needs from the perspective of organization space. Yet Pine had tacitly adopted the perspective of the standard enterprise logic, from which demand factors are remotely perceived and imperfectly assessed. It is likely that the "new uncertainty" and "instability" Pine ascribed to end consumers would have been more accurately construed as the "new confusion" of producers, as their aims and practices had become increasingly less relevant to the new individuals.

By 1996, a review of mass-customization efforts concluded that the real trend set into motion by the new techniques was not from standardization toward customization, but rather from standardization and from customization toward a middle range of what is called "customized standardization."[51] Modular design and modular production had made it possible to specify architectural features in a high-rise building, mayonnaise on a hamburger, the readings in a textbook, the configuration of a computer system, or the color of an automobile and the size of its engine—all at prices that were generally competitive with pure mass production.[52]

When such variations can be achieved cost-effectively, they probably do constitute an improvement for end consumers who know their own tastes and want to take the time to specify them. But they do not fundamentally alter the standard enterprise logic or the distance it describes between producers and consumers. Scholars and business analysts alike have also begun to question how deep and widespread the demand for customized products really is.[53] While some examples of customized standardization apply to significant consumer durables such as computer systems and automobiles, most are in the realm of novelty products like CDs, soap, cookies, cosmetics, fragrances, greeting cards, and running shoes.[54] Many analysts have noted that it takes time, focus, and perseverance for a person to go through the steps of customizing a product. As we have seen, one of the hallmarks of the new individual is the stress created by the shrinkage of discretionary time. The question arises, is this really how the new individual wants to spend the little free time she has? For example, the online customization of Barbie dolls was a media favorite in its coverage of mass customization, until it was eliminated by Mattel—only 0.2 percent of the people who took the time to go through the painstaking customizing process actually purchased the doll because they were too young to have a credit card. Similar dropout rates have been observed in the online customization of beauty products.[55]

As careful case studies began to emerge, they revealed the ways in which the standard enterprise logic laid siege to mass customization's initial aim of customer responsiveness. For example, a study of one IBM division revealed that managers were reluctant to offer custom modules of their products and services for fear that customers would no longer choose the more comprehensive, and more expensive, standard packages.[56] Others reported conflicts between the goal of manufacturing variety and the "lean production" approaches that had been adopted to increase manufacturing efficiencies.[57] These findings were echoed in detailed studies of the "factory of the future" that suggested the ways in which the new impetus toward manufacturing variety became embroiled in the time-honored efforts of manufacturing managers to control labor; reduce lead times, inventory, and direct operating costs; realize higher rates of machine utilization; and emphasize economies of scale rather than scope.[58]

Similarly, a team of Belgian researchers led one of the few larger-scale empirical studies to consider the effects of the new production techniques, generally known as flexible specialization, designed to respond to fragmented markets with increased product variety. They concluded that the amazing new levels of production flexibility were not accomplished by integrating "thinking and doing," establishing "autonomous teams," or creating a "boundaryless organization" with widely diffused customer contact and responsibility, as Pine and others had advocated. Instead, these organizations achieved their goals through "the more intensive control of the overall production flow made possible by information technology, in which all parts have to switch simultaneously like cogs in a cogwheel." The "new manufacturing" turned out to be another "extension of scientific management, as the process of standardization includes not merely the execution of predetermined tasks, but also the frequent changeovers between them."[59] The initial impetus to reach out to the individual end consumer was mired in a struggle for acceptance as a low-cost, high-variety, tightly controlled manufacturing strategy.

The mass-customization movement quickly fell prey to the syndrome of the "horseless carriage," in which a remarkable invention (for example, the automobile) is made comprehensible and acceptable through its containment within an old framework (for example, a horsedrawn carriage). But comprehension and acceptance come at a price. When they were considered to be replacements for the horsedrawn carriage, the early runabouts and touring cars never demonstrated their utility as a truly new mode of transportation.[60] Only when Henry Ford recast the automobile as part of a new pattern—a wholly new form of transportation capable of outperforming a team of horses but within the financial reach of the ordinary person—was its explosive potential unleashed.[61]

In the case of mass customization, an important new idea about individuals as the building blocks of the new economy was made acceptable and accessible by an immediate integration into the old framework of the standard enterprise logic, in which value is created in organization space through low-cost products and services. The new idea was intended to transform the old framework, but as in the case of the horseless carriage, the old framework submerged and fatally limited the new idea. Gradually it became clear that mass customization was a manufacturing strategy that could be quite significant under certain product and market conditions. It was not, however, a vehicle for comprehensive transformation, let alone for integrating the individual end consumer into the center of the commercial solar system. In short, it was no match for the reproductive power of the standard enterprise logic.

RELATIONSHIP MARKETING

"Relationship" marketing and "one-to-one" marketing have ridden a parallel wave to mass customization and with a similar aim: the rediscovery of end consumers with a panoply of new marketing approaches intended to integrate them into the producer's orbit and ensure their ongoing loyalty. Introduced in the late 1980s by the Boston Consulting Group (BCG) and popularized in the early 1990s by marketing consultants such as Regis McKenna, Martha Rogers, and Don Peppers, relationship marketing and its cousins signified a resurgence of interest in marketing and what it could contribute to stronger "relationships" between sellers and buyers.[62] Unraveling the reasoning and practices behind relationship marketing reveals the ways in which, like mass customization, it was a prisoner of the standard enterprise logic from the very start.

Relationship marketing began with an important but once again unelaborated insight into the centrality of the individual in the late-century marketplace. As two BCG consultants put it back in 1989, "Ten years ago marketers discovered they could narrow their focus and create products for specific customer segments. Now a segment can be trimmed down to an individual."[63] This insight did not emerge from an analysis of social changes and the markets they produce, but rather from an interest in exploiting new technical capabilities. First, there were the rapidly diminishing price of data storage, the proliferation of data-capture opportunities through electronic point of sale, bar-coding, and loyalty cards, and the increasing ease and sophistication of data-management and analysis tools. This made it possible to collect and store customer data in previously uneconomic quantities and refine them down to the level of a single customer. These trends, already strong in the late 1980s, continued to develop at a rapid clip. In addition, the Internet provided a powerful new and inexpensive channel for amassing already digitized customer data. For example, in 1989 it cost $15 to store one megabyte of customer information; by 2001 that was down to a mere 15 cents.[64]

Second, the proponents of one-to-one marketing insisted that their approach was the result of a "technological discontinuity" that would "compel" businesses to compete in a new way. The technology in question was that of marketing media. The old mass-media approaches were being supplanted by new media that were "individually addressable," interactive, and inexpensive. Peppers and Rogers had come to the conclusion that "totally individualized media would not only make totally individualized marketing possible, it would *require* it."[65] As in Stan Davis's formulation, there seemed to be an inevitable march—driven by new technologies and understood from the perspective of organization space—from mass markets, to segmented markets, to "segments of one."

New technologies shaped the early formulations of relationship marketing in another important way. The programmability of the new information technologies was understood as the source of unprecedented product variety and consumer choice. Even without the added spin of mass customization, product lines were already exploding into scores of variations aimed at every conceivable consumer segment. Between 1985 and 1989, the number of new products grew by 60 percent to an all-time high of 12,055 per year.[66] Even venerable Tide detergent, which had served its market steadfastly for nearly forty years, had by 1984 begun to morph into a variety of new identities: unscented, with bleach, liquid, ultra. This explosion of choice was occurring during exactly the same time frame that the new realities of global competition were finally beginning to be absorbed by business executives.

For those watching these trends, it seemed clear that customers confronted by this new cornucopia of choice would no longer be won over by mass-market offerings alone. Instead, it was believed, they would seek products that appealed to their individuality. Global competition assured that there would be more than enough to choose from. In this fierce new marketplace, marketing gurus warned that business as usual would not suffice. Companies needed to establish "unique positions" in the marketplace.[67] This positioning was no longer simply a matter of clever advertising—it required much more. As Regis McKenna put it, "In a world where customers have so many choices, they can be fickle. This means modern marketing is a battle for customer loyalty. Positioning must involve more than simple awareness of a hierarchy of brands and company names. It demands a special relationship with the customer."[68]

Peppers and Rogers underscored the urgency of this new approach. Forging a "relationship" with a customer was said to be a firm's last best hope for protecting margins on its own products or services. "One-to-one relationships" were to be the arena in which producers learned more about their customers in order to customize, however trivially, their offerings. Since the whole point of customization was that it entailed little or no additional cost to producers, the way was cleared, at least conceptually, for companies to buy individual loyalty at mass-market prices. This was a critical piece of the equation for retaining, or even increasing, margins. "Now, even if a competitor offers the same type of customization and interaction," they gloated, "your customer won't be able to get back to the same level of convenience until he reteaches the competitor what he's already spent time and energy teaching you."[69]

In other words, relationship marketing and its one-to-one cousin were from the start strategies to limit consumer choice. They were intended to erect "barriers of inconvenience,"[70] which would raise the cost to the customer of switching from one producer to another, whether or not that was in the consumer's best interests. While customization could be achieved on the cheap—Peppers and Rogers assured their readers that "you can use mass customization to reduce your costs"[71]—the cost to the consumer of defection would be high. "Loyalty" was to be the barometer of these switching costs. The intent, however dressed up in Sunday clothes, was not to support the end consumer but to make sure "they" buy "our" stuff and *only* "our" stuff for as long as possible. But, as we saw in the discussion of little murders, when the economic equation of "cheap for dear" fails and the cost of servicing the relationship rises, the so-called relationship can quickly revert to relationship mimicry.

It is not surprising that relationship marketing concealed this zero-sum game between producers and individual end consumers. Because these strategies continued to revolve around a single firm's products or services, more choice for the end consumer had to mean less revenue for "us." This predicament underscores the fact that the new approach never challenged the standard enterprise logic. Once again, an important new insight about individuals was quickly packaged in the commercial status quo, despite a blizzard of oratory about paradigm shifts and discontinuity. As in the case of the horseless carriage, the new idea was lodged in the old framework of the standard enterprise logic that focuses on products and services, and places producers' interests above all else.

And as in the case of the horseless carriage, the conditions that ensured its acceptance also defined its limitations. That is why a search of the literature for examples of one-to-one relationship practices reveals nothing that most people would regard as having anything to do with a relationship. Instead, there are marketing tactics and technology tools designed and launched from organization space. Most rely on database technologies to integrate and track customer data. These efforts may result in personalized marketing letters, using the customer's name during a call-center transaction, price incentives, personalized Web content, frequent-user programs, preferred-customer programs, customer-referral benefits, invitations to product-oriented parties and seminars, or customization efforts, from "customized standardization" of a product to tailored billing, packaging, or delivery.[72] Such efforts may produce benefits for sellers. They may even shield some buyers from the worst excesses of the transaction crisis. They remain, however, a solar system away from the dreams of today's individuals and their expression in the new markets for deep support.

In fact, relationship marketing could have been more accurately labeled "convenience marketing." As Peppers and Rogers exhorted their readers, "Learning relationships . . . do not depend on emotional attachments. . . . Emotional attachments are not the primary mechanism at work in securing customer loyalty. Convenience is."[73] And "convenience" is a consequence of data banks, analysis tools, and reliable operations. As technology sustains the strategy of cheap for dear, end consumers do not have "relationships" with people, but with databases, Web sites, and so on. These interactions must retain their focus on selling the firm's products and services if they are to be cost-efficient, which further ensures that the borderlands leading to individual space are never traversed. As Peppers and Rogers caution, "To make interactions more efficient, drive them into more automated, cost efficient channels. Push call-center interactions toward your Web site, and push personal sales calls more to the call center. To improve the effectiveness of each interaction, gather only relevant information."[74]

A new type of software product known as customer relationship management (CRM) quickly rose to the technology challenge. Such systems were intended to consolidate all the transaction information about each customer so that it could be universally accessed by anyone from sales representatives to call-center operators. In theory, the software provided managers with new ways to analyze customer transactions. By 2000, the Gartner Group estimated CRM sales at $20 billion. Implementation costs probably added another $30 billion. Sales climbed to $25 billion in 2001 and were expected to top $64 billion by 2005.[75] The research group International Data

Corporation predicted an annual compounded growth rate for CRM products of 29 percent between 1999 and 2004, significantly outpacing the information technology market as a whole.[76] The systems are expensive. Software alone tends to be priced at $3 million and up for a large company, with additional expenses for consultants, time, and training.

Not surprisingly, given the hegemony of transaction economics, the rationale for these pricey systems has tended to rely on the promise of cost reduction. Firms seek to cut the cost of acquiring new customers and retaining old ones. They want their call centers to handle more calls per day, with more automation and less personnel, while reducing the duration of each call. But CRM systems have become notorious for their complexity and the time-consuming nature of their installation. Much of the difficulty revolves around social-psychological barriers associated with the standard enterprise logic. For example, division heads balk at relinquishing customer data. Employees are not convinced of the system's utility and anyway lack the training to use it properly.[77] According to the *Financial Times*, CRM applications have among the highest failure rates of all corporate information technology projects.[78] In 2001, one research group reported a 55 percent to 75 percent failure rate of CRM projects. Another survey of 226 CRM users in 2001 reported that one-quarter saw no significant improvement in company operations, while half experienced only minor improvement.[79] The Gartner Group estimated CRM failures at 50 percent.[80] It would appear that CRM systems are failing to create value, even within the limited terms of transaction economics.

Beyond the failures of CRM, relationship management clearly falls wide of the mark when it comes to rediscovering the end consumer.[81] Researchers interested in assessing relationship marketing report on the wide gap that exists between the simplistic bait that companies offer—personally addressed direct-mail offers, frequent-purchase programs—and the real experiences of end consumers. One set of interviews with people who participated in such "relationships" found that 81 percent were motivated by cost savings. Sixteen percent mentioned liking the personal recognition afforded by programs such as those based on frequent purchase. Seven percent cited the added convenience of shopping. Not a single respondent cited any interest in reducing the number of choices available to them.[82] When *Marketing* magazine convened a senior panel of consultants to debate relationship marketing, they noted that it was held back by a number of obstacles, especially the reality that "what is meant to be a dialogue with customers is all too often one way."[83]

When another team of researchers interviewed consumers about their responses to relationship-marketing techniques, they concluded, "Relationship marketing is powerful in theory but troubled in practice." They wondered why "the very things that marketers are doing to build relationships with customers are often the things that are destroying those relationships." In considering relationship marketing from the end consumer's perspective, they noted the flood of "personalized" advances from companies that look like meaningless junk mail to most end consumers. Many people received "personal" overtures from a company that were clearly concocted by a computer system and were perceived as irrelevant to their real lives. Customers were badgered by companies for more personal data, while they saw no return on their investment of time and information, and they complained about the "one-way" nature of the so-called relationship. As one end consumer told the researchers, "Companies claim that they're interested in the customer. But the focus is not on the customer—it's on the company." Customers complained about the impossibility of getting their names deleted from mailing lists. They reported being annoyed by the mindless proliferation of products in almost every category, from cereals to painkillers.

The researchers concluded that the end consumer's experience was characterized by loss of control, vulnerability, stress, and victimization. Newly acquired products were more often a source of frustration than of pleasure. They found that consumers were more likely to view companies as enemies than as allies and that the presumptuous, largely impersonal techniques of relationship marketing had exacerbated and intensified these feelings. "Relationship marketing . . . has sent us further afield. . . . Consumers don't welcome our advances," they warned, instead "they arm themselves to fight back."[84]

Once again, the very techniques touted as a solution to the transaction crisis only seemed to make things worse. Relationship marketing, like other innovations aimed at rediscovering the end consumer, did not venture beyond the light from the lamppost to challenge the fundamental assumptions of the standard enterprise logic or propose any alternative to it. Instead, it traded the power of its insights for easy acceptance within the terms of the old logic and so drew upon itself the fate of the horseless carriage.

Proponents of relationship marketing and the one-to-one concept, like those of mass customization, insist that shortfalls in their results are explained by a firm's failure to achieve the "transformational" change necessary to "truly" implement the new marketing approach. "It's impossible to simply 'strap on' a 1 to 1 marketing campaign and continue to do business in a traditional manner," counsel Peppers and Rogers.[85] "A true 1:1 marketing philosophy can't be implemented without integrating it into the entire organization. Your firm must embrace significant change, affecting virtually every department, division, officer, and employee, every product, and every function."[86] Others have emphasized the need for cross-functional alignment, observing that interactions with nonmarketing functions are probably the most significant determinants of whether a customer wants to keep doing business with a company.[87] Still others stress the notion that relationship marketing requires everyone in the firm to undertake a marketing approach. "Relationship marketing represents a fundamental transformation in approach from traditional marketing," admonishes one proponent, requiring new roles for managers, customers, and suppliers.[88] Blaming the inadequacy of transformational change might be a plausible explanation for limited results, were it not for one important issue: There is little evidence that business organizations operating under the monopoly of the standard enterprise logic can systemically transform themselves from within to create sustainable change. Any innovation packaged with fine print that conditions its success on such change must be regarded with some caution. An examination of transformational change efforts over the last thirty years shows just how elusive that goal can be.

ORGANIZATIONS DO NOT TRANSFORM THEMSELVES

Between the 1940s and the 1960s a new breed of social scientists emerged whose focus of interest was "the organization." From Elton Mayo to Douglas McGregor, their work began to uncover the social dimensions of the workplace and the other-than-rational organizational behaviors that formed its context.[89] For the first time, the workplace came to be viewed as more than an economic system. Gradually, it came to be understood as a complex social system, shaped by attitudes and values. These observers exhorted managers to improve communication with their workforce and to further develop their range of interpersonal skills.

By 1973, as the new society of individuals was gathering force, a report published by a task force to the U.S. secretary of health, education, and welfare called *Work in America* described the blue-collar blues, white-collar woes, and managerial malaise that seemed to have infected the entire labor force. It declared that just about everyone was alienated from their work and concluded that workers wanted to feel in control of their immediate environment and to feel that their work was important. The stagnating productivity, poor quality, and high levels of absenteeism and turnover that characterized the turbulent U.S. economy of the 1970s were blamed, in part, on this new alienation.

A new generation of social scientists and consultants, building on the work of their predecessors, developed an approach to "work reform" aimed largely at the now more educated manufacturing workforce. The new perspective migrated from academia to the factory floor, becoming the basis for a widespread effort to transform the workplace by reversing many of the fundamental axioms of the mass-production model of work organization. The sometimes implicit, sometimes explicit, goal was to increase productivity and ultimately competitiveness. Throughout the 1970s, social scientists and management consultants were invited to advise, design, and evaluate new forms of work organization that emphasized holistic task cycles, skill upgrading, varied task content, responsibility for results, regular feedback, and autonomy. Some called for self-managing work teams, participatory management, reduced levels of hierarchy, and organization-wide social system redesign.[90] Many of the efforts originally went under the banner of "quality of work life," which became known as a "movement." Later these innovations generally became known as "high-performance" work systems.

As had been the case throughout the twentieth century, corporations appeared to be more or less "normally" distributed in their ability to engage reforms.[91] There was a progressive minority of firms that invested a great deal of money in experimenting with new, plant-wide social systems design, often with the additional motive of keeping those plants union-free. Most firms adopted a more cautious approach, embracing discrete elements of the innovations, such as job enrichment or problem-solving teams or, later, quality circles. And then there was the group that clung to the status quo with ever-renewed fervor.

Yet even when companies made strong commitments to implementing innovative work arrangements, there were serious limitations. Only a small minority of firms institutionalized the new approaches to factory work, and even there, the new design principles rarely migrated beyond the walls of the factory. The rest of the firm continued as before, with managerial functions cleaving and multiplying at a prodigious rate. Most of the firms that did venture into the new approaches could not sustain them for long. Well-intentioned efforts were regularly undermined by turnover in top or plant-level management, poorly informed work-system designs, lack of middle-management commitment, acrimonious labor relations, and knee-jerk cost-reduction responses to short-term fluctuations in market conditions.[92]

By 1993, a careful study of "workplace transformation" surveyed 694 U.S. manufacturing establishments to determine the incidence of the new high-performance work practices.[93] Not surprisingly, the study reported that the companies most likely to adopt such practices were also most likely to be oriented toward the sort of managerial strategies that we have labeled "revenue enhancement," emphasizing skills, service, and quality over cost. The survey analysis concluded that about 35 percent of private-sector manufacturing establishments with fifty or more employees made use of the new approaches to plant-level work organization. However, closer inspection of the survey revealed that the standard for inclusion in that 35 percent was set very low. Employers were interviewed by phone and asked whether they used self-directed work teams, job rotation, employee problem-solving groups or quality circles, or total quality management. Employers were included in the 35 percent if they identified two out of these four already modest components. A simple ratcheting up of the bar to include three of the four elements reduced the percentage from 35 percent to 13 percent.[94] And as we have already seen, some of these innovations, such as quality circles, were destined to fade away almost as quickly as they appeared on the scene.

Most other surveys have come to a similar conclusion. A 1990 survey conducted by the Commission on the Skills of the American Workforce found that 80 percent of employers emphasized the importance of workers' attitudes and work ethic, while only 5 percent emphasized cognitive abilities and growing skill demands.[95] A 1991 study commissioned by the Secretary of Labor estimated that only about 10 percent of U.S. employers utilized aspects of the high-performance work organization model, despite growing data reflecting its superior returns in productivity and other outcomes related to a firm's competitiveness.[96] A study conducted by the American Society for Training and Development of its member firms also concluded that about 13 percent of firms had employed high-performance work systems. Based on such figures, it was calculated that only about 2 percent of U.S. workers would have had any exposure to such practices.[97]

Some researchers, puzzled by the apparent irrationality of the cycles of investment in and then rejection of innovation, have offered new ways of understanding the phenomenon, such as the psychology of fads ("They are doing it, so I should too") or the psychology of fashion trends ("The leaders are doing it, so I should too").[98] In a 1995 article, leadership expert John Kotter attempted to explain "why transformation efforts fail," citing his own observation that "few corporate change efforts have been successful." His answer was, not surprisingly, to improve the quality of change leadership.[99] In a 1998 essay, Harvard Business School professor Chris Argyris, a foundational thinker in management behavioral science, stated flatly, "Despite all the best efforts that have gone into fostering empowerment, it remains very much like the emperor's new clothes. . . . There has been no transformation in the workforce, and there has been no sweeping metamorphosis." He blamed managers who feel most comfortable with a command-and-control management model.[100]

After an extensive review of all the current surveys on the topic of high-performance work systems, two well-known labor economists determined that "linear movement from mass production to a unique successor is not evident from these surveys." They concluded that the increased efficiency of the new "high performance" approaches was not enough to encourage firms to migrate from the old mass-production model to the new high-performance one. "The institutional framework of the United States," they observed, "was developed to support the old mass-production system. . . . Now that the basis of competitive advantage in the advanced industrial economies has changed, U.S. economic development is constrained by the very institutions that previously assured its competitive success."[101]

Others have looked at the record of organizational transformation in a more general way. Their emphasis has been on progressive employment policies that enable a firm to attract and retain the best workers and thus enhance its competitiveness. These policies typically include flexible, family-friendly work arrangements, open and fair management practices, opportunities for education and career development, and generous benefits, perks, and amenities. The focus tends to center more on white-collar, managerial, and professional employees—knowledge workers—and less on the factory floor. Typically, these progressive employers are praised for being less hierarchical and political. They develop a spirit of community among employees, who work and play together as colleagues and friends. The problem is that such firms represent only a tiny fraction of the U.S. labor force. For example, in 1998, *Fortune* magazine began publishing an annual survey of the "100 Best Companies to Work For." In 1999 only forty-eight of the best companies to work for were listed in the *Fortune* 1000. The total employment of those forty-eight companies was somewhat short of 2.5 million, or only 8.42 percent of the total employment in the *Fortune* 1000.

Media reports tend to give the impression that whole industrial sectors, such as the high-tech sector, can be characterized by "new age" progressive employment practices. The numbers tell a different story. For example, in 1999, at the height of the high-tech boom, none of the best companies to work for that were also in the *Fortune* 1000 came from the "computer and data-services" sector. Those "best" companies that were related to high-tech accounted for only 0.27 percent of employment in computer peripherals, 1.97 percent of employment in computer software, and 6.52 percent of employment in computers and office equipment.[102] In 2000, the top 706 publicly traded U.S. Internet firms, generally hyped as progressive workplaces, employed only 971,500 people, fewer than the total employment of Wal-Mart that year, which was 1.1 million.[103]

Another problem with this approach takes us back to the swinging pendulum discussed in our exploration of the transaction crisis. Just as companies ricochet between resource-reduction and revenue-enhancement strategies, routinely changing their attitudes toward end consumers, they can just as quickly change their policies toward their own employees. When times are good and revenue enhancement is on the rise, firms want to attract the best people, invest in employee development, empower members to serve customers better, and all the rest. When economic retrenchment threatens markets and labor supply becomes more plentiful, many companies shift to resource reduction, which typically translates into layoffs, more control-oriented management practices, less investment for training and development, and less inclination to foster commitment. As the *Wall Street Journal* put it, "As much as executives bemoan sliding stock prices and slowing corporate profits, they are happy about one consequence of the economic slowdown. For the first time in years, they are not at the beck and call of employees' 'gimme more' demands."[104]

For example, sociologist Arlie Hochschild wrote an in-depth study of the "time bind" issue as it affected employees at a firm she called Amerco. That company had set up a Work-Life Balance Program to assist its employees, and the work of that program figured prominently in Hochschild's report. But in 1995, while Hochschild was still completing her study, Amerco began a reengineering process. Everyone was sent to workshops to learn about the fierce global competition that threatened Amerco. Next came downsizing: Employees were "de-hired," and the Work-Life program, along with many other progressive employee benefits, was eliminated.[105] Another emblematic example of the pendulum swing is the Silicon Valley software company PeopleSoft. In 1999, it was listed sixth on *Fortune*'s list of "100 Best Companies to Work For." But in 2000, the firm had vanished from the list.[106] A 78 percent stock dive, disappointing acquisitions, and top-management defections led to significant reversals for a company that was known for its "aggressively informal and sensitive corporate culture." Shortly after the manager for employee communications insisted that layoffs "could never happen at PeopleSoft" because "we are a family," 430 people were terminated— some by voice-mail message.[107]

We conclude that organizations do not transform themselves from within, at least not in any way that is sustainable. If the innovations aimed at rediscovering the end consumer depend upon such transformations, then this provides another way of accounting for their shortcomings. Why is transformation so elusive? Each of the explanations that we have reviewed has merit: failures of leadership, managers wedded to command and control, institutional barriers, short-term financial pressures. But each is also danger-ously incomplete. A more comprehensive explanation lies in the proposition that change in the deep structure of the organization cannot occur without change in the deep structure of the enterprise logic in which it must operate. This means that as long as the orbits of interest remain fixed, as long as value is assumed to be created inside the firm for shareholders at the expense of end consumers, as long as transaction economics institutionalizes these pre-suppositions on a daily basis, and as long as the forces of organizational nar-cissism remain in place, transformational change will remain an illusion. Organization critics, vendors, consultants, and idealists alike throw them-selves at the star called producers, the centerpiece of the commercial solar system. Perhaps occasionally they dent its crust, carving out a hill or valley. But none of this affects the star's position or trajectory as it continues to oc-cupy its century-old place of honor.

IF BOYS LIKED GIRLS BETTER, WOULD THEY BE RICHER?

One last place to look for evidence that firms are truly rediscovering their end consumers involves the culture of management and its male identifica-tion. In the first half of the twentieth century, that culture was enforced and refreshed by a sexualized contempt toward end consumers, considered to be primarily female. This contributed to organizational narcissism as it helped to define and maintain the distance between producers and consumers. Today, as we have seen, women are once again in the vanguard of the new individuated consumption. It is reasonable to suppose that a strong presence of women in management, and a more androgynous managerial culture, might also be associated with a new capacity to bridge the distance between producers and consumers, and even integrate end consumers into the pro-ducers' orbit. The underlying linkages between women's presence and role in management, the transaction crisis, the ignorance of relationship value, and the lost possibilities of wealth creation are difficult to track, because they are rarely illuminated. On occasion, though, it is possible to catch a glimpse of the connections among these phenomena, and these clues are tantalizing.

For example, a survey of women at the level of vice president or higher in *Fortune* 1000 companies asked, "Why should women be in charge?" Eighty-one percent agreed or strongly agreed with the reason that "women are a large part of the consumer base," and 93 percent agreed or strongly agreed because "women contribute a unique perspective."[108] The *Wall Street Journal* has linked the proliferation of cut-price furniture stores to the fact that women make 80 percent of furniture-purchasing decisions but are nearly absent from that industry's executive ranks.[109] Success in the industry depends upon predicting the colors and styles that will appeal to female consumers, but the men get it wrong so frequently that they end up with warehouses of inventory that must be sold at discount prices. In 1999, the board of the senior executive forum known as the American Furniture Manufacturers Association had forty-nine members, all male. Even the marketing director of La-Z-Boy, Inc., one of the nation's best-known furniture makers, which long resisted promoting women to top positions or recruiting them for its corporate board, was forced to concede: "We need a female perspective because we're dealing with a female customer."[110] The *Journal* reported on an ailing furniture company that finally hired a woman as vice president of marketing. Despite the firm's abysmal record in the marketplace, its CEO remained skeptical of the remedy. "We don't think having sawdust on your pants is all bad," he told a reporter. "All this warm and fuzzy stuff, and women, won't do anything for our shareholders."[111]

A similar disconnect was documented within the women's sportswear chain The Limited. In 1999, after reporting more than $90 million in operating losses, the company launched an internal campaign called WAR (Winning at Retail). The campaign included a lot of tough talk aimed at employees. The company newsletter provided "battle briefings," and store managers were flown each week to motivational "battle summits" where they were seated in order of their performance. But the campaign's centerpiece was a motivational video in which clips of graphic battle scenes—replete with exploding bombs, shells, and fallen bodies—were interspersed with those of executives exhorting their troops to war. "It is a war," the CEO told his employees, "and in wars people really do live and people do die." "Make the critical and key decisions effectively and efficiently . . . then move in for the kill," intoned another. Many employees complained about the approach, and some managers quit the chain, including Andrea Weiss, the well-known director of store operations. But the company was undeterred: "This is not a mission for people who need developing or the weak-hearted," an executive warned. In the meantime, analysts blamed The Limited's troubles on large, impersonal, out-dated stores and products that were no longer meaningful to the firm's end consumers. The Limited's executives, however, refused to invest in the stores until the business showed signs of improvement.[112]

A British historian has written a detailed analysis of the British advertising industry in the 1980s. His research revealed creative teams that functioned as "sites of male bonding, in which teamwork was secured through forms of homosociability. . . . Departments openly boasted that they contained outright misogynists." He carefully demonstrates the links between this internal masculine culture and a predominant advertising style that depicted women only in the roles of sex object and clotheshorse, "contemptuously ignoring femininity," as one frustrated magazine subscriber put it.[113]

In Stanford Business School professor Joanne Martin's in-depth account of a Silicon Valley high-tech company she called Link.com, the connections flash to the surface, if only briefly.[114] Through interviews and observations, she tells the story of an executive she calls Natalie Kramer, hired in 1989 as Link.com's vice president of marketing and the only woman on its executive team. Martin documents Natalie Kramer's efforts to conform to the masculine culture and its implicit expectations of her. The CEO made it clear that he did not like aggressive women (he called them "pushy broads"). She reigned in her language and tried not to appear too opinionated, working long hours and traveling, despite her young children.

It was clear, nevertheless, that Natalie did not fit the organization culture. She took exception to the "rape and pillage" language executives used to describe their moves against the competition. She spoke up against pay inequities and other unjust behavior toward women in the company. She went out of her way to hire more women and support their careers. Her quiet and humane management style contrasted with the angry outbursts and raised voices in the executive committee. "The culture was . . . very 'old boy,'" she reflected, "so, the dominant culture was one in which I was marginal. There were people in the organization who were threatened by me. . . . The behavior I was modeling was not behavior that my male colleagues on the executive staff were going to emulate." In spite of these difficulties, Natalie was able to see the ways in which her outsider status contributed to her success as a marketing professional:

> Sometimes if you are marginalized, or an outsider . . . you have a borderline identity that permits you to think outside the usual paradigms and make creative contributions. I really liked and understood our customers. I understood how to use symbols to communicate with them.

Maybe what I was able to do in marketing, and in positioning the company, was seen as creative because I didn't share the usual paradigms. I wasn't an engineer. I wasn't a man. I was drawn to and identified with our customers partly because I was an iconoclast like them.

Natalie was able to escape the centrifugal forces of organizational narcissism and connect with the firm's end consumers in a unique way. She paid a price to do so. Despite her accomplishments, she experienced years of social isolation and recognized how hard it was to have a lasting impact on deeply ingrained attitudes and practices. The other executives who helped the company ride the wave of the Silicon Valley high-tech boom never regarded the presence of women in general, or Natalie in particular, as in any way related to Link.com's performance. Within the terms of the standard enterprise logic, they may well have been correct.

Sociologists have long demonstrated that numbers make a difference in group life. The group that holds the majority determines the overall culture.[115] This continues to be the case for men and women in the corporate world, much as it was in 1977 when sociologist Rosabeth Moss Kanter published her well-known study *Men and Women of the Corporation*, and much as it was in 1920. There is ample evidence from a variety of industries and countries that women continue to be the extreme minority in most managerial groups, and as a result they continue to experience sexually charged patterns of separatism and exclusion that reinforce the prevailing values of the dominant masculine culture and its stance toward the end consumer.[116]

Readers of the *New York Times* who picked up a fat Sunday edition well into the first year of the new millennium may have been intrigued to find the front page of its "Money & Business" section covered with thirty-one passport-size photos of middle-aged men, thirty white, one of color. A closer inspection revealed that these thirty-one men represented the top management of one of the world's most respected corporations, General Electric. While in 1999 women accounted for only 11.9 percent of corporate officers in the *Fortune* 500, at GE that number turned out to be an even more modest 6.4 percent.[117] With a rapidly growing number of women graduating from colleges, business schools, and professional schools since the 1970s, there was a widespread expectation that the demographic profile of management, especially top management, would soon begin to change. GE was a powerful example that this was not the case.

In 1970, the U.S. Census found that one in six managers was a woman. By 1989, that proportion had shifted to two in five. Most women managers, however, remained concentrated in the lower and middle ranks. A 1990 *Fortune* magazine survey of the 799 largest service and industrial companies found only nineteen of the more than 4,000 highest-paid officers and directors were women. That's fewer than 0.05 percent. Of the next echelon down, only 5 percent were women.[118] Another survey at that time conducted by the research organization Catalyst found that fewer than 3 percent of the top executives in *Fortune* 500 companies were women.[119] In the United Kingdom, the numbers of women in lower- and middle-management ranks were fewer, around 16 percent, but there too women accounted for only about 3 percent to 5 percent of directors and senior executives.[120]

Further investigation of the surge in U.S. women managers from 17 percent to 40 percent between 1970 and 1989 revealed many interesting patterns. For example, in the 1970s and early 1980s, under the threat of oversight from the Equal Employment Opportunity Commission and the pressure of affirmative action regulations, some researchers reported a tendency for women's positions to be retitled in order to have them counted as "managerial."[121] Others noted a trend toward "resegregation," in which women were accepted into an occupational niche just as its skill requirements were diminishing and men were exiting to higher-paying jobs. Researchers found that the decline of an occupation's status generally began before women entered but was then reinforced by their presence.[122] This process had already occurred in other occupations, including clerical work, bookkeeping, and teaching. Now it was occurring within the ranks of lower-level managers. For example, one 1990 study documented this process in detail as it applied to bank branch managers.[123] Another substantial study published in 1992 found evidence of real, if slow, progress, but concluded that women "continued to trail their male counterparts in both earnings and authority," with "a long way to go" before they reached parity.[124]

As the 1990s progressed, there was more change in the sex composition of the hierarchy, though still at the lower and middle levels. Between 1993 and 1998, the number of women in management jobs increased by 29 percent, compared to a 19 percent increase for men. Closer inspection, however, revealed that women held only 7 percent of the "line" positions, where there is profit-and-loss responsibility. These are the jobs that routinely lead to executive promotion. It appeared that women were still being shuffled into staff jobs in areas like public relations and human resources.[125] Similarly, Catalyst found that the percentage of women corporate officers grew steadily from 8.7 percent in 1995 to 11.9 percent in 1999, but when the focus was narrowed to so-called clout titles—chairman, chief executive, vice chairman, president, chief operating officer, senior executive vice president, and executive vice president—the proportion dropped to 5.1 percent, up from 2.4 percent in 1995.[126] Pay disparity persisted. In 1983, women managers earned 64 percent of what men did; in 1998 that had grown to only 68 percent.[127] A team of labor economists found that the top executive compensation gender gap was around 45 percent. At least half of that was accounted for by the absence of women in these clout jobs. Another 15 percent was attributed to women's under-representation in large corporations where salaries are higher.[128]

A 2001 survey of corporate boards showed 12 percent female composition among large companies where public scrutiny is greatest, but only 5 percent at small companies.[129] Even these numbers, though, concealed an important pattern. When one looks strictly at the numbers of women "inside" directors on corporate boards—top executives promoted to board-level appointments and typically the source of future CEOs—the numbers fall dramatically. In 1987 there were ten such women on U.S. corporate boards in the *Fortune* 500. In 1997 there were eight, or just over 0.05 percent of all inside board member positions. Is the picture any different in small companies? During the same ten-year period the number of women serving as CEOs in *Inc.* 100 firms increased from zero to one. In fact, the number of *Inc.* 100 firms with any female board representation actually declined during that period, from 16.9 percent to 16.7 percent.[130]

The evidence suggests that these minority-majority dynamics are reflected in the culture of management. One recent study found that men's organizational commitment and job satisfaction were significantly reduced by the presence of women in the workplace and concluded that the fact that men preferred to work with other men went a long way toward explaining the inequality of the sexes in the workplace.[131] Other studies have found consistent patterns of men preferring male colleagues and the ways in which those attitudes marginalized women from formal as well as informal networks of coworkers.[132] Women managers have been found to experience significantly less interaction with executives compared to their male peers.[133] The interactions they do have are reported to be more problematic than those of their male counterparts. They are "tested" in a variety of informal ways to see if they are "man" enough to succeed in the organization, and then are often penalized for not being womanly.[134]

Sexual demographics may influence culture, but this is decidedly a two-way street. Masculine organizational cultures limit women's advancement, discourage their participation, and, in the end, cause many women to depart the scene altogether. Another Catalyst survey in 1997 asked male and female senior executives, "What prevents women from advancing to positions of corporate leadership?" The answers they received reveal sharp differences among men and women in their interpretation of the two-way street between culture and numbers. Eighty-two percent of the men cited the "lack of experience" among women as the key reason for lack of advancement, compared to only 47 percent of the female respondents. Sixty-four percent of men cited "not enough women in the pipeline," compared to only 29 percent of the women. When it came to an appraisal of the cultural barriers, the numbers were solidly reversed. Fifty-two percent of women cited "male stereotyping and preconceptions," compared to 25 percent of the men. Forty-nine percent of women cited "exclusion from informal networks," compared to 15 percent of men, and 35 percent of women cited "inhospitable corporate culture" compared to 18 percent of men.[135]

A follow-up survey revealed a significant number of women entrepreneurs citing "the glass ceiling" as their reason for leaving their former employers. In 1998 this study showed that 29 percent left their previous companies because of a glass ceiling, and another 22 percent said it was because they were not sufficiently challenged in their previous jobs. For those who remain in the corporate environment, however, their strategies for advancement tend to emphasize conformity and stealth. For example, women managers at GE formed a Women's Network only after they observed the "success" of such a group among the company's African-American managers. They were careful to steer the network's agenda away from matters explicitly related to sex and gender, such as exclusionary practices or work-family issues, for fear of further marginalization.[136] This fearful silence of women managers brings us back full circle to the individual end consumer, as the silence of one group mirrors and reinforces the lack of structured opportunities for voice that plagues the other.

THE PRODUCER GOES EXPLORING, AGAIN

The dawn of a new millennium finds the new individuals driving a new structure of consumption, convening new markets for deep support, and ferreting out what they need at the margins of the mainstream economy. Meanwhile, despite some surface turbulence, the other planets in the commercial solar system remain unperturbed, sailing serenely in their well-worn orbits.

In that system, producers' remoteness from end consumers is fixed by the standard enterprise logic, constrained by the assumptions of transaction economics and sustained by organizational narcissism. Billions of dollars have been spent on innovations aimed at bridging the frozen distance between producers and end consumers, but with little effect. This is because none of those efforts confronted the standard enterprise logic or developed an alternative to it.

Recall that the featured article in a 1923 *Saturday Evening Post* was titled "The Producer Goes Exploring to Find the Consumer." After what we have learned about the revolving door of consumer-oriented innovations, it should come as no surprise that producers are still "going exploring." Since 1988, spending on for-profit market research services has grown by an average of 9 percent each year. In 2000 alone, U.S. companies spent more than $5 billion on market research, and that number does not include either the hundreds of millions spent by government agencies and directed toward not-for-profit research groups or the many millions more spent in-house by firms.[137]

And there is a new and even more expensive twist. Today, companies like Procter & Gamble, American Express, Honda, Philip Morris, Toyota, AT&T, MTV, and many others, frustrated by traditional research techniques, are hiring anthropologists, ethnographers, filmmakers, and video specialists to seek out end consumers in their bedrooms, living rooms, kitchens, and bathrooms as if they were an undiscovered tribe, hidden for centuries in a faraway rain forest. Other "retail anthropologists" discern the "gimmicks" that draw shoppers into the most lucrative sections of a store.[138] One such "consumer anthropologist" plainly states the purpose of this undertaking: "Our goal is to put the consumer back into the equation." The anthropologists promise a deeper understanding of the end consumer's language, experience, and interests in order to improve the corporation's ability to market what it has to sell.[139] Typically, a company hires an ad agency, which in turn employs the anthropologists or has them on staff. As in the case of department store clerks, the new researchers are usually female, in order to enhance the connection with the all-important female end consumer.[140] Then the research—in the form of films, videos, live Web cams, interviews, and so on—is funneled back to marketing and product-development teams inside the firm so they can figure out the most effective marketing strategies for the products that are already on the shelves and in the pipeline.

In other words, after all the money that has been spent—on quality initiatives, reengineering, relationship marketing, and organizational transformation—all in the name of rediscovering the end consumer, the producer must still go exploring. More accurately, producers must hire yet another group of people—women—to bridge the distance for them. And in the end, the goal that drives the search for information has nothing to do with responding to the needs for sanctuary, voice, and connection. The goal is to uncover the secrets of consumption that can enhance the effectiveness of marketing products that exist or are slated for production. And so the pattern continues, marked by a bottomless appetite for addressing the symptoms of the transaction crisis and a complete aversion to addressing its cause.

AFTER INSTITUTIONS

Observers of the business world, long steeped in the assumptions of neoclassical economics, tend to view organizations and managers as rational actors who seek to optimize the firm's performance. After all, isn't this freedom to follow the path of rational self-interest the hallmark of a free-market economy for individuals as well as for corporations? But another kind of theoretical perspective gaining ground in economics and organizational studies emphasizes the unique properties of institutions and their preference for behavior that promotes stability and continuity over optimization. This institutional perspective, imbued with the insights of evolutionary studies, economic history, systems theory, and social psychology, holds an important key to the tenacity of the standard enterprise logic.

From this new perspective, organizational inventions—like, for example, the elements of an "enterprise logic"—are considered "institutionalized" when they have a long history, when they draw legitimacy from other organizations using similar inventions, when they are explicit and codified, and when they are interdependent in complex networks, to the extent that a change in one set of inventions requires changes in many others. The more institutionalized an element is, the more it appears to be a "given" that is "taken for granted" by people acting in the system. The more this occurs, the greater the effort that goes into maintaining the invention.[141]

Organizational elements with low levels of institutionalization may be fairly easy to change. Those are the adaptations that occur at the margins of the organization. But elements with high degrees of institutionalization exhibit a relentless resistance to change.[142] They compose what we have been

referring to as the "deep structure" of the living system. The institutionalization of these elements creates a coherent deep structure that operates to produce stability, coherence, and continuity. This tends to increase efficiency
by relying on the proven routines. But it works against efficiency when different, newer structures could achieve higher levels of performance. The
problem is that such alternatives are not just ignored, they cannot even be
perceived.[143] Another way of saying this is that "institutionalization" explains the behavior that does not conform to "rational" market dynamics.
Institutionalized behavior conforms to the dictates of established authority,
not to the laws of the marketplace. This is why processes of institutionalization can be helpful when they consolidate new inventions but inevitably become obstacles to change later, when they block the application of even
newer and more effective inventions.[144]

We have said that the standard enterprise logic expresses the deep structure of managerial capitalism. It is a coherent, interlocking set of inventions
that have defined commercial activity for a century, and it certainly exhibits
all the characteristics of institutionalization. Inside that logic there are always bits and pieces that are relatively easy to change. For example, new
jobs will appear, such as "CRM programmer" or "supply chain coordina-
tor." These jobs are not highly institutionalized and are fairly easy to
change. But elements that are central to the logic are highly institutionalized.

Consider the professional managerial hierarchy as an example. It is a
core element of the standard enterprise logic. It also fulfills all the criteria of
a thoroughly institutionalized invention: To begin with, it first emerged as a
response to the demands of mass production, so by now it has a nearly
century-old history. Second, it is a feature of most organizations—from large
corporations to government agencies, small companies, not-for-profits, and
service providers—granting it immense legitimacy. Third, it is extensively
codified in job titles, promotional criteria, internal career ladders, work rules,
employment contracts, and so on. Finally, changes to the managerial hierarchy have ripple effects in every direction inside and outside the organization,
from the division of labor to the conceptualization of careers, the legal relationship between a company and its shareholders, and federal pay standards.
This kind of depth of institutionalization helps to explain why this and other
core elements of the standard enterprise logic appear to be infinitely robust
in the face of so-called transformational change efforts.[145]

Economists utilizing institutional analysis stress the strength of routines, habits, and norms in creating self-reinforcing behavior.[146] They have
noted a phenomenon called "weak selection." It means that, contrary to traditional economic assumptions, environments do not necessarily punish

suboptimal performance. This is especially true when there are many organizations exhibiting the same performance routines, and when the environment itself is changing, uncertain, and complex. As we said in Chapter One, challenges to the deep structure do not necessarily result in revolutionary change. Actors in the system do not typically recognize discontinuity. There is no natural impetus to leave the light from the lamppost. People assume that the immediate future will follow from the immediate past. In fact, as conditions become more uncertain, behavioral rules become even more restrictive, finally constraining behavior to the simplest and least sophisticated patterns, which are easiest for people to recognize and predict.

The case of Northwest Airlines provides an example. Its customer-satisfaction ratings had been in decline throughout the 1990s, even as it improved its financial position through intensive cost reductions. But by July 2001, following a downturn in the U.S. economy, the airline reported second-quarter losses of $55 million. The company's response to this fresh set of wounds was more resource reductions. First, it announced that 1,500 employees would be laid off. Then more cost cuts were announced, including the elimination of meal service for children and others with special dietary needs, winning the ire of passenger groups and a derisive front-page story in the *Financial Times*.[147] As one economic theorist concludes, "Greater uncertainty will cause rule-governed behavior to exhibit increasingly predictable regularities, so that uncertainty becomes the basic source of predictable behavior."[148]

One of the most infamous examples of this tendency involves the events at the Three Mile Island nuclear power plant, near Harrisburg, Pennsylvania. There, on March 28, 1979, the United States had its closest encounter with nuclear catastrophe. Dozens of panels and committees conducted exhaustive investigations and produced thousands of pages of analysis in an attempt to unravel what happened that day. At the heart of the mess lay buried one definitive, crippling pattern. Highly trained control-room operators monitored dozens of instruments and technical readings on the state of the plant. There is a range of normal output for such instrumentation, and the readings are nearly always within that range, indicating a steady state. At 3:55 A.M., a series of alarms signaled that key instrument readings were climbing out of normal range. That marked the beginning of the nearly fatal meltdown in the reactor core. But operators did not imagine that catastrophe was possible. They could not conceive of a discontinuity from the steady state. Instead, they continued to make decisions as if they were responding to normal conditions. As they clung to their performance routines, a challenging situation turned into a full-fledged nuclear emergency.

For example, pumps were shut down to prevent water spilling onto the floor when they were urgently needed for emergency cooling. Routines were followed that pumped water out of the containment building into an auxiliary building, without considering that the water might have carried unsafe levels of radioactivity. Other pumps were shut down because they were vibrating under strain. Correct procedure under normal conditions, this decision turned out to be disastrous within the context of the unfolding emergency. The pumps were vitally needed to cool the reactor, and without them high temperatures in the reactor led to exposed fuel rods and the possibility of serious radiation leakage. As the control-room supervisor would later tell a congressional committee, "Once a man gets on a track, it's hard for him to step back and become objective."[149]

In most cases, the intractability of performance routines does not result in horrible catastrophe. Organizations can limp along for quite a while with substantial suboptimization, especially if everyone else is doing the same. Traditional economics has long assumed that when institutional forms like this persist, it is because they are efficient. Institutional change has been regarded as the process of moving from one efficient equilibrium to another as a consequence of external changes, such as a new technology. But economists and historians working from the new institutional perspective have shown that "inefficient equilibria" can and do persist for long periods of time. We are suggesting that the persistence of the standard enterprise logic in the face of the new society of individuals is just such a case. Inefficiency, it turns out, is not a sufficient condition for deep structure change.[150]

The institutionalization processes we have described can successfully maintain inefficient equilibria because they complement another set of processes that occur in people's heads and in their relationships with one another. Actors within the organizational system use their skills, intelligence, and cunning to evade deep structure change. There are three big reasons why: conceptual limitations, lack of motivation, and the desire to maintain current relationships.[151]

The first reason is cognitive: People simply do not grasp the fact of discontinuity. As in the case of Three Mile Island, they assume a linear path from the present to the future. People take refuge in a kind of cognitive bunker, protected by expectations and assumptions that have worked well enough in the past. The way they interpret new experiences is limited by these old assumptions. Thomas Kuhn described a related phenomenon among scientists. Quite frequently, he noted, scientific observations that contradict an established theory are simply not perceived at all, because they do not fit the framework of old assumptions.[152]

United States Federal Reserve chairman Alan Greenspan pointed to the same syndrome operating in the world economy, when he described the failure of economists, governments, and markets around the world to anticipate the meltdown of the Asian economies in 1997. "I suspect that the very nature of the process may make it virtually impossible to anticipate. It's like water pressing against a dam. Everything appears normal until a crack brings a deluge."[153] Well, maybe some could have noticed the strain on the dam, but not if they were enjoying the comforts of their cognitive bunkers. John Maynard Keynes described this dilemma in his preface to *The General Theory of Employment, Interest, and Money*, where he wrote, "The composition of this book has been for the author a long struggle of escape, and so must the reading of it be for most readers if the author's assault upon them is to be successful,—a struggle of escape from habitual modes of thought and expression. . . . The difficulty lies, not in the new ideas, but in escaping from the old ones, which ramify, for those brought up as most of us have been, into every corner of our minds."[154] And what is it that makes that cognitive bunker such a comforting place?

That question brings us to reason number two, which has to do with human motivation. Letting go of the past is painful. The dissolution of old values, beliefs, priorities, and meanings is a real cause for grief. That grief is compounded by uncertainty. What lies beyond the light from the lamppost? How will I meet new challenges and construct new answers? Am I up to the risk? Am I up to the challenge? Will I be able to find new sources of satisfaction and reward? Similar processes are at work on the group and organizational levels. People know how to operate in the system that already exists. They know how to compete and how to succeed in that system. Changing the deep structure of the system is threatening to everyone. There will be new winners and losers, new skills to learn, and new ranking rules.

These fears are compounded by the fact that many people have invested their entire careers in the old structures. Revolutionary change belittles their lifetime achievement. It diminishes all that they have sacrificed. Kuhn observed scientists who would readily devise "ad hoc modifications" to their theories in an effort to eliminate contradictions that could otherwise call into question their life's work. One of the most famous examples of this involves the century or so leading up to what has come to be known as the "Copernican Revolution." Astronomers had for some time encountered real difficulty in accommodating their actual observations of the movement of planets to the still-reigning paradigm of the geocentric universe. But instead of postulating a new model, as Copernicus finally did, they made ever more bizarre and arcane adjustments to the old one.[155]

There is still a third set of reasons to explain why people evade deep structure change. It involves the relationships and commitments that people have developed both inside and outside the system. Individuals frequently find it hard to change because they are afraid of disappointing the people closest to them, such as marital partners or professional colleagues. If a person has been valued by important others, he tends to fear the loss of that positive regard as he undergoes change and possibly develops in new directions. In organizations and professions, patterns of career lineage and loyalty can also freeze any impetus toward change. Kuhn noted how scientific communities promote inertia, carefully socializing students, legitimizing the study of only certain problems, and ignoring or deriding scientific findings that fall outside the paradigm.[156] These social processes continue to be documented in every professional domain.[157] It is easy to see how the same processes of career channeling and legitimization occur in MBA programs, economics departments, and other forms of graduate and professional education that prepare people for participation in the standard enterprise logic.

A final key to the puzzle of the transaction crisis is found in the work of one of the early architects of the institutional analysis of organizations. In a classic essay written in 1965, Arthur Stinchcombe offered evidence to illustrate the way in which the structural characteristics of organizations reflect their time of origin.[158] This means that the "organizational inventions" that are made at a particular time in history reflect what he called the "social technology"—norms, ideas, values, attitudes, behaviors, assumptions, roles, and techniques—of that period. According to Stinchcombe, in any given historical period these social resources are the raw materials from which organizational inventions are shaped. This means that social conditions make certain organizational forms possible. It also means that organizational inventions to address new purposes emerge only when social resources make it possible to address those purposes efficiently. In other words, fundamentally new inventions emerge when there are fundamentally new kinds of social resources to draw upon.

Stinchcombe also recognized a lag between society and its organizations. Organizational inventions are institutionalized and tend to remain stable, even as society continues to change. The organizational inventions of any given period end up outliving the social resources from which they were drawn. These forms persist because they tend to work "well enough," but also because both the institutional and social-psychological processes we have described exert a profound impulse toward the reproduction of the status quo. In this way, he explained the existence of "inefficient equilibria," long before they became a focus of institutional economics.

Stinchcombe's insights shed more light on the supermonopoly of the standard enterprise logic and the puzzle of the transaction crisis. The standard enterprise logic expresses the social realities of the early twentieth century: the emphasis on the mass; the elitism and threatened masculinity that led to a sexualized contempt for end consumers, enforced their lack of voice, fixed their distance from producers, and supported the tendency to extol male producers as the creators of value over female consumers as the destroyers of value; the romance with products and technology; the faith in "systems" and science that led to an emphasis on control, centralization, and bureaucracy; the vast disparities in education that were used to underscore and legitimate the need for a managerial hierarchy. Despite many adaptations and much added complexity, the standard enterprise logic continues to reflect those social realities. They are perpetuated in the commercial world, even though the rest of society has moved on.

It is only now—with the rise of the new society of individuals, the emergence of the individuation of consumption, and the new markets for deep support—that the institutionalized elements of the standard enterprise logic can be seen to exist in an inefficient equilibrium. The transaction crisis is the expression of this inefficiency. But the supermonopoly of the standard enterprise logic yields weak selection processes, which are in turn exacerbated by environmental change and uncertainty. For these reasons the inefficiencies of the standard enterprise logic have endured.

But as we have also seen, economic revolutions do occur. They depend first of all upon the presence of new markets, illuminated by a new quality of human yearning. This condition is fulfilled by the new society of individuals, with their insistent demands for psychological self-determination and their hunger for relationships of deep support. They seek organizational inventions that reflect the realities of their lives, not those of their parents, grandparents, and great-grandparents. They are first among the new social resources that make it possible to consider wholly different organizational inventions that effectively and efficiently address this wholly new commercial purpose.

Such new inventions do not spring to life on their own. As in the case of Henry Ford, they depend upon people who see what is still invisible to the rest. Their imaginative leaps of faith, through trial and error, eventually find the way to combine technologies and people in a wholly new framework to address the new purposes dictated by new markets. Their successes attract imitators, who ultimately can turn an experiment into a social movement. This is how a new enterprise logic is forged. As in the case of managerial capitalism, it succeeds in much the same way any social movement does, because it speaks to the needs and longings of people better than what went before.

Who are these inventors? The evidence we have reviewed strongly suggests that the failures arising from inadequate deep structures will almost certainly elude the efforts of organization members to correct them. The only hope of revolutionary change for these systems rests with newcomers and outsiders unwilling to yield to the siren song of the horseless carriage. Kuhn described this pattern in the scientific profession, when the persistence of apparently unresolvable anomalies attracts the attention of new thinkers to these "trouble spots." They are not the experts but rather outsiders and novices who, "being little committed by prior practice to the traditional rules of normal science, are particularly likely to see that those rules no longer define a playable game and to conceive another set that can replace them."[159] This suggests that continued efforts by agents of the standard enterprise logic to rediscover the end consumer under the lamppost are unlikely to make economic history. The new revolutionaries are more likely to emerge from outside that circle of light.

In summary, then, managerial capitalism and its handmaiden, transaction economics, have sown a harvest that they cannot reap. They helped to set into motion the large-scale historical forces of mass literacy, extended education, mass consumption, increased health, universal communication, and unlimited information access that propelled people toward lives of greater richness, diversity, longevity, and ultimately individuality. They created the conditions that yield wholly new dreams. But like Moses leading his people only to the edge of the promised land, the enterprises of managerial capitalism can go no further. Their allegiance to the confining precepts of transaction economics, their pernicious inward focus, and their intractable contempt for individual end consumers render them institutionally incapable of reaping the new wealth that arises from this changing structure of consumption. It is not just that the time for a new enterprise logic and a new episode of capitalism has finally come. It is, in fact, long overdue.

PART THREE

EMERGENCE

THE NEW ENTERPRISE LOGIC

TEN

The Digital Bridge

Two decades of customer-oriented innovations failed to integrate the end consumer into the producer's self-centered orbit. As a result, in the late 1990s pent-up demand for sanctuary, voice, and connection exploded upon the new digital medium called the Internet, driving a frenzy of innovation and expansion.

THE DIGITAL DREAM

Some aspects of this great commercial drama in the twentieth century's last decade are well known. Internet start-up companies became financial behemoths in record time as customers fled the transaction crisis, flocking to the relatively benign atmosphere of e-commerce to make their purchases. Some of the new e-firms garnered stunning valuations that dwarfed the market capitalization of larger and more established "bricks and mortar" corporations.[1] By 2001, these premiums, along with many of the companies in question, had vanished. The excitement and panic over this bubble—how it grew, how it burst—have obscured the three most important issues that it raised. First, what made e-commerce so full of promise for so many people? Second, why did the first generation of e-commerce applications fall short of its aspirations, disappointing consumers and investors? Third, what is to be done next?

In this chapter, we propose that e-commerce disappointed not because it was revolutionary, but because it was not revolutionary enough. Remember that in the early twentieth century the economic revolution associated with managerial capitalism arose from the confluence of <u>three</u> forces. There were new markets ripe for mass consumption. There were also production, communication, and transportation technologies to stimulate and enable that consumption. (Many of the equities in those new technology companies rose to unprecedented heights, but that too was not to last.) But it took a third force, a new enterprise logic that came to be known as managerial capitalism, to effectively link the new technologies to the new markets. These three forces in combination were the foundation for sustainable wealth creation that transformed the economy and society in the United States, and eventually in much of the rest of the world too.

While the conditions we face today are poised for the same kind of explosive and discontinuous growth, the so-called Internet revolution failed to provide the crucial foundation for economic revolution. Instead, the dotcoms exploited a new technology medium to service the same enterprise logic as their established competitors, often at the expense of the same end consumers. This amounted to little more than old behavior in a new medium, but with too little of the financial or operational expertise to make even that work effectively. As a result, the great potential of the new medium was overshadowed by the financial turbulence it created when, in the absence of a new enterprise logic, it could not discover adequate new sources of sustainable value.

Despite these difficulties, we regard the Internet—and the new generations of technologies and network capabilities, such as broadband, interactive Web services, and the "semantic Web," that will modify, augment or replace the Internet in the years to come—as an essential bridge from the old capitalism to the new. Why? The individuation of consumption will place immense demands on the new enterprise logic for the ceaseless coordination of complexity and multilayered collaboration across far-flung networks. Only the new digital medium—with its potentially infinite embrace of complexity, connection, detail, intelligence, ubiquity, immediacy, transparency, lightness, and plasticity—can meet these demands. It will provide the economies of infrastructure convergence and the smart coordination and collaboration capabilities necessary to provide affordable deep support to millions of individuals.

The new markets for deep support now coexist alongside this emerging technology medium. So far, though, there is little that unites them. They are like two people destined for one another, just before they've met. What will join them and so fulfill the destiny of each? That missing link is the new enterprise logic of distributed capitalism, which will once again reinvent the purpose and organization of commerce. It is this combination of the new markets for deep support, the new digital medium, and a new enterprise logic aligned with individuals that will result in the next leap forward in wealth creation. In other words, the new digital medium is essential to the realization of distributed capitalism, which in turn imbues it with the historic purpose for which it has been searching. In this chapter, we will explore the growth and popularity of the new medium, how the standard enterprise logic limited its early development, and the truly explosive economic potential that awaits the marriage of the new digital technologies to the new enterprise logic of distributed capitalism.

UNIQUE CHARACTERISTICS OF THE NEW DIGITAL MEDIUM

The new digital medium is composed of wires and microwaves, cables and satellites, servers, networks, routers, sensors, wireless receivers, Web appliances, personal computers, mobile phones, microprocessors, mainframes, supercomputers, and software. These have thus far found their most powerful expression in the network known as the Internet and its leading application, the World Wide Web—a medium for an ever-widening array of electronic commerce, communication, and connection. The Internet continues to evolve in interactivity, immediacy, richness, intelligence, functionality, complexity, and suppleness. At some point, it probably won't even be called "the Internet." For the purposes of this discussion, though, we do not want to focus on particular technological innovations, but rather on the general characteristics of this rapidly evolving medium that distinguish it from earlier generations of technology.

Digital technologies—the combination of computers and communication networks—bestow a new and global *transparency* on everything they touch. Processes, objects, and events are translated into information (data, text, image, and sound) and connected to a wider network, thus making them visible and accessible anywhere, anytime. This transparency contributes to what has been called the unique "informating" capacity of digital technologies, when a complex, three-dimensional world that includes everything from factories to blood cells can be digitized and transformed into information, becoming visible, knowable, shareable, mobile, and manageable in wholly new ways. If it can be sensed, it can be measured. If it can be measured, it can be connected. If it can be connected, it can be communicated.[2]

No detail is too small to be captured in this net. Information that was formerly isolated, fragmented, and private—within heads, desks, machines, bodies, departments, automobiles, companies, households, industrial sectors, communities, governments, or countries—can now be made available for inspection, communication, integration, and analysis. This transparency challenges hierarchical boundaries, functional boundaries, and the boundaries that have defined public and private realms. Information seeps across old borders, cascades from the top to the bottom, and washes from the center to the periphery and back again. All this creates the opportunity for knowledge to be more widely shared. It paves the way for more horizontal, less hierarchical forms of social organization, as well as methods of distributing authority and power that emphasize coordination and collaboration over administration and fragmentation.

The earliest generations of information technology were contained within the organization. But the current wave of technological change is a very different matter. It extends far beyond the organization to encompass its markets, suppliers, and competitors. Indeed, the essence of today's digital medium is that it *informates* all the constituencies in the commercial solar system. In industry after industry, matters that were once the private domain of top managers and product experts—comparative information on prices, product knowledge, inventories, supply chain efficiencies, quality— are now transparent. They spill beyond the firm and engulf all its stakeholders. It is now possible for end consumers, business customers, suppliers, and competitors to know almost as much or more about many aspects of the organizations they are buying from, and the things they are buying, as its managers do. As one General Motors executive put it, "When you link the consumer into the same systems as the dealership, you're tying them into legacy production systems"—manufacturing operations that were once invisible to the consumer.[3]

Most technological innovation throughout history has been designed to save labor and simplify work. Tools, machines, and automated systems have replaced the human body. Work has been continually simplified and standardized—broken down into the tiniest fragments so that machines can do it. In this way, complexity has been continually eliminated from the "lower levels" of organizations, and simple inputs were reaggregated later as information for "higher levels" of managers. In contrast, the new digital medium moves decisively away from the logic of simplification and its counterpart in hierarchical oversight. Here for the first time is a technology that *preserves and coordinates complexity*. It can enable the immediate comprehension, communication, and coordination of immensely complex activities, while rendering transparent even the most evanescent details necessary to bring vast producer networks to heel in the support of individual lives. Increasingly, it can bring a kind of autonomous and proactive *intelligence* to bear upon tasks and problems. Indeed, its ability to metabolize complexity far exceeds any human capacity. As the medium continues to develop, the information thus metabolized can be turned into purposeful accomplishments.

The new medium creates the opportunity for *comprehensive under-standing*. Overviews, composites, trends, comparisons, and forecasts are as easy to achieve as the most detailed and nuanced appreciation of the tiniest fragment of activity in real time. Qualities that have always been held in op-position are united in the new world of the digital medium. In this way, it is *synthetic*, capable of both customization and speed, quality and volume, in-dividualization and connection, sharing and ownership, flexibility and preci-sion, operational perfection and low cost, knowing the whole and knowing the part, being one place and being every place, serving one at the cost of serving one million. Rather than being diluted, the value of information can increase as it is *distributed*, allowing more people to do more with more, as it enables collaboration and coordination across space and time. And the new medium provides *immediacy*, redefining the parameters of action and com-munication as these migrate from the physical to the virtual. Amazon's "one click" is not only a patent-protected business method, but also a metaphor for the experiences of conduct, exchange, and discourse in the new digital space.

The new medium lends itself to infinite *plasticity*. Industrial technology was used to create a fixed base, or "infrastructure," upon which higher-order activities could be built. But those activities were constrained by the very in-frastructure upon which they depended. For example, factories produced a limited range of one type of product. Physical distribution systems went some places but not others. Forms of coordination around these earlier tech-nologies tended to be fixed. There was one best way to organize, very much like a jigsaw puzzle where the pieces can fit together only one way. But digi-tal technologies do not simply create platforms for a fixed range of action. Instead, they introduce an all-encompassing new kind of action space in which structures can form, dissolve, and reassemble in unlimited configura-tions. As digits replace atoms in the methods available for work, consump-tion, communication, and exchange, the parameters that shape action are transformed.

The guiding metaphor of the new medium is no longer that of a jigsaw puzzle but of a *kaleidoscope*. Not only are there infinite ways that the pieces can fit together, but those patterns can change fluidly, lending themselves to what one scholar has called the "nomadic" nature of action in networks.[4]

This means that it is also a *ubiquitous* technology. In the world of mass markets, people had to be where the technology was. In the digital medium, the new technology travels with you as you travel through it, creating a connected world of immediately connected individuals.

TAKING MY LIFE IN MY OWN HANDS: SELF-SUPPORT THROUGH INFORMATION AND COMMUNITY

Decades of frustrated yearning for psychological self-determination drove millions of the new individuals onto the Internet in retreat from the conflicts of the transaction crisis. Once there, they marshaled its commercial and noncommercial resources in an effort to fulfill their needs for sanctuary, voice, and connection. In this way, the exponential growth of Internet participation in general, and e-commerce in particular, can be explained by the way in which the new medium, however unwittingly, offered itself as an antidote to the experience of a persistently thwarted individuality. If psychological self-determination was problematic in an institutional world dominated by the standard enterprise logic, the Internet could at least provide some relief in the form of *self-support*. This helps to explain why Internet participation has grown rapidly and why it quickly came to reflect the population at large. It makes sense that Internet use would eventually be as widely distributed as the demand for psychological self-determination and the disappointments arising from the transaction crisis.

By 2001 the Internet encompassed about 4 billion static Web pages and provided access to about 600 billion more pages of dynamic content in libraries and databases around the world.[5] Internet growth rates have continually outpaced expectations and can reasonably be compared to those associated with the expansion of the rail system and the rise of the telephone and automobile.[6] Internet usage has increased by about 20 percent annually in the United States since 1998.[7] In 1996 only about 10 percent of U.S. households were online.[8] That percentage climbed to 50.5 percent by 2001.[9] In 1996 there were about 37 million U.S. Internet users.[10] By 2001 that number had risen to just over 143 million, representing about 54 percent of the U.S. population.[11] Outside the United States, Internet participation was calculated at 44 percent in Europe in late 2001[12] and 36 percent in Japan.[13] In terms of absolute numbers, more people currently use the Internet in Europe than in the United States.[14] International Data Corporation calculates that between 2001 and 2006 worldwide Internet usage will double from 500 million to 1 billion users, with most of that growth coming from outside the United States.[15]

As early as 1998 it was clear that the population of U.S. Internet users was changing. What had begun as a medium dominated by young, well-educated, and technologically savvy men had turned into a close approximation of mainstream America. One study that year concluded that the "buying habits, behaviors, and attitudes of Internet users increasingly mirror those of the general population."[16] By 2001 the U.S. Commerce Department concluded that computer and Internet use was well established in every demographic and socioeconomic segment of the society. While Internet use was still more likely among higher-income households, the growth rate at lower-income levels had accelerated dramatically. For example, among the lowest-income households ($15,000 or less) Internet use grew at an annual rate of 25 percent between 1998 and 2001, compared to a growth rate of 11 percent in households with income above $75,000.[17] In 1998 gender differences had begun to diminish, yielding virtually identical aggregate rates of Internet use by men and women in 2000.[18] Internet use within households headed by single women had also accelerated, reaching near parity with male single-parent households by 2001.[19]

While men's and women's aggregate rates of Internet use are similar, women exceed men in many key self-support activities. This should come as no surprise, given the stress of the daily grind to which women are particularly subject and their consequent role at the forefront of the new markets for deep support. For example, women were more likely than men to report spending more time online in 2001 than they did in 2000.[20] Women are more likely than men to be Internet users during the peak wage-earning years between age twenty and fifty, when the pressures of the daily grind are greatest.[21] Women are more likely to be e-mailers,[22] and they are more likely to join a group they have encountered online.[23] Women have also taken the lead in online purchasing, constituting 52 percent of online shoppers in 2001 and 58 percent of online shoppers during the 2001 Christmas season.[24]

Online information resources and communities have enabled individuals to support themselves, or find support among peers, when traditional organizations failed to meet their needs. The Internet has enabled self-support for those engaged in home-based work and education as they seek to take control of those critical activities within individual space. Still more people, dissatisfied with their quality of health care, have turned to the Internet as a means to self-support in their efforts to care for themselves and their families. In 2001 about 52 million Internet users sought health information on Web sites or in chat groups and bulletin boards—that is more than those who shopped online, looked up stock quotes, or checked sports scores.[25] There are Web sites that support people taking care of aging parents, as well as others devoted to expert and group advice on particular illnesses.[26] More than half the people who accessed these medical resources said it improved their ability to get health information, about half said it improved their self-care efforts, and a little less than half said it influenced their treatment decisions.[27] The claim of sanctuary was evident in their motivations for support, as they repeatedly cited online convenience (93 percent), the fact that they could get more information than is available from other sources, such as their doctors (83 percent), and the welcome anonymity of their search and query activity (80 percent).[28]

Self-support in the quest for connection has flourished through e-mails, chat rooms, and online communities. By March 2001 some 100 million people were sending and receiving e-mails, up 33 percent from the prior year.[29] Ninety million people had contacted groups, and most of those sustained high levels of involvement, discussing issues and developing relationships. While some online communities represent associations or professional groups already established in the physical world, many are constituted online as individuals with similar needs opt into conversations with each other. This is reflected in the fact that almost half of those who have contacted groups (43 percent) use those connections to support their efforts to cope with personal issues such as job loss, parenting, health, or even the frustrations and injustices associated with consumption and the transaction crisis.[30] More than half (56 percent) connect with groups to support their religious and spiritual needs (more than those who have gambled online, attended Web auctions, traded stocks online, placed phone calls, done online banking, or used Internet dating services),[31] and 28 percent use the Internet to find support among others with similar lifestyles and interests.[32] New forms of associational activity have been stimulated in the search for connection, including online participation in civic groups (45 percent), relationships with people from different generations (37 percent), and relationships with people from different economic and ethnic backgrounds (27 percent).[33]

TAKING MY LIFE IN MY OWN HANDS: SELF-SUPPORT AND E-COMMERCE

More than any other single factor, it is the transaction crisis—squarely located in the physical world of Main Street, the mall, the airport, and the telephone—that best explains the abrupt rise of e-commerce and its sustained growth, even long after the demise of so many dot-com firms. Fleeing the transaction crisis, people have found their way online in search of self-support—the first substantial alternative to the little murders encountered daily in the physical world of commerce. Here is a way to remain safely within the comfort of one's sanctuary and still get things done. Self-support means hassle-free, rapid, and reliable transactions. The experience may be devoid of the human touch, but for many kinds of purchases—the books, CDs, airline flights, and software that dominated the first phases of e-commerce growth—that's just fine. No one is helping you, but no one is humiliating you either. As long as individuals' needs for deep support are ignored in the physical world of commercial activity, there is little to be lost—and much to be gained—by switching to the digital medium for self-supported purchases of goods and services. Indeed, above and beyond the limitless polyglot of goods and services available on the Internet, its defining product is the opportunity for self-support.

The pervasiveness of the transaction crisis and the hunger for an alternative to it helps to explain the stunning growth rates in e-commerce. A few figures are illustrative. In 1997 about $3 billion worth of retail goods were sold through the Internet in the United States, compared to nearly $15 billion in 1999.[34] In 2001 that number rose to $33.3 billion, a 31 percent increase in online sales over 2000.[35] In 2001, online Christmas sales rose to about $10 billion, a 12 percent increase over holiday sales in 2000.[36] By some research estimates, total e-commerce activity reached about $480 billion in the United States in 2001, and about $1.2 trillion worldwide.[37] According to a variety of sources using disparate forms of measurement, the volume of commercial transactions over the Internet just keeps growing. Within the United States, the Commerce Department found that the percentage of the U.S. population making online purchases had increased substantially from 13 percent in 2000 to 21 percent in 2001,[38] despite worries about economic downturn and the collapse of many Internet companies. Other studies have also found an across-the-board increase in online commercial transactions during that period, when the number of Internet users who purchased goods rose by 45 percent, those who bought travel services increased by 59 percent, and those who used banking services grew by 79 percent.[39]

Despite these healthy rates of growth, the commercial consolidation and spread of the digital medium remains in its very early stages. If around half of U.S. households are online, then half are not. In 1999 U.S. online retail sales accounted for only 1.4 percent of all retail sales.[40] By 2001 it was up to 2 percent.[41] Even the celebrated success of the 2001 Christmas online shopping season amounted to only 3.5 percent of holiday retail purchases.[42] In 2000 U.S. shoppers committed less than 15 percent of their discretionary spending to the Internet.[43] Even in the heady days of 1999, when Forrester Research calculated that Web-based retail revenues would grow at a compound annual growth rate of 69 percent, Forrester projected online retail sales at only 6 percent of total U.S. retail sales for 2003 and 7 percent for 2004.[44] In the United States alone, 2 million new participants are coming online each month.[45] Among worldwide consumers who have not yet purchased online, 63 percent said they planned to do so.[46] Sharp increases in the number of cell phones worldwide also mean that China, India, Latin America, and other regions with poor telecommunication infrastructures will be able to leapfrog the development curve and plug right in to the evolving digital medium. In other words, the data suggest that most of the people in the world who may one day routinely operate in the digital medium haven't even used it yet.

If online consumers are seeking respite from the transaction crisis through self-support, then one would predict that convenience would be a key factor in shaping their online choices. In fact, convenience is repeatedly cited as the number-one reason that people shift purchasing to the Internet. That word "convenience" tells a big story. First, it says that "inconvenience" is a taken-for-granted feature of most transactions in the physical world of consumption. Inconvenience is composed of the logistical impositions of shopping, the time it costs, and the knowledge that sellers are likely to be indifferent to individual needs. Making the process convenient is simply not part of their job, and support that reaches beyond the transaction is not in the picture. As one report concluded: "Online consumers want a new type of shopping experience. They seek out merchants that can take the time and hassle out of the purchase process." Consumers want "to take greater control of the retail experience," these researchers said. "People want convenience first and foremost. Forty-five percent of online consumers cite this reason for choosing an online vendor. It easily outdistances the other reasons for merchant selection."[47]

A 1999 marketing survey found that 64 percent of Internet users were ready to try shopping online as an alternative to the traditional back-to-school trek and were open to purchasing items such as computers, clothing, and school supplies over the Web. Their reasons were a chronicle of the transaction crisis: Competing with crowds, bare shelves and out-of-stock items, the need to traipse from store to store, and "price come-ons" ranked highest among them.[48] By 2001 these dispositions were taking a toll on physical store traffic. Researchers found that 29 percent of all online purchasers reported that they were indeed spending less time shopping in stores.[49] Another survey found that consumers were far more interested in the utilities of the Internet—"tools that enhance or facilitate tasks such as information gathering or errands consumers often face in the real world"—than its entertainment features. And consistent with the theme of self-support, it found that "online vendors seem to have little influence on online shopping behavior. Consumers are shopping for intended purchases rather than making impulse buys. Shoppers are finding their own way to commerce sites instead of being steered by banner ads and buttons."[50]

A report from the Georgia Institute of Technology found that "convenience" was the most frequently cited of all reasons for using the Web, especially among women. Other frequently cited reasons were saving time, the presence of vendor information, and the absence of sales pressure. They noted that "in 76.9% of the cases, females, more than any other group, cited the absence of sales pressure as a reason for using the Web."[51] And sales pressure is, of course, just one feature of the contempt and alienation that has come to be regarded as an inescapable feature of the transaction crisis. A 2001 study of online consumption in twelve countries (Australia, Brazil, Canada, France, Germany, Israel, the Netherlands, South Africa, Spain, Switzerland, the United Kingdom, and the United States) concluded that convenience and price dominated the online purchase decision across its sample of more than 7,000 respondents.[52]

Consider AOL. When network browsers and free Internet access first emerged, many analysts no longer saw a viable business model in AOL's services. Today it is one of the largest Internet businesses. When asked to explain its success, AOL's president, Robert Pittman, summarized: "It is all about convenience. Convenience is king."[53] The same motives exist in the case of business-to-business transactions. As a Dell Online executive put it, "The Web's real power is that it helps customers help themselves. . . . Our job is to put people in charge of the buying process."[54] Customers at Dell do their own selection, configuration, comparative pricing, purchasing, data entry, information reconciliation, and order tracking. Dell backs up its Web sales with relentless efficiencies and high levels of automation designed to strengthen the self-support experience.[55]

THE RISE OF NINJA SHOPPING

A small group of scholars and practitioners anticipated the processes that would accompany the transparency of electronic markets.[56] Some described these processes as the basis for a new "frictionless" form of commerce.[57] The reasoning was powerful. It had long been established in classical economics that differences in prices for similar products could be explained primarily by consumer ignorance—people simply could not know that the same product existed elsewhere at a lower price.[58] But in the electronic markets of the Internet, end consumers needed to be able to assess product characteristics and prices to make their choices. The one-click immediacy of the new medium was expected to enable buyers to use that transparency to compare products and prices across many sellers. This would force sellers to reduce prices and so diminish apparent differences between their offerings. In the process, complex products and services—like mortgages, consumer electronics, brokerage services, and even automobiles—come to be regarded as undifferentiated commodities. These dynamics intensify competition and put continuous pressure on margins.

A growing body of research on the economics of electronic markets shows that the transparency of prices in the digital medium did indeed result in lower prices, as compared to conventional outlets.[59] Informed consumers were an important factor in maintaining these lower prices, along with the lower entry and operational costs that characterized the early stages of e-commerce activity. But as experience with e-commerce widened, many studies did not conform to the theory, surprising analysts, observers, and practitioners alike.

The new studies showed that while prices on the Internet tended to be lower than those in traditional retail channels, the e-commerce businesses with the highest market share did not necessarily have lower prices than their e-commerce competitors.[60] Online consumers, it turned out, shopped with the company they trusted to actually get them the goods. Trusting the purchase process took precedence over price, within the context of a general expectation of lower prices in the digital medium. Some greeted these findings with relief, taking them as evidence that e-commerce businesses would be able to sustain or even increase their margins, without fatal consequences for market share.[61] In fact, these findings spelled out something a lot gloomier for the digital seller. They signaled only a brief respite, rather than a permanent escape, from the relentless pressures of automation and commoditization.

Much of the paradox of price and market share on the Web can be explained by the requirements of self-support. That means fast, reliable, trustworthy, no-hassle acquisition. While the physical product offered by a variety of e-tailers might be exactly the same, the larger experiential product that we are calling self-support can differ substantially. These differences were reflected in the high levels of fragmentation that characterized the earliest stages of e-commerce. In 1999 there were 34,000 secure Web sites, with 2,000 more being added to the Web each month. Many of the sellers represented in those numbers consisted of nothing more than a Web site and a distribution agreement. Others represented super-thin retail niches for products as diverse as boxer shorts, refrigerator magnets, and mustards.[62] A study by the University of Texas randomly sampled 3,400 of those companies. It found that the top ten companies in the sample accounted for only 27 percent of all Internet revenue. What distinguished the dominant brands, however, were their investments in the business processes that could reliably deliver self-support: physical infrastructure, inventory, navigation tools, information content, organization, management, partnerships, logistics, server capacity, customer service systems, site design, and so on.[63]

In the context of the self-support product, "trust" was not an emotional factor that was external to the product. Rather, trust was an intrinsic product feature. This helps to explain another anomaly that confounded many researchers: Internet consumers appeared to be highly sensitive to prices in conventional outlets but not as price-sensitive online.[64] That's because when they were shopping in the mall, they were shopping for things. When they were shopping on the Internet, they were shopping for self-support and so were willing to pay more than they would have at a less-reliable online alternative.

Reliable self-support became the implicit criterion against which much of the consolidation of e-commerce occurred. In 1999 advertisers spent about $4.4 billion on the Internet, with 2,560 sites and networks competing for those revenues. But 87 percent of the available ad revenues were taken up by the top fifty sites, leaving only 13 percent for the remaining 2,510, or just $228,000 per site.[65] Obviously, these were not revenues upon which any viable business model could be based. To make matters worse, customer acquisition costs rose steeply. Getting started in e-commerce once looked cheap, compared to bricks-and-mortar installations, but that changed quickly. In late 1999 Forrester Research found that it cost between $2 million and $20 million to launch a new e-commerce site, with operating budgets being driven by ballooning marketing costs in the fierce scramble for "eyeballs" and an attractive Internet multiple, as well as a new appreciation of the infrastructure investments (warehouses, call centers) that would be necessary to deliver self-support.[66] These escalating costs help explain the cash crisis that many Internet firms faced in early 2000, and the reluctance of venture capitalists to invest more.

As e-commerce underwent the inevitable consolidation associated with its infancy, the only e-commerce businesses left "standing" were those that dependably delivered self-support. By mid-2000 the top fifty online retailers represented about two-thirds of all online sales.[67] But for all of the success of e-commerce based on self-support, that business model quickly revealed an ominous flaw. The end consumer's ability to acquire self-support was becoming an expectation like clean dishes in a restaurant or a dial tone in a telephone receiver. Self-support was itself being commoditized as the value in the self-support transaction was rapidly vanishing.[68] What happens when every online business reliably gets out the goods and self-support is a taken-for-granted experience?

One important dimension of what can happen next is what we call *ninja shopping*: a ruthlessly effective approach that insists upon the best deal for all transactions, anywhere, all the time. Once online consumers no longer have to pay a premium for self-support, they are free to home in on price, using a sophisticated arsenal of shopping weaponry. In order to attract and retain their business, producers and merchants find themselves in the unusual situation of having to aggressively support ninja shopping activities.

One way that ninja shopping is expressed is in the automation of comparison shopping. Today, sophisticated protocols can instantaneously compare prices and other important product information across the Web. Many of these protocols have become integrated into routine search processes. By 2001 59 percent of online shoppers simply typed a product name and let their search engine find the best purchase site.[69] Other specialty services have emerged based on advanced shopping "bots," each with a unique twist on ninja shopping. Some search the best price, comparing online retailers as well as auction sites and even classified ads. Others include availability information. Still others provide appraisals from merchants or gather product feedback from end consumers. Some of the new software also supports dynamic pricing. It will search the lowest price and give the merchant an opportunity to lower its price rather than lose the sale. Other software agents allow companies to monitor and adjust prices in real time, in order to pre-serve a sale or ensure the best rates from a vendor. More new shopping tools are arriving on the scene each month. Increasingly, they not only automate price transparency, and thus inform end consumers, but they are actually au-tomating and accelerating ninja shopping.

In this way, ninja shopping becomes a taken-for-granted expectation that infects all consumers and governs all purchases, driving commoditiza-tion in ever more complex products and services. This helps to explain why the magical new world of e-tailing ran out of cash before it ever saw puberty, as its vaunted productivity gains from automation accrued to customers rather than to the bottom line. Once self-support is commoditized, ninja shopping means that achieving "customer satisfaction" is synonymous with achieving product commoditization, as the transparency of prices and costs is ubiquitous. The traditional sources of value—low prices, product quality, availability, complexity, on-time delivery, and eventually even customiza-tion—implode when they meet the highly informed end consumer who can know it all and have it all, from any source, any time. To quote the innova-tive computer manufacturer Michael Dell, "You [now] have transparency of pricing. You can't trick the consumer anymore."[70] Still, this was only the be-ginning of the bad news for merchants and producers in the digital medium.

NINJA SHOPPING IN THE OLD SUPPLY CHAIN

The new technologies associated with the Internet were not in and of them-selves sufficient to sustain a viable new kind of e-commerce. The same costly lesson would be repeated among more conventional companies. By the early 1990s it had become evident that the traditional economies of scale associ-ated with volume production and intensive physical assets were more or less exhausted. They were no longer regarded as a source of sustainable competi-tive advantage. As we have already explored, many firms looked to "reengi-neering" and automation as the way to achieve new economies. Eventually, most of these companies came to believe they had exhausted the savings po-tential in "reengineering," or they became disillusioned with its results. The search for new sources of cost reduction began again in earnest, just as the Internet made its appearance on the business scene. Many companies saw an opportunity to escape the impacts of commoditization by de-emphasizing the economies of vertical integration in favor of the economies of networks. Information technology, and especially the Internet, were to play a major role in forming new business "webs" that would create new opportunities for dramatic cost reduction by virtually linking producers with their suppliers and customers.[71]

Investors too were seeking protection from the wildfires of commoditization. Fleeing the difficulties already evident in the world of business-to-consumer e-commerce, they turned their attention to a newly emerging set of Web firms known as business-to-business, or B2B, exchanges.[72] Like the companies in search of new network economies, they recognized that the nearly universal drive of the standard enterprise logic—to create transaction value by reducing cost and resources—had found a powerful ally in the new technology medium. The new enthusiasm for "webifying" transactions within supply chains in order to lower costs mirrored the earlier frenzy over "reengineering." Both used automation to integrate and rationalize business processes in order to reduce costs and resources. The difference was that reengineering focused within the firm, whereas the Internet enabled companies to seek these efficiencies across their supply chains and industries through the use of electronic markets.[73] In other words, B2B was ninja shopping for business. The result was that business trade poured into the digital medium as firms sought ways to lower the costs of procurement and supply chain coordination, and investors saw a new opportunity to make money with a business model they thought they knew well—increased efficiency and reduced cost.[74] There was a growing number of public electronic markets in which immediacy and transparency seemed to promise buyers new opportunities to gain margin from suppliers,[75] while reducing the internal costs of purchasing.[76]

But there was a paradox: In the past, lower costs from suppliers did not necessarily translate into lower prices for end consumers. Instead, they could be exploited for higher margins further up the chain and never be passed on to consumers. The new electronic market mechanisms, however, provided unprecedented price transparency and choice to business customers in their transactions as buyers *and* sellers, just as they did to end consumers. One firm could demand price transparency among its suppliers and find itself exposed to exactly the same pressures as it sold on to its own business customers. This new nakedness demonstrated as never before the zero-sum qualities of the traditional supply chain, in which one firm's transaction value creation, and eventual profit, translated into another firm's costs—costs that ultimately found their way into the price of goods. It began to dawn on firms that the cumulative effect of the new electronic market mechanisms would be to squeeze out inefficiencies and excess working capital, and thus sellers' price advantages, within old, industry-based supply chains and eventually across the economy. As a result, businesses that competed further down the supply chain, instead of being shielded from automation and commoditization, would end up facing exactly the same pressures as retailers. As one industry analyst put it, "A lot of the early rhetoric around e-marketplaces was that they would allow buyers better pricing. What would be the incentive for the suppliers to get involved?"[77]

The specter of falling margins and price wars caused many companies to pull back from their plans to collaborate in public exchanges, resulting in a loss of liquidity and contributing to the collapse of most B2B initiatives.[78] By 2001 the 1,000 to 2,000 online exchanges that had formed in the United States had attracted only 1 percent of direct business purchases.[79] Similarly, a 2002 survey of thirty large European firms found that 80 percent sold fewer than 1 percent of their goods through an exchange. The study concluded that the zero-sum relationships among equity holders in industry exchanges forced them to fight for control of strategy and objectives, each with competing requirements for its own top management and shareholders.[80] Most business-to-business Internet trading retreated to private exchanges between established buyers and suppliers. This, presumably, shielded buyers from upstream pressures on their own margins while still enabling them to practice ninja shopping on their own suppliers.[81] Both the retreat from public networks and the regrouping action around private exchanges were a predictable consequence of the standard enterprise logic and its zero-sum directives.

Despite these failures, the market for collaborative software is expected to more than double between 2000 and 2004, rising to more than $4 billion.[82] A new generation of Web services will, it is said, make it truly possible for firms to collaborate. Because Web services technologies enable distinct forms of software to work together, it is assumed that organizations will follow suit. As one analyst forecasts, "By 2005, Web services technology and adoption will coalesce to dramatically lower the cost of business interactions and recast firms and industries in more specialized interoperating, and agile, forms."[83] But the predictions for collaborative commerce follow the same technology-driven reasoning that led to the rise and fall of B2B exchanges, as well as many earlier software trends, from groupware to enterprise planning software.[84] In each case, it is assumed that new technologies will lead to new behaviors, whether that means sharing information across functional boundaries within a firm or across firm boundaries within a supply chain or an industry. And in each case, human behavior falls short of the potential for change created by the new technology. This is because new technologies are implemented within the standard enterprise logic, which remains the overarching force in shaping the behavior of every constituency inside and outside the firm.

THE NOT-SO-NEW ECONOMY

Our examination of the first phase of commerce in the digital medium suggests two propositions. First, everything that can be automated will be automated. Second, everything that can be commoditized will be commoditized. First movers in the wide-open spaces of the new medium were able to attract millions of people searching for the respite of self-support. The Internet exploded the possibilities of connection, communication, and knowledge across time and space, both appealing to and intensifying the individuation of consumption. But as they stumbled onto the new medium and pressed Go, the dot-coms unleashed an irreversible force that could radically accelerate the rate of cost reduction, while bringing down margins too. As we have seen, automation and commoditization did not require decades, but years and, in some cases, months or days. Indeed, these processes ripped through the e-world like wildfire through a parched wilderness. On the way through, the flames sucked a good deal of oxygen from the atmosphere of transaction value.

Not even the attractiveness of self-support could offer sufficient protection from the onslaught of value depletion, as many companies were forced to seek out market share by selling products at substantially lower prices than they, or others, sold them in the physical world.[85] Worse yet, the accelerated development curve associated with the new medium, so-called Internet-time, also accelerated the rate of value depletion. Where it once took fifty years to exhaust a source of transaction value, it now required much less. Cost reduction remained, as ever, a finite resource, and it became evident that this familiar wellspring of transaction value could eventually be depleted.

As Internet-based companies invested heavily in expanding their customer base but failed to generate operating profit, they turned to venture capital and the public markets as the primary source of cash. That increased the pressure to succeed in terms of traditional financial metrics based on margins and profits. Similarly, as bricks-and-mortar firms climbed into the Net, they also imported the financial standards and disciplines of the standard enterprise logic.[86] With mounting doubts about their business skills, serious competition from established brands, an increasingly volatile stock market that decreased the flow of venture capital, and rapidly diminishing transaction value, e-commerce firms came under significant pressure to generate revenue.[87] How were new sources of revenue and value to be found?

It was in answering this question that the utter conventionality of the supposed "new economy" was most vividly exposed to reveal the strong beating heart of the standard enterprise logic. Ultimately, the means that many firms adopted to generate additional revenues began to threaten the very experience of self-support that had attracted people in the first place. In the frenzy for revenue, the new tactics drew the transaction crisis online, turning a once benign vending machine and forum for community and exchange into an increasingly sordid carnival of intrusive marketing ploys, privacy violations, blowzy rhetoric, exploitation, and fake friendship.

THE TRANSACTION CRISIS GOES DIGITAL

Many Web-based businesses shared the mystique of operating in the interests of end consumers in some new way. But ninja shopping had forced them to relinquish productivity gains to their customers. Under pressure to find new sources of value, they reverted to the long-established syndrome we call organizational narcissism—an inward focus that can only see the end consumer as the means to a self-satisfying end. Indeed, many of the new tactics aimed at transaction value creation depended upon end consumers being manipulated, massaged, lured, and hoodwinked in all the usual ways. One such tactic involved Internet companies that gave away free services and then depended heavily on advertising revenues. These companies offered their customers a trade-off—we will give you free stuff if you give us personal information we can sell to advertisers. Instead of homing in on the opportunity to discover an entirely new source of value in individual space, they chose to turn their money-losing customer accounts into money-making databases. Many sold detailed profiles of their customers' shopping behavior to marketers and sometimes directly to producers themselves.

Advertising proved to be one of the most popular short-term strategies for generating revenue, and it continued to illuminate the acrimonious distance between producers and end consumers, even as it softened the blow with the electronically enhanced experience of self-support. At Buy.com, for example, executives described discounted goods as the lure used to attract "eyeballs." This made Buy.com an attractive target for brand-name advertisers eager to put their message in front of people in the act of buying something. Meanwhile, most other products at Buy.com were sold well above cost, and revenues were generated from inflated shipping costs as well as from installation and service charges related to its high-end products.[88] At Onsale.com, the chief executive acknowledged using price to "drive the customer base." Low-price offerings increased the volume of sales, but revenues derived instead from $5 to $10 fees charged on items sold at wholesale cost, from advertising, and from inflated shipping charges.[89]

The president of one ad agency observed the differences between traditional and online advertising: "Traditional marketing focuses on learning as much as possible about your target audience. Then you hurl your marketing spear and impale your customer. But on-line, the key is to hold the spear and let the customer impale himself."[90] With self-service impaling, the goal was to make ads more engaging and interactive, including games, full video, and high-quality audio. Some of these "rich media" ads were already programmed to play on a Web site whenever a user clicked to move to a new page.

New software gave retailers an unprecedented opportunity to learn about their customers, and to use that learning to discover new sources of value from the individual's point of view. Instead, the data tended to be used as a tool for supercharging the advertising message.[91] For example, companies like MatchLogic maintained data on tens of millions of Web users, including information on what sites a user had visited and how long they spent there. With a new generation of software, sites could analyze what someone did on a page and reconfigure themselves, in real time, to sell more effectively. Using "cookies"—bits of code that a site downloads to the user's computer—the sites could recognize users when they visited again, so their pages would automatically come up configured to a person's tastes.[92]

Retailers could also use their highly refined data about customers to exploit differences in shopping styles. It became possible to identify value-conscious shoppers and offer them discounts, while raising prices for those who were less sensitive to price. Other Web merchants learned to adjust the pages that customers viewed, based on the products they purchased. Then, depending on what a shopper put in her cart, the site could flash promotions for related items. Software was developed to help companies classify people when they came to a Web site. For example, people coming from a ".com" address might get higher priority than those coming from an ".edu" address, on the assumption that the former have more money to spend. Other software could configure ads and product offerings in real time, based on an analysis of the most recent sites that a customer had surfed. So an appliance seller might offer a bread maker to someone who has just surfed a bakery site. With the new software, expecting parents who had visited a baby-oriented site might find diaper ads when they logged on to check their stock portfolio.[93]

Most experts insisted that customer data had to be gathered "automatically," which is to say secretly. Why? Because lots of people resisted volunteering the very information that e-companies were seeking. One marketing vice president explained that consumers didn't want to fill out forms, and they "always bail when they get to the field that asks their annual income." The chairman of an Internet consulting firm cited an even more compelling motive: "The new paradigm is of friendship, where you aren't overly intrusive, but you aren't treating them like everyone else, either."[94] E-firms thus found it necessary to create the illusion of friendship and personal relationship by surreptitiously subjecting each customer to permanent, detailed, covert surveillance of every accessible aspect of their behavior.[95]

It is not surprising, then, that privacy concerns have consistently remained one of the leading reasons that people avoid the Internet or limit their usage. In 1998 a *Business Week*/Harris Poll found that privacy was the top reason cited for not going online, and 78 percent of those who did use the Internet said that they would use it more if they were not concerned about privacy.[96] By 2001 the picture had not changed much. That year 72 percent of Internet users said they were concerned about giving out personal information and credit card numbers online.[97] An even more dramatic 89 percent of those seeking health information online voiced concern that Web sites might sell or give away information about their online behavior.[98] So much for the new paradigm of friendship.

Advertising helped to fan the transaction crisis in another way. Most analysts agreed that the need to invest in marketing and advertising had drained investment dollars from the "back room" arenas of physical infrastructure and service that had been critical to the self-support experience.[99] This occurred in parallel with a substantial expansion of consumer expectations. A survey by BizRate.com in mid-1999 showed that customer service was the top factor in determining whether a customer returned to a particular merchant, beating out on-time delivery, price, and other concerns. A late 1999 Forrester survey showed that 90 percent of online shoppers considered customer service to be critical when choosing a Web merchant.[100]

It was already evident, however, that customer satisfaction with online retailers was dropping precipitously. One 1999 Jupiter Communications study identified a drop of nearly twenty percentage points as compared to 1998 (62 percent to 43 percent) in the numbers of online shoppers reporting that they were highly satisfied, and a rise of five points—from 3 percent to 8 percent—in those who reported low satisfaction. By the end of that year, message boards all over the Internet bemoaned the travails of "online shopping hell."[101] In 2001 the numbers were similar, with 48 percent of Internet users reporting high levels of satisfaction and 13 percent reporting low satisfaction.[102] Of 117 consumer-oriented business sites reviewed by Forrester Research in 1999 and 2000, the average user-experience score was –3 on a scale of –50 to +50 (a passing grade was +25).[103]

The growing numbers of beleaguered customers reflected the erosion of the self-support experience. Of forty-one companies surveyed in 1999 by the Yankee Group, fewer than 30 percent responded to customer queries within twenty-four hours. After forty-eight hours only 60 percent had responded, and still only half of those provided a straight answer to the original query.[104] In 1999 Jupiter found that 46 percent of the top Web sites in the content, consumer brands, travel, retail, and financial services categories took five or more days to respond to a request, never responded, or did not post an e-mail address on the site. In 1998 that failure rate had been 38 percent. Among shopping sites, 40 percent took more than a day to respond to customer inquiries in 1999 up from 28 percent in the 1998 survey.[105] Three years later, in 2002, that 40 percent had risen, rather than declined, this time to 46 percent.[106] During the crucial 1999 Christmas shopping season only 74 percent of online orders were delivered on time.[107] Things were not significantly different during the 2000 season, when only 78 percent of orders reached their destinations on time.[108]

Some merchants moved toward "live-help" software that allowed shoppers to "chat" with helpers as they decided on their purchases. But most e-tailers adopted a view of customer service that was based on the worst possible model—customer service in the physical world of commerce. They emphasized remote call centers, automated e-mail responses, and software that rated customer queries so that rapid real-time response was reserved for the best "customers" (ensuring that anyone who wasn't in that group would never be motivated to join).[109] In many cases, e-companies used software in an approach, known as "up-leveling," that was designed to lower the cost of customer service by providing low-cost automated interfaces and offering real-time service only as a last resort. One Forrester Research report on the subject of customer satisfaction with the online experience insisted that shoppers would remain loyal only to "high-touch retailers." What was a high-touch retailer? It was the merchant who offered "better customer service via regular updates to FAQs, constant improvements to the home page, and proactive e-mail order notification."[110] Service to customers remained a problem to be automated, relegated, and delegated.

THE E-COMMERCE SEXUAL DIVIDE

In our earlier discussion of the historical roots of organizational narcissism, we saw that the contempt of producers toward consumers evolved with a strong sexual charge. Perhaps then, it is more than coincidental that advertising activity online heated up at around the same time that advertisers became aware of the large presence of women participating in e-commerce. In 1999 Nielsen Media Research declared that the driving force in the explosive growth of e-commerce was the rapid increase in the proportion of women executing online purchasing and comparative shopping. Data from the 1999 Christmas season showed that women made a full 50 percent of all purchases.[111] By early 2000, Media Metrix found that women accounted for 48 percent of all Internet users but dominated commercial activity in most retail categories. AdRelevance, offering online analysis to the advertising community, crowed the news to its clientele: "Women Emerging as Coveted Audience Among Online Advertisers." Their report translated a century-old axiom to a new generation of Net executives: "Why is a female audience so desirable? Recent studies show women exert a great deal of purchase power, controlling 75 percent of family finances and 80 percent of purchase decisions. So it's no wonder that with the influence and purchase power that women wield, targeting women online is a growing trend. . . . The birth of the new millennium marks the emergence of women as a lucrative online market."[112]

On the back of such "insights," the old lines of force were redrawn in the new territory of the digital medium. This trend was facilitated in part by the fact that the top management of e-commerce firms displayed more or less the same sex ratios as those at the top of the *Fortune* 500, leaving the way open for a perpetuation of the traditionally inward-focused masculine culture. For example, in early 2000 at the height of the dot-coms, the 156 board members and senior managers in the top ten e-commerce businesses, as measured by market capitalization, included only eighteen women, for 11.54 percent of the total. That year the 305 people at the top of the *Fortune* 10 included only thirty-two women, or 10.49 percent of top management and directors. If a new producer social psychology was emerging among the new economy pioneers, then perhaps it was within those firms known as e-commerce "builders"—the companies that helped advise and build new Web-based businesses, often regarded as paradigms of the Internet firm. But a random selection of ten companies from a list of the top e-builders in 2000 revealed similar sex ratios, with only 11.29 percent of top managers or directors who were women.[113]

The dot-com leaders had found their way to a mostly male-identified organization on the one hand, set off against an increasingly female-identified end consumer on the other. The distance between them was mediated by advertisers, and distributors, and profiling software aimed at "them." Clearly, populating senior management and boards of directors with women is not enough to bridge the distance between producers and end consumers. The inward focus of the standard enterprise logic depends upon many factors, not just sex. At the same time, though, and considering the examples we reviewed in Chapter Nine, bringing the outside sex inside can make a vital contribution to bridging that distance.

GLIMMERS OF THE DIGITAL BRIDGE

Even in the first years of the online transaction crisis, there were tantalizing hints that things could be different. These involved efforts at revenue generation that, however crudely, began to acknowledge the end consumer as an individual. Most notable among such efforts was the way producers used the Internet to accelerate customization. End consumers could design or specify their own product configurations on the Internet for a range of goods that included dolls, hats, jeans, personal computers, CDs, vitamin pills, beauty products, golf clubs, newspapers, and more. One company even offered customized romance novels—one chose the names of the hero and heroine and indicated the preferred level of sensuality.

Customized products and services are surely welcome news for many end consumers, but the model is limited in three ways. First, business models based on customization are vulnerable, as automation inevitably reduces the margins on customized products. Second, the daily grind means that it is unrealistic to suppose that many people can take the time to design very many of their own consumption objects. And third, in the new context of individuated consumption, products and services are not substitutes for relationships of deep support, no matter how individually tailored they may be.

E-merchants also tried to enhance the buyer's experience with what has come to be known as "personalization." Personalization depends upon software that recognizes an e-mail address and "greets" the user with his or her name on the screen. Sites like Amazon.com offer recommendations on new products based on their software's analysis of past purchases. Amazon receives well-deserved kudos from many analysts for what one research group calls "smart personalization": the use of rich profile information to provide services to customers. Other popular forms of personalization include e-mail messages with reminders, updates, sale notifications, or other tailored promotional content, customized pricing, and configurable home pages.

Personalization can certainly heighten convenience, but in the end there is little that is "personal" about software that knows your electronic address, can spell your name, or configure information in light of automated analyses. There is no I–You relationship with interactive software. When consumers are moved to enthusiasm over personalization, it is simply fresh testimony to the depth of the transaction crisis. So much commercial interaction is anonymous or degrading that even something as impersonal as automatic personalization can make an individual feel recognized and welcomed.

In any case, superficial as it may have been, personalization was only a fond hope for most online businesses. Referring to their survey of major retail sites, interactive architects, and software vendors, one Forrester Research study lamented: "With simple personalization and data mining vexing our interviewees, a broader strategy for meeting the rising tide of consumer demands seems beyond their reach." One executive from an online financial site explained, "So much of our effort has to go into the transactional aspects of our site—scale and reliability issues—so personalization will have to wait."[114]

In the cases of customization and personalization, important innovations aimed at individuals were ultimately circumscribed by the standard enterprise logic: they were designed from the point of view of organization space, emphasized products and services, and focused on transaction value. While they contributed to the higher-order product that we call self-support, in most cases even that product cannot sustain a viable business model, as it remains at the mercy of the relentless commoditizing pressures of the digital medium. While self-support will surely continue to have an important role to play in the larger context of deep support, there are still other reasons why it has lost much of its original allure.

As we have seen, self-support had a strong beginning. It had immediate appeal for time-starved individuals with complex, modern lives who wanted to get things done quickly, efficiently, and without hassle. What could be better than buying books with one click and having them show up at your door, or tracking your own parcels, rather than waiting in a telephone queue listening to a recording telling you how important your business is? But as self-support became more widely available, it also reflected the fragmentation of the commercial world that was offering it. People who began by gleefully one-clicking up the volume of their libraries or monitoring the flight path of their holiday gifts were soon booking their own hotel rooms and airline reservations, managing their own stock portfolios, researching their own insurance policies and automobile purchases, and custom-designing their own newspapers, magazines, beauty products, radio broadcasts, CDs, dolls, hats, cars, personal computers, and more. Simultaneously, more information—whether it's about autos or antiques, books or bonds, insecticide or insurance, socks or software—also means more choices. This increases the amount of time required to complete a self-support transaction.

According to Jupiter Communications, Internet users were already spending an average of seven to eight hours a week online at home in 1999, as compared to 4.4 hours per week in 1998.[115] User self-reports indicated that eight of the top ten online activities were "utilitarian," including using search engines, researching products and services, purchasing from online stores, and downloading software.[116] In 2002, Pew Research reported that the average Internet user spent about 9.68 hours a week in nonwork online activity. That's more than an entire workday, each week, spent online. Again, of the top ten activities, only three were entertainment-related.[117] Yet when Saturday rolled around, there was still the hardware store, dry cleaning, shoe repair, mail-order returns, car wash, shoes for the kids, and every other intensely real-world errand that couldn't be crammed into the workweek. Self-support was not reclaiming life after all, but sucking up more of it.

Moreover, self-support quickly lost much of its appeal for end consumers as it began a quiet shift from being an option to being a requirement. For instance, by the late 1990s some airlines began to slash their fees to travel agents, and others closed down their reservation offices, including those at airports, in order to shift most of their bookings to the Internet. In other cases, people with access to full travel information realized how poorly they had been served by their travel agents and felt it necessary to book their own arrangements in order to achieve the best value.[118] Some companies drove their telephone customer service systems to such levels of automation that consumers were forced onto the Internet out of sheer frustration. For example, the availability of toll-free phone service on financial services sites dropped from 92 percent of sites in 1996 to 50 percent of sites in 1999.[119]

It became increasingly clear that self-support was becoming a way for companies to shift labor from employees to end consumers, in an all too familiar resource reduction strategy. Self-support was becoming yet another way to control and reduce costs within the organization, as more transactions relied on end consumers for data entry, quality control, and monitoring. This meant that there was no way to get some things done if you didn't do them yourself. In the language of classical political economics, self-support was being used to externalize key aspects of the labor process—tasks once accomplished by employees were now performed by customers, much as drivers now often pump their own gasoline at the service station. What had begun as a time-saver was turning into a time swamp. Once again individuals were left to shoulder their burdens alone, hounded by the transaction crisis even in the quiet of their own rooms as they sat before a flickering screen.

Thanks to ninja shopping and these other factors, self-support alone can no longer be considered a foundation for sustainable wealth creation in most cases. New sources of value must be discovered, value that cannot be overtaken by the rampant forces of automation and commoditization. But as a new generation of software and Web devices is coming online, their extraordinary new capabilities are already being channeled into the self-support proposition, leaving their new applications prey to the same vulnerabilities as their immediate predecessors. For instance, as companies adopt Web services, "software designed to be used by other software via Internet protocols and formats," there is a good deal of excitement about the new consumer services that can be offered. One example is an online travel service whose computers can automatically send an e-mail to friends and family, alerting them to your arrival time, or send you instant messages, informing you about a sale to travel destinations in which you have shown an interest. Another example is a banking service that "lets consumers handle savings, investments, and credit card payments from various financial institutions on one Web site," as behind-the-scenes software "travels among the different sites gathering data and completing transactions."[120]

Similarly, those who are writing about the eagerly anticipated "semantic Web" have typically cast its consumer applications in the mold of self-support. The semantic Web will vastly extend the capabilities of the current Web as intelligent software agents that understand the meaning and context of language are able to carry out complex tasks. A widely read article by Tim Berners-Lee, semantic Web architect and creator of the World Wide Web, begins with the example of "Pete and Lucy" using an intelligent software agent to find their mother a doctor covered by her insurance and to schedule a series of appointments that enable the two siblings to share the driving.[121] Another typical example is that of the software agent that can replace a travel agent, gathering relevant information about flights, prices, locales, and lodgings and then presenting choices and making reservations.[122]

These examples are all quite exciting. Who wouldn't want a software agent to take over the drudgery of routine tasks? But the technology-driven examples that people are imagining today do not resolve the commercial limitations of the self-support model. They do not ensure that commercial activity is aligned with the interests and needs of the end consumer. They do not assume accountability and responsibility for the consumption experience. The new technology tools may reduce the time involved in any single self-support activity, especially the searching and sorting of information that can be so time-consuming. But as long as producers stay locked in the standard enterprise logic, in which consumers' interests are a solar system away, these innovations cannot address the fundamental needs for psychological self-determination that animate the new individuals. The new tools may extend the self-support model for a limited period of time, but they too will eventually capitulate to the forces of commoditization. Along the way, end consumers will be as much on their own as they are today. Relationship value will remain undiscovered, as the new markets for deep support—and the opportunity for wealth creation they represent—remain invisible, wrapped in the silence of individual space.

Our scenario is a different one. In it, the greatest promise of the new digital technologies lies in their ability to enhance the capabilities and productivity of advocates charged with providing deep support, making their work efficient, effective, and affordable. In the world of individuated consumption, support is required not just when you book a trip but to ensure that when you arrive at your hotel you do not find that your room has been given away or is not what you expected. Support is required not just to find an insurance company but to guarantee that the company does not reject a legitimate claim and that it provides speedy service. Support is required not simply to book a doctor's appointment but to ensure that your doctor never feels the misaligned financial pressures that result in fragmented and superficial care. Support is required not simply to configure and order the correct personal computer but to make certain that it arrives, that it always works, and that you know how to use it. It is the assumption of accountability and responsibility for every phase of the consumption experience that defines advocacy and distinguishes deep support from mere goods and services. This is why deep support cannot be commoditized. On the contrary, when exposed to the illuminating fires of transparency, it only becomes more effective and thus capable of realizing more value.

FROM SELF-SUPPORT TO DEEP SUPPORT

The vast new potential of the digital medium cannot, on its own, break free of the standard enterprise logic to connect with the new sources of value lodged in the markets for deep support. Yet without the intelligence and complexity of the new medium, the breakthrough to the support economy is unthinkable. The new digital medium and its continuing enhancements represent the first technologies capable of enabling an enterprise to meet the demands of individuated consumption, with its requirements for sustained deep support across time and space and multiple domains of activity. Indeed, deep support is neither economically feasible nor practically achievable without the specific characteristics that define this new medium.

Thus far, however, the unique potential of the new digital medium has been subverted to serve standard commercial goals. Even the ever more compelling self-support experience does not provide an alternative to the standard enterprise logic. Without a new enterprise logic to link this immense new technological capability to the new markets, even the brilliant innovations slated to transform the Internet will not supersede the standard enterprise logic to embrace the equally immense potential for new wealth creation associated with deep support.

The goal, then, should not simply be "going digital," even when that means supercharged self-support at lower cost. The new goal should be to utilize the powerful new capabilities of the digital medium to liberate the vast, but suppressed, reserves of relationship value in individual space waiting to be turned into cash through the advocacy and relationship of deep support. Going digital is thus essential to the development of distributed capitalism, and distributed capitalism is the more complex purpose, packed with untapped economic value, to which the new medium is uniquely suited. The essential combination of new markets, new technologies, and a new enterprise logic suggests that the digital medium is not the destination; it is, rather, the bridge to the next episode of capitalism. The fire is laid. What's needed is the match. Watch the flames when these three forces finally combine. They will mark the real discontinuity between the economy of the twentieth century and that of the twenty-first.

ELEVEN

Conceptualizing the New Enterprise Logic

The Metaprinciples of Distributed Capitalism I

This chapter begins a discussion of the new enterprise logic that we call distributed capitalism. In this new logic, we seek the kind of irreversible revolution in perspective that can alter the fitful standoff between individuals and organizations, as it transforms the glacial inevitability of the transaction crisis into the next leap forward in wealth creation.

A COPERNICAN INVERSION FOR COMMERCE

The old worldview of managerial capitalism and its standard enterprise logic is in a crisis that cannot be resolved from within. The structure of consumption has shifted toward individuals and their needs for deep support, but so far the wealth associated with relationship value has been left on the table, a straight flush that cannot be played until a new worldview emerges. Such a new worldview must be capable of reconstructing the old problems from "new fundamentals," rendering them available to wholly new solutions.[1] The standard for this kind of revolution in worldview was set on an unusually warm and fragrant spring day in 1543, in Frauenburg, Poland, when, only hours before his death, Nicolas Copernicus saw the just-published copy of his life's work for the first time.

It was a treatise that would change forever the assumptions we hold about ourselves and the universe we inhabit. Copernicus is revered for his discovery that Earth and the other planets in our solar system revolve around the sun, though astronomy was a field that he merely dabbled in as he pursued other studies. He was the kind of man toward whom today's scholars might feel more than a touch of skepticism—a man of the church who had also mastered his era's knowledge of mathematics, medicine, philosophy, theology, and astronomy. He published only twenty-seven astronomical observations, but it was the breadth of his knowledge—his reading of the ancient Greeks, his mathematical skill—that allowed him to frame new questions and to question old answers.

Thirteen hundred years earlier, Ptolemy had worked out a very different conception of the heavens, in which Earth was the center of the universe, the point around which the sun and all planets orbited. This model of a geocentric universe remained dogma, though its empirical roots had been deeply compromised and its propositions had become increasingly arcane. By the time Copernicus was born in the late fifteenth century, the model had been buffeted for decades by observations it could not explain. As new tools allowed for ever more precise observations, reconciling those new data with the reigning model became more challenging and predicting the movements of the planets ever more difficult. Astronomers posited increasingly complicated and awkward concepts to shore up the model instead of questioning their fundamental assumptions—that is, until Copernicus synthesized a new conception that not only helped to explain actual observations but laid a solid foundation for the further development of scientific observation in astronomy and physics. His genius lay in his ability to reconsider the same elements in a wholly new relationship to one another. His mental act of inverting periphery and center, Earth and sun, remains one of the defining moments in the history of science.

Commerce today is like astronomy then. The standard enterprise logic, like Ptolemy's geocentric model, enjoys a supermonopoly over the human imagination and the practice of commerce, despite the fact that the firm is bombarded by ruptures on all key fronts: in the nature of the people it would serve and employ, in the technologies it would utilize, and in the competition it can expect. The firm under managerial capitalism has struggled to implement adaptations in the face of these ruptures, while carefully avoiding "cutting into the cloth" and altering the deep structure of the enterprise. In the process, today's enterprise has become as arcane, burdensome, and bizarre as the ancient conception of the heavens. And just as Ptolemy's model weighed on the progress of science, so has the standard enterprise logic become a weight on the progress of wealth creation and individual well-being. Individual consumers and employees find it impossible to get what they really need from the corporations upon which they depend. At the same time, those organizations appear incapable of freeing themselves from the self-mutilating cycles of commoditization that have infected the global competitive environment and are intensified by the special character-istics of the digital medium. If it is no longer sufficient to try to fix the sys-tem, then it is time to discover the inversion that can reveal a new one.

THE METAPRINCIPLES

We know that if distributed capitalism is to emerge as a true third force, it will require much more than can be accomplished on these pages. Those in the vanguard of mass consumption one hundred years ago pioneered a new social movement for the production of plenty that came to be known as managerial capitalism. It did not come with an instructional manual. Rather, they invented it as they went. And so it will be now, as the new indi-viduals in their roles as business leaders and entrepreneurs, end consumers and employees, mothers and fathers, elected officials, investors, and tech-nologists use their vision to grope, push, join forces, cheerlead, stumble, exhort, devise, innovate, and dream their way toward a new kind of econ-omy. A new enterprise logic must capture the imagination of many people from many different perspectives who see it as a superior alternative to today's practices: a way to make more money, a better way to work, and an opportunity to live a more self-determining life enriched by family and friends *and* by the people upon whom one depends for any aspect of con-sumption.

What we can offer is the beginning of a conversation. Hoping that ours is the first word but not the last, our intention is to lay a foundation that others can build upon in theory and practice. Ours is not a prescription for action; we offer no "steps" toward a new way of doing business. Our em-phasis is on the framework that helps make sense of a new way forward to-ward the support economy, a framework that can be applied successfully in many different ways. In that spirit, the "metaprinciples" of distributed capi-talism are intended to convey the architecture of a higher-order commercial logic, one that integrates, but is much more than, what went before.

In this chapter, all the metaprinciples are listed for consideration. We then explore the first seven principles in more detail, as they provide a conceptual overview of the new enterprise logic. Later, in Chapter Twelve, we return to Lillian and Carlos Acero to further explore the changing face of consumption in the support economy as a young family experiences the possibilities and potential of the new enterprise logic. With their example in mind, an examination of the remaining metaprinciples helps illuminate the inner workings of the new enterprise logic.

1. All value resides in individuals.

This is the fundamental inversion that reveals a wholly new system and entails the *distributed imperative*. Individuals are recognized as the source of all value and all cash flow. This value is realized through relationships of deep support with individuals and is distributed in individual space. Distributed capitalism thus entails a shift in commercial logic from consumer to individual, as momentous as the eighteenth-century shift in political logic from subject to citizen.

2. Distributed value necessitates distributed structures among all aspects of the enterprise.

Value is distributed, lodged in individuals in individual space. This is the common origin for corresponding distributed structures in every aspect of the enterprise. It necessitates distributed production, distributed ownership, and distributed control.

3. Relationship economics is the framework for wealth creation.

Distributed capitalism creates wealth from the essential building blocks of relationships with individuals. Using the new framework of relationship economics, enterprises and their federations invest in commitment and trust in order to maximize realized relationship value. Wealth is created in the realization of relationship value in individual space and depends upon the quality of deep support.

4. Markets are self-authoring.

Markets for deep support are formed in individual space as individuals opt into fluid, dynamic *constituencies* that hold the possibility of community for individuals as well as for the federation advocates who provide deep support.

5. Deep support is the new "metaproduct."

In the support economy, relationship value is realized as the enterprise assumes total accountability and responsibility for every aspect of the consumption experience. Products and services are merely the vehicles for the delivery of deep support, which is the "metaproduct" that defines the new commerce.

6. Federated support networks are the new competitors.

Under distributed capitalism, enterprises are linked into *federated support networks.* These dynamic and fluid federations are the new competitors. They achieve economies and differentiation through the configuration, quality, and consolidation of deep support in each relationship, while providing unique aggregations of products and services.

7. All commercial practices are aligned with the individual.

Under distributed capitalism, commercial practices are aligned with the interests of individuals and the requirements of deep support. This is operationalized by a strict dictate that cannot be compromised: *No cash is released into the federation and its enterprises until the individual pays.* This aligns the interests of all enterprises participating in a federation with one another as it aligns each and all with the individual. Cash flow is thus the essential measure of value realization.

8. Infrastructure convergence redefines costs and frees resources.

Under distributed capitalism, a wholly new approach to utilizing the digital medium makes it possible to merge infrastructure activities within and across all federated networks, by eliminating the replication of functional and administrative activities that exist within today's organizations. *Infrastructure convergence* dramatically lowers operating costs and working capital, enabling equally dramatic cost reductions in the delivery of deep support. As a result, infrastructure convergence puts deep support, along with goods and services formerly considered "premium," within the reach of individuals across income levels, and it frees human and economic resources for reinvestment in the new complexities of deep support.

9. Federations are infinitely configurable.

Under distributed capitalism, federations can use intellectual, emotional, digital, and physical assets to produce *infinite configurations* of deep support by and for individuals. No single template provides a universal formula for realizing relationship value, because each individual, or constituency, determines the right configuration for deep support in his life now. These unique configurations are an endlessly renewable resource for competitive advantage.

10. New valuation methods reflect the primacy of individual space.

New approaches to valuation emphasize the intellectual, emotional, behavioral, and digital assets that enable infinite configuration, sustain alliances among enterprises, and nourish relationships of deep support with individuals. A federation's competitiveness depends upon its ability to nurture and leverage these intangibles, alongside its physical assets.

11. A new consumption means a new employment.

The distributed imperative that arises from the individuation of consumption also leads to the distributed characteristics of responsibility and authority. This necessitates a new "employment" relationship, including new *career rights* and a new managerial canon based upon *collaborative coordination.* These new processes are not discretionary, but rather a necessary consequence of the distributed requirements of relationship economics, the intricacy of deep support, and the complexity of the federated support network.

THE DISTRIBUTED IMPERATIVE: DISTRIBUTED VALUE IS THE ORIGIN OF ALL STRUCTURES (PRINCIPLES 1 & 2)

Distributed capitalism derives from the principle that all value originates in individuals, who are the source of all the cash that flows through the enterprise and its federations. Value is thus lodged in individual space and expressed in markets for deep support. Here is the Copernican inversion that defines the new capitalism. We no longer look toward the producer in the center of the solar system as the source of value and the fount of wealth. Instead, we look outward, to the very individuals who have been spurned by the standard enterprise logic. This is the fundamental tenet that breaches the old logic. As we have illustrated, no amount of adaptation can stretch the standard enterprise logic enough to accommodate this new challenge. Just as managerial capitalism grew out of the exigencies of mass production, so distributed capitalism will grow out of the demands of deep support and the challenges of value realization in individual space.

The new enterprise logic is the commercial equivalent of the Vietnam Veterans Memorial Wall. The Wall reflects the great psychological reformation of the second half of the twentieth century that created individuals with an urgent hunger for psychological self-determination. It expressed this reformation as it distributed the rights and responsibilities associated with "the creation of meaning" from the designers of the monument to all the individuals who would experience it. Here was a new kind of Copernican inversion, one that made individuals the center and source of their own meanings. Traditionalists saw this as an abdication of authority. They feared a leap into the void—a meaningless monument. Instead, that inversion dramatically increased the depth and breadth of meanings associated with the Wall. Indeed, the experience of the Wall, rather than the Wall itself, became a boundless cornucopia of meaning, making it the most popular monument anywhere, ever.

Distributed capitalism, like the Wall, embodies the social shift from masses to individuals. It expresses a shift in the rights and responsibilities associated with the realization of value—from decision-makers in organization space to individuals and their advocates in individual space. Once again, the same pattern of inversion is evident. Under managerial capitalism, value is concentrated. It is created inside firms, agglomerated in supply chains, and delivered to customers. But under the conditions of individuated consumption, value is distributed. Once value is deemed to reside in individuals, everything changes. Firms no longer "create" value; they can only strive to realize the value that already exists in individual space.

The distribution of value is the bedrock from which every other structure is derived. It implies an inversion of managerial capitalism's structures, which have their origins in concentration. Recall that managerial capitalism was itself a revolutionary shift in the concept of ownership. Under its new aegis, ownership was dispersed among many shareholders, but the very dispersal of ownership diluted its authority. As a countermeasure, the standard enterprise logic led to greater concentration than had ever been known before. The property rights of shareholders were vested in managers, allowing control to be concentrated in the managerial hierarchy. Managers, especially top managers, enjoyed many of the rights and responsibilities associated with ownership, as they controlled the process of value creation. Value was concentrated in organization space, where it was "created" and "added to" through the production process, which was also concentrated there. The fact that organizations could be centralized or decentralized should not be confused with this fundamental structure of concentration. Decentralization merely means that concentrated authority is delegated. But delegated authority can also be recentralized. Large organizations often go through these pendulum swings, but both ends of the spectrum are simply different manifestations of concentrated authority.

The new enterprise logic derives from the distributed structure of relationship value, and as such it is the inversion of the old logic. This foundational principle creates an imperative in which every aspect of the new enterprise logic must mirror the distributed form, including its systems of production, ownership, authority, and social relations. In this new world, production is synonymous with relationship value realization. The process of production is distributed, because relationship value is distributed. Advocates are called upon to produce the behavioral, emotional, and intellectual innovations that can realize relationship value in their engagements with individuals. Naturally, they leverage network resources in the production process, including physical, digital, and collegial assets. But advocates and other federation members must realize value in parallel throughout individual space.

The distribution of value thus leads to a more extensive distribution of ownership than was the case under managerial capitalism. In addition to shareholders who own equity in federations, individuals "own" the sources of value, as all value originates in their needs, and all cash flows from their trust. As the origins of value, people can no longer be written off as faceless consumers who sit at the far end of the value chain, devouring the value created by managers and underwritten by shareholders. No longer an anonymous abstraction, the individual as the owner of all value and the source of all cash co-determines relationship value realization. This distribution of ownership creates structurally based opportunities for individuals to exercise voice in federation management and governance, adding to the operationally enforced pressures to align all behavior around successful relationship value realization and thus wealth creation. In the new enterprise logic, mutuality and interdependence replace the old zero-sum rules. We liken this development to the shift *from subject to citizen* wrought by the spread of democracy and universal enfranchisement. Distributed capitalism announces a similar shift *from consumer to individual* wrought by the new distributed structure of ownership.

The distributed nature of ownership is further enriched by the fact that advocates "own" important aspects of the "means of production." Specifically, federations rely largely upon intangible assets in the production of deep support. Preeminent among these intangibles are the behavioral, emotional, and intellectual innovations that advocates must produce in the service of deep support. Advocates produce these intangibles from their own personal resources of empathy, integrity, intelligence, skill, and so on, even as they leverage the wider resources of the support network.

As we shall discuss more fully in Chapter Twelve, distributed production and ownership also lead to the necessity of distributed authority. Federation members enjoy significant new rights and obligations as they now have responsibility, and accountability, for every aspect of the individual consumption experience to which they have contributed. The authority to solve problems and to innovate must be distributed throughout individual space—in parallel, in real time—or advocates risk abdicating responsibility and destroying relationship value. Mutual gains sustain distributed control: Individuals attain the support they need, advocates develop meaningful and successful careers, and realized relationship value turns into positive and sustainable cash flows for the federation and its enterprises. This will necessitate a new managerial canon and new forms and qualities of social relations that mirror the realities of distributed authority. As we shall see in more detail in Chapter Twelve, we expect these to emphasize collaboration and coordination over supervision and administration. There will be a need for new qualities of consensual leadership and new kinds of managerial roles and practices that are consistent with the distributed form.

RELATIONSHIP ECONOMICS AND THE DISCIPLINE OF CASH (PRINCIPLE 3)

Relationship economics is the new source code, the new DNA, from which every aspect of behavior in the new commercial solar system is derived. The value lodged in individuals is what we have called relationship value. All the relationship value that can exist at any given moment already does exist—though still implicitly—in the hearts and minds of individuals as they face the challenges of daily life. Management can neither create nor destroy relationship value. That value originates in individuals to be either realized or suffocated through the experience of relationship. Realized relationship value is dynamic. It leads to new experiences that in turn create new layers of implicit needs and desires awaiting new opportunities for expression and realization.

The purpose of commercial activity under distributed capitalism is not to create relationship value but rather to realize it with and for individuals. This means a profound realignment of the commercial system around individuals and the value that is locked up in the travails and challenges of their daily lives. No longer is there an organization deciding what it will or will not do to or for the end consumer. No longer is there an organization oriented toward—or indifferent to—its end consumers. All wealth derives from one source: realized relationship value. All cash flows from one source: realized relationship value. We mean this quite literally. Surplus cash derives only from the individual's willingness to pay more for realized value than it took to achieve.

Relationship economics describes mutually beneficial reciprocities between enterprises and the individuals who choose them for support. Firms make money when realized relationship value flows through a federated support network, enriching all its partners and investors according to their role in its realization. In contrast, suffocated relationship value reduces the federation's access to that cash, possibly forever. Relationship economics unifies the interests of each enterprise in a federation around value realization for individuals, eliminating the zero-sum conflicts of the old supply chain. It also supersedes the age-old adversarialism between buyers and sellers. In this new regime, no one will have to look for a correlation between financial performance and the realization of relationship value, and no one will be able to ignore it. They will be one and the same.

The relation between transaction economics and relationship economics is one of "hierarchical integration," a term often used in science to refer to the developmental patterns of complex systems. It means that later and more differentiated systems include but are also "more than" the earlier and simpler systems from which they evolved. Later systems can do all the things that earlier systems could do, but much more as well. More important, elements of the earlier system are organized in a wholly new way in the context of a new more intricate and capacious system. One obvious example of this process is the relation between childhood and adulthood. The simpler cognitive systems of childhood are reorganized in new ways in the context of adult systems that entail greater complexity, scope, and ability. In relationship economics many of the elements of transaction economics—supply and demand, profit, return on investment, return on capital, operating cash flow, etc.—continue to exist, but they are now organized in a more complex system that is oriented toward a wholly new purpose: relationship value realization through deep support.

One of the factors that most distinguishes the simpler system of transaction economics from the more complex system of relationship economics is the way that each treats the opportunity to enact commitment and engender trust. In transaction economics, commitment is almost always considered purely as a cost. Because each transaction is an end in itself for which profits must therefore be maximized, the cost of commitment is nearly always viewed as prohibitive. While firms advertise their devotion to customers, it is, in fact, the fear of too-high commitment costs, in both the short and the long terms, that accounts for most of how end consumers are really treated. In relationship economics, each transaction is a vital opportunity to begin or continue to nurture a relationship of deep support. The cost of commitment is therefore regarded as an investment opportunity. *Accrued trust*, which rises with the commitment that is invested, enables long-term value realization through deep support. For this reason, measurements of "intangibles" like accrued trust, repeat purchase, repeat content, and realized relationship value will become a vital dimension of every balance sheet and financial statement.

According to the new competitive demands of individual space, federations that do a better job of supporting and extending relationships with individuals will be the most successful entities in the global economy, and human societies that do the best job of supplying federations with smart and relationship-oriented human beings will be the most prosperous. The rural and small-town cultures that survive in the so-called backwaters of the developed world have long held relationship at the center of commercial activity. These remnants of the past may also be fragments of the future: important sources of the kinds of people who can pioneer individual space and help drive the economic powerhouses of distributed capitalism.

INDIVIDUAL SPACE AND SELF-AUTHORING MARKETS (PRINCIPLE 4)

Individual space has been invisible because it is the opposite of organization space. It can be found only beyond the light from the lamppost, outside the territory that has been mapped by managerial capitalism. Though uncharted, this space is replete with unrealized relationship value. It is where needs are felt, needs that grow in subtlety and particularity as people's lives grow more complex and demanding. Individual space cannot be reduced to a physical location. Individual space is psychological space; it is the subjective space in which an individual creates and assigns meaning to objects, activities, and experiences. Individual space is in my head, not just in my house. That means individual space is wherever I am, wherever I have been, and wherever I am going.

The content of individual space is a function of "how I make sense of my life." It is dictated by what an experience means to me. It is a subjective universe of values and priorities, dreams and desires. This is why relationship value can be assigned only from the vantage point of individual space. There have been many companies that have tried to get a foothold in the home. They had the right intuition but the wrong model. They treated individual space as if it were a place to which they could deliver more stuff. They sought to create dependencies and lock consumers into new sales channels. Because they approached the home with the standard enterprise logic, relationship value and individual space remained hidden in plain sight.

Individual space is always the individual's space, and the choices that exist there are always the individual's choices. Each individual sets the rules of relationship, which help define the unique configuration that reflects his or her individuality. These relationships cannot be constructed mechanistically. They are necessarily intimate and authentic. They build over time, based on mutual respect and interpersonal trust. They do not arise from loyalty cards, frequent usage points, or other relationship-marketing formulae. Federations will not give points to individuals, but individuals will expect federations to earn points from them for the privilege of continuing to provide them with deep support.

In the new enterprise logic, markets are no longer targeted, attacked, penetrated, or saturated by organizations and their products or services. Instead, markets are self-selected and self-defining. They are composed of constituencies that arise voluntarily as individuals opt into similarly designed configurations of deep support that best suit their needs at that time. In the standard enterprise logic, companies target markets or market segments for their products or services. Segmentation is an act of interpretation and definition conducted in organization space. It is something done to markets, rather than something that arises from them. In contrast, constituencies are organic groupings that arise from individual space and are therefore consistent with the subjective logic of individual space. Constituencies are not defined by federations but are supported by them. Individuals define constituencies by intentionally opting in and out of the dialogues that lend them coherence. Deep support is thus addressed to individuals and the relevant constituencies that define themselves through the aggregation of individual choices. Such constituencies are fluid, temporary, and porous groups that constitute new economic, social, and psychological opportunities for their individuals and the advocates who support them.

DEEP SUPPORT (PRINCIPLE 5)

In the support economy, the relationship value embedded in individual yearning is unlocked by the federation's assumption of total accountability and responsibility for every aspect of the consumption experience and its related activities. This is what we call deep support. Business is no longer about selling a product, a service contract, or a doctor's appointment. Now it is about the advocacy, authentic relationship, mutual trust, interdependence, intimate knowledge, and practical consolidation that ensures the quality of everything that precedes and everything that follows the "transaction." Relationship value realization depends upon providing individuals with the deep support they require to develop and sustain the activities, experiences, processes, and material requirements associated with their ever-individuating lives.

Today, the only commercial operations in individual space are those based on self-support. While self-support is likely to remain an important option for some people, some of the time, it offers only a modest solution to the problems associated with the stress of the daily grind, provides only weak protection from the transaction crisis, and remains vulnerable to automation and commoditization. The new individuals yearn to take their lives into their own hands, but that doesn't mean they want to take all the work into their own hands too. Individuals want enterprises to work for them. They want to retrieve their lives from the stresses of the daily grind. They want time in which their lives can unfold, time that has been usurped by the fragmentation of commerce, the complexity of modern life, and the intrinsic adversarialism of consumption and employment.

Individuals need more than things. While deep support may be punctuated with the delivery of goods and services, it cannot be reduced to either. Deep support can be thought of as a "metaproduct" that includes, but is much more than, goods and services. It means perpetually adaptive and proactive attention to the dynamic needs of an individual. It is not a marketing gimmick, a slogan, an advertising campaign, or a fortuitous way to acquire data about end consumers. There is nothing ironic about deep support. Deep support cannot exist without an I–You relationship in which individuals cease to be merely means to ends and become ends in themselves. It means that the duality of producers and consumers is synthesized in a new dynamic interdependency in which cynicism and instrumentality are replaced by a common interest and a mutual regard among individuals. "Buyer beware" gives way to "United we stand," as little murders are converted to daily acts of life-enhancing, wealth-generating relationship value realization.

Deep support can be defined only in individual space because it connects to each individual's meaningful construction of his or her needs. As an end consumer, deep support is "for me." It enables me in ways that I consider valuable and eliminates what I consider to be valueless. The forms of advocacy, activity, experience, goods, and services that compose the ever-changing content of the ongoing and durable relationship that is deep support arise from each individual's meanings. In this sense, deep support and relationship value realization are always and only experiential—in other words, they can be judged only by the individual and from his or her point of view. Dialogue replaces marketing, because only through real dialogue can the other's meanings be known. Dialogue is an important dimension of value realization, as it builds trust and interdependency, identifies emerging arenas of support, monitors quality, and anticipates needs for products and services.

Deep support requires a combination of two worlds: One is local and physical, the other is global and digital. On the one hand, deep support will leverage the resources of a vast, federated, switched-on network that operates on behalf of individuals. It must transcend time and space, connecting support to people wherever and whenever they need it. These capabilities of deep support are not possible outside the digital medium. But deep support is always implemented locally. Deep support must finally connect with "where I am now," both in terms of my subjective sense of value and in terms of my actual physical location. No matter how vast a federation might be, the extensiveness of the information and knowledge it commands, or the excellence of its systems, deep support will always be only as good as its immediate, here-and-now, local implementation.

Deep support can range from reactive to proactive. It can also vary in terms of the actual depth of support—basic support is at the "shallow" end of the spectrum, relying heavily on automated systems and remote dialogue for problem-solving, while "deeper" levels of support will build on those automated platforms, adding complexity, functionality, and a more prominent interpersonal dimension. We anticipate that individuals will be able to choose the scale and style of deep support that best suit them at any point in time and for different aspects of their consumption needs. At the most basic level of deep support, a federation's automated systems, content providers, and local service aggregators can take over most of the valueless activities that plague daily life, from personal finances to grocery shopping to simply navigating the world in order to identify the best resources for one's needs. Deeper levels of support will address increasingly subtle and nonroutine aspects of daily life and thus require a greater degree of interdependency. Advocates will play a role at every level. At the basic levels of support they will assign responsibilities, monitor quality, oversee online performance, and initiate corrective action when necessary. At more complex levels, teams of advocates will coordinate deep support, leverage federation resources, link to other federations and enterprises as needed, and blend virtual and physical contact in highly interdependent relationships with individuals and constituencies.

FEDERATED SUPPORT AND THE NECESSITY OF ALIGNMENT (PRINCIPLES 6 & 7)

Once we invert the enterprise system and inspect each set of activities within it from the point of view of individual space, certain matters, once settled, become problematic in a new way. The once distinct realms of production and consumption now merge and blend around the nexus of deep support. Instead of supply and demand, the new enterprise logic of distributed capitalism is based on *need and support*. Instead of a supply chain or a value chain, there are federated support networks that integrate a wide range of enterprises, each offering its distinctive approach to deep support, bundled with the goods and services in which it specializes. Federations offer unique configurations of these tangible and intangible assets, suited to the demands of their constituencies.

When deep support is the purpose of commercial activity, the institutional landscape changes radically. It is no longer sensible to ask what kind of organization is best suited to provide deep support, because deep support is not something that organizations as we know them can provide. Modern organizations were invented to command and control physical, human, and, now, virtual assets in organization space. They do best when they are making things, and they struggle to maintain similar levels of quality when they are providing services. But deep support is neither a product nor a service. It does not originate in organization space, nor is it enacted there. Deep support requires perpetual relationship and it occurs in individual space. Deep support is an ongoing resource that can be drawn upon according to the rhythms and necessities of the individual's experience.

Thinking about the enterprise in a support economy thus puts new demands on the imagination. Gone are the simple and universal methodologies. Gone are the boxes and arrows that neatly map the hierarchical territory under the lamppost. Euclidean space gives way to fractal geometry, as we learn how to invent and sustain dynamic complexity, both in the fluid operations of federated support networks and in the dynamic interplay of their ongoing relationships with individuals.

The image that best expresses the relationship between individuals and federations is no longer that of a solar system—a central, organizational sun ringed by increasingly distant planets in fixed orbits—but rather of a *coast-line*, enduring but ever-changing, stable but turbulent. The coastline is a complex dynamic system that is orderly but radically adaptive, "webbed with positive feedback" as it appears distinct yet is a merger of ocean and land. This is not "organization" as we have known it. Mathematicians refer to systems like this as "nonlinear" or "fractal." Such systems combine chaos and order in arrangements of extreme complexity and infinite intricacy to create "meaningful patterns of uncertainty."[2]

Euclidean geometry conceived of space as blank distances composed of points, lines, circles, rectangles, triangles, cubes, and spheres. These Euclidean concepts offer a fictional but still useful way of imposing orderly relations on points in space, much as the standard logic of our organizations imposes an artificial but useful order for the administration and control of production and distribution. In contrast, fractal geometry expresses an implicit and demanding truth—the world is not a tidy composition of boxes and arrows. Rather it is filled, twisted, kinked, crinkled, wrinkled, folded, and pocked.

This geometry, first elucidated by Benoit Mandelbrot in 1967, became the basis for a new understanding of natural forms such as clouds, trees, mountain ranges, and coastlines. As one interpreter of fractal geometry explains, "Most natural objects, including ourselves, are composed of many different types of fractals woven into each other, each with 'parts' that have different fractal dimensions. For example, the bronchial tubes in the human lung have one fractal dimension for the first seven generations of branching, and a different dimension for the branching after that. In the complex environment of nature, intricate patterns of self-similar, scaled detail were laid down by the dynamical forces affecting evolution, growth, and function."[3] Mandelbrot wrote of the intuitive logic of fractal patterns and saw his new geometry as part of "a shift away from a strict qualification of nature—measuring objects and processes in terms of degrees, lengths, and calibrated time durations—and toward an appreciation of the qualities of nature such as roughness, openness, branchiness."[4]

Linear and nonlinear systems differ in a number of important ways. For one thing, nonlinear systems emphasize uniqueness, varying with the nature of their initial conditions. With a linear equation, solving for one value provides a good idea of how the equation will behave in general when any other value is used. In contrast, nonlinear equations can vary significantly with different values.[5] Another feature of nonlinear systems is that everything is connected to everything else through feedback. As a result, the form in which any "part" of such a system starts out will have an enormous impact on where it ends up. Two specks of ice drifting in the upper atmosphere might start out at almost exactly the same place, but the microscopic differences in each speck's initial conditions will lead each to a vastly different fate. "The complex and subtle dynamical forces acting on each individual snowflake as its crystal grows will result in very dissimilar final forms."[6] In a fractal world, all outcomes are individual outcomes. These new insights into the intricacy of real life and the uncontrollable but not out-of-control dynamism of natural systems begins to bridge the stale distance between what science can say and what human beings already know. In other words, individuality and dynamic interdependence are inherent to this way of ordering, rather than being challenges to its fundamental precepts.

The organization as it has evolved in the twentieth century is a Euclidean masterpiece. It carved a single spacious order of boxes and arrows, flow charts and hierarchies, from a messy fragmented world of craftsmen and merchants and small producers. Standardization was necessary to maintain this artificial order; for the parts to work together smoothly, variation in raw materials, finished goods, employees, or end consumers had to be identified, rooted out, and obliterated. The new enterprise logic will continue to need elements of these organizations and their capacity for economy and efficiency. But those organizational elements will now be integrated into a new enterprise system that embraces individual variation in order to support the intricacy of real lives.

When we look at the coastline more carefully, we see that it actually represents a merger of several distinct elements: the ocean, the surf, the beach, and the land beyond. And so it is in the relationship between individuals and federations. Individuals, advocates, and their federated support networks are like the beach, the surf, and the ocean. They are utterly interpenetrated and merged, while maintaining their distinctness. At the point of contact where the surf meets the beach are the federation advocates and the individuals they support, as well as the wider constituencies to which they may belong. Advocates are the vanguard of their federations, the immediate source of relationship for deep support, and the guardians of cash flow. Beyond them are the federated support networks they represent and the enterprises that participate in them. The image of a coastline expresses the fluidity and interdependence among all of these stakeholders. And therein lies the more intricate future of the once obvious duality that was production and consumption. That duality now gives way to a new experience of mutuality, in which individuality not only matters but is vital to all outcomes. In this new economic order, unique and complex needs are the catalysts for relationship, which is the source of value realization. In this inverted universe, variation and complexity are treasured and nurtured, not banished. They are the new sources of wealth.

THE OCEAN: FEDERATED SUPPORT NETWORKS AND THEIR ENTERPRISES

In the middle of the nineteenth century, before the rise and consolidation of the corporation and its new managerial hierarchy, the economy was composed of autonomous business units "monitored and coordinated by market mechanisms."[7] In many instances, the owners of these independent businesses combined into "federations"... "to control competition between units or to assure enterprises of sources of raw materials or outlets for finished goods."[8] Frequently they agreed on common buying, pricing, production, and marketing policies. According to business historian Alfred Chandler, such federations were able to achieve modest reductions in information and transaction costs, but they could not achieve the productivity improvements that could lead to dramatically lower unit costs. That breakthrough awaited the new corporate form, which internalized these once independent units. The corporate form necessitated the creation of the professional managerial hierarchies that finally enabled administrative coordination of the flow of goods, more intensive use of facilities and personnel, increased productivity, reduced costs associated with information and transactions as well as production and distribution, more certain cash flow, and more rapid payment.[9] One hundred years later, as we have explored in some detail, the obligatory inward focus that characterizes these hierarchies also spells the limits to their adaptive range.

In today's world, the continued growth of the managerial hierarchy represents a productivity drag, not an enhancement. Computer and communications technologies make it faster and easier to coordinate complexity with fewer people, and without the disadvantages of the inward focus that leaves

firms vulnerable to organizational narcissism. The presence of more educated people at every organizational level makes it possible to distribute information and decision rights more widely. The transparency of real-time
systems reduces the risks of distributed information and authority, enabling
the automation of decision parameters, monitoring, and rapid problem identification. All this means that vertical integration of the various sources of
products and services that contribute to deep support is not feasible. Instead, we think it is most likely that enterprises will link together in twenty-
first-century versions of the federation, in which autonomy no longer
comes at the expense of the economies associated with coordination and
communication.

The necessity of such federations also derives from the new commercial
purpose of the enterprise. As we have seen, deep support cannot be reduced
to a single product, service, or industry. The metaproduct of deep support
draws its form from an individual's needs, not from the organization of
commerce by product line, industry, or sector. On any given day, the deep
support an individual requires might also convey a dozen distinct products
and services drawn from a range of commercial sectors. In other words, deep
support is not fragmented; it is a holistic and seamless experience. That
means no single company can fulfill its constituencies' needs for deep support. Under distributed capitalism, new enterprises would offer deep support bundled with their particular products or services. While this scenario
would constitute an improvement over the old commercial logic, it means
that deep support would be just as fragmented as self-support is today.

To create integrated deep support, companies would have to be linked in
cross-industry multienterprise support networks, each and all aligned with
the individuals they support. These federated support networks combine
and integrate the fragmented support offerings of a range of enterprises,
along with their distinct products and services. The support network's
unique strategy to meet the needs of its constituency is reflected in the innovative ways in which it combines the tangible and intangible assets of participating enterprises, as well as the ways in which it chooses and develops
relationships with these participants. In the world of distributed capitalism,
these federations are the new competitors.

It is likely that most enterprises will, at any given time, be participants in
more than one federation and will receive distinct revenue streams from each
participation. In this way, enterprises must exhibit a kind of modularity, in
which they enjoy an integrity of internal operations but are also organized
for smooth linkage and interdependence with one or more federations. A

"proto" example of such relationships can be seen in today's components manufacturers—highly efficient contractors who produce manufactured goods for a variety of branded industrial companies such as Hewlett-Packard, IBM, and Cisco Systems.[10]

The mass-production values of efficiency, low cost, return on capital, etc., are still extremely important for participating enterprises, but now they are part of a larger and more complex framework based on the logic of relationship economics. For example, from the point of view of individual space, the so-called value chain, whether virtual or physical, is actually a "cost chain": The multiplication of effort and profit-taking up and down the traditional supply chain has meant added cost, not just added value, to the end consumer. When a firm achieves cost reductions, those savings normally accrue to that individual firm, not to the supply chain as a whole, and typically not to end consumers. Thus, conflicts across the supply chain derive from each organization's efforts to maximize its own interests at the expense of other participants in the chain and its end consumers.

These sources of conflict are eliminated in the new federation, as the entire network is aligned with the requirements of deep support and depends upon value realization in order to initiate the flow of cash. The commitment to this alignment is a critical factor that distinguishes relationship economics from transaction economics. That commitment is expressed in the commercial entity's complete assumption of accountability and responsibility for every aspect of consumption-related activity and experience. It is operationalized by an iron-fisted discipline that cannot be compromised: No cash is released into the federation and its enterprises until the individual pays. This aligns the interests of all enterprises within the federation with one another, as it aligns each with the individual. It is this fundamental operational criterion that protects enterprises and federations from the old narcissistic behaviors associated with the standard enterprise logic—behavior that would spell financial ruin under distributed capitalism. With the discipline of cash alignment, every strategy, every act of resource allocation, every activity, every choice, every behavior, and every judgment is undertaken from the point of view of individuals in individual space. It ensures that alignment never degenerates into mere platitudes. Only when the individual pays more for deep support than it took the federation to provide it does the federation generate surplus cash.

Cash is thus the key indicator of commercial success and is directly correlated with realized relationship value. All federation-related activities, from governance to investment valuation, are conducted according to this principle of alignment, which is to say, from the point of view of the individual in individual space and the metrics that reflect the quality of deep support. This is facilitated by assuring that the individual is always the unit of analysis, whether in data capture and manipulation, financial analysis, or operations and metrics.

As a result of this alignment with the individual, each participant in a federated support network, and each level within the participant organization, is concerned about one and the same thing—the cash that flows from ongoing value realization as individuals draw upon deep support. Each participant strives to realize the same value: the relationship value embedded in the network's relationship to each individual. In this new order, all the operating cash that flows through the federation derives from one source—the individual. No participants in the federation are paid for their contributions to deep support until the individual pays. The financial interests of all federation participants are immediately aligned with one another, as they are defined by their shared alignment with the individual.

In this new framework, operating cash flow becomes a primary indicator for each enterprise, as well as for the network as a whole, of the quality of the relationship with individuals and constituencies and the extent to which value is being realized. Partners will share information, knowledge, and experience, because their survival depends upon their collective ability to optimize realized relationship value. As cash flow aligns all interests, loyalty will have to be focused on the individual rather than the enterprise. Irrespective of who pays the employee, everyone will know that the cash comes from individuals.

Federations are not defined by what they make, what they sell, or what services they perform. Federations are defined by the constituencies that select them for support and by the ways they invent to provide that support. Some federations may specialize in supporting certain constituencies, others may specialize in providing only certain levels of deep support, and still others might specialize in their ability to aggregate support through various levels. At the deepest levels of support, federations will leverage cross-federation alliances to meet the most extensive range of their individuals' needs. All federations will have to be flexible, agile, and operationally excellent. The qualities that distinguish them will be far more subtle. Federations will be differentiated by their ability to effectively invent and consolidate new practices and social relations that are appropriate to the distributed nature of the commercial undertaking. They will also be distinguished by the style, creativity, imagination, authenticity, and consistency with which they enter into relationship with and provide deep support for individuals. Indeed, we anticipate that the quality of the I–You relationship associated with a federation and its reserves of accrued trust will become an important factor in the ways it is valued by investors, as well as the ways it is evaluated by individuals and constituencies.

A federation is likely to be mobilized by a lead enterprise or alliance of enterprises that have recognized a dimension of individual space in which they can realize value. The perceived opportunity to provide unique configurations of deep support to particular individuals and constituencies drives the formation of the federation. This mobilization creates an immense opportunity for brand development and extension. Federations add to the value-realizing potential of their participating enterprises through the unique values, style, and meaning that are reflected in the ways they provide deep support, including the strategic choices related to configuration and consolidation. One can easily imagine a lead enterprise, such as UPS or Apple Computer, organizing a federation that provides deep support in ways that express, reflect, and extend their brand. An Apple Federation, for example, would appeal to individuals and constituencies drawn to its style of brainy but whimsical panache and its empowering creative and high-tech values. These values would be expressed in the people it employs, the ways it invests in the development of those members, the ways it invents to support individuals, the quality of the partnerships and alliances it sustains, and so on. Or imagine a Wal-Mart–mobilized federation that specializes in low-cost, 100 percent reliable automated support and product replenishment. It would also be possible for enterprises to coalesce in a federation and form a new brand. Or federations might unite around a particular individual or symbol whose values and appeal suggest unique support characteristics that can draw participation from particular constituencies.

Relationship value is realized and converted into wealth through the federated network's relentless, imaginative, and unbounded pursuit of deep support for individuals, their families, friends, acquaintances, colleagues, extended kinship networks, neighborhoods, communities, organizations, affinity groups, and so on. The limits of relationship value are the limits of the imaginations of all who are involved in its realization. Value realization is infinite and enduring; it accrues to all the contributors in the federated support network, starting with individuals. In contrast, the limits on the creation of transaction value are always finite, especially when those efforts depend upon cost reduction as the primary method of achieving profit. The burdens of historical transformation are now disproportionately shouldered by individuals. They want help with their burden, and the evidence suggests that they are willing to pay for that help. By assuming accountability and responsibility for every aspect of the consumption experience, the federated support network shares that burden. It is precisely this sharing that becomes the source of future wealth for the network.

ADVOCATES: THE SURF

Advocates are like the surf, merging with individuals but flowing from and drawing upon the wider ocean of the federated support network. Teams of advocates operate in individual space using digital and physical channels to provide deep support. Advocates are accountable for the operational challenges associated with deep support. Advocates never "own the customer." Instead, they earn the right on a daily basis to participate in interdependent relationships with individuals.

These relationships define the heart, both literally and figuratively, of the new commercial system. Advocates are gatekeepers with considerable influence over the generation of cash and thus the wealth of the federation. The quality of their relationships with individuals is an important factor in determining the success of the federation. The federation's skill in organizing, supporting, and developing advocates is a source of competitive differentiation.

Advocates are individuals and exist in dialogue with individuals. They create community together. More than anyone else, they take responsibility, and have accountability, for the integrity of the I–You relationship. Advocates' individuality and authenticity enable them to identify with other individuals and provide a foundation for dialogue, inquiry, and empathy. No longer is it acceptable to formally ignore large sectors of one's own experience while "at work." Advocates draw on their humanity as they integrate all of their personal experience—as parents, family members, and individuals who are themselves in need of deep support—into their daily work on behalf of others. Federations, therefore, have a critical stake in the development and well-being of their advocates. Investing in the people who help shape the coastline cannot be optional and cannot be cyclical. It is essential, and it is compulsory.

In today's world many people are trapped as employees behind the barbed wire of resource-starved transactions. As employees they are asked to ignore who they are and what they know in order to squeeze themselves into the narrow roles provided by the standard enterprise logic. Instead of acting on their wholeness, they surrender essential pieces of themselves—

their common sense, their judgment, their empathy—in the forced march to the drumbeat of organizational narcissism. This is what most people do, and who can blame them?

What's really fascinating, though, is to take a very careful look at those rare individuals who do not succumb to the demands of organization space. Occasionally, they survive inside the standard enterprise logic and by their stubborn presence manage to humanize activities that would otherwise be devoid of real life. Frequently, they leave large organizations in order to run their own businesses according to a more personal model that preserves and honors what they know as human beings. We are very interested in these people. While their experiences often reflect the limits of the old logic, they also impart a glimpse of different and vital possibilities. No one has taught us more about the role of advocate, and the vast potential of that role as the cornerstone of a new economy, than our friend Faith.

FAITH'S STORY: THE ORIGINS OF ADVOCACY

We preface Faith's story with an account of a scientific anomaly. In 1977 molecular biologist J. A. Leigh isolated an organism from a sediment sample scraped from the seafloor at the base of a 2,600-meter-deep volcanic vent on the East Pacific Rise. This organism thrived in those near-boiling waters (optimally at 85°C or 185°F) while keeping its own temperature stable. It grew under pressures that would flatten most submarines. At first, scientists believed the organism was an ancient form of bacteria. After further study, it was found to have more commonalities with the only other known life-form, eukaryotes, which include plants, animals, and humans. For twenty years, this organism, known as Archaeon for its ancient origins, remained an intriguing and unresolved scientific mystery.

In 1996 the mystery was resolved, and in a way that no one would have predicted. In a major scientific breakthrough, scientists announced that they had decoded the first complete set of genetic instructions from a micro-organism—none other than Archaeon. They were astonished to find that two-thirds of its genetic structure did not look like anything ever before seen in biology. Archaeon was in fact an example of a wholly new life-form, confirming the existence of a third major branch of life on Earth. "These findings represent the scientific equivalent of opening a new porthole on Earth and discovering a wholly new view of the universe," explained Dr. J. Craig Venter, then director of the Institute for Genomic Research, which participated in the study. Venter and the other geneticists regarded Archaeon as the likely precursor to all the life-forms on the planet. And though it was originally assumed that Archaeon lived only in extreme environmental conditions of temperature and pressure, scientists now think that Archaeon is far more common, composing a significant part of the world's biomass and playing an important, though still unknown, role in Earth's ecology, especially its carbon and nitrogen cycles.[11]

Archaeon had once been regarded as an intriguing but obscure anomaly, an ambiguous protobacteria dependent upon the odd and highly specialized environment of deep-sea volcanic gases. Now it may hold the secret of all life. Faith is just like that. What distinguishes Faith is that she lives in individual space, which is, from the organization's point of view, about as remote, exotic, and irrelevant as some place 2,600 meters below the sea adjacent to a "white-smoker" chimney at 21° north on the East Pacific Rise. As she stubbornly clings to those depths, maintaining equanimity in the heat and unruffled under pressure, she must be watchful for the submarine patrols that are eager to haul her back to organization space. She is as diminutive as a porcelain figurine, as quiet as a prayer. It's easy for a manager to write her off as an obscure anomaly—quirky, eccentric, problematic, marginal, and simply not one of "us."

Faith is an airline agent who works in the frequent-flier lounge of an American airline in the Rome airport. She has faced the pendulum swings of organizational support (more like benign neglect, really) and organizational opposition. During that time she has pioneered individual space, with no one to applaud or even take notes. She does it because her heart and brain tell her to. The relationships she has with her "customers" give meaning to her work and to her life. Supporting them makes her feel alive, useful, and worthy. It also means, she believes but cannot prove, more revenue for her company—or at least it would if others were encouraged to operate out there in individual space, which they are not. So she perseveres, dodging bullets, weary of the conflict, but buoyed by her network of close personal relationships with other individuals.

When Faith began her work in the early 1980s, her role was largely ceremonial. Her job was to meet and greet people, to make sure they felt recognized. But Faith's instincts told her to do more. Her customers needed help getting real problems solved, but no one was empowered to help them. Throughout the 1980s, she watched various management programs come and go, each intended to improve customer service. What struck her was how disconnected they were from real life. "Nothing ever related to what really went on at the airport. It was just slogans like 'go the extra mile.' This approach simply isn't relevant to the real issues my customers have."

By the late 1980s, under the aegis of a new customer service program,

Faith was given access to a customer database that maintained detailed profiles of frequent-flier cardholders. Faith could download data to a laptop, work with the data, and then hand off data cards to the flight crew. Faith knew what she wanted to do for her customers. What she sought from the company was some assurance that she wouldn't get into trouble for "going out on a limb." The new program created the necessary legitimacy for Faith's efforts.

> I could work on a problem and stay with it until it was resolved. That follow-through is the most important thing. I took on a lot of problems, from sales to ticketing and baggage. Technically, I did things that you were not supposed to do, but there are ways of playing with it and getting around it. It is kind of bending the rules and knowing what you can get away with for the customer. I saw my work grow into something that became recognized by the customer as of value. I have received tons of letters saying, "Listen, my bags are missing again, but I want you to know that you really handled it professionally. You are the reason I am coming back. I know you are there for me." The customers know that they can call me. I say, "Here is my card and here is my number. If you have a problem anywhere in the world, just call me." I am their friend within the company.

Faith had found her niche as an advocate for her customers. Frequently that advocacy required her to defend her customers' interests over and against the company's own rules and regulations. Ethically, she found this acceptable, because Faith also saw her work as contributing to the airline's best interests by building accrued trust, even when the company was too myopic, political, and bureaucratic to know it. Her exploits were legendary. First, there were the matters related to air travel. Faith would stand out on the curb, boarding passes in hand, waiting for a couple who were chronically late for their flight to New York. She would have everyone standing by to whisk them onto the plane as soon as they drove up.

Faith knew how to pull seats and upgrades from thin air, juggle tickets to keep parents and children together, and change itineraries at a moment's notice. One couple reported that while wandering around the airport terminal in Johannesburg, they heard their names being paged. It was Faith. She had been tracking their round-the-world itinerary and found that one flight had been canceled. She had rebooked them on another flight, even making sure that they had their preferred seat assignments.

Faith could have stopped right there and set a new world's record in any standard metric of customer service. But Faith was into her customers' lives, not just their air travel. She understood her customers as people, not as ticket holders or frequent fliers. In her case, she went more than the extra mile. She went right through the looking glass to the other side. There she began to explore individual space. "I regarded my job as really about maintaining an ongoing relationship with the people who were traveling and finding out what was going on with them. I identified with them. I cared about them."

She arranged a birthday party for the nine-year-old son of one customer, including specially printed invitations, a tour of the airport, and lunch on a plane. When she learned that one of her customers was fighting a cancerous brain tumor, she made sure that relatives from Istanbul and Geneva could visit him frequently, shuffling around frequent-flier miles to pay for their trips. She visited his sickbed regularly to tell him jokes and bring him humorous cards. She attended his funeral in Milan and his memorial service in London. In several instances, she introduced customers to one another, knowing that they had similar business interests. Many of these matchmaking efforts turned into commercial ventures and new business partnerships. Anyone lucky enough to know Faith would have entrusted her with just about any aspect of their lives and cheerfully let the airline take a cut of the action. But that was not to be the case.

By 1992, the pendulum began to swing at the airline, and it hit Faith right in the head:

> Instead of doing what was necessary for the customer, the new priority was budgets, budgets, and budgets. Everything you did came under the scrutiny of what budget it was falling under. Everything from cheese for the lounges to delivery of lost baggage had to be scrutinized and cut. I still had my laptop and continued to download information, but when my boss found out she was livid. She made me send it back to New York. Eventually they sent me back the laptop, but I can no longer use it to access data. It's just sitting on the floor in my office, unplugged and gathering dust.

With the new emphasis on cost reduction, organization space was once again front and center. Now, instead of dealing with all her frequent fliers, Faith was faxed lists from New York each day telling her which passengers were to be "touched." The fax would specify which four passengers should be "touched" in the lounge and which two should be "touched" on the plane, by the flight crew. It didn't matter if the last two on the list were the first to check in, or if the first ones on the list arrived late and never even made it to the lounge.

> If a customer is sitting in front of me for three hours, but they are not on my list, then I am not supposed to speak with them, because they have been identified for a cabin crew touch. If the person who is on my list shows up five minutes before the gate closes, then I have to run alongside them down to the airplane so that I can have this dialogue.

Just when Faith thought it couldn't get any worse, it did. The faxes from New York gave way to a new program. Now the customer service effort was outsourced to a market research firm in the Midwest. They employed various criteria for identifying daily "touch targets"—birthdays, a long hiatus since a last flight, a recent upgrade or downgrade in frequent-flyer status, or the anniversary of the date the customer joined the Frequent Flier Club. The decisions about what "we" do to "them" had retreated even deeper into organization space, leading to even more ridiculous outcomes.

> They fax me a series of forms that I have to fill out and fax back to them. Then they update the file and tell me who to "touch." It is like a kindergarten now, with everyone fighting among themselves and trying to do the least amount of work. The poor customer is the last one to get help. The customer is way out there shouting, "Hello? Hello?"

Faith continues to try to keep at least one foot in individual space, but it's hard and she is often in trouble. She's been called on the carpet by her bosses, forced into meetings with her supervisors and her shop steward, and disciplinary letters have been placed in her personnel file. She hasn't given up her relationships, but there is less and less that she can do to support them. In the world of the standard enterprise logic, Faith looks to her managers the way Archaeon looked to scientists twenty years ago. They see only two life forms: First there is everything that exists inside the organization—that's called "us." Then there are customers—that's called "them." Faith is an odd sort of creature whose DNA is linked to both groups. While supposedly an employee, she appears better suited to the rarefied conditions of individual space than to organization space, where real business is conducted. Her membership in the organization appears ambiguous; her loyalty is a cause for concern.

Today, Faith is not only trapped in the organization, she is limited to the frequent-flier lounge dominated by first-class and business-class passengers. But in the new world of federations, the economics of infrastructure convergence will mean that everyone will be able to afford some version of Faith—not just for air travel, but for deep support from an extended federation across a wide, if not infinite, array of activities. Faith and her colleagues, together with the electronic and physical infrastructure they can leverage and the federations that enable them, will be there to advocate and support the complex activities and material requirements of individual lives each day to the degree that one desires, and in exactly the way one prefers.

As individual space becomes every place that value is realized and wealth is created, Faith will begin to look more like the Archaeon of 1996. She will be seen as the mother of the new life-form we call advocate as it emerges from the implosion of organization space. This Faith organism will survive that cataclysm, precisely because it knows how to thrive in individual space. Once individual space becomes the central cornucopia of wealth creation, Faith, like Archaeon, will be reinterpreted as both ubiquitous and essential to the biomass of the new commercial system. As our understanding of the real potential of deep support becomes more sophisticated, no enterprise or federation will fear being "Amazoned" or "Delled," but it will fear being "Faithed"—watching someone else win the race to establish the I–You relationship that provides the best support at the best price to the right individual in the right constituency for the longest period of time.

*   *   *   *

The old order and the new order each harbor their own paradox. In the old logic, the standardization required to serve the mass created a divergence of interests between producers and consumers and among all participants in the supply chain. In the new order, supporting individuals uniquely creates a convergence of interests between advocates and individuals, as well as among participants in federated support networks. This is not merely a transformation of the organization. This is a transformation of the entire commercial system and with it the forging of a new phase of economic evolution. We are out from under the lamppost now. This is a revolt in the heavens, a new Copernican inversion.

TWELVE

The Inner Workings of the New Enterprise Logic

The Metaprinciples of Distributed Capitalism II

In this chapter, we first travel full circle, back to Lillian and Carlos Acero, the young couple in a not-too-distant future whom we met in Chapter One, as they learn the new pathways and possibilities of the support economy. In the scenarios provided here, we examine their experiences with a federated support network in greater detail in order to more fully illustrate how one might operate. This example is offered in the spirit of a single act of imagination, knowing that the principle of infinite configuration invites illustrations but prohibits any definitive template of future practice. The chapter then continues with a discussion of those metaprinciples that help explain the inner workings of a federated network. The ideas and illustrations we develop here represent only one configuration, among the hundreds and thousands that are waiting to be created. They represent what *can* happen, rather than what *must* happen, as we consider the concrete innovations that can bring the new enterprise logic to life.

EXPERIENCING THE FEDERATED SUPPORT NETWORK

Recall Lillian and Carlos—she's a librarian and he is a software engineer. They are a hard-working middle-class couple who joined the rural renaissance in the 1990s, eager to reassert control over the quality of their lives.

They have two young children. Carlos works primarily from home, in part to ensure that at least one parent is there with the children after school. When Carlos is not working on a professional project, he enjoys checking and updating the systems in their "automated intelligent house." Lillian heads up library services for the State University's main campus, forty miles from their home. When Lillian's father died, her mother moved to be near them. They enjoy being close to her and are very concerned about her health and well-being.

The Aceros have opted into several federations. The federation they use for basic services is called SweetSupport. Its brand is based on a 100 percent service guarantee, backed by accuracy and timeliness metrics that are refreshed every twenty minutes and carry financial penalties when targets are missed. Carlos had been reluctant to concentrate all his family's information with one federation, but their security guarantees and authentication software allowed him to overcome those misgivings. SweetSupport uses complex, interactive, intelligent software to carry out routine functions. It is one of the largest automated federations, providing "base functions" for its participants and a digital platform for other, more specialized federations with which it shares alliances.

SweetSupport, like other platforms of its type, is responsible for ensuring that all its enterprise participants, as well as those of other allied federations, are paid when cash is released from its individuals. Once an individual pays, payments are made using the product and service autobiographies, which contain unique identifiers for each transaction and track each enterprise's contribution to the individual's final purchase. These payments are fully automated; they can be made and reconciled in real time. While SweetSupport provides the digital platform for many federations, its complex information is manageable because the individual is the unit of analysis for all information storage and manipulation across the platform and across all alliances.

SweetSupport uses next-generation Web services to gain access to relevant databases and common standards and protocols for transmitting data to home systems, electronic "filofaxes," and mobile PDAs, ensuring that individuals can have their data accessible when and where they require. SweetSupport is accountable and responsible for problem resolution. There is also a Web-based support area, where problems are resolved online with SweetSupport advocates. They meet daily with leadership advocates to review the issues raised by individuals and identify performance-improvement opportunities. They also meet with strategic advocates and enterprise advocates to review the performance of participant enterprises as well as of federations with which they have alliances. They make use of online voting and discussion groups among all types of advocates and individuals when considering new alliances. There are also monthly performance reviews that use the online polling systems.

Leadership advocates report against agreed benchmarks and note new trends. Performance results are constantly updated online for all enterprise participants. SweetSupport displays a time clock on all its interfaces with individuals that shows how much time was saved each day, week, and month, based on family profiles. These ratings are continually aggregated in real time. They are a primary source of performance feedback and provide another important federation metric, as the more time they save, the more valuable the support they offer, and the higher the valuation of the federation.

The Aceros use SweetSupport for all their purchase, payment, and information-management activities, which are recorded in their home data system, as well as their electronic Filofax, their PDAs, and other data-capture sites they value. The federation pays all their routine bills, including telephone, electricity, mortgages, credit lines, and local taxes. It also pays their credit cards and provides a monthly reconciliation of expenditures, separating out business and personal expenses where relevant, and maintains cumulative records that can be used for tax purposes. SweetSupport also renews memberships, makes insurance payments, pays subscriptions, and stores personal information about passwords, pin numbers, etc. Forty-eight hours before a payment is made or an appointment is pending, SweetSupport checks with the Aceros to confirm payment amounts, what credit card or debit line they want to use for payment, or if they want to maintain the appointment schedule. Using the electronic Filofax, the federation maintains information on birthdays and other important dates, as updated by the Aceros. These are reconciled with the calendars of the children's schools as well as Lillian's and Carlos's personal diaries, updating schedules and communicating "alerts" for potential conflicts.

SweetSupport offers various payment options for large and small purchases, including credit cards, lines of credit, loans, leases, and mortgages. It collects bids for these financial services, lists all costs and interest rates, and recommends the most cost-effective options. The federation also maintains a warranty and product usage function. When a new product is purchased, its autobiography, including warranty and instructions, is immediately sent to the family's file and can be easily accessed. These records are also used for payment to the enterprises that assembled the product. SweetSupport is linked to UPS for parcel delivery, instructions, and tracking, and this information also appears in the family's Filofax.

SweetSupport's core skills are software development and integration. It guarantees the highest metric of all the automated federations (99.9 percent up time, 100 percent accuracy, and thirty-minute problem resolution), and its fees reflect a premium for this level of quality. Its aggressive and innovative product development keeps it competitive, as it works on razor-thin margins and is constantly exposed to the threat of ninja shopping. It relies on scale for its revenue, as well as fees for supporting the thousands of federations with which it shares alliances. As a digital platform alone, SweetSupport's valuation would be low, but its valuation increases substantially in consideration of the number and quality of its alliances. Its value also depends upon the amount of time saved, repeat purchase rates, repeat content, realized relationship value, accrued trust, and online voting and evaluation by the individuals who use its support, whether they are exclusive to Sweet-Support or relate to it through an allied federation.

Lillian and Carlos also opt into the GoldenApple federation, a unique support network derived from the earlier Apple Computer company. Their decision to participate in this federation was based on recommendations from families with similar patterns of needs, the qualities of support available, and their appreciation of the federation's distinctive style and values. GoldenApple is allied with SweetSupport and their systems are fully aligned. That means that all of SweetSupport's basic support functions are hierarchically integrated into GoldenApple's support, though from the individual's point of view, the two are seamless, sharing accountability and responsibility for the Aceros' support. (Typically, the "highest order" federation in which an individual participates assumes ultimate responsibility for all activities in which it plays a role, even when another "lower order" federation's systems may also be involved. In this case, GoldenApple assumes accountability and responsibility for the resolution of any problems the Aceros encounter that are related to any activity in which it played a role.) GoldenApple provides interactive displays of all SweetSupport functions, though they appear in its characteristic three-dimensional bright green, gold, and red fonts and video-graphics.

GoldenApple offers high-quality deep support aimed at saving, on average, ten to twenty hours per week. Its support includes personal advocates that develop and maintain relationships with individuals and play an important role in supporting complex consumption activities. Its advocates are uniquely skilled in supporting working couples with children and elderly parents. It maintains an extensive network of local service providers, a feature that is particularly attractive for dual-career families. GoldenApple is also distinguished by its small-business hub, which supports individuals who run their own small businesses or are self-employed. When Carlos does freelance work, GoldenApple provides all the accounting, bookkeeping, secretarial, report-generation, and design services support through its small-business support hub. He can buy this support in a package or on an hourly or daily basis. The federation sends out invoices and collects outstanding balances for Carlos.

With summer approaching, Lillian is anxious to find a summer camp for their oldest child. GoldenApple offers three levels of support in this area. The first level is modified self-support. Lillian can visit a variety of recommended interactive sites, as well as relevant chat rooms that GoldenApple can identify. At the next level of support, GoldenApple assists her with search and evaluation activities. Using its Web-based support, Lillian can build a profile of the kind of camp she is looking for, and the federation will undertake a search. It quickly delivers extensive information on various options, including availability, parent and child evaluations, independent evaluations, and so on. Finally, GoldenApple also offers expert support through one of its allied enterprises, HERE4U, which specializes in expert advice in more than one hundred family-oriented categories. In this fee-for-support engagement, Lillian would ask an expert in the subject, who listens to her needs, executes research, makes recommendations, and is available for follow-up quality monitoring throughout the summer.

In this case, Lillian opts for the expert, and a video appointment is immediately scheduled for the time she requests. Within twenty-four hours of their video dialogue, they have a second meeting. At that time she is presented with three recommendations, including performance metrics for each. There are streaming videos of each camp, links to other families happy to discuss their evaluations of one or more camps, and links to discussion groups on each camp. Lillian confers with Carlos and their children, and a decision is made the next day. GoldenApple completes the application and reservations process, sending deposits, doctor's reports, and other required material. All entries are posted in the Filofax, including the camp schedule. Lillian receives a communication alerting her to the fact that the camp's first visiting day conflicts with her doctor's appointment and asking permission to reschedule the appointment.

Lillian and Carlos also have a relationship with a GoldenApple advocate, David, who supports their more complex consumption needs. David and his three team partners (advocate teams are typically composed of two women and two men) also support anywhere from 300 to 400 other families. They are leveraged by intelligent software agents that can be used to accomplish most of an advocate's routine tasks. The Aceros consider David a member of their extended family. He has earned their trust, acting as a champion for their well-being in many situations. He consistently fulfills his charter, accepting accountability and responsibility for every aspect of the activities associated with his support. David also represents his individuals within the federation, using their experiences to direct his strategic advocates toward new forms of support, services, and products.

When the Aceros travel, David monitors in-journey care, home oversight, and communications, each according to instructions from the couple and subject to their input and control. When David arranges a business trip for Lillian, she often elects to have the concierge service. This means that she is supported throughout the journey: Cancellations or other deviations from the schedule are managed proactively with alternative reservations, in-air food selections, and reading or video material; ground transportation and hotel accommodations are assigned and monitored; Lillian's luggage is shipped separately, and her clothes are stowed in her hotel room before arrival. Lillian communicates with David and the federation's systems through her PDA, which alerts her when new arrangements appear.

David notifies the Aceros that the hot-water tank has signaled that its service period has expired (a feature of their automated house) and that the in-home service call has been arranged. GoldenApple guarantees all contractors and repair services, using allied agents who are bonded and must conform to the federation's performance metrics. If there are service problems, they are immediately corrected without question and at no additional cost. David also reminds Carlos that his car is due for service next week. He has arranged a loan car from the dealer, which will be left at the house when the car is picked up. David advises the Aceros that he has moved them to a new local service provider for their groceries and other errands, as recent performance reviews have shown it to be superior in service and product quality to the earlier provider with whom GoldenApple had been allied. Later, Lillian receives a message from the new provider that the semi-weekly food order will be delivered at four, as requested. There is a query as to whether she wants the concierge service, which unpacks and stows the groceries, or a simple drop-off. Lillian selects the drop-off option. At 4:05 the delivery person arrives. She leaves the groceries, along with a pick list and price analysis that shows itemized costs compared to other options, so that Lillian can determine if she is receiving the most delivered value from her federation. Just before dinner, Lillian notices that David has recommended three new films that he thinks the couple will enjoy and has downloaded them to their home network.

Lillian and Carlos agree they want to trade in their second car. Once they decide their brand and model preferences, they access federation-vetted consumer reports and chat rooms where they can talk to other owners. Thanks to GoldenApple's unique software, they can also see three-dimensional models of the car in various configurations and colors. The couple has strong feelings about additional options. Lillian wants to buy an "SRV," or socially responsible vehicle. She does not want any part of the car, including the raw material, to be sourced from countries where there is child labor. She also wants it 40 percent recyclable. Carlos wants all the high-tech gear, including the global positioning system with concierge support.

Once the general specifications have been agreed upon, their federation creates an electronic product specification and purchase order that is sent out across a distributed network to the federation's participant enterprises. Each enterprise reads the request and decides if it can fill the specification, as it contacts its own federated suppliers as to feasibility and availability. To ensure there are no child-labor inputs, all object biographies must be traced back to their raw materials. If a specification cannot be met through the federation, the request is broadcast to enterprises outside the federation. If one of these enterprises is tapped for supplies, it is automatically hooked into the payment, delivery, and quality-control systems of the federation, which also guarantees its performance. When the information on components and costs is assembled, it is indexed under Carlos's and Lillian's unique identifiers. Payment systems are specified, along with delivery dates and carriers.

Finally, David communicates the final cost and delivery dates to the couple. To verify that the Aceros are receiving the best possible deal, David also asks a competing federation to price the vehicle. Though both federations use the SweetSupport platform, David is surprised that his competitor is able to generate a lower price for the new car. David confers with his cluster of leader advocates, as well as several enterprise advocates. They identify the price variance in the higher cost of the global positioning systems from the GoldenApple allied manufacturer. They also note that this supplier has missed several key performance metrics during the past month, through late deliveries and unusually high costs. They agree to review the status of this supplier, investigate its problems, and examine alternatives in the next few days. In the interim, the Aceros are offered the vehicle at the lower price, and the difference is absorbed by the federation as an investment in accrued trust.

Lillian queries the trade-in value being assigned to their current vehicle. She is immediately shown all the relevant data, including the online bids from the enterprises that buy used cars. The federation also calculates what the Aceros might expect to receive if they were to sell their car privately, including the cost of advertising and the cost of holding the car for an extra twenty-one days (the average time it takes to sell a car of that make and model in their area). The additional data persuade Lillian that they are receiving a fair price. While this is going on, the federation uses SweetSupport to gather outside quotes for financing the new car. These are compared to the quotes from GoldenApple's three allied banks. As the allied banks are able to meet or exceed market rates, the Aceros are offered a choice among the three, as well as information on the other quotes that were gathered. The Aceros select their lender from within the federation, based on earlier experiences with its financial services.

When the Aceros decide to purchase the vehicle with the designated price and financing package, all the participating enterprises are notified that the order is live. Within seconds, the couple receives a message indicating their new car will be delivered in three weeks and the old one picked up on the same day. It also confirms their car loan and locks in the low rate. The components for the car are gathered for modular and, later, final assembly. In every phase, all parts are electronically tagged with Lillian's unique identifier. During this process, David receives daily updates, as do all the enterprises involved. The vehicle is completed and sent to a delivery point near the Aceros' home within eighteen days, from which it is delivered to their house on the twenty-first day, fully taxed, insured, and with all documentation completed. Their old car is taken away. The Aceros inspect the new car and test-drive it. When they are satisfied, they notify David and their account is credited with the used car value, debited with the new car cost, and all participating enterprises are issued payment, which is received within hours.

As Lillian's mother begins treatment for a blood disorder, David determines which aspects of the treatment are covered by the mother's existing insurance policies and which will be picked up by Medicare. Because she is the unit of analysis for all her personal information, these links can easily be determined. GoldenApple's health-support systems will ensure that all payments are made from the insurance company and all account reconciliations are appropriately recorded. As treatment progresses, David works with the mother's medical team to determine the in-home support that she will require. The Aceros are already considering GoldenApple's in-home care package, which offers home monitoring, prescription deliveries, and various levels of home care, most of which is covered by their mother's insurance carrier, also a GoldenApple enterprise.

GoldenApple operates on healthy margins and a relatively high valuation. Its effectiveness and success depend upon the quality of its constantly evolving dialogue with the individuals who opt into its offerings. All of GoldenApple's economics and brand characteristics are geared to the unique pattern of needs voiced by this constituency. These individuals are working moms and dads with at least one elderly parent. Usually one of the adults is self-employed or owns a small business. They have—or want to have—automated houses and are technologically competent. They seek high levels of local service and want to free up one to two days, on average, each week. GoldenApple is continually developing its offerings to support this pattern of needs. Members of its constituency who are happy with its support are constantly pulling in new families. Its strategic advocates track the evolving needs and new trends that emerge from their constituents, based on ongoing analyses of their utilization patterns and feedback from individuals, advocates, and allied enterprises.

INFRASTRUCTURE CONVERGENCE (PRINCIPLE 8)

Deep support is for individuals at every income level. Today, anything that remotely approximates deep support is typically available only to the very rich, either because they can afford to hire many people to support their needs, or because their attractiveness as wealthy customers leads to special service and consideration. Everyone else has equally great needs for deep support but fewer resources to secure it. In the new enterprise logic, levels of deep support can be developed so that they are widely affordable. The baseline? A majority of individuals should be able to purchase the kinds of supported experiences that, were they even to exist today, would be sold in fragments and at a very high premium. Beyond that baseline, deep support would increase in complexity, depth, and scope.

The economies that make deep support affordable are based, in part, on infrastructure convergence. In the new enterprise logic, the need to lower the cost of commitment while increasing accrued trust, effectiveness, speed, and coordination will force federation participants toward hitherto unthinkable infrastructure solutions. In today's world, infrastructure costs arise from the basic activities and functions replicated in every company—accounting, legal, payroll, auditing, warehousing, logistics, etc. In a federated support network, the opportunity for a radically redefined cost structure arises from the elimination of most, if not all, of these replicated activities.

As long as firms operate in the standard enterprise logic, this solution is not feasible. As we have already seen, each entity in the supply chain must operate according to its own strategy and the diverse interests of its top management and shareholders. Each requires "ownership" of accounting, logistics, inventory control, payments processing, and so on. Supply chain management (from planning production levels to sourcing and procurement, inventory management, and delivering products to market) costs the average manufacturer more than 14 percent of its annual revenue.[1] Companies frequently turn to the outsourcing of discrete activities, which reduces some complexity but does not have a radical impact on the cost structure of the firm or its supply chain. It has been estimated that in the automobile industry alone, "webification" of various supply chain, procurement, and manufacturing activities could provide cost savings of around 13 percent.[2] But as we have seen, the dynamics of ninja shopping limit the competitive advantage from such productivity improvements and drive the commoditization of ever more complex products. And in any case, as long as the savings represented by such estimates are pursued in the context of the standard enterprise logic, they can accrue only to a single firm, locked in a zero-sum game with its own supply chain and end consumers.

When these savings opportunities are considered in the framework of the new enterprise logic, a very different horizon opens up. Consider the elimination or virtualization of infrastructural activities, and multiply that effect across an entire support network. The result is infrastructure convergence, the key to lowering infrastructure costs across a federation by many orders of magnitude. Once this occurs, cost and working capital can literally be vacuumed out of the support network, and its speed of execution will reach new standards. This opens up once unimaginable possibilities associated with newly liberated working capital, as it enables the increased levels of reinvestment in deep support and the operational quality necessary to raise the levels of accrued trust. In the new logic, cost reduction through automation no longer leads to an endgame of commoditization or zero-sum dynamics. Instead, it reorients concepts of infrastructure ownership as it reconfigures the cost base of the enterprise and the federation. This dramatically lowered cost profile and redeployment of assets make deep support both feasible and widely affordable. In this way, infrastructure convergence is a critical success factor in the creation of new wealth through value realization in individual space—wealth that is shared among participant enterprises and their federations.

The merger of infrastructure activities will occur as they migrate to a ubiquitous digital platform. The individual is the common denominator for all data. That means the individual is at all times the fundamental unit of analysis for data capture, data operations, and data retrieval. All transactions and all payments are identified by the individual. The digital platform can act as a giant pipeline, capturing all relevant transactions and other necessary data. It could automate everything that can be automated, while integrating processes and functions across enterprises and federations. All federations could access all relevant information directly from this pipeline. This means that there could be one inventory system, cash-based accounting system, payments system, integrated logistics system, etc., all based on common protocols and shared by participant enterprises of federations. Ultimately, such a platform could be used by many, or even all, federations, linking federation enterprises and their respective networks, while providing the basis for integrating a federation's strategically designed range of products and services.

The new platforms can track all materials that are, in any form, ultimately destined for an individual. This tracking is more than a logistical exercise. It aggregates information about a material's composition and history, not just its location. Every unit could carry its own permanent electronic attachment that provides a cumulative history of all its physical, intellectual, and digital inputs. The precise tracking of the aggregated inputs on all goods, documents, and other materials can provide an empirical basis for the cash distribution that will ultimately flow back through the federation and is therefore the basis for federation payments and governance. We anticipate electronic tags that aggregate inputs as well as all other related details, accumulating an always current autobiography of all materials. Such autobiographies could include sourcing, inputs, delivery notes, payment terms, credit lines, damage and return histories, automatic reconciliations, etc.

We think that payment, accounting, finance, audit, and other administrative services can be ubiquitous, bundled, and consolidated in every digital platform. This vital element can enable cost savings and standardization within and across federations. In addition to tracking the physical transactions, the areas of payments, accounting, and finance would be critical for easy and universal consolidation. Today there are financial accounts, management accounts, cash accounts, and statutory accounts. Each must be created and reconciled on a monthly or quarterly basis. With the digital platform, it would be feasible to move all accounting to a cash accounting basis. When this is combined with standard accounting formats, electronic reconciliation, payroll systems, payments, etc., one can imagine a single set of cash accounts that track all cash transactions and even make accruals for non-cash items. These can be processed through a common code of accounts (no more U.S. GAPP, U.K. GAPP, Napoleonic code, etc.) and provide balanced books on a daily basis, and eventually in real time. The basic audit can also be standardized and completed electronically with variances easily identified.

Routine administrative processes can also be absorbed by the platform. For example, human resource administration has already begun moving to the Web. Large software companies like PeopleSoft and SAP have entered the Web-based market, offering comprehensive human resource management systems on the Internet.[3] Other administrative activities subject to automation on the new platforms include travel services, personal concierge services, telecommunications and systems administration, logistics, and tax payments. Most of the routine legal and secretarial functions will also be automated. Existing exchanges have already automated most purchasing functions right down to consumables like pencils and paper clips. Administrative processes are now typically fragmented, but it is not difficult to imagine how such systems could be consolidated on ubiquitous digital platforms whose design reflects the new enterprise logic.

Infrastructure convergence is essential to the seamless integration of the federation, in order to support every aspect and phase of the individual's experience. Individuals will not experience deep support in fragments. From the point of view of individual space, deep support is one continuous stream, and the federation is one entity. The end consumer's experience is unique, holistic, and seamless, requiring a similarly comprehensive and distributed structure in the systems that support that experience. The new platforms can integrate the activities related to support-network coordination, logistics, and financing that provide the foundation for transactions. They can also integrate the processes necessary for supporting the employment, growth, and development of advocates and all employees, as well as the communication, administrative processes, social interaction, feedback, and metrics that stream through the network. We anticipate common systems on ubiquitous Web-based or distributed platforms that support all the participant enterprises and advocates in a federation, their constituencies, and their relationships with individuals.

In all likelihood, these common platform services like SweetSupport will evolve rather quickly in size and reliability, enabling them to support many, if not all, federations. Basic platform services are likely to be commoditized, offering efficient and reliable information flows. But platform providers will distinguish themselves in part by their degree of flexibility in offering federations' customized interfaces, protocols, processes, and security. Each would be integrated with a range of federations and their brand experience as they reflect the unique requirements of their constituencies and the kinds of needs they intend to support.

Infrastructure convergence not only eliminates redundant activity across the entire federation; it also creates an environment of complete transparency and shared data, allowing everyone in the federation to see the same reality. Everyone sees the same flow of feedback through a variety of measures, including the ultimate performance metric: the release of cash. Interdependencies are made visible in real time. Partnerships, alliances, and relationships are nurtured, supported, and enriched by this environment of jointly owned valid information. This shared reality helps to support a culture based on distributed ownership and control, in which anyone who sees a problem feels compelled to fix it quickly, rather than to find someone to blame for it.

Infrastructure convergence is not a science fiction view of a distant future. Many of the technical components of infrastructure convergence are already developed on Web-based platforms, in distributed computing, or in hybrid forms. We see prototypes emerging in the work of firms known as "Internet enablers." These are the companies that are inventing the early technologies designed to support the processes associated with generating, executing, and fulfilling today's commercial transactions on the Web. They are also developing the hosting networks, the applications, the Web services, the wireless devices, and the satellite networks upon which all this digital activity depends. We see prototypes in the new Web-based business services that offer everything from accounting to human resource management, as well as in the new collaborative working environments explored by early movers such as Groove and Alibra.

New technologies are also being developed to coordinate today's supply chains beyond the traditional point-to-point model, ensuring timely production, assembly, and shipping of orders. Such coordination depends upon forecasting demand and tracking demand fulfillment. Important lessons for the large-scale platforms associated with infrastructure convergence can be learned from these early efforts.[4]

An even more dramatic contemporary approach to the supply chain is peer-to-peer technology, which has been used to develop a new generation of supply chain management software that allows collaborative processes to be embedded at any and every point in a network, improving the real-time flow of information, creating shared information repositories, and amalgamating multiple business functions using "agents" or "sitelets." The goal here is to distribute information throughout supply chains, enabling them to be truly collaborative and to operate seamlessly across enterprise boundaries. Described as "collaborative commerce," such new solutions represent some of the first building blocks of the technological platform that can enable a federated support network and the possibility of order-of-magnitude shifts in managing complexity while reducing costs and freeing working capital.[5]

In today's environment, these new technologies are fragmented, each aimed at a different point in the transaction process or at a distinct functional area—informing end consumers, allowing them to customize products, increasing the efficiency of their transactions, coordinating supply chains, managing payment and financing, tracking orders, providing customer service, managing the logistics of inventory and delivery, managing employee benefits, analyzing data on customer behavior, etc. This fragmentation obviously mirrors the assumptions of the standard enterprise logic. Under distributed capitalism, adaptations of these early applications can be integrated to form the high-speed digital backbone of the federation. These platforms will be combined with powerful new technologies that support easy, real-time, lifelike interaction and "reflexive software" that teaches people how to better utilize the systems with which they work. Such multilevel platforms can enable federations to eliminate their own valueless activities and unnecessary complexity, while providing the means to manage the intricacies of deep support and federation governance.

We see another precursor of infrastructure convergence in the logistics platforms being pioneered by UPS. Its unique combination of digital and physical assets is being used to assemble the platforms that make it both the logistics intermediary and the financial guarantor of goods in transit. UPS Logistics operates hundreds of distribution facilities and offers an integrated range of logistics service and solutions, including supply chain management, transportation, service/parts logistics, and reverse logistics. UPS Capital offers a range of financial services and products such as COD enhancement, distribution finance, electronic invoicing and payments, foreign exchange, equipment leasing, insurance, trade finance, and merchant services.

Considered in isolation, none of these UPS offerings is remarkable, but taken together they represent a significant step toward infrastructure convergence, and, intentionally or unintentionally, toward deep support. By drawing upon a base of physical transactions that make up the sales ledger of any organization, they can offer a range of systems and solutions that provide companies or individuals with transparency and control of end-to-end activities. UPS Capital can act as a banker, offering financing of these activities and the secure electronic interfaces that allow these financial transactions to be completed, recorded, and verified with a range of third parties. By bundling financial and logistical services, they have blurred industry boundaries, but more important, they have created a platform that any company can use anywhere to transact business. From this vantage point, it is easy to imagine UPS adding the accounting, cash management, and even planning, forecasting, and budgeting that could transform their platform into a universal infrastructure shared by many enterprises. In other words, UPS could become part of the operational core of a wide range of enterprises and, ultimately, federations.

INFINITE CONFIGURATION (PRINCIPLE 9)

Mass production owed only efficiency to its mass consumers. It was organized like an equation. Every detail of the production process had to be specified a priori. Time and motion studies of workers on assembly lines measured fractions of seconds. Machinery was fixed in place and tools were finely calibrated. Supervisors and managers had rigid plans, production goals, and behavioral rules to enforce. The best operations ran with military precision. Unlike the mass-production machine, there is no universal template for a successful federation. If there were, then federations themselves would quickly become commoditized. Instead, federations operate in individual space precisely to escape the inevitability of commoditization associated with the exhaustion of transaction value.

Thus, federations would vary in scale and scope, style and spirit, according to the constituencies that choose them and the imagination with which the evolving demands of their individual relationships are supported. Differentiation among federations arises from their unique approaches to marshaling resources and executing deep support. Their actual design may vary with each individual relationship, because individuals can dynamically assemble and reassemble the activities and resources that best fit their experience of value. In this sense, federations are characterized by infinite possibilities of configuration and content, and the ingenuity behind those choices is a critical source of competitive advantage.

This principle of infinite configuration reflects the new market structure of individuated consumption. Federations owe uniqueness and flexibility to their individuals and constituencies. They are less like an equation and more like a haiku poem. Haiku requires a set number of syllables in a set number of lines, yet tens of thousands, perhaps millions, of haiku poems have been written, and each one is utterly unique. That is because the structure of the poem underdetermines its content. And so it is with the federated support network. The distributed structure provides a small number of limiting conditions: Federations are collaborative, informed networks characterized by shared ownership and control and aligned with individuals in individual space. They use the economies derived from infrastructure convergence to realize relationship value by providing deep support to individuals and their self-defining constituencies. Inside these conditions, infinite variation, subtlety, and innovation are competitive necessities.

From the point of view of the individual in individual space, infinite configurability is a requirement, because it is an important mechanism through which individuality is developed and expressed. As individuals make time and money trade-offs and design the forms of deep support they require, they are giving definition to what is valued and what is valueless in their lives now. When individuals transfer cash to a federation, part of what they are paying for is precisely this flexibility: the fact that "I" is the template for the support I receive, not some rigid notion conceived by the marketing department in the nether reaches of organization space, for whom "I" is merely another anonymous transaction. Once premium service has been redefined as standard, individuals no longer pay a surcharge for operational excellence, quality products, or effective services. They pay for variations in the realization of relationship value, which implies the intimacy and flexibility of infinite configuration.

NEW FORMS OF VALUATION (PRINCIPLE 10)

As products and services reach nearly universal commodity status, the quality of intellectual, emotional, behavioral, and digital assets—as reflected in unique configurations and relationships—will constitute the preeminent dimension against which federations and their participant enterprises are valued. In today's environment most management information systems are exclusively geared to measuring and reporting "industrial-age physical and labor inputs."[6] Still more problematic is the fact that the supermonopoly of transaction economics has made it difficult to perceive, let alone measure, intangible results like realized relationship value or intangible products like deep support. Indeed, true relationship value is incalculable by today's methods of financial measurement and valuation. But in the new enterprise logic, mapping, measuring, and monitoring the flows of content, experience, and realized relationship value will be critical to assessing the value of any enterprise or federation.

New valuation methodologies will be enabled by the transparency of the digital medium. We expect balance sheets and financial statements to reflect the "public" flow of data and feedback that permeates the federation network, especially the assessments of individuals through polling, structured feedback, and other formats. The perpetual flow of polling and feedback from all directions in the network, along with the streams of "public" data that flow through the ubiquitous platforms, will make it possible to assess the critical input and output of "intangibles" that bear on the growth and durability of value-realizing relationships with individuals.[7] Ultimately, it will fall to the investment community to invent and refine the valuation parameters that can effectively measure, assess, and predict realized relationship value. Our purpose here is to point out some general directions for debate and innovation.

A federation's competitiveness will ultimately depend upon the extent to which it can develop, nurture, and leverage the intangibles that are the inputs to realized relationship value—intellectual, emotional, behavioral, and digital assets. These assets are the primary sources of innovation, as they can be infinitely reconfigured in new and unique patterns, according to the changing requirements of individuals and constituencies. In the context of these new businesses, the intangible assets that enable and sustain alliances among enterprises and relationships with individuals are essential to a federation's success, far more so than the products or services it provides. Indeed, products and services, whether digital or physical, are merely the delivery mechanisms for the important subjective experiences of mutual trust and commitment that arise from the application of intangible assets.

The plasticity of intangible assets also means that they can be deployed in many different ways in conjunction with physical assets, and these kaleidoscopic patterns result in the creation, destruction, and re-creation of new and different businesses and forms of deep support. The majority of federations will face the challenge of blending tangible and intangible assets in many changing combinations, a process that will breathe new life into "old" assets. Stripped of their redundancies and overhead, preexisting physical assets can enter into relationships with more than one federation, where they can be bundled with intangible assets that link them to the unique constituencies served by that federation. In this way, physical assets can have many faces and play many roles, as they contribute to a variety of federations and serve multiple constituencies. Given the presence of ubiquitous systems and the universal efficiencies they imply, sustainable competitive advantage will arise from the intelligence and creativity that lead to these unique alliances and partnerships.

A key valuation challenge for investors and federations alike will be how to translate the balance sheet and financial statements into individual space.

This entails a significant mind-shift, as the assets that are critical to success in individual space are intangible and do not reflect conventional forms of ownership. For example, in today's world, real option valuation (ROV) is used by analysts to capture the value of decision-making in the standard enterprise logic and is a powerful tool in organization space. Imagine translating this kind of tool into individual space and emerging with a new metric—call it "real individual option valuation" (RIOV). That new metric would place a value on the individual's decision to stay with or abandon a federation. It would capture the value-realizing potential inherent in these decisions and could be reflected in decision trees similar to those employed for ROV analysis.

Another example of translating financial analysis into individual space involves the way that the value of a network is considered. Some business analysts are already seeking ways to measure the value of "community" and the value of "interconnectivity," observing that the value of a network is a geometric function of the number of nodes on the network. Networks become more valuable as they include more people with whom to communicate for pleasure, professional exchange, or commerce. Certainly, there will be some federations that are more or less fully automated and operate as commodities. In these cases, pure network characteristics, such as the number of nodes, may indeed be legitimate quantitative indicators of value. But for many federations operating in individual space, assessments of the value in the network will be more complex, involving a substantial subjective and experiential component.

Value will arise in federations because people will have intentionally opted into them. Their interconnectivity will be a function of shared experience and shared desires, which will enable the federation to realize value far beyond the cost of providing deep support. The tighter these linkages, the greater the opportunity for value realization. As a result of these new dynamics, federations cannot be valued only by their number of connections; they must also be valued by the *embedded value* at each point of intelligence. This embedded value, when realized, becomes the source of the federation's cash flow. In this way, federations can be quantifiably measured in terms of their size, as well as qualitatively measured in terms of their potential embedded cash flow, irrespective of their size.

With today's valuation methods, even measures that purport to be about relationship, such as "lifetime revenue" or "share of wallet," merely measure transactions across time or product/service categories. In contrast, relationship economics will require a new and far more detailed focus on the dimensions and sources of realized relationship value, such as cost of commitment, accrued trust, operating cash flow, ratios of reinvestment in deep support, the cost of deep support per individual, advocate quality, advocate tenure, partner tenure, levels of investment in human development, and operational gearing. It will also be possible to value partnerships and alliances by determining their contributions to the overall performance in value realization.

Output-oriented metrics like realized relationship value (RRV) and realized relationship value per individual (RRVI) describe the extent of interdependency between the individual and the federation. Techniques to measure these outputs will have to be invented based on the number of individuals supported, the percent of content aggregated for each, and the time span of the relationship. RRV will have subjective components derived from individual polling and feedback, as well as objective components derived from cash flows, behavior patterns over time, the number of federations serving an individual, and so on. Such a figure would need to both quantify cash flows and qualify them in terms of the vested interdependency, trust, and delegation that they represent. Investors and advocates alike will want to understand ratios such as the cost of deep support as a percentage of RRV and reinvestment as a percentage of RRV. Federations will also be valued in terms of the amount of time that they save per individual—a federation that saves one hour has less embedded value and is likely to be more vulnerable to competition than a federation that saves ten or twenty hours per week per individual.

A NEW CONSUMPTION MEANS A NEW EMPLOYMENT (PRINCIPLE 11)

The individuation of consumption wants far more than just efficiency from "producers" and their "employees." Indeed, in this commoditized world of products and services, efficiency is taken for granted. The absence of it means a costly competitive debacle, but the presence of it alone buys little. Instead, the new consumption wants assistance in the lifelong pursuit of psychological self-determination, as expressed in the needs for sanctuary, voice, and connection. In the support economy, the central product is itself intangible—the deep support in which accountability and responsibility for every aspect of the consumption experience are bundled with each cash expenditure. This product in turn draws upon the intangible inputs of the advocacy relationship like integrity, empathy, authenticity, trust, creativity, dialogue, and collaboration—none of which can be specified a priori. Rather, they must be actualized in the here and now by real people in relationship to other real people. The questions arise, then, what does this new consumption mean for the individual-as-employee? What does it mean for the nature of the employment relationship?

In this section we highlight two overarching themes that point to a reinvention of the employment relationship in the support economy. The first of these involves the redistribution of rights and responsibilities associated with employment. We call this theme career rights. The second concerns the new processes of collaborative coordination that absorb and redefine the accepted professional canon of managerial capitalism's managerial culture.

CAREER RIGHTS VERSUS CAREER TAXIDERMY

Under distributed capitalism, the challenges of distributed value will affect every employee of every federated enterprise who must consistently think and act from the point of view of individual space. The interdependence of the individual-as-consumer and the federation is mirrored in the interdependence between the federation, its enterprises, and those whom they "employ." This interdependence is exemplified in the preeminence of intangibles as the source of competitiveness, the ways in which such intangibles are "produced," and the ownership issues to which they give rise.

Many economists have recognized the substantially increased significance of "intangibles" for business success, especially since the 1980s. This is attributed to the combined effects of intensified competition, due primarily to globalization, and the accession of information technologies, especially the Internet.[8] In 1955 tangible assets (real estate, equipment, inventories) accounted for 78 percent of the assets of U.S. nonfinancial corporations. In 2000 that proportion had dropped to 53 percent. Investment in intangibles such as research and development, software, and brand equity rose from 4 percent of gross domestic product in 1978 to nearly 10 percent in 2000.[9] In another calculation, market services and intangibles accounted for more than two-thirds of gross domestic product in the United States in 1995.[10] Despite this trend, the canon of professional management under the standard enterprise logic—including everything from its culture and behavioral repertoire to its formal policies, information systems, and methods of financial analysis—has remained ill-suited to the effective "management" of intangibles.

In the shift toward a support economy and the new enterprise logic of distributed capitalism, the preeminence of intangible assets is even more dramatic. It will demand an equally dramatic reinvention of the managerial canon geared to the effective distributed production and nourishment of intangible assets. Indeed, in the support economy physical products and services are generally treated as commodities. In consequence, the unique configuration of intellectual, emotional, behavioral, and digital intangibles carries the weight of a federation's competitive success. This configuration of intangibles defines the federation's brand. These intangibles do not spring full-blown to life. Most are painstakingly wrought from "employees'" intelligence, effort, and commitment in the production of deep support. They are what make the federation come alive; they are what make it active and receptive—a safe haven for individuals.

The standard enterprise logic has difficulty embracing the management of intangibles because its assumptions about property rights were institutionalized when assets were mainly physical and financial.[11] These "hard" assets lend themselves to highly specifiable contracts and forms of measurement. In contrast, the intangibles that are the critical success factors for a federated support network challenge once-settled notions of property rights. They are not only "produced" by individual "employees," but they arise from the "employee's" own personal resources of intelligence, feeling, empathy, commitment, creativity, and so on. In other words, they are fabricated from an "employee's" self. In the march toward wealth creation, however, these fabrications exist in a highly interdependent relationship with the wider context of the enterprise and federation, as they must be leveraged by federation investments in digital and physical assets as well as in "employee" development, education, and training.

The idea that an "employee's" selfhood is now an intrinsic factor in wealth creation is itself an inversion of the standard enterprise logic, in which the employee was not expected to be an individual at work, but rather a means to a specific and predetermined objective. Employees could also use these boundaries between work and life as a form of self-protection, keeping their "private" self, with its insights and ethical judgment, well separated from the commercial zone of the workplace. There are many cases in which this fragmentation, both imposed and internalized, has led people to embrace different standards for their workplace and personal behavior. During the media exposé of the Enron Corporation in 2001 and 2002, for example, many news stories focused on the gap between the unsavory business dealings of executives who appeared to lead exemplary private lives.

The new enterprise logic asks something altogether different from "employees." If every commercial practice is aligned with individuals in individual space, then every single human being contributing to those practices must call upon his or her own awareness as individuals in the execution of every aspect of their work. This is essential for advocates, but it is equally true for the person who works in a factory making furniture, or monitors keyboard fabrication in a modular plant, or treats cancer patients, or resolves insurance claims, or attends to airline passengers, or designs buildings, or invents financial products, or sells, well, anything. In the support economy, work calls upon the whole self. It is no longer acceptable to leave one's life at the door, replete with its special knowledge, experience, common sense, and empathy. In work, these are critical resources that people have to draw upon in achieving alignment with individuals, realizing value with them, and ultimately creating wealth.

Once employees become individuals too, they can no longer be regarded as "plug and play" parts in the ongoing exercise of producing goods and services. True to the observations of fractal geometry, their individuality now matters. Indeed, it is essential to all outcomes, because through the medium of that individuality, they learn to produce the intangibles that are the critical inputs to competitive success. Work cannot be a question of managing false emotional displays in the service of some kind of "customer satisfaction."[12] The work of nourishing relationships with individuals cannot be cynical. The I–You relationship requires two individuals, each imperfect but committed to honestly doing their best. These things simply cannot be faked. They want real people, freed to act on what they can learn in the pursuit of real relationship and supported in this effort by every federation system, practice, policy, and colleague.

The role of the federation is to create the larger context in which all of this intellectual, emotional, and behavioral effort translates into wealth creation. It is the individual-as-employee, especially in the role of advocate, who possesses the most extensive repertoire of tacit, as well as explicit, knowledge about the individuals he or she supports. Successful advocates will have earned the trust of their individuals over time through the efficacy of their support. Even where explicit knowledge is transparent, this relationship-based trust is not easily transferred. Advocates gain power with the trust they hold, but only to the extent that the individuals they support are themselves empowered by their efforts, all of which leads directly to greater value realization and more wealth. If advocates leave, they not only take with them knowledge and skills, which represent investment dollars, but they take these vital repositories of trust. This requires a new emphasis on the critical importance of retention and the search for new forms of remuneration.

Thus the people once called "employees" are now one of the most valuable sources of the intangibles that determine competitive success. They must create those intangibles from their own personal resources, and produce and reproduce them consistently, always innovating and always learning how to increase their effectiveness. They share responsibility, as well as ownership and control. While they are nourished, developed, and leveraged by federation investments, they no longer depend upon their "employers" so much as they enter into interdependent relationships with their enterprises and federations. Instead of the subordinate-superior connotations of the employee-employer vocabulary, something new is needed to convey this interdependency. We think it is more accurate to describe these co-owners, co-creators, and co-managers as *members* of enterprises and federations. The membership relationship is quite different from the employment relationship that preceded it.

Clearly, the traditions of property rights associated with the standard enterprise logic no longer adequately describe this new relationship. In a distributed structure, authority follows responsibility. We have already seen that production, ownership, and control must be distributed when individuals-as-consumers own the sources of value. Now it is possible to deepen our appreciation of this distributed imperative. As the members who compose the surf and the ocean are the source of the federation's critical success factors—especially its intellectual, emotional, and behavioral assets—new obligations and rights accrue to them.

Members have new obligations. First and foremost, each member must assume responsibility for every aspect of the consumption experience in which he or she has played a role. Closely linked to responsibility is the fact that the assumption of authority is now an obligation, not a choice. That means the member or members who are most responsible for a problem must also accept, and be granted by other members, the decision-making authority necessary to resolve that problem. Their assumption of authority extends to their obligation to innovate in the service of continually improving deep support.

Members also have an obligation to develop appropriate mechanisms to sanction peers who violate the principle of alignment or other key principles and norms. Another new obligation is that members must bring the totality of themselves to work. They have the obligation to utilize all of their experience, judgment, and values—as sisters and brothers, children and parents, friends, consumers, skateboarders, spiritual seekers, patients, students—in the service of the deep support they provide. They also have the obligation to continue to develop themselves—their empathy, communication skills, self-awareness, systems knowledge, and practical knowledge—in order to continuously improve their effectiveness.

In fulfilling these new obligations, members also win new rights. Chiefly, they assume the rights to their own careers. Career rights mean that careers are converted into intellectual property and owned by the member. Career rights carry with them decision rights over those matters for which a member has assumed responsibility. In other words, career rights are an essential mechanism for the distribution of authority among members. They convey authority for innovation and problem-solving activities. The career as intellectual property includes the vital intellectual, emotional, and behavioral assets that are now key to a federation's competitiveness. As the owners of this intellectual property, members also enjoy decision rights over the structure, content, and pacing of their careers. Careers are no longer stuck to an organizational framework that remains stationary as employees step in and out. Now careers belong to their incumbents, and federations and enterprises compete to invest in those intellectual properties.

Career rights also have obvious implications for the logic of compensation. As owners of their careers, as the creators and producers of key intangibles, and as decision-makers, members would also have a greater claim on the wealth derived from the value they help to realize. These new rights and obligations are essential to the "distributed" nature of distributed capitalism. Ownership is shared with individuals who are its sources of value and with members who are the sources of the intangibles that help realize that value. Control is distributed as members and individuals pursue relationships in individual space, uniting value and the means to realize it in the here-and-now production and sustenance of the intangibles that enable deep support and determine competitiveness.

Enterprises and their federations also face a changing balance of obligations and rights. Under the standard enterprise logic, investing in employees was a variable cost. The levels of these investments varied according to a firm's managerial philosophy, strategy, business cycle, and economic resources. In the new enterprise logic, federations are obligated to invest in their members. This is an unalterable consequence of the relentless necessity of aligning all commercial practices with the interests of individuals in individual space, which in turn requires the nourishing and development of intellectual, emotional, and behavioral assets. Federations are also obligated to accommodate members' rights to development and education, to their career-related choices, and to their claims on wealth creation. Indeed, we would expect federations to use the interdependencies reflected in career rights and new approaches to compensation as an opportunity to differentiate themselves in ways that attract the best members for their constituencies.

These new obligations are also balanced with important new rights. The federation now has a right to hold members responsible for the quality of deep support and for the effectiveness of their authority. Federations have the right to expect the member community to apply sanctions for behavior that threatens, undermines, or obstructs value realization. The federation has the right to require the participation of the "whole person" in the creation and production of critical intangible assets. Instead of asking people to leave their brains and hearts at the door, they can now insist that effective membership requires holistic participation. Clearly, distributed capitalism entails new costs and new benefits for all parties in the membership relationship. Given the new possibilities of wealth creation and human development associated with this new enterprise logic, however, it appears to us that the benefits for all parties far outweigh the costs.

The career rights associated with federation membership have disastrous implications for the practices of career taxidermy that penalize women, and sometimes men too, who do not conform to anachronistic career norms. Under the standard enterprise logic, outside forces tried to exert pressure for change in the institutionalized routines of career taxidermy, but the very organizational narcissism they sought to influence is what buffered managers from profound discomfort. Those practices, which have been impervious to exhortation and even legislation, are more likely to collapse from the sheer intensity of the market dynamics that drive the new enterprise logic. The migration of commercial activity to individual space and the consequent alignment of that activity with the needs and interests of individuals are indigenous economic forces that not only necessitate career rights but eliminate the sources of sexual contempt that surreptitiously fed the old distance between producers and consumers. Were that contempt to reappear in the new federated support network, it would sour the federation's appeal to individuals, cripple its ability to attract competent members, and strike a fatal blow to its competitiveness. Indeed, if organizational narcissism was fed, in part, by the self-sealing dynamics of men in groups, then the federated support network operating in individual space will of necessity summon a new sexual politics.

COLLABORATIVE COORDINATION

The salience of intangible assets as the source of innovation and competitiveness creates new pressures for a reinvention of the managerial canon and the social relations it reflects, including roles, structures, policies, practices, norms, and values. These pressures express the importance of the intangibles we have cited for a federation's success, as well as the degree to which the dependence on intangible assets presents an unavoidable and irreversible source of competitive vulnerability.

Even in the current environment, it is obvious that when a firm's viability depends less on hard assets than on the integrity and trustworthiness of its practices, it is highly vulnerable to the competitive consequences of management lapses. The Arthur Andersen accounting firm is one such example. A criminal conviction for obstruction of justice, in response to its shredding documents related to the Enron Corporation, caused the dissolution of the nearly century-old partnership. Even hard-asset companies are not immune to this vulnerability, as Firestone discovered when it was suspected that it allowed substandard tires to be shipped and installed on Ford Explorers.

As we have already examined in some detail, the managerial hierarchy arose as a response to the administrative complexity of overseeing the production and distribution of things, and was later, fitfully, adapted to the delivery of services. That hierarchy came with its own inward focus, which helped to ensure efficiency, while also creating and maintaining a distance from the very markets it was intended to serve. The professional managerial canon and its social organization were first formulated under societal and market conditions far different from those that exist today, a vanished reality that nevertheless continues to be expressed in its institutionalized routines and assumptions. As a result, today's managers are constantly exhorted to do many sensible things—like make customers their most valuable asset, or collaborate with colleagues across functions and company boundaries—that the institutional arrangements of the standard enterprise logic fundamentally preclude. Rational as such exhortations might be, they defy the true incentive structure of the standard enterprise logic. In our view, the difficulties of creating and sustaining intellectual, emotional, and behavioral intangibles have less to do with human predilection than with the institutional logic in which they are supposed to unfold. Under distributed capitalism, a wholly new kind of management would be required. It would have to be capable of nurturing delicate but precious intangibles, enabling them to develop unassailable strength.

The distributed nature of value, production, ownership, responsibility, and control in the new enterprise logic means that managerial practices based on collaborative coordination would have to replace top-down "command and control" management as it has evolved in the twentieth century. Today, collaborative behaviors are notoriously difficult to achieve and, it would seem, almost impossible to sustain within the standard enterprise logic. Organizations play a zero-sum game with one another, in much the same way that individuals within organizations find it prudent to hoard information or knowledge for their individual competitive advantage. As an example, nearly every article about the importance of integrating supply chains or forging strategic alliances concludes by lamenting the difficulties entailed by collaboration and trust.[13] One consulting group estimated that the global value of alliances will reach between $25 trillion and $40 trillion in 2004, with alliances accounting for as much as 15 percent of a typical company's market valuation.[14] (As federations supplant individual enterprises as economic agents and competitors, figures like these will be a gross underestimation of the value embedded in the quality of a support network.) Yet the same study also estimated that fewer than 40 percent of alliances actually achieve the expectations set for them, however modest those may be.

We think that the human capabilities associated with collaborative coordination can evolve and thrive only when they are consistent with the enterprise logic in which people must operate. In the new enterprise logic of distributed capitalism, all commercial practices must exhibit total alignment with the individual in every respect, including the flow of cash. The distribution of ownership and control associated with that alignment, together with the complexity of infrastructure convergence and virtual communication, necessitate collaborative coordination, in much the same way that life on Earth necessitates breathing. There simply is no other way to survive. That is why distributed capitalism makes it possible to imagine a new management canon based on very different social relations, in which peer-to-peer collaboration replaces hierarchical supervision and multidimensional coordination replaces executive administration and direction.[15] These are the kinds of managerial orientations that will be necessary to nurture, leverage, and safeguard the federation's now critical intangible assets. In this scenario, the skills associated with nurturing and sustaining collaborative relationships—dialogue, respect for the individual, listening, dispute resolution, negotiation, and empathy—can no longer be regarded as an afterthought, relegated to a lower status than other "hard" skills.

The centrality of collaborative coordination can evolve in proportion to the devolution of institutionalized routines. Recall that we described institutional routines as those aspects of organizational behavior that reproduce established authority, independent of the influence of rational market forces. The self-protective dynamics associated with organizational narcissism are, by definition, buffered from the rational demands of the marketplace. But the devolution of such routines is an inescapable consequence of the unprecedented public transparency of the action environment in a federated support network. Transparency results from at least three factors: the continuous

requirements of alignment and the necessity of metrics that enable the federation to monitor performance on this all-important dimension; the necessity
of networked action in the service of deep support and the information flows
required to enable that coordination; and the flow of information associated
with infrastructure convergence. That these information flows are also public
is necessitated by the distributed nature of ownership and control in the realization of relationship value in individual space. Many people need to know
many things all the time.

As a result of these requirements, a federation's information systems
could provide a transparent and universally accessible flow of feedback arising from individuals, members, investors, and others. Women and men in individual space would evaluate the success of advocates, of enterprises, and of
federations. They would vote on that success hourly and daily, with their
feedback and with their cash. Each network member would be swimming in
a rich feedback soup, filled in real time from its sources on the beach, in the
surf, and in the wider ocean of the support network. This transparent flow
of feedback and interaction, in conjunction with increasingly sophisticated
collaboration software tools, would be used as a foundation for collaborative
and coordinated action and decision-making. Complex coordination can be
thus enabled, without recourse to the costly hierarchies built for that purpose a century earlier.

The transparent flow of information provides the framework that enables distributed responsibility and accountability, as well as distributed
control over innovation and problem-solving. It is also the source from
which multiple metrics are drawn in the ongoing processes of evaluating and
valuing the performance of members, teams, enterprises, and whole federations. One can easily imagine at least four levels of metrics, including: individuals' and constituencies' experience of the federation, of advocates, and of
participating enterprises; advocates' assessments of their relationships with
individuals, with one another, with enterprises, and with the federation; enterprise assessments of their relationships with individuals, with advocates,
with one another, with investors, and with the federation; and federation assessments of their relationships with participant enterprises, with advocates,
with individuals, with investors, etc.

In the world of organization space, managers frequently use a political
process to make decisions, especially where there isn't much data or its interpretation can be disputed. In the world of the federated support network,
many decisions should be easier to make, and a lot more objective. This
would be enabled by the public transparency of information flow as well as
by the clarity and universally shared decision rules associated with the align-

ment of all commercial practices with relationship value realization for individuals. Information flows could be translated into metrics with automated analyses and summarized through feedback loops embedded in all interactions. Every relationship would have full access to complete information as to its quality and the quality of each of its components. The metrics would permeate network discussions and deliberations. The evaluations that arise from these metrics should be subject to less acrimony than would be typical in organization space, because of their overwhelming face validity. In the end, advocates, enterprises, and federations that ignore the data would also reduce the flow of cash, which is the ultimate metric.

While relationships in the new support networks should be highly self-regulating, due to the transparency of information flows, there inevitably will be situations where data are subject to competing interpretations and a priori guidelines are inadequate. Consequently, we anticipate that federations will require a variety of member roles, in addition to those roles that provide direct support to individuals, that specialize in the tasks of leadership, strategy, and adjudication. For example, *leadership advocates* would provide the connective tissue for the network, creating consensus as to its direction and its governance. These advocates would ensure that the federation exists only as a derivative of individual space and that all choices, activities, and behaviors are coordinated and evaluated from that point of view. They ensure that every member has the ability to judge every action from the point of view of individual space.

Most important, though, would be the creation of a style of leadership that is consistent with the realities of the distributed imperative. For example, a variety of observers have tried to characterize the quality of leadership exerted by Linus Torvalds within the open source software community that formed around the Linux operating system he originated in 1990.[16] While a federated support network is different from an open source community in many respects, it does share similar characteristics, especially as regards the distributed form. Indeed, the successful growth and diffusion of the Linux system suggest that it may hold some clues to the nature of leadership in a federated support network. Torvalds has an obvious claim to leadership in his community, deriving from his status as the Linux "founder" and the associated respect he commands. Despite this fact, he has been portrayed as acutely aware of the contentious, skeptical, independent-minded nature of the Linux software developers, and, as is the case in all "open source" communities, the fact that they participate on a voluntary basis. As a result, his leadership approach is described as one that seeks to justify itself and its decisions to the wider community. "Torvalds goes to great lengths to document and justify his decisions about controversial matters. He admits when he is wrong. It is a kind of charisma that has to be continuously re-created through consistent patterns of behavior."[17]

In addition to leadership advocates, we can also imagine a role for *strategic advocates.* They are the avant-garde of the federation. They provide its eyes and ears, dwelling deeply in individual space and tracking technological innovation. Strategic advocates channel recommendations for innovation, improvement, and differentiation from individuals, direct-support advocates, and other members, and they also work to create consensus and to coordinate innovation. *Adjudicating advocates* have a special role to play in managing conflict and the new complexity of relationships—intra-enterprise, intra-federation, federation to advocate, enterprise to advocate, advocate to individual, individual to advocate, individual to federation, constituency to enterprise, constituency to federation, and so on—that now define the support network. In a thriving federation, the incentives for positive, self-regulating conflict resolution are high because the interdependencies that characterize every direction and level of relationship increase the network's value for each member. Nevertheless, there will always be conflicts that cannot be settled through peer-to-peer processes. Adjudicators have special responsibility for due process and dispute resolution in these cases, where the mechanisms of distributed authority cannot achieve resolution of competing claims. New rules of engagement would have to be invented that provide a recourse to formal lines of authority in ways that contribute to, rather than detract from, the importance of distributed control. The quality of that invention and its implementation are important sources of differentiation for a federation.

We anticipate that each enterprise would also have its own *enterprise advocates* who would have special responsibility for keeping the enterprise aligned with the requirements of individual space as they apply to each of the federations in which the enterprise is a participant, as well as engaging with direct-support advocates and individuals. Enterprises will differentiate themselves in terms of how well they are organized to contribute to a federation's value-realizing activities. For example, as an enterprise achieves new efficiencies in a particular domain, those benefits accrue to the entire support network and enhance the attractiveness of that enterprise as a long-term federation participant. Conversely, participant enterprises that fail to continuously improve will be less attractive to successful federations. When realized relationship value releases cash into the federation, payments are made to participant enterprises based on the contribution they have made to value realization and the risk they have undertaken. Under distributed capitalism, the fates of all network participants are inextricably linked, and all are defined by the same value: the value of the federated support network's relationship with its individuals and constituencies.

Governance processes would absorb, but transform, the current roles of boards of directors and senior management. A governing body would need to include representatives from all federation stakeholders: individuals, direct-support advocates, enterprise advocates, specialist advocates, other members, and independents. Again, governance criteria are perpetually transparent and public. This body would have ultimate responsibility for a federation's policies, configuration, and composition, the application of metrics, and the distribution of wealth from realized value. It would also have responsibility for the statutory reporting of the federation. Like every other set of actors in the federation, the governing body must remain rooted in individual space and consistent with the distributed imperative. This could translate into rotating memberships and open debate that depends upon the elaborate feedback loops that connect all parties in the network.

The evolution of a new managerial canon that emphasizes collaborative coordination in correspondence with the distributed imperative would naturally occur as the result of trial-and-error experimentation over time. The distinctions we offer here are intended to be suggestive, rather than exhaustive. There are many more innovations that would need to be made and many more systemic issues to tackle as coordination demands expand without recourse to the expansion of "administrative overhead." In addition to the general challenges of innovation, federations would have to evolve their own unique versions of this new canon, based on the qualities associated with their brand of deep support. A federation's capacity to nourish its vital intangibles through these new processes, skills, roles, structures, policies, and practices would naturally be an important factor in its ability to attract and retain participant enterprises and talented members as well as the individuals and constituencies upon which its wealth ultimately depends.

LIFEBOATS TO INDIVIDUAL SPACE

If enterprises were ships, then those built according to the specifications of the standard enterprise logic would be structurally incapable of sailing the waters of individual space. As we have said repeatedly, the standard enterprise logic can stretch and can adapt, but only so far. Like any system, it is adaptable within a range, and that range also implies limits. Horses can accommodate to the sparse grasses of the high country, but they can't fly or climb a tree to reach its leaves. In our view, the organizations spawned and nurtured by managerial capitalism, however plastic they may be, will not be able to adapt to the individuation of consumption and the new enterprise logic of distributed capitalism. Like Moses, they have led the way toward a new land but are not destined to lead within it. We think that the new territory of individual space is more likely to be laid open by the twenty-first-century equivalents of Josiah Wedgwood, Henry Ford, and Alfred Sloan. They will be entrepreneur leaders who understand individuals and the changing structure of consumption. Their insights into the new markets for deep support and the potential of the new digital medium will allow them to invent the practical action that brings the new enterprise logic to life. The forms they create will be uniquely suited to unlocking the wealth that is hiding in plain sight in individual space.

Having said this, we also recognize that the "old" organizations are the source of vast and precious human, physical, digital, and economic assets that will need to be reconfigured and redeployed. The skill, speed, and creativity with which this is accomplished will be an important source of competitive advantage for the new federations. We think that this redeployment will occur in at least two ways. First, existing organizations will have to release *lifeboats* capable of charting a course into and through individual space and staking their claim there. The crew will represent the best of the "parent" organization, but also a mix of others who bring the skills that are most crucial to this undertaking. The challenge for lifeboaters will be to define the coastline: the ways and means of establishing vital interdependencies with individuals in individual space. The crew will require a broad vision that transcends industrial boundaries and geographic borders.

Lifeboats could issue from other sources too. They could be launched by individual entrepreneurs, by venture capitalists and others seeking new investment opportunities, by universities and not-for-profits, and even by government agencies. Lifeboaters will need to identify the constituencies they hope to attract, determine the capabilities they need to provide them with support, and be ready to participate in the landgrab that is likely to ensue once they hit the beach. They will need to evaluate who else they should invite to their landing party, which means having the judgment to determine the partners who can rapidly make a contribution to relationship value realization and who have the skills to form alliances and joint ventures. They must be able to learn how to learn about individuals and constituencies. They will need to experiment and observe the results of their and others' experiments. They will need to codify their learning and quickly develop standards, goals, and metrics. They will have to know how to identify failure and quickly abandon efforts that don't measure up to the new standards. They will have to establish the governance mechanisms that ensure independence from their enterprise of origin, while forming new interdependencies with individuals, constituencies, other lifeboats, and new start-ups in individual space.

Eventually they will be ready to begin the process of *grafting*, which will entail migrating carefully chosen resources from the old organization to the emerging enterprise. Those resources may include people, capital, brands, customers, databases, suppliers, and systems. The key to grafting is hierarchical integration. Again, that means that these resources are integrated into a new entity according to the terms of a wholly new enterprise logic. The old skills and resources are reorganized as part of a larger and different kind of organism. Once investors begin to understand the true potential of a successful lifeboat operation, lifeboating and grafting will quickly form a new focus for investment. Not all segments of the old organization will be grafted onto the new lifeboating operation. This means that other lifeboats and start-ups in individual space will be searching out assets from "old" organizations that can productively be integrated into their emerging enterprises.

As new enterprises combine into federations, they will continue to need a supply of goods and services that are produced with quality and efficiency. Businesses that operate with a high degree of excellence, but in the transaction model, will continue to have an important role to play in the new networks. In these cases, the internal logic that governs efficient production will have to be subordinated to the necessity of alignment with the individual and thus the distributed imperative. These enterprises will develop new strengths as they respond to the new disciplines and participate in the feedback loops and economics of the new federation. The efficiency they can achieve in this new context will make them valued participants of the federations in which they participate, even as it increases their claim on the wealth they help to create. Lifeboaters will be able to advise their old organizations on how to salvage old assets and steer them toward the formation of new partnerships. New experts will also emerge who specialize in rearranging old assets and developing the linkages to new federations.

Joseph A. Schumpeter's image of "creative destruction" experienced popular renewal in the heady days of the Internet revolution. Later, after so many Internet companies failed, many wondered if revolutionary discontinuous change, such as we are describing here, is truly feasible after all. If history is a teacher, then the answer is yes. Economies do renew themselves through discontinuity. Capitalism, in particular, has proven its unique capacity for just this sort of renewal. But change of this magnitude does not occur in "Internet time." If the notion of "creative destruction" was discredited, it's because the temporal expectations that people had were naive.

Consider the time frame for another, similarly profound phase change—what historian Martin Sklar calls "the corporate reconstruction of American capitalism" that introduced and consolidated most of the features of the standard enterprise logic. Sklar reckons that revolution took about thirty years. He uses legislative benchmarks, starting with the passage of the Sherman Antitrust Act in 1890, to the completion of the legislative agenda that defined the modern corporation in 1916.[18] Other scholars vary that estimate, but not by much.[19] A narrower example of "creative destruction" concerns the rise of the automobile, which extinguished the use of horses for transportation. Carl Friedrich Benz and Gottlieb Daimler (independently) built the first gasoline-powered vehicles in 1885, but it wasn't until twenty-three years later that Ford's Model Ts began to roll off the assembly line.[20] For those accustomed to operating in Internet time, a quarter of a century may seem too long to qualify for revolutionary change, but in the more languorous rhythms of history, these examples signify creative destruction par excellence. There is a hitch, though. The kind of phase change that we have examined is ignited only under certain conditions. There must be new markets ripe for a new approach to consumption, technologies able to meet their needs, and, most important, a third force—a new enterprise logic that organizes people, markets, and technologies in a wholly new way.

THE THIRD FORCE

The enterprise logic of distributed capitalism is the third force that can marry the new markets for deep support with the new digital medium and ignite a new era of wealth creation. In doing this, it will also produce better life and better work for the individuals who compose society today. The distributed imperative set into motion by the individuation of consumption leads to many new economic and social practices. Nevertheless, it continues to draw on the essential insight upon which all capitalism since Adam Smith has rested, that "the natural effort of every individual to better his own condition . . . is so powerful a principle, that it is alone, and without any assistance, not only capable of carrying on the society to wealth and prosperity, but of surmounting a hundred impertinent obstructions."[21]

In the world after managerial capitalism, though, the pursuit of "self-interest" is more complex than ever before. Education and experience have allowed those born of a postscarcity society to develop as self-aware individuals who, despite all their diversity, share a hunger for psychological self-determination. Fulfilling this yearning has become as much a part of their sense of "self-interest" as the accumulation of more things. When Adam Smith wrote about "impertinent obstructions," he was vehemently fighting a government whose monetary and trade policies allowed merchants to enrich themselves at the expense of their consumers and their societies. That government favored the self-interest of the few over the many and reduced the pursuit of that self-interest to mere corruption, insolence, and vanity.

Today, the "impertinent obstructions" that prevent the many from pursuing their new and broader sense of self-interest do not arise from Smith's "folly of human laws" so much as from the practices of the old capitalism itself. The very system that succeeded in making new people now obstructs their ability to have what they want in life and work. What is more, and this is the central notion that would rivet even Smith's attention, there is a great deal of data to suggest that these new people are willing to pay for what they want, if only there was someone to sell it to them. That is the simmering pain we have called "the transaction crisis," and that is the opportunity for the next leap forward in wealth creation represented by the support economy.

Some will read our description of the federated support network—with its distributed structures of value, production, ownership, responsibility, and control—and will wonder if people can really work this way. Historical perspective is also useful here. There have been times when an enterprise logic leaped ahead of those whom it needed to employ, and other times when it lagged far behind. In the first industrial revolution of eighteenth-century Britain, for example, workers were loathe to harness themselves to the disciplines of factory work. A preindustrial people accustomed to the sensual rhythms of agricultural life was repelled by the clock tower, the relentless demands of machinery, the perpetual supervision of the mill owner. The highlander, it was said, "never sits at ease at a loom; it is like putting a deer in the plough."[22] In time, though, the requirements of factory work would become the central metaphor for life in an industrial society, its once peculiar rites now as taken for granted as the presence of clock time strapped to our wrists that it bequeathed to us all.

In contrast, consider the transition to private enterprise in Eastern Europe. In Poland, for example, when the newly elected democratic government took the first bold steps to encourage free markets by legitimating private enterprise, eliminating price supports, and abandoning protectionist trade policies, it took days and weeks, not years, for urban streets to be converted into open bazaars of new enterprise, with a wide variety of once scarce goods ready for sale. In that case, the enterprise logic was merely catching up to where the population was yearning to be.

We think this last scenario is suggestive of the situation today. The requirements of the distributed structure are a much more accurate reflection of how today's individuals actually live their lives. They routinely manage high levels of complexity, they balance many competing claims, and, in the context of the transaction crisis, they must absorb all responsibility for all their activities, even when that responsibility should be lodged with the corporations that sell them things. They somehow contrive to accomplish all of this without the resources and support that the new federations would provide for them as members, let alone as individual consumers.

Add to this mix the fact that psychologically aware individuals are compelled to seek meaning in their activities. According to sociologist Robert Wuthnow's 1991 study of the voluntary sector, 80 million Americans were engaged in 1990 in some kind of "voluntary caring activity"; that's 45 percent of all U.S. adults.[23] We can only wonder how many more might be involved in these caring activities, but for the stress of the daily grind. As Wuthnow found in a 1998 study of civic engagement, people deeply want to connect with one another, but today they tend to do so "around specific needs and to work on projects that have definite objectives."[24] Add the growing attention in the management literature to the ways in which employees seek meaning in their work. Management scholars Christopher Bartlett and Sumantra Ghoshal have, for example, written extensively on the need for leaders to assert a higher purpose with which employees can identify as the key to commitment and retention.[25] Consistent with our earlier analysis, the new individuals do not find fulfillment in the old communities of the mass, but they do create and seek their own communities of meaning.

We think that distributed capitalism would have a liberating effect on the new individuals as regards their working lives, and their potential to operate in the ways we have described already far exceeds the institutional arrangements with which they now contend. There is much to suggest that they are interested in caring, perhaps as much as they want to be cared for, but the standard enterprise logic has proven itself to be a very effective editor of these impulses. To borrow once again from the software community, today's individuals lead "open source" lives. These sensibilities and capacities are suppressed only when they go to work. Indeed, the institutional arrangements of an economy are unusually powerful in their ability to evoke or subdue the many potentialities that comprise the human range in any given epoch. This fact preoccupied Adam Smith himself and was the subject of much of his analysis. "Where the inferior ranks of people are chiefly maintained by the employment of capital," he observed, "they are in general industrious, sober, and thriving. . . . [Where] the inferior ranks of people are chiefly maintained by the spending of revenue, they are in general idle, dissolute, and poor."[26]

A new episode of capitalism does not arise by fiat. Nor is it mounted like a new marketing promotion, to be indulged in and discarded when fashion moves on. The new enterprise logic of distributed capitalism associated with the support economy would have to take hold in the manner of a social movement. It would mobilize proponents drawn to the possibilities of new wealth and new well-being, people who feel compelled to seize what seems to be a better road to their dreams. Many of the specific manifestations of distributed capitalism's operating practices that we have imagined here may never come to life. Its principles, though, can be a beacon to the new individuals in their various roles as consumers and employees, managers and executives, entrepreneurs, technologists, investors, and public officials. Each of these constituencies will have a major role to play in the arduous but exhilarating experimentation and risk-taking that can carve a road and build a city in the rich but still unmapped territory beyond the lamppost.

Chapter One

1. The first poll cited on public trust in institutions was conducted by the *Wall Street Journal* and NBC News. It appeared in John Harwood, "Americans Distrust Institutions in Poll," the *Wall Street Journal*, June 13, 2002, p. A4. The survey data on how corporations serve the interests of employees and customers is from the Pew Research Center for the People and the Press, "Views of Business and Regulation," February 21, 2002.

2. Ipsos-Reid/*Business Week* poll, published in *Business Week*, February 25, 2002, p. 108.

3. MORI Polls and Surveys, 1999. MORI House, 79–81 Borough Road, London SE1. www.mori.com.

4. "Eurobarometer: Public Opinion in the European Union," European Commission, Brussels, Report Number 56, April 2002. It is interesting to note that while the public's trust in the army, the police, and the United Nations somewhat increased in the post-September 11, 2001, environment, the most recent Eurobarometer survey conducted before that date also ranked corporations last in public trust, with only 34 percent indicating a tendency to trust big companies.

5. *Interim Report on Airline Customer Service Commitment*, June 27, 2000; Office of the Inspector General, U.S. Department of Transportation, Washington, D.C., figures on pp. 1–3.

6. Fox, Susannah, et al., "The Online Health Care Revolution," Pew Internet & American Life Project, November 26, 2001.

7. Eisenberg, David, et al., "Trends in Alternative Medicine Use in the United States, 1990–1997," *Journal of the American Medical Association*, 280:18, November 11, 1998, pp. 1569–1575.

8. Lines, Patricia, "Homeschoolers: Estimating Numbers and Growth," U.S. Department of Education, Spring 1999.

9. Johnson, Kenneth M., "Renewed Population Growth in Rural America," *Research in Rural Sociology and Development*," Vol. 7, pp. 23–45, data on p. 27.

10. Pfleeger, Janet, "U.S. Consumers: Which Jobs Are They Creating?" *Monthly Labor Review*, June 1996.

11. *International Financial Statistics Yearbook*, International Monetary Fund, Washington, D.C., 2001.

12. Gersick, Connie, "Revolutionary Change Theories: A Multilevel Exploration of the Punctuated Equilibrium Paradigm," *Academy of Management Review*, 16:1, 1991, pp. 10–36; see p. 19.

13. Ibid.

14. For the classic portrayal of the new enterprise logic known as managerial capitalism, see Alfred Chandler, *The Visible Hand: The Managerial Revolution in American Business*, Harvard University Press, Cambridge, Mass.: 1977. For a summary of these principles, see pp. 6–12. See also Martin Sklar, *The Corporate Reconstruction of American Capitalism, 1890–1916*, Cambridge University Press, Cambridge: 1988.

15. Elias, Norbert, *The Civilizing Process*, Urizen Books, New York: 1978.
16. Shoshana Zuboff's decade-long study of eight organizations in transition to information technology, *In the Age of the Smart Machine*, came to precisely this conclusion. No matter what innovation was thrown in its path, the organizational status quo was able to undermine it, absorb it, and finally use it as just another medium to reproduce itself. Many other serious studies of institutional economics and innovation lead to the same conclusion.
17. Kuhn, Thomas, *The Structure of Scientific Revolutions*, University of Chicago Press, Chicago: 1970.
18. Davis, Donald Finlay, *Conspicuous Production: Automobiles and Elites in Detroit, 1899–1933*, Temple University Press, Philadelphia: 1988.
19. Gersick, op. cit., p. 22.

Chapter Two

1. For critical appraisals of the concept of the "new economy," see Jeff Madrick, "The Treadmill Economy," *The American Prospect*, November 1998; Paul Krugman, "America the Beautiful," *Foreign Affairs*, May 1998; Dean Baker, "The New Economy Does Not Lurk in the Statistical Discrepancy," *Challenge*, July 1998; Alan Greenspan, "Is There a New Economy?" *Vital Speeches*, October 1998; J. Bradford DeLong, "What New Economy?" *The Wilson Quarterly*, October 1998. See also the *New York Times* coverage of "new economy" proselytizers as they try to cope with the bursting of the Internet bubble, Amy Harmon, " 'Getting Amazoned' and Other Fantasies," *New York Times*, May 13, 2001, section 3, p. 1.
2. See, for example: Neil McKendrick, "The Consumer Revolution of Eighteenth-Century England," in Neil McKendrick, John Brewer, and J. H. Plumb, *The Birth of a Consumer Society: The Commercialization of Eighteenth-Century England*, Indiana University Press, Bloomington: 1982; Neil McKendrick, "Home Demand and Economic Growth," in *Historical Perspectives: Studies in English Thought and Society*, Neil McKendrick, ed., Taylor & Francis, London: 1974; Joan Thirsk, *Economic Policy and Projects: The Development of a Consumer Society in Early Modern England*, Oxford University Press, Oxford: 1978; D.E.C. Eversley, "The Home Market and Home Demand: 1750–1780," in *Land, Labour, and Population in the Industrial Revolution*, E.L. Jones and E.E. Mingay, eds., Edward Arnold, London: 1967; Jan de Vries, "Peasant Demand Patterns and Economic Development: Friesland 1550–1750," in *European Peasants and Their Markets*, William N. Parker and Eric L. Jones, eds., Princeton University Press, Princeton, N.J.: 1976; Fernand Braudel, *The Wheels of Commerce*, Harper & Row, New York: 1982; Simon Schama, *The Embarrassment of Riches: An Interpretation of Dutch Culture in the Golden Age*, Knopf, New York: 1987; Ben Fine and Ellen Leopold, "Consumerism and the Industrial Revolution," *Social History*, 15, May 1990; Grant McCracken, *Culture and Consumption*, Indiana University Press, Bloomington: 1988; Stuart Ewen and Elizabeth Ewen, *Channels of Desire*, University of Minnesota Press, Minneapolis: 1992, especially Chapter 2, "Consumption as a Way of Life"; Rosalind Williams, *Dream Worlds: Mass Consumption in Late Nineteenth Century France*, University of California Press, Berkeley: 1982; Nancy Koehn, *Brand New: How Entrepreneurs Earned Consumers' Trust From Wedgwood to Dell*, Harvard Business School Press, Boston: 2001; William Roseberry, "The Rise of Yuppie Coffees and the Reimagination of Class in the United States," *American Anthropologist*, 98:4, 1996, pp. 762–775; Richard Langlois, "The Coevolution of Technology and Organization in the Transition to the Factory System," in *Authority and Control in Modern Industry*, Paul L. Robertson, ed., Routledge, London: 1999; and, with slightly different emphasis, Paul Romer, "Why, Indeed, in America?: Theory, History, and the Origins of Modern Economic Growth," *American Economic Association Papers and Proceedings*, May 1996.

3. Mukerji, Chandra, *From Graven Images: Patterns of Modern Materialism*, Columbia University Press, New York: 1983.

4. Weber, Max, *General Economic History*, Collier, New York: 1961, p. 230.

5. Appleby, Joyce, "Consumption in Early Modern Social Thought," in *Consumption and the World of Goods*, John Brewer and Roy Porter, eds., Routledge, London: 1993. Most of the essays in this collection are relevant to the new history of consumption and its role in initiating the first industrial revolution. See especially Jean-Christophe Agnew, "Coming Up for Air: Consumer Culture in Historical Perspective"; Jan de Vries, "Between Purchasing Power and the World of Goods"; Peter Burke, "Res et Verba: Conspicuous Consumption in the Early Modern World"; Carole Shammas, "Changes in English and Anglo-American Consumption from 1550–1800"; Lorna Weatherill, "The Meaning of Consumer Behavior in Late Seventeenth- and Early Eighteenth-Century England"; T.H. Breen, "The Meaning of Things: Interpreting the Consumer Economy in the Eighteenth Century"; and Amanda Vickery, "Women and the World of Goods: A Lancashire Consumer and Her Possessions, 1751–81."

6. McKendrick, "Consumer Revolution," p. 9.

7. See also the description of the new consumption in Koehn, op. cit., pp. 24–25.

8. See, for example, Weatherill, op. cit. See also Williams, op. cit., and Mukerji, op. cit.

9. McKendrick, "Consumer Revolution," p. 9. See also Roy Porter, *English Society in the Eighteenth Century*, Penguin, New York: 1982. The point is also made by Nancy Koehn in her review of Wedgwood's marketing techniques, op. cit., pp. 33–35.

10. Forster, Nathaniel, *An Enquiry into the Causes of the Present High Price of Provisions*, J. Fletcher and Co., London: 1767, p. 41. Also quoted in Koehn, op. cit., p. 33.

11. McKendrick, "Consumer Revolution," p. 24.

12. Williams., op. cit., pp. 23, 31.

13. For a seminal statement of this relationship, see McKendrick, "Home Demand," p. 209, and "Consumer Revolution," p. 11, in which he concludes that it was this new "propensity to consume . . . unprecedented in the depth to which it penetrated the lower reaches of society and unprecedented in its impact on the economy" that was the salient force behind the first industrial revolution.

14. McKendrick also writes: "It was consumer demand which attracted the attention of the textile entrepreneurs and made the fortunes of the manufacturers of mass consumer goods. And it was the despised labour of women and children which helped to finance that new consumer demand. It was the fact that she took the consumption decisions which decided the direction of those earnings; it was her control of a larger portion of the family income—that earned by herself and her children—which decided where this extra prosperity was to be released into the economy; and the very fact of her increasing employment outside the home ensured that her demand for manufactured goods would increase because she could no longer make them herself" (McKendrick, "Home Demand," pp. 169, 208–209).

15. Economic historian Richard Langlois summarized the major debates on the origins of the factory system. "Did the factory system emerge because of its organizational form," he asked, "or did it spring from new technology, notably centralized motive power? . . . Did the factory system emerge because it was more efficient than what went before, or did it emerge because capitalists found themselves able to use factory organization as a mechanism for worker exploitation?" (Langlois, op.cit., p. 2). A careful review of the empirical evidence leads him to a conclusion overlooked in most discussions of a subject to which many thousands of pages have been devoted. This new analysis reveals that the factory system was the result of the growth of new mass markets that created the need for entrepreneurial innovations capable of producing high-volume throughput: "The factory system arose

because growth in the extent of the market (for textiles principally, but eventually most other goods as well) opened up entrepreneurial possibilities for high-volume throughput. This meant not only an extended division of labor, but also investment in new capabilities ... that, by making production more routine, permitted lower unit costs. ... These new capabilities implied high fixed costs, at least initially, and it was these fixed costs that called for the 'factory' mode of organization" (Langlois, op. cit., p. 4).

16. See Neil McKendrick's description in "Josiah Wedgwood and the Commercialization of the Potteries," in McKendrick, et al., *The Birth of a Consumer Society*. See also Nancy Koehn's depiction of Wedgwood, op. cit., pp. 11–42, quote on p. 34.

17. Koehn, op. cit. See also Sidney Pollard, *The Genesis of Modern Management: A Study of the Industrial Revolution in Great Britain*, Harvard University Press, Cambridge, Mass.: 1965.

18. Koehn, op. cit., p. 35.

19. See Pollard, op. cit. There are many good sources that describe this period in British economic history and its paradigmatic innovations. Some of the classic accounts include T.S. Ashton, *The Industrial Revolution 1760–1830*, Oxford University Press, London: 1948; Paul Mantoux, *The Industrial Revolution in the Eighteenth Century*, Macmillan, New York: 1961 (first edition London: 1928); Karl Polanyi, *The Great Transformation*, Farrar & Rinehart, New York: 1944; W.O. Henderson, *Britain and Industrial Europe, 1750–1870*, Leicester University Press, Leicester, England: 1972; E.J. Hobsbawm, *The Age of Revolution*, Times Mirror, New York: 1962; Phyliss Dean, *The First Industrial Revolution*, Cambridge University Press, Cambridge: 1969; Eric Pawson, *The Early Industrial Revolution*, Barnes & Noble, New York: 1979; and Robin Reeve, *The Industrial Revolution, 1750–1850*, University of London Press, London: 1971. See also the essays in *Industrial Revolution, 1700–1914*, Carlo Cipolla, ed., Harvester Press, Hassocks, England: 1976; David Landes, "The Industrial Revolution in Britain," in his *The Unbound Prometheus: Technological Change and Industrial Development in Western Europe from 1750 to the Present*, Cambridge University Press, Cambridge: 1969, pp. 41–123; Robert Gordon, "Paradoxical Property," in John Brewer and Susan Staves, *Early Modern Conceptions of Property*, Routledge, London, New York: 1995, pp. 95–110, esp. p. 107–108; and N.F.R. Crafts, "The Industrial Revolution," in *The Economic History of Britain since 1700*, R. Floud and D. McCloskey, eds., Cambridge University Press, Cambridge: 1994.

20. See also Weber, op. cit., p. 227.

21. The most comprehensive account of the meaning of the first industrial revolution for workers, the experience of work, and the imposition of a new labor discipline is E.P. Thompson, *The Making of the English Working Class*, Random House, New York: 1966. See also his essay, "Time, Work-Discipline, and Industrial Capitalism," in his *Customs in Common*, New Press, New York: 1993, pp. 352–403. There are many other good sources on this subject, including Pollard, op. cit., esp. pp. 160–208; Sebastian de Grazia, *Of Time, Work and Leisure*, Twentieth Century Fund, New York: 1962; Douglas Reid, "The Decline of Saint Monday," in *Past and Present*, 71, 1976; and Rhodes Boyson, *The Ashworth Cotton Enterprises*, Oxford University Press, Oxford: 1970.

22. Max Weber identified the concentration of ownership as the critical accomplishment of this phase of capitalism: "The real distinguishing characteristic of the modern factory is in general ... not the implements of work applied, but the concentration of ownership of workplace, means of work, source of power, and raw material in one and the same hand, that of the entrepreneur. This combination was only exceptionally met with before the 18th century" (*General Economic History*, p. 224).

23. See Pollard's discussion of this crucial point, op. cit., pp. 6–23.

24. For example, in a famous passage Smith denies the ability of salaried managers in joint-stock companies to honestly administer the deployment of capital: "The directors of such companies, however, being the managers rather of other people's money than of their own, it cannot well be expected that they should watch over it with the same anxious vigilance with which the partners in a private co-partnery frequently watch over their own. Like the stewards of a rich man, they are apt to consider attention to small matters as not for their master's honour, and very easily give themselves a dispensation from having it. Negligence and profusion, therefore, must always prevail, more or less, in the management of the affairs of such a company" (*The Wealth of Nations*, Edwin Cannan, ed., Modern Library, Random House, New York: 1994; Book V, p. 800). See also Gordon, op. cit.

25. This discussion of modern pleasure and its relationship to the expansion of capitalism and the rise of modern consumption is based largely on Colin Campbell's brilliant historical discourse in *The Romantic Ethic and the Spirit of Modern Consumerism*, Basil Blackwell, London: 1987.

26. Veyne, Paul, "The Roman Empire," in *A History of Private Life: From Pagan Rome to Byzantium*, Paul Veyne, ed., Belknap Press of Harvard University Press, Cambridge, Mass.: 1987, p. 205. See also V.S. Naipaul's essay, "Our Universal Civilization," 1990 Wriston Lecture, The Manhattan Institute; his depiction of traditional society follows Veyne's description of the ancient Romans.

27. See Edward Shorter, *The Making of the Modern Family*, Basic Books, New York: 1975, esp. pp. 22–78; and John Demos, *Past, Present, and Personal: The Family and the Life Course in American History*, Oxford University Press, Oxford: 1986, esp. pp. 27–30.

28. Shorter, op. cit.

29. This process is also documented in Philippe Aries's seminal *Centuries of Childhood: A Social History of Family Life*, Random House, New York: 1962.

30. Shorter, op. cit.

31. Aries, Philippe, op. cit., pp. 398–400.

32. Aries, Philippe, *Western Attitudes Toward Death: From the Middle Ages to the Present*, Johns Hopkins University Press, Baltimore: 1974.

33. Corbin, Alain, "Backstage," in *A History of Private Life: From the Fires of Revolution to the Great War*, Vol. IV, Belknap Press of Harvard University Press, Cambridge, Mass.: 1990, esp. pp. 457–547.

34. Campbell, Colin, *The Romantic Ethic and the Spirit of Modern Consumerism*, Basil Blackwell, London: 1987.

35. Ibid., p. 90. "This dynamic interaction between illusion and reality," writes Campbell, "is the key to the understanding of modern consumerism . . . that dissatisfaction with existence and the consequent readiness to seize whatever pleasures are promised, which characterize the modern attitude of longing."

36. Patten, Simon, *The Consumption of Wealth*, New York: 1892, p. 51.

37. Bushman, Richard L., *The Refinement of America: Persons, Houses, Cities*, Knopf, New York: 1992, p. 404. See also Richard L. Bushman and Claudia L. Bushman, "The Early History of Cleanliness in America," *Journal of American History*, 74:4, March 1988, pp. 1213–1238; John F. Kasson, *Rudeness and Civility: Manners in Nineteenth Century America*, Hill and Wang, New York: 1990; and Stuart M. Blumin, *The Emergence of Middle Class: Social Experience in the American City 1760–1900*, Cambridge University Press, Cambridge: 1989, esp. chapters 4 and 5.

38. Bushman, *The Refinement of America*, p. xiii.

39. Ibid., pp. 442–445.

40. Ibid., pp. 406–407. It must be noted that these manufacturing efforts did not yet meet the standard of mass production, with truly dramatic reductions in unit costs coupled with almost unimaginable increases in throughput.

41. For the most authoritative description of this phase in manufacturing development, see David Hounshell, *From the American System to Mass Production, 1800–1932*, Johns Hopkins University Press, Baltimore: 1984, pp. 1–216.

42. Bushman, op. cit., pp. xiii, xviii–xix, 406–407. See also Fine and Leopold, op. cit.

43. See the discussion of corporate capitalism as a social movement in Martin J. Sklar, *The Corporate Reconstruction of American Capitalism, 1890–1916*, Cambridge University Press, Cambridge: 1988, esp. pp. 13–14, 20–33. See also William G. Roy, *Socializing Capital: The Rise of the Large Industrial Corporation in America*, Princeton University Press, Princeton, N.J.: 1997, and Louis Galambos, "The U.S. Corporate Economy in the Twentieth Century," in *The Cambridge Economic History of the United States, Vol. III: The Twentieth Century*, Stanley L. Engerman and Robert E. Gallman, eds., Cambridge University Press, Cambridge: 2000, pp. 927–968.

44. For a few of the more prominent sources on Henry Ford, see Allan Nevins with Frank Ernest Hill, *Ford: The Times, The Man, The Company*, Scribners, New York: 1954; Allan Nevins and Frank Ernest Hill, *Ford: Expansion and Challenge, 1915–1933*, Scribners, New York: 1957; Anne Jardim, *The First Henry Ford: A Study in Personality and Business Leadership*, MIT Press, Cambridge, Mass.: 1970; Keith Sward, *The Legend of Henry Ford*, Atheneum, New York: 1968; David L. Lewis, *The Public Image of Henry Ford*, Wayne State University Press, Detroit: 1976; Thomas K. McCraw, "Henry Ford and Alfred Sloan," in *Management, Past and Present*, Alfred Chandler, Jr., Thomas K. McCraw, and Richard Tedlow, eds., South-Western College Publishing, Cincinnati: 1995; and Richard Tedlow, *Giants of Enterprise*, Harper Business, New York: 2001, pp. 119–177.

45. Davis, Donald Finlay, *Conspicuous Production: Automobiles and Elites in Detroit, 1899–1933*, Temple University Press, Philadelphia: 1988, pp. 209–210.

46. Ibid., p. 209.

47. Ibid., esp. pp. 117–143 and 209–210.

48. See Tedlow, op. cit., pp. 124–125.

49. Nevins with Hill, *Ford: The Times*, pp. 576–577.

50. Tedlow, pp. 153–154.

51. Finlay, op. cit., pp. 118–120.

52. Tedlow, op. cit., p. 154.

53. See Hounshell, op. cit., on the American system, pp. 15–123.

54. Tedlow, op. cit., pp. 161–162.

55. Hounshell, op. cit., pp. 221, 241.

56. Ibid.; see detailed account on pp. 220–259.

57. Ibid., p. 248.

58. Tedlow, op. cit., p. 163.

59. Hounshell, op. cit., p. 255.

60. Ibid., p. 10.

61. See Shoshana Zuboff, "Work," *Encyclopedia of the United States in the Twentieth Century*, Stanley I. Kutler, ed., Charles Scribner's Sons, New York: 1996, pp. 1091–1126.

62. Hounshell, op. cit., p. 9.

63. Tedlow, op. cit., pp. 159–160.

64. Finlay, op. cit., p. 122.

65. Drucker, Peter, *Concept of the Corporation*, Transaction Publishers, New Brunswick, N.J.: 1995, pp. 219–221. See also Galambos, op. cit., p. 937.

66. Hounshell, op. cit., p. 237.

67. Ibid., p. 257; and Sward, op. cit., p. 49.

68. Hounshell, op. cit., pp. 258–259.

69. For a critique of the Ford Motor Company's use of the five-dollar day for social control and worker screening, see Stephen Meyer III, *The Five Dollar Day*, State University of New York Press, Albany: 1981.

70. Tedlow, op. cit., pp. 163–165.
71. Hounshell, op. cit., p. 259.
72. Lazonick, William, and Mary O'Sullivan, "Big Business and Skill Formation in the Wealthiest Nations: The Organizational Revolution in the Twentieth Century," in *Big Business and the Wealth of Nations*, Alfred D. Chandler, Jr., Franco Amatori, and Takashi Hikino, eds., Cambridge University Press, Cambridge: 1997, pp. 502–503.
73. For more on the standardization of this employment relationship, see Peter Cappelli, *The New Deal at Work*, Harvard Business School, Boston: 1999, esp. Chapter 2, "The Arrangements We Left Behind," pp. 49–68.
74. For more on Ford's autocratic behavior and reluctance to delegate management, see Hounshell, op. cit., p. 293, and Peter Drucker, *Management*, Harper & Row, New York: 1973, p. 381. For more general discussions of the shift to a managerial model, see Alfred D. Chandler, Jr., *The Visible Hand: The Managerial Revolution in American Business*, Harvard University Press, Cambridge, Mass.: 1977; Alfred D. Chandler, Jr., *Scale and Scope: The Dynamics of Industrial Capitalism*, Harvard University Press, Cambridge, Mass.: 1990; and Alfred D. Chandler, Jr., *Big Business*, pp. 30, 33. See also Lazonick, op. cit., p. 501.
75. Ford, Henry, *My Life and Work,* Ayer, North Stratford, N.H.: 1999, p. 96.
76. Ibid., p. 91.
77. Ibid., p. 92.
78. See, for example, Richard Tedlow, *New and Improved: The Story of Mass Marketing in America*, Basic Books, New York: 1990, p. 163. See also Peter Drucker, *Management*, pp. 380–388.
79. Finlay, op. cit., p. 122.
80. See Hounshell, op. cit., for extensive discussion of this phase at Ford, on pp. 263–301.
81. Ibid., pp. 264–267.
82. See Tedlow, *Giants of Enterprise*, pp. 159–160.
83. Chandler, *Visible Hand*, p. 486.
84. Ibid., p. 459.
85. Ibid., p. 457.
86. Ibid., p. 463.
87. For the classic portrayal of this new enterprise logic known as managerial capitalism, see Chandler, *Visible Hand;* for a summary of these principles, see pp. 6–12. See also Sklar, op. cit.
88. For more on the origins and early history of the corporation see Chandler, *Scale and Scope*, esp. pp. 1–90; Roy, op. cit.; Galambos, op. cit.; and Sklar, op. cit. Roy is especially thorough on the preindustrial origins of the corporate form and its evolution in law and practice.
89. See Roy, op. cit., pp. 151–154.
90. Chandler, *Scale and Scope*, pp. 75–77. See also Galambos, op. cit., pp. 930–932.
91. Chandler, *Scale and Scope*, pp. 75–76.
92. See the remarkable letter setting out this reasoning written by a DuPont associate, Albert Moxham, to Coleman du Pont in 1903. Quoted in Chandler, *Scale and Scope*, p. 76. See also Galambos, op. cit., pp. 936–937.
93. According to Chandler, though, their influence waned once firms could fund growth primarily from retained earnings; see *Scale and Scope*, p. 81.
94. Roy, op. cit., pp. 144–175.
95. See Chandler, *Scale and Scope*, pp. 85–86. Typically these rights to manage were revoked only when the company faced crisis or failure at the hands of management or when major strategic decisions threatened the perceived interests of major shareholders. It should also be noted that the dilution of owners' control typically affected average shareholders differently than large shareholders. See also Roy, op. cit., pp. 172–173.

 96. See Roy, op. cit., pp. 254–256. See also Chandler, *Visible Hand*, pp. 468 and 9–10.
 97. Ford's well-known article, "Mass Production," in the 1926 *Encyclopedia Britannica*, 13th ed., Vol. 2, Chicago, 1926 (actually ghostwritten by William Cameron), reflects this understanding: "Mass production is not merely quantity production . . . nor is it merely machine production. . . . Mass production is the focussing [*sic*] upon a manufacturing project of the principles of power, accuracy, economy, system, continuity, and speed. The interpretation of these principles, through studies of operation and machine development and their co-ordination, is the conspicuous task of management."
 98. Chandler, Alfred, "The United States: Engines of Economic Growth in the Capital-Intensive and Knowledge-Intensive Industries," in *Big Business*, p. 77.
 99. For a useful and concise description of Sloan's innovations and their relationship to Ford's, see Thomas McCraw, *American Business, 1920–2000: How It Worked*, Harlan Davidson, Wheeling, Ill.: 2000, pp. 10–27.
100. For the classic portrayal of this new enterprise logic known as managerial capitalism, see Chandler, *Visible Hand*, pp. 6–12.
101. Much of this discussion of the new capitalism as a social movement relies on the extensive historical investigation of the "corporate reconstruction of American capitalism" in Sklar, op. cit. The interested reader should see his chapter on corporate capitalism and corporate liberalism, pp. 1–42; see also pp. 431–461.
102. See also Roy, op. cit., pp. 268–269.
103. See Chandler, *Scale and Scope*, p. 79. Also Galambos, op. cit., p. 933.
104. Galambos, op. cit., pp. 934–937.
105. Ibid., p. 934.
106. Sklar, op. cit., pp. 21, 26.
107. Galambos, op. cit., p. 938. Recent work by Philip Scranton, Michael Piore, and Charles Sabel underscored the presence of many types of firms for whom a more flexible and customized approach to production remained most sensible. Even here, however, most of these firms incorporated and evolved organizational structures, and many work practices, consistent with the standard enterprise logic. See Philip Scranton, *Endless Novelty*, Princeton University Press, Princeton N.J.: 1997; *Worlds of Possibilities*, Charles Sabel and Jonathan Zeitlin, eds., Cambridge University Press, Cambridge: 1997; Michael Piore and Charles Sabel, *The Second Industrial Divide*, Basic Books, New York: 1984.
108. As Harvard historian Alfred Chandler put it, "The wealth of nations during the past hundred years has been based more on organization and technology—on how technologies of production have been created or improved. It rested on the ability of industrial enterprises to adopt and to develop these technologies and to devise administrative structures to coordinate the flow of materials from the raw materials through the processes of production and distribution to the final consumer" (*Big Business*, p. 63).
109. Wiebe, Robert, *The Search for Order, 1877–1920*, Hill and Wang, New York: 1967. Wiebe continues: "The ideas that filtered through and eventually took the fort were bureaucratic ones, peculiarly suited to the fluidity and impersonality of an urban-industrial world. . . . Instead of likening society to a clock's simple gears in perpetual motion, men were now thinking in terms of a complex social technology, of a mechanized and systematized factory. . . . Now education implied the guidance of behavior in harmony with social processes." The point is echoed by Sklar, op. cit., in his description, on p. 437, of the new principles of corporate-liberal thought, well established by 1920, that designated "the organized group (corporation, trade union, cooperative) as the basic unit of the economy." It is also regarded as the central theme of the individual's life by cultural historian Martha Banta, in her *Taylored Lives: Narrative Productions in the Age of Taylor, Veblen, and Ford*, University of Chicago Press, Chicago: 1993, p. 281: "The relation of parts to wholes was both the leading principle in the standardization pro-

cedures considered necessary to modern industrial production and the guiding trope for lives led within a culture of management"; see also pp. 145–149. For another discussion of this theme, see Jean B. Quandt, *From the Small Town to the Great Community: The Social Thought of Progressive Intellectuals*, Rutgers University Press, New Brunswick, N.J.: 1970.

110. Roy, op. cit., p. 273.
111. Ibid., p. 134.
112. See general discussion in Wiebe, op. cit., Chapter 7, "Progressivism Arrives," pp. 164–195; the quote is on p. 164.
113. Ibid., pp. 182–183.
114. Putnam, Robert, *Bowling Alone: The Collapse and Revival of American Community*, Simon & Schuster, New York: 2000, p. 383.
115. Skocpol, Theda, et al., "How Americans Became Civic," in *Civic Engagement in American Democracy*, Theda Skocpol and Morris P. Fiorina, eds., Brookings Institution Press, Washington, D.C.: 1999.
116. See Putnam, op. cit., p. 437; see also Stephanie Coontz, *The Social Origins of Private Life*, Verso, London: 1988, pp. 339–342.
117. Putnam, op. cit., pp. 389, 342. See also the vivid discussions in Robert Schrank, *Ten Thousand Working Days*, MIT Press, Cambridge, Mass.: 1976, and Robert Schrank, *Wasn't That a Time?: Growing Up Radical and Red in America*, MIT Press, Cambridge, Mass.: 1998.
118. See Zuboff, op. cit.
119. Putnam, op. cit.
120. Burnham, John, "The New Psychology," in *Change and Continuity in Twentieth Century America: The 1920s*, John Braeman, Robert Bremner, and David Brody, eds., Ohio State University Press, Columbus: 1968, pp. 323–350.
121. *Historical Statistics*, U.S. Bureau of the Census, Washington, D.C.: series H, pp. 412–432.
122. See Zuboff, op. cit.
123. See Warren Susman, "Culture and Civilization: The 1920's," in *Culture as History: The Transformation of American Society in the Twentieth Century*, Pantheon Books, New York: 1973. Regenia Gagnier describes a similar shift in the function of the upper-class English public school, in *Subjectivities: A History of Self-Representation in Britain, 1832–1920*, Oxford University Press, Oxford: 1991; see esp. "The Making of Middle Class Identities: School and Family," pp. 171–199.
124. Coontz, op. cit., p. 338. French historian Antoine Prost makes a similar observation: "The prolongation of schooling actually stems from far deeper changes in society. The phenomenon reflects not so much the socialization of apprenticeship as the need for an apprenticeship in the ways of society. In the past this kind of teaching was carried on within the family, and for that reason it was possible to characterize the family as society's 'basic cell.' . . . The liberalization of family education shifted the burden of educating youngsters for their future life in society from the family to the school. The schools assumed responsibility for teaching young people to respect the realities of time and space and the rules of social life as well as how to relate to other people" ("The Family and the Individual," in *A History of Private Life*, Vol. V, Antoine Prost and Gerard Vincent, eds., Belknap Press of Harvard University Press, Cambridge, Mass: 1991, p. 71).
125. Frederick, Christine, *Selling Mrs. Consumer*, The Business Bourse, New York: 1929. See also Stuart Ewen, *Captains of Consciousness: Advertising and the Social Roots of the Consumer Culture*, McGraw-Hill, New York: 1976.
126. Coontz, op. cit., p. 351.
127. Susman, op. cit.
128. Hounshell, op. cit., pp. 318–320.
129. Coontz, op. cit., p. 347.

130. Coontz, Stephanie, *The Way We Never Were: American Families and the Nostalgia Trap*, Basic Books, New York: 1992, p. 24.
131. Ibid., pp. 24–25.
132. "The Fortune Survey," *Fortune*, August 1943, p. 10. The survey interviewers were told to rate each respondent according to her level of attractiveness. Later, survey responses were correlated with these attractiveness scales to see if pretty women held different attitudes about their gender roles than homely women.
133. Coontz, *The Way We Never Were*, p. 25.
134. Parsons, Talcott, and Robert F. Bales, *Family, Socialization and Interaction Process*, Free Press, New York: 1955, pp. 16–17.
135. Coontz, *The Way We Never Were*; see discussion on pp. 35–38, quote on p. 36.
136. See Marynia Farnham and Ferdinand Lundberg, *Modern Woman: The Lost Sex*, Harper & Brothers, New York: 1947; Susan Hartmann, *The Home Front and Beyond: American Women in the 1940's*, Twayne, Boston: 1982; Carol Warren, *Madwives: Schizophrenic Women in the 1950's*, Rutgers University Press, New Brunswick, N.J.: 1987; Douglas Miller and Marion Nowak, *The Fifties: The Way We Really Were*, Doubleday, Garden City, N.Y.: 1977.
137. Friedan, Betty, *The Feminine Mystique*, Norton, New York: 1963.

Chapter Three

1. Erikson, Erik, *Childhood and Society*, New York: 1963, p. 16.
2. As one visitor was quoted in the *Congressional Quarterly*, "This is the only monument I've ever been to where there is total silence, even when it's crowded" (*CQ Researcher*, February 18, 2000).
3. As one scholar put it, "The Vietnam Veterans Memorial willfully relinquishes the traditional role to speak as the official voice of the community, explaining the meaning of past events, reassuring us that these deaths had meaning, celebrating the virtue of sacrifice. . . . Rather than electing 'speech' through a traditional form of symbolic expression, it opts for silence. It . . . places both the burden and the freedom upon us to discover what these past events mean, whether these deaths do have meaning, what virtue is to be found in sacrifice, and what our own relationship should be to our political institutions" (Peter Ehrenhaus, "Silence and Symbolic Expression," *Communication Monographs*, 55, p. 55).
4. Those commissioned to create a Vietnam memorial appreciated the Wall because it did not pretend to offer an artificial consensus about a war that was distinguished, above all, by an acrimonious absence of consensus. Social conservatives were outraged that the memorial did so little to beatify the nation's sacrifice in Vietnam. Eventually, the conservative secretary of the interior, James Watt, gave his permission for the memorial to be built but insisted on the addition of the American flag, as well as a more traditional sculpture, elsewhere on the memorial site.
5. The Wall has been televised and reproduced on postcards, T-shirts, buttons, brochures, and posters. Books and articles have been written about it. A portable version of the Wall travels around the country, and numerous new memorials have been built that echo its design.
6. Wagner-Pacifici, Robin, and Barry Schwartz, "The Vietnam Veterans Memorial: Commemorating a Difficult Past," *American Journal of Sociology*, 97:2, September 1991, pp. 379–420, quotation is on p. 405.
7. Other useful articles on the Vietnam Veterans Memorial include Lora Senechal Carney, "Not Telling Us What to Think: The Vietnam Veterans Memorial," *Metaphor and Symbolic Activity*, 8:3, 1993; and Carole Blair, Marsha S. Jeppeson, and Enrico Pucci, Jr., "Public Memorializing in Postmodernity: The Vietnam Veterans Memorial as Prototype," *Quarterly Journal of Speech*, 77, 1991.

8. Pyle, Ernie, "Brave Men," Scripps-Howard Newspaper Alliance, 1943, pp. 17–18, republished by Aeonian Press, Mattituck, N.Y.: 1978.
9. Tobin, James, *Ernie Pyle's War*, University Press of Kansas, Lawrence, Kan: 1998, p. 4.
10. Hannity, Sean, Alan Colmes, Fox News Network, March 31, 1999, transcript no. 033102cb.253; Bob Deans, Cox News Service, March 31, 1999; *All Things Considered*, 9:00 P.M. ET, March 31, 1999.
11. Cushman, John H., Jr., "Crisis in the Balkans: The Ambush," *New York Times*, April 1, 1999; Mimi Hall and Paul Hoversten, "Serbs: We Have U.S. Soldiers on Mission near Yugoslav Line," *USA Today*, April 1, 1999; "Clinton Warns Milosevic on Soldiers," UPI, April 1, 1999; Michael Clarke and Tim Moynihan, "Clinton Warns Milosevic over Trial of Captured Soldiers," Press Association Newsfile, April 1, 1999.
12. Defense Department Regular News Briefing, "Ken Bacon Holds Defense Department Regular News Briefing," FDCH Political Transcripts, April 1, 1999; *CBS This Morning*, 7:00 A.M. ET, April 1, 1999.
13. *CBS Morning News*, 6:30 A.M. ET, April 2, 1999; George Ramos, "Crisis in Yugoslavia," *Los Angeles Times*, April 2, 1999; Brett Pulley, "Crisis in the Balkans," *New York Times*, April 2, 1999.
14. Williams, Daniel, "Serbs Release POWs to Jackson," *Washington Post*, May 2, 1999; Anne-Marie O'Connor, "Crisis in Yugoslavia," *Los Angeles Times*, May 3, 1999.
15. See, for example, "ABC News Special Report: America Under Attack," 8:00 P.M. EST, September 12, 2001.
16. See, for example, *Rivera Live*, 9:00 P.M. EST, September 14, 2001; "Mourning Begins as Hope Fades," *Daily Telegraph*, London, September 14, 2001; "ABC News Special Report: America Under Attack," 10:00 P.M. EST, September 13, 2001; "CNN Live Event Special," September 13, 2001.
17. "Five Lives," *Wall Street Journal*, Thursday, October 11, 2001, p. A1, and "The Human Toll," p. C1.
18. The *New York Times* reported nearly two thousand of these "obituaries," which continued well into 2002. Editors said they would end the project only when they ran out of families to talk with.
19. "Honoring the Rescuers," *New York Times*, Sunday, September 23, 2001, p. B8.
20. On October 20, 2001, a Blackhawk helicopter crashed while trying to land in Pakistan, after supporting Special Forces in a nighttime raid inside Afghanistan. By October 21, the national news services reported the identities of the two soldiers who died in the crash, John Edmunds, from Wyoming, and Kris Stonesifer, of Montana. By the next day, the press was delving into each man's biography and high school highlights and interviewing family members. On November 26, 2001, news leaked that an American adviser had been killed in a prison revolt outside Mazar-e Sharif. By November 28, once the American's body had been recovered, the CIA took the unusual step of announcing that the dead man was Johnny Michael Spann. He had been one of their operatives, presumably in Afghanistan to interview and recruit Taliban prisoners. While many of his colleagues complained about the breach of secrecy, CIA Director George Tenet had apparently decided that it was necessary to satisfy public interest in the fallen American. Once again, the national news services quickly unearthed his biography, interviewed hometown friends in Winfield, Alabama, and conducted a news conference with his grief-stricken father. A similar process ensued with the "first death of an American soldier in Afghanistan" on Friday, January 4, 2002. That afternoon, General Tommy Franks informed reporters of the death of Green Beret sergeant Nathan Chapman of San Antonio, Texas, killed in a gunfight in eastern Afghanistan. The next morning the print media and early talk shows featured Chapman's family—including interviews with his parents, friends, and colleagues—

and discussed his boyhood, fatherhood, hobbies, attitudes, and military experience. By Sunday, the *New York Times* featured a front-page article on the man, his family, personality, and background, as well as a large color photo of Nathan Chapman's casket as it was carried by eight solemn soldiers from an air force plane. For records of this coverage see: "NBC News, Saturday Today," 7:00 A.M. ET, October 20, 2001; "Bombing Resumes in Afghanistan," Bloomberg News Service, Sunday, October 21, 2001, 5:49 A.M. ET; Chris Georgy, "War Claims Cheyenne Son," *Wyoming Tribune Eagle*, October 22, 2001; AP, "The War on Terror," *Newsday*, October 22, 2001, p. A6; Carlotta Gall, "An American Is Said to Be Killed," *New York Times*, November 26, 2001, p. A1; Pamela Hess, "CIA Officer's Body Recovered from Riot," UPI, November 28, 2001; Hugh Doherty, "Tributes to CIA Hero Who Died in Action," Press Association Limited, November 28, 2001; Tom Gjelten, *Talk of the Nation*, National Public Radio, November 28, 2001, 3:00 P.M. ET; Drew Jubera, "Agent's Death Leaves a Town in Shock," Cox News Service, November 28, 2001; Pamela Hess, "Soldier Dead, CIA Officer Hurt in Ambush," UPI, January 4, 2002; "Ft. Lewis Soldier Killed in Action," *Seattle Times*, January 5, 2002; Eileen Flynn, "Gentle Father of Two Embraced Duty as Soldier," Cox News Service, January 5, 2002; "Comrades Remember Chapman," *CNN Saturday*, 12:00, January 5, 2002; "Family, Friends Have Fond Memories of Chapman," *CNN Tonight*, 22:00, January 5, 2002; Jim Yardley, "A Soldier and Son Who Thrived on Risk and Army Discipline," *New York Times*, January 6, 2002.

21. Williams, Molly, "Many Americans Try to Join the Military, But Not So Many Measure Up," *Wall Street Journal*, October 25, 2001, p. B1. See also Ellen Gamerman, "Many Calling, Few Are Helping," *Baltimore Sun*, November 21, 2001; Scott MacKay, "War on Terrorism," *Providence Journal*, November 8, 2001; Harry Levins, "Recruiters Find Many Willing to Talk, But Not Enlist," *St. Louis Post-Dispatch*, October 30, 2001.

22. Leo, John, "One Tin Slogan," *U.S. News & World Report*, January 22, 2001; James Dao, "Ads Now Seek Recruits for 'An Army of One,'" *New York Times*, January 10, 2001; Mark Shields, "Here's a New One: Uncle Sam Wants Your Personal Growth," *Seattle Post-Intelligencer*, January 22 2001; Clyde Haberman, "Army of One Is Missing Sense of Duty," *New York Times*, January 20, 2001; "New Army Slogan Tribute to 'Tribalism,'" *USA Today*, January 16, 2001; Lucian K. Truscott IV, "Marketing an Army of Individuals," *New York Times*, January 12, 2001; Jennifer Harper, "Army's Slogan Centers on 'One' 'Me-now' Message Set to Lure Recruits," *Washington Times*, January 11, 2001; Thomas Evans, "The Wrong Campaign," *Advertising Age*, January 29, 2001; *CNN Early Edition*, interview with Louis Caldera, January 10, 2001.

23. The work of sociolinguist Basil Bernstein is a testament to this idea. See his *Class, Codes, and Control: Theoretical Studies Toward a Sociology of Language*, Schocken Books, New York: 1975.

24. The discussion focuses primarily on the U.S. case. While there are important variations on these trends in other developed countries, there are even more pronounced similarities, particularly among the industrialized nations of Western Europe and the Commonwealth countries.

25. DeLong, J. Bradford, "Cornucopia: The Pace of Economic Growth in the Twentieth Century," Working Paper no. 7602, National Bureau of Economic Research, March 2000, pp. 11–12. For background, see also his "The Shape of Twentieth Century Economic History," Working Paper no. 7569, National Bureau of Economic Research, February 2000. Note: Gross domestic product is a measure of all the final goods and services produced and bought by households, businesses, and government agencies.

26. DeLong, "The Shape of Twentieth Century Economic History," pp. 12–13.

27. Ibid. As DeLong notes, this burgeoning wealth has been most pronounced in the

advanced economies, especially the United States, but has not been strictly confined to them. Even as early as 1987, 97 percent of households in Greece owned a television set. In Mexico that year, there was one automobile for every sixteen people, one television for every eight, one telephone for every ten.

28. Ibid., p. 17.

29. Ibid., see discussion pp. 14–26.

30. Abramovitz, Moses, and Paul A. David, "American Macroeconomic Growth in the Era of Knowledge-Based Progress: The Long-Run Perspective," in *The Cambridge Economic History of the United States, Vol. III: The Twentieth Century*, Stanley Engerman and Robert Gallman, eds., Cambridge University Press, Cambridge: 2000, pp. 1–92. See the collection of essays in Timothy F. Bresnahan and Robert J. Gordon, *The Economics of New Goods*, University of Chicago Press, Chicago: 1997. One analysis in this collection ("Do Real Output and Real Wage Measures Capture Reality?", pp. 29–70) addresses the discontinuity in real wealth by looking at the true cost of lighting. It concludes that nearly three-quarters of today's consumption is radically different from its counterpart in the nineteenth century. The study suggests that the growth of real wages and the availability of remarkable new consumption opportunities has been substantially understated by traditional indices, just as prices have been substantially overstated.

31. DeLong, "Cornucopia," p. 26. DeLong's analysis of the wealth effect compensates for earlier understated measurements of the value of new goods, while recognizing that the value of those new goods will vary with personal income, which represents the ability to access them. See also Dora Costa, "American Living Standards, 1888–1994: Evidence from Consumer Expenditures," Working Paper no. 7650, National Bureau of Economic Research, April 2000.

32. DeLong, "Cornucopia" pp. 30–31.

33. Ibid., p. 32.

34. Pfleeger, Janet, "U.S. Consumers: Which Jobs Are They Creating?" *Monthly Labor Review*, June 1996.

35. "The Changing American: Life Style Trends 1975–1996," DDB Needham Worldwide, Inc., Chicago: 1996.

36. "General Social Survey," National Opinion Research Center, University of Chicago: 1994.

37. Gray, Maureen Boyle, "Consumer Spending on Durables and Services in the 1980's," *Monthly Labor Review*, May 1992; quote on p. 18.

38. Riesman, David, *The Lonely Crowd: A Study of Changing American Character*, Yale University Press, New Haven, Conn.: 1950; John Kenneth Galbraith, *The Affluent Society*, Houghton Mifflin, Boston: 1958; Daniel Bell, *The Cultural Contradictions of Capitalism*, Basic Books, New York: 1976; Christopher Lasch, *The Culture of Narcissism*, Norton, New York: 1979; Juliet Schor, *The Overspent American: Upscaling, Downshifting, and the New Consumer*, Basic Books, New York: 1998. For an overview of the early literature of this type, and a general sense of the historical persistence of desire and its denouncers, see Daniel Horowitz, *The Morality of Spending: Attitudes Toward the Consumer Society in America, 1875–1940*, Johns Hopkins University Press, Baltimore: 1985.

39. See Cass Sunstein and Edna Ullmann-Margalit, "Solidarity in Consumption," The Law School, University of Chicago, Working Paper no. 98, April 28, 2000; Metin M. Cosgel, "Consumption Institutions," *Review of Social Economy*, LV:2, Summer 1997; Elizabeth Hirschman, "Primitive Aspects of Consumption in Modern American Society," *Journal of Consumer Research*, 12, September 1985; Susan Schultz Kleine, et al., "How Is a Possession 'Me' or 'Not Me'?" *Journal of Consumer Research*, 22, December 1995; Marsha Richins, "Special Possessions and the Expression of Material Values" and "Valuing Things: The Public and Private Meanings of Possessions," *Journal of Consumer Research*, 21, December 1994;

Stephen J. Gould, "The Self-Manipulation of My Pervasive, Perceived Vital Energy through Product Use," *Journal of Consumer Research*, 18, September 1991; Craig Thompson, et al., "The Lived Meaning of Free Choice," *Journal of Consumer Research*, 17, December 1990; M. Joseph Sirgy, "Self-Concept in Consumer Behavior," *Journal of Consumer Research*, 9, 1982; Morris Holbrook and Elizabeth Hirschman, "The Experiential Aspects of Consumption: Consumer Fantasies, Feelings, and Fun," *Journal of Consumer Research*, 9, 1982; Craig Thompson, "Caring Consumers: Gendered Consumption Meanings and the Juggling Lifestyle," *Journal of Consumer Research*, 22, March 1996; John Schouten, "Selves in Transition: Symbolic Consumption in Personal Rites of Passage and Identity Reconstruction," *Journal of Consumer Research*, 17, March 1991; Russell Belk, "Possessions and the Extended Self," *Journal of Consumer Research*, 15, September 1988; William Havlena and Morris Holbrook, "The Varieties of Consumption Experience: Comparing Two Typologies of Emotion in Consumer Behavior," *Journal of Consumer Behavior*, 13, December 1986; Douglas B. Holt, "How Consumers Consume," *Journal of Consumer Research*, 22, June 1995; and Grant McCracken, *Culture and Consumption: New Approaches to the Symbolic Character of Consumer Goods and Activities*, Indiana University Press, Bloomington: 1990.

40. Enrollments in secondary and higher education increased dramatically, especially in the second half of the twentieth century. The modern high school was established at the turn of the century and showed spectacular growth between 1910 and 1940, when graduation rates increased from 9 percent of American youths to nearly 50 percent. By 1996 they had reached 82 percent. According to Harvard economists Claudia Goldin and Lawrence Katz, about 70 percent of the increase in years of education in the U.S. adult population between 1900 and 1970 was due solely to the rapid rise of high school education. See: Claudia Goldin and Lawrence F. Katz, "Human Capital and Social Capital: The Rise of Secondary Schooling in America, 1910–1940," *The Journal of Interdisciplinary History*, XXIX, Spring 1999; and Claudia Goldin, "America's Graduation from High School: The Evolution and Spread of Secondary Schooling in the Twentieth Century," *Journal of Economic History*, 58:2, June 1998.

41. Mare, Robert D., "Changes in Educational Attainment and School Enrollment," in *State of the Union: America in the 1990's*, Reynolds Farley, ed., Russell Sage Foundation, New York: 1995; *Digest of Education Statistics*, "American Education 1870–1991"; *Statistical Abstract of the United States; Historical Statistics of the United States*; Colin B. Burke, *American Collegiate Populations*, New York University Press, New York: 1982; Arthur B. Cohen, *The Shaping of American Higher Education*, Jossey-Bass, San Francisco, 1998. For the GI Bill, see Clark Kerr, "Expanding Access and Changing Missions: The Federal Role in U.S. Higher Education," *Educational Record*, Fall 1994; Theda Skocpol, "The G.I. Bill and U.S. Social Policy, Past and Future," *Social Philosophy & Policy*, 1997, 14:2, pp. 95–115; John Bound and Sarah Turner, "Going to War and Going to College: Did World War II and the G.I. Bill Increase Educational Attainment for Returning Veterans?" National Bureau of Economic Research, Working Paper no. 7452, December 1999.

42. U.S. Department of Education, National Center for Education Statistics, "Earned degrees conferred by institutions of higher education, by level of degree and sex of student," in *Digest of Educational Statistics*, Washington, D.C., 2000.

43. Ibid.

44. Lind, Joellen, "Symbols, Leaders, Practitioners: The First Women Professionals," *Valparaiso UL Review*, 28, 1994.

45. Ibid.

46. Ibid. See also the discussion in Sharon Hartman Strom, *Beyond the Typewriter: Gender, Class, and the Origins of Modern American Office Work, 1900–1930*, Uni-

versity of Illinois Press, Urbana: 1992, esp. "Gender and Masculine Business Professions," pp. 63–108.

47. See Suzanne Bianchi, "Changing Economic Roles of Men and Women," in Farley, ed., *State of the Union*; Suzanne Bianchi and Daphne Spain, *American Women in Transition*, Russell Sage Foundation, New York: 1986, p. 122; Mare, op. cit.

48. *Vital Statistics of the United States*, U.S. National Center for Health Statistics, Washington, D.C., 2000.

49. Ibid. A number of other industrialized countries have achieved even higher rates of life expectancy, such as 79.1 years in Canada, 79.9 years in Japan, and 78.7 years in France. See *U.N. Human Development Report 1998*, Oxford University Press, New York: 1998.

50. For a potential eighteenth-century parallel, see Philippe Aries, *Centuries of Childhood: A Social History of Family Life*, Random House, New York: 1962.

51. For an overview of these trends, see Claudia Goldin, "Labor Markets in the Twentieth Century," in *The Cambridge Economic History of the United States, Vol. III: The Twentieth Century*, pp. 549–624.

52. For an extensive discussion of the abstraction of work, and its antecedents, consequences, and relationship to the spread of computerization, see Shoshana Zuboff, *In the Age of the Smart Machine: The Future of Work and Power*, Basic Books, New York: 1988. See also Zuboff's history of work in the United States in the twentieth century: "Work," in *Encyclopedia of the United States in the Twentieth Century*, Vol. III, Stanley I. Kutler, ed., Charles Scribner's Sons, New York: 1996, pp. 1091–1126.

53. Franklin, James C., "Industry Output and Employment Projections to 2006," *Monthly Labor Review*, November 1997. See also Manuel Castells, *The Rise of the Network Society*, Blackwell Publishers, Oxford: 1996, pp. 201–230.

54. Weinberg, Bruce, "Computer Use and the Demand for Women Workers," Working Paper, Department of Economics, Ohio State University, January 1999.

55. For an extensive discussion of these dynamics, see Zuboff, *In the Age of the Smart Machine*.

56. Oppenheimer, Valerie Kincade, *The Female Labor Force in the United States: Demographic and Economic Factors Governing Its Growth and Changing Composition*, Greenwood Press, Westport, Conn.: 1976.

57. Shank, Susan E., "Women and the Labor Market: The Link Grows Stronger," *Monthly Labor Review*, March 1988.

58. Ibid.

59. International Labour Organization, *Breaking Through the Glass Ceiling: Women in Management*, Geneva: 1997.

60. Judy, Richard, and Carol D'Amico, *Workforce 2020: Work and Workers in the 21st Century*, Hudson Institute, Indianapolis: 1997. Also Shank, op. cit.

61. Mitchell, Susan, *Generation X*, New Strategist, New York: 2001 (calculations based on data from National Opinion Research Center).

62. Costa, Dora, "From Mill Town to Board Room: The Rise of Women's Paid Labor," National Bureau of Economic Research, Working Paper no. 7608, March 2000.

63. Goldin, Claudia, "Career and Family: College Women Look to the Past," in *Gender and Family Issues in the Workplace*, Francine Blau and Ronald Ehrenberg, eds., Russell Sage Foundation, New York: 1997. See also Goldin's related article: "Marriage Bars: Discrimination against Married Women Workers from the 1920's to the 1950's," in *Favorites of Fortune: Technology, Growth, and Economic Development Since the Industrial Revolution*, Patrice Higonnet, David Landes, Henry Rosovsky, eds., Harvard University Press, Cambridge, Mass.: 1991.

64. Weinberg, op. cit.

65. Putnam, Robert, *Bowling Alone: the Collapse and Revival of American Community*, Simon & Schuster, New York: 2000, p. 197.

66. "General Social Survey," National Opinion Research Center, University of Chicago, Chicago: 1994.
67. Mishel, Lawrence, Jared Bernstein, and John Schmitt, *The State of Working America: 1998–1999*, Cornell University Press, Ithaca, N.Y.: 1999, pp. 47, 72.
68. "Women: The New Providers," Whirlpool Foundation Study, Part One, Families and Work Institute, New York, 1995.
69. See also Howard Hayghe, "Developments in Women's Labor Force Participation," *Monthly Labor Review*, September 1997.
70. *Statistical Abstract*, U.S. Bureau of the Census, Washington, D.C., Table no. 915, 1998.
71. *Statistical Abstract*, U.S. Bureau of the Census, Washington, D.C., no. 386; *Historical Statistics*, U.S. Bureau of the Census, Washington, D.C., Series r, no. 192–217.
72. Edgington, Denise, "Reading Between the Lines," *Business Record*, Des Moines, Iowa, January 1, 1996.
73. *Drug Store News*, September 22, 1997, p. 106.
74. Pogrebin, Robin, "Magazines Multiplying As Their Fortunes Narrow," *New York Times*, January 2, 1997, p. C16.
75. Miffin, Laurie, "As Band of Channels Grows, Niche Programs Will Boom," *New York Times*, December 28, 1998, p. A1; Joe Schlosser, "Cable's Little Engines That Might," *Broadcasting and Cable*, 13:127, p. 62.
76. "Consumer Goods: Online Projections," *Jupiter Communications*, I, July 1999.
77. "E-Mail Outpaces the Web," *Industry Standard*, December 4, 2000, p. 168. See also Mark Levitt, "Email Usage Forecast and Analysis, 2000–2005," International Data Corporation Report no. W23011, September 2000.
78. *Statistical Abstract*, Census Bureau, Washington, D.C., no. 401, "Personal Consumption Expenditure for Recreation in Real (1992) Dollars: 1970–1994," 1996.
79. *Statistical Abstract*, Census Bureau, Washington, D.C., no. 914, "Media Usage and Consumer Spending: 1990–2001," 1998.
80. Costa, Dora, "Less of a Luxury: The Rise of Recreation Since 1888," National Bureau of Economic Research, Working Paper no. 6054, June 1997.
81. "America Is Becoming a Nation of Culture," *Wall Street Journal*, September 17, 1998.
82. McGuigan, Cathleen, and Peter Plagens, "State of the Art," *Newsweek*, March 26, 2001.
83. Norval, A. J., *The Tourist Industry: A National and International Survey*, Isaac Pitman & Sons, London: 1936.
84. Figures for 1929 and 1950 are taken from "Survey of International Travel," U.S. Department of Commerce, Washington, D.C., 1953, table 3, chart 4, pp. 9–10. Figures for 1996 are found in *Statistical Abstract of the United States*, U.S. Census Bureau, Washington, D.C., 1998, no. 455, p. 274.
85. See Gautam Naik, "Vacationing with the Vermin," *Wall Street Journal*, September 8, 2000; and Robin Knight, "Back on Track," *Time*, September 21, 1998.
86. Opdyke, Jeff, "Charitable Escapes," and Michael and Laura Murphy, "Getting Started," *Wall Street Journal*, October 22, 2001, p. R11.
87. Klein, Debra, "Hard Work Holidays," *Newsweek*, July 10, 2000.
88. "Survey of International Travel," table xix, p. 50; *Statistical Abstract of the United States*, U.S. Bureau of the Census, Washington, D.C., 1998, no. 457, p. 275.
89. "Travel and Tourism," *The Economist*, January 10, 1998.
90. Bryson, Ken, "Household and Family Characteristics: March 1995," U.S. Department of Commerce, U.S. Census Bureau, 1996.
91. Ibid.
92. "Profiles of General Demographic Characteristics: 2000 Census of Population and Housing," U.S. Census Bureau, May 2001, Table DP-1.
93. Bryson, op. cit.
94. "Profiles."
95. "The Young Adult Market," MarketResearch.com, New York: July 2001.

96. Casper, Lynne, and Ken Bryson, "Household and Family Characteristics: March 1998," U.S. Department of Commerce, Census Bureau, May 2000; Bryson, op. cit.
97. Anderton, Douglas, et al., *The Population of the United States*, Free Press, New York: 1997.
98. Edwards, Tamala, "Flying Solo," *Time*, August 28, 2000.
99. Casper and Bryson, op. cit.
100. Ibid.
101. "Profiles."
102. Anderton, op. cit. See also James Wetzel, "American Families: 75 Years of Change," *Monthly Labor Review*, March 1990.
103. Lugaila, Terry, "Marital Status and Living Arrangements: March 1996," U.S. Commerce Department, U.S. Census Bureau. Washington, D.C.
104. Holloway, Lynette, "In Schools, Family Tree Bends with Times," *New York Times*, February 7, 1999.
105. For another discussion of this topic, and those who celebrate it and those who despair of it, see Andrew Hacker, "The War Over the Family," *New York Review of Books*, December 4, 1997.
106. Sorrentino, Constance, "The Changing Family in International Perspective," *Monthly Labor Review*, March 1990. See also Sarah Lyall, "For Europeans, Love, Yes; Marriage, Maybe," *New York Times*, March 24, 2002, p. 1.
107. Lyall, op. cit.
108. *Generations and Gaps: A Global Study*, EURO RSCG Worldwide, New York: 2001, pp. 6–7.
109. Aries, op. cit.
110. Demos, John, *Past, Present, and Personal: The Family and the Life Course in American History*, Oxford University Press, New York: 1986.
111. Ibid.
112. Prost, Antoine, "The Family and the Individual," in *A History of Private Life*, Vol. V, Antoine Prost and Gerard Vincent, eds., Belknap Press of Harvard University Press, Cambridge, Mass: 1991.
113. Gorman, Christine, "Stressed-out Kids," *Time*, December 25, 2000.
114. Jacobsen, Mary H., *Hand Me Down Dreams: How Families Influence Our Career Paths and How We Can Reclaim Them*, Harmony Books, New York: 1999; quotes on p. xix.
115. *The Graduate* was one of the most honored films of that period. It won four Oscars, including best director, actor, and actress, and three additional Oscar nominations; five BAFTA awards and two additional nominations; the Director's Guild Award; five Golden Globe Awards and two more nominations; a Grammy Award; a New York Film Critics Circle Award; and a Writers Guild of America Award.
116. "The Sound of Silence," Paul Simon, Paul Simon Music.
117. Ibid.

Chapter Four

1. Beck, Ulrich, *The Risk Society: Towards a New Modernity*, Sage, London: 1992, pp. 92–95. The specific conditions he has in mind are those concerning the increasingly complex experiences of people in the modern labor market, especially those experiences associated with education, mobility, competition, increased wealth, and consumption.
2. Beck, Ulrich, "The Reinvention of Politics: Towards a Theory of Reflexive Modernization," in *Reflexive Modernization: Politics, Tradition, and Aesthetics in the Modern Social Order*, Ulrich Beck, Anthony Giddens, and Scott Lash, eds., Stanford University Press, Stanford, Calif.: 1994, p. 3. See also Anthony Giddens, *Modernity and Self-Identity: Self and Society in the Late Modern Age*, Stanford University Press, Stanford, Calif.: 1991.

3. Inglehart, Ronald, *Culture Shift in Advanced Industrial Society*, Princeton University Press, Princeton: 1990. In this volume, Inglehart drew his data from three separate large-scale surveys: the Eurobarometers, sponsored by the Commission of the European Communities, which has measured attitudes, values, and behavior among the publics of twelve Western nations for nearly two decades; the World Values Survey, carried out in twenty-five countries in 1981 and 1982 by the European Value Systems Study Group; and a three-nation panel study carried out by Professor Inglehart and a prestigious international team of scholars between 1974 and 1981.

4. Ibid., p. 135.

5. Evaluating American and Western European data collected from 1970 to 1988, Inglehart concluded that both regions became significantly more postmaterialist during that period. For example, in 1970 materialists outnumbered postmaterialists by four to one. By 1988, that ratio had shifted to four to three (ibid., p. 103).

6. Ibid., p. 103.

7. Inglehart, Ronald, *Modernization and Postmodernization: Cultural, Economic, and Political Change in 43 Societies*, Princeton University Press, Princeton, N.J.: 1997.

8. Ibid., p. 8.

9. Ibid., pp. 326–328.

10. Ibid., pp. 156–158. Inglehart cautions that values at any point in time reflect the long-term processes of generational replacement as well as short-term period effects like high inflation, political instability, or high unemployment, which can make people temporarily revert to a greater emphasis on traditional materialistic values associated with order, stability, and economic security.

11. Ibid., p. 158.

12. To complicate this statement a bit: We know from adult developmental psychology that adults who continue to develop are better equipped to act on these values than adults who remain fixated on more adolescent concerns of group-oriented identity. Adolescents and "adolescent adults" may assert the claim to psychological self-determination without being able to implement it effectively, as they have not yet developed the necessary cognitive and emotional resources. Further, the meanings of psychological self-determination are likely to develop a deeper resonance and a more wide-ranging application with greater maturity. Thus, we would expect an important interaction effect between cohort and life stage. For sources on adult development that provide context and foundation for these observations, see note 50, p. 404.

13. Inglehart, *Modernization*, pp. 143–159.

14. Franck, Thomas, *The Empowered Self: Law and Society in the Age of Individualism*, Oxford University Press, New York: 1999, pp. 101–149.

15. Ibid., pp. 123–132.

16. Ibid., p. 135.

17. Ibid.

18. The quote is from William Blackwell's commentaries and is discussed in Franck, op. cit., p. 180. It should be noted that other Western countries shared this legal perspective on women. In France, for example, the married woman was a "femme couvert," who existed under "the protection of her husband, her baron or lord, and her condition during marriage is one of coverture." She could not own or inherit property, enter into contracts, or sue or be sued. See Lind, Joellen, "Symbols, Leaders, Practitioners: The First Women Professionals," *Valparaiso UL Review*, 28, 1994.

19. For more on the legal and cultural conditions of U.S. women at that time, see Porter, Susan, ed., *Women of the Commonwealth: Work, Family, and Social Change in Nineteenth-Century Massachusetts*, University of Massachusetts Press, Boston: 1996; Frances B. Cogan, *All-American Girl: The Ideal of Real Womanhood in Mid-Nineteenth-Century America*, University of Georgia Press, Atlanta: 1989; Allison M. Parker, ed., *Women and the Unstable State in Nineteenth Century America*, Texas A&M University Press, 2000; Jill K. Conway, *The Female Ex-*

perience in Eighteenth and Nineteenth Century America: A Guide to the History of American Women, Princeton University Press, Princeton: 1985; Stephanie Coontz, *The Social Origins of Private Life*, Verso, London: 1988; Geoffrey C. Ward and Ken Burns, *Not for Ourselves Alone*, Knopf, New York: 1999. For the U.S. and European perspective, see Geneviève Fraisse and Michelle Perrot, eds., *A History of Women: Emerging Feminism from Revolution to World War*, Harvard University Press, Cambridge, Mass.: 1993.

20. Eliot's comments are taken from the Page-Barber Lectures, delivered at the University of Virginia and published in his *After Strange Gods: A Primer of Modern History*, Harcourt Brace, New York: 1934, pp. 19–20.

21. Franck, op. cit., pp. 115–116: As Franck puts it, "Even in the most individuated Western societies there are today still remnants of a lively culture of enforced social coherence and not inconsiderable social pressures to conform."

22. There is a compelling literature to choose from on this subject. For a few outstanding examples, see Bernard Lewis, *What Went Wrong?* Oxford University Press, New York: 2002; V.S. Naipaul, *Beyond Belief*, Vintage, New York: 1998; Fouad Ajami, *The Arab Predicament*, Cambridge University Press, Cambridge: 1981. Thomas Franck also discusses the human rights records of the Muslim countries and finds a far more diverse set of viewpoints than a stereotypical view of these nations implies. He concludes that rather than being homogeneous, most of these countries harbor dynamic conflicts between progressives who advocate individual autonomy and conservative forces who champion communitarian social rights. Franck, op. cit., pp. 101–122. See also Amartya Sen, *Development as Freedom*, Anchor Books, New York: 1999.

23. Franck, op. cit., pp. 107, 123.

24. Ibid., p. 144. As Franck puts it, "It is a civilization of tolerance, freedom, and personal self-determination that is no more inherently Western than was the civilization of communitarian conformity and enforced subordination of the individual to state and church, which until so recently held sway in the West. Rather, what is emerging is a civilization of modernity, in which the needs of urbanizing, industrializing, communicating, and information-networking have provoked a demand for civil society in which is clearly demarked a large area reserved for private choice and action."

25. Much of our discussion of these developments in international law is based on the incisive work of legal scholar Thomas Franck in *The Empowered Self*; for these references, see pp. 117, 173; also pp. 101, 122.

26. Ibid.

27. Ibid., pp. 103, 141, 146.

28. Ibid., pp. 151–195.

29. Ibid., p. 3.

30. While there have been other societies in which people routinely exhibited multiple loyalties—including many phases of the Roman, Ottoman, and Hapsburg Empires—those loyalty referents were imposed on people by virtue of who they were and where they lived. A Jew in Roman Judea is one such example of a person allowed to be loyal to Judaism while also expected to be loyal to Rome. Ibid., p. 62.

31. Ibid., p. 65.

32. Ibid., pp. 62–73.

33. These consist of binding treaties and "a nimbus of non-binding declarations." By late 1996, ninety-two states had also accepted an optional protocol that permits the Commission to consider petitions from individuals against their own nations for violations of their rights.

34. Franck, op. cit., p. 206.

35. Walker, Samuel, *The Rights Revolution: Rights and Community in Modern America*, Oxford University Press, New York: 1998, pp. 41–44.

36. See, for example, Daniel Bell, *The Cultural Contradictions of Capitalism*, Basic Books, New York: 1976; Christopher Lasch, *The Culture of Narcissism*, Warner Books, New York: 1979; Richard Sennett, *The Fall of Public Man*, Knopf, New

York: 1977. For useful critiques of these analyses see Jesse F. Batten, "The 'New Narcissism' in 20th-Century America: The Shadow and Substance of Social Change," *Journal of Social History*, 1983, 17:2, pp. 199–220; Bruce Mazlish, "American Narcissism," *Psychohistory Review*, 10:3/4, Spring/Summer 1982; and Peter Clecak, *America's Quest for the Ideal Self: Dissent and Fulfillment in the 60s and 70s*, Oxford University Press, New York: 1983.

37. Crozier, Michel, Samuel P. Huntington, and Joji Watanuki, *The Crisis of Democracy: Report on the Governability of Democracies to the Trilateral Commission*, New York University Press, New York: 1975.

38. Gendlin, Eugene, "A Philosophical Critique of the Concept of Narcissism," in D. M. Levin, ed., *Pathologies of the Modern Self: Postmodern Studies on Narcissism, Schizophrenia, and Depression*, New York University Press, New York: 1987. Available on www. focusing.org; John L. Schimel, et al., "Changing Styles in Psychiatric Syndromes," *American Journal of Psychiatry*, 130, 1973, pp. 146–155; Abram de Swaan, "The Politics of Agoraphobia: On Changes in Emotional and Relational Management," *Theory and Society*, 10, 1981; Nathan Hale, Jr., "From Berggasse XIX to Central Park West: The Americanization of Psychoanalysis, 1919–1940," *Journal of the History of the Behavioral Sciences*, 14, 1978.

39. Putnam, Robert, *Bowling Alone: The Collapse and Revival of American Community*, Simon & Schuster, New York: 2000.

40. Ibid, p. 63; see discussion in Chapters 2 and 3, pp. 31–64.

41. Ibid., pp. 250–255. "Political interest and participation, church attendance, community projects, charitable giving, organization involvement . . . all these forms of civic involvement and more besides have declined largely, if not exclusively, because of the inexorable replacement of a highly civic generation by others that are much less so. . . . Each generation that has reached adulthood since the 1950's has been less engaged in community affairs than its immediate predecessor. . . . In short, the decades that have seen a national deterioration in social capital are the very decades during which the numerical dominance of an exceptionally civic generation was replaced by the dominion of 'postcivic' cohorts."

42. Ibid., p. 258.

43. Ibid., p. 259.

44. Ibid.

45. Ibid., p. 261.

46. Ibid., p. 263.

47. Ibid., pp. 272–274.

48. Ibid., pp. 274–275.

49. Ibid., p. 256.

50. We refer the interested reader to the many books and articles by path-breaking adult developmental psychologists like Lawrence Kohlberg, Robert Kegan, Carol Gilligan, and Jane Loevinger. For a good overview of this extensive literature, see Charles N. Alexander and Ellen J. Langer, eds., *Higher Stages of Human Development*, Oxford University Press, New York: 1990; and Jane Loevinger, "Stages of Personality Development," in *Handbook of Personality Psychology*, Robert Hogan, John Johnson, and Stephen Briggs, eds., Academic Press, San Diego, Calif.: 1997, pp. 199–208.

51. Inglehart, *Culture Shift*, p. 339.

52. Ibid., Chapter 10, "From Elite-Directed to Elite-Directing Politics: The Role of Cognitive Mobilization, Changing Gender Roles, and Changing Values," pp. 335–370.

53. Dalton, Russell, "Value Change and Democracy," in *Disaffected Democracies: What's Troubling the Trilateral Countries?* Susan Pharr and Robert Putnam, eds., Princeton University Press, Princeton, N.J.: 2000.

54. Peter Hart Research Associates, "New Leadership for a New Century," Washington, D.C., August 28, 1998.

55. Electronic voting technology already exists and is being utilized in some U.S. districts with stunning speed, efficiency, and accuracy. The step from centralized to distributed electronic voting would pave the way for direct democracy. For a recent example of electronic voting, see Katherine Seelye, "County in California Touches Future of Voting," *New York Times*, February 12, 2001.

56. See Ian Budge, *The New Challenge of Direct Democracy*, Polity Press, Cambridge, Mass.: 1996; and Wolf Linder, *Swiss Democracy: Possible Solutions to Conflict in Multicultural Societies*, St. Martin's Press, New York: 1998.

57. See Enrique Larana et al., eds., *New Social Movements: From Ideology to Identity*, Temple University Press, Philadelphia: 1994.

58. Tarrow, Sidney, "Mad Cows and Social Activists," in *Disaffected Democracies*, pp. 270–290; quote on p. 281. See also Peter Gundelach, "Grass Roots Activity," in *The Impact of Values*, Jan W. Van Deth and Elinor Scarbrough, eds., Oxford University Press, Oxford: 1995.

59. Tarrow, op. cit., p. 280. See also David Meyer, "Social Movements: Creating Communities of Change," in *Feminist Approaches to Social Movements, Communities and Power*, Mary Ann Tetreault and Robin Teske, eds., University of South Carolina Press, Columbia: 1998.

60. "2001 Report on Socially Responsible Investing Trends in the United States," Social Investment Forum, Washington, D.C., November 28, 2001, pp. 3–4. The description of the Web site is in "Looking to Get a Righteous Return by Doing Right," *Newsweek*, November 13, 2000, p. 94.

61. Once considered a fringe element in West German politics, "the Greens" have a style and substance that resonated with the new individuals, eventually winning them legitimacy and a voice in the German parliament. Unlike conventional political parties, the Green Party acted from a sense of global interdependency. A powerful expression of postmaterialist values that transcends national boundaries, it was just as concerned to influence policy in New Zealand as in West Germany. The Greens' emphasis on global direct action has drawn a highly educated membership around the world. Most recently, they were able to attract a candidate of the stature of Ralph Nader and undertake a serious run at third-party status in the U.S. presidential election of 2000.

62. Franck, op. cit., p. 88.

63. Boulding, Elise, *Building a Global Civic Culture*, Syracuse University Press, Syracuse, N.Y.: 1988, p. 35.

64. Also cited in Franck, op. cit.

65. *Yearbook of International Organizations*, Vol. 5, Union of International Associations, Brussels: 2000.

66. Sancton, Thomas, "Distinguished Service: Médicins sans Frontières Receives the Nobel Peace Prize," *Time*, October 25, 1999.

67. Mellgren, Doug, "Humanitarian Doctors' Group Wins Nobel Peace Prize," Associated Press Newswires, October 15, 1999. Today the MSF vigilantly guards its independence from governments and large bureaucratic organizations, even though it has had, by all accounts, a significant impact on the UN and international foreign policy. In 1999 when MSF was awarded the Nobel Peace Prize, James Orbinski, president of MSF International, accepted the prize with a mixture of gratitude and reticence that expressed the attitude toward organizational participation so characteristic of the new individuals. "We are pleased to have received the prize; we accept it with honor," he said, then added that in some ways the prize was "a risk for the MSF because it reinforces the institutionalization of humanitarian assistance." He described the group's resolve to "not let borders, laws, or rules stand in the way of the basic dignity of people and their right to humanitarian aid." Sancton, op. cit.; Kerry Gillespie and Chris Hondros, "Doctors Prize Inner Peace More than Coveted Nobel," *Toronto Star*, October 16, 1999.

68. Veroff, Joseph, Elizabeth Douvan, and Richard A. Kulka, *The Inner American: A Self-Portrait from 1957 to 1976*, Basic Books, New York: 1981, p. 529. For other studies that illustrate and discuss the rise of subjectivity and the experience of psychological individuality, see Joel Pfister and Nancy Schnog, eds., *Inventing the Psychological: Toward a Cultural History of Emotional Life in America*, Yale University Press, New Haven: 1997; Michael M. Sokal, ed., *Psychological Testing and American Society, 1890–1930*, Rutgers University Press, New Brunswick, N.J.: 1990; Ray Fuller et al., eds., *A Century of Psychology: Progress, Paradigms, and Prospects for the New Millennium*, Routledge, London: 1997; Nikolas Rose, *Inventing Ourselves*, Cambridge University Press, Cambridge: 1996; Michael Stone, *Healing the Mind: A History of Psychiatry from Antiquity to the Present*, W. W. Norton, New York: 1997; Carl Graumann and Kenneth Gergen, eds., *Historical Dimensions of Psychological Discourse*, Cambridge University Press, Cambridge: 1996; Clecak, op. cit.

69. Veroff et al., op. cit., pp. 534–535: "We hesitate to interpret the change simply as a regression to primary or secondary narcissism. Rather, we see it as a social development in a very affluent society. Concerns about self-development occur when society moves to a level of complexity that makes ease in social integration more difficult. To the degree that work life and family life have been no longer simply and ritually worked out for people, to the degree that more choices are open to people in selecting careers or family situations to which they can see themselves committed over a lifetime, there is an inevitable refocusing on the self. We do not see it as a disintegration of values, but as an adaptation that people have made to a complexity of choice in a heterogeneous society. Indeed a heightened concern about choice, self-direction, and self-sufficiency can be a potential positive contributor to subjective well-being in many ways. From 1957 to 1976 there are significant changes in the following: seeing oneself as different from other people in a more positive light, seeing oneself as less needy of being liked by others, seeing oneself as less needy of having other people listen to what one is saying, seeing oneself as generally more efficacious. This pattern seems to indicate a much more positive regard for oneself and a much less involved interest in how other people react to the self . . . a value which has been directly espoused in our society from a very early point in American life. Indeed, many more people in the 1976 population look at their own independence as a source of their well-being."

70. Ibid., pp. 530, 534.

71. Ibid., pp. 530–531.

72. Ibid., pp. 531–533. "It is clear from the data that men and women have become much more psychological in their thinking about themselves and attempting to understand their own lives. The most dramatic findings illustrating this theme come from two sources: the increase in formal help-seeking and the decrease in people's denial of problems in their lives."

73. The quote is from the study's director, Dr. Mark Olfson, and appears in "Study Details Steep Rise in Depression Therapy," *Los Angeles Times*, January 9, 2002, p. A14. For the actual study, see Mark Olfson et al., "National Trends in the Outpatient Treatment of Depression," *Journal of the American Medical Association*, 287:2, January 8, 2002, pp. 203–209.

74. Putnam, op. cit., p. 264.

75. Shorter, Edward, *From Paralysis to Fatigue: A History of Psychosomatic Illness in the Modern Era*, Free Press, New York: 1992, pp. 320–321.

76. Cherlin, Andrew, "I'm OK, You're Selfish," *New York Times Magazine*, October 17, 1999.

77. Wolfe, Alan, *One Nation, After All*, Viking, New York: 1998.

78. "How America's Faith Has Changed Since 9/11," Barna Research Online, Barna Research Group, Ventura, Calif., 2001.

Chapter Five

1. For a discussion of the changing employment relationship, its origins, and conse-
quences, see Peter Cappelli, *The New Deal at Work*, Harvard Business School
Press, Boston: 1999. See also the collection of essays in Paul Osterman, ed., *Broken
Ladders: Managerial Careers in the New Economy*, Oxford University Press,
Oxford: 1996; and Louis Galambos, "The U.S. Corporate Economy in the Twenti-
eth Century, in *The Cambridge Economic History of the United States, Vol. III:
The Twentieth Century*, Stanley L. Engerman and Robert E. Gallman, eds., Cam-
bridge University Press, Cambridge: 2000, esp. p. 961–965.
2. Cappelli, op. cit., pp. 82–85.
3. For a discussion of nonstandard jobs and their economic consequences, see Arne
Kalleberg et al., *Nonstandard Work, Substandard Jobs*, and Roberta M. Spalter-
Roth et al., *Managing Work and Family: Nonstandard Work Arrangements Among
Managers and Professionals*, both published by the Economic Policy Institute,
Washington, D.C., 1997.
4. See Cappelli, op. cit., pp. 113–136.
5. For a good discussion of the reworking of the effort bargain, its effect on employees, and the renewed emphasis on efficiency, see Eliezer Geisler, *Managing the Aftermath of Radical Corporate Change*, Quorum Books, Westport, Conn.: 1997,
esp. Chapter 6, "The Aftermath of Reengineering"; see also the discussion of efficiency values on pp. 101–102.
6. Schor, Juliet B., *The Overworked American*, Basic Books, New York: 1992; quote
on p. 81.
7. Hochschild, Arlie, *The Second Shift*, Viking Penguin, New York: 1989; and *The
Time Bind*, Metropolitan Books, New York: 1997.
8. Robinson, John P., and Geoffrey Godbey, *Time for Life*, Pennsylvania State University Press, University Park, Penn.: 1997.
9. Rones, Phillip L., Randy E. Ilg, and Jennifer M. Gardner, "Trends in Hours of
Work since the Mid-1970s," *Monthly Labor Review*, April 1997.
10. Jacobs, Jerry A., and Kathleen Gerson, "Who Are the Overworked Americans?"
Review of Social Economy, December 1998. For another noteworthy analysis, see
Barry Bluestone and Stephen Rose, "The Macroeconomics of Work Time," *Review of Social Economy*, December 1998.
11. In 2000 a U.K. government-sponsored study, "Work-Life Balance 2000," combined a survey of 2,500 employers with another of 7,500 employees in a nationwide
sample. While nearly all the employees surveyed agreed that people should have
the right to balance home and work life, 80 percent reported working more than
their standard hours, and 39 percent of those did so without extra pay. Fourteen
percent of fathers reported working more than sixty-hour weeks, and two-thirds
of the men surveyed felt that working less would damage their chances for career
progression. Among employers, 49 percent offered stress counseling, but only 9
percent offered assistance with basic child-care needs. Only about one-fifth were
aware of increased maternity and paternal leave rights. "Work-Life Balance 2000,"
Institute for Employment Research, University of Warwick, November 2000.
12. Bond, James T., Ellen Galinsky, and Jennifer E. Swanberg, *The 1997 National
Study of the Changing Workforce*, Families and Work Institute, New York: 1997.
13. See, for example, Empirica GMBH Consultancy, *Electronic Commerce and Telework Trend Survey*, Bonn, 1999; J.H. Pratt, *1999 Telework America National Telework Survey*, International Telework Association and Council, Wakefield, Mass.:
1999; Ekos Research Associates, *Canadians and Telework*, Toronto, November 1998.
14. Van Horn, Carl, and Herbert Schaffner, "Work Trends: Americans' Attitudes
About Work, Employers, and the Government." This was a national study conducted jointly by the Center for Workforce Development at Rutgers University

and the Center for Survey Research and Analysis at the University of Connecticut in March 1999.

15. See Ekos Research, op. cit.

16. Doherty, Sean, Jean Andrey, and Laura Johnson, "The Economic and Social Impacts of Telework," U.S. Department of Labor, Washington, D.C., February 2001. The variations among estimates reflect the different definitions and standards of telecommuting used by different studies.

17. For commentary on renewed interest in telecommuting after September 11, 2001, see Sue Shellenbarger's *Wall Street Journal* column, "Work and Family," January 23, 2002. For insight into employer resistance, see Doherty et al., op. cit. See also Jenny C. McCune, "Telecommunicating Revisited," *Management Review*, February 1998. The anecdotal evidence suggests that the reasons for this resistance lead straight back to the standard enterprise logic. For example, CareerEngine.com, a network of career Web sites, surveyed 650 employers on this subject. Most indicated that they would be hiring fewer people who wanted to work from home, citing resentment from other colleagues and weakened corporate loyalty. The *Wall Street Journal* tracked the experiences of several well-qualified job candidates in search of telecommuting opportunities. It found that some companies place help-wanted ads that falsely promise telecommuting to portray themselves as sensitive to family issues. One candidate reported haggling with several potential employers who were eager to hire her but opposed to her working from home. "They're all saying the same thing," she lamented. " 'We want you in here at a desk where we can watch you and trust that you're doing your job.' " Kemba Dunham, "Telecommuters' Lament," *Wall Street Journal*, October 31, 2000.

18. McCune, op. cit.

19. 1997 figures. See Howard Hayghe, "Developments in Women's Labor Force Participation," *Monthly Labor Review*, September 1997.

20. For an overview of recent theories on women's developmental patterns at midlife, see Laurel Lippert, "Women at Midlife," *Journal of Counseling and Development*, 76, Winter 1997, pp. 16–22. See also the collection of research essays in Margie E. Lachman and Jacquelyn Boone James, eds., *Multiple Paths of Midlife Development*, University of Chicago Press, Chicago: 1997.

21. Women's Bar Association of Massachusetts, "More Than Part-Time," Boston: 2000.

22. Zappert, Laraine T., *Getting It Right*, Pocket Books, New York: 2001, pp. 120, 154.

23. The research was conducted by Marin Clarkberg and Phyliss Moen of Cornell University and was based on 4,554 married couples questioned in 1988 and 1994 as part of the National Study of Families and Households. See Marin Clarkberg and Phyllis Moen, "Understanding the Time Squeeze: Married Couples' Preferred and Actual Work-Hour Strategies," *American Behavioral Scientist*, 44:7, March 2001.

24. Van Horn and Schaffner, op. cit.

25. Cafferata, Patricia, Martin Horn, and William Wells, "Gender Role Changes in the United States," in *Values, Lifestyles, and Psychographics*, Lynn R. Kahle and Larry Chiagouris, eds., Lawrence Erlbaum Associates, Mahwah, N.J.: 1997, pp. 258–259.

26. Center for Policy Alternatives and Lifetime Television, *Women's Voices 2000*, Connecticut Permanent Commission on the Status of Women, Hartford, Conn.: 2000.

27. Ibid., pp. 4, 10, 13, 26, 27.

28. A small sample of recent popular books that treat this subject includes Michele Bolton, *The Third Shift*, Jossey-Bass, San Francisco, 2000; Ellen Galinsky, *Ask the Children*, Morrow, New York: 1999; Alvin Rosenfeld, *Hyper-Parenting*, St. Martin's Press, New York: 2000; Katherine Goldman, *Working Mothers 101*, Harper-Collins, New York: 1998; Leslie Perlow, *Finding Time*, ILR Press, Ithaca, N.Y.: 1997; William Doherty, *Take Back Your Kids*, Sorin Books, Notre Dame, Ind.,

2000; and William Doherty, *The Intentional Family*, Addison-Wesley, Reading, Mass.: 1997.

29. The quote is from William Doherty, a University of Minnesota professor of family social science and author of *The Intentional Family*. The quote is found in "Busy Around the Clock," *Newsweek*, July 17, 2000, p. 49. The mother is quoted in the same article. For other popular press, see Sue Shellenbarger, "For Harried Workers, Time Off Is Not Just for Family Affairs," *Wall Street Journal*, November 11, 1998. See also Hochschild, *The Second Shift*.

30. Robinson and Godbey, op. cit., p. 305.

31. Freedman, Samuel, "Part of Bridge on Route I-95 Falls into River in Greenwich, Killing 3," *New York Times*, June 29, 1983; Samuel Freedman, "Repairs Start on I-95 Span Amid Inquiry," *New York Times*, June 30, 1983.

32. Kugelmann, Robert, *Stress: The Nature and History of Engineered Grief*, Praeger, Westport, Conn.: 1992, pp. 15–16.

33. Wheaton, Blair, "The Domains and Boundaries of Stress Concepts," in *Psychosocial Stress: Perspectives on Structure, Theory, Life-Course, and Methods*, Howard B. Kaplan, ed., Academic Press, San Diego: 1996, pp. 29–67.

34. Kaplan, Howard B., "Perspectives on Psychosocial Stress," in Kaplan, ed., op. cit., quote on p. 45.

35. Kugelmann, op. cit., p. 17.

36. Burke, Peter J., "Social Identities and Psychosocial Stress," in Kaplan, ed., op. cit., pp. 141–168.

37. Lachman, Margie, and Suzanne Weaver, "The Sense of Control as a Moderator of Social Class Differences in Health and Well-Being," *Journal of Personality and Social Psychology*, 74:3, 1998, pp. 763–773.

38. Krause, Neal, and Benjamin Shaw, "Role-Specific Feelings of Control and Mortality," *Psychology and Aging*, 15:4, December 2000.

39. While this study was conducted with older adults, the researchers rely on other studies and theoretical frameworks that are derived from, or equally applicable to, adults in general. They suggest that similar studies need to be conducted with other age groups in order to track similarities and differences across the life span.

40. In his dramatic book *Man's Search for Meaning* (Simon & Schuster, New York: 1963), psychoanalyst Victor Frankl describes his experiences in the Nazi death camps of World War II. He observed that the people who were able to survive were those most able to find meaning in the face of so much suffering and tragedy. For other studies that link hope, optimism, and health, see K.P. Nunn, "Personal Hopefulness: A Conceptual Review of the Relevance of the Perceived Future to Psychiatry," *British Journal of Medical Psychology*, 69, 1996, pp. 227–245; and C. Peterson, M. Seligman, and G. Vaillant, "Pessimistic Explanatory Style Is a Risk Factor for Physical Illness: A Thirty-Five-Year Longitudinal Survey," *Journal of Personality and Social Psychology*, 55, 1988, pp. 23–57.

41. Elder, Glen H., Jr., et al., "Psychosocial Stress over the Life Course," in Kaplan, ed., op. cit., p. 250.

42. Even casual observation drives this message home. The number of citations for stress-related research in the Social Science Citation Index has risen steadily since 1975, with sharp increases since 1990. The number of stress-related citations in 2000 was five times greater than in 1990, twenty times greater than in 1975, and seventy-two times greater than in 1956. Given the lag between developments in real life and social-science research, this suggests that stress issues probably increased sharply in real life around 1980, during the period when masses of highly educated baby-boomer women and men entered the labor market in full force.

43. Kugelmann, op cit., p. 8.

44. New York Business Group on Health, "Stress Among Working Women," New York: September 1993.

45. Princeton Survey Research Associates, Princeton: July 1997.

46. National Institute for Occupational Safety and Health, "Stress and the American Worker," Washington, D.C., January 1999.
47. Gallup Organization, "Women's Most Pressing Concerns," Princeton, N.J., March 17, 2000.
48. "Time Is Worth Money," Circles Press Release, Boston, August 24, 2000.
49. "Stress," ABC News Special Report, March 10, 2001.
50. "Getting All Stressed Out," *Maclean's*, 112:47, November 22, 1999.
51. Dolliver, Mark, "Life's Not All That Simple North of the Border," *Adweek*, November 6, 2000.
52. Williamson, Janet and Phillippa Vine, "Run Down, Stressed Out," *The British Journal of Administrative Management*, January/February 1998.
53. "Heavy Workload Blamed for Increasing Levels of Stress," *Management Accounting*, 76:1, January 1998, p. 11.
54. The U.K. Survey was conducted at Bristol University and sponsored by the British Health and Safety Executive. It is reported in "Work Stress Survey," *Worklife Report*, 12:1, London, January 1, 1999, p. 16.
55. Aldred, Carolyn, "Stress Levels Growing," *Business Insurance*, March 13, 2000.
56. "Focus on Health and Safety," Trades Union Congress, London: December 2000.
57. Sparks, K., C.L. Cooper, Y. Fried, and A. Shiron, "The Effect of Hours of Work on Health: A Meta-analytic Review," *Journal of Occupational and Organizational Psychology*, 70: 4, 1997.
58. European Foundation for the Improvement of Living and Working Conditions, *Precarious Employment and Health Related Outcomes in the European Union*, Office for the Official Publications of the European Communities, Luxembourg: 1999.
59. Harris, Stephaan, "Worldwide, Women Feel More Stress Than Men," *USA Today*, August 4, 1999.
60. Beck, Ulrich, "Das Eigene Leben In Die Eigene Hand Nehmen," *Padagogik*, 48.Jahrgang, Heft 7–8/1996, unpublished trans. by Indra Reinbergs, Harvard University, Cambridge, Mass.: 1999.

Chapter Six

1. Machalaba, Daniel, "Car-Pool Lanes Merge Poorly with Modern Lifestyle," *Wall Street Journal*, August 27, 1998.
2. Stapinski, Helen, "Let's Talk Dirty," *American Demographics*, November 1998, p. 50.
3. The song "Bali Hai" is from Rodgers and Hammerstein's musical *South Pacific*.
4. Bulkeley, William M., "Office-Supply Superstores Find Bounty in the Boonies," *Wall Street Journal*, September 1, 1998.
5. Johnson, Kenneth M., "Renewed Population Growth in Rural America," *Research in Rural Sociology and Development*, 7, pp. 23–45; data on p. 27.
6. Ibid., p. 34.
7. Berg, Steve, "The New Migration," *Star Tribune* (Minneapolis), May 24, 1998.
8. See Louis Uchitelle, "Economic View," *New York Times*, June 10, 2001.
9. U.S. Census Bureau, "Characteristics of New Privately Owned One-Family Houses Completed: 1970–1997," 1200 *Statistical Abstract of the United States*, U.S. Census Bureau, Washington, D.C., October 5, 1998.
10. Uchitelle, op. cit.
11. *SGMA Sports Participation Trends Report*, North Palm Beach, Fla.: 1997. See John Robinson and Geoffrey Godbey, "Has Fitness Peaked?" *American Demographics*, September 1993.
12. Mayer, Caroline, "A Showcase with All the Advantages," *Washington Post*, February 1, 1996.
13. Edmonds, Patricia, "The New American Dream Home," *USA Weekend*, August 3, 1997.

14. "The Home Report 2001," Unity Marketing, Stevens, Penn.: 2001.
15. Deming, William, "Work at Home: Data from the CPS," *Monthly Labor Review*, February 1994.
16. Porter, Mary, and Raymond Boggs, "U.S. Home Office Forecast and Analysis, 1999–2004," International Data Corporation, Document no. 22450, June 2000. Note that the number of distinctly utilized home offices adds up to more than the total number of home-office households. This is because many home offices are used by more than one person, for different purposes. Of the home offices in 2000, IDC estimates that more than 20 million were "income generating." Other estimates are even higher. The National Association of Home Based Businesses says that many surveys fail to count home-based firms that do not have business licenses. According to their own surveys, there were 50 million people working at least part-time from home-based businesses in 1998. Indeed, half of all the new businesses registered in the state of Texas in 1997 were based at home. See Steve Bates, "Following Their Homing Instinct," *Nation's Business*, U.S. Department of Commerce, June 1998.
17. Doherty, Sean, Jean Andrey, and Laura Johnson, "The Economic and Social Impacts of Telework," U.S. Department of Labor, Washington, D.C., February, 2001.
18. "Telework 2001," International Telework Association and Council, Washington, D.C., 2001.
19. In 1990, self-employed women were most likely to work in retail, or in business, personal, and professional services. Men were most likely to be found in construction and retail, or in business and professional services. More women than men tended to be in unincorporated business ventures. For more detailed information on the profiles of self-employed women and men, see the source for these figures: Theresa Devine, "Characteristics of Self-employed Women in the United States," *Monthly Labor Review*, March 1994. It should also be noted that a 2000 study using late-1990s data from the U.S. Current Population Survey found a decline in the absolute numbers of self-employed, as well as among women and men. However, other research suggests that these declines are a result of an increased incidence of incorporation among self-employed business ventures, especially after 1994. Once a self-employed person incorporates her business, the survey no longer counts her as "self-employed." Thus comparisons between the early and late 1990s on these figures are difficult to make. See Marilyn Manser and Garnett Picot, "The Role of Self-Employment in U.S. and Canadian Job Growth," *Monthly Labor Review*, April 1999, pp. 10–25. The 2000 study also noted that the occupational and industry distributions of male and female self-employment were more similar than they had been in 1990. However, within industries and occupations there continued to be significant divergence between the sexes. For example, in the industrial category of "professional and related services," about half the self-employed men offered legal services or were dentists or doctors. Among women, 36 percent offered child-care services, 7 percent education services, and 10 percent bookkeeping and auditing services. See Yannis Georgellis and Howard Wall, "Who Are the Self-Employed?" Federal Reserve Bank of St. Louis, November/December 2000.
20. Jurik, Nancy, "Getting Away and Getting By: The Experiences of Self-Employed Homeworkers," *Work and Occupations*, 25:1, February 1998, pp. 7–35.
21. Carr, Deborah, "Two Paths to Self-Employment? Women's and Men's Self-employment in the United States," *Work and Occupations*, 23, 1999, pp. 26–53.
22. Boden, Richard, "Flexible Working Hours, Family Responsibilities, and Female Self-employment: Gender Differences in Self-employment Selection," *American Journal of Economics and Sociology*, January 1, 1999, pp. 71–83.
23. According to a paper presented at the Women in Technology International Conference in Santa Clara, California, June 1998, the failure rate of new female-owned businesses was 39 percent compared to 80 percent for all new businesses. The study was reported in Laura DiDio, "Women in High-Tech Opt More and More to Run Own Business," *Computerworld*, Framingham, Mass., 32:25, June 22, 1998, p. 14.

Another study by Richard Boden sheds some light on this finding. He discovered that "women's lower wage returns to observed worker characteristics have a positive and significant effect on women's decision to switch from wage employment to self-employment." In other words, when well-qualified women find that they are underrewarded for their work, are paid less than comparably skilled men, or cannot achieve the flexible arrangements they require, they are more likely to leave corporate life and become self-employed, and their higher initial qualifications lead to higher-than-average success rates. Richard Boden, Jr., "Gender Inequality in Wage Earnings and Female Self-Employment Selection," *Journal of Socio-Economics*, 28:3, 1999, pp. 351–364.

24. Mayberry, Maralee, et al., *Home Schooling: Parents as Educators*, Corwin Press, Thousand Oaks, Calif.: 1995, pp. 9–17. See also Suzanne Buchanan, "Evolution of Parental Rights in Education," *Journal of Law and Education*, 16:3, Summer 1987; and Diana Buell Hiatt, "Parent Involvement in American Public Schools: An Historical Perspective 1642–1994," *School Community Journal*, 4:2, Fall/Winter 1994.

25. Lines, Patricia, "Homeschoolers: Estimating Numbers and Growth," U.S. Department of Education, Washington, D.C., Spring 1999, pp. 1, 8.

26. Bielick, Stacey, et al., "Homeschooling in the United States: 1999," NCES 2001-033, U.S. Department of Education, National Center for Education Statistics, Washington D.C., August 2001.

27. This estimate is based on the work of Dr. Brian Ray, who heads an advocate group, the National Home Education Research Institute. It has been quoted by many sources, including David Scott of the Associated Press, in "Home Schooling Had Bee Champion Under Its Spell," *The Commerical Appeal*, Memphis, Tenn., June 9, 2000; "Academics—How to Spell Success," *Cincinnati Enquirer*, June 6, 2000; and Klicka, Christopher J., "Issue Analysis," Home School Legal Defense Association, March 9, 2000. Analyses have shown that past home-schooling estimates by the U.S. Department of Education were somewhat low, while Dr. Ray's estimates were somewhat high.

28. Lines, op. cit.

29. Bunday, Karl, "Homeschooling Is Growing Worldwide," 1995, published on the Web by the advocacy group Learn in Freedom, see learnfreedom.org. See also Andrea Billups, "Home School Movement Goes Global," *Washington Times*, September 19, 2000.

30. Home-schooling parents have incomes slightly below the national median, and their levels of education are higher than the national norm. See Daniel Golden, "Class of Their Own," *Wall Street Journal*, February 11, 2000. See also James Muncy, "The Home Schooling 'Market': Results and Implications of Current Research," *Journal of Marketing for Higher Education*, 7:3, 1996.

31. Bielick, op. cit., p. 9.

32. Martin, Margaret, "Homeschooling: Parents' Reactions," ERIC Reports, ED367040, U.S. Department of Education, Office of Educational Research and Improvement, Washington, D.C., 1997. See also the featured article "Home Sweet School," by John Cloud and Jodie Morse, *Time*, August 27, 2001. One suburban mother explained that she chose home schooling because she was afraid her children's needs "might get lost in the crowd" (quoted in Clarence Page, "Success of Home Schooling Spelled Out," *Houston Chronicle*, June 12, 2000). A Nevada mother reflects, "I think children should have time to concentrate on what is meaningful to them. . . . I consider that our children attend school in a sense—it's just that we choose our own subjects" (quoted in Mayberry, op. cit., p. 1). "In school, you're told what to study. I discover my own interests and pursue them," said one homeschooler (quoted in Barbara Kantrowitz and Pat Wingert, "Learning at Home," *Newsweek*, October 5, 1998). "In homeschooling, you don't have to sit for half a year studying something you already know. If you're prepared to go to the next level, you take it to the next level," reports another (quoted in Golden, op. cit.).

33. Home-school families have an increasing variety of consumption options to choose from in designing their unique approach to education. There are dozens of newsletters and magazines filled with ads for home-schooling textbooks, videos, software, seminars, and camps. Amazon.com recently added an online store especially for home-schooling families. There are home-schooling cooperatives and collaborative relationships with community organizations, libraries, colleges, and local school systems, many of which have appointed special coordinators to act as liaisons and provide support to home-schoolers. Home-schoolers are estimated to have nearly twice the rate of Internet access as U.S. households in general—93 percent compared to about 50 percent. A vast range of content and services is available to them on the Web. They can download course material from NASA, the Discovery Channel, PBS, or a university library. There are virtual schools that produce curricula, reading lists, books, CDs, study guides, and exams. Thousands of course packages are available on the Internet, including every subject from algebra to ancient Kush. Internet-based services also offer parent networks, chat groups for parents and kids, lists of "safe sites," links, and books on home schooling. Distance-learning organizations offer online classes for all ages, as well as online mentors and tutors. One Internet site lets visitors build their own courses and hosts tens of thousands of classes. Another provides templates for people to create and post their own lesson plans, which are then shared across the Web and rated by other homeschoolers. See Steffan Heuer, "Putting the Home in Homework," *Industry Standard*, October 2000; Kristine L. Angelis, "The Evolving Relationship between Home Schoolers and Their Local Public Schools," ERIC Reports, ED417483, U.S. Department of Education, Office of Educational Research and Improvement, Washington, D.C., 1998.
34. Sewall, Gil, et al., "Private School Boom," *Newsweek*, August 13, 1979, p. 83.
35. Brimelow, Peter, "Private School Surge," *Forbes*, November 27, 2000, p. 104. See also Bruce Cooper et al., "The Latest Word on Private School Growth," *Teachers College Record*, 85:1 1983, pp. 88–98; Bruce Cooper, "The Changing Demography of Private Schools: Trends and Implications," *Education and Urban Society*, 16:4, pp. 429–442. These articles all discuss and predict current trends.
36. Hanson, D., et al., *Distance Education: Review of the Literature*, Second edition, Association for Education Communications and Technology and Research Institute for Studies in Education, Washington, D.C., and Ames, Iowa: 1997.
37. U.S. Department of Education, National Center for Educational Statistics, "Distance Education at Postsecondary Education Institutions: 1997–98," Washington, D.C., December 1999.
38. Burger, Jill, et al., "Distance Learning in Higher Education: Market Forecast and Analysis, 1999–2004," International Data Corporation, Needham, Mass., 2000.
39. U.S. Distance Learning Association, 2001.
40. Burger, op. cit. p. 9.
41. Ibid.
42. Lau, Sau, and Stephen Webber, "Education Markets Research Update," International Data Corporation, April 2000.
43. Fox, Susannah, et al., "The Online Health Care Revolution," Pew Internet & American Life Project, Washington, D.C., November 26, 2001, p. 3.
44. "Natural Sensibility: A Study of America's Changing Culture and Lifestyle," Hartman Group, Bellevue, Wash.: 1999.
45. Parkman, Cynthia, "Alternative Therapies Are Here to Stay," *Nursing Management*, 32:2, February 2001, pp. 36–39.
46. Eisenberg, David M., et al., "Trends in Alternative Medicine Use in the United States, 1990–1997," *Journal of the American Medical Association*, 280:18, November 11, 1998, pp. 1569–1575.
47. The telephone survey is described in Scott Marber, "Putting the Squeeze on Traditional Medicine," *Managed Healthcare*, 10:2, February 2000.

48. Mirasol, Felizia, "Nutritional Industry Gains Market-Driven Momentum," *Chemical Market Reporter*, June 5, 2000.
49. "Natural Sensibility" Hartman Group, op. cit.
50. The survey was conducted by HealthFocus and was the subject of the Foundation for Innovation in Medicine's eleventh annual nutraceutical conference held in New York City in 2000. It is described in Sandra Levy, "Self-Care Trend Alive and Well—And Growing," *Drug Topics*, March 6, 2000.
51. "Organic Foods Report 2001," *Nutrition Business Journal*, San Diego, Calif., September 2001.
52. Vaczek, David, "The Health Store Within," *Supermarket Business*, September 15, 2000.
53. Thompson, Stephanie, "Healthy Foods Sector Attracts Powerhouse Seeking Growth Spurt," *Advertising Age*, 71:40, Chicago, September 25, 2000, p. 24.
54. Vaczek, op. cit.
55. Meadows, Susannah, "Kindler, Gentler Clinics," *Newsweek*, February 26, 2001, p. 52.
56. Sharpe, Anita, "Boutique Medicine: For the Right Price, These Doctors Treat Patients as Precious," *Wall Street Journal*, August 12, 1998, p. 1.
57. Chase, Marilyn, "Critics Chafe as More Doctors Offer Only Extra-Fee 'Concierge Care,'" *Wall Street Journal*, July 27, 2001.
58. Freudenheim, Milt, "Paying Someone Else to Talk Back to Your Doctor," *New York Times*, January 6, 2002.
59. See Alger, Alexandra, "Is There a Doctor in the House?" *Forbes*, September 20, 1999.
60. Muscat, Michael, "Docs in Your Living Room," *Alternative Therapies in Health and Medicine*, November 2000.
61. "Florida Firm Makes House Calls Its Business," *American Medical News*, October 11, 1999.
62. Alger, op. cit.
63. Rundle, Rhonda, "In Stores Now: Full Body Scans," *Wall Street Journal*, July 24, 2001. See also Nancy Hass, "Scared Sick: The $900 Antidote," *New York Times*, August 26, 2001.
64. See, for example, Thomas Weber, "A Doctor, 700 Patients and the Net: Inventing the Virtual House Call," *Wall Street Journal*, January 17, 2000.
65. "Market Engineering Research for the Total U.S. Home Diagnostic and Monitoring Device Market," Frost & Sullivan, New York, 1998. For 2001 figures, see Daniel Costello and Lisa Gubernick, "The Worried Well," *Wall Street Journal*, October 26, 2001.
66. Costello and Gubernick, op. cit.
67. Miller, Lisa, "Boomers Begin to Look Beyond the Good Life to the 'Good Death,'" *Wall Street Journal*, February 25, 2000, p. 1.
68. "Home Service Store to Address Home Improvement Needs," *Air Conditioning, Heating, and Refrigeration News*, February 7, 2000.
69. Tice, Carol, and Don Longo, "Diagnosing the Home: Baby Boomers Will Spark Home Services," *National Home Center News*, August 10, 1998.
70. Cited in Maria Osborn Howard, "Too Busy for the Little Stuff?" *Richmond Times Dispatch*, May 1, 1998.
71. "Time Is Worth Money," Circles Press Release, Boston, August 24, 2000.
72. Clark, Paul, "Servicing the Workaholics," *Asheville Citizen-Times*, August 20, 2000.
73. Richter, Marcie, "Hiring out the Chores: Services Boom," *Dallas Morning News*, February 14, 1999.
74. Cole, Wendy, "Personal Chefs," *Time*, April 2002.
75. Hecker, Daniel, "Occupational Employment Projections to 2010," *Monthly Labor Review*, 124:1, November 2001, Table 3.
76. Ibid.

77. "The Consumer Expenditure Survey: Personal Consumption," Bureau of Labor Statistics, U.S. Department of Labor, Washington, D.C., 2001.

78. For a sampling of such articles, see Pamela Rohland, "Get My Batsuit, Alfred!" *Business Start-Ups Magazine*, March 2000; "Online Concierge Service Secures Funding," VIPdesk.com, press release, March 10, 2000; Paul Katzeff, "Corporate Concierges Can Save You Valuable Time," *Investor's Business Daily*, October 8, 1999; Marc Ballon, "Concierge Makes Hay in Corporate Fields," *Inc.*, September 1998; Michelle Gordon, "Concierge Among New Job Incentives," *Arizona Republic*, April 26, 1999; Sabrina Jones, "Concierges Answer Cries for Help," *News and Observer* (Raleigh, N.C.), August 12, 1999; Lauren Chambliss, "Need a Helping Hand?" *Evening Standard*, London, July 14, 1999; Susan Port, "Making Arrangements for Concierge Service," *Newsday*, July 8, 1999; Kenneth Harney, "Need Help at Home?" *Washington Post*, July 30, 1999; Clarke Canfield, "Concierge Services Are Getting Paid to Do Things That Time-Starved Clients Cannot," *Portland Press Herald*, March 23, 1999; Shari Caudron, "At Your Service," *Industry Week*, January 18, 1999; Debra Phillips et al., "Hot Stuff," *Entrepreneur*, January 1999; Sandra Livingston and Corwin Thomas, "On-the-Job Concierges Do-It-All Service for Workers Catching on in Cleveland," *Plain Dealer*, November 15, 2000; Charlene Oldham, "To the Rescue: Corporate Concierges a Godsend for Busy Office Workers During Holidays," *Dallas Morning News*, December 23, 2000; "Concierge Services a New Employee Benefit," *Healthcare Financial Management*, April 10, 2001.

79. Lauerman, Connie, "Leave the Details of Living to Them," special from *Chicago Tribune*, reprinted in *The Record*, May 10, 1999, p. L4.

80. Lauerman, op. cit.

81. Fromartz, Samuel, "The Face of an Emerging Industry," *Inc.*, September 1998, p. 24.

82. Research file 6-3-41; personal communication, April 24, 2001.

83. Goldfine, Melissa, "Personal Services Demand Still High," *Washington Post*, March 4, 2001.

84. Cohan, Peter, "Crisis Manager," *Industry Standard*, August 7, 2000. See also "Evolution of Work/Life Initiatives," *Benefits Quarterly*, April 1, 1998; Joanne Gordon, "The New Paternalism," *Forbes*, November 2, 1998; and Web site www.lifecare.com for background on significant companies in the work/life industry.

85. Fletcher, Lee, "Online Work/Life Resources: Web Expands Benefits," *Business Insurance*, March 26, 2001.

86. Ibid. See also Gregory Weaver, "Firms Use Corporate Concierges to Help Employees Accomplish Personal Tasks," *Indianapolis Star and News*, December 25, 2000. One major player in the work/life services industry offers a combination of online and telephone support, claiming that "employees can request assistance with both day-to-day tasks or major life events and receive highly personalized attention regardless if the request is for service around the corner or around the world . . . pet care, travel, convenience/errands, gift giving/shopping, entertainment and home services, as well as routine tasks and extraordinary or unusual requests." PR Newswire, "LifeCare.com Introduces Full Complement of Concierge Services to Round Out Already Extensive Portfolio of Work/Life Products," September 25, 2000. Another work/life services provider offers options that include a twenty-four-hour health-care help line, wellness services, a management help line, backup dependent-care reimbursement, temporary on-site child care, resource and counseling services for lower-wage workers and management employees, eldercare support, education referrals and support, legal and financial referrals, and concierge and home services, including referrals, dispatch, and delivery. Its 1997 customer survey showed that the highest level of service usage was for "personal and relationship issues" at 34 percent, followed by parenting and child care at 17 percent, legal concerns at 15 percent, work issues at 9 percent, and so on. "We've

seen a significant increase in the demand for 'personal services,'" observes the president of another company specializing in providing corporations with information about work/life services. "Tomorrow's Work/Life Provider," *Employee Benefit Plan Review*, September 1, 1998. A 2001 survey conducted by the management consultancy Hewitt Associates found that the percentage of companies offering work/life benefits increased in 2000, despite an economic downturn that year, though they found that only about 3 percent of the largest 1,200 U.S. companies offered benefits that included concierge services. "Hewitt Study Shows Work/Life Benefits Continue to Grow Despite Slowing Economy," *Business Wire*, April 23, 2001. A recent study published by the Society for Human Resource Management that surveyed nearly 800 human resource professionals also reported work/life programs on the rise. Patricia Kitchen, "Flexible Benefits Flourish Despite Economic Downturn," *Newsday*, April 18, 2001.

87. Levitt, Mark, "E-mail Usage Forecast and Analysis, 2000–2005," International Data Corporation, Report no. W23011, September 2000.
88. Horrigan, John B., "Online Communities," Pew Internet & American Life Project, Washington, D.C., October 31, 2001.
89. Rainie, Lee, "The Commons of the Tragedy," Pew Internet & American Life Project, October 10, 2001; quote on p. 2.
90. Terry, Sara, "Tell-All Culture Wonders, What Are the Limits?" *Christian Science Monitor*, October 8, 1998.
91. Ibid.
92. Quoted in James Atlas, "Confessing for Voyeurs," *New York Times Magazine*, May 12, 1996.
93. Gale, Elaine, "My Life as a Book," *Star Tribune* (Minneapolis), January 25, 1998.
94. Terry, op. cit.
95. Quoted in John Balzar, "Making the Most of the Memoir," *Los Angeles Times*, August 1, 1996.
96. Pennebaker, James, et al., "Disclosure of Traumas and Immune Function: Health Implications for Psychotherapy," *Journal of Consulting and Clinical Psychology*, 56, 1988, pp. 239–345; S.P. Spera, E.D. Buhrfeind, and J.W. Pennebaker, "Expressive Writing and Coping with Job Loss," *Academy of Management Journal*, 37, 1994, pp. 722–733; K.P. Petrie, R.J. Booth, and J.W. Pennebaker, "The Immunological Effects of Thought Suppression," *Journal of Personality and Social Psychology*, 75, 1998, pp. 1264–1272. See also J.W. Pennebaker, "Writing About Emotional Experiences as a Therapeutic Process," *Psychological Science*, 8, 1997, pp. 162–166; R.J. Booth, K.J. Petrie, and J.W. Pennebaker, "Changes in Circulating Lymphocyte Numbers Following Emotional Disclosure: Evidence of Buffering?" *Stress Medicine*, 13, 1997, pp. 23–29; James Pennebaker and J. Seagal, "Forming a Story: The Health Benefits of Narrative," *Journal of Clinical Psychology*, 55, 1999, pp. 1243–1254; James Pennebaker, *Opening Up: The Healing Power of Expressing Emotion*, Guilford Press, New York: 1997.
97. Stout, Hilary, "Historians for Hire Chronicle Lives of Ordinary Folks," *Wall Street Journal*, December 29, 1998.
98. Hendrick, Bill, "An Epidemic of Memoir Fever," *Atlanta Constitution*, February 15, 1999.
99. Fulkerson, Jennifer, "Climbing the Family Tree," *American Demographics*, December 1995.
100. Ibid.
101. Hornblower, Margot, "Roots Mania," *Time*, April 19, 1999, p. 55.
102. Price, Christopher, "Hunt for Family Tree Felled by Log-On Overload," *Financial Times*, May 28, 1999.
103. Reported on *ABC Evening News*, April 27, 2001.
104. Schoemer, Karen, "Pop That's Produced Alone at Home Gets Personal," *New York Times*, October 24, 1999.

105. Sawhill, Ray, "Self-Publishing Made Easy," *Newsweek*, October 25, 1999; Peter Gumbel, "A New Creative Order," *Wall Street Journal*, January 1, 2000.

106. Goff, Lisa, "Don't Miss The Bus!" *American Demographics*, August 1999; Philip Connors, "The Best Way to Entertain the Teens," *Wall Street Journal*, December 6, 1999.

107. Robinson and Godbey, op. cit.

108. "Growth in Youth Sports Participation," *Journal of Physical Education, Recreation, & Dance*, Reston, 70:9, November/December 1999, p. 6. According to figures from the National Sporting Goods Association in 1996, the number of people age seven and older who participated in tennis declined from 18 million in 1986 to 11.5 million in 1996. In volleyball the figures were 20.7 million in 1986, 18.5 million in 1996. See *NSGA Research*, 1996, available at the Sports Business Research Network, www.sbrnet.com.

109. "14th Annual Superstudy of Sports Participation," American Sports Data, Hartsdale, N.Y., May 2002.

110. Shellenbarger, Sue, "A Skateboarder Hero Becomes Unlikely Icon of the Family Man," *Wall Street Journal*, August 30, 2000.

111. "X Marks the Spot for Riders at Mount Snow," *New York Times*, February 3, 2000, p. D5. See also "Smaller Companies and Extreme Sports Conquer the Sporting-Goods Industry," *Wall Street Journal*, February 14, 2000.

112. Dortch, Shannon, "Skiing, Skating, and Shredding," *American Demographics*, February 1996.

113. "14th Annual Superstudy." See also Mike Troy, "Rush of New Sports Interests X-actly What Industry Needed," *Discount Store News*, February 7, 2000. Skiers declined from 12 million to 7.5 million in the same decade, and in most of the large ski resorts snowboarding now accounts for as much as half the business.

114. Heath, Rebecca, "You Can Buy a Thrill," *American Demographics*, June 1997.

115. Wise, Jeff, "Manufacturing the Next Extreme Sport," *New York Times Magazine*, March 21, 1999.

Chapter Seven

1. For a detailed description of this historical process, see Alfred Chandler, *The Visible Hand: The Managerial Revolution in American Business*, Harvard University Press, Cambridge, Mass.: 1977; these propositions are summarized on pp. 6–11. For example: "As the multiunit business grew in size and diversity and as its managers became more professional, the management of the enterprise became separated from its ownership. The rise of modern business brought a new definition of the relationship between ownership and management and therefore a new type of capitalism to the American economy. Before the appearance of the multiunit firm, owners managed and managers owned. . . . In many modern business enterprises neither bankers nor families were in control. Ownership became widely scattered. The stockholders did not have the influence, knowledge, experience, or commitment to take part in the high command. Salaried managers determined long-term policy as well as managing short-term operating activities. They dominated top as well as lower and middle management. Such an enterprise controlled by its managers can properly be identified as managerial and a system dominated by such firms is called managerial capitalism. . . . In many industries and sectors of the American economy, managerial capitalism soon replaced family or financial capitalism" (pp. 9–10). See also Shoshana Zuboff, *In the Age of the Smart Machine: The Future of Work and Power*, Basic Books, New York: 1988, especially Chapter 6, "What Was Managerial Authority?" and Chapter 3, "The White Collar Body in History." See also her essay "Work," in *Encyclopedia of the United States in the Twentieth Century*, Stanley Kutler, ed., Vol. III, Charles Scribner's Sons, New York: 1996, pp. 1091–1126.

2. For a similar point, see William G. Roy, *Socializing Capital: The Rise of the Large Industrial Corporation in America*, Princeton University Press, Princeton, N.J.: 1997, p. 275.

3. See, for example, the *Wall Street Journal*'s special section on executive compensation: "Executive Pay," April 8, 1999. Another example is the wave of corporate mergers in the 1990s. Despite ample evidence that mergers tend to diminish share price and punish consumers, merger mania continued unabated on an increasingly large scale. Mergers tend to reward top managers with large bonuses and payouts, as well as increase the size and importance of their businesses. See, for example, "Merger Mania, Sobering Statistics," *The Economist*, June 20, 1998; "After the Deal," *The Economist*, January 9, 1999; Lucian Arye Bebchuk and Christine Jolls, "Managerial Value Diversion and Shareholder Wealth," *Journal of Law, Economics, and Organization*, 15:2, Summer 1999; "Big Mergers of '90s Prove Disappointing to Shareholders," *Wall Street Journal*, October 30, 2000.

4. As Alfred Chandler put it in *The Visible Hand*: "The hierarchies that came to manage the new multiunit enterprises had a permanence beyond that of any individual or group of individuals who worked in them. When a manager died, retired, was promoted, or left an office, another was ready and trained to take his place. Men came and went. The institution and its offices remained" (p. 8).

5. Even the most generous employers guard these rights with the utmost vigilance. For example, Motorola, widely known as a progressive employer, carefully limited the amount of authority it would delegate to so-called self-managing, empowered work teams. Their much-publicized efforts to educate and develop teams of workers were constantly monitored by the company's legal staff, lest the devolution of responsibility to the teams became the de facto basis for an alteration of the employment relationship and the distribution of rights within it. As one senior executive explained, "We didn't want anyone to be able to argue that we had effectively created a union within our own company." Personal communication, vice president for organizational development, Harvard Business School/Motorola Research, File Note no. 69, Winter 1991.

6. Tyndall, Gene, Christopher Gopal, Wolfgang Partsch, John Kamauff, et al., *Supercharging Supply Chains*, Wiley, New York: 1998, p. 131. The authors were all partners in Ernst & Young's global supply chain practice.

7. Fink, Ronald, "Forget the Float," *CFO*, July 2001, pp. 54–62.

8. Banham, Russ, "Caught in the Middle," *CFO*, May 2001; quotes on pp. 72–73. Loyalty can break down even in the Japanese system, where economic pressures have sometimes forced firms to sacrifice their suppliers. As land values decrease in Japan, some firms have even turned back to warehouse construction as a way of lowering the coordination and transportation costs associated with just-in-time inventories. See Fred Kuglin, *Customer-Centered Supply Chain Management*; AMACOM, New York: 1998, p. 1.

9. "Want to increase your company's stock price? Perhaps bring the options above water? . . . The greatest positive effect on stock price comes from implementing high-impact operational improvement programs on an enterprise-wide basis. . . . Inventory turns and DSO (days-of-sales-outstanding) can have a material impact on stock valuation and market capitalization" (Tyndall et al., op. cit., pp. 1–8).

10. A recent survey by KPMG Peat Marwick and the University of Tennessee points to "a significant gap between perception and reality. Despite the industry buzz around supply chain management, many companies have a long way to go to improve their supply chain performance and efficiency." Forty-three percent of all companies surveyed said their inventories were the same as or higher than five years earlier. See Deborah Asbrand, "Squeeze Out Excess Costs with Supply Chain Solutions," *Datamation*, March 1997. Another study by Deloitte Consulting makes the same point: 97 percent of the companies surveyed said supply chain management was critical to their long-term success, but only 1 percent considered their own supply chains to be of a world-class standard. Few companies had been

able to implement electronic data interchange to support information flow among supply chain "partners." See "Survey Spotlights Need to Improve Capabilities," *Modern Materials Handling*, April 1998.

11. See, for example, Maurice Dobb, *Theories of Value and Distribution since Adam Smith: Ideology and Economic Theory*, Cambridge University Press, Cambridge: 1973.

12. For examples of this literature, see Andrew Campbell et al., "The Value of the Parent Company," *California Management Review*, 38:1, Fall 1995; Tony Grundy, "Strategy Acquisitions and Value," *European Management Journal*, 14:2, April 1996; Philip Berger and Eli Ofek, "Bustup Takeovers of Value-Destroying Diversified Firms," *Journal of Finance*, LI:4, September 1996; Sudip Datta and Mai Iskandar-Datta, "Who Gains from Corporate Asset Sales?" *Journal of Financial Research*, XIX:1, Spring 1996; and David Collis and Cynthia Montgomery, "Creating Corporate Advantage," *Harvard Business Review*, May/June 1998.

13. See "A Star to Sail By?" *The Economist*, 344:8028, August 2, 1997, pp. 53–55; Shawn Tully, "America's Greatest Wealth Creators," *Fortune*, November 9, 1998, pp. 193–204; and Ronald B. Lieber, "Who Are the Real Wealth Creators?" *Fortune*, December 9, 1996, pp. 107–116.

14. Three articles that articulate the revenue-generating path to transaction value are Gary Hamel, "Strategy Innovation and the Quest for Value," *Sloan Management Review*, Winter 1998; Sumantra Ghoshal, Christopher Bartlett, and Peter Moran, "A New Manifesto for Management," *Sloan Management Review*, Spring 1999; and Michael Porter, "What Is Strategy?" *Harvard Business Review*, 74, November/December 1996.

15. See for example, Sanford M. Jacoby, *Employing Bureaucracy*, Columbia University Press, New York: 1985, pp. 173, 188–189, 198–199; Sanford M. Jacoby, *Modern Manors*, Princeton University Press, Princeton, N.J.: 1997, pp. 20, 26, 31.

16. For recent examples, see Adam Bryant, "The Candid Mr. Fix It of the Skies: Continental's Chief Shifts Focus from Cutting Costs," *New York Times*, November 12, 1996; and Alex Taylor III, "Pulling Delta Out of Its Dive," *Fortune*, December 7, 1998.

17. For one typical example, see Bruce Orwall, "Disney Says Profit Tumbled by 41%, Promises Further Cost-cutting Efforts," *Wall Street Journal*, April 28, 1999.

18. Anderson, Eugene, Claes Fornell, and Roland Rust, "Customer Satisfaction, Productivity, and Profitability: Differences between Goods and Services," *Marketing Science*, 16:2, 1997.

19. Fornell, Claes, Michael Johnson, Eugene Anderson, Jaesung Cha, and Barbara Everitt Bryant, "The American Customer Satisfaction Index: Nature, Purpose, and Findings," *Journal of Marketing*, 60, October 1996.

20. Ittner, Christopher D., and David Larcker, "Measuring the Impact of Quality Initiatives on Firm Financial Performance," in *Advances in the Management of Organizational Quality*, Vol. 1, Soumeh Ghosh and Donald Fedor, eds., JAI Press, Greenwich, Conn.: 1996, pp. 1–37.

21. Fornell, Claes, Christopher D. Ittner, and David F. Larcker, "The Valuations Consequences of Customer Satisfaction," Working Paper, National Quality Research Center, Ann Arbor, Mich.: 1996.

22. Fornell, Claes, "Transportation, Communications, and Services—Commentary," American Customer Satisfaction Index, Quarter 1, 2001, May 21, 2001.

23. Fornell, Claes, "Q4: Retail & Finance/Insurance Company Scores by Year—Commentary," American Customer Satisfaction Index, February 22, 2000.

24. See American Customer Satisfaction Index Sector/Industry/Company Scores Quarter 4, 1999 and Quarter 1, 2000.

25. American Customer Satisfaction Index National Scores: 1994–2001; "Q4 2001," American Customer Satisfaction Index, February 19, 2002.

26. Fornell, Claes, "Q1: Transportation, Communications, and Utilities/Services— Commentary," American Customer Satisfaction Index, May 15, 2000.

27. Fornell, Claes, "Customer Satisfaction and Expectations," *American Customer Satisfaction Index*—Commentary, Quarter 3, 1999, November 22, 1999.

28. For a recent and well-publicized report that reflects these assumptions, see "Close to the Customer," American Society for Quality Control, Milwaukee, Wisc.: 1997.

29. For three classic and well-publicized examples of this sort of gyration, each in a different industry and separated by nearly a decade, see Robert Tomsho, "Real Dog: How Greyhound Lines Re-Engineered Itself Right into a Deep Hole," *Wall Street Journal*, October 20, 1994, p. 1; Laura Johannes, "Vital Signs Improve at Texas Cancer Center After Radical Measures," *Wall Street Journal*, August 29, 2000, p. 1; and Barbara Martinez, "Making Amends: Aetna Tries to Improve Bedside Manner in Bid to Help Bottom Line," *Wall Street Journal*, February 23, 2001, p. 1.

30. We will explore Web-based customer contact in detail in Chapter 10, "The Digital Bridge."

31. See for example, Rebecca Gunzel, "Customer Service Is Getting Worse?," *Training*, July 1998, p. 25. There are some notable exceptions to this dominant strategy, for example, Federal Express and Vanguard. Thomas H. Davenport and Nitin Nohria, "Case Management and the Integration of Labor," *Sloan Management Review*, winter 1994, 35:2, pp. 11–23.

32. Solomon, Deborah, "AT&T Will Pay Accenture Ltd. $2.6 Billion in Deal," *Wall Street Journal*, January 16, 2002.

33. While the United States leads the world in the number of call centers and rate of growth in tele-services, the trend is well established in Europe too. Increasingly, the call center's telephone activities are augmented by or blended with Web-based response systems. It is estimated that U.S. companies spend roughly $60 billion to answer the phone each year, and those numbers are growing fast. But the fastest-growing part of the tele-services industry involves companies that provide outsourced call centers. As of 1997, the U.S. call-center business was growing by 50 percent annually, and Europe's by 40 percent. Between 1992 and 1997, the number of companies in this industry in the United States doubled to about 1,200, and by some estimates they employ about 2 million people. One in every thirty-three Nebraskans already wears a headset for a living. U.K. experts calculated that in 1997, some 250,000 people worked in call centers, about 1.2 percent of the workforce, and that percentage was expected to double by the end of 2002, according to Datamonitor. See Mary E. Thyfault, "MicroAge: Call Center Outsourcing Spurs Growth," *InformationWeek*, December 1, 1997; Dorothy G. Young, "Study Reveals the Financial Impact of Outsourcing," *Telemarketing and Call Center Solutions*, March 1998; Robert Taylor, "Call Centres Expected to Employ 1M by 2000," *Financial Times*, June 24, 1997; and "Technology May Reduce Jobs," *Financial Times*, August 1, 1999.

34. Thyfault, op. cit.

35. Young, op. cit.

36. Taylor, op. cit.

37. Dawe, Tony, "Dialing Up Some Help from the Outside," *The Times* (London), June 3, 1998.

38. Thurston, Charles, "Outsourced or In-house? Service Call Centers," *Public Utilities Fortnightly*, June 15, 1998.

39. Fishman, Charles, "Inside the 1-800 Factory," *Los Angeles Times Magazine*, August 3, 1997.

40. For an overview of these issues, see James C. Robinson, *The Corporate Practice of Medicine: Competition and Innovation in Health Care*, University of California Press, Berkeley: 1999.

41. Lagnado, Lucette, "Intensive Care: Ex-Manager Describes the Profit-Driven Life Inside Columbia/HCA," *Wall Street Journal*, May 30, 1997.

42. Freudenheim, Milt, "Bedside Visits, on the Telephone," *New York Times*, February 17, 2002.

43. Many of these examples are drawn from the report "Home Recovery," *Jim Lehrer News Hour*, May 13, 1997.

44. Himmelstein, David, et al., "Quality of Care in Investor-Owned vs. Not-for-Profit HMOs," *Journal of the American Medical Association*, July 14, 1999. For the role that managerial incentives—and the disconnect between relationship value and measures of wealth creation—may play in these differences, see Myron Roomkin and Burton Weisbrod, "Managerial Compensation and Incentives in For-Profit and Nonprofit Hospitals," *Journal of Law, Economics, and Organization*, 15:3, Fall 1999.

45. Levine, Carol, ed., *Always on Call: When Illness Turns Families into Caregivers*, United Hospital Fund, New York: 2000.

46. Levine is quoted in Ian Fisher, "Health Care Comes Home," *New York Times*, June 7, 1998.

47. Levine, Carol, "The Loneliness of the Long-Term Caregiver," in Levine, ed., op. cit., pp. 78, 74.

48. Levine, Carol, "The Many Worlds of Family Caregivers," in Levine, ed., op. cit., p. 5. A midrange estimate of $196 billion is based on an assumed wage of $8.18 per hour. The higher estimate of $288 billion is based on wages of $11.20 per hour.

49. See Daniel Gitterman, "The President and the Power of the Purchaser: Consumer Protection and Managed Care in the United States," *California Management Review*, 43:1, Fall 2000, pp. 103–120.

50. As quoted in Fisher, op. cit.

51. As quoted in J. Taylor Buckley, "Flying for Peanuts," *USA Today*, February 19–21, 1999.

52. Pedersen, Daniel, "Dissing Customers," *Newsweek*, June 23, 1997. See also the extremely low ratings that airlines have received each year in the ACSI.

53. U.S. Department of Transportation, Office of the Inspector General, *Interim Report on Airline Customer Service Commitment*, June 27, 2000; see pp. 1–3 for figures cited. For recent articles on air travel that provide many examples of the transaction crisis, especially transaction starvation, see Scott McCartney, "Airlines Find a Bag of High Tech Tricks to Keep Income Aloft," *Wall Street Journal*, January 20, 2000; Wendy Bounds and Lauren Lipton, "Mom, the Airlines Don't Like Me!" *Wall Street Journal*, February 11, 2000; Martha Brannigan, "Flight or Fight," *Wall Street Journal*, August 29, 2000; Joni James, "The Airport Waiting Game," *Wall Street Journal*, May 24, 2001; and *New York Times* coverage in a special "Travel" section, " 'We Hope You Enjoy Your Flight,' " June 25, 2000.

54. Cordes, C.L., and T.W. Dougherty, "A Review and an Integration of Research on Job Burnout," *Academy of Management Review*, 18, 1993, p. 644.

55. See, for example, Gilbert Churchill et al., "The Determinants of Salesperson Performance: A Meta-Analysis," *Journal of Marketing Research*, 22, May 1985, pp. 103–18; Gilbert Churchill and O. Walker, Jr., "Measuring the Job Satisfaction of Industrial Salesmen," *Journal of Marketing Research*, 11, August 1974, pp. 254–260; James Donnelly and John Ivancevich, "Role Clarity and the Salesman," *Journal of Marketing*, 39, January 1975, pp. 71–74; A. Dubinsky and B. Mattson, "Consequences of Role Conflict and Ambiguity Experienced by Retail Salespeople," *Journal of Retailing*, 55, Winter 1979, pp. 70–86; Annetta Miller, et al., "Stress on the Job," *Newsweek*, April 25, 1988, pp. 40–45.

56. Singh, Jagdip, et al., "Behavioral and Psychological Consequences of Boundary Spanning Burnout for Customer Service Representatives," *Journal of Marketing Research*, XXXI, November 1994, pp. 558–569, esp. p. 564.

57. "Big Banks, Bigger Fees: The 1999 PIRG Bank Fee Survey," U.S. Public Interest Research Group, Washington, D.C., 1999, p. 1.

58. Ibid., p. 3.

59. Ibid., pp. 7–8.
60. See Paul Beckett, "Citibank Hitches Itself to Primerica's Team to Peddle Accounts," *Wall Street Journal*, April 19, 1999.
61. This discussion is based on Nicki Chesworth, "Advance of the Banking Brigands" *Sunday Telegraph*, May 23, 1999.
62. If your U.K. bank has closed its local branch (thousands have been closed in the past decade) and you need to use another bank to clear your check, that has also become costly. Barclays charged £5 just for putting a check into an account in another bank. Using another bank's cash machine can cost £1.50. Some credit card issuers charge £2 for acknowledgment of payment, and all will charge stiff penalties in late fees for delayed payments, even on very small amounts.
63. Miller, Lisa, "Want Insurance? Car-Rental Industry Promises That Things Will Improve. Really," *Wall Street Journal*, July 17, 1997.
64. James, op. cit.
65. Hwang, Suein, and Michelle Green, "Restaurants Get Rude!" *Wall Street Journal*, February 26, 1999.
66. Gubernick, Lisa, "The Little Extras That Count (Up)," *Wall Street Journal*, July 12, 2001, p. B1.
67. See the analysis of yield management in Laurence Zuckerman, "Musical Fares," *New York Times Magazine*, March 8, 1998.
68. Templin, Neal, "Your Room Costs . . . ," *Wall Street Journal*, May 5, 1999.
69. Ibid.
70. Drucker, Jesse, "Hotel Rage: Losing It in the Lobby," *Wall Street Journal*, February 16, 2001, p. W1.
71. Noonan, David, "The Frequent-Flier Economy," *New York Times Magazine*, March 8, 1998.
72. Wiener, Jon, "The 548-Mile Marathon," *New York Times Magazine*, March 16, 1997.

Chapter Eight

1. Geyelin, Milo, "Lasting Impact," *Wall Street Journal*, September 29, 1999, p. 1.
2. Smith, Rebecca, "Fastow Memo Defends Enron Partnerships and Sees Criticism as Ploy to Get His Job," *Wall Street Journal*, February 20, 2002.
3. See the discussion of corporate capitalism as a social movement in Martin J. Sklar, *The Corporate Reconstruction of American Capitalism, 1890–1916*, Cambridge University Press, Cambridge: 1988, esp. pp. 13–14, 20–33.
4. Arendt, Hannah, *Eichmann in Jerusalem: A Report on the Banality of Evil*, Penguin, New York: 1963.
5. Milgram, Stanley, *Obedience to Authority*, Harper & Row, New York: 1974.
6. Of course, the mother of all cases of organizational narcissism must be Enron. The tale has unfolded in hundreds of news stories. See, for example, Kurt Eichenwald and Diana Enriques, "Enron Buffed Image to a Shine, Even as It Rotted from Within," *New York Times*, February 10, 2002, p. 1. For other material that illustrates the same syndrome, see the many stories that covered Yahoo!'s plunge, including Mylene Mangalindan and Suein Hwang, "Coterie of Early Hires Made Yahoo! a Hit But an Insular Place," *Wall Street Journal*, March 9, 2001, p. 1; Saul Hansell, "Red Face for the Internet's Blue Chip," *New York Times*, March 11, 2001. See also the example of AT&T in Cynthia Crossen and Deborah Solomon, "Once a Corporate Icon, AT&T Finally Yields to a Humbler Role," *Wall Street Journal*, October 26, 2000, p. 1. The many articles covering the Ford/Firestone debacle over faulty tires are also instructive; for one early piece that illustrated the dynamics of organizational narcissism, see "How Ford, Firestone Let the Warnings Slide by as Debacle Developed," *Wall Street Journal*, September 6, 2000, p. 1. See also Norihiko Shirouzu et al., "Driving Lessons: Beyond Explorer Woes, Ford Misses Key Turns in Buyers, Technology," *Wall Street Journal*, January 14, 2002,

p. 1. Another tale of organizational narcissism is behind the demise of Webvan, according to Miguel Helft, "The End of the Road," *Industry Standard*, July 23, 2001.

7. Ford, Henry, *My Life and Work*, Doubleday, New York: 1922, p. 75.

8. We note that recent scholarship has revealed a number of interesting exceptions to the mass-production model, as well as earlier industrial alternatives that were sidelined by the spread of mass production. These cases are very important historically, though they complicate rather than undermine the story of mass production as the principal template in the worldwide diffusion of the modern principles of work organization. For examples of this "alternative history," see Charles Sabel and Jonathan Zeitlin, eds., *World of Possibilities: Flexibility and Mass Production in Western Industrialization*, Cambridge University Press, New York: 1977; and Philip Scranton, *Endless Novelty: Specialty Production and American Industrialization, 1865–1925*, Princeton University Press, Princeton, N.J.: 1997.

9. Couzens, James, "What I Learned About Business from Ford," *System*, 40, September 1921.

10. Ford, op. cit., p. 71.

11. Ibid., p. 72.

12. Couzens, op. cit.

13. Urwick, Lyndall, *Elements of Administration*, Pitman, London: 1943, p. 29.

14. See Paul Osterman, *Broken Ladders: Managerial Careers in the New Economy*, Oxford University Press, New York: 1996, Chapter 1.

15. Melman, Seymour, "The Rise of Administrative Overhead in the Manufacturing Industries of the United States 1899–1947," *Oxford Economic Papers*, 1951. For more detail, see Shoshana Zuboff, "Work," in the *Encyclopedia of the United States in the Twentieth Century*, Stanley Kutler, ed., Vol. III, Charles Scribner's Sons, New York: 1996, pp. 1091–1126.

16. Melman, op. cit.

17. Osterman, op. cit., p. 5.

18. See, for example, Paul Milgrom and John Roberts, *Economics, Organizations, and Management*, Prentice Hall, Englewood Cliffs, N.J.: 1992.

19. U.S. Department of Labor, Bureau of Labor Statistics, "Employment and Earnings," Washington, D.C. 1981. See also Mauro Guillen, *Models of Management*, University of Chicago Press, Chicago: 1994.

20. Attewell, Paul, "Skill and Occupational Changes in Manufacturing," in *Technology and the Future of Work*, Paul Adler, ed., Oxford University Press, New York: 1992, pp. 46–88. A similar conclusion was reached by Eli Berman, John Bound, and Zvi Griliches in "Changes in the Demand for Skilled Labor within U.S. Manufacturing," *Quarterly Journal of Economics*, CIX:2, May 1994, pp. 367–397.

21. U.S. Department of Labor, Bureau of Labor Statistics, "Employment Outlook, 1996–2006: A Summary of BLS Projections," Bulletin 2502, Washington, D.C., February 1998, p. 58.

22. Osterman, op. cit., p. 11. Another study by Peter Cappelli came to a similar conclusion regarding moderately increased churning in managerial careers; see his "Examining Managerial Displacement," *Academy of Management Journal*, 35:1, 1992.

23. U.S. Department of Labor, "Employment Outlook 1996–2006." These projections were upheld in the Bureau of Labor Statistics' subsequent analysis by Daniel Hecker, "Occupational Employment Projections to 2010," *Monthly Labor Review*, November 2001, p. 58.

24. U.S. Department of Labor, Bureau of Labor Statistics, "Employment and Earnings," Washington, D.C., 2002.

25. Miller, Eugene, *Barron's Guide to Graduate Business Schools*, Barron's Educational Series, Woodbury, N.Y.: 2001. Paul Hugstad, *The Business School in the 1980s*, Praeger, N.Y.: 1983. However, their predictions of slower growth are based on the assumption that "restructured" organizations will require fewer middle managers. There was anecdotal evidence throughout the 1990s, though, that raised questions about the BLS's assumption of slower growth in the numbers of managers. The

Association of Executive Search Consultants reported that between 1997 and 1998 searches for general managers below the division-head level increased by 58 percent. The *Wall Street Journal* reported that "after years of downsizing and 'delayering' the management hierarchy, [people] are hot again. Companies that once bragged about their re-engineered work processes and new quality measurements now are extolling the importance of human beings. . . . Many companies are spotlighting managers in an effort to rebuild cultures disrupted by mergers and cost cutting." Shortly after the BLS projections were issued, the president of a large executive search firm, Management Recruiters International, noted, "There is higher demand for middle managers today than I have seen in my 33 years in this business. There are more middle-management job openings than there are people to fill them—and this has never happened before." Cited in Hal Lancaster, "Middle Managers Are Back—But Now They're 'High Impact' Players," *Wall Street Journal*, April 14, 1998. See also Geoffrey Colvin, "Revenge of the Nerds," *Fortune*, March 2, 1998; and Hal Lancaster, "Hiring a Full Staff May Be the Next Fad," *Wall Street Journal*, April 28, 1998.

26. For this discussion of court society we rely on Norbert Elias's *Power and Civility: The Civilizing Process*, Vol. 2, Pantheon, New York: 1976, esp. pp. 270–274.

27. La Bruyère, Jean de, "De la Cow," *Caractères*, *Oeuvres*, Vol. 2, Hachette, Paris: 1922. We have relied here on Elias's translation.

28. Elias, op. cit., p. 271.

29. Fowler, Nathaniel C., *The Boy: How to Help Him Succeed*, Oakwood, Boston: 1902, pp. 101–102.

30. Weiss, Janice, "Educating for Clerical Work: The Nineteenth Century Private Commercial School," *Journal of Social History*, 14, 1981, p. 415.

31. Barnard, Chester, *The Functions of the Executive*, Harvard University Press, Cambridge, Mass.: 1938, pp. 121, 220.

32. Mills, C. Wright, *White Collar*, Oxford University Press, New York: 1951.

33. Whyte, William H., *The Organization Man*, Simon & Schuster, New York: 1956.

34. Dalton, Melville, *Men Who Manage*, Wiley, New York: 1959.

35. Whyte, op. cit., p. 152.

36. Dalton, op. cit., p. 250.

37. Rosabeth Moss Kanter, in her description of corporate life, *Men and Women of the Corporation* (Basic Books, New York: 1977), stressed the salience of face-to-face communication in managers' work. She concluded that the manager's ability to win acceptance and to communicate was often more important than any substantive knowledge of the business. Henry Mintzberg's empirical study of top managers' work (*The Nature of Managerial Work*, Harper & Row, New York: 1973) emphasized the ways in which actual leadership activity is inseparable from the daily flow of interaction and communication. "In virtually everything he does, the manager's actions are screened by subordinates searching for leadership clues. In answering a request for authorization, he may encourage or inhibit a subordinate, and even in his form of greeting, messages (perhaps nonexistent ones) may be read by anxious subordinates." John Kotter's studies of top managers have stressed the work of developing networks of relationships that provide the insights for their strategic agenda. Their mental road maps are composed more of "people" issues than of systematic formal information. Chris Argyris has spent most of his career meticulously documenting the "self-sealing" action systems of the managerial hierarchy that emphasize the need for subtle attunement to the behavioral and conversational boundaries of managerial discourse and the ways they are geared to maintain the status quo. He has shown how violation of these boundaries is highly unusual and carries the stiff penalty of exclusion. Most ethnographies of organizational life echo the same themes. Time and again they document the longing and anxiety that afflict managers as they parry and thrust their way through the political maze on the way toward career advancement. See Robert Jackall, *Moral Mazes*, Oxford University Press, New York: 1988; Shoshana Zuboff, *In the Age of the Smart Machine: The Fu-*

ture of Work and Power, Basic Books, New York: 1988; Vicki Smith, *Managing in the Corporate Interest*, University of California Press, Berkeley: 1990; Claudio Ciborra, *Groupware and Teamwork*, Wiley, New York: 1996.

38. Nadler, David, *Champions of Change*, Jossey-Bass, San Fransisco: 1998, p. 96.
39. The quote is attributed to Murray Rothbard, author of the textbook *Man, Economy, and State*, Van Nostrand, Princeton, N.J.: 1962. The attribution is found in John Blundell, "Any Schmuck Can Consume," *Economic Affairs*, 20:3, September 2000, p. 49. (The word "schmuck" is Yiddish slang for "undistinguished person.")
40. Smith, Adam, *The Wealth of Nations*, Modern Library, Random House, New York: 1994, p. 715.
41. Marchand, Roland, "Customer Research as Public Relations: General Motors in the 1930s," in *Getting and Spending: European and American Consumer Societies in the Twentieth Century*, Susan Strasser, Charles McGovern, and Matthias Judt, eds., Cambridge University Press, Cambridge: 1998, p. 87.
42. Our discussion of Buck Weaver's work is largely based on the historical research of Roland Marchand, op. cit.
43. Ibid., pp. 90–92.
44. Ibid., p. 92.
45. Ibid., p. 93.
46. Ibid., p. 102.
47. Ibid., p. 105.
48. Ibid.
49. Bernays, Edward L., *Biography of an Idea: Memoirs of Public Relations Counsel Edward L. Bernays*, Simon & Schuster, New York: 1965, p. 552.
50. Sloan, Alfred P., *My Years with General Motors*, Doubleday, New York: 1990, pp. 239–240.
51. Marchand, Roland, *Advertising the American Dream: Making Way for Modernity 1920–1940*, University of California Press, Berkeley: 1985, p. 2.
52. Ibid., pp. 6–7.
53. Ibid., p. 7.
54. Ibid., p. 13.
55. According to Marchand: "The term 'businessman' connoted efficiency, self-control, rationality, practical common sense, and a hatred of waste. Most businessmen treasured this self-image. . . . They clung to a producer ethic. Whatever compromises with the consumption ethic they forged out of opportunism, they wished to hold themselves aloof from its complicity in catering to the weak-willed self-indulgence of the consumer masses. For advertising agents of that era, the apparent popular enthusiasm for the consumption ethic created a potentially agonizing dilemma. . . . They shared with other businessmen a deep suspicion of the impulses toward what could be considered self-indulgence, frivolous wastefulness, and decadent extravagance . . . which directly negated or undermined the values of efficiency and the work ethic on which the system was based. . . . Like their businessmen clients, they saw themselves as producers, not consumers. They sought self-fulfillment in hard work, in carrying out what they instinctively defined as serious, purposeful tasks. *They shared the producer's almost ascetic contempt for the weak-willed, dependent consumer* [the emphasis is ours]. . . . Much of the advertising elite looked down upon the throng of consumers with bemused contempt: these masses were ignorant, tasteless, emotionally foolish. . . . Drawing pay and professional prestige from their association with the (presumably) rational elite, they could hardly escape sharing some of their clients' scorn, as producers, for the less rational . . . consumer. Ibid., pp. 158, 84. See also Pamela Walker Laird, *Advertising Progress*, John Hopkins University Press, Baltimore: 1998, pp. 312, 317, 327, 336, 370–371; the author details advertisers' identification with their clients and disdain for consumers, especially female consumers.
56. Marchand, *Advertising the American Dream*, p. 85.
57. Ibid., p. 67.

58. Ibid., p. 68.
59. Ibid., p. 74.
60. Bushman, Richard L., *The Refinement of America: Persons, Houses, Cities*, Knopf, New York: 1992, p. 424.
61. Ibid., pp. 442–443.
62. Leach, William, *Land of Desire: Merchants, Power, and the Rise of a New American Culture*, Random House, New York: 1993, p. 147.
63. It is worth noting that there is much recent historical research that illuminates the "borderlands" of the newly separated female and male territories called home and work. Women had a presence in the business world, though they were concentrated in the so-called feminine industries—making and selling hats, beauty products, women's clothing, small retail shops, and so on. This new, more multifaceted understanding is vital; it provides a more nuanced view of how men and women participated in each world, though it does not undermine the larger story of the way in which men and women split off into the two distinct spheres of production and consumption. For an excellent overview, see Angel Kwolek-Folland, *Incorporating Women: A History of Women and Business in the United States*, Simon & Schuster, New York: 1998. See also Ava Baron, ed., *Work Engendered: Toward a New History of American Labor*, Cornell University Press, Ithaca, N.Y.: 1991; Wendy Gamber, "A Gendered Enterprise: Placing Nineteenth-Century Businesswomen in History," *Business History Review*, 72, Summer 1998; Kathy Peiss, " 'Vital Industry' and Women's Ventures: Conceptualizing Gender in Twentieth-Century Business History," *Business History Review*, 72, Summer 1998; and Joan W. Scott, "Comment: Conceptualizing Gender in American Business History," *Business History Review*, 72, Summer 1998. See also the discussion on "mapping the borderlands" in Steven Lubar, "Men/Women/Production/Consumption," in *His and Hers: Gender, Consumption, and Technology*, Roger Horowitz and Arwen Mohun, eds., University Press of Virginia, Charlottesville: 1998.
64. *Advertising Age*, July 12, 1937, p. 15.
65. Marchand, *Advertising the American Dream*, p. 66. See also Christine Frederick, *Selling Mrs. Consumer*, The Business Bourse, New York: 1929. See also Stephanie Coontz, *The Social Origins of Private Life: A History of American Families, 1600–1900*, Verso, London: 1988, pp. 348–354.
66. See the discussion in Leach, op. cit., p. 148. See also the 1912 article written by an economics professor at the University of California lamenting women's lack of training and systematic knowledge in their new roles as consumers: Wesley C. Mitchell, "The Backward Art of Spending Money," *American Economic Review*, 2:2, pp. 269–281.
67. Benson, Susan Porter, "Living on the Margin," in *The Sex of Things*, Victoria de Grazia and Ellen Furlough, eds., University of California Press, Berkeley: 1996; Joan Wallach Scott and Louise Tilly, "Women in the Family Consumer Economy," in their *Women, Work, and Family*, Methuen, New York: 1987; Neil McKendrick, "Home Demand and Economic Growth," in *Historical Perspectives: Studies in English Thought and Society in Honour of J.H. Plumb*, Neil McKendrick, ed., Europa, London: 1974; Judith G. Coffin, "Consumption, Production, and Gender: The Sewing Machine in France," in *Gender and the Reconstruction of European Working-Class History*, Laura Frader and Sonya Rose, eds., Cornell University Press, Ithaca, N.Y.: 1995.
68. Benson, op. cit., p. 220.
69. Scott and Tilly, op. cit., pp. 209–210. Considering the lives of early-twentieth-century women in the United Kingdom and France, these historians have written: "Clearly, the economic situation and smooth functioning of the household depended on the woman's ability to 'manage.' Over and over again accounts refer to the wife as a good or bad manager. It may well be that the self-denial which seems to have been characteristic of working-class women was related to their sense of themselves as responsible for shortages. . . . Studies well into the 1930s showed that

mothers bore the brunt of nutritional deprivation. . . . If she could not manage to provide enough for everyone, the manager herself had to do without."

70. Marchand, *Advertising the American Dream*, p. 70.
71. Ibid.
72. Ibid., p. 343.
73. Ibid., pp. 67, 69.
74. Bushman, op. cit., p. 443. "They conveyed a sense that the household existed on the margins of life's serious work. The stereotypical caricatures of women and women's work offer clues to male thinking about household gentility. The humorous comments often assumed that efforts at refinement were frills. Genteel women were charged with a slavish devotion to fashion, an excessive love of balls and fine clothes, a squandering of their husbands' money on needless fripperies. . . . The 'master's' wealth had created a space that was foreign to his tastes, and his wife had turned the house into a place where he was not at home."
75. Parr, Joy, "Shopping for a Good Stove," in Horowitz and Mohun, eds., op. cit., p. 174.
76. Ibid.
77. Ibid.
78. Ibid, pp. 168–170.
79. Fischer, Claude, *America Calling: A Social History of the Telephone to 1940*, University of California Press, Berkeley: 1992, pp. 234–236.
80. Fischer, Claude, " 'Touch Someone': The Telephone Industry Discovers Sociability," *Technology and American History*, Stephen Cutcliffe and Terry Reynolds, eds., University of Chicago Press, Chicago: 1997, pp. 271–300; see discussion on p. 286.
81. Marchand, Roland, *Creating the Corporate Soul: The Rise of Public Relations and Corporate Imagery in American Big Business*, University of California Press, Berkeley: 1998, p. 72.
82. Fischer, in Cutcliffe and Reynolds, op. cit., pp. 295–296.
83 For extensive descriptions, see Leach, op. cit., and Susan Porter Benson, *Counter Cultures: Saleswomen, Managers, and Customers in American Department Stores, 1890–1940*, University of Illinois Press, Urbana: 1986.
84. Benson, *Counter Cultures*, pp. 94–95.
85. Ibid., p. 99.
86. Frederick, Christine, op. cit., pp. 295, 298.
87. Reekie, Gail, "Impulsive Women, Predictable Men: Psychological Constructions of Sexual Difference in Sales Literature to 1930," *Australian Historical Studies*, 97, October 1991, pp. 364, 370.
88. There are many useful discussions of this topic. See, for example, E. Anthony Rotundo, *American Manhood: Transformations in Masculinity from the Revolution to the Modern Era*, Basic Books, New York: 1993, esp. Chapter 11 and pp. 248–274; Gail Bederman and John Charles Pettigrew, *The Origins of the Masculine Mystique*, University of Wisconsin Press, Madison: 1994; Michael Kimmel, *Manhood in America: A Cultural History*, Free Press, New York: 1996; Tom Pendergast, "Horatio Alger Doesn't Work Here Anymore," *American Studies*, 38:1, Spring 1997, pp. 55–80; Robyn Muncy, "Trustbusting and White Manhood in America, 1898–1914," *American Studies*, 38:3, Fall 1997, pp. 21–42.
89. For more detail, see Shoshana Zuboff, "Work," in *Encyclopedia of the United States in the Twentieth Century*, Stanley Kutler, ed., Vol. III, Charles Scribner's Sons, New York: 1996, pp. 1091–1126.
90. Marchand, *Creating the Corporate Soul*, p. 44. The "western" as a literary form developed in the early twentieth century as a kind of antidote to the threatened masculinity of the new corporate urban life. As one historian has described it, "As a genre, the western represented the apotheosis of masculinist fantasy, a revolt not against women but against feminization." See Kimmel, op. cit., p. 150; see also pp. 117–188 for further discussion of the late-nineteenth- and early-twentieth-century crisis of masculinity.

There is a similar relationship to the rise of scouting: See Jeffrey Hantover, "The Boy Scouts and the Validation of Masculinity," *Journal of Social Issues*, 34:1, 1978, pp. 184–195; and Allen Warren, "Popular Manliness: Baden Powell, Scouting, and the Development of Manly Character," in *Manliness and Morality: Middle Class Masculinity in Britain and America, 1800–1940*, J.A. Mangan and James Walvin, eds., St. Martin's Press, New York: 1987, pp. 199–216; other essays in this collection are also instructive on the general topic of the "masculinity crisis."

91. Marchand, *Creating the Corporate Soul*; see, for example, the discussion on p. 44: "Patterned roughly on Charles Dana Gibson's drawing of Richard Harding Davis, the dauntless, romantic war correspondent and symbol of the independent adventurer, this jutting-jaw image of the business executive would predominate. . . . In describing Marshall Field as a 'born commander' among captains of industry, a reporter in 1906 noted particularly that Field's 'dominant quality was expressed in a jaw of extra-ordinary width.' That was exactly the image adopted in the standardized vignettes of exemplary businessmen that accompanied each major article in the magazine of business modernization, *System*."

92. Zuboff, "Work."

93. Kwolek-Folland, Angel, "Gender, Self, and Work in the Life Insurance Industry," in Ava Baron, ed., *Work Engendered*, pp. 176–177. In this detailed study of Metropolitan Life Insurance, one sees some of the tactics that managers used to reassert their masculinity, protecting themselves from the onslaught of uncertainty and self-doubt evoked by their new circumstances. "Corporate organization generally muted individual choice and autonomy, a phenomenon heightened by the feminized persona of a life insurance corporation." As an antidote, "The life insurance product, as opposed to the producing company itself, was couched in masculine terms. Companies emphasized life insurance sales as a masculine calling, much like the clergy or the law. . . . Sales pitches aimed life insurance primarily at male breadwinners and played on the desire for what one historian has called 'economic immortality.' Life insurance removed death from the feminized regions of sentimentality and . . . demonstrated that death could be tabulated, categorized, predicted, and given a cash value" (p. 181).

94. Ibid., p. 174.

95. Ibid., pp. 181–182.

96. For a compelling historical excursion into the detailed practices that accomplished this kind of "sexual purity" within the management hierarchy and other business professions, see Sharon Strom, *Beyond the Typewriter: Gender, Class, and the Origins of Modern American Office Work, 1900–1930*, University of Illinois Press, Urbana: 1992, esp. Chapter 2, "Gender and the Masculine Business Professions," and Chapter 6, "High School, Office Work, and Female Ambition." As Strom concludes at the close of her Chapter 2, "Men who dominated elite business professions were happy to recruit women as assistants as long as they respected the central rule: men were in charge and would remain in charge. Women could not be in charge, not because they lacked qualifications or proper educational training, but because they were women. . . . Discrimination guaranteed a large pool of capable women who could be hired as secretaries and assistants. Male college graduates and executives could be guaranteed a separate career ladder and an assurance that the virility of the masculine business professions had not been diluted" (pp. 95–96). Other historians have begun to explore the diverse and less easily categorized commercial undertakings of women excluded from the mainstream of managerial capitalism. For an excellent overview of this new perspective, see Wendy Gamber, op. cit., pp. 188–218; and Kathy Peiss, op. cit., pp. 219–241.

97. Kwolek-Folland, Angel, *Engendering Business: Men and Women in the Corporate Office 1870–1930*, Johns Hopkins University Press, Baltimore: 1994, pp. 177–179.

98. Marchand, *Creating the Corporate Soul*, p. 14.

99. Similar patterns existed in French department stores. See Theresa M. McBride, "A Woman's World: Department Stores and the Evolution of Women's Employment,

1870–1920," *French Historical Studies*, 10, Fall 1978, pp. 664–683. The practice of hiring women to mediate between producers and their (largely female) end consumers had caught on in other businesses too. Just as managers had delegated communications with end consumers to ad men and, later, marketing experts, this ploy allowed managers to remain comfortably ensconced in organization space, attending to their careers in production and the production of their careers. It also, and incidentally, created employment opportunities for women. Home economists were hired to oversee customer service training or advise on sales techniques. In some cases, they advised manufacturers on technical design, based on their knowledge of how women used specific products. For example, the advice of home economists was used in the development of a refrigerator that was suited for residential kitchens. Women were used as demonstrators for a variety of products, including many home appliances. In showrooms, in advertisements, and in power company offices, they instructed other women in the use of electric ranges, irons, lamps, and other "power tools." Trained "domestic science experts" explained the use of products at local demonstrations, but "salesmen" were on hand to collect the names and addresses of those whose interest warranted follow-up. Mass consumer businesses hired women to represent them, going so far as to have them impersonate the company owner, an industry expert, or even the role model for a brand name. In some cases fictitious female identities were created in order to more effectively sell products into a female market: Think Betty Crocker. Kwolek-Folland, *Incorporating Women*, p. 143; Lubar, op. cit., p. 29; James Williams, "Getting Housewives the Electric Message: Gender and Energy Marketing in the Early Twentieth Century," in Horowitz and Mohun, op. cit., p. 106; Peiss, op. cit., p. 229.

100. White, Harrison, "Where Do Markets Come From?" *American Journal of Sociology*, 87:3, November 1981.

Chapter Nine

1. Webster, Frederick E., *Market-Driven Management*, Wiley, New York: 1994, p. 8.
2. Drucker, Peter, *The Practice of Management*, Harper & Row, New York: 1954, pp. 37–41.
3. Webster, op. cit., p. 10.
4. As quoted in Stephen Greyser, "Janus and Marketing: The Past, Present, and Prospective Future of Marketing," in *Reflections on the Futures of Marketing: Practice and Education*, Donald Lehman and Katherine Jocz, eds., Marketing Science Institute, Cambridge, Mass.: 1997, pp. 4, 6.
5. Webster, op. cit., p. 15. According to Webster's history of this period, "Instead of true customer orientation, managing for profitability, and integrated marketing at the business unit level, what was often found was continued product and manufacturing orientation, continued emphasis on sales volume rather than long-term profitability based on customer satisfaction, and weak integration . . . of marketing with other functions."
6. Ibid., p. 21.
7. Coles, Robert E., "Learning from the Quality Movement," *California Management Review*, 41:1, Fall 1998, p. 43.
8. Ibid., p. 70.
9. Ibid., p. 59.
10. Ibid., p. 69.
11. Both surveys and the FP&L story are reviewed in "The Cracks in Quality," *The Economist*, 323:7755, April 18, 1992, p. 67.
12. Coles, op. cit., p. 59.
13. Ibid., pp. 60–61.
14. Hammer, Michael, "Reengineering Work: Don't Automate, Obliterate," *Harvard Business Review*, 68:4, July/August 1990, pp. 104–112.

15. Hammer, Michael, and James Champy, *Reengineering the Corporation*, Harper-Collins, New York: 1993.
16. Hammer, Michael, "Reengineering the Corporation," *Insights Quarterly*, Summer 1993, pp. 3–19.
17. Hammer and Champy, op. cit., p. 53
18. Ibid., p. 32.
19. Ibid., pp. 20, 74.
20. Ibid., p. 31.
21. Hammer, "Reengineering Work."
22. Hammer, Michael, and S.A. Stanton, *The Reengineering Revolution*, Harper Business, New York: 1995, p. 183.
23. Strassman, Paul, "The Hocus-Pocus of Reengineering," *Across the Board*, 34:6, 1994, p. 38.
24. Conti, R.F., and M. Warner, "Taylorism, Teams, and Technology in 'Reengineering' Work-Organization," *New Technology, Work, and Employment*, 9, 1994, pp. 93–102.
25. Thackray, J., "Fads, Fixes, and Fictions," *Management Today*, June 1993, pp. 40–42.
26. Grint, K., and L. Willcocks, "Business Process Reengineering in Theory and Practice: Business Paradise Regained?" *New Technology, Work, and Employment*, 10, 1995, pp. 99–109.
27. Geisler, Eliezer, *Managing the Aftermath of Radical Corporate Change*, Quorum Books, Westport, Conn.: 1997, p. 39.
28. Champy, James, *Reengineering Management*, Harper Business, New York: 1995.
29. Vogl, A. J., "Reengineering: A Light That Failed?," *Across the Board*, March 1995, pp. 27–31.
30. A small sampling of articles extolling the Levi Strauss management approach includes Robert Howard, "Values Make the Company," *Harvard Business Review*, September/October 1990; Tracy Benson, "Robert Haas' Vision Scores 20/20," *Industry Week*, April 2, 1990; and Jon Berry, "Keeping a Shiny Corporate Image," *San Francisco Chronicle*, January 29, 1990.
31. Bill Eaton interview, file note no. 139, HBS/MIT–Levi Strauss Research, 1990. (Shoshana Zuboff led a research effort at LS & Co. between 1989 and 1992.)
32. HBS/MIT–Levi Strauss research, "CSSC Convening Meeting," file note 150, 1991.
33. This recounting of events at Levi Strauss is based on Nina Munk, "How Levi's Trashed a Great American Brand," *Fortune*, April 12, 1999.
34. Hausman, Tamar, "Seeking a Good Fit," *Wall Street Journal*, March 9, 1999; Del Jones and Lorrie Grant, "What Caused Levi's Blues?" *USA Today*, February 23, 1999.
35. Munk, op. cit.
36. Ibid., p. 84.
37. Letter to the editor by Richard Unger, *USA Today*, March 2, 1999.
38. Knights, David, and Darren McCabe, "When 'Life Is But a Dream': Obliterating Politics Through Business Process Reengineering?" *Human Relations*, 51:6, 1998; Tom Rose, "Notes from the Front," *National Productivity Review*, Spring 1998; Varun Grover, "From Business Reengineering to Business Process Change Management: A Longitudinal Study of Trends and Practices," *IEEE Transactions on Engineering Management*, 46:1, February 1999; Dennis Jaffe and Cynthia Scott, "Reengineering in Practice," *Journal of Applied Behaviorial Science*, 34:3, September 1998; Donna Stoddard et al., "The Reality of Business Reengineering," *California Management Review*, 38:3, Spring 1996.
39. Grint, Keith, and Peter Case, "The Violent Rhetoric of Re-Engineering: Management Consultancy on the Offensive," *Journal of Management Studies*, 35:5, September 1998; Christian De Cock and Ian Hipkin, "TQM and BPR: Beyond the Beyond Myth," *Journal of Management Studies*, 34:5, September 1997. See also Allen Sloan, "The Hit Men," *Newsweek*, February 26, 1996.

40. Jarrar, Yasar, and Elaine Aspinwall, "Business Process Reengineering: Learning from Organizational Experience," *Total Quality Management*, 10:2, 1999.
41. "Meet the New Consumer," *Fortune*, Autumn/Winter 1993, pp. 6–7.
42. "Change Management: Striving for Customer Value," Conference Board Research Report no. 1167-96-RR, 1996, p. 5.
43. Davis, Stan, *Future Perfect*, Addison-Wesley, Reading, Mass.: 1987, p. 138.
44. Ibid., p. 169.
45. Ibid.
46. Pine, B. Joseph, *Mass Customization*, Harvard Business School Press, Boston: 1993.
47. Pine, B. Joseph, et al., "Making Mass Customization Work," *Harvard Business Review*, September/October 1993, p. 108.
48. Pine, op. cit., pp. 213–214.
49. Ibid., pp. 55–61.
50. Pine et al., op. cit., p. 108.
51. Lampel, Joseph, and Henry Mintzberg, "Customizing Customization," *Sloan Management Review*, 38:1, Fall 1996.
52. See, for example, B. Joseph Pine II and Thomas Pietrocini, "Standard Modules Allow Mass Customization at Bally Engineered Structures," *Planning Review*, 21:4, July/August 1993.
53. Zipkin, Paul, "The Limits of Mass Customization," *Sloan Management Review*, 42:3, Spring 2001. See also Evie Dykema, "Mass Customization Apparel Lacks Mass Appeal," Forrester Brief, June 28, 1999.
54. See, for example, Matthew Mirapaul, "Made Especially for You, in Industrial Quantities," *New York Times*, March 11, 2001; and Bruce Horovitz, "In 1999, You'll Have It Your Way," *USA Today*, December 29, 1998.
55. Examples drawn from Mirapaul, op. cit., p. 11.
56. Peters, Linda, and Hasannudin Saidin, "IT and the Mass Customization of Services," *International Journal of Information Management*, 20, 2000, pp. 103–119.
57. Alford, Dave, et al., "Mass Customisation—An Automotive Perspective," *International Journal of Production Economics*, 65, 2000, p. 105.
58. See Bryn Jones, *Forcing the Factory of the Future*, Cambridge University Press, Cambridge: 1997; and Richard Delbridge, *Life on the Line in Contemporary Manufacturing*, Oxford University Press, Oxford: 1998.
59. Huys, Rik, et al., "Toward Less Division of Labor?" *Human Relations*, 52:1, 1999, p. 87. See also Jayashankar M. Swaminathan, "Enabling Customization Using Standardized Operations," *California Management Review*, 43:3, Spring 2001, pp. 125–135.
60. Davis, Donald Finlay, *Conspicuous Production: Automobiles and Elites in Detroit, 1899–1933*, Temple University Press, Philadelphia: 1988, pp. 43–44, 73, 79. As early as 1910, Detroit's elite families had become reluctant to continue investing in the auto industry, believing that "the automobile had reached the limit of its possibilities" and that it might be a fad, like bicycles in the 1890s, whose sales would quickly stagnate as the public turned toward fresh diversions.
61. Ibid., pp. 121–122.
62. The original work at BCG is attributed to Richard Winger and David Edelman, who coined and copyrighted for their firm the phrase "segment-of-one." Also see Don Peppers and Martha Rogers, *The One to One Future*, Doubleday, New York: 1993; and Regis McKenna, *Relationship Marketing*, Perseus Books, Reading, Mass.: 1991.
63. David Edelman is quoted in Simon London, "Messages That Never Go Wide of the Mark," *Financial Times*, August 8, 2001.
64. Ibid.
65. Peppers and Rogers, op. cit., pp. 6–10; quote on p. xxviii.
66. McKenna, op. cit., p. 2.
67. Ibid.
68. Ibid.

69. Peppers, Don, and Martha Rogers, *The One to One Fieldbook*, Doubleday, New York: 1999, p. 3.
70. Peppers, Don, and Martha Rogers, *Enterprise One to One*, Doubleday, New York: 1997, p. 179.
71. Peppers and Rogers, *Fieldbook*, p. 126.
72. Berry, Leonard, "Relationship Marketing of Services," *Journal of the Academy of Marketing Science*, 23:4, 1995, pp. 236–245.
73. Peppers and Rogers, *Enterprise One to One*, p. 179.
74. Peppers and Rogers, *Fieldbook*, p. 5. This helps to explain the headlines in a recent advertisement announcing the "most highly acclaimed, talked-about event of the year!". The event was a business conference on "Customer Intimacy" featuring popular speakers such as Peppers and Rogers, Joseph Pine, and others. Among the "leading edge strategies" to be discussed at the conference, the ad promised, were expert guidance on how to "reduce and control the cost of 'customer touches' " as well as how to "transform customer data into seductive intimacy strategies." The ad appeared in *Business 2.0*, October 2000.
75. Boslet, Mark, "CRM: The Promise, the Peril, the Eye-Popping Price," *Industry Standard*, August 6, 2001, p. 65.
76. Menzigian, Katrina, "Worldwide CRM Services," International Data Corporation, 2000.
77. Boslet, op. cit., pp. 62–63.
78. London, op. cit.
79. Boslet, op. cit., p. 62.
80. Platerink, Mary, "The Truth Behind the Failure of CRM," *Computer Weekly*, June 14, 2001.
81. As one marketing scholar told the *Financial Times*, business processes were designed to avoid dealing with individual customers. "The challenge is not so much acquiring the tools, but creating an organization mindset that it is better to treat people as individuals."
82. Peterson, Robert, "Relationship Marketing and the Consumer," *Journal of the Academy of Marketing Science*, 23:4, 1995, p. 280.
83. Gofton, Ken, "Seeds of a Revolution," *Marketing*, November 1997, p. 7.
84. Fournier, Susan, et al., "Preventing the Premature Death of Relationship Marketing," *Harvard Business Review*, January/February 1998.
85. Peppers and Rogers, *Fieldbook*, p. 6.
86. Peppers, Don, and Martha Rogers, "Better Business—One Customer at a Time," *Journal for Quality and Participation*, March/April 1998, p. 30.
87. Gronroos, Christian, "From Marketing Mix to Relationship Marketing," *Management Decision*, 32:2, 1994, pp. 10–11; Tom Duncan and Sandra Moriarty, "A Communication-Based Marketing Model for Managing Relationships," *Journal of Marketing*, 62, April 1998, pp. 1–13.
88. Gruen, Thomas, "Relationship Marketing," *Business Horizons*, 40:6, November/December 1997, pp. 33, 34, 35, 37.
89. For some classic examples of what became a burgeoning literature, see Elton Mayo, *The Human Problems of an Industrial Civilization*, Harvard Business School, Boston: 1946; Eli Chinoy, *Automobile Workers and the American Dream*, Doubleday, New York: 1955; Chris Argyris, *Personality and Organization*, Harper and Brothers, New York: 1957; Frederick Hertzberg et al., *The Motivation to Work*, Wiley, New York: 1959; Douglas McGregor, *The Human Side of Enterprise*, McGraw-Hill, New York: 1960; and Rensis Likert, *The Human Organization*, McGraw-Hill, New York: 1967.
90. See Richard Walton, "How to Counter Alienation in the Plant," *Harvard Business Review*, 50, November/December, 1972, pp. 70–81.
91. See the discussion in Sanford Jacoby, *Employing Bureaucracy*, Columbia University Press, New York: 1985, pp. 173, 188–189, 198–199, and his *Modern Manors*, Princeton University Press, Princeton, N.J.: 1997, pp. 20, 26, 31.

92. Walton, Richard, "The Topeka Work System," in *The Innovative Organization*, Robert Zager and Michael Rosow, eds., Pergamon Press, New York: 1982.

93. Osterman, Paul, "How Common Is Workplace Transformation and Who Adopts It?" *Industrial and Labor Relations Review*, 47:2, January 1994, pp. 173–188.

94. Teixeira, Ruy A., and Lawrence Mishel, "Skills Shortage or Management Shortage?" in *The New Modern Times*, David Bills, ed., State University of New York Press, Albany: 1995, pp. 193–206.

95. Ibid.

96. Ibid. See also Casey Ichniowski et al., "The Effects of Human Resource Management Practices on Productivity," Working Paper, Graduate School of Business, Columbia University, New York: July 1993.

97. Applebaum, Eileen, and Rosemary Batt, *The New American Workplace*, Cornell University Press, Ithaca, N.Y.: 1994, p. 61.

98. Abramanson, Eric, "Managerial Fads and Fashions: The Diffusion and Rejection of Innovations," *Academy of Management Review*, 16:3, July 1991, pp. 586–612.

99. Kotter, John, "Leading Change: Why Transformation Efforts Fail," *Harvard Business Review*, March/April, 1995.

100. Argyris, Chris, "Empowerment: The Emperor's New Clothes," *Harvard Business Review*, May/June, 1998.

101. Applebaum and Batt, op. cit., p. 68; quote at p. 147.

102. Figures are calculated from "Best Companies to Work For," *Fortune*, January 11, 1999.

103. *Industry Standard*, October 16, 2000, p. 43.

104. Hymowitz, Carol, "Managers Are Starting to Gain More Clout Over Their Employees," *Wall Street Journal*, January 30, 2001.

105. Hochschild, Arlie Russell, *The Time Bind*, Metropolitan Books, New York: 1997, p. 239.

106. The 2000 list is found in *Fortune*, January 10, 2000.

107. Hardy, Quentin, "A Software Star Sees Its Family Culture Turn Dysfunctional," *Wall Street Journal*, May 5, 1999, p. 1. For other recent media coverage of the pendulum swing among progressive high-tech companies, see: Kim Girard, "The Return of the Crummy Job," *Business 2.0*, February 6, 2001, p. 75; Alyda Wheat, "This Little Diatribe," *Fortune*, April 16, 2001, p. 58; and Erika Brown, "Fear.com," *Forbes*, April 16, 2001, p. 108.

108. Townsend, Bickley, "Room at the Top?" *American Demographics*, July 1996.

109. Hagerty, James, "A Female Executive Tells Furniture Maker What Women Want," *Wall Street Journal*, June 25, 1999, p. A1.

110. Ibid.

111. Ibid.

112. Quick, Rebecca, "Retail, Like War, Is Hell at The Limited," *Wall Street Journal*, April 21, 1999, p. B1. By March 2001, The Limited announced that it would miss its profit target for the fourth quarter in a row, with earnings off as much as 20 percent, high inventories, and sales increases of barely 3 percent. Analysts remained skeptical of the company's plans for more restructuring. See Kelly Barron, "Limited Expectations," *Forbes*, March 5, 2001, p. 145; and Teri Agins and Erin White, "As Founder Trims, Limited Tries to Live Up to Its Name," *Wall Street Journal*, March 2, 2001, p. B4.

113. Mort, Frank, *Cultures of Consumption*, Routledge, London: 1996; quotes on pp. 118, 82.

114. Martin, Joanne, and Debra Meyerson, "Executive Women at Link.Com: Part Two, Natalie Kramer's Story," Case study, Stanford University, Graduate School of Business, September 1997.

115. The best discussion of this syndrome among men and women in the corporate environment is still Rosabeth Moss Kanter's *Men and Women of the Corporation*, Basic Books, New York: 1977.

116. For a small sample of recent work on this subject in the United States, see Joan Williams, *Unbending Gender*, Oxford University Press, Oxford: 2000; and Herminia Ibarra, "Personal Networks of Women and Minorities in Management," *Academy of Management Review*, 18:1, 1993, pp. 56–87. See also the discussion in Virginia Valian, *Why So Slow?* MIT Press, Cambridge, Mass.: 1998, esp. Chapter Ten, "Women in the Professions," pp. 187–216. Though it refers to sex inequality in academia, Stanford Business School professor Joanne Martin's essay "The Organization of Exclusion" describes the way formal and informal organizational practices express and reinforce sexual differences, creating significant career barriers for women; it is in *Organization*, 1:2, 1994, pp. 401–431. See also the study of Stanford women MBAs, discussed in our Chapter Five; Laraine Zappert, *Getting It Right*, Pocket Books, New York: 2001. For the case in the United Kingdom, see, for example, T. Coe, *The Key to the Men's Club*, IM, London: 1992; S. Maddock and D. Parkin, "Gender Cultures," in Davidson and Burke, eds., *Women in Management*, Paul Chapman, London: 1994; J. Marshall, *Women Managers Moving On: Exploring Career and Life Choices*, Routledge, London: 1995. See also Ruth Simpson, "Have Times Changed?," *British Journal of Management*, 8, June 1997, pp. 121–130. Note that these matters are not confined to blue-collar settings. Far from it. Recent class-action suits against Wall Street giants, such as Merrill Lynch, Morgan Stanley, and Salomon Smith Barney, cited hundreds of cases of sexual harassment and discrimination. A survey of women on Wall Street found that 60 percent believed that their gender had held back their careers; cited in "The Color (and Sex) of Money," *The Economist*, June 19, 1999, pp. 78–79.

117. Walsh, Mary, "Where GE Falls Short: Diversity at the Top," *New York Times*, September 3, 2000, section 3, p. 1.

118. Fierman, Jaclyn, "Why Women Still Don't Hit the Top," *Fortune*, July 30, 1990, p. 42.

119. Ball, Karen, "Study Finds Few Women Hold Top Executive Jobs," *Washington Post*, August 26, 1991, p. A-11.

120. Simpson, Ruth, "Have Times Changed?" *British Journal of Management*, 8, June 1997, pp. 121–130. The patterns are similar around the world. Women's share of management jobs rarely exceeds 20 percent, while their share of the labor force averages about 40 percent. The higher one looks in the hierarchy, the fewer women there are. In 1991, 3 percent of top executives in Brazil were women. A 1995 survey of the 70,000 largest German companies found 1 percent to 3 percent of top executives and board members were women. See Linda Wirth, "Women in Management," *International Labour Review*, 137:1, 1998, pp. 93–102.

121. Smith, James, and Finis Welch, "Affirmative Action and Labor Markets," *Journal of Labor Economics*, 2, 1984, pp. 269–301; Ann Miller, "Occupational Statistics and Labor Force Analysis," *Proceedings of the American Statistical Association*, Social Statistics Section, 1980, pp. 108–115.

122. Reskin, Barbara, and Catherine Ross, "Jobs, Authority, and Earnings Among Managers: The Continuing Significance of Sex," *Work and Occupations*, 19:4, November 1992, pp. 342–365.

123. Bird, Chloe, "High Finance and Small Change," in *Job Queues, Gender Queues*, Barbara Reskin and Patricia Roos, eds., Temple University Press, Philadelphia: 1990, pp. 145–166.

124. Jacobs, Jerry, "Women's Entry into Management," *Administrative Science Quarterly*, 37, 1992, pp. 282–301. See also Clair Brown and Joseph Pechman, eds., *Gender in the Workplace*, Brookings Institution, Washington, D.C., 1987.

125. Armas, Genaro, "New Census Figures Show Cracks in the Glass Ceiling," *St. Louis Post-Dispatch*, April 25, 2000.

126. "Catalyst Census," Catalyst, New York: November 11, 1999.

127. Bowler, Mary, "Women's Earnings," *Monthly Labor Review*, December 1999, pp. 13–21, figures on p. 19.

128. Bertrand, Marianne, and Kevin Hallock, "The Gender Gap in Top Corporate Jobs," NBER [National Bureau of Economic Research] Working Paper 7931, October 2000.

129. "No Gains for Women on Corporate Boards," *New York Times*, June 24, 2001, p. B4.

130. Dalton, Dan, and Catherine Daily, "Not There Yet," *Across the Board*, November/December 1998, pp. 16–20.

131. Appold, Stephen, et al., "The Employment of Women Managers and Professionals in an Emerging Economy: Gender Inequality as an Organizational Practice," *Administrative Science Quarterly*, 43, 1998, pp. 538–565. The study was conducted in Thailand among U.S., Japanese, and Thai corporations. The authors persuasively argue the relevance of their findings to developed as well as emerging economies.

132. Ibarra, Herminia, "Homophily and Differential Returns," *Administrative Science Quarterly*, 37, 1992, pp. 422–447, and "Paving an Alternative Route," *Social Psychology Quarterly*, 60:1, 1997, pp. 91–102.

133. Walsh, Ann, "Gender Differences in Factors Affecting Health Care Administration Career Development," *Hospital and Health Services Administration*, 40:2, Summer 1995.

134. Traves, Joanne, et al., "Careers of Women Managers in the Retail Industry," *Service Industries Journal*, 17:1, January 1997; Belle Rose Ragins, et al., "Gender Gap in the Executive Suite," *Academy of Management Executives*, 12:1, 1998; Herminia Ibarra and Brooke Harrington, "Deference and Demeanor: Gender, Demography and Self-Presentation in Professional Careers," Harvard Business School Working Paper, July 10, 1997.

135. "Workplace Equity," *Harvard Business Review*, November/December 1997, p. 16.

136. Walsh, Mary, op. cit.

137. Honomichl, Jack, "Annual Business Report on the Marketing Research Industry," *Marketing News*, June 4, 2001.

138. Osborne, Lawrence, "Consuming Rituals," *New York Times Magazine*, January 13, 2002.

139. "Field Trip to Your Medicine Cabinet," *Time*, July 23, 2001, p. 47. See also Emily Nelson, "P&G Checks Out Real Life," *Wall Street Journal*, May 17, 2001, p. B1; Melanie Wells, "New Ways to Get into Our Heads," *USA Today*, March 2, 1999; Joshua Macht, "The New Market Research," *Inc.*, July 1998; Barbara Perry, "Seeing Your Customers in a Whole New Light," *Journal for Quality and Participation*, November/December 1998; Lynn Smith, "What Do Consumers Want?" *Los Angeles Times*, March 21, 1996; and Katie Hafner, "Coming of Age in Palo Alto," *New York Times*, June 10, 1999.

140. Osborne, op. cit.

141. Zucker, Lynne G., "Where Do Institutional Patterns Come From?" in Institutional Patterns and Organizations, Lynne G. Zucker, ed., Ballinger, Cambridge, Mass.: 1988, pp. 23–52.

142. For a detailed elaboration of this perspective, see Zucker, op. cit., and her "The Role of Institutionalization in Cultural Persistence," *American Sociological Review*, 42:5, October 1977, pp. 726–743.

143. Zucker, Lynne, "Institutional Theories of Organization," *Annual Review of Sociology*, 13, 1987, pp. 443–464; reference on p. 446.

144. See discussion in William Roy, *Socializing Capital: The Rise of the Large Industrial Corporation in America*, Princeton University Press, Princeton, N.J.: 1997, pp. 265–276, esp. at p. 269.

145. Zucker, "Where Do Institutional Patterns Come From?" p. 35.

146. Waller, William, Jr., "The Concept of Habit in Economic Analysis," *Journal of Economic Issues*, XXII:1, 1988. See also Geoffrey Hodgson, *The Economics of Institutions*, E. Elgar, Brookfield, Vt.: 1993.

147. Foster, Lauren, "Northwest Flies into Flak for Junking Kids' Food," *Financial Times*, August 16, 2001, p. 1.
148. Heiner, Ronald, "The Origin of Predictable Behavior," *American Economic Review*, 73:4, September 1983, pp. 560–595; quote on p. 570.
149. A chronology of events is found in Laurence Stern et al., "A Pump Failure, a Claxon Alert, a Nuclear Crisis," *Washington Post*, April 8, 1979, p. A1. The supervisor's quote is found in Thomas O'Toole, "Plant Operators Dispute NRC Version of Mishap," *Washington Post*, May 8, 1979, p. A1. See also Thomas Moss and David Sills, eds., "The Three Mile Island Nuclear Accident," *Annals of the New York Academy of Sciences*, 365, 1981; and Philip Starr and William Pearman, *Three Mile Island Sourcebook: Annotations of a Disaster*, Garland Publishing, New York: 1983.
150. Binger, Brian, and Elizabeth Hoffman, "Institutional Persistence and Change: The Question of Efficiency," *Journal of Institutional and Theoretical Economics*, 145, 1989, pp. 67–84.
151. Gersick, Connie, "Revolutionary Change Theories: A Multilevel Exploration of the Punctuated Equilibrium Paradigm," *Academy of Management Review*, 16:1, 1991, p. 18.
152. Kuhn, Thomas, *The Structure of Scientific Revolutions*, University of Chicago Press, Chicago: 1970, p. 24. Psychologists have labeled this phenomenon "selective perception."
153. Greenspan, Alan, "Is There a New Economy?" *California Management Review*, 41:1, Fall 1998, p. 80.
154. Keynes, John Maynard, *The General Theory of Employment, Interest, and Money*, Harcourt Brace, New York: 1964, p. viii.
155. See Kuhn, op. cit., Chapter 7, "Crisis and the Emergence of Scientific Theories," p. 66–76.
156. Kuhn, op. cit., pp. 37, 168–173.
157. See, for example, the archaeological controversy over "Clovis Man," popularly summarized in Sharon Begley and Andrew Murr, "The First Americans," *Newsweek*, April 26, 1999.
158. Stinchcombe, Arthur, "Social Structure and Organizations," in *Handbook of Organizations*, James March, ed., Rand McNally, Chicago: 1965, pp. 142–193. See also John Kimberly, "Environmental Constraints and Organizational Structure," *Administrative Sciences Quarterly*, 20, 1975, pp. 1–9.
159. Kuhn, op. cit., p. 90. Similarly, organizational researchers have observed that when a company faces serious troubles, externally recruited top managers are more than three times more likely than the existing top managment team to initiate change that challenges the existing business model or strategy. See M. Tushman and E. Romanelli, "Organizational Evolution: A Metamorphosis Model of Convergence and Reorientation," in L.L. Cummings and B.M. Staw, eds., *Research in Organizational Behavior*, Vol. 7, JAI Press, Greenwich, Conn.: 1985, p. 179.

Chapter Ten

1. Recent articles on this include Andrew Barry, "Investors Say Yahoo! to Yahoo!, Ho-Hum to GE," *Barron's Market Week*, April 12, 1999; Justin Fox, "Net Stock Rules," *Fortune*, June 7, 1999; "Valuation of the Internet Industry," *Weekly Corporate Growth Report*, March 22, 1999. In 1999, the 294 companies doing the most business on the Internet had an average market capitalization of $18 billion, thirty times the average $600 million market capitalization for all the 5,068 companies listed on the Nasdaq. "Measuring the Internet Economy," Center for Research in Electronic Commerce, Graduate School of Business, University of Texas at Austin, October 1999. See also "About Those Internet Wipeouts . . ." *Fortune*, July 5, 1999.

2. For an elaboration of the "informate" concept and its wider implications, see Shoshana Zuboff, *In the Age of the Smart Machine: The Future of Work and Power*, Basic Books, New York: 1988.

3. As quoted in John Dodge, "Shifting Gears," *Wall Street Journal*, July 12, 1999.

4. Dahlbom, Bo, "Postface: From Infrastructure to Networking," in Claudio U. Ciborra et al., *From Control to Drift: The Dynamics of Corporate Information Infrastructures*, Oxford University Press, Oxford: 2000, pp. 212–226. Dahlbom also describes the difference between "infrastructure" and a networking medium.

5. "The X Internet," Forrester Research, May 2001.

6. See U.S. Department of Commerce, *The Emerging Digital Economy*, Washington, D.C.: 1998.

7. U.S. Department of Commerce, "A Nation Online," Washington, D.C., February 2002, p. 10.

8. "Consumer Goods: Online Projections," Vol. 1, Jupiter Communications, July 1999.

9. U.S. Department of Commerce, "A Nation Online," p. 3.

10. Jupiter, op. cit.

11. U.S. Department of Commerce, "A Nation Online," pp. 3–4.

12. "Consumer Technographics Europe," Forrester Research, March 21, 2002.

13. International Data Corporation, "The Global Market Forecast for Internet Usage and Commerce," 2002.

14. Ibid., p. 17.

15. Ibid.

16. Maguire, Tom, "Web Nets the Masses," *American Demographics*, December 1998.

17. U.S. Department of Commerce, "A Nation Online," pp. 11–12.

18. 1998 data from the Jupiter/NFO Consumer Survey, Vol. 2, "Attitudes, Behaviors, and Demographics of the Online User," Jupiter Communications, August 1999. 2000 data from U.S. Department of Commerce, "A Nation Online," p. 15.

19. U.S. Department of Commerce, "A Nation Online," pp. 15–16.

20. Fox, Susannah, et al., "Time Online," Pew Internet & American Life Project, Washington, D.C., 2001, p. 4.

21. U.S. Department of Commerce, "A Nation Online," p. 16.

22. Horrigan, John, et al., "Getting Serious Online," Pew Internet & American Life Project, Washington, D.C., 2002, p. 13.

23. Horrigan, John, "Online Communities," Pew Internet & American Life Project, Washington, D.C., 2001, p. 15.

24. Rainie, Lee, "Women Surpass Men as E-Shoppers," Pew Internet & American Life Project, Washington, D.C., 2002, p. 4.

25. See Susannah Fox and Lee Rainie, "The Online Health Care Revolution," Pew Internet & American Life Project, November 26, 2001; figures on p. 9.

26. See, for example, Sue Shellenbarger, "Some Internet Sites That Can Help Ease Burdens of Elder Care," *Wall Street Journal*, February 27, 2002.

27. Fox and Rainie, op. cit.; figures on p. 9.

28. Ibid., p. 10.

29. Horrigan et al., "Getting Serious Online," p. 21.

30. Horrigan, "Online Communities," p. 20. See also Hilary Appelman, "I Scream, You Scream: Consumers Vent Over the Net," *New York Times*, March 4, 2001.

31. Larsen, Elena, "Cyberfaith," Pew Internet & American Life Project, Washington, D.C., 2001, p. 2.

32. Ibid., p. 21.

33. Ibid., pp. 22, 11.

34. 1997 and 1999 figures from "Shopping: Online Projections," Vol. 2, Jupiter Communications, November 1999.

35. 2001 figures from BizRate.com, December 2001.

36. Brown, Jeanette, "Shoppers Are Beating a Path to the Web," *Business Week*, December 24, 2001, p. 41.

37. "The X Internet," op. cit.
38. U.S. Department of Commerce, "A Nation Online" p. 30.
39. Horrigan, et al., "Getting Serious Online," p. 3.
40. "The Online Retail Market," Boston Consulting Group and Shopping.org, Boston, April 2000.
41. Brown, op. cit.
42. "Business to Consumer Commerce," Gartner Group, January 18, 2002.
43. "Global Online Retailing," Ernst & Young, 2001, p. 9.
44. "Online Retail Strategies: Retail's Growth Spiral," Forrester Research, November 1998; "Post-Web Retail," Forrester Research, September 1999.
45. U.S. Department of Commerce, "A Nation Online," p. 10.
46. "Global Online Retailing," p. 9.
47. Morrisette, Shelley, et al., "The Retail Power Shift," Forrester Research, August 1998.
48. "Back to School Shopping Report," Market Facts, Inc., August 13, 1999.
49. Horrigan et al., "Getting Serious Online," p. 20.
50. "Shopping: Online Projections" Jupiter Communications.
51. "GVU WWW User Survey," Graphics Visualization and Usability Center, College of Computing, Georgia Institute of Technology, Atlanta, Ga., May 14, 1999.
52. "Global Online Retailing," p. 10.
53. Henig, Peter, "Is AOL Insulting Our Intelligence?" *Red Herring*, September 17, 1998.
54. "How Dell Sells on the Web," *Money*, September 1998.
55. For some insight into Compaq's difficulties in competing with Dell on the Web, see "Compaq vs. Dell," *Money*, January 1999.
56. See, for example, Yannis J. Bakos, "Reducing Buyer Search Costs: Implications for Electronic Marketplaces," *Management Science*, 43:12, December 1997; "The Emerging Role of Electronic Marketplaces on the Internet," *Communications of the ACM*, August 1998; Eric Clemons et al., "The Nature of Competition in Electronic Markets," Working Paper, Wharton School of the University of Pennsylvania, June 1999; and Ho Geun Lee, "Do Electronic Marketplaces Lower the Price of Goods?" *Communications of the ACM*, 41:12, January 1997.
57. See Bill Gates's *Business @ The Speed of Thought*, Warner Books, New York: 1999; Erik Brynjolfsson and Michael D. Smith, "Frictionless Commerce? A Comparison of Internet and Conventional Retailers," Working Paper, MIT Sloan School of Management, August 1999.
58. Stigler, George, "The Economics of Information,"*Journal of Political Economy*, 69:3, June 1961.
59. Empirical work on this subject is found in Brynjolfsson and Smith, "Frictionless Commerce?". The authors examined prices of books and CDs, and found that a straight comparison of product prices between online and physical outlets produced prices on the Internet that averaged about 16 percent lower than in the physical world. They then attempted a comparison between prices based on the cost "for consumers to have the product in their living room." In this comparison they added the cost of shipping, handling, taxes, and transportation. These comparisons yielded prices that were 9 percent to 13 percent lower on the Internet. As the researchers noted, however, these comparisons tended to understate the cost of goods from conventional outlets, based on very conservative estimates of transportation costs, and a failure to consider other associated costs such as parking, time allocation, etc. More realistic comparisons might yield an even wider spread between Internet and conventional pricing.
60. Ibid.
61. "The Bottom Line," *Wall Street Journal*, July 12, 1999; "Frictions in Cyberspace," *The Economist*, November 20, 1999.
62. De Lisser, Eleena, "Online Retailers Slice and Dice Niches Thinner Than Julienne Fries," *Wall Street Journal*, November 29, 1999.

63. "Measuring the Internet Economy."
64. See the discussion in Austan Goolsbee, "In a World without Borders: The Impact of Taxes on Internet Commerce," Working Paper, University of Chicago, 1998. Rajiv Lal and Miklos Sarvary have begun to sketch out a related point in their distinction between digital and nondigital product attributes. See their paper "Does the Internet Always Intensify Price Competition?" Stanford Graduate School of Business Research Paper no. 1457R, April 2, 1998.
65. "Slim Pickings Likely for Small Start-Ups," *Financial Times*, January 21, 2000.
66. Dykema, Evie Black, "Ringing Up Web Store Costs," Forrester Research, August 1999. In 1999 Internet pure-play retailers spent an average of $42 per customer, compared to $22 for multichannel retailers. During the 1999 Christmas season, new Internet retailers were spending $108 for each customer, as opposed to an average of $29 per customer by established retailers. "Online Customer Acquisition Costs," *Business 2.0*, November 1999.
67. "The Online Retail Market."
68. On this point it is instructive to note that Amazon.com lowered its prices when Barnesandnoble.com entered the market.
69. "E-Commerce Report Digest," *Financial Times*, December 10, 2001.
70. "Dell to Detroit," *Wall Street Journal*, December 1, 1999.
71. See discussion in Baruch Lev, *Intangibles*, Brookings Institution Press, Washington, D.C.: 2001, pp. 8–13.
72. Ip, Greg, "Internet Business Stocks Replace Consumer Issues as Hot Favorites," *Wall Street Journal*, November 15, 1999.
73. As a Goldman Sachs study of B2B commerce concluded, "Companies are adopting B2B solutions since they present cost savings up front. . . . By pursuing more B2B implementations, we estimate that B2B solutions can reduce the process costs (of procurement) between 10% and 25%, thereby reducing total costs between 3% and 12.5%. . . . B2B solutions also offer potential savings on the product side of procurement. The typical purchasing manager is not an effective researcher. Due to poor research, an estimated 20% of suppliers are awarded 90% of purchases. One of the key weaknesses of procurement is poor information flow. B2B solutions automate the information process, maximizing the cost efficiencies. . . . The product side of costs can be reduced more than 20%, adding to further efficiencies won on the process side of total cost calculation. *Significant cost savings offer a demonstrable ROI that compels management to embrace B2B as a means to gain competitive advantage*" (the emphasis is theirs).
74. "B2B: 2B or Not 2B?" Goldman Sachs Investment Research, November 12, 1999. Goldman Sachs reported that U.S. intercompany trade of hard goods over the Internet, the so-called business-to-business or B2B sector, increased from about $18 billion in 1997 to $114 billion in 1999, and was expected to reach $1.5 trillion in 2004. International Data Corporation calculated only $516 billion in business-to-business Internet trade in 2001 but expected that figure to reach $4.3 trillion by 2005 (International Data Corporation, 2002, op. cit.). AMR Research forecast an even higher figure of $5.7 trillion. A University of Texas study calculated that between 1995 and 1998, the Internet economy grew at an annual rate of 174.5 percent. Its assessment was based on an inclusive definition of the Internet economy—companies providing infrastructure, applications, intermediaries, and e-commerce. It concluded that the entire Internet economy generated $301.4 billion in revenue in 1998 and $507 billion in 1999. That growth was fueled in large measure by the spectacular growth in Internet commerce, which increased by 127 percent between the first quarter of 1998 and the first quarter of 1999 ("Measuring the Internet Economy"). But even these growth rates represent the very earliest stages of activity. Business-to-business trade represented 0.2 percent of all intercompany trade in the United States in 1997, 0.4 percent in 1998, 1.1 percent in 1999, 2.6 percent in 2000, and 4.4 percent in 2001, and it was predicted to reach levels of 10.9 percent in 2004. Analysts expected Western Europe to closely trail those growth rates. (1997–1999

figures are cited in Goldman Sachs report, op. cit.; 2000–2004 figures are cited in "Current Technology Trends," Community B2B.com, December 15, 2001.) The trajectory in Japan was not dissimilar, rising from 1.6 percent online penetration in 1998 to 4.9 percent in 2001 and an anticipated 11.1 percent in 2003 (Japanese Ministry of International Trade, Andersen Consulting, 1999). For an intriguing account of the rise of Internet use in Japan, see Stephanie Strom, "Rising Internet Use Quietly Transforms Way Japanese Live," *New York Times*, May 14, 2000. In 1999, the Yankee Group, a technology consultancy, surveyed 250 large- and medium-sized U.S. companies across a broad range of industries about their views on e-commerce. Not surprisingly, they found that 58 percent of top corporate decision-makers considered the Web to be important or very important to their business strategy. However, 75 percent indicated that their companies did not yet have Web sites that would support online transactions or tie in with their customer databases or those of their suppliers. Similarly, DHL interviewed executives from 621 businesses around the world and found that 79 percent were not yet trading over the Internet, 74 percent had no e-commerce department, and 40 percent of all the e-commerce directors had never bought goods over the Internet. (As quoted in "The Net Imperative," *The Economist*, June 26, 1999.) A study in 2000 by MORI, a British research firm, polled 702 U.S. and European firms. A full 51 percent of the executive respondents said that e-business was either "not at all important" or "not very important," while only 7 percent thought it was "essential." A leading provider of online procurement software found only 8 percent of global companies were using e-procurement "B2B . . ."; The DHL and MORI studies are described in Carlos Grande, "Business 'Unready' for Boom in Online Trading," *Financial Times*, December 21, 1999, p. 8.

75. See for example, Caroline Daniel, "Keeping the Wheel of E-Commerce Turning Smoothly," *Financial Times*, January 6, 2000. See also Jacob Schlesinger, "Will the Real Economy Please Stand Up?" *Wall Street Journal*, March 22, 2000; "Vertically Challenged," *The Economist*, November 26, 1999; "Steelmakers Face Online Threat from Auto Industry," *Wall Street Journal*, November 26, 1999; "Trading Metal in a Virtual Marketplace," *Financial Times*, October 13, 1999; "E-muscle," *Forbes*, March 9, 1998; "How Should CIOs Deal with Web-Based Auctions?" *Communications of the ACM*, 41:7, July 1998; Richard Waters, "Wringing New Potential Out of the Old Economy," *Financial Times*, April 19, 2000; "Shell Plans Internet Market," *Financial Times*, January 14, 2000, as cited in "B2B. . . ."; Clare Ansberry, "Let's Build an Online Supply Network!" *Wall Street Journal*, April 17, 2000; "Airlines Unite to Buy Over the Web," *Financial Times*, April 28, 2000, as cited in "Cars/Internet," The Lex Column, *Financial Times*, February 26/27, 2000; Notihiko Shirouzu, "Matsushita Aims to Unite Suppliers Via Internet," *Wall Street Journal*, January 28, 2000; "Virtual Auctions Knock Down Costs," *Financial Times*, November 3, 1998; and David Patton, "Supply Side," *Wall Street Journal*, November 15, 1999.

76. One early report noted that 53 percent of wholesalers surveyed moved to the Internet to reduce costs. The study summarized its findings this way: "Pursuing market share via the Net reaps a windfall: Nearly half of the wholesalers told us their operating margins are higher on-line. They use less labor and send fewer paper catalogs because customers get the information on the Web instead. . . ." ("Middlemen on the Net," Forrester Research, January 1998).

77. Kirby, Carrie, "B2B Exchanges Dying Off Fast," *San Francisco Chronicle*, May 21, 2001.

78. As an example, Internet Commerce Group saw its share price drop from around $300 a share to 70 cents.

79. Rombel, Adam, "The Internet B2B Market Shake-Up," *Global Finance*, January 1, 2001.

80. Metcalfe, David, "eMarketplaces: Rebound and Deliver," Forrester Research, March 2002.

81. Sanders, Matthew, "eBusiness Propels Productivity," November 2001. See also "Time to Rebuild," *The Economist*, May 19, 2001; Fiona Harvey, "Back to Basics," *New Media Age*, February 22, 2001; Ken Berryman, "Is the Third Time the Charm?" *McKinsey Quarterly*, March 22, 2001; Carol Vinzant and Neil Irwin, "To B2B or Not to B2B?" *Washington Post*, June 20, 2001; Ted Doyle, "B2B Web Exchanges," *Journal of Business Strategy*, May 1, 2002; Nuala Moran, "Fallout Is Far from Over in Electronic Marketplaces," *Financial Times*, March 13, 2002.

82. "Collaborative Customer Relationship Management," Yankee Group, February 2002. Also quoted in Eric Pfeiffer, "Friendly Foes," *Red Herring*, April 2002.

83. "Web Services: The Next Technology Thunderstorm," Forrester Research, March 18, 2002. For a similar viewpoint, see other Forrester reports on this subject, such as Simon Yates, "The Web Services Payoff," Forrester Research, December 2001; and Bruce Temkin, "Web Services Boost B2B Collaboration," Forrester Research, February 2002.

84. For an overview of the chronic failure of the technology imperative, see Shoshana Zuboff, op. cit. For a compelling set of case studies that illustrate this dynamic as it relates to "groupware," see Claudio Ciborra, *Groupware and Teamwork: Invisible Aid or Technical Hindrance?* Wiley, New York: 1996.

85. Johannes, Laura, "Competing Online, Drugstore Chains Virtually Undersell Themselves," *Wall Street Journal*, January 10, 2000. Some Internet companies relied on the auction mode, so prices were set by the market of buyers at any given time. Others set prices based on real-time inventory levels, and still others offered products for sale or bid at or less than wholesale prices, based on their own volume buying and a willingness to trade margins for advertising revenue. Some offered products at the lowest price, guaranteed against the findings of their own shopping engines. More dabbled in the advantages of pricing based on yield management, just like the airlines. And there were many others who decided on the ultimate modification—no price at all; some Web-based companies simply gave away their electronic products and sought revenue from other sources. In some cases, their new business models changed whole industries in a matter of days. For example, in the United Kingdom, subscription-free Internet services completely replaced a once robust market for paid service. Within a year of that sea change, nearly 200 companies were competing to give away their services. E-Trade began to give away stock market information that companies had always paid hundreds of dollars for. Suddenly, an entire business simply vanished. The Internet was quickly rife with free services for everything from long-distance calling to voice mail, e-mail, and CD downloads. This approach paid off for some. Yahoo! didn't charge for its Internet directory service, yet it attracted enough users to command a $29.7 billion stock valuation in 1999. Netscape decided to give away its Internet browser and a few years later was acquired by AOL for $10 billion. Hotmail's strategy included free e-mail services, and Microsoft acquired it in 1998 for $400 million. Egreetings was struggling to find customers for its e-mail birthday cards, until it decided to give them away. It grew from 300,000 registered users to 7 million in less than a year. eFax launched a free service that merges voice and e-mail, eliminating any premiums for the new technology. *Slate* magazine increased its readership five-fold in a matter of months when it stopped charging for the privilege of readership. Prestigious newspapers gave up trying to charge for their electronic versions. User fees for business information services went into sharp decline. "Good-Bye to Fixed Pricing?" *Business Week*, May 4, 1998; "Free for All," *Wall Street Journal*, July 28, 1999; Jim Nail, "The New Business Portals," Forrester Research, February 1999.

86. "The Age of Net Pragmatism," Forrester Research, December 1998.

87. "Behind Web Sector's Moderate Decline Lie Tales of Woe, with Some Celebrity Issues Down 75%," *Wall Street Journal*, January 20, 2000.

88. Bank, David, "A Site-Eat-Site World," *Wall Street Journal*, July 12, 1999.

89. See ibid. and Lisa Bransten, "The Bottom Line," *Wall Street Journal*, July 12, 1999.

90. "The New Brand Experience—Journal Entries," Forrester Research, February 3, 1999.

91. See Andrea Petersen, "Now It's Time for a Commercial," *Wall Street Journal*, November 22, 1999.

92. Bulkeley, William M., "We're Watching You," *Wall Street Journal*, November 22, 1999. See also Petersen, op. cit.

93. Petersen, op. cit.

94. See Bulkeley, op. cit.

95. The specter of covert surveillance was at issue when RealNetworks' CEO Rob Glaser was forced to apologize to his customers. An Internet security consultant had revealed that RealJukebox monitors its users—preferred music storage format, the number of songs on a person's hard disk, favorite type of music, type of portable music player—and sends the information back to RealNetworks. The company insisted it was using the information only to provide customized service for its users, but customer reactions forced a contrite admission of error and a "patch" to prevent any future data gathering. ("A Few Problems for RealNetworks," *Newsweek*, November 15, 1999.) The same mistrust spilled into the headlines when Web advertising distributor DoubleClick announced plans to merge a newly acquired database of individual names, addresses, and buying habits for millions of consumers with its own volumes of data on Web-site traffic. The company became the object of intense public backlash and was eventually forced to halt its plans, pending the development of clear public standards on privacy. (Andrea Petersen, "DoubleClick Reverses Course after Privacy Outcry," *Wall Street Journal*, March 3, 2000.) AOL has come under increasing scrutiny as it probably sits on more detailed consumer data than any other single company. ("With So Much Subscriber Data, AOL Walks a Cautious Line on Privacy," *Wall Street Journal*, March 15, 2000.)

96. "A Little Privacy, Please," *Business Week*, March 16, 1998.

97. Rainie, "Women Surpass Men," p. 5.

98. Fox and Rainie, "The Online Health Care Revolution," p. 12.

99. See, for example, "You'll Wanna Hold Their Hands," *Business Week*, March 22, 1999; and "Getting the Goods," *Wall Street Journal*, November 22, 1999.

100. Kelley, Christopher, "Driving Sales with Service," Forrester Research, November 1999.

101. See Katrina Brooker, "The Nightmare Before Christmas," *Fortune*, January 24, 2000.

102. Rainie, "Women Surpass Men," pp. 4–5.

103. "The X Internet," op. cit.

104. As cited in "Online Shoppers on E-mail Hold," *ComputerWorld*, August 30, 1999.

105. Jupiter/NFO Consumer Survey. See also "Online Customer Service: Strategies for Improving Satisfaction and Retention," Jupiter Communications, 1999.

106. "Key Statistics," *E Marketer*, January 20, 2002.

107. Chen, Christine Y., and Treg Lindsay, "The Straight Dope," *Fortune*, February 21, 2000. As one market research executive put it, "The service experience was broken." His firm shop-tested the top fifty e-commerce sites. They were unable to place an order 25 percent of the time, 20 percent of packages arrived late or never, and 36 percent of sites had busy or unhelpful customer-service numbers.

108. PricewaterhouseCoopers, "Transactions and Spending," Shop.org, January 22, 2001.

109. For a sample description, see "Serving the Customer," *Upside*, November 1999.

110. Ibid. See also Timothy Hanrahan, "Price Isn't Everything," *Wall Street Journal*, July 12, 1999.

111. "Cyber-Santa's Sleigh Ride," *Newsweek*, January 10, 2000.

112. AdRelevance, January 17, 2000.

113. The *Fortune* top ten drawn from its 1999 list were Citigroup, Boeing, General Electric, IBM, General Motors, Philip Morris, AT&T, Ford, Exxon Mobil, and Wal-Mart. E-commerce companies, drawn from the *E-Commerce Times'* top ten list, January 26, 2000, were Amazon.com, Barnesandnoble.com., Beyond.com, eBay, Egghead.com, eToys, E*Trade Group, Open Market, Inc., Priceline.com, and ShopNow.com. The e-builders were drawn from Forrester's list of the top firms consulting in this area in January 2000. We included ten randomly selected from a list of twenty. Data were publicly available on only nine of those selected: Agency.com, AppNet.com, Cambridge Technology Partners, Diamond Technology Partners, Sapient Corporation, Scient Corporation, Proxicom, Inc., Viant Corporation, and Zefer Corporation.
114. Butt, Joseph, Jr., "Empowered Consumers," Forrester Research, October 1999.
115. "Consumer Goods: Online Projections," Jupiter Communications, July 1999.
116. "Online Customer Service: Strategies for Improving Satisfaction and Retention," Jupiter Communications, 1999.
117. Horrigan et al. "Getting Serious Online," pp. 19, 21.
118. See, for example, Barbara Boydston "That's the Ticket," *Wall Street Journal*, July 17, 2000.
119. Jupiter Webtrack, October 1999.
120. Kerstetter, Jim, "The Web at Your Service," *Business Week*, March 18, 2002.
121. Berners-Lee, Tim, James Hendler, and Ora Lassila, "The Semantic Web," *Scientific American*, May 2001; for more on the semantic Web, see Mark Fravenfelder, "A Smarter Web," *Technology Review*, 104:9, November 2001, pp. 52–59; Seth Grimes, "The Semantic Web," *The Intelligent Enterprise*, 5:6, March 28, 2002, p. 16; Henry Kim, "Predicting How Ontologies for the Semantic Web Will Evolve," *Communications of the ACM*, 45:2, February 2002, p. 48.
122. One version of this example is found in Otis Port, "The Next Web," *Business Week*, March 4, 2002.

Chapter Eleven

1. See Thomas Kuhn's discussion in *The Structure of Scientific Revolutions*, University of Chicago Press, Chicago: 1970, Chapter 8, "The Response to Crisis," pp. 77–91; quotes on p. 85.
2. Briggs, John, *Fractals: The Patterns of Chaos*, Simon & Schuster, New York: 1992, p. 34.
3. Ibid., p. 71.
4. Ibid.
5. Ibid., p. 45.
6. Ibid., p. 59.
7. Chandler, Alfred D., *The Visible Hand: The Managerial Revolution in American Business*, Harvard University Press, Cambridge, Mass.: 1977, p. 7.
8. Ibid.
9. Ibid.
10. Thurm, Scott, "Some Manufacturers Prosper by Facilitating Rise of 'Virtual Firm,'" *Wall Street Journal*, August 18, 1998.
11. Bult, Carol J., et al., "Complete Genome Sequence of the Methanogenic Archaeon, Methanococcus jannaschii," *Science*, 273:23, August 1996.

Chapter Twelve

1. These figures are based on a study conducted by a supply chain management consultancy—Pittiglio, Rabin, Todd, & McGrath, Stamford, Conn., 1997—as cited in Jeff Moad, "Forging Flexible Links," *PC Week*, September 15, 1997.
2. Fine, Charles, and Daniel Raff, "The Automotive Industry: Internet-Driven Innovation and Economic Performance," in Robert Litvan and Alice Rivlin, eds.,

The Economic Payoff from the Internet Revolution, Brookings Institution Press, Washington, D.C., 2001.

3. Richards, Bill, "Employer Benefits," *Wall Street Journal*, November 15, 1999.

4. For example, at Sun Microsystems, which sources electronic components rather than manufacturing them, supply chain forecasting and fulfillment software from I2 Technologies allows a network of 150 supplier links around the world to share demand forecasts and manufacturing schedules. According to one observer, "The idea is for Sun to be air-traffic controller of its supply chain—not flying any of the planes, but knowing which are in the air, where they're headed, if they're on schedule." "A Better Mousetrap Catalog," *Business 2.0*, February 2000.

5. Magi Corp has been a pioneer in this peer-to-peer technology, which has been used by Global Etech in supply chain software development. For a perspective on these developments, see also "The Emergence of Distributed Content Management," Gartner Group, Stamford, Conn., 2001.

6. Lev, Baruch, *Intangibles*, Brookings Institution Press, Washington, D.C.: 2001, p. 33.

7. In today's accounting environment, regulators are reluctant to qualify such intangibles as assets, because they are not subject to strict legal control by the enterprise. In consequence, corporate investments in these areas are treated as expenses rather than investments, leading to what Baruch Lev has called "the deterioration in the usefulness of financial information to managers and investors." He has pioneered the financial analysis of intangibles in ways that are extremely relevant to the development of metrics for the support economy. See Lev, op. cit., p. 36.

8. See Lev, op. cit., pp. 8–18. Also see Margaret Blair and Steven Wallman, *Unseen Wealth*, Brookings Institution Press, Washington, D.C.: 2001.

9. Nakamura, Leonard, "What Is the US Gross Investment in Intangibles?" Federal Reserve Bank of Philadelphia, Working Paper no. 01–15, October 2001.

10. Blair and Wallman, op. cit., p. 7.

11. See also Lev, op. cit., p. 32.

12. See Arlie Hochschild, *The Managed Heart*, University of California Press, Berkeley: 1983.

13. There are always many examples in the popular and academic press that describe the obstacles to collaboration, both within and across organizations. Recent articles extolling the opportunities of shared electronic infrastructures for supply chain management or electronic market-making have cited the so-called cultural problems of mistrust that are difficult to overcome. In our view, these are not merely cultural roadblocks but predictable consequences of the standard enterprise logic and the behavioral patterns it mandates. For a few such examples, see "The Net Imperative," *The Economist*, June 26, 1999; "Supply Traffic Control," *Business 2.0*, February 2000; Penelope Ody, "Collaborative Planning and Forecasting," *Financial Times*, September 1, 1999; Joseph B. White, "Getting into Gear," *Wall Street Journal*, April 17, 2000; and Clare Ansberry, "Let's Build an Online Supply Network!" *Wall Street Journal*, April, 17, 2000.

14. As cited in *Business 2.0*, February 2000, p. 139.

15. On the subject of "coordination theory," see Thomas Malone and Kevin Crowston, "The Interdisciplinary Study of Coordination," *ACM Computing Surveys*, 26:1, March 1994.

16. "Open source" refers to a genre of software that is freely distributed, includes its full source code, and allows anyone to modify and redistribute their own versions under the same terms. See Steven Weber, "The Political Economy of Open Source Software," in *Tracking a Transformation: E-Commerce and the Terms of Competition in Industries*," Brookings Institution Press, Washington, D.C.: 2001, pp. 406–407.

17. Weber, op. cit., pp. 428–429.

18. Sklar, Martin, *The Corporate Reconstruction of American Capitalism, 1890–1916*, Cambridge University Press, Cambridge: 1988, pp. 1–40.

19. Alfred Chandler's dating of the same accomplishment extends to 1925 or so. He emphasizes the adjustments made to the managerial canon in the wake of the recession that followed World War I. See Alfred Chandler, *The Visible Hand: The Managerial Revolution in American Business*, Harvard University Press, Cambridge, Mass: 1977, pp. 455–475.

20. See Amar Bhide, *The Origin and Evolution of New Businesses*, Oxford University Press, Oxford: 2000, pp. 330–336.

21. Smith, Adam, *The Wealth of Nations*, Edwin Cannan, ed. Modern Library, Random House, New York: 1994, p. 581.

22. Thompson, E.P., *The Making of the English Working Class*, Random House, New York: 1966, p. 291.

23. Wuthnow, Robert, *Acts of Compassion*, Princeton University Press, Princeton, N.J.: 1991.

24. Wuthnow, Robert, *Loose Connections*, Harvard University Press, Cambridge, Mass.: 1998.

25. Bartlett, Christopher and Sumantra Ghoshal, *The Individualized Corporation*, Harper Business, New York: 1997.

26. Smith, op. cit. See also Nathan Rosenberg, "Some Institutional Aspects of *The Wealth of Nations*," *Journal of Political Economy*, LXVIII:6, December 1960.

INDEX